MANAGING CULTURAL DIFFERENCES

The world of business for all organizations in the twenty-first century is global, interdependent, complex, and rapidly changing. That means sophisticated global leadership skills are required more than ever today. Individual and organizational success is no longer dependent solely on business acumen. Our ability to understand, communicate, and manage across borders, countries, and cultures has never been as important as it is now. The understanding and utilization of cultural differences as a business resource is a key building block as companies rely on their global reach to achieve the best profit and performance.

For this reason, international business and cross-cultural management are key topics in undergraduate business, MBA, and executive education programs worldwide as companies and institutions prepare current and future business leaders for the global marketplace. This exciting new edition of the highly successful textbook, *Managing Cultural Differences*, seeks to guide students and any person with global responsibilities to understand how culture fits in a changing business world and how to gain a competitive advantage from effective cross-cultural management, and gives practical advice for doing business across the globe.

With updated content, new case studies, and a new author team, *Managing Cultural Differences* is required course reading for undergraduates, postgraduates, and MBA students alike as well as being of significant value for anyone who sells, purchases, travels, or works internationally.

Robert T. Moran is Professor of International Management, Emeritus and Former Interim Chair of the International Studies Department at Thunderbird School of Global Management, USA.

Neil Remington Abramson is Associate Professor of Management in the Strategy Area Group of the Beedie School of Business, Simon Fraser University, Vancouver, British Columbia, Canada. He is the recently elected president of the Simon Fraser Faculty Association (2013–2014), a position he has held in the past (2001–2002). In 1991–1992, he was an assistant professor at the Richard Ivey School of Business in London, Ontario, Canada.

Sarah V. Moran has a masters degree in Intercultural Communication from Arizona State University and has successfully completed all required course work at McGill University for a Ph.D. in Management. Following her masters degree, she worked for four years in Asia.

MANAGING CULTURAL
DIFFERENCES
NINTH EDITION

Robert T. Moran, Neil Remington
Abramson and Sarah V. Moran

Routledge
Taylor & Francis Group

LONDON AND NEW YORK

Eighth edition published 2011
by Butterworth-Heinemann

Ninth edition published 2014
by Routledge
2 Park Square, Milton Park, Abingdon, Oxon OX14 4RN

and by Routledge
711 Third Avenue, New York, NY 10017

Routledge is an imprint of the Taylor & Francis Group, an informa business

British Library Cataloguing in Publication Data
A catalogue record for this book is available from the British Library

Library of Congress Cataloging in Publication Data
Moran, Robert T.,
Managing cultural differences / Robert T. Moran, Neil Remington Abramson
and Sarah V. Moran. – 9th edition.
  pages cm
Earlier editions published as: Managing cultural differences / Philip R. Harris,
Robert T. Moran.
Includes bibliographical references and index.
1. International business enterprises–Management. 2. Management–Cross-cultural
studies. 3. Acculturation. 4. Cross-cultural studies. I. Abramson, Neil R.,
II. Moran, Sarah V. (Sarah Virgilia), III. Harris, Philip R. (Philip Robert), Managing
cultural differences. IV. Title.
HD62.4.H37 2014
658.1'8–dc23

2013033933

ISBN: 978-0-415-71734-2 (hbk)
ISBN: 978-0-415-71735-9 (pbk)
ISBN: 978-1-315-87141-7 (ebk)

Typeset in Berthold Akzidenz Grotesk
by RefineCatch Limited, Bungay, Suffolk
Printed and bound by Ashford Colour Press Ltd

To Philip R. Harris who first suggested writing a book on Managing Cultural Differences in 1977. Since then he has been a consistent contributor and valued colleague.

Robert T. Moran

With special thanks to my family for your constant support: Haruyo, Karen, Ikkei, Ryoko, Tomoka, and Sumire. In faith, hope, and love.

Neil Remington Abramson

To my parents, whose global humanitarian lives have influenced me profoundly, and to every person who has crossed my path whose diversity of backgrounds, ethnicities, cultures, and world views have opened my eyes and mind. You have all taught me that through respect and developing a deep understanding of what makes each of us unique, that humankind, in all our wonderful diversity, can find ways to harmoniously live and work together.

Sarah V. Moran

CONTENTS

CONTENTS ▪▪▪▪

EXHIBITS

FOREWORD

Each day I drive down the road to my office: the route that connects New Delhi, the capital city of India, to the home of the Taj Mahal, Agra. From the humble bullock cart to the technological and engineering marvel, the latest limousine; from the farmer carrying his harvest to the market to the Ivy League educated executive; from the cows, to the trucks and the crowded buses, everyone seemingly has equal right to space on the road. Yet in all of this chaos, each person seems to be headed somewhere with intent.

One often wonders what overseas visitors, especially businesspersons, would think of this on their first visit to India. Would the Westerners, who are perhaps "goal-focused" ponder how they will meet their objectives in this chaos? Would the Chinese, who are perhaps used to "order," contemplate how they will achieve their goals? What is the Indian, who is used to "ambiguity," thinking? What if they are actually members of the same global company, perhaps part of the same team that has been tasked to execute a time-bound project?

Having worked with Japanese, Indian, American, and British MNCs, I am often reminded of my early days in one of the first Indo-Japanese JVs in India almost three decades ago, when the Indian and the Japanese teams prepared two entirely different time plans for setting up the same project in India. One of the major points of contention, fairly simple it may seem, was the time it would take to bring component parts from the south to the north of India, a journey of over 2,000 km. The Indian team had ten days, and the Japanese five, in their respective estimates. This variance applied to most other activities in the project plan as well, with the overall project estimate varying from 18 to 30 months depending on who one asked. The matter was resolved amicably at 26 months after both teams were asked to experience the 2,000 km journey by traveling together.

After this episode, which is described below in greater detail, all other issues of contention fell into place, as both teams made it a point to experience all areas of differences together and develop countermeasures for each activity. A joint team made the presentation to the Indo-Japanese Board. The JV went on to become a huge success. What brought this about was the underlying, unwritten, understanding of one anothers' point of view taken in the context of culture.

India is a land where there are 1.2 billion people, with 22 official languages, 1,596 dialects, 7 major religions, where chaos seems the only order; where day after tomorrow could mean any day after two; where people are comfortable with making improvisations based on context on a continual basis to accommodate the constantly changing plans of others. And yet, within this chaos there are world class companies, extremely successful, operating in India.

So, I return to the 2,000-km journey from the south to the north. On the very first day, we had to postpone our departure because of a "bandh" (a general strike) called by a Southern State to protest a river water sharing dispute that went back over five decades. We did set off on the second day and had several interesting experiences together. Road signages in India are difficult to come by, so one often had to stop to ask local passers-by for directions. The directions are "approximate" — turn right from the yellow house with the clothes line, left from the small biscuit shop, etc. Also, since we in India often speak only three languages each, and there is often no overlap in script amongst the 22 languages officially recognized, communication cannot therefore be taken for granted.

We passed trucks with broken axles, not because their quality was sub-standard, but because overloading was the norm and not the exception. We were invited into homes for meals, though we were complete strangers and of course we accepted some invitations. Food was often served on banana leaves or in "thaalis" (a round steel tray). The entire meal was served simultaneously including the dessert. Our Japanese guests noticed that the food was mixed by the person eating it in the proportion that he or she liked it best. It was therefore "approximate." In contrast, in the West and even in Japan, precise quantities are served — by course.

Our Japanese colleagues being used to "precision, tight tolerances, just-in-time," began to understand that at least within the new JV and its supply chain, an enormous cultural change from "approximation" to "precision" would be required. It was this understanding that was the critical factor that laid the foundation to a successful JV. Needless to say, our Japanese colleagues made extensive notes at every stage.

I first had the privilege of meeting Professor Moran in India and later in the United Kingdom during modules that he was conducting for our future global leadership team based on the title of his book *Managing Cultural Differences*. In a program comprising seven distinct modules covering finance, strategy, operation, etc., his module was rated as the very best — the most appropriate and relevant and he personally as the most articulate Professor — by the participants, our future leaders representing, Brazil, China, India, the United Kingdom, and the United States. It enabled the participants to better understand one another especially from a cultural context and therefore arrive at synergistic decisions during these discussions. The unspoken "whys" of the opinions of one another were much better appreciated. Most participants recommended that this be the very first module in the future!

Most global managers, aspiring or otherwise, are challenged by a highly dynamic environment even in the land of their own birth, which only becomes more complex as they step on to the shores of others. It is how they are able to empower themselves to leverage the power of culture to maximize organizational performance in a cross-cultural environment that will determine their ultimate success. To my mind, it is not humanly possible or even necessary to be an expert in all cultures, but it is important for us to develop a local cultural sensitivity within an overall global context.

In its ninth edition, the authors maintain the theme that our global world is changing; complex and sophisticated skills are not only helpful but necessary for today's global leaders, managers, and travelers. However, most chapters have been reorganized and there is significant new material. A sampling includes new sections on how parents, teachers, and society influence the factual knowledge and attitudes of children, how non-violent communication can reduce cross cultural misunderstandings and ways organizational and individual learning is impacted under crisis change conditions. Women, in roles as global leaders, have made progress but the world in which they live and work is not equal. Diversity in all aspects with integration results in high performance and a competitive advantage are themes in two chapters. Suggestions for more skillfully planning global transitions and leading teams to become "high performing" are new sections. There is a new chapter on the emerging markets. The second part of the book covers the cultural factors including what to do and what not to do as well as what visitors should know in order to work or travel in many countries.

Finally, I would like to thank the authors, Professor Robert Moran, Dr. Neil Remington Abramson, and Sarah Moran; with special thanks in particular to Professor Moran for giving me the opportunity of penning the Foreward to *Managing Cultural Differences*, ninth edition.

The subject of *Managing Cultural Differences* is a must-learn and must-read text for every business school; in fact for every aspiring and practicing business leader. The book is perhaps the most comprehensive, easy to relate to and therefore to understand, that I have had the pleasure of reading. I am sure all readers, will benefit immensely from it as much as I have!

Vipin Sondhi
MD and CEO
JCB India Limited
New Delhi
India

PROLOGUE

In a recent private sale of "everything in the house" the owner who was a man in response to a question of a buyer "why are you selling everything?" said "I have just been divorced and my new wife said to me 'get rid of everything old, we want to start with all new things.'"

In the ninth edition we have kept a lot of the old because we believe the material is good and many readers and reviewers have agreed. Dr. Neil Remington Abramson, Associate Professor of Strategy at Simon Fraser University in Vancouver is adding much new. We welcome him to our team.

With all old and new material we continue to strive for balance between theory and practice and for readers to find immediate application and relevance to their studies or to their global responsibilities.

Robert T. Moran, Ph.D.
Paradise Valley, Arizona, United States
Neil Remington Abramson, Ph.D.
Vancouver, British Columbia, Canada
Sarah V. Moran, M.A.
Chicago, Illinois, United States

ACKNOWLEDGMENTS

When one begins any project, it is difficult to predict, with accuracy, subsequent successes, challenges, or failures. The first edition of *Managing Cultural Differences* was published in 1979. We did not anticipate the success of our book.

As authors we are humbled and grateful to all readers who have honored us by allowing us to influence them by considering the ideas in the various editions. We thank you.

Vipin Sondhi, Managing Director and CEO, JCB India Limited, is unusual among the many executives we have worked with over the years. He is brilliant. In this he is not so unique, as most executives are quite smart. But he has emotional intelligence to a very high degree and always leads with his head and with his heart. We thank you for writing the Foreword.

Georgia Lessard is a very valued colleague at Thunderbird who again was supportive in all ways as we produced a document to send to the publisher. David Varley, Nicola Cupit, and Emily Davies were among the best in providing support and direction we have experienced in any previous publishing venture. Thank you.

We acknowledge and thank Haruyo Abramson who solved complex formatting difficulties.

Jonathan Piskor checked facts in several chapters and made a number of suggestions for changes and drafted ideas for additional paragraphs. We wish you success in your career.

We also thank the many professors and other readers of previous editions who gave us feedback which we hope have strengthen this edition.

Robert T. Moran, Neil Remington Abramson, Sarah V. Moran

1 GLOBAL LEADERS, CULTURE, AND A CHANGING WORLD

The world has changed, and so must people living in this changed global world. But not everything has changed.

The premise of this book is simple: just as no two individuals are exactly the same, neither are two nations of societies. However, the people in the same culture share certain things in common which are not necessarily shared by people of another culture. This is the reality.

Our goal is to help readers think or rethink many aspects related to the attitudes and skills we all need to survive and thrive in today's global environment. Or, to write it more simply: to learn to live and work with differences. Hence, the title of our book, *Managing Cultural Differences*.

In the early stages of socialization, the parents or caregivers of children from all cultures have a major influence on how their children behave and their values and attitudes. The parental influence example illustrates this point.[1]

AN EXAMPLE OF PARENTAL INFLUENCE

When I began delivering executive seminars for a particular large global company about eight years ago with a professional colleague, his presentations to executives were good but not great according to the ratings of attendees. Feedback was that they were a little too academic in contrast with a different style which included "stories" to illustrate academic points. Over the years, he has included more and more stories to illustrate what he wants participants to remember and use.

I suspect some of his stories have fabricated elements, but he recently told the following, which illustrated to me the influence of parents on children.

"My wife is Republican and listens regularly at home and in the car to conservative talk shows. Often, our two boys are in the car with her. I am registered Independent but often vote for a Democrat, and I voted for Obama. My wife voted for McCain, the Republican candidate in 2008.

On election day, the boys went to bed at the regular time, but I stayed up till it was clear Obama would win. I was thrilled. My wife was depressed.

My younger son, who was nine years old at the time, got up first and asked me, 'Dad, who won?' When I told him Obama won, he began to weep uncontrollably. I hugged him and told him it is going to be OK that Obama won, and don't worry.

He then said, 'But Obama will tax my allowance.' When I told him that Obama was not going to tax his $2.00-a-week allowance, he stopped crying."

Parents, indeed, influence their children.

As parents and caregivers gradually lose their ability to influence us, teachers, religious leaders, and textbooks, as well as our children's friends and peers, become increasingly major influences in their lives. The following examples are from textbooks in several different countries taken from an article in *The Economist*. They are illustrations of how governments and school districts in selected countries attempt to control ideology by the textbooks they allow and what is written in them. The examples cited are from the Georg Eckert Institute,[2] which studies textbooks from 160 countries covering history and geography.

- From Saudi Arabian textbooks, "The Jews and Christians are enemies of the true believers" is written and probably results in intolerance towards Jews and Christians.
- In China, there was an attempt to introduce a curriculum of national education which omitted the events of the Cultural Revolution and Tiananmen Square.
- In Japan, textbooks whitewash and gloss over Japanese World War II war crimes.

- In the United States, many textbooks play down slavery and the killing of many Indian tribes.
- In an Israeli textbook, Palestinians are depicted as refugees, farmers, and terrorists.
- In the United States in 2012, about 25 percent of students in public schools are Hispanic, yet most of the main characters in children's texts read by Hispanics are white.

We believe that children are not born with prejudice but it is learned, and bias and the resulting xenophobia are present in most, if not all, cultures. In fact, we could say we live in xenophobic times — for proof, just pick up any newspaper and we can see prejudice towards people who are not quite like us and minority groups that is often accompanied by cruelty.

In Andrew Solomon's wonderful book, *Far from the Tree*,[3] he writes that most children share some traits with their parents or caregivers. He calls these "vertical identities" which are passed down through strands of DNA and cultural/family traditions. Solomon cites skin color, language, religion, and nationality as examples.

There are also acquired traits which he refers to as horizontal identities which are different from one's parents and are acquired from a peer group. Being gay is a horizontal identity, as most gay kids are born of straight parents.

Some things have NOT CHANGED or changed very little over the past few years.

Russia is still the largest country in the world by size. Everest is the tallest mountain, and the Nile is the longest river — which is 179 miles longer than the Amazon. The Sahara is the largest desert by far. Greenland is the largest island, and China has the most people. Tokyo is the world's largest city by population: 38,000,000. But did you know the facts in the Did You Know box?

DID YOU KNOW?

- Twenty-five percent of the population in China with the highest IQs and 28 percent in India are greater than the total population of North America. Implication for parents, teachers, and politicians — China and India have more honor kids than most, if not all countries.
- China will soon be the number one English-speaking country in the world.
- Every 6 minutes, 60 babies will be born in the United States, 244 babies will be born in China, and 351 babies will be born in India.
- In the United States, one out of two people are working for a company for whom they have worked less than five years.
- The top 10 jobs that are in demand in 2010 didn't exist in 2004, according to a former U.S. Secretary of Education.
- One out of eight couples married in the United States in 2006 met online.

■ If *MySpace* were a country, it would be the 11th largest in the world.
■ There are over 2.7 billion searches performed on Google each month.
■ The amount of new technical information is doubling every two years.

Source: From *Did You Know?* By Karl Fisch and Scott McLeod. Adapted by Sony BMG. Full presentation can be viewed at http://www.youtube.com/watch?v=jpEnFwiqdx8.

Vérité en-deçà des Pyrénées, erreur au delà. (There are truths on this side of the Pyrenees that are falsehoods on the other.)[4]

In 1492, Christopher Columbus set sail for India, going west . . . he called the people he met "Indians" and came home and reported to his king and queen, "The world is round." I set off for India 512 years later . . . I went east . . . I came home and reported only to my wife and only in a whisper, "The world is flat."[5]

The real voyage of discovery consists not in seeking new landscapes but in having new eyes.

Marcel Proust, French novelist, 1871–1922

The important thing is not to stop questioning. Curiosity has its own reason for existing.

Albert Einstein

ENCOURAGING CURIOSITY IN CHILDREN

Although I wouldn't encourage my two-year-old to stick his fingers down a spider hole in the African soil where he is being raised, I try and foster his sense of curiosity and his desire to learn. Can he climb to the top of the water tank? Sure; I will be right behind him. What does that flame feel like? Let's find out; I'll guide his fingers close enough to it so he won't get burned.

Today, academics, psychologists, teachers, parents, and even business leaders are being encouraged to not only be curious themselves but to nurture curiosity in their employees. Curiosity is linked to innovation, exploration, drive, growth, and solving challenges . . . and to learning about other people and cultures.

Most people are comfortable with what they know and with ideas and people that are very much like themselves.

Curiosity leads to learning and to seeing with new eyes what is in our rich resource world.

Source: Rebecca Moran, pilot in Tanzania, 2004–2013.

In the twenty-first century, leaders in business, government, and the professions cope with the phenomenon of globalization. It prompts them to cross borders more frequently and to communicate with persons from other cultures, either in person or electronically.

This chapter provides a rationale and an imperative for all individuals working "globally" to understand and respect their counterparts, and to develop the skills required to work effectively in today's complex world. Ways to analyze and understand other cultures are presented, along with how to use the suggested strategies. Seeing global issues through "multiple lens" or "by hearing with new ears" is also important.

Why does the world appear flat to some, round to others, and what are the advantages or disadvantages of either? Thomas Friedman writes about his insights during an interview with Nandan Nilekani, CEO of Infosys Technologies Limited:

> "Outsourcing is just one dimension of a much more fundamental thing happening today in the world," Nilekani explained. "What happened over the last (few) years is that there was a massive investment in technology, especially in the bubble era, when hundreds of millions of dollars were invested in putting broadband connectivity around the world, undersea cables, all those things." At the same time, he added, computers became cheaper and dispersed all over the world, and there was an explosion of software e-mail, search engines like Google, and proprietary software that can chop up any piece of work and send one part to Boston, one part to Bangalore, and one part to Beijing, making it easy for anyone to do remote development. When all of these things suddenly came together around 2000, added Nilekani, they created a platform where intellectual work, intellectual capital, could be delivered from anywhere. It could be disaggregated, delivered, distributed, produced, and put back together again — and this gave a whole new degree of freedom to the way we do work, especially work of an intellectual nature. ... And what you are seeing in Bangalore today is really the culmination of all these things coming together.[6]

The point is, the playing field in the global marketplace is being leveled for some, and thus "flat." That is an advantage for many and a disadvantage for others. In either view, cultural competing is a requirement. Culture does count.

The coauthors of this book have worked for global organizations for many years. In the 1960s and early 1970s, we had to convince many business and government leaders that "culture counts." From the industrialized world, the perspective often voiced was, "We tell them what to do, and if they want to work with us, they do it." This is rarely or never the situation today.

We no longer have to convince anyone with any global experience that *culture counts*. And when organizations, nongovernmental organizations (NGOs), and political organizations ignore, dismiss, or minimize culture, the costs are often significant. This

LEARNING OBJECTIVES

chapter will present proven frameworks, models, and paradigms relevant to working skillfully in today's global business and geopolitical world. We believe managing cultural differences skillfully for all individuals, organizations, NGOs, and governments from all countries is a human and business imperative. Understanding the environment is a fundamental requirement for maintaining a competitive advantage. To successfully adapt to changes in the environment is a requirement for survival. Culture impacts relationships and business operations. Schein states it profoundly:

> Consider any complex, potentially volatile issue — Arab relations, the problems between Serbs, Croats, and Bosnians, corporate decision-making, getting control of the U.S. deficit, or healthcare costs, labor/management relations, and so on. At the root of the issue, we are likely to find communication failures and cultural misunderstandings that prevent the parties from framing the problem in a common way, and thus make it impossible to deal with the problem constructively.[7]

Also supporting the notion that "culture" is important is Alan Greenspan, former chairman of the U.S. Federal Reserve. Greenspan stated that he originally believed that capitalism was "human nature."[8]

After the collapse of the Soviet economy, however, he concluded that "it was not human nature at all, but culture." Culture is finding its place of significance in the experience of global individuals.

Cultures have always been distinct, mostly separate and independent. Over the past 100 years, and especially during the last 25, cultures and nations have remained unique, but have become increasingly more interconnected in complex and nonobvious ways. This book covers many topics, but the threads of culture, differences, and leadership run throughout.

> In the early 1990s, I happened to come across early 1960s economic data on Ghana and South Korea, and I was astonished to see how similar their economies were at that time. These two countries had roughly comparable levels of per capita gross national product (GNP); similar divisions of their economy among primary products, manufacturing, and services; and overwhelmingly primary product exports, with South Korea producing a few manufactured goods. They were also receiving comparable levels of economic aid. Thirty years later, South Korea had become an industrial giant with the fourteenth largest economy in the world. No such changes had occurred in Ghana, whose per capita GNP was now about one-fifteenth that of South Korea's. How could this extraordinary difference in development be explained? Undoubtedly, many factors played a role, but it seemed to me that culture had to be a large part of the explanation. South Koreans value thrift, investment, hard work, education, organization, and discipline. Ghanaians had different values.[9]

In short, culture counts.

Diamond's[10] statement that, "We all know that history has proceeded very differently for peoples from different parts of the globe," is one we can all agree with. The specific data that humans all came from Africa are not disputed. Diamond questions, why did different people develop in different ways? His answer, "History followed different courses for different peoples because of differences in peoples' environments, not because of biological differences among peoples themselves."[11]

Change is also a part of our daily lives, and impacts all. If culture counts, managing cultural differences or skillfully leading in a global world becomes of paramount importance. Most of the following events took place after the year 2000 and share aspects of culture, differences, conflict, consequences, and leadership.

"An internationalist without being indifferent to members of one's tribe." — Albert Einstein wrote the words in a letter to a friend in 1919. Einstein was a genius, but these words suggest he was also quite wise.

The following examples are relevant and from the experiences of Robert Moran.[12] He was born in Canada, where he lived for 25 years, then moved to Japan and later settled in the United States. His stories, therefore, have a North American flavor.

Example 1: *A friendly encounter*

In our neighborhood, trash is picked up every Monday and Thursday. I was born and spent my early years in Canada, and everyone then called the trash "garbage." One of my early chores as a young boy was to take out the garbage.

I still take out the garbage, usually on a Sunday night for an early Monday morning pickup. One Sunday, as I left a full bucket on our street, I met a neighbor who was taking her dog for a walk. We exchanged friendly pleasantries, and she asked about our adult children. She was genuinely interested.

"Elizabeth is still living and working in France," I said, "and we are about to have a second American/French grandchild." I told her that Sarah was working in Taiwan, Molly was in San Francisco working for the Gap, Rebecca was a volunteer bush pilot in Tanzania flying medical personnel to the Masaai, and Ben, our youngest, was in West Africa finishing his first year as a Peace Corps volunteer.

Our neighbor looked at me, and in a matter-of-fact way responded, "Well, at least you have one 'normal' one."

We believe our five adult children are all "normal," at least most of the time. Working and living in San Francisco — and working in Taiwan — are equally "normal" in today's world.

Example 2: *You can't trust the French*

Many years before the above encounter, around the 1990s, I took a sabbatical from the Thunderbird School of Global Management, where I have been a faculty member since

L
E
A
R
N
I
N
G
O
B
J
E
C
T
I
V
E
S

1976. With two stuffed duffel bags each, my spouse and I left for France with our five young children. I was going to teach at a grande école — a French Ivy League university — in the suburbs of Paris. We wanted our children to learn another language and have a genuine experience of another culture.

For several weeks, we had not yet met any other foreigners as we tried to find an affordable used car, a house to rent, and schools for our children. We had only met French people who, without exception, helped us figure out how things worked in their sometimes-bureaucratic country.

Our youngest child, Ben, however, who was seven at the time, had met an American whose name was Jack, and he asked if Jack could come over and have dinner with us. We immediately agreed. As it was my turn to cook, with the help of my eldest daughter, we decided that fish — four trout from the local marché — would be the entree.

As Jack was our guest, I presented the fish on a platter to him first. As I did this, my daughter said, from across the table, "Be careful, everyone, there may be some small bones in the fish." Jack, also seven years old, looked at me and responded, "Okay … (sigh) … You know, you just can't trust the French."

Surprised at his comment, I asked him where he had first heard it.

"My mother says that all the time," he responded.

Later that night, when I was dropping him off at his home, I met Jack's mother. She told me that she hated living in Europe and wanted to go home to the United States. She was lonesome, missed her friends, and did not really like living in France.

Of course, there is nothing abnormal about being lonely and finding a new environment difficult to adapt to. But her feelings and attitudes clearly influenced Jack, who might have been less disparaging and closed to his new environment had she felt differently.

Example 3: *The all-American girl*

Last spring, as my work at the university slowed down, my spouse and I were able to spend a little more time together, and we were ready for a new adventure. So we rented a small house in the French countryside, thinking that we would spend our time studying French, the first language of two of our grandchildren.

When my spouse told one of her friends that we were leaving for several weeks, her friend responded, "That's not for me — I'm an all-American girl!"

Remaining an "all-American" would be a safe bet, I suppose, if the world in which we live had not changed drastically since the 1990s from huge forces of globalization. In fact, leading economists comfortably predict that in a generation, the center of worldwide economic activity will shift out of the United States and into Asia, where countries are already preparing to take over this role.

Our world has been most influenced by the victors of a war that concluded over half of a century ago — namely, the United States, Western Europe, and Russia — but rising economic powers such as India, Brazil, and China are increasingly asserting themselves in the international arena. The United States will no longer be able to maintain its role as sole superpower.

But many people, including global businessfolks, to my great alarm, believe otherwise.

In order for all people to better prepare themselves for this tectonic shift, a new way of thinking is necessary. Those who learn new ways of living in a globalized world will have the tools necessary to step forward and participate, and even lead. Those who stick to being "all-American," however, will in all likelihood be left out of the process altogether.

Indeed, being a *global American* is, in many ways, just as important for all Americans as being a *global company* is for most, if not all, of American organizations, if they are to succeed in today's world. Companies that were late in adapting to the new global economy are struggling to catch up. The same must also be true for Germans, Japanese, Saudis, Indians, Nigerians, and people of all nations.

Such a shift in paradigm is not impossible. About five hundred years ago, after the earth was discovered to rotate around the Sun, humanity had to give up the then-held belief that the earth was at the center of the universe. It simply wasn't. Giving up old ideas or ideas that don't work, or ideas that are inaccurate, is difficult.

New skills and attitudes are required for businesspeople, students, and all individuals to find our way in a new and rapidly changing world. Being at ease in other cultures, and having the global awareness and curiosity that is necessary to follow the rapid transformations taking place outside our borders — *and even inside of them —* are important ingredients in a global psyche.

Global people are already active in the fields of politics, business, academics, healthcare and in other professions and walks of life. Indeed, millions — yes, millions — of individuals already live and work in countries other than their own. But today, it is increasingly important that every person develop a global attitude as well. We can no longer leave this to government or business leaders.

Importantly, the major issues that the world may be facing in this century, that is, tectonic shifts in the global economy, terrorism, global warming and increased pollution, mass migration, and the threat of global epidemics (just to name a few), are not issues that any country, even if it wanted to, could deal with alone. An increased collaboration with other countries and organizations across a wide spectrum of cultures will be fundamental to overcoming these challenges.

Not only global Americans, but also global French, Saudi, Chinese, and others

One final incident demonstrates an important motivation that I have held since the 1990s.

LEARNING OBJECTIVES

During executive business seminars that I teach, I am often asked, "Is it only Americans who have to be global? What about the rest of the world?" I usually respond by relating the following incident.

Many years ago, in New York, I was in the office of a senior vice president of a very large U.S.-based company. A person who reported to the senior vice president, and who had just returned from Asia to conclude an important contract, was invited to meet me. During the meeting, he told me that the deal in Asia should be canceled, as he explained, "they don't understand us, or our business, and they are arrogant."

The senior vice president, in my presence, responded angrily, "If they are arrogant, don't understand us — or whatever — I expect you to be that much more skillful. If you tell me how bad anyone else is again, I'll fire you."

Talk about tension!

A global person

Warren Buffett, the CEO of Berkshire Hathaway and one of the world's most successful, influential, and wealthy individuals, is quoted as saying, "Only when the tides goes out do you find out who is not wearing a bathing suit."

Globalization is exposing most countries to more interactions and relationships with people and products from other countries, yet many people from different countries are not prepared to work, live, and prosper in a global and highly competitive new world.

In an Apple white paper,[13] the authors cited a 2002 National Geographic Study as follows:

> Eighty-five percent of 18- to 24-year-old Americans were unable to locate Afghanistan and Iraq on a map, despite the fact that the United States was at war or publicly preparing for war in both countries. Sixty-nine percent were unable to locate Great Britain, and 29 percent were unable to find the Pacific Ocean.

But what is a global person? A global person does not believe that his/her nation is the best at everything and that everyone else wants to be just like him/her — rather he/she is aware that other cultures of the world have lives and viewpoints different from his/her own. A global person may not speak more than one language or have lived in another country. He/she may not even own a passport. However, a global person is aware of and interested in the issues of people around the world. He/she is empathetic and sensitive, and has skills in interacting with people who may not look like, talk like, smell like, or act like him/her.

"Worldmindedness" — a global awareness of other cultures and people (in many ways, the opposite of hate and fear) — is a trait that can be taught, just like language.

The growing importance of other countries in the global arena should not be a threat, but an opportunity for cultural education, growth, and creativity.

In the *Sage Handbook of Intercultural Competence*,[14] many models and paradigms are identified to describe an interculturally competent individual. In most models, there are a knowledge component (knowledge of self, knowledge of other cultures, etc.), a skill component (showing respect, listening, accurately interpreting meanings, etc.), and an attitudinal component (globally minded, not believing one's way is the best or only way, etc.). All can be learned. Knowledge is easier to acquire than a skill to act on. Learning a skill is easier than transforming an ethnocentric attitude. We will start with culture and a short definition: "culture is the way we do things here."

It is important to remember the following, however:

1   All people are to some extent like all other people. This is the universal aspect which all humans share. All people are to some extent unique. This is the individual aspect, and no two human beings are exactly the same. All people are to some extent like some other people. This is the cultural aspect which we share, in part, with people from our own tribe (as Einstein said).

2   Culture is learned. This learning is on the basis of the following statements: An individual's early childhood experiences exert a lasting effect on his/her personality. Psychologists, sociologists, anthropologists, and others accept this. The issues being studied are the critical ages and the specific experiences. The early childhood experiences and parenting practices vary from culture to culture. As a result, if a child of a U.S. white woman were to be adopted by a Chinese couple living in a village in China, that child would learn to speak, read, and write Chinese, and behave like most of the other children in the village, but look more like the U.S. mother than any others in the village. He or she would behave like a Chinese boy or girl and learn Chinese values.

We begin with culture.

CULTURE

Culture is a distinctly human means of adapting to circumstances and transmitting this coping skill and knowledge to subsequent generations. Culture gives people a sense of who they are, of belonging, of how they should behave, and of what they should be doing. Culture impacts behavior, morale, and productivity at work, and includes values and patterns that influence company attitudes and actions. Culture is dynamic. Cultures change . . . but slowly.

Culture is often considered the driving force behind human behavior everywhere. The concept has become the context to explain politics, economics, progress, and failures. In that regard, Huntington[15] has written:

It is my hypothesis that the fundamental source of human conflict in this new world will not be primarily ideological or primarily economic. The great divisions among human-kind and the dominating source of conflict will be culture.

Culture and cultural identities are shaping the patterns of cohesion, disintegra-tion, and conflict in the post-cold war world. Global politics is being reconfigured along cultural lines . . . peoples and countries with similar culture are coming together. Peoples and countries with different cultures are coming apart.

Prior to entering a new market, forming a partnership, or buying a company, organiza-tions spend time and money on "due diligence." What is forgotten or minimized in both busi-ness and politics is "cultural due diligence." The following models or frameworks on cultural analysis might be important in any due diligence exercise that has a cultural component. Chomsky et al.,[16] for example, demonstrate the ability to master an incredible wealth of factual knowledge, and these skills exemplify political due diligence. Lewis[17] demonstrates the impor-tance of cultural due diligence for business. Globally minded individuals did this routinely.

The following 10 categories are a means for understanding either a macroculture or a microculture, and can be useful for studying any group of people, whether they live in the rural south of the United States, India, the bustling city of Hong Kong, Bangalore, Arusha in Tanzania, or Baghdad in Iraq.

Sense of self and space. The comfort one has with self can be expressed differently by culture. Self-identity and appreciation can be manifested by humble bearing in one culture and by macho behavior in another. Americans have a sense of space that requires more distance between individuals than Latins or Arabs.

Communication and language. The communication system, verbal and nonverbal, distinguishes one group from another. It is estimated that there are less than 7,000 human languages today.[18] Apart from the multitude of "foreign" languages, some nations have 15 or more major spoken languages (within one language group there are dialects, accents, slang, jargon, and other such variations). The meanings given to gestures, for example, often differ by culture (see examples in Chapter 3).

Dress and appearance. This includes the outward garments and adornments, as well as body decorations that tend to be culturally distinctive. We are aware of the Japanese kimono, the African headdress, the Englishman's umbrella, and the Polynesian sarong.

Food and feeding habits. The manner in which food is selected, prepared, presented, and eaten often differs by culture. One man's pet is another person's delicacy. Americans love beef, yet it is forbidden to Hindus, while the forbidden food in Muslim and Jewish culture is pork, eaten extensively by the Chinese and others. Using one's hands, chopsticks, or knives and forks to eat also vary by location.

Time and time consciousness. Sense of time differs by culture – some are exact and others are relative. Generally, Germans are precise about the clock, while many Latins are more casual. In some cultures, promptness is determined by age or status. Thus, in some countries, subordinates are expected on time at staff meetings, but the boss is the last to arrive. Yet, there are people in some other cultures who do not bother with hours or minutes, but manage their days by sunrise and sunset.

A FRIENDLY SOLUTION

Guillaume is a fast-paced expatriate pilot originally from Paris. He drives quickly and walks with purpose. Naturally friendly, he chats with locals — when he has time. On his way to work, he is often late and rarely has time; he blames this on the local pace.

Rebecca, also an expatriate pilot, understands the local culture and works with it. Without rush and little effort, she moves mostly unhindered.

On her drive to work, she slows down to give an airport worker a ride. It is here that Guillaume goes zipping by.

A minute later, Guillaume comes to a skidding halt at the airport gate, where his morning's frustrations begin.

The guard is stirring his tea. He waits until the dust settles, then looks up to see an expatriate in a hurry. He puts down his mug and stretches his arms. He checks the weather, slides on his jacket, and strolls out to open the gate. The process takes no more than two minutes, but it drives the fast-paced pilot crazy every morning.

When the gate finally swings open, it is for Rebecca, who coasts through with a wave and friendly smile. The guard is still inspecting Guillaume's car.

Guillaume will check in at his plane four minutes late again. For him, working in this culture is frustrating and full of unnecessary delays.

The pace at which different cultures operate varies drastically across the globe. For most Westerners, time is money and life is rushed; but far from Wall Street, Swahili culture moves with the saying, "Hurry, hurry, and you'll lose the blessings."

A hurried expatriate in Africa can expect to be slowed down.

Rebecca, who has lived all over the world, has found a solution that seems to work for her everywhere. Regardless of her rush, she takes time to greet people. As a result, when the guard at the gate sees her coming, he has the gate open before she arrives.

By slowing down to be friendly she is able to maintain her fast pace. Unlike Guillaume, she arrives at her plane smiling and on time.

When it comes to dealing with cultural differences, there is nothing more important than being friendly.

Source: Jay, Ezra, *Tanzania*, 2013.

Relationships. Many cultures fix human and organizational relationships by age, gender, status, and degree of kindred, as well as by wealth, power, and wisdom. The family unit is the most common expression of this characteristic, and the arrangement may go from small to large — in a Hindu household, the joint family may include under one roof, mother, father, children, parents, uncles, aunts, and cousins. In fact, one's physical location in such houses may also be determined, with men on one side of the house, women on the other.

Relationships between and among people vary by category – in some cultures, the elderly are honored, whereas in others they are ignored; in some cultures, women must wear veils and appear deferential, while in others the woman is considered the equal, if not the superior, of the man.

Values and norms. The values of a culture, or subculture, determine behavior.

From the value system, a culture sets norms of behavior for that society. These acceptable standards for membership may range from work ethic or pleasure to absolute obedience or permissiveness for children; from rigid submission of the wife to her husband to a more equal relationship. The globalization process and telecommunications are leading to the development of some shared values that cross borders and express planetary concerns, such as protection of the environment.[19]

Beliefs and attitudes. Possibly the most difficult classification is ascertaining the major belief themes of a people, and how this and other factors influence their attitudes toward themselves, others, and what happens in their world. People in all cultures seem to have a concern for the supernatural that is evident in their religions and religious practices. Western culture seems to be largely influenced by the Judeo-Christian-Islamic traditions, while Eastern or Asian cultures have been dominated by Buddhism, Confucianism, Taoism, and Hinduism. Religion, to a degree, expresses the philosophy of a people about important facets of life and is influenced by culture, and vice versa.

Mental process and learning. Some cultures emphasize one aspect of brain development over another, so that one may observe striking differences in the way people think and learn. Anthropologist Edward Hall maintains that the mind is internalized culture, and the mental process involves how people organize and process information. Life in a particular locale defines the rewards and punishment for learning or not learning certain information or in a certain way, and this is confirmed and reinforced by the culture. For example, Germans stress logic, while logic for a Hopi Indian is on the basis of preserving the integrity of his/her social system and all the relationships connected with it.

Work habits and practices. Another dimension of a group's culture is its attitude toward work – the dominant types of work, the division of work, and the work habits or practices, such as promotions or incentives. Work has been defined as exertion or effort directed to produce or accomplish something. Some cultures espouse a work ethic in which all members are expected to engage in a desirable and worthwhile activity. In other societies, this is broadly defined to include cultural pursuits in music and the arts or sports. For some cultures, the worthiness of the activity is narrowly measured in terms of income produced, or the worth of the individual is assessed in terms of job status.

These ten general classifications are a basic model for assessing a particular culture. It does not include every aspect of culture, nor is it the only way to analyze culture. This approach enables one to examine a people systemically. The categories are a beginning means of cultural understanding as one travels and visits different cultures. Likewise, the model can be used to study the microcultures within a majority national culture. All aspects of culture are interrelated, and to change one part is to change the whole. There is a danger in trying to compartmentalize a complex concept like culture, while trying to retain a sense of its whole. Culture is a complex system of interrelated parts that must be understood holistically.

SYSTEMS APPROACH TO CULTURE

There are many different anthropological approaches to cultural analysis, and many prefer to use a coordinated systems approach as an alternative to understanding other cultures. A system, in this sense, refers to an ordered assemblage or combination of correlated parts that form a unitary whole.[20]

Kinship system. The family relationships and the way a people reproduce, train, and socialize their children, and the typical North American family is a nuclear and rather independent unit. In many countries, there may be an extended family that consists of several generations held together through the male line (patrilineal) or through the female line (matrilineal). Such families have a powerful influence on child rearing, and often on nation building.

Educational system. How young or new members of a society are provided with information, knowledge, skills, and values may be formal and informal within any culture. How people learn varies by culture.

Economic system. The manner in which the society produces and distributes its goods and services is in some ways an extension of the family and in Japan is group-oriented. Until recently, the world was divided into capitalistic or socialistic economic blocs, and economies were labeled *First World* (advanced free enterprise systems); *Second World* (socialist or communistic societies based on centralized planning and control); and *Third World* (developing nations moving from the agricultural to industrial or postindustrial stages). These categories are now outdated. Today, economies are mixed – some supposed Third World economies have high technology sectors, as in India and China; and Second World, formerly in the European Eastern Bloc, are in transition to free market systems, such as in Poland or Lithuania. Another trend beyond national economies is toward regional economic cooperatives or associations that cut across national and ideological boundaries, such as is happening with the North American Free Trade Agreement (NAFTA) and the European Union. Macroeconomics is the study of such systems.

Political system. The dominant means of governance for maintaining order and exercising power or authority, and in some cultures it is tribal where chiefs rule; others have a ruling royal family with an operating king, while some prefer democracy

Religious system. The means for providing meaning and motivation beyond the material aspects of life, that is, the spiritual side of a culture or its approach to the supernatural, may lift a people to great heights of accomplishment, as is witnessed in the pyramids of Egypt and the Renaissance of Europe. It is possible to project the history and future of India, for instance, in terms of the impact of its belief in reincarnation, which is enshrined in its major religion.

Diverse national cultures can be somewhat unified under a shared religious belief in Islam or Christianity, for example. In some countries, Islam is becoming the basis for governance, legal, and political systems. In others, religion dominates legal and political systems, such as Judaism in Israel. Unfortunately, history demonstrates that in the name of religion, zealots and extremists may engage in culturally repressive behavior, such as religious persecutions, ethnic cleansing, terrorism of nonbelievers, and even "holy" wars. Many religions also teach that their religious beliefs are the correct ones and other religious beliefs are wrong.

Association system. The network of social groupings that people form, whether in person or electronically may range from fraternal and secret societies to professional/trade associations. Some cultures are very group-oriented and create formal and informal associations for every conceivable type of activity (e.g., the culture in the United States). In some countries, families organize into clans, finding it difficult to work together for the common national good, as in Afghanistan and Iraq.

Health system. The concepts of health and wholeness, well-being, and medical problems differ by culture. Some countries have witch doctors, spiritual remedies, and herb medications. Others, like India, have fewer government-sponsored social services, while Britain has a system of socialized medicine. The United States is in the midst of a major transition in its healthcare and delivery system, and there is increasing emphasis on universal coverage, prevention, and wellness health models. Medical practitioners can be culturally biased. For example, Western medicine tended to ignore folk medicine, especially in Asia and Africa.

Recreational system. What may be considered play in one culture may be viewed as work in another, and vice versa. In some cultures, "sport" has considerable political implications; in others, it is solely for enjoyment; while in still others, it is big business. Some cultures cherish the creative and performing arts, providing financial support for artists and musicians. Certain types of entertainment, such as a form of folk dancing, seem to cut across cultures.

KEY CULTURAL TERMINOLOGY

The specialists who make a formal study of culture use terms that may be helpful to those trying to comprehend the significance of this phenomenon in business or international life.

Tradition

This is a very important aspect of culture that may be expressed in unwritten customs, taboos, and sanctions. Tradition can program a people as to what are proper behavior and procedures relative to food, dress, and to certain types of people, and what to value, avoid, or deemphasize. As the song on the subject of "tradition" from the musical *Fiddler on the Roof* extols:

Because of our traditions, we keep our sanity. ... Tradition tells us how to sleep, how to work, how to wear clothes. ... How did it get started? I don't know – it's a tradition. ... Because of our traditions, everyone knows who he is and what God expects of him![21]

Traditions provide a people with a "mindset" and have a powerful influence on their moral system for evaluating what is right or wrong, good or bad, and desirable or not. Traditions express a particular culture, giving its members a sense of belonging and uniqueness. But whether one is talking of a tribal or national culture, or of a military or religious subculture, traditions should be reexamined regularly for their relevance and validity. Mass global communications stimulate acquisition of new values and behavior patterns that may more rapidly undermine ancient, local, or religious traditions, especially among women and young people worldwide.

The following struck the authors' imagination when a manager for a high tech company brought it to our attention, namely, tradition and superstition express themselves when numbering floors in a hotel. We added some observations of our own as well (see Exhibit 1.1).

EXHIBIT 1.1 COUNTING ELEVATOR FLOORS

It is quite normal in the United States to see the 13th floor absent in the selection of floors on the elevator directory panel. This is due, of course, to our cultural bias regarding the number 13 being "unlucky." By omitting it in the numbering sequence of the hotel floors, one avoids the anxiety of a superstitious customer. After entering the Hai-Li Hotel elevator in China and punching in my floor selection, I quickly noticed that not only was number 13 absent, but 14 was as well. As one rose to the higher floors in the hotel, one passed from floor number 12 to floor number 15. I mentioned this to my friends, and they assured me that the Chinese culture had an aversion to an unlucky number as well, only it was number 14. So our culturally astute hotel had decided to delete both numbers, thus showing their sensitivity (and respect) to both cultures, while showing favor to neither. Similarly in some countries, the custom is to designate the entrance floor as the "ground" floor, while the next floor becomes labeled the "first" floor, as the numbering continues upward. This is confusing to foreigners from countries where the entrance area from the street is known as the "first floor"; the problem worsens when more floors are being built underground, as when entering the visitor may find him or herself on the second or even third floor. Even basements are being built downward in levels 1, 2, 3, etc., and may be given exotic names after fruit or flowers. All this shakes up the staid, but makes the world more interesting.

EXHIBIT 1.1

17 ■ ■ ■

Some of these cultural variables have been researched and a "cultural profile" developed by Schmitz[22] for many countries. There are ten concepts in the model:

1 *Environment*. Social environments can be categorized according to whether they view and relate to people, objects, and issues from the orientation of *control* (change environment), *harmony* (build balance), or *constraint* (external forces set parameters).

2 *Time*. A *past* orientation is indicated by placing a high value on preestablished processes and procedures. A *present* orientation is indicated by placing a focus on short-term and quick results. A *future* orientation is indicated by placing a focus on long-term results.

3 *Action*. Social environments can be distinguished by their approach to actions and interactions. An emphasis on relationships, reflection, and analysis indicates a *being* orientation. A focus on task and action indicates a *doing* orientation.

4 *Communication*. An emphasis on implicit communication and reliance on nonverbal cues indicates *high-context* orientation. A *low-context* orientation is indicated by a strong value on explicit communication.

5 *Space*. Cultures can be categorized according to the distinctions they make between *public* and *private* spaces.

6 *Power*. Social environments can be categorized by the way they structure power relationships. A *hierarchy* orientation is indicated by a high degree of acceptability of differential power relationships and social stratification. An *equality* orientation is indicated by little tolerance for differential power relationships and the minimizing of social stratification.

7 *Individualism*. An emphasis on independence and a focus on the individual indicate an *individualistic* orientation. An emphasis on affiliation and subordination of individual interest to that of a group, company, or organization indicates a *collectivistic* orientation.

8 *Competitiveness*. An emphasis on personal achievements, individual assertiveness, and success indicates a *competitive* orientation. Valuing quality of life, interdependence, and relationships indicates a *cooperative* orientation.

9 *Structure*. Environments that value adherence to rules, regulations, and procedures are considered *order* oriented and prefer predictability and minimization of risk. Environments that value improvisation exhibit a *flexibility* orientation and tend to reward risk-taking, tolerate ambiguity, and value innovation.

10 *Thinking*. Cultures can expect, reinforce, and reward either a *deductive* approach (an emphasis on theory, principles, concepts, and abstract logic) or an *inductive* approach (emphasis on data, experience, and experimentation). They may also either emphasize a *linear* approach (analysis and segmentation of issues) or a *systemic* approach (synthesis, holism, and the "big picture").

Of course, it is important to keep in mind that these constructs are not rigid and material diversity illustrates this. Thought of the concepts along a continuum, where extremes are unlikely and placement is relative, it is this which leads us to Hofstede's research.

Hofstede's early research

To create opportunities for collaboration, global leaders must learn not only the customs, courtesies, and business protocols of their counterparts from other countries, but they must also understand the national character, management philosophies, and mindsets of the people. Dr. Geert Hofstede, a European research consultant, has helped identify important dimensions of national character. He firmly believes that "culture counts" and has identified four dimensions of national culture:

1   *Power distance* – indicates "the extent to which a society accepts that power in institutions and organizations is distributed unequally."
2   *Uncertainty avoidance* – indicates "the extent to which a society feels threatened by uncertain or ambiguous situations."
3   *Individualism* – refers to a "loosely knit social framework in a society in which people are supposed to take care of themselves and of their immediate families only." Collectivism, the opposite, occurs when there is a "tight social framework in which people distinguish between in-groups and out-groups; they expect their in-group (relatives, clan, organizations) to look after them, and in exchange for that owe absolute loyalty to it."
4   *Masculinity* – with its opposite pole, *femininity*, expresses "the extent to which the dominant values in society are assertiveness, money and material things, not caring for others, quality of life, and people."[23]

A significant dimension related to leadership in Hofstede's original study of 40 countries is the power distance dimension. He assigned an index value to each country on the basis of mean ratings of employees on a number of key questions.[24]

Exhibit 1.2 shows the positions of the 40 countries on the power distance and uncertainty avoidance scales, and Exhibit 1.3 shows the countries' positions on the power distance and individualism scales.

The United States ranked 15th on power distance, 9th on uncertainty avoidance (both of these are below the average), 40th on individualism (the most individualist country in the sample), and 28th on masculinity (above average).

In Hofstede's study, the United States ranked 14th out of 40 on the power distance dimension. If this had been higher, then the theories of leadership taught in the United States might have been expected to be more Machiavellian. We might also ask how U.S. leaders are selected. Most are selected on the basis of competence, and it is the position of the person that provides his or her authority in the United States, which is, theoretically

EXHIBIT 1.2 POSITIONS OF 40 COUNTRIES ON THE POWER DISTANCE AND UNCERTAINTY AVOIDANCE SCALES

E X H I B I T 1.2

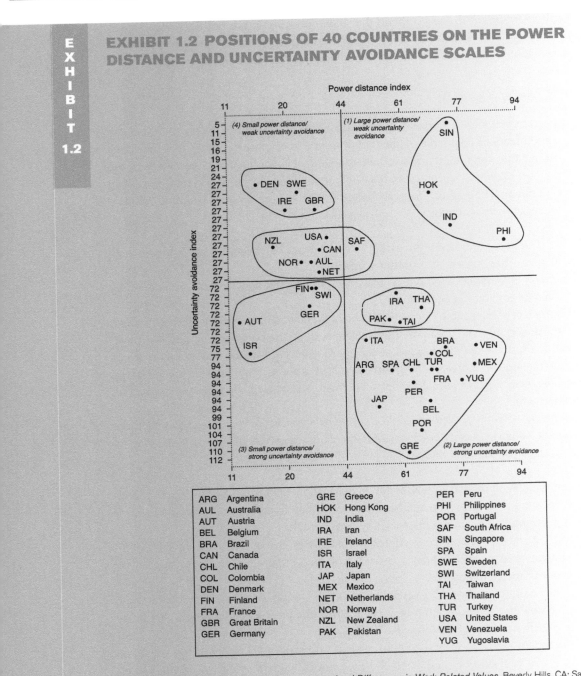

ARG	Argentina	GRE	Greece	PER	Peru
AUL	Australia	HOK	Hong Kong	PHI	Philippines
AUT	Austria	IND	India	POR	Portugal
BEL	Belgium	IRA	Iran	SAF	South Africa
BRA	Brazil	IRE	Ireland	SIN	Singapore
CAN	Canada	ISR	Israel	SPA	Spain
CHL	Chile	ITA	Italy	SWE	Sweden
COL	Colombia	JAP	Japan	SWI	Switzerland
DEN	Denmark	MEX	Mexico	TAI	Taiwan
FIN	Finland	NET	Netherlands	THA	Thailand
FRA	France	NOR	Norway	TUR	Turkey
GBR	Great Britain	NZL	New Zealand	USA	United States
GER	Germany	PAK	Pakistan	VEN	Venezuela
				YUG	Yugoslavia

Source: Hofstede, G. *Cultures Consequences: International Differences in Work-Related Values.* Beverly Hills, CA: Sage Publications, 1984.

EXHIBIT 1.3 POSITIONS OF 40 COUNTRIES ON THE POWER DISTANCE AND INDIVIDUALISM SCALES

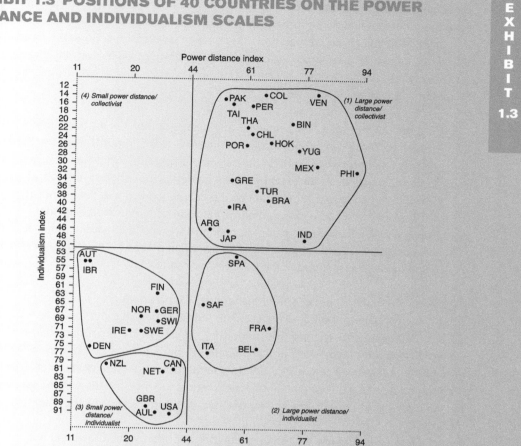

Source: Hofstede, G. *Cultures Consequences: International Differences in Work-Related Values.* Beverly Hills, CA: Sage Publications, 1984.

at least, an egalitarian society. In France, which has a higher power distance index score, there is little concern with participative management but great concern with who has the power.

Even today, French industry and the managers who run it are a mixture of the old and the new. France is still, in some ways, a country of family empires with many paternalistic traditions. There is also a remnant of a feudalistic heritage that is deeply rooted within the French spirit, which could account for the very conservative and autocratic nature of their business methodology. Hofstede has shown that in countries with lower power distance scores than the United States, such as Sweden and Germany, there is considerable acceptance of leadership styles and management models that are even more participative than those that presently exist. Industrial democracy and codetermination is a style that does not find much sympathy in the United States.

Hofstede has demonstrated that in Germany there is high uncertainty avoidance and, therefore, industrial democracy is brought about first by legislation. In Sweden, where uncertainty avoidance is low, industrial democracy was started with local experiments. Hofstede[25] continues as follows:

> The crucial fact about leadership in any culture is that it is a complement to subordinateship. The Power Distance Index scores ... are in fact based on the values of people as *subordinates*, not on the values of superiors. Whatever a naive literature on leadership may try to make us believe, a leader cannot choose his style at will; what is feasible depends to a large extent on the cultural conditioning of his/her subordinates. I therefore show ... a description of the type of subordinateship that, other things being equal, a leader can expect to meet in societies at three different levels of Power Distance, and to which his/her leadership has to respond. The middle level represents what most likely is found in the U.S. environment.

Where does this leave us as global managers? Perhaps we pick and choose, and adopt what is appropriate in the home culture. The matter is brought into focus as we examine a specific management system. The underlying assumptions regarding leadership in the United States are clearly seen in the practice of management by objectives (MBO). This assumes that a subordinate is independent enough to negotiate meaningfully with a superior (not too high of a power distance), that both the superior and the subordinate are willing to take risks (a low uncertainty avoidance), and that performance is important to both (high masculinity).

Hofstede continues to demonstrate the importance of cross-cultural research as MBO is applied to Germany.

> Let us now take the case of Germany. This is also a below-average Power Distance country, so the dialogue element in MBO should present no problem. However, Germany scores considerably higher on Uncertainty Avoidance; consequently, the tendency towards accepting risk and ambiguity will not be present to the same extent. The idea of replacing the arbitrary authority of the boss by the impersonal authority of mutually agreed-upon objectives, however, fits the low Power Distance, high Uncertainty Avoidance cultural cluster very well. The objectives become the subordinates' "superego."[26]

The consequences of Hofstede's conclusions are significant. Leadership, decision-making, teamwork, organization, motivation, and in fact everything managers do are learned. Management functions are learned, and they are on the basis of assumptions about one's place in the world. Managers from other business systems are not "underdeveloped" American managers.

Bond's Confucian cultural patterns

Another researcher, Michael H. Bond, believes that the taxonomies developed by Western scholars have a Western bias.[27] In his research, he found four dimensions of cultural patterns: integration, which refers in a broad sense to the continuum of social stability. Human-heartedness, which refers to values of gentleness and compassion, people who score highly on this dimension value patience, courtesy, and kindness towards others. Moral discipline refers to a sense of moderation in daily activities and the Confucian work dynamic indicates an individual's orientation to life and work. According to Bond, the behaviors that are exhibited along this continuum are consistent with the teachings of Confucius.

Kong Fuzi, renamed Confucius by Jesuit missionaries, was a Chinese civil servant who lived during the Warring States Period about 2,500 years ago. He sought to determine ways in which Chinese society could move away from fighting among themselves so that through discipline, human relationships, ethics, politics, and business relationships are more harmonious. He was well known for his wisdom and wit and was regularly surrounded by followers who recorded his teachings. Confucianism is a set of practical principles and ethical rules for daily life.

Confucius taught that people should be educated, skilled, hard-working, thrifty, modest, patient, and unrelenting in all things. Human nature is assumed to be inherently good, and it is the responsibility of the individual to train his or her character in these standards of behavior.

Exhibit 1.4 represents a framework for understanding cultural differences along several dimensions and will be valuable for any person working in the global world.

EXHIBIT 1.4 CONTINUUM OF CULTURAL VARIABLES

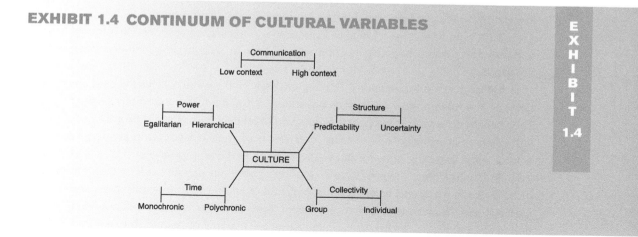

Many other researchers, including Fons Trompenaars and Charles Hampden-Turner, have studied culture and written persuasively on culture's impact on global business in the twenty-first century.

CULTURAL UNDERSTANDING AND SENSITIVITY

And does culture explain everything?

As one works and lives in other cultures, most come to realize there are no good cultures or bad cultures in every aspect. Most also come to believe there are no perfect cultures, including their own.

The recent book, *Why Nations Fail*,[28] by Daron Acemoglu and James Robinson, asks the question, "Why are there significant differences in the standard of living between rich countries and poor countries?"

The authors begin by describing theories and realities that do NOT answer the question adequately. The first inadequate answer, according to the authors, is the "geography hypothesis" which purports to explain the differences between rich and poor countries by differences in geography. "Many poor countries, such as those in Africa, Central America, and South Asia, are between the tropics of Cancer and Capricorn. Rich nations, in contrast, tend to be in temperate zones." Many social scientists and well-known authors use this as an explanation, arguing that people in warm or hot areas of the world tend to be lazy and don't work hard.

The other widely promoted theory to explain national differences in prosperity is the "cultural hypothesis." Acemoglu and Robinson write that culture explains, in part, world inequality. "Yes, in the sense that social norms, which are related to culture, matter and can be hard to change, but mostly no, because those aspects of culture often emphasized — religion, national ethics, African or Latin American values — are just not important for understanding how we got here and why the inequities in the world persist."

The "ignorance theory" is also inadequate to explain differences. This theory asserts that inequality exists because no one knows how to help poor countries become more prosperous.

So what is the explanation? The authors demonstrate that nations fail because nations differ on the rules of how an economy works and the incentives that motivate their people. They cite the following to support their answer. Most people in North Korea are poor without entrepreneurial initiative or creativity, and much of their education is propaganda. After school, most enter the army for ten years. They cannot own property or own a business.

In South Korea, most receive a good education (in recent studies, their students at most levels in math and science are among the world's best); they can borrow money to start a business or build a home on property they own. The authors call economic institutions in South Korea "inclusive," as they allow the majority of people to make the best use of their talents and skills in their economic activities; and this results in advances in technologies and innovation. North Korea's economic institutions are referred to as "extractive" because "such institutions are designed to extract income and wealth from one subset of society to benefit a different subset." They use many examples from different centuries in different geographical locations to explain *why nations fail*.

The global leader, sensitive to cultural differences, appreciates a people's distinctiveness and effectively communicates with individuals from different cultures. A global leader does not impose his/her own cultural attitudes and approaches. Thus, by respecting the cultural differences of others, we will not be labeled as "ethnocentric," defined in *The Random House Dictionary* as follows:

> Belief in the inherent superiority of one's own group and culture; it may be accompanied by a feeling of contempt for those considered as foreign; it views and measures alien cultures and groups in terms of one's own culture.

Through cross-cultural experiences, we become more broad-minded and tolerant of cultural "uniqueness." When this is coupled with some formal study of the concept of culture, we not only gain new insights for improving our human relations, but we become aware of the impact of our native culture. Cultural understanding may minimize the impact of culture shock and maximize intercultural experiences, as well as increase professional development and organizational effectiveness. Cultural sensitivity should teach us that culture and behavior are relative and that we should be more tentative, and less absolute, in human interaction.

The first step in managing cultural differences effectively is increasing one's general cultural awareness. We must understand the concept of culture and its characteristics before we can fully benefit from the study of cultural specifics and a foreign language.

Further, we should appreciate the impact of our specific cultural background on our own mindset and behavior, as well as those of colleagues and customers with whom we interact in the workplace.[29] This takes on special significance within a more diverse business environment, often the result of increasing migration from less developed to more developed economies.

In the March 20, 2009, *Herald Tribune*, article by Nicholas D. Kristof, he wrote:

> That's because there's pretty good evidence that we generally don't truly want good information — but rather information that confirms our prejudices. We may believe intellectually in the clash of opinions, but in practice we like to embed ourselves in the reassuring womb of an echo chamber.

He ended his article:

> So perhaps the only way forward is for each of us to struggle on our own to work out intellectually with sparring partners whose views we deplore. Think of it as a

daily mental workout analogous to a trip to the gym: if you don't work up a sweat, it doesn't count.

What follows are some ideas on how to learn and get good information.

CROSS-CULTURAL LEARNING

To increase effectiveness across cultures, *training* must be the focus of the job, while *education* thought of with reference to the individual, and *development* reserved for organizational concerns. Whether one is concerned with intercultural training, education, or development, all employees should learn about the influence of culture and be effective cross-cultural communicators if they are to work with minorities within their own society or with foreigners encountered at home or abroad. For example, there has been a significant increase in foreign investments in the United States − millions of Americans now work within the borders of their own country for foreign employers. All along the U.S.–Mexican border, twin plants have emerged that provide for a flow of goods and services between the two countries.

A new reality of the global marketplace is the Information Highway and its impact on jobs and cross-cultural communications. Many skilled workers in advanced economies are watching their positions migrate overseas, where college educated nationals are doing high technology tasks for less pay. The Internet has changed how global business is and will be conducted for many decades.

Not considering computer language, most international exchanges take place with individuals using English as a second language. While a few corporate representatives will travel abroad, the main communication will occur by means of satellites on the Internet through modems connected to laptop or personal computers. Offshore operations done electronically in developing countries are stimulated by growing software applications that turn skilled tasks into routine work. Cross-cultural sensitivity is essential when participating in teleconferences or video conferences. Electronic media also require appropriate etiquette and protocols to create cultural synergy.

GLOBAL TRANSFORMATIONS

To stay globally competitive, more and more corporations are increasing their investments and activities in foreign countries. U.S. engineers can work on a project during the day, and then send it electronically to Asia or elsewhere for additional work while they sleep. Such trends represent an enormous challenge for cross-cultural competence. C-Bay Systems in Annapolis, Maryland, for instance, transmits U.S. physicians' dictations about patients to their subsidiary operations in India where they are transcribed into English, sent back to headquarters by computer, and then the completed version is sent on to the medical office from which the communication originated.

Another example of "going global" is seen in personalized service firms such as law and accounting. These professions are increasingly engaging in cross-border activities, hiring local practitioners who comprehend their own unique culture, language, and legal or accounting systems. The need for international expertise and capital is one reason for this trend. Companies of professionals are forming alliances with their foreign counterparts such as the Alliance of European Lawyers. To be successful, the acquisition process then requires an integration of *national, organizational*, and *professional cultures*. Under these circumstances, culture becomes a critical factor ensuring business success, particularly with the twenty-first century trend toward economies of scale favoring large, multidisciplinary, and multinational professional service organizations.[30]

In only 10 percent of 191 nations are the people ethnically or racially homogenous. Never before in history have so many inhabitants traveled beyond their homelands, either to travel or work abroad, or to flee as refugees. In host countries, the social fabric is being reconfigured and strained by massive waves of immigrants, whether legal or illegal.[31]

Many corporate and government leaders, business students, and citizens still operate with dated mindsets regarding the world, the people in various societies, the nature of work, the worker, and the management process itself. The Industrial Age has given way to the Information Age, and we can only speculate on its replacement in the next hundred years. Possibly the Space Age? Capra and Rast[32] state as follows:

> Now, in the old paradigm, it was also recognized that things are interrelated. But conceptually you first had the things with their properties, and then there were mechanisms and forces that interconnected them. In the new paradigm we say the things themselves do not have intrinsic properties. All the properties flow from their relationships. This is what I mean by understanding the properties of the parts from the dynamics of the whole, because these relationships are dynamic relationships. So the only way to understand the part is to understand its relationship to the whole. This insight occurred in physics in the 1920s and this is also a key insight of ecology. Ecologists think exactly in this way. They say an organism is defined by its relationship to the rest.

Thus, today's leaders are challenged to create new models of management systems. For that to happen, managers and other professionals must become more innovative and recognize the contribution of each individual or unit to the effective workings of the whole.

As the late Peter Drucker consistently observed, the art and science of management is in its own revolution, and many of the assumptions on which management practice was based are now becoming obsolete.

Foreign competition and the need to trade more effectively overseas have forced most corporations to become more culturally sensitive and globally minded. Managing people from different cultures is receiving the attention of business students as well as those in education and human resource development. Global management is a component in most executive education training programs worldwide.

According to Rhinesmith:[33]

Global managers must reframe the boundaries of their world . . . of space, time, scope, structure, geography and function; of functional, professional, and technical skills from a past age; of thinking and classification relative to rational to intuitive, national versus foreign, we versus they; of cultural assumptions, values and beliefs about your relations with others, and your understanding of yourself.

How do companies foster and create effective global managers? What is a global manager? Companies with worldwide operations are pondering these questions, plus many others. They find that the human resource component of the answer is, at times, more limiting than the capital investment in globalization. Bartlett and Ghoshal[34] state:

Clearly, there is no single model for the global manager. Neither the old-line international specialist nor the more recent global generalist can cope with the complexities of cross-border strategies. Indeed, the dynamism of today's marketplace calls for managers with diverse skills. Responsibility for worldwide operations belongs to senior business, country, and functional executives who focus on the intense interchanges and subtle negotiations required. In contrast, those in middle management and front-line jobs need well-defined responsibilities, a clear understanding of their organization's transnational mission, and a sense of accountability.

Percy Barnevik, former President and CEO of Asea Brown Boveri (ABB), responded when asked if there is such a thing as a global manager:[35]

Global managers are made, not born. This is not a natural process. We are herd animals. We like people who are like us. But there are many things you can do. Obviously, you rotate people around the world. There is no substitute for line experience in three or four countries to create a global perspective. You also encourage people to work in mixed nationality teams. You *force* them to create personal alliances across borders, which means that sometimes you interfere in hiring decisions.

You also have to acknowledge cultural differences without becoming paralyzed by them. We've done some surveys, as have lots of other companies, and we find interesting differences in perception. For example, a Swede may think a Swiss is not completely frank and open, that he doesn't know exactly where he stands. That is a cultural phenomenon. Swiss culture shuns disagreement. A Swiss might say, "Let's come back to that point later, let me review it with my colleagues." A Swede would prefer to confront the issue directly. How do we undo hundreds of years of upbringing and education? We don't, and we shouldn't try to. But we do need to broaden understanding.

Sheridan[36] found three clusters of leadership competencies and included intrapersonal competencies, interpersonal competencies, and social competencies. The following seven C's apply not only to U.S. leaders but to any global leaders also. Her summary is shown in Exhibit 1.5.

Self-perception and others' perception of you

Intentions are important but, like culture, perceptions count. And for the present and fore-seeable future, what happens in our global world will be to a large extent influenced by the United States. China is increasingly becoming a world power. The United States is involved in many global economic, political, and religious disputes and conflicts. But in this complex, rapidly changing yet interconnected global world, the influence of even the most powerful is highly limited.

EXHIBIT 1.5 INTERCULTURALLY COMPETENT LEADER

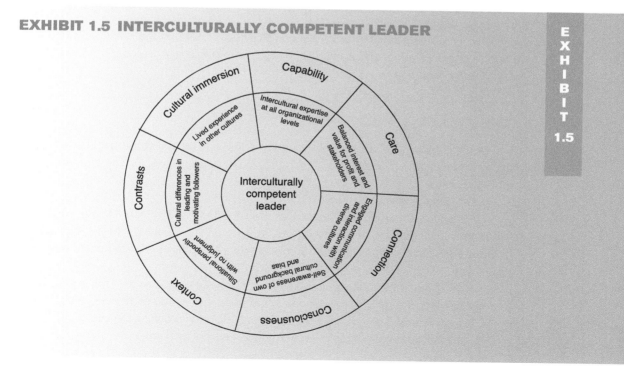

Now consider these comments, which provide a contrast.[37]

> Americans almost alone in the world, have a serious . . . even simplistic belief that their country is a force for enduring good. They acknowledge it does not always get it right, that at times its antics fall far short of its highest ideals, but all but the most hardened cynics really believe in America as a force for freedom and prosperity and in the universality of these goals. This belief is born of the country's history, religion, and culture. . . . It is this self-faith as much as anything that defines and differentiates Americans from most of the rest of the world. There is not much doubt that outside the United States, American intentions, especially under the Bush administration, are regarded with a degree of suspicion and resentment . . . it is not hard to see why this self-belief evinces such cynicism around the world. The United States' record – supporting tyrants, even in places such as Iraq – where it eventually topples them – is hardly unblemished. At times, America's commitment to liberty has looked a little selective.

Denial

Most individuals, at some time in their lives, deny realities. In families, children deny that their parents are alcoholic, and women deny that their husbands are abusive. Similarly, in business organizations and academic institutions, "realities" are suppressed, "feelings" and emotional reactions are not considered, and intellectualization exercises force new realities into old paradigms.

The humorous parody in the American Way box illustrates the denial of a country's competitiveness problem and a misdiagnosis. This example is American, but it can easily apply to most countries.

THE AMERICAN WAY

The Americans and the Japanese decided to engage in a competitive boat race. Both teams practiced hard and long to reach their peak performance. On the big day they both felt ready.

The Japanese won by a *mile*.

Afterward, the American team was discouraged by the loss. Morale sagged. Corporate management decided that the reason for the crushing defeat had to be found, so a consulting firm was hired to investigate the problem and recommend corrective action.

The consultant's findings: the Japanese team had eight people rowing and one person steering; the American team had one person rowing and eight people steering.

After a year of study and millions spent analyzing the problem, the consulting firm concluded that too many people were steering and not enough were rowing on the American team.

So, as race day neared again the following year, the American team's management structure was completely reorganized. The new structure: four steering managers, three area steering managers, one staff steering manager, and a new performance review system for the person rowing the boat to provide work incentive.

That year the Japanese won by *two* miles.

Humiliated, the American corporation laid off the rower for poor performance and gave the managers a bonus for discovering the problem.

In this oversimplification, in the first race the Americans were overconfident and denied they had a competitiveness problem. In preparation for the second race, there was a serious misdiagnosis. Hamel states it well:

> To fully understand our competitive advantage/disadvantage, we have to go deeper, and look at our "genetic Coding" — that is, our beliefs, our managerial frames. It is these beliefs that restrict our perceptions of reality and degrees of freedom. To be successful, a company needs "genetic variety." Our challenge must be to get outside our restrictive managerial frames.

If you want to enlarge your managerial frames, you must be curious about how the *rest of the world thinks* — and you must *have humility*. The real competitive problem is not that our institutional environment is hopelessly unhelpful, but that our managerial frames are hopelessly *inappropriate to the next round of global competition*.[38]

CONCLUSIONS

Two additional skills are of fundamental importance today for global people. The first skill is *listening* to understand (see additional concepts in Chapter 2). Many global leaders, particularly of nation-states, do not seem to possess this skill to a high degree. Listening is a symbol of respecting the dignity of others.

The second is the skill of locating and using many very sophisticated *cultural interpreters*. It is impossible for any individual, given the complexity of culture, to have a full understanding of other systems. However, cultural interpreters, individuals from each culture, can teach leaders. Having listened and been a student with cultural interpreters as teachers, the global leader is equipped to face the many opportunities and challenges that will be continually presented.

Having a sense of culture and its related skills is a unique human attribute. Culture is fundamentally a group of problem-solving tools for coping in a particular environment. It enables people to create a distinctive world around themselves, to control their own destinies, and to grow. Sharing the legacy of diverse cultures advances our social, economic, technological, and human development. Culture can be analyzed in a macrocontext, such as in terms of national groups, or in a micro sense, such as within a system or organization. Increasingly, we examine culture in a global sense from the perspective of work, leadership, or markets.

Because management philosophies and practices are culturally conditioned, it stands to reason that there is much to be gained by including cultural studies in all management or professional development. This is particularly relevant during the global transformation under way. Culturally skilled leaders are essential for the effective management of emerging global corporations as well as for the furtherance of mutually beneficial world trade and exchange. In these undertakings, the promotion of cultural synergy by those who are truly global managers will help us to capitalize on the differences in people, while ensuring their collaborative action.

Learning to manage cultural differences is a means for all persons to become more global in their outlook and behavior, as well as more effective personally and professionally. When cultural differences are understood and utilized as a *resource*, then all benefit.[39] When they are not, the costs are significant.

MIND STRETCHING

1   How did your parents/caregivers influence you?
2   Can you have a global mindset and be a proud Canadian or French or …?
3   What was your reaction to the points in "Did You Know"?
4   Do you believe the world is really "flat," and what does this mean?
5   How can you see events and issues through multiple lens?
6   When confronted with cultural differences, why do we often dig in and believe our way is right rather than listen?
7   What is your opinion regarding the Prophet Mohammed cartoon controversy?
8   In five years, with your "futurist hat" on, how would you describe our "global world"?
9   What is your opinion on the two words, "culture counts"?

NOTES

1   Moran, Robert T. Journal notes, 2013.
2   "It Ain't Necessarily So," *The Economist*, October 13, 2012.
3   Solomon, Andrew. *Far from the Tree: Parents, Children and the Search for Identity*. New York: Scribner, 2012.
4   Pascal, B. *Pensées*, Vol. 60, 1670, p. 294.
5   Freidman, T. "It's a Flat World, After All," *The New York Times Magazine*, April 3, 2005.
6   Freidman, T. *The World Is Flat, a Brief History of the Twenty-First Century*. New York: Farrar, Strauss and Giroux, 2005, pp. 6–7.
7   Schein, E. H. "On Dialogue, Culture and Organizational Learning," *Organizational Dynamics*, Vol. 22, No. 2, 1993, pp. 40–51.
8   Brooks, D. "It's Culture That Counts," *International Herald Tribune*, February 21, 2006.

9   Harrison, L. and Huntington, S. P. (eds). *Culture Matters*. New York: Basic Books, 2000, p. 111.

10 Diamond, J. *Guns, Germs, and Steel*. New York: Norton and Company, 1999, p. 13.

11 Ibid. p. 25.

12 Moran, Robert T. Personal journal, 2010.

13 *Global Awareness and Education: American's Test for the 21st Century*. Apple Inc., February, 2007.

14 Deardorff, D. K. (ed.). *The Sage Handbook of Intercultural Competence*. Thousand Oaks, CA: Sage, 2009.

15 Huntington, S. *The Clash of Civilizations and the Remaking of World Order*. New York: Simon & Schuster, 1996.

16 Chomsky, N., Mitchell, P. R., and Schoeffel, J. (eds). *Understanding Power*. New York: Vintage, 2002.

17 Lewis, R. D. *The Cultural Imperative*. Yarmouth, ME: Intercultural Press, 2003.

18 *Science & Culture*, January/February 2008.

19 Freidman, *The World is Flat, a Brief History of the Twenty-First Century*.

20 Miller, J. G. *Living Systems*. Niwot, CO: University Press of Colorado, 1994. See also *Systems Research and Behavioral Science*. Wiley Interscience, online.

21 Stein, J. "Tradition," *Fiddler on the Roof*. Harnick, S., lyrics, Bock, J., music, 1964.

22 Schmitz, J. *Cultural Orientations Guide*. Princeton, NJ: Princeton Training Press, 2003, pp. 10–12.

23 *Science & Culture*, January/February 2008.

24 Ibid.

25 Hofstede, G. *Cultures Consequences: International Differences in Work-Related Values*. Beverly Hills, CA: Sage, 1984. See also Hofstede, G. *Cultures and Organizations: Software of the Mind*. London: McGraw-Hill, 1991.

26 Hofstede, *Cultures and Organizations*.

27 Lustig, M. W. and Koester, J. *Intercultural Competence: Interpersonal Communication Across Cultures*, 5th edn. New York: Allyn and Bacon, 2005.

28 Acemoglu, D. and Robinson, J. *Why Nations Fail*. New York: Crown Business, 2012.

29 Thiederman, S. *Bridging Cultural Barriers to Success: How to Manage the Multicultural Workforce*. Lexington, MA: Lexington Books, 1990; Thiederman, S. *Profiting in America's Multicultural Workplace*. Lexington, MA: Lexington Books, 1991.

30 *The Economist*, August 29, 1998, p. 59.

31 Harris, P. R. in, Simons, G., Abramms, B., Hopkins, A., and Johnson, D. (eds). *The Cultural Diversity Handbook*. Princeton, NJ: Pacesetter Books, 1996.

32 Capra, F. and Rast, D. S. *Belonging to the Universe*. San Francisco, CA: Harper, 1991.

33 Rhinesmith, S. H. *A Manager's Guide to Globalization*, 2nd edn. Chicago, IL: Irwin/ASTD, 1996, p. x.

34 Bartlett, C. A., and Ghoshal, S. "What Is a Global Manager?" *Harvard Business Review*, September/October, 1992, p. 131.

35 Taylor, W. "The Logic of Global Business: An Interview with ABB's Percy Barnevik," *Harvard Business Review*, March/April, 1991, p. 95.

36 Sheridan, E. *The Global Business Leadership*. Burlington, MA: Elsevier, 2009.

37 Baker, G. "The Land of the Free Enjoys the Thrill of Being a Force for Good," *Financial Times*, April 12–13, 2003.

38 Hamel, G. "Pushing the Envelope of Global Strategy and Competitiveness," A summary of remarks by Gary Hamel for the Executive Focus International 1993 Executive Forum, February 12, 1993.

39 Gesteland, R. R. *Cross-Cultural Business Behavior: Marketing, Negotiating, and Managing Across Cultures*. Copenhagen: Copenhagen Business School Press (Handelshojskolens Forlag), 1999.

ADDITIONAL FEATURES

Please visit the companion website at: www.routledge.com/cw/Moran where you will find additional case studies, study aides, and instructor resources.

2 GLOBAL LEADERS AND INTERCULTURAL COMMUNICATIONS

GMs develop a network of relationships with those the job makes them dependent on and then use that network to help create, implement, and update an organizational agenda. As such, the whole approach to the job involves interacting with people.

John P. Kotter[1]

Cross-cultural communication looks at how people from differing cultural backgrounds communicate, in similar and different ways among themselves, and how they endeavor to communicate across cultures.[2] Intercultural communication studies situations where people from different cultural backgrounds *interact*.

Wikipedia[3]

We know that most leaders of organizations spend upwards of 70 to 90 percent of their time communicating with others, and only about 25 percent of their time alone.[4] These days, with smartphones, pads, email, texting, and interactive electronic media, much of our "alone" time is spent with others as well. We also know that all business undertakings are comprised of communication. We have learned from experience, and from extensive interaction with expatriates from all over the globe, that participating in these cross-cultural communications and interactions while working internationally can be very challenging. This may be especially true when living or working in a foreign cultural environment. We, however, exchange email, text messages, or phone calls with our business associates in China, Japan, Korea, or almost anywhere worldwide at any moment, engaging in cross-cultural communication without being aware of it. Electronic communication may be very culturally conditioned especially in ways we are not conscious, so we must always be on guard against culturally inappropriate interactions.

It is for these reasons that this chapter provides an overview of interpersonal and intercultural communication. It is hard enough to communicate successfully, and stay out of misunderstandings or conflicts with one's own work colleagues, friends, and family. It can be much more challenging when differing culturally based assumptions or behaviors make interpretation on either side more difficult. People used to believe that if you learned the language, you could make yourself understood in a foreign culture. It is very valuable to learn the language, but communications experts know that people communicate in ways that are outside of their awareness — unconsciously if you like. Edward Hall, the founder of the intercultural communication field, argued as much as 80 to 90 percent of the message we communicate or receive is nonverbal.[5] Any culture is primarily a system for identifying and processing relevant information so most cultural behavior entails communication whether we realize it or not.[6]

At the same time, we should not allow our focus on the effects of cultural differences blind us to cross-cultural similarities that may be used to reduce the effect of cultural differences.[7] For example, humans as a species have been observed to have the same set of personality dimensions across cultures, and the effects of personality are independent from those of culture. Personality similarities across cultures may be used to reduce the complexity and effects of cultural differences. In addition, evolutionary psychology teaches that there are styles of *self-interested* and *altruistic* interaction strategies common to humans-as-species that have similar effects across cultures. The same pattern has been observed in the field of business philosophy concerning I/It versus I/Thou relationships.[8] Intercultural cooperation is more likely with altruistic or I/Thou interaction. Intercultural defensiveness and resistance is more likely with self-interested or I/It interaction. And altruistic I/Thou relationships may be achieved through a communication technology called Nonviolent Communication (NVC) demonstrated effective for any cross-national negotiations and resolution of international conflicts.[9]

INTRODUCTION

When we study international business, we might have a tendency to believe that the cultures in North America, Europe, and Japan are the most important to consider in terms of achieving effective communication. Many of the most successful multinational enterprises (MNEs) have originated from these areas. However, the odds are that you will have to communicate far beyond this circle of cultures over the course of your management career. Our world's population exceeds 7 billion. If, however, the global population was only 1,000 people, it would have the following composition:[10]

■ 52 North Americans (including 47 Americans and 5 Canadians)
■ 150 Europeans (including Western, Eastern, and Russian)
■ 6 Australians and New Zealanders
■ 584 Asians (including 200 Chinese and 167 Indians)
■ 124 Africans
■ 84 Latin and South Americans.

In addition, when we hear that English is the international language of commerce, it is all too easy to forget how few speak it as their native language. If the global population again was only 1,000 people, about 50 percent of the people would speak the following as their first languages:

■ 165 Mandarin
■ 86 English
■ 83 Hindi/Urdu
■ 64 Spanish
■ 58 Russian
■ 37 Arabic.

The other 50 percent speak Bengali, Portuguese, Indonesian, Japanese, German, French, and two hundred other languages. Communication, indeed, can be challenging in this global village.

For sure, some nations and cultures are more important for international business. Most international trade (exports + imports) is currently conducted by 20 nations. These are indicated in Exhibit 2.1. Most of us will find that our international business related careers will involve doing business with managers and companies from these nations. However, these nations do business throughout the world and there is no guarantee where you will be assigned, or with whom you will have to conduct business.

With our globally interdependent economy, it is essential that we appreciate and understand the perspectives and goals of our world trade partners. This is especially true when these trade partners are trying to work together for certain agreed-upon objectives.

EXHIBIT 2.1 BIGGEST TRADING NATIONS (WORLD TOTAL = US$ 27,567 BILLION)

Rank	Nation	Total international trade (B$)	% value of world trade	Cumulative value (B$)
1	USA	3,825.0	13.9	3,825.0
2	China[a]	3,561.0	12.9	7,386.0
3	Germany	2,882.0	10.5	10,268.0
4	Japan	1,595.5	5.8	11,863.5
5	France	1,263.0	4.6	13,126.5
6	United Kingdom	1,150.3	4.2	14,276.8
7	Netherlands	1,091.0	4.0	15,367.8
8	South Korea	1,084.0	3.9	16,451.8
9	Italy	1,050.1	3.8	17,501.9
–	Hong Kong	944.8	3.4	18,446.7
10	Canada	910.2	3.3	19,356.9
11	Russia	843.4	3.1	20,200.3
12	Singapore	818.8	3.0	21,019.1
13	India	792.3	2.9	21,811.4
14	Spain	715.2	2.6	22,526.6
15	Mexico	678.2	2.5	23,204.8
16	Belgium	664.4	2.4	23,869.2
17	Taiwan	623.7	2.3	24,492.9
18	Switzerland	607.9	2.2	25,100.8
19	Australia	502.3	1.8	25,603.1
20	Brazil	470.4	1.7	26,073.5
	Total Top 20		94.8%	

Source: CIA, The World Factbook, 2013, http://www.cia.gov/library/publications/the-world-factbook.
Note: [a]China + Hong Kong = 16.2% of world trade.

We recognize that we are most comfortable communicating with those who are the most similar to us. This comfort level tends to decrease as dissimilarity increases. Research has demonstrated that communication openness tends to be a precursor to different group members' response to conflict which can impact a diverse groups' performance.[11] Reasons cited[12] include that members prefer to communicate and are more open with others who are most similar to themselves, and perceived dissimilarity tends to negatively impact communication. People are often unaware when misunderstandings occur or "errors" are committed while working with persons from different cultures. A cross-cultural faux pas results when we fail to recognize that persons of other cultural backgrounds have certain goals, customs, thought patterns, and/or values different from our own. This is particularly true in a diverse workforce with increasing numbers of expatriate workers not familiar with others' home cultures, languages, and communication systems. Conflict tends to result from any of these kinds of misunderstandings and it becomes more challenging to integrate the diverse viewpoints to achieve positive outcomes.

Effective communication across cultural and linguistic boundaries is difficult. It involves learning to use flexible approaches to listen, observe, and speak according to the specific situation at hand. Before a person is able to communicate effectively with people from different cultures, it is important to know about their culture, language, history, and where they live. The following is a list of questions that require a little more knowledge and sophistication. They are adapted from the booklet, *So You're Going Abroad: Are You Prepared?*[13] These are the kinds of questions you want to be able to answer as part of your preparations for an international assignment that could facilitate your communicating effectively with locals. Can you answer the questions for any country in which you have worked or done business in the past?

1   There are many contemporary and historical people of whom a country is proud. Can you name a politician, a musician, a writer, a religious leader, a sports figure?
2   Are you familiar with that country's basic history? Date of independence? Relationship to other countries?
3   What are some routine courtesies that people are expected to observe in that country?
4   How do they greet each other? Foreigners?
5   What do you know about their major religions?
6   Are there role differences between men and women?
7   What kinds of foods are traditional?
8   What kind of humor is appreciated?
9   What is the relationship between that country and your country?

THE COMMUNICATION PROCESS

Effective communications is difficult enough even with your spouse and loved ones. For that reason, it makes sense for us to review the communication process in general before considering the added complications of effective intercultural communications.

Communication is a process of circular interaction involving a sender, receiver, and message. In the most basic terms, the sender sends a message to the receiver. When the receiver understands what the sender means, successful communication has occurred. In human interaction, the sender or receiver may be a person or a group of people. The message conveys meaning through the medium or symbol used to send it (the how), as well as in its content (the what). Essentially, people tend to selectively perceive information, and judge its relevance and importance in the context of their own perceptual preferences. An individual's self-image, needs, values, expectations, goals, standards, cultural norms, and personality affect the way input is received and interpreted. Two people can thus receive the same message and understand it as having two entirely different meanings. They actually perceive the same object or information differently. Communication, then, is a complex process of linking up or sharing perceptual fields between sender and receiver. The effective communicator builds a bridge to the world of the receiver. When the sender is from one cultural group and the receiver from another (and in the communication process, this is reciprocal), the human interaction is intercultural communication.

Once the sender sends the message, the receiver analyzes the message in terms of his or her particular field of experience and pattern of ideas. He/she essentially decodes the message, interpreting it for meaning, and encoding and sending back a response. Thus, communication is a circular process of interaction.

The communicator, whether as an individual from a cultural group or as a member of an organization, exhibits or transmits many kinds of information. First, the intended message is communicated on verbal and nonverbal levels. We also communicate unintended, or unconscious messages, on verbal and nonverbal levels. The latter includes a whole "silent language" including voice tone, gestures, facial expressions, and body language. According to Hall,[14] 80–90 percent of the message you send, or interpret as the receiver, is based on this silent language. The person is both a medium of communication and a message. This silent language is particularly influenced by culture in ways people are often not aware.

Listening

Listening is at the heart of all successful communications. We listen to both the words and the nonverbal signaling. We learn to listen and talk before we read and write.

Listening is a complex activity. The average person speaks approximately 12,000 sentences every day at about 150 words per minute, while the listener's brain can absorb around 400 words per minute. This means the listener always has the capacity to understand. What do we do with this spare capacity? We become bored. We assume we know what is being said. We think about what we are going to say whenever he/she is finished speaking. We interrupt. A good listener understands that without good listening, there will be poor results. He/she uses this extra capacity to listen to the entire message and to more fully analyze the meanings behind the words.

Listening means different things to different people. It can mean different things to the same person in different situations. There are two types of positive listening behaviors:

1   *Information gathering* is a form of listening. Its purpose is the absorption of information, both stated and nonverbally signaled. Information gathering is not the same as interpretation. As soon as we start interpreting what someone is saying, it is possible to lose track of anything else he/she is saying.

2   *Active listening*[15] requires that the listener demonstrate to the speaker that he/she really understands what is being said. We *paraphrase* the speaker by saying what we think he/she means. We *perception check* how we understand the speaker to be feeling about what he/she is saying. We *summarize* briefly before making our own response, so the speaker will understand we are discussing the points he/she has made. Active listening is what our normal listening mode should be, but we rarely do it fully because it is work, and because it feels artificial if we are not used to doing it.

There are also some negative forms of listening that are more likely to cause difficulties and result in poor outcomes. These include:

1   *Polite listening* is listening just enough to meet the minimum social requirements by being able to make a relevant response or changing to a relevant alternate topic. If we are thinking what to say next, then we are not really listening.
2   *Defensive listening* is based on finding points that can be disputed in order to maintain our own positions against whatever the speaker is saying.
3   *Offensive listening* looks for opportunities to trap or trip up an opponent with his/her own words. A lawyer, when questioning a witness, listens for contradictions, irrelevancies, and weakness.

The positive forms of listening, especially active listening, are above all a sharing of oneself with another. It is impossible for one to become an active listener without becoming involved with the speaker. Listening demonstrates a respect and concern that words alone cannot fully express. It has the unique power of diminishing the magnitude of potential communication problems. By speaking to someone who actively listens, a speaker has the sense of, already accomplishing something. He/she knows that the message has been successfully transmitted. And the listener exerts some influence over the speaker when it is the listener's turn to speak. Both know that they are talking about the same topic and that the listener has understood the speaker's points. This makes the speaker more interested in what the response will be when it is his/her turn to listen.

INTERCULTURAL COMMUNICATION

Intercultural communication is a process whereby individuals from different cultural backgrounds attempt to share meanings. In the classical anthropological sense, culture refers to the range of human phenomena that cannot be attributed to genetic outcomes. Specifically, "culture" has two meanings.[16] First, it comprises the evolved human capacity to classify and represent experience symbolically, and to act with imagination and creativity. Second, it includes all the distinct ways in which people in different geographic locations classify and represent their experiences and act creatively. *Material* culture includes physical artifacts.

Intangible culture includes language, customs, beliefs, values, mores, and so on, passed on from generation to generation. With communication, we are most concerned with the intangible. Lustig and Koester[17] provide definitions of communications. For example, intercultural communication is "the presence of at least two individuals who are culturally different from each other on such important attributes as their value orientations, preferred communication codes, role expectations, and perceived rules of social relationship."

Models of intercultural communication

Traditional Western models of communication were a reflection of Western cultural and philosophical thought. The early models depicted communication as a linear process, and were deemed process models including the source, message, channel, and receiver.[18] The sender was regarded as the one responsible for the success of the communication because he/she took responsibility for the contents of the message.[19]

Current models tend to be more sociological and to highlight the effect of culture. For example, one model includes the sender, message, channel, noise, receiver, feedback, and cultural context.[20] Noise is defined as the perceptions of, and the cultural backgrounds of, each communicator. Cultural filters are the noise for both the sender and receiver.[21] We agree, however, with recent research[22] asserting that the language and signaling used in communication are not separable from its cultural context. Therefore, culture should not be viewed as noise, but rather as a key ingredient within the practice of communication. Culture influences how language is formed, how the linguistic communication is understood, and impacts how the language is constructed.[23] Because we do not view culture as peripheral to communication, the values[24] that are espoused as part of one's culture become highly salient. One's values are the basis for judging whether actions are considered "right or wrong." So, failing to understand predominant values within a society as well as failing to concede that an individual person has a particular set of beliefs will both lead to poor communication.[25]

Our own view is that intercultural communication seeks to understand how people from different countries and cultures act, communicate, and perceive the world around them. On the one hand, it considers the effect of culture in determining how individuals encode messages, the mediums they choose to transmit messages, and the ways they interpret messages. On the other hand, it also studies situations where people from different cultural backgrounds interact. While language is an important component, intercultural communication also focuses on social attributes, thought patterns, and cultural contents. The fields of anthropology, cultural studies, linguistics, psychology, and even philosophy all participate in identifying its key attributes.

There are many theories in all these disciplines that seek to explain how intercultural communications works and how to do it successfully. Our own approach recognizes that individuals engage in culturally moderated behaviors that may be consciously adopted as normative patterns of everyday life, or unconsciously adopted as habitual patterns of communicating within their own particular cultural group. Our approach also recognizes that, while in the past, the identification of cultural differences was the paramount concern, more recently the role of cultural similarities in simplifying communication challenges has become a more important consideration.

Variables in the communication process

Samovar and Porter[26] identified a number of variables in the communication process whose values were determined to some extent by culture. Each variable influences our perceptions, which in turn influence the meanings we attribute to behavior. In order to work effectively in a multicultural environment, one should recognize these and study the cultural specifics of the country or area to be visited.

Values are abstract and generalized principles defining appropriate and inappropriate behavior, believed to apply in all situations. Members of a cultural group feel a strong and emotionally toned commitment that becomes a standard for judging others' actions. Values provide the generalized standards of behavior that are expressed in more specific and concrete ways in social norms. For example, Western Christian and Middle Eastern Islamic societies have a strong value commitment to the principle of charity offered to monetarily or socially disadvantaged individuals.

Social norms define rules or standards for evaluating what behavior is considered socially acceptable. Norms are guidelines as to the ranges of behavior considered appropriate and applicable in particular situations. In the example offered above, Western Christian and Middle Eastern Islamic societies accept a generous range of what constitutes acceptable expressions of charity, including nonfinancial contributions.

Attitudes are emotionally toned psychological states that predispose us to behave in certain ways. Attitudes differ from values in being situational in their application while values are understood to apply in all cases.

Stereotypes are sets of attitudes that cause us to attribute qualities or characteristics to a person on the basis of the group to which that individual belongs. Stereotypes are outsiders' beliefs about groups. They constitute assumptions and/or generalizations, based on experience, that allow an educated guess about how someone or some group will behave that allow us to organize and understand our environment. Stereotypes aid us in predicting behavior and reduce our feelings of uncertainty. Stereotypes may be dangerous, however, when we apply them to any individual member from that group. This is especially a concern in cross-cultural communication. We can say that a stereotype is useful in suggesting how we should approach an unknown stranger, but as we learn about that person we should abandon general assumptions for specific individual knowledge. There is no guarantee that any individual from a specific culture will behave as members of that culture generally behave according to the stereotype.

The *social organization* of cultures is another variable that influences one's perceptions. Hofstede and Hofstede[27] developed a cultural dimensions theory based on five value dimensions and their impact on national cultural organizational culture (see Chapter 1 for Hofstede's earlier work). They argued that these five values dimensions strongly influenced social organization (and individual behavior) in predictable directions.

Roles in a society are expectations within a culture concerning behavior that may affect communication. Some roles have very prescriptive rules. Gender is an obvious example. In Western business, there is an expectation of gender equality that may not be found in various conservative cultures. Western companies typically send female expatriates to conservative societies, Saudi Arabia for example, where the rights of women are not as well established. These female expatriates are usually treated as foreigners rather than as women, assuming they are not members of the ethnic group to which they have been sent. Merchant[28] observed that the role of female expatriates may be affected by their gender; as much by their own stereotypical expectations about the culture they have been sent to, as by how they are actually treated.

Language skill in a host country is acknowledged as important. Many believe, however, that a competent interpreter can be helpful and, at times, necessary even if we speak the native language. A competent interpreter may help us understand the deliberations of those we negotiate with. An interpreter is also helpful to ensure that the opposite side's translator is providing an accurate translation of our own statements. An interpreter may, therefore, be useful even if you do speak the local language.

NONVERBAL COMMUNICATION

Earlier in this chapter, we noted that 80 to 90 percent of communication was nonverbal in that it involved no exchange of words.[29] Hall, an anthropologist generally acknowledged as the founder of the intercultural communications field,[30] observed that much of what anyone communicated was done unconsciously. There was an "out-of-awareness" level of communication[31] on the part of the "speaker" that was received at an out-of-awareness level by the receiver. Intercultural communications could be influenced profoundly and negatively without the conscious awareness of either side. Because neither side was aware of this level of communication, it represented an uncontrolled dimension of interpersonal communication operating at the level of the unconscious.[32] The purpose of the following sections is to acquaint you with these unconscious media and their effects on intercultural communication.

Low- and high-context communication

Hall makes a vital distinction between high- and low-context cultures, and how this impacts communications. A *high-context culture* uses more vague forms of (or high-context) communications. Information is either understood to be in the physical context or internalized in the person so that less has to be communicated in the explicit words or message. Japan, Saudi Arabia, and Spain are cultures characterized by high-context communications.

On the other hand, a *low-context culture* employs more direct (or low-context) forms of communications. It is assumed that receivers need the context around the communication and so most information is contained in explicit codes, such as words. Canada and the United States, as well as many European countries, regard low-context communications as the norm.

When individuals communicate, they attempt to find out how much the listener knows about whatever is being discussed. In a low-context communication, the listener is assumed to know very little and must be told practically everything. In high-context cultures, the listener is already "contexted" and therefore does not need to have much background information.

When communicating with individuals of our own culture, we can more readily assess the communication cues so that we know when our conversation, our ideas, and

E X H I B I T 2.2

EXHIBIT 2.2 MIDDLE EAST LOW/HIGH CONTEXT COMMUNICATION

"How many days did it take?" I asked.

"I will tell you. We watered at al Ghaba in the Amairi. There were four of us, myself, Salim, Janazil of the Awamir, and Alaiwi of the Afar; it was in the middle of summer. We had been to Ibri to settle the feud between the Rashid and the Mahamid started by the killing of Fahad's son."

Musallim interrupted, "That must have been before the Riqaishi was Governor of Ibri. I had been there myself the year before. Sahail was with me and we went there from…"

But al Auf went on, "I was riding the three-year-old I had bought from bin Duailan."

"The one the Manahil raided from the Yam?" Bin Kabina asked.

"Yes. I exchanged it later for the yellow six-year-old I got from bin Ham. Janazil rode a Batina camel. Do you remember her? She was the daughter of the famous gray which belonged to the Harahaish of the Wahiba."

Mabkhaut said, "Yes, I saw her last year when he was in Salala, a tall animal; she was old when I saw her, past her prime but even then a real beauty."

Al Auf went on, "We spent the night with Rai of the Afar."

Bin Kabina chimed in, "I met him last year when he came to Habarut; he carried a rifle, 'a father of 10 shots,' which he had taken from the Mahra he had killed in the Ghudun. Bin Mautlauq offered him the gray yearling, the daughter of Farha, and 50 riyals for this rifle, but he refused."

Al Auf continued, "Rai killed a goat for our dinner and told us …," but I interrupted: "Yes, but how many days did it take you to get to Bai?" He looked at me in surprise and said, "Am I not telling you?"

Source: Thesiger, W. *Arabian Sands*. London: Penguin Books, 1991.

words are being understood and internalized. However, communication between high- and low-context people is often fraught with impatience and irritation on both sides. Low-context communicators may provide more information than high-context receivers feel necessary, and be regarded by the latter as repetitive or even disrespectful of others' time. High-context communicators may not provide enough information or background for low-context listeners, and be regarded as difficult to understand, or even as holding back important information. High-context communicators may feel that they are expected to be blunt to an almost disrespectful level just to get their messages across to low-context listeners.

When communicating across cultures, communication misunderstandings can occur, but they are usually not serious and can be rectified. Exhibit 2.2 is an excellent example of low-context question responded to by a very high-context Middle-Eastern communicator.

When communicating across cultures, communication misunderstandings can occur, but they are usually not serious and can be rectified. Exhibit 2.3 illustrates a communication misunderstanding that had grave results. It is the transcript of the conversation between the captain, copilot, and controller on the Avianca flight that crashed on Long Island, New York, in 1991.

The communication misunderstanding involves the high- and low-context communication styles. It can be seen from this dialogue between the pilot, copilot, and controller (Exhibit 2.3) that there was a critical misunderstanding between the copilot who was

EXHIBIT 2.3 AN EMERGENCY

Captain to Copilot: "Tell them we are in emergency."

Copilot to Controller: "We are running out of fuel."

Controller: "Climb and maintain 3,000."

Copilot to Controller: "Uh, we're running out of fuel."

Controller: "I'm going to bring you about 15 miles northeast and then turn you back …. Is that fine with you and your fuel?"

Copilot: "I guess so."

The jet ran out of fuel and crashed.

E
X
H
I
B
I
T

2.3

Colombian (native language Spanish and high context), and the American controller, who was a low-context communicator. "Emergency" is low context. "We are running out of fuel" is more high context (literally, all airplanes, once they take off, are running out of fuel). The controller's last question, "Is that fine with you and your fuel?" is more high context. The controller could have asked, "Are you declaring a fuel emergency?" If the controller had asked this question, perhaps the copilot would have responded "yes" because he or she had just heard the pilot say, "Tell them we are in emergency."

Unless global leaders are aware of the subtle differences, communication misunderstandings between low- and high-context communicators can result. Japanese communicate by not stating things directly, while Canadians usually do just the opposite – often declaring, "spell it all out, please." The former looks for meaning and understanding in what is not said – in the nonverbal communication or body language, in the silences and pauses, in relationships and empathy. The latter is not as used to interpreting nonverbal communication and emphasizes sending and receiving accurate messages directly, usually by articulating words.

Slow versus fast messaging preferences

There has been a tremendous emphasis on fast messaging in Euro-North American cultures in last few years. The days of "snail" mail, telephones with or without answering machines, pagers, and even taking your time answering email, are receding quickly into the past. These days we carry smartphones and tablets to ensure we get and reply to email ASAP. And younger folks often prefer texting, allowing a rapid exchange of instant messages in "real" time. One study showed that the predominant form of communication for people between ages 35 and 50 was email, but for people younger than 35, texting was the preferred means of communication. Even telephone conversations are becoming passé; reserved for telephone salespersons, and older folks who haven't really discovered the electronic age. Why take the time to phone and possibly have to leave a message when usually a text message will be received and responded to almost instantly. If someone is not instantly available, we often find ways to work around him/her. We find someone else more readily accessible.

Even slow-message-preferring cultures like China and Japan are getting into the act. In China, for example, text messaging is a way to get around the state censors that try to monitor and restrict freedom of speech, and do a pretty thorough job with the Internet and email.

Hall and Hall[33] observed, however, there were both fast and slow frequencies by which messages could be sent, and that there were cultural preferences as to which were preferred. Exhibit 2.4 indicates sources for fast and slow messaging. Note that the fast and slow equivalents are given side by side.

Hall and Hall[34] observed that part of the difference between the fast- and slow-message cultures was the quality of interpersonal relationships that cultures valued. In

EXHIBIT 2.4 FAST AND SLOW MESSAGES

Fast messaging	Slow messaging
Prose	Poetry
Headlines; news summaries	Books
A communiqué	An ambassador
Propaganda	Art
Cartoons	Etchings
TV commercials	TV documentaries
Television and radio and Internet	Print
Quick, easy, familiarity	Slow, deep relationships
Ideologies	Culture
Telephone (becoming slower)	Telephone answering machines
Email	Mail from the post office
Texting	Telephone

Japan, personal relationships tended to take a long time to develop and solidify, and were based on knowing a lot about, and having a lot in common with another.

The same was true in China. Kipnis[35] observed that there were three levels of relationship in Chinese culture. The people you trusted most were your family members about whom you knew everything, good or bad. Almost as good were the network of close friends you built up at school – your "old boys or girls" network. These were friends you had a special emotional commitment to ("ganqing") because you shared a lot of personal context with. The least valuable were "meat and potato" friends who hoped to ingratiate themselves, and become instrumental friends, by buying you lunch.

Western businesspeople understood that to build valuable relationships in China, you had to spend the time to develop trust and personal feeling for each other, through cooperation, finding shared interests and goals, handling disagreements constructively, and being reliable over a long period of time. Otherwise, you were just a "meat and potatoes" friend to the Chinese and achieved worse outcomes in China.[36] Fast messaging would be more commonly directed to "meat and potatoes" friends.

These considerations pose a red flag for twenty-first-century Euro-North American businesspeople. Fast messaging has become the norm in these cultures. It is, however, a very culture laden practice. Even though business cultures in other cultures – China, or India, for example – have adopted it as well, it may not build effective relationships in slow messaging cultures. We need to remember to take the time and trouble to write more fully and allow the time for our Asian associates to digest our messages and respond in their own way. And if they respond quickly, we should not be surprised, remembering that we should not stereotype in individual cases, as we learn more about each of our associates.

Space preferences

Hall and Hall[37] consider perceptions of appropriate spatial boundaries in terms of territoriality and personal space. Territoriality in animals is the act of laying claim to and defending a physical territory. China's claim to the Republic of Taiwan as an integral part of Chinese territory is an example. In restaurants near our university, groups of Chinese and Taiwanese students argue about what territory belongs to whom. Both sides regard their positions as entirely rational and obvious to anyone. One needs to be sensitive to all these strong feelings. The territorial dispute between Japan and China over the Sendaku Islands (or Diaoyu Islands for the Chinese – Taiwan and South Korea also have claims) may be another example, moderated by the belief that possession will result in undersea oil and gas riches.

Different cultures also have different conceptions about what constitutes an appropriate amount of personal space. This is the "bubble" of space left between individuals, for example, who are communicating with each other. In northern Europe, these bubbles are quite large, but as you go south to France, Italy, Greece, and Spain, the expected size decreases. A space considered "intimate" in northern Europe, or for Americans of northern European ancestry – less than two feet separating – would be considered normal conversing distance between bodies in southern Europe. In Japan and China, people accept levels of crowding in public spaces that would be considered unacceptable in Europe or North America. Violation of these norms – too close or too far apart – may produce a feeling of discomfort whether you are conscious of it or not.

Time preferences

Hall and Hall[38] distinguish between monochronic and polychronic time. In monochromic cultures such as in the United States, Canada, Western Europe, and Japan, time is experienced as linear, like a road that goes from past to future. Time naturally divides into segments, and is efficiently scheduled. There is a strong emphasis on using time efficiently and saving it wherever possible. It's almost sinful to lose or waste time. People burdened with priorities learn at time management courses how to handle less important tasks in as little time as possible.

Latin America and southern Europe are examples of polychromic cultures. They are in almost every way the antitheses of monochromic cultures. A much greater emphasis is placed on involvement with people, and one's schedule is often sacrificed to complete individual transactions or interactions. Japan is an interesting combination because the culture is monochromic in the way schedules are kept with foreigners, and public transport runs exactly on time. However, interpersonal relationships are often conducted polychronically. Exhibit 2.5 highlights the major differences between the two.

There are tremendous opportunities in monochromic cultures to employ electronic communication (texting, email, social media, websites, and so on) to save time by completing tasks quickly and efficiently. We should be aware, however, that individuals in polychromic

EXHIBIT 2.5 MONOCHRONIC VERSUS POLYCHRONIC PEOPLE

Monochronic people	Polychronic people
Do one thing at a time	Do many things at once
Focus intently on their work	Easy to distract; constantly interrupted
Committed to the job	Committed to people and relationships
Deadlines and schedules rigidly kept	Schedules are objectives, to be kept if possible
Emphasize and expect promptness	Need for promptness depends on the relationship
Tend to be low-context and need lots of background information and context	Tend to be high-context and already know or think they know
Adhere to plans with determination	Plans may change easily
Used to short-term relationships	Build lifelong relationships

E
X
H
I
B
I
T

2.5

Source: Hall, E. T. and Hall, M. R. *Hidden Differences.* Garden City, NY: Anchor Doubleday, 1985, pp. 18–19.

cultures could feel uncomfortable with these technologies or see them as emanating from people that they did not have significant relationships with. Therefore, they might not respond as efficiently as we hoped, or might not place as much value on relationships with us because we had not spent the time they preferred in face-to-face contact. Despite the historical tensions Chinese feel about Japan, Chinese businesspeople have reported that they preferred to do business with Japanese sellers because the latter took the time to build personal relationships. If North American sellers sold the Chinese a product, that was the last you saw of them for years until they thought maybe you might need something else. The Chinese called this approach, "disposable relationships."[39] It was also a difference between polychronic and monochronic relationship building.

International body language

Do your actions really speak louder than your words? A study by Ting-Toomey[40] found that up to 65 percent (Hall had observed 90 percent) of a message's meaning is sent through nonverbal cues. A significant component of this is body language, or physical signaling. It contributes to at least three reasons for cross-cultural conflict. First, the same signal has different meanings in different cultures. Second, many nonverbal signals are sent in each interaction, making interpretation ambiguous. Third, personality, gender, socioeconomic status, and the situation may all produce variants in bodily signaling adding to potential confusion.[41] Exhibit 2.6 lists the many types of nonverbal communication.

Nonverbal signals or gestures are used in all cultures, and understanding the differences can help us become better cross-cultural communicators. Furnham[42] reported an example of similar body language cues having different cultural reactions. He said,

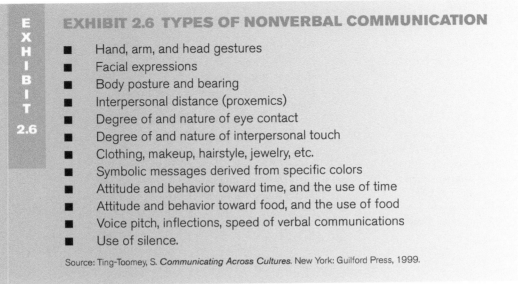

EXHIBIT 2.6 TYPES OF NONVERBAL COMMUNICATION

- Hand, arm, and head gestures
- Facial expressions
- Body posture and bearing
- Interpersonal distance (proxemics)
- Degree of and nature of eye contact
- Degree of and nature of interpersonal touch
- Clothing, makeup, hairstyle, jewelry, etc.
- Symbolic messages derived from specific colors
- Attitude and behavior toward time, and the use of time
- Attitude and behavior toward food, and the use of food
- Voice pitch, inflections, speed of verbal communications
- Use of silence.

Source: Ting-Toomey, S. *Communicating Across Cultures*. New York: Guilford Press, 1999.

"Research in the United States has shown that tips tend to be larger if the waiter touches the diner . . . and if the waiter gives a big and 'authentic' initial smile." However, in the UK that same body language exhibited by a waiter may result in no tip at all. Body language is frequently culturally distinct.

International body language can fall under three categories, the first two of which can create problems.

1   A gesture can mean something different to others than it does to you. For example, the A-OK gesture, as used in the United States, means that things are fine, great, or that something has been understood perfectly. But Brazilians interpret it as an obscene gesture, and to the Japanese it means money.

2   A gesture can mean nothing to the person observing it. Scratching one's head or drawing in breath and saying "saa" are common Japanese responses to embarrassment. One can miss these cues as these gestures may have no particular meaning in one's own native culture.

3   A gesture can mean basically the same in both cultures and the meaning is accurately communicated with few possible misunderstandings.

Hand and arm gestures

Most persons use their hands when speaking, to punctuate the flow of conversation, refer to objects or persons, and mimic and illustrate words or ideas. Often, gestures are used in place of words. Generally, Japanese speakers use fewer words and fewer gestures than Canadian speakers. French, including French-Canadians, use more of both. Italians use much more.

In Canada, patting a small child on the head usually conveys affection. But in Malaysia and other Islamic countries, the head is considered the source of one's intellectual and spiritual powers. It is sacred and should not be touched. Australians signal "time to drink up" by folding three fingers of the hand against the palm, leaving the thumb and little finger sticking straight up and out. In China, the same gesture means six.

To get someone's attention or to summon a waiter or waitress is often a problem. This task requires different gestures in different countries. For example, in restaurants in North American countries, one would call a waiter or waitress quietly, "sir," "miss," or "waiter," raise a finger to catch his or her attention, or tilt one's head to one side. Do not snap your fingers. In the Middle East, clapping one's hands is effective. In Japan, extend your arm slightly upward, palm down, and flutter your fingers. In Spain and Latin America, extend your hand, palm down, and rapidly open and close your fingers. In Brazil, make a "hissing" sound.

Eye contact

In many Western cultures, a person who does not maintain good eye contact is regarded as slightly suspect. Those who avoid eye contact are unconsciously considered unfriendly, insecure, untrustworthy, inattentive, and impersonal. By contrast, Japanese children are taught in school to direct their gaze at the region of their teacher's Adam's apple or tie knot. As adults, Japanese lower their eyes when speaking to a superior as a gesture of respect. In Canadian First Nations' cultures, those who seek and maintain eye contact are the ones considered suspicious and questionable.

In Latin American cultures and some African cultures, such as Nigeria, prolonged eye contact from an individual of lower status is considered disrespectful. In the United States, it is considered rude to stare — regardless of who is looking at whom. By contrast, the polite English person is taught to pay strict attention to a speaker, to listen carefully, and to blink his or her eyes to let the speaker know he or she has been understood as well as heard. Americans signal interest and comprehension by bobbing their heads or grunting.

INTERCULTURAL COMMUNICATION GUIDELINES

Achieving successful intercultural communication can be a challenging — even daunting — task. Interculturally, you need to study the culture you will be working with, and to understand the key ways it is different from your own. When you are the speaker, you have to be sensitive to values, norms, and attitudinal differences so that you don't make your receiver uncomfortable. You need to be informed and watch to provide the right context (high or low), and the right messaging speed, without intruding on your receiver's personal space bubble. You need to be sensitive as to how he/she regards the time you are taking, making sure your gestures are appropriate, and whether you should make eye contact or not, or some. There are skilled international personnel who can do all this and more as easily as we might ride a bicycle. They have been doing it a long time. It takes a long time to get good at intercultural communication. And it's difficult to prescribe what each individual reader needs to concentrate on because each one of us is different.

There are, however, some general guidelines that anyone should be aware of while building up one's sensitivity to all the potential pitfalls in intercultural communication. Exhibit 2.7 summarizes a number of behaviors research has identified as useful for intercultural effectiveness.

Guidelines using English with non-English speakers

On average, most Europeans speak more than one language. For example, Switzerland, a relatively small country, has three official languages; French, German, and Italian. Canada has two official languages, English and French, and while not nearly all citizens are bilingual it sure is helpful if an Anglo-Canadian can speak passible French in the province of Quebec where only French is officially recognized. The typical Japanese studies English as well as other languages. English is becoming a second language in China and most Chinese students coming to study in North America are reasonably fluent or working hard to become so. This is not the case for most U.S. citizens who, even when they study a foreign language, often lack fluency. Americans generally expect to conduct their business in English, either because their local contacts have learned English or through the use of interpreters.

EXHIBIT 2.7

EXHIBIT 2.7 RESEARCH IDENTIFIED BEHAVIORS MOST IMPORTANT FOR INTERCULTURAL EFFECTIVENESS

- Demonstrate respect (verbally and nonverbally)
- Respond to people in a nonjudgmental, non-evaluative manner
- Recognize that your exact knowledge, beliefs, and perceptions are unique and valid only for yourself
- Demonstrate empathy
- Listen carefully and try to show you've understood by saying what you think the speaker has said
- Have tolerance for ambiguity
- Turn off your behavioral auto-pilot and actively manage how you interact with others
- Demonstrate a willingness to adopt different roles and adapt your behaviors

The good news for these Americans and other native English-speaking people is that English has become a global language and is recognized in many places around the world as the language of commerce. Many international businesspeople have learned English as a second language (ESL). The bad news is that even though ESL people are usually doing their best to function in English, they may not have as good a command of the language as you might hope. And the pronunciation accents of some ESL English speakers may require a lot of practice to understand.

You could rely on interpreters if one is available or affordable. Translation does, however, have downsides. It is slow since what one says in English must be translated bit by bit, so less detail may be communicated. Translators often do not provide a full translation of what is being said. Sometimes translators lack the specialized vocabulary to accurately translate business concepts. There is also the problem of equivalence of concepts between languages. The same word may mean something quite different from language to language. For example, in English, "consensus" means that everyone agrees. In Japanese, it means that the other party is willing to agree but expects you to compromise on some other later point. Sounds like compromise, but if you didn't know, you could get in trouble later not realizing the other side believed you owed them one in return.

In any event, you will often find yourself doing intercultural communication with ESL people whose command of English may not be as good as a native English speaker. This can easily lead to misunderstandings. You may only discover these when the final contract is produced in both native languages, and you have the one in their language back-translated into English (a good practice). Riddle and Lanham[43] proposed some guidelines for handling these kinds of situations, and others are based on the authors' experience.

1   Use simple English. Practice using the most common 3,000 words in English; that is, those words typically learned in the first two years of language study. Avoid uncommon words; for example, use "witty" rather than "jocose," or "effective" rather than "efficacious."

2   In writing, use maximum punctuation; for example, use commas that help clarify the meaning, but that could technically be omitted.

3   Conform to basic grammar rules more strictly than is common in everyday conversation. Make sure that sentences express a complete thought, that pronouns and antecedents are used correctly, and that subordination is accurately expressed. A Japanese associate finds the lack of rigid English grammatical and pronunciation rules frustrating because both are clearly defined in Japanese.

4   Avoid the use of idiom and slang.

5   Avoid terms borrowed from sports (e.g., "struck out," "field that question," "can't get to first base"), the military (e.g., "run a tight ship"), or literature (e.g., "catch-22"). With international associates, you may have to explain the game.

6   When speaking or writing to someone you do not know well, use their last name and keep the tone formal while expressing personal interest or concern. In

Germany, people are often uncomfortable with the American practice of using only first names.

7   Oral presentations should be made plainly, clearly, and slowly, using visual aids whenever possible.

8   Important face-to-face or telephoned international business communications should be confirmed by email, fax, or letter, preferably in both languages.

9   Written brochures, proposals, and reports should be translated into the native language of the receiver or client. However, you should send both the English material and its translation. In China for example, carrying an English brochure is a status symbol that others may envy even if no one can read it. Too often, it is only the English brochure that is sent, communicating nothing but ignorance.

10 Communication by email, texting, or through websites has the disadvantage that you do not know the receiver's culture, values, norms, and so on. You don't see the nonverbal response. As fast messages from a monochromic culture, possibly high context if little context is provided, with a strong expectation of a fast response, there are many possibilities for ineffective communications. If it is important, it is best to stick with email and provide considerably more context than would be normal within North American electronic communication.

Companies work hard not only to ensure accurate translations, but also to achieve fortuitous translations. Accurate and fortuitous translation is dependent upon knowledge of the intended group's culture and how their cultural values influence their perceptions. For example, Sang and Zhang[44] provide examples of English corporate names translated into Mandarin Chinese. The goal in each case was to achieve a sound similar to that of the English, while highlighting positive Chinese values to create a basis for corporate trust:

■   Ford = Fu Te, or Fortune and Uniqueness;
■   Nike = Nai Ke, or Endurance and Victory;
■   Desis (a Pesticide company) = Di Sha Si, or Enemy, Kill, Dead.

When Exxon first entered Japan it chose "Enco" as its name. This turned out to mean "stalled car" in Japanese. Coca-Cola's first name in Asia employed Chinese characters that produced the right sounds but meant "Bite the wax tadpole."

MANAGING THROUGH INTERCULTURAL SIMILARITY

The traditional approach to intercultural communication has followed Hall's differences-focused approach by comparing and contrasting cultural communication practices between cultures.[45] More recently, researchers have noted that the problem with this focus on comparative differences has been the neglect of observed similarities between cultures,[46] and the reinforcement of the inaccurate view that all cultures are entirely unique.[47] Often, because of Hall's influence, there has been little effort to specify how cross-cultural similarities could be used to facilitate intercultural communication.[48]

We can understand Hall's bias in favor of identifying cross-cultural differences. He was an anthropologist in the tradition of Franz Boas who contended that every culture was unique and that no commonalities existed across all cultures. Hall worked for years in an institution, the Foreign Service Institute, whose purpose was to prepare diplomats to serve at specific cultural locations throughout the world. It made perfect sense to acquaint students with all the cultural differences they would encounter in the culture they were to be dispatched.

There are, however, reasons that would support the strategy of identifying cultural similarities that could be used to improve intercultural communications as well. In certain industries, the hospitality industry for example, managers and staff in a particular location may encounter individual customers from a wide range of cultural backgrounds. It would be difficult to prepare them in detail for all possible cross-cultural differences they might experience. Similarly, a competent hospitality industry manager might be promoted to a new location and encounter novel cultural conditions for which he/she was entirely unprepared.

Modern twenty-first-century electronic and Internet based communications have expanded the seriousness of these problems. We routinely communicate by email (or texting, or Twitter, or Facebook) with colleagues and strangers in the United States, Japan, China, Korea, First Nations (in Canada), and parts of Europe – all over the world. It is a daunting task to be "up" on cultural differences related to values, norms, attitudes, stereotypes, roles, contexts, messaging speeds, space bubbles, timing, body language and eye contact (via Skype), and how our words will be interpreted by ESL people in any culture from which we could send or receive electronic communication. And it is not possible to read up on all these variables before responding to an email when common email etiquette requires an almost instantaneous response.

What we need to know are some common cross-cultural similarities that will improve our odds of successful communication, especially with individuals from cultures with which we are not immediately familiar. Now, if we discovered that we were going to have a lot of business to do with people in that culture, we would want to become familiar with the cultural differences but we would also continue to rely on our knowledge of cultural similarities as well. Relying on general cultural similarities to improve communications may not be the most effective approach in individual cases, but it helps us stay out of trouble – it offers a more satisficing approach.

In the following sections, we will propose three well-known areas of cultural similarity that could serve these purposes. First, there are common *personality dimensions*, demonstrated by much research to be characteristic of humans as a species regardless of which culture they belong. Understanding personality dimensions helps us because they provide a useful stereotype about how people from a specific culture tend to process information, communicate about it, and make decisions. This knowledge can even be used to select expatriates with personality dimensions similar to those predominant in a particular culture. Research shows that effective selection can reduce some of the effects of cultural differences.[49]

Second, evolutionary psychology tells us that there are two interpersonal relationship strategies inherent in humans-as-species. These are called *self-interested* and *altruistic* in this literature,[50] or I/It and I/Thou in the philosophy and business literature.[51] Research has shown that altruistic or I/Thou relationships are far more likely to achieve trust and genuine cooperation than are self-interested or I/It relationships even though the latter as far more common in business.

Third, there is an interpersonal communication process called *Nonviolent Communication* (NVC), built upon and enhancing active listening, that may be considered as a technology for building altruistic or I/Thou relationships. It is a proven method for conducting successful cross-cultural negotiations in antagonistic situations, such as between the Hutu and Tutsi in Rwanda, or Palestinians and Israelis in the Middle East.[52]

Personality similarities and cultural differences

Personality psychology research[53] has consistently observed that the same personality dimensions exist in humans as a species, and that the effects of personality are independent of culture.[54] Different personality models contain different numbers of dimensions. The well-known Big Five[55] includes five dimensions whereas the Jungian model[56] (including the Myers-Briggs MBTI, and Keirsey Temperament versions) contains four dimensions. See Exhibit 2.8 for a comparative overview of these two models.

EXHIBIT 2.8 THE BIG FIVE AND JUNGIAN PERSONALITY DIMENSIONS

Big Five dimensions	Description	Jungian dimensions
Extraversion	Sociable vs. retiring; fun-loving vs. sober; interactive vs. reserved	Extravert/Introvert
Openness	Imaginative vs. down-to-earth; preference for variety vs. routine.	Sensing/Intuiting
Agreeableness	Softhearted vs. hardhearted; helpful vs. analytical; merciful vs. just	Thinking/Feeling
Conscientiousness	Well-organized vs. disorganized; careful vs. careless; fast vs. slow	Judging/Perceiving
Neuroticism	Worried vs. calm; insecure vs. secure; self-pitying vs. self-satisfied	

Source: Ting-Toomey, S. *Communicating Across Cultures.* New York: Guilford Press, 1999.

While advocates of the Big Five have condemned the Jungian model for missing the Neuroticism dimension, various researchers have proposed models ranging from three to as many as 16 factors. One three-dimensional model that has received much attention related to intercultural communication, particularly between North America and Asia, is the Human Dynamics model.[57] We will discuss how the Human Dynamics approach facilitates intercultural communication through the identification of similarities, and add specific examples from other research using the Jungian (Keirsey[58]) model.

Human dynamics

The personality dimensions, or principles, of Human Dynamics have been verified with extensive studies in six nations (the USA, Canada, England, Sweden, Israel, Singapore), and interview/observational studies in twenty other nations. All individuals in every study represent either the *mental, emotional*, or *physical* principle in the centering of their psychology, though in different distributions by national culture.

The names of these principles are derived from the strengths they confer on those illuminated by them. Individuals characterized by the *mental* principle are rational ahead of all else. They may seem a bit like Mr. Spock of the starship *Enterprise*. They focus on logical understanding of concepts and ideas. Those characterized by the *emotional* principle are above all else relational. They are most concerned with interpersonal interaction and relationships. Those characterized by the *physical* principle are especially practical and applied in their thinking. Exhibit 2.9 differentiates these three principles in detail.

EXHIBIT 2.9 THREE UNIVERSAL PRINCIPLES

	Mental principle	Emotional principle	Physical principle
Overview Emphasizes	Ideational Concepts and ideas Structures	Interpersonal Relationships Social organization	Operational Action Operations
Process	Linear, logical, sequential	Lateral through emotional association, rather than logical connection	Systemic through comprehensive gathering, linking and seeing connections between data
Functions	Seeing the overview Establishing values and principles Maintaining objectivity Conceptualizing	Feeling, connecting, relating, personalizing, empathizing Communicating, organizing, harmonizing	Doing, making, concretizing, detailing, making operational Synthesizing Ensuring practicality Cooperating

Source: Derived from Seagal, S. and Horne, D. *Human Dynamics: A New Framework for Understanding People and Realizing the Potential in Our Organizations*. Waltham, CA: Pegasus, 1997.

EXHIBIT 2.9

In addition to this central principle for organizing personality, individuals also have a secondary principle; again *mental, emotional*, or *physical*. "The central principle determines to a large degree *how* one processes information, and the secondary principle drives *what* kind of information one tends to process."[59] While this model would in theory produce nine personality types (3 central × 3 secondary), in practice only five have been generally observed in human cultures. Each of these five has characteristic sets of preferences and rhythms in their communication patterns. The five personality types and their preferred communication patterns are summarized in Exhibit 2.10.

EXHIBIT 2.10

EXHIBIT 2.10 HUMAN DYNAMICS: COMMUNICATION "RHYTHMS"

Dynamic	Communication rhythms
Emotional mental (Em)	Prefer to discuss issues interactively. Use brainstorming process with individuals quickly offering ideas. Expressing an idea is a way of beginning a discussion. They appreciate others expanding or challenging, feeling this represents openness and forward momentum. Their goal is to achieve a plan for immediate actions and general directions for the future.
Emotional physical (Ep)	Prefer a highly interpersonal process. Likely to begin with someone giving a dramatic account of a personal experience. Others will recount what they consider related experiences. Process may appear chaotic to non Ep. Usual result is creative and multifaceted conclusions accounting for all participants' personal needs. Their goals are both an appropriate plan and a satisfying interpersonal process.
Physical emotional (Pe)	Prefer to discuss with an even, steady, and deliberate quality. Likely to begin with one person laying out context, often historical antecedents. Each person lays out whole pieces of information; context, continuity between past and present. Speak one at a time with silences for processing. May appear overly detailed and methodical to non Pe. Goal is a highly practical and comprehensive plan of action.
Physical mental (Pm)	As with Pe, pacing is even and one speaks at a time, laying out whole pieces of information. Prefer to establish context and accumulate factual data but in less detail than Pe. Language is precise and the flow of discussion logical like Mp. Focus is generally on the end purpose, clarifying it early. This makes their process faster than Pe. The goal is a clear strategic plan, often illustrated with models, diagrams, and charts.
Mental physical (Mp)	Prefer to discuss issues abstractly. Speak one at a time; precisely, logically, orderly. Even paced speech with silences for processing. Their goal is to establish guiding principles, and a clear and long range plan.

Source: Seagal, S. and Horne, D. *Human Dynamics*. Waltham, CA: Pegasus, 1997.

These personality types are interesting for intercultural communications because of the systematic differences in distributions of predominant personality types from culture to culture. Euro-North American samples have been predominantly characterized by the emotional principle. Euro-North American corporate culture tends to be dominated by the Emotional-mental (Em) mindset. Individuals are far more likely, however, to be characterized by the Emotional-physical (Ep) mindset. In the past, Seagal and Horne asserted that up to 80 percent of North Americans were characterized by the emotional principle, with 20 percent Emotional mental, and 60 percent Emotional physical.

By contrast, only about 10 percent of Euro-North Americans were identified as either mentally centered or physically centered. The physically entered were approximately 5 percent Physical emotional (Pe), and 5 percent Physical mental (Pm). More recently, Seagal and Horne[60] have found somewhat more physically centered in North America but the predominance of the emotional principle is unchallenged.

By contrast, Asian samples have been predominantly physically centered with only a relatively small minority of emotionally or mentally centered. Chinese samples, including Singapore, have been predominantly Physical emotional (Pe). Japanese samples have been predominantly Physical mental (Pm). Euro-North Americans who spend the bulk of their careers in East Asia tend to be physically centered. They feel particularly at home in these physically centered cultures – more so than in their own home cultures.

This characteristic personality difference between Euro-North America and Asia – emotional versus physical centering – has resulted in some significant Western versus Asian differences that affect intercultural communications. These are summarized in Exhibit 2.11. Should you find yourself trying to communicate with someone from China or Japan (or

EXHIBIT 2.11 WESTERN VERSUS ASIAN DIFFERENCES

	Emotional centering (Western)	Physical centering (Asian)
Orientation	Individualistic (I, me, my)	Collectivistic (we, us, our)
Time focus	Present and immediate future	Continuity of past and present into the long-term future
Learning process	Derived from individual experiences and interpretations. Requires dialogue, interaction with others, opportunities for experiment and self-expression	Through individual study of detailed texts; hands-on experiences; memorization; repetition
Physical movements	Spontaneous	Deliberate
Communication process	Expressive of individual personality, ideas, feelings, and subjective awareness	Factual; detailed; expressive of group decision-making

Source: Seagal, S. and Horne, D. *Human Dynamics*. Waltham, CA: Pegasus, 1997.

Euro-North America), you could use Exhibits 2.9, 2.10, and 2.11 to predict issues that could negatively effect your communication process. Obviously, you couldn't ask them to fill out a questionnaire, and Human Dynamics has been designed to allow you to type someone through simple observation.

In addition to these general differences, each of the Emotional (mental and physical) and Physical (emotional and mental) personality types had characteristic needs for specific styles of communication process. As well, each has functional strengths they contribute to communication process and outcomes. These are summarized in Exhibit 2.12. In this exhibit, the Mental-physical mindset was left out because it has not been found to be more than a very small minority of individuals in any culture except the United Kingdom, where it still remained a somewhat larger minority. For Euro-North Americans engaged in intercultural communications with Asians, the Emotional/Physical mindset differences are key.

EXHIBIT 2.12 COMMUNICATION NEEDS AND STRENGTHS

Dynamic	Communication needs	Functional strengths
Emotional mental (Em)	■ Direct ■ Goal directed	■ Forward movement ■ Innovation
(Western corporate mindset)	■ Giving general picture ■ Interplay of ideas	■ Create models ■ Short-range planning
Emotional physical (Ep)	■ Personal connection ■ Sensitive to others' feelings	■ People issues ■ Processing feelings ■ Personal communication
(Predominant North America mindset)	■ Sincere feeling expression ■ Process oriented	■ Create new organizational forms
Physical emotional (Pe)	■ Considerable context and detail	■ Ensure practicality ■ Ensure continuity
(Predominant Chinese mindset)	■ Factual, practical and applied ■ Allowing sufficient time to process	■ Operationalization ■ Create comprehensive interrelated systems
Physical mental (Pm)	■ Purpose established from beginning	■ Strategic planning ■ Modeling plans
(Predominant Japanese mindset)	■ Sufficient context and detail ■ Factual and structured ■ Allowing sufficient time to process	■ Ensure practicality and continuity ■ Operationalization ■ Create systems

Source: Seagal, S. and Horne, D. *Human Dynamics*. Waltham, CA: Pegasus, 1997.

The Emotional-mental mindset, characterizing Western corporate culture, is experienced as pushy and controlling by other mindsets. It prefers "direct" and unvarnished communication which is an issue in both China and Japan where a loss of "face" through feeling disrespected is a major concern.

A senior Chinese manager at Nortel Beijing once reported that he and his Chinese colleagues found their Western counterparts very difficult because they did not respect Chinese "face." The Americans would suggest a practice based on how things were done in the United States or elsewhere in the world. The Chinese would say it wouldn't work in China for whatever cultural or practical reasons. The Americans would argue, and challenge the Chinese to provide evidence. The Chinese would fall silent, feeling a loss of face because their experience had been disrespected, and aware that whatever they said would be further challenged. The Americans would implement their plan and it wouldn't work, and then they would complain that the Chinese had not warned them. From the point-of-view of the American Emotional-mental person, however, the Chinese Physical-emotional person is perceived as too slow, and insisting on too great a level of contextual detail as part of his/her discussions. The Em mindset strongly prefers forward momentum and speedy decisions. It does not like to get bogged down in too much detail.

By contrast, the Emotional-physical mindset, characteristic of the majority of North American expatriates, is experienced as "touchy-feely" by other mindsets. Most Chinese and Japanese businesspeople are very restrained in physical expressions of camaraderie in negotiations. American negotiators who squeeze your hand hard in shaking hands and then won't let go, or who slap you on the back, or are perceived as inappropriately personal, are generally not appreciated. Japanese counterparts, often Physical mental, are often perceived by Emotional physicals as aloof and uncaring because they want to focus on the problem and not the interaction dynamics. The Ep believes he/she can build a firm relationship on the spot through sincerity. The Pm believes sincere relationship takes a long time to build.

This Human Dynamics model is useful in simplifying the complexities of intercultural communications in two ways. First, it offers a simplified stereotype of a relatively small number of key information processing differences, and proposes how, for example, the pitfalls for a Euro-North American doing intercultural communication with Chinese counterparts would be different than with Japanese counterparts. Similar research using, for example, the Jungian/MBTI/Keirsey personality model, has offered the same kind of useful simplification for doing business with Thai,[61] and Korean[62] counterparts.

We should, however, reiterate that stereotypes cut both ways. They are useful as an initial estimation of the foreign counterpart you are meeting for the first time. We say, "the Chinese are predominantly Physical emotional," for example, meaning often. The actual Chinese person you communicate with may also be Physical mental, Emotional mental, Emotional physical, or even Mental physical but the probabilities are much lower. You begin with the stereotype but if it does not produce the anticipated results, you vary your communication style looking for positive reactions.

Seagal and Horne's book[63] offers a compendium of behavioral signs of their five universal mindsets and can be a very helpful resource. One purpose of *Human Dynamics International*, Seagal and Horne's company, is to teach international team building between individuals with these five mindsets.

Second, because the effects of universal personality types and national culture are independent (neither causes the other), we can use personality mindset as a selection criterion for sending expatriates who will be more effective at intercultural communication in that location. The important thing to realize is that because of the differential distribution of personality types across nations, everyone is likely to be effective somewhere.[64]

For example, in our own research using Keirsey model of personality,[65] we found that 72 percent of Korean managers were characterized by the same Keirsey temperament mindset (called SJ or Logistical). By contrast, only 52 percent of Canadian managers shared this mindset. Even though there were the anticipated strong cultural differences in behavioral preferences between the two, there were significantly less cultural differences between the Koreans and Canadians that shared the same mindset. By contrast, there were much stronger cultural differences between the Koreans and those Canadians from one of the other three Keirsey temperament mindsets. It was evident that if the Canadian expatriates sent to Korea to negotiate shared the predominant Korean information processing mindset, their intercultural communications problems would be much reduced.

I/Thou (altruistic) versus I/It (self-interested) relationships

Evolutionary psychology is the analysis of biologically based mental mechanisms characteristic of all humans-as-species, developed through evolution, and their influence on human behavior.[66] These mental mechanisms are understood to influence behavior in consistent ways, and to be culturally and historically invariable,[67] representing stereotypical information processing preferences that result in typical sets of action.[68] Evolutionary psychology is based on Darwin's original theory of natural selection, stating that evolution affected both physiological and psychological functions and capabilities.[69]

For example, if humans encountered strangers from unfamiliar groups or cultures uncountable numbers of times over many generations, certain ways of interacting with them would emerge as more (or less) effective. Individuals better able to respond in these more effective ways would have greater psychological fitness and this would confer a survival advantage. Over time, those having a survival advantage would become more numerous and eventually this fitness advantage would become characteristic of all humans.

Evolutionary psychology research has identified two characteristic interaction strategies for relationship building common to all humans. All humans are capable of approaching interaction with others using either *self-interest* or *altruist* strategies. All humans have a tendency to prefer either the one or the other depending on their personal experience in achieving the desired outcome of effective relationships.

Self-interest is a strategy for using power to influence a weaker other to provide what one wants even at the other's expense. Altruism is a strategy for helping a weaker other by providing what he/she needs in order to build a cooperative relationship where the other will help in return if or when needed.

There are two kinds of altruist strategies. *Reciprocal altruism*, commonly found in Chinese guanxi relationships, expects that the person who has been helped will provide a reciprocal return of similar and/or equivalent value within an anticipated timeframe. *Costly signaling*, commonly found among close friends, provides unlimited support for a weaker other as long as it is needed, intending to signal that one may be trusted and would make a good friend. Good friends typically support each other "through thick and thin." According to evolutionary psychology, any intercultural communication may find its basis either in self-interest, or in one of the altruism strategies.

The same dichotomy of interaction strategies has been observed in existential philosophy. Both Buber[70] and Marcel[71] observed that there were two ways that people interacted. I/It relationships were based on one's own self-interest. One treated the other person as an object that could be grasped and made to provide whatever outcomes were desired. This is the common approach to most sales' interaction between a seller and a buyer. The seller attempts to use his/her influence to persuade the buyer to purchase the product or service. The problem with this approach was that it provoked resistance on the part of the buyer, and sellers had to learn how to overcome buyer objections to try to close the deal.

By contrast, I/Thou relationships were based on altruism, generally *costly signaling*. One accepted that the other was a self-determining subject like oneself, as opposed to an object to be grasped for a self-interested purpose. One accepted that the other was in charge of his/her own intentions, goals, and actions. One's initial purpose was to success-fully *be* with the other, rather than *acting upon* the other. Being-with was achieved through successful communication that did not attempt to influence. Over time, as mutual coopera-tion and trust developed, the buyer, for example, would come to understand that the seller placed the buyer's needs ahead of his/her own. At the same time, the buyer would start to value the seller's needs more highly than his/her own. A relationship like this eventually became illuminated by love and consideration for the other person, as opposed to trying to have power over each other. When Fisher, Ury, and Patton[72] observe that the easiest nego-tiations are those in which you focus on helping the other solve his/her own problems rather than trying to make the other help solve yours, they are highlighting the difference between I/It and I/Thou.

When we engage in intercultural communications, we have the choice between pursuing our own self-interest, or selecting a more altruistic strategy. We can try to grasp the other person as if he/she was an object – like a screwdriver to help us screw down our objectives. That approach usually provokes resistance no matter how interculturally aware and skillful you are. Or, we can recognize that the other person is a subject like ourselves and in control of his/her own agenda. Then we can work to build cooperation, mutual consideration, and eventually trust. This approach may provoke disbelief in your counterpart at first because so many business interactions are based on self-interest. You have to keep at it until the other person begins to suspect that you might be sincere.

Nonviolent Communication (NVC) is a communication technology that may be used to build altruistic I/Thou relationships. NVC is an interpersonal communication process that, according to Rosenberg,[73] allows altruistic compassion to flourish by guiding practitioners to reframe how they express themselves, and how they listen to others. Using NPC, one focuses one's attention sequentially on four areas of communication.[74]

1   We observe what is actually happening in a situation; what we are observing others to be saying or doing. The "trick" in this first step is to state what we are observing without offering any judgment or evaluation that would imply to the other that we were trying to use our power to make them behave differently.

2   Next, we state how we feel when we observe this action; hurt, scared, irritated, et cetera. Again, this is not a judgment against what the other person is saying or doing but simply how we are relating to the situation.

3   Then, we say what needs we have that are connected to the feelings we have identi-fied in ourselves.

4   Finally, we make a specific behavioral request. This is not a demand because the other person is free to refuse. If he/she does refuse, then the discussion that ensues may be about what he/she is willing to do. Or we may discuss what we ourselves are willing to do in relation to them to improve how we feel or to satisfy our needs.

At the same time, NVC communications entails our own willingness to receive these four pieces of information from the other person including their requests of us. Rosenberg has demonstrated the effectiveness of this approach in intercultural situations including diplomatic and business situations including problem-solving negotiations between hostile groups of Israelis and Palestinians in Israel.

One key to successful NVC is to avoid judgments that appear to others as blame, insults, put-downs, labels, criticisms, comparisons, or diagnoses. Judgments are likely to cause resistance and defensiveness in the form of anger, resentment, fear, guilt, or even shame. They move the communication from being about actual situations or events, to being about the feelings engendered by the discussion. Rosenberg offers an extended example in Exhibit 2.13.

A second key is that a request for change must be very specific and not appear to be a demand. A request is a demand when the receiver hears that he/she will be inconve-nienced, blamed, or punished should he/she fail to comply. One perceives only two options in relation to a demand: submission or rebellion. Either way, the person making the request is seen as coercive, and the receiver's ability to respond compassionately is greatly reduced leading to a conflictual rather than cooperative interaction.

EXHIBIT 2.13 "MURDERER, ASSASSIN, CHILD-KILLER"

Rosenberg relates the story of making a presentation to 170 Palestinian Muslim men at a mosque in a Palestinian refugee camp in Bethlehem. Attitudes towards Americans like Rosenberg were not positive because of the United States' support for Israel. As he was speaking, he heard a commotion in the back of the crowd. His translator warned, "They're whispering that you are an American." Then one man leaped to his feet and shouted, "Murderer," and a dozen voices behind him shouted, "Assassin! Child-killer! Murderer!"

Rosenberg (R) addressed the man (M) who shouted first:

"R: Are you angry because you would like my government to use its resources differently? (*I didn't know whether my guess was correct — what was critical was my sincere effort to connect with his feeling and need.*)

M: Damn right I'm angry! You think we need tear gas? We need sewers, not your tear gas! We need housing! We need to have our own country!

R: So you're furious and would appreciate some support in improving your living conditions and gaining political independence?

M: Do you know what it's like to live here for twenty-five years the way I have with my family — children and all? Have you got the faintest idea what that's been like for us?

R: Sounds like you're feeling very desperate and you're wondering whether I or anybody else can really understand what it's like to be living under these conditions. Am I hearing you right?

M: You want to understand? Tell me, do you have any children? Do they go to school? Do they have playgrounds? My son is sick! He plays in open sewage! His classroom has no books! Have you seen a school that has no books?

R: I hear how painful it is for you to raise your children here; you'd like me to know that what you want is what all parents want for their children — a good education, opportunity to play and grow in a healthy environment…

M: That's right, the basics! Human rights — isn't that what you Americans call it? Why don't more of you come here and see what kind of human rights you're bringing here?

R: You'd like more Americans to be aware of the enormity of the suffering here and to look more deeply at the consequences of our political actions?

"The dialogue continued with him expressing his pain for nearly twenty more minutes, and me listening for the feeling and need behind each statement. I didn't agree or disagree. I received his words, not as attacks, but as gifts from a fellow human willing to share his soul and deep vulnerabilities with me.

"Once the gentleman felt understood, he was able to hear me express my purpose for being at the camp. An hour later, the same man who had called me a murderer was inviting me to his home for a Ramadan dinner."

Source: Rosenberg, M.B. *Nonviolent Communication: A Way of Life.* Encitas, CA: PuddleDancer, 2003, pp. 12–14.

We must be aware of our objective in making a request. If our goal is only to change the other person, or to get our own way, then we are motivated by self-interest and NVC is not an appropriate tool. "The objective of NVC is to establish a relationship based on honesty and empathy"[75] that freely accepts that all parties have the right to refuse any solution and look for a compromise that all may agree with.

CONCLUSIONS

The most basic skill that global leaders must cultivate is learning how to effectively communicate and listen cross-culturally. To facilitate our interactions with persons who do not share our values, assumptions, or learned ways of behaving requires new competencies and sensitivities so that those very cultural differences become resources. The complexities of the communication process have been reviewed here from the perspectives of cross-cultural behaviors and factors. We have considered listening, and foreign language skill levels, and variables when interacting such as body language and gestures.

Some of these aspects of communication represent conscious choices based on cultural preferences. Some are unconscious and habitual behaviors, also based on culture, but more challenging to be aware that we are doing them. This chapter has emphasized the possibilities and the pitfalls in intercultural communication, whether in personal or electronic encounters. Learning to take account of all these factors can be mind stretching (see below), and will take years to achieve proficiency.

The study of cultural similarities shows that there are shortcuts that you may employ in the short run, or when you work in a global industry like hospitality where there are too many cultures to learn in depth. Personality dimensions are universal to all humans regardless of their culture. If you understand the predominant personality types in a culture where you are doing business, and you understand your own personality predilections, you may have a useful and simplified stereotype to work with. Self-interested (I/It) and altruistic (I/Thou) relationships are two universal bases for intercultural communication. Humans in all cultures resist communications intended to force others' interests onto them, and respond with greater cooperation to altruism. NVC is a communication technology that has been proven successful for building cooperation, trust, and altruism even among sworn enemies.

MIND STRETCHING

Not only is the field of intercultural communication changing, but the relationship between culture and communication is — and probably always will be — complex and dynamic. We live in a rapidly changing world in which cross-cultural contracts will continue to increase, creating heightened potential for both conflict and communication.[76]

As you have read in this chapter, you of course understand yourself as formed in large part by your socialization in a particular culture. Therefore, we have a list of questions for you to consider. We ask that you take the time and look into the mirror to become better acquainted with your own style of communication and the societal and cultural influences that influence who you are. Ask yourself, what do you communicate about? How do you communicate your thoughts? In this manner, you will best understand how to improve yourself as a cross-cultural communicator within the global business context.

1   How does your culture tell you how to communicate and behave, and what are the messages that you feel are consistently reinforced?
2   How do you prefer to communicate? Directly? Indirectly?
3   How does your religion influence your values? Your beliefs? Your behavior? Who do you prefer to associate with?
4   In your personal life, do you have many friends who are different from you? How are they different? Are they different in personality, ethnicity, culture, or are most of your friends of your own cultural background? Why?
5   How much time do you spend to understand another person's perspective? Or do you prefer to try to persuade others to change and adopt your own perspective?

Everyone finds it easier to communicate and interact with people who have a similar personality, ethnicity, and culture. We also prefer to be around people who share our religion, our beliefs, and our worldview. The challenge is to learn how to move beyond the inherent conflict that arises when two different people interact, and ultimately create an environment where all parties can find the common ground. The first step is to understand your own culture and communication style, and what barriers you may have toward positive cross-cultural communication interaction.

NOTES

1   Kotter, J. P. "What Effective General Managers Really Do," *Harvard Business Review*, Vol. 60, No. 6, 1982, pp. 156–167.
2   en.wikipedia.org/wiki/Cross-cultural_communication.
3   en.wikipedia.org/wiki/Intercultural_communication.
4   Kotter, "What Effective General Managers Really Do,", p. 158.
5   Hall, E. T. *The Silent Language*. Garden City, NY: Anchor/Doubleday, 1959.
6   Ibid.
7   Rogers, E. M., Hart, W. B., and Miike, Y. "Edward T. Hall and the History of Intercultural Communication: The United States and Japan," *Keio Communication Review*, Vol. 24, 2002, pp. 3–26.
8   Marcel, G. *The Mystery of Being, Volume I: Reflection and Mystery*. South Bend, IN: St. Augustine's, 2001.

9 Rosenberg, M. B. *Nonviolent Communication: A Language of Life,* 2nd edn. Encinitas, CA: PuddleDancer, 2003.

10 Meadows, D. H. "If the World Were a Village of 1,000 People," in D. Aberley (ed.), *Futures by Design: The Practice of Ecological Planning.* Philadelphia, PA: New Society Publishers, 1994.

11 Ayoko, O. B. "Communication Openesss, Conflict Events, and Reactions to Conflict in Culturally Diverse Workgroups," *Cross-Cultural Management*, Vol. 14, No. 2, 2007, pp. 105–124.

12 Ibid.

13 Moran, R. T. *So You're Going Abroad: Are You Prepared?* Self-Published, 10th printing, 2003.

14 Hall, *The Silent Language.*

15 Gordon, T. *Lwader Effectiveness Training: L.E.T. (Revised).* New York: Perigee Trade, 2002.

16 Macionis, G. and John, L. *Sociology,* 7th Canadian edn. Toronto, ON: Pearson Canada, 2010, p. 53.

17 Lustig, M. W. and Koester, J. *Intercultural Competence.* New York: Addison-Wesley, 1998.

18 Clausen, L. "Corporate Communication Challenges: A 'Negotiated' Cultural Perspective," *International Journal of Cross-Cultural Management*, Vol. 7, No. 3, 2007, pp. 317–332.

19 Ibid.

20 Jandt, F. E. *Intercultural Communication: An Introduction,* 2nd edn. Thousand Oaks, CA: Sage, 1998.

21 Ibid.

22 Liddicoat, A. J. "Communication as Culturally Contexted Practice: A View from Intercultural Communication," *Australian Journal of Linguistics*, Vol. 29, No. 1, 2009, pp. 115–133.

23 Ibid.

24 Nordby, H. "Values, Cultural Identity and Communication: A Perspective from Philosophy of Language," *Journal of Intercultural Communication*, Vol. 17, No. 6, 2008, p. 1.

25 Ibid.

26 Samovar, L. A. and Porter, R. E. *Intercultural Communications: A Reader.* Belmont, CA: Wadsworth Publishing, 1988.

27 Hofstede, G. and Hofstede, G. J. *Cultures and Organizations: Software of the Mind*, 2nd edn. New York: McGraw-Hill, 2005.

28 Merchant, H. "Olly Racella in Bangkok," in H. Merchant (ed.), *Competing in Emerging Markets: Cases and Readings.* New York: Routledge, 2007, pp. 139–155.

29 Hall, *The Silent Language.*

30 Rogers, Hart, and Miike, "Edward T. Hall."

31 Hall, op cit., p. 62.

32 Rogers, Hart, and Miike, "Edward T. Hall."

33 Hall, E. T. and Hall, M. R. *Hidden Differences: Doing Business with the Japanese.* Garden City, NY: Anchor Press/Doubleday, 1987.

34 Ibid.

35 Kipnis, A. B. *Producing Guanxi: Sentiment, Self, and Subculture in a North China Village.* London: Duke University, 1997.

36 Abramson, N. R. and Ai, J. X. "Using Guanxi-Style Buyer–Seller Relationships in China: Reducing Uncertainty and Improving Performance Outcomes," *International Executive*, Vol. 39, No. 6, 1997, pp. 765–804.

37 Hall and Hall, *Hidden Differences.*

38 Ibid.

39 Abramson and Ai, "Using Guanxi-Style Buyer–Seller Relationships in China."

40 Ting-Toomey, S. *Communicating Across Cultures.* New York: Guilford Press, 1999.

41 Ibid.

42 Furnham, A. "Actions Speak Louder than Words," *Financial Times*, April 4, 1999.

43 Riddle, D. L. and Lanham, Z. D. "Internationalizing Written Business English: 20 Propositions for Native English Speakers," *Journal of Language for International Business*, 1985.

44 Sang, J. and Zhang, G. "Communication across Languages and Cultures: A Perspective of Brand Name Translation from English to Chinese," *Journal of Asian Pacific Communication*, Vol. 18, No. 2, 2008, pp. 225–246.

45 Rogers, Hart, and Miike, "Edward T. Hall."

46 Hirai, K. "Intercultural Communication Education: What to Teach," *Speech Communication Education* (Journal of the Communication Association of Japan), Vol. 1, pp. 1–26.

47 Rogers, Hart, and Miike, "Edward T. Hall."

48 Miike, Y. "Beyond Eurocentrism in the Intercultural Field: Searching for an Asiacentric Paradigm," Paper presented at the National Communication Association, Atlanta, GA, 2001.

49 Abramson, N. R. "Measuring the Independent Effects of Culture and Personality on Marketing Behavior: A Canadian–Korean Comparison Using the Cognitive Theory of Strategy," *Journal of Current Research in Global Business*, Vol. 9, No. 14, 2006, pp. 1–19.

50 Barkow, J. H., Cosmides, L., and Tooby, J. *The Adapted Mind: Evolutionary Psychology and the Generation of Culture.* New York: Oxford University Press, 1992. See also Buss, D. M. *Evolutionary Psychology: The New Science of the Mind*, 3rd edn. Boston, MA: Pearson, 2008.

51 Buber, M. *I and Thou.* New York: Charles Scribner's Sons. See also Marcel, *The Mystery of Being*.

52 Rosenberg, *Nonviolent Communication*.

53 Burger, J. M. *Personality*, 6th edn. Toronto, ON: Thompson Wadsworth, 2004.

54 For example, see McCrae, R. R., Costa, P. T. Jr., and Yik, M. S. M. "Universal Aspects of Chinese Personality Structure," in M. H. Bond (ed.), *The Handbook of Chinese Psychology.* Hong Kong: Oxford University, 1996, pp. 189–207.

55 Nettle, D. *Personality: What Makes You the Way You Are.* Oxford: Oxford University Press.

56 There are many sources for the Jungian, Myers-Briggs, and Keirsey models. One of the most readable is Bayne, R. *Ideas and Evidence: Critical Reflections on MBTI Theory and Practice.* Gainesville, FL: CAPT, 2005. Jung's original discussions are found in Jung, C. G. *Psychological Types.* Princeton, NJ: Princeton University, 2013.

57 Seagal, S. and Horne, D. *Human Dynamics: A New Framework for Understanding People and Realizing the Potential in Our Organizations.* Waltham, CA: Pegasus, 1997.

58 Keirsey, D. *Please Understand Me: Temperament, Character, Intelligence.* Del Mar, CA: Prometheus, 1984.

59 Seagal and Horne, *Human Dynamics*, p. 32.

60 Seagal, S. and Horne, D. Personal conversations with the author.

61 Abramson, N. R. and Keating, R. J. "Knowledge Management through the Lens of the Cognitive Theory of Strategy: American, Chinese, and Thai Decision-Making Capabilities," *Journal of Global Business*, Vol. 17, No. 34, 2006, pp. 27–42.

62 Abramson, "Measuring the Independent Effects."

63 Seagal and Horne, *Human Dynamics*.

64 Massey, B. *Where in the World Do I Belong? Which Country's Culture Fits Your Myers-Briggs Personality Type?* Gainesville, FL: Jetlag Press ebook, 2006.

65 Abramson, N. R. "Comparing the Effects of Evolutionary Psychology and National Culture on Canadian–Korean Buyer–Seller Relationships: A Study of Temperament," Working paper.

66 Buss, *Evolutionary Psychology*.

67 Saad, G. "Applying Evolutionary Psychology in Understanding the Representation of Women in Advertising," *Psychology & Marketing*, Vol. 21, 2004, pp. 593–412.

68 Hantula, D. A. "Guest Editorial: Evolutionary Psychology and Consumption," *Psychology & Marketing*, Vol. 20, 2003, pp. 757–763.

69 Darwin, C. *The Origin of Species.* New York: Penguin, 1985.

70 Buber, *I and Thou*.

71 Marcel, *The Mystery of Being*.

72 Fisher, R., Ury, W., and Patton, B. *Getting to Yes: Negotiating Agreement Without Giving In*. New York: Penguin, 2011.

73 Rosenberg, *Nonviolent Communication*.

74 A workbook has been developed for learning and practicing NVC in conjunction with Tosenberg's (2003) book. See Leu, L. *Nonviolent Communication Companion Workbook: A Practical Guide for Individual, Group, or Classroom Study*. Encinitas, CA: PuddleDancer, 2003.

75 Ibid., p. 81.

76 Martin, J. N. and Nakayama, T. K. *Intercultural Communication in Contexts*. Boston, MA: McGraw-Hill, 2004, p. xviii.

ADDITIONAL FEATURES

Please visit the companion website at: www.routledge.com/cw/Moran where you will find additional case studies, study aides, and instructor resources.

3 NEGOTIATING LONG TERM FOR MUTUAL BENEFIT

In the game theory or economic theory, a zero-sum negotiation occurs when one participant's benefit (gain) or loss is balanced by the losses or benefits (gains) of the other participant. The result is zero. One gains 100, and the other loses 100, or vice-versa.

A non-zero sum negotiation occurs when the gains or losses of the participants in a negotiation are either less than or more than zero.

Skillful negotiators build trust and negotiate for mutual long-term benefit of all.[1]

Negotiating is not a theoretical activity. It is a face-to-face activity, kind of like a dance where partners in the dance influence each other. Behaving as an effective negotiator involves great skill. A good example of a skillful negotiator is Abraham Lincoln,[2] the 16th president of the United States. The skills he demonstrated in discussion leading to the Emancipation Declaration demonstrate the importance of the skills of "resilience, forbearance, emotional intelligence, thoughtful listening, and the consideration of all sides of an argument," as well as "staying true to a larger mission."

Another author[3] writes, "Classically trained negotiators take a win-at-all-costs approach based on concealment, camouflage, and deception."

To understand the importance of "culture" when negotiating with individuals in today's global world: dealing with conflicts, having a high degree of emotional intelligence, and being able to "profile" accurately one's negotiating counterparts are significant ingredients in negotiating success. It is also important for negotiators to develop a "partnership mindset" as each approaches a negotiation to achieve long-term mutual benefits.

The chapter is intended to be conceptual and immediately useful whether negotiating at home or abroad, and to persuade readers that skillful global negotiating is a necessary learned skill in today's business world.

There is a significant increase in business travel to and from the United States, China, India, Russia, Brazil, and many other countries. Globalization has resulted in increased business travel to many countries in order to buy, sell, form mergers or acquisitions, build relationships, and for many other activities. Most of these business relationships will involve some form of negotiation.

Today's leaders seek business ventures in the global arena, crisscrossing the world to negotiate and bargain. Many claim the success rate of mergers and acquisitions to be less than 50 percent for successful integration, although few hard data are available, but state that these mergers typically failed to achieve the targeted results.

Appreciating the complexities of labor negotiations in one's home country or negotiating a contract in a foreign country has made leaders understand the competency and skill needed to effectively work out these partnerships to mutual benefit.

In the twenty-first century, global leaders increasingly do their negotiating *electronically*, by telephone, fax, email, and video conferencing. One of the most powerful communication tools for this purpose is the Internet. It offers quick and easy negotiation opportunities with manufacturers, suppliers, customers, and even government regulators. But it also requires more openness, transparency, and trust.

TWO EXAMPLES OF "CULTURAL BAGGAGE"

A United States example

Graham and Herberger[4] describe a combination of characteristics typical of American negotiators. They are part of the cultural baggage such nationals bring to the negotiating table and, according to Graham and Herberger, typify the American "John Wayne" style of negotiating.

"I can go it alone." Many U.S. executives seem to believe they can handle any negotiating situation by themselves, and they are outnumbered in most negotiating situations.

"Just call me John." Americans value informality and equality in human relations. They try to make people feel comfortable by playing down status distinctions.

"Pardon my French." Americans aren't very talented at speaking foreign languages.

"Check with the home office." American negotiators get upset when, halfway through a negotiation, the other side says, "I'll have to check with the home office." The implication is that the decision-makers are not present.

"Get to the point." American negotiators prefer to come directly to the point, getting to the heart of the matter quickly.

"Lay your cards on the table." Americans expect honest information at the bargaining table.

"Don't just sit there, speak up." Americans don't deal well with silence during negotiations.

"Don't take no for an answer." Persistence is highly valued by Americans, and is part of the deeply ingrained competitive spirit that manifests itself in every aspect of American life.

"One thing at a time." Americans usually attack a complex negotiation task sequentially; that is, they separate the issues and settle them one at a time.

"A deal is a deal." When Americans make an agreement and give their word, they expect to honor the agreement no matter what the circumstances.

"I am what I am." Few Americans take pride in changing their minds, even in difficult circumstances.

These comments on American negotiators may appear to be harsh. They are not intended to isolate Americans as lacking in global negotiating skills. In today's marketplace, other nationalities can learn, as well as Americans, how to negotiate more effectively and skillfully.

A European example

A German Swiss buyer of goods is visiting a Chinese entrepreneur, trying to close a contract. The Chinese sits inscrutably while the Swiss expostulates his detailed proposal. The Swiss finishes his speech, a bit nervous at receiving so little feedback. Finally, the Chinese speaks: "This is not good for us." And then, "Let me take you for dinner."[5]

According to the German Swiss, the relationship may be in trouble, but the Chinese, in fact, may be keenly interested and wants to strengthen the relationship with a social event.

In Exhibit 3.1, Acuff[6] is not complimentary in his report card on American negotiators' skills.

We hope, as our horizons are widened by the global experience, that we are getting better at understanding the national character of our negotiating counterparts, confronting cultural stereotypes, and putting the negotiating process into a cultural context.

E
X
H
I
B
I
T

3.1

EXIBIT 3.1 THE U.S. NEGOTIATOR'S GLOBAL REPORT CARD

Competency	Grade
Preparation	B−
Synergistic approach (win-win)	D
Cultural IQ	D
Adapting the negotiating process to the host country environment	D
Patience	D
Listening	D
Linguistic abilities	F
Using language that is simple and accessible	C
High aspirations	B+
Personal integrity	A−
Building solid relationships	D

Source: Adapted from Acuff, F. L. *How to Negotiate with Anyone Anywhere Around the World.* New York: Amacom, 1993, Exhibit 8.1, p. 192.

NEGOTIATING ACROSS CULTURES

Negotiation is a process in which two or more entities come together to discuss common and conflicting interests in order to reach an agreement of mutual benefit. In international business negotiations, the negotiation process differs from culture to culture in language, cultural conditioning, negotiating styles, approaches to problem-solving, and building trust, among many other factors.

National character

Studies of national character call attention to both the patterns of personality that negotiators tend to exhibit and the collective concerns that give a nation a distinctive outlook in international relationships. Foreign negotiators concerned with international image may be preoccupied with discussions of their national heritage, identity, and language. Cultural attitudes, such as ethnocentrism or xenophobia, may influence the tone of the argument.

Foreign negotiators often display many different styles of logic and reasoning. They frequently find that discussions are impeded because the two sides seem to be pursuing different paths of logic. Negotiation breakdown may result from the way issues are conceptualized, the way evidence and new information are used, or the way one point seems to lead to the next.

During the discussions, the foreign counterpart may pay more attention to some arguments than to others. Greater weight may be given to legal precedence, expert opinion, technical data, amity, or reciprocal advantage. A good international negotiator will discover what is persuasive to the foreign counterpart and use that method of persuasion.

Negotiators may place different values on agreements and hold different assumptions about the way contracts should be honored. The negotiator must find out what steps the counterpart intends to take in implementing the agreement. A signature on a piece of paper or a handshake may signify friendship rather than the closing of a contract.

Cross-cultural noise

Noise consists of background distractions that have nothing to do with the substance of the foreign negotiator's message. Factors such as gestures, personal proximity, and office surroundings may unintentionally interfere with communication. The danger of misinterpretation of messages necessitates analysis of various contextual factors.

Interpreters and translators

There are limitations in translating certain ideas, concepts, meanings, and nuances. Subjective meaning may not come across through words alone. Gestures, tone of voice, cadence, and double entendres are all meant to transmit a message. Yet these are not included in a translation.

Sometimes a negotiator will try to communicate a concept or idea that does not exist in the counterpart's culture. For example, the American and English concept of "fair play" seems to have no exact equivalent in any other language. How, then, can an English national expect "fair play" from a foreign counterpart?

Interpreters and translators may have difficulty transmitting the logic of key arguments. This is especially true in discussions of abstract concepts such as planning and international strategy. The parties may think that they have come to an agreement when, in fact, they have entirely different intentions and understandings.

Fisher's five-part framework provides scholars and consultants with a launching pad for both theory building and practical applications. Two working papers, "Assess, Don't Assume, Part 1: Etiquette and Material Culture in Negotiation" and "Assess, Part II: Cross-Border Differences in Decision Making, Governance, and Political Economy" are also excellent in identifying the cultural variables in global negotiations.[7]

In Chapter 2, we covered some of the complexities in communicating effectively across geographical and cultural boundaries. Consider, however, the following Anglo-EU translation guide of phrases which are routinely used in face-to-face negotiations and could easily lead to misunderstandings.

ANGLO-EU TRANSLATION GUIDE

What the British say	What the British might mean	What others might understand
I hear what you say	I disagree and do not want to discuss it further	He accepts my point of view
With the greatest respect...	I think you are an idiot	He is listening to me
That's not bad	That's good	That's poor
That is a very brave proposal	You are insane	He thinks I have courage
Quite good	A bit disappointing	Quite good
I would suggest...	Do it or be prepared to justify yourself	Think about the idea, but do what you like
Oh, incidentally/by the way	The primary purpose of our discussion is...	That is not very important
I was a bit disappointed that	I am annoyed that	It doesn't really matter
Very interesting	That is clearly nonsense	They are impressed
I'll bear it in mind	I've forgotten it already	They will probably do it
I'm sure it's my fault	It's your fault	Why do they think it was their fault?
You must come for dinner	It's not an invitation, I'm just being polite	I will get an invitation soon .
I almost agree	I don't agree at all	He's not far from agreement
I only have a few minor comments	Please rewrite completely	He has found a few typos
Could we consider some other options?	I don't like your idea	They have not yet decided

Source: http://www.scribd.com/doc/55551980/Anglo-EU-Translation-Guide.

ASSUMPTIONS AND NEGOTIATING

When people communicate, they make certain assumptions about the other's process of perceiving, judging, thinking, and reasoning patterns. These assumptions are made without realization. Correct assumptions facilitate communication, but incorrect assumptions lead to misunderstandings, and miscommunication often results.

The most common assumption is projective cognitive similarity; that is, one assumes that the other perceives, judges, thinks, and reasons the same way he or she does. Persons from the same culture, but with a different education, age, background, and experience, often have difficulty communicating. American managers experience greater difficulties communicating with managers from other cultures than with managers from their own culture. However, in some contexts, American managers share more interests with other members of the world managerial subculture than with their own workers or union leaders. The effects of our cultural conditioning are so pervasive that people whose experience has been limited to the rules of one culture can have difficulty understanding communication based on another set of rules.

To create cultural synergistic solutions to management problems and international negotiating, U.S. managers must identify and understand what is American about America, what common cultural traits are shared by Americans, and what values and assumptions form their foundation.

Awareness of cultural influences is essential for transferring concepts, technology, or ideas. Depending on the cultures, there may be an overlap of values in a specific area, and therefore the problems related to transferring ideas will be minimal. However, in some instances, the gap will be significant and cause serious problems. According to Graham,[8] there are four problems in international business negotiations: (1) language, (2) nonverbal behavior, (3) values, and (4) thinking and decision-making.

The problems increase in importance and complexity because of their subtle nature. For instance, it is easy to ascertain the language differences between the French and the Brazilians. The solution is either state-of-the-art translating headsets or interpreting/translating teams to accommodate each side. The problem is obvious and relatively easy to address.

Cultural differences concerning nonverbal behavior are often not as obvious; we are not as aware of these behaviors. In face-to-face negotiations, we give and receive nonverbal behavioral cues. Some argue that these cues are the critical messages of a negotiation. The nonverbal signals from our counterparts can be so subtle that we may feel a sense of discomfort but may not know exactly why. For example, when a Japanese negotiator fails to make eye contact, it may produce a sense of unease in the foreigner, but it may simply be shyness on the part of the Japanese. Often, nonverbal intercultural friction affects business negotiations, but goes undefined and more often uncorrected.

Laver and Trudgill in Scheu-Lottgen and Hernandez-Campoy also point out that, during conversations, one must act almost as a detective, not only considering the words and speech but also attempting to establish, from an array of clues, the state of mind and the profile and perspective of the other's identity.[9]

The difference in values is even more obscure and harder to understand. For example, Americans value objectivity, competitiveness, equity, and punctuality, and often presume that other cultures hold the same values in high esteem. Regarding punctuality, Graham states, "Everyone else in the world knows no negotiation tactic is more useful with Americans. Nobody places more value on time. Nobody has less patience when things slow down."[10]

Generally, during a complex negotiation, Westerners divide the large tasks up into smaller ones. One can move through the smaller tasks, finishing one and moving on to the next, sensing accomplishment along the way. Issues are resolved at each step in the process, and the final agreement is the sum of the sequence. However, in Eastern thinking, all issues are discussed, often with no apparent order, and concessions, when made, occur at the conclusion of negotiations. The Western approach is sequential and the Eastern is holistic – the two are worlds apart. Therefore, American negotiators have difficulty measuring progress during negotiations with the Japanese, and the differences in the thinking and decision-making processes can result in blunders. For the Japanese, the long-term goal is a mutually beneficial ongoing business relationship.

FRAMEWORK FOR INTERNATIONAL BUSINESS NEGOTIATIONS

A successful negotiation is a "win-win situation" in which both parties gain. Many factors affect a negotiation's outcome.

There are varied negotiation postures, bases from which to negotiate. One framework by Weiss and Stripp[11] maintains that there are 12 variables in every international negotiation that impact the negotiation, and can therefore significantly influence the outcome, either positively or negatively.

- *Basic conception of negotiation process.* There are two opposing approaches to the concept of negotiation: strategic and synergistic. In the strategic model, resources are perceived as limited. The sides are competitive and, as a result of bargaining, one side is perceived as getting a larger portion of the pie. In the synergistic model, resources are unlimited. Each party wants to cooperate so that all can have what they want. Counterparts look for alternative ways to obtain the desired results.
- *Negotiator selection criteria.* These criteria include negotiating experience, seniority, political affiliation, gender, ethnic ties, kinship, technical knowledge, and personal attributes (e.g., affability, loyalty, and trustworthiness). Each culture has preferences and biases regarding selection.
- *Significance of type of issue.* Defining the issues in negotiation is critical. Generally, substantive issues focus on control and use of resources (space, power, property). Relationship-based issues center on the ongoing nature of mutual or reciprocal interests. The negotiation should not hinder relationships and future negotiations.
- *Concern with protocol.* Protocol is the accepted practices of social behavior and interaction. Rules of protocol can be formal or informal. Americans are generally less formal than Germans, for example.
- *Complexity of language.* Complexity refers to the degree of reliance on nonverbal cues to convey and interpret intentions and information in dialogue. These cues include distance (space), eye contact, gestures, and silence. There are high- and low-context

communications. Cultures that are high context in communication (China) are fast and efficient communicators, and information is in the physical context or preprogrammed in the person. Low-context communication, in contrast, is information conveyed by the words, without shared meaning implied. The United States has a low-context culture.

■ *Nature of persuasive arguments*. One way or another, negotiation involves attempts to influence the other party. Counterparts can use an emotional or logical approach.

■ *Role of individuals' aspirations*. The emphasis negotiators place on their individual goals and need for recognition may also vary. In some cases, the position of a negotiator may reflect personal goals to a greater extent than corporate goals. In contrast, a negotiator may want to prove he or she is a hard bargainer and compromise the goals of the corporation.

■ *Bases of trust*. Every negotiator, at some point, must face the critical issue of trust. One must eventually trust one's counterparts; otherwise, resolution would be impossible. Trust can be based on the written laws of a particular country, or it can be based on friendship and mutual respect and esteem.

■ *Risk-taking propensity*. Negotiators can be perceived as either "cautious" (low risk-takers), or "adventurous" (high risk-takers). If a negotiator selects a solution that has lower rewards but higher probability of success, he or she is not a risk-taker. If the negotiator chooses higher rewards, but a lower probability of success, then he or she is "adventurous" and a risk-taker.

■ *Value of time*. Each culture has a different way of perceiving and acting on time. Monochronic cultures emphasize making agendas and being on time for appointments, generally seeing time as a quantity to be scheduled. Polychronic cultures stress the involvement of people rather than preset schedules. The future cannot be firm, so planning takes on little consequence.

■ *Decision-making system*. Broadly understood, decision-making systems can be "authoritative" or "consensual." In authoritative decision-making, an individual makes the decision without consulting with his or her superiors. However, senior executives may overturn the decision. In consensual decision-making, negotiators do not have the authority to make decisions unless they consult their superiors.

■ *Form of satisfactory agreement*. Generally, there are two broad forms of agreement. One is the written contract that covers possible contingencies. The other is the broad oral agreement that binds the negotiating parties through the quality of their relationship.

Negotiation insights for India, China, Brazil, South Korea, Germany, and Russia[12]

Can statements that are mostly accurate be made about a group of people or a "culture"? Is there a "national character" of a people, that is, a system of beliefs, attitudes, and values that are dominant in a country or nation as a result of common experiences?

In the definition of national character, there are three assumptions: (1) all people belonging to a certain culture are alike in some respects; (2) they are somewhat different from other cultures in the same respects; and (3) the characteristics ascribed to them are in some way related to the fact that they are citizens of a given country.

During negotiations, however, all anyone can observe is human behavior. We see what people do. What are the determinants of human behavior? We believe one has to consider three factors: culture (a national character); personality (no two people from the same culture are exactly alike); and context (where does the behavior take place — in New York? Sao Paulo? Tokyo? Jeddah?).

What follows is a summary of aspects of Indian, Chinese, Brazilian, South Korean, German, and Russian "national character." Remember that "personality" and "context" are also determinants of behavior.

Framework applied to Indian negotiators

1 Basic Concept of the Negotiation Process
   - Building relationships and establishing rapport
   - Having conversations important
   - "Facilitation payments" often requested
   - Correct manners a requirement
2 Negotiator Selection Criteria
   - Technical experts always present
   - Status differences among team members a factor
   - Decisions made by senior management
3 Significance of Type of Issue
   - Price bargaining, reliability, credit, and local service important
   - Working rapport important
4 Concern with Protocol
   - Formality a norm
   - Friendly atmosphere
5 Complexity of Language
   - Concern with maintaining harmony
   - When Indians say "no problem," this is not to be taken literally
6 Nature of Persuasive Arguments
   - Maturity, wisdom, and self-control are valued behaviors
7 Role of Individuals' Aspirations
   - No attempt to "stand out"
   - Decision-making at higher levels
8 Bases of Trust
   - Trust must be earned

9   Risk-Taking Propensity
- ■   Many are fatalists and are willing to take risks

10   Value of Time
- ■   Punctuality is important, but patience is often required

11   Decision-Making System
- ■   Highly centralized with only modest responsibility delegated to lower levels

12   Form of Satisfactory Agreement
- ■   Detailed agreements are the norm

Framework applied to Chinese negotiators

1   Basic Concept of the Negotiation Process
- ■   Intelligence gathering
- ■   Statements emphasizing "friendship"
- ■   Hard bargaining

2   Negotiator Selection Criteria
- ■   Technical expertise
- ■   In times of turbulence/change political reliability

3   Significance of Type of Issue
- ■   Relationship-based issues receive attention
- ■   Connections (guanxi) important

4   Concern with Protocol
- ■   High concern with proper etiquette
- ■   Use "home court" as advantage

5   Complexity of Language
- ■   Very high context with implicit and unstated desires and approaches

6   Nature of Persuasive Arguments
- ■   "No compromising" to establish economic value

7   Role of Individuals' Aspirations
- ■   Individual aspirations are resurfacing but "standing out" is unusual

8   Bases of Trust
- ■   Past record is important

9   Risk-Taking Propensity
- ■   High avoidance of risk-taking resulting in meticulous and tough negotiating tactics and strategy

10   Value of Time
- ■   Long view of time, and masters at the art of stalling

11   Decision-Making System
- ■   Appearance of participative decision-making, but in reality is an authoritative system with higher levels always controlling

12   Form of Satisfactory Agreement
- Carefully worded contracts, but legal infrastructure lacking

Framework applied to Brazilian negotiators

1   Basic Concept of the Negotiation Process
- Verbal facility, harmony, and eloquence are valued
- Negotiating is often a long process
- Establishing trust is critical to success

2   Negotiator Selection Criteria
- Seniority is important
- Oratory skills, social and political connections, and academic training are significant

3   Significance of Type of Issue
- Early in the discussion, building relationships is important

4   Concern with Protocol
- Formal in social hierarchy and ceremony
- Dress is important

5   Complexity of Language
- Less direct and high context

6   Nature of Persuasive Arguments
- Inference, indirection, but with common sense

7   Role of Individuals' Aspirations
- Brazilians are individualistic, and outshining one's colleagues is acceptable

8   Bases of Trust
- Trust is built slowly

9   Risk-Taking Propensity
- Basically low on risk-taking

10   Value of Time
- Not hurried . . . a more polychronic approach to schedules

11   Decision-Making System
- Bureaucratic and hierarchical

12   Form of Satisfactory Agreement
- A handshake and words of honor are followed by details which are formalized by lawyers

Framework applied to South Korean negotiators

1   Basic Concept of the Negotiation Process
- Maintaining harmony and setting the stage for establishing the right kibun (feeling) of both sides is important

2　Negotiator Selection Criteria
- ■　　Status, knowledge, and expertise

3　Significance of Type of Issue
- ■　　Maintaining a positive business relationship is important but haggling over many aspects of the deal is typical

4　Concern with Protocol
- ■　　Basic rules of exchange must be followed
- ■　　Title, position, and formality are norms to be recognized

5　Complexity of Language
- ■　　High context and indirect

6　Nature of Persuasive Arguments
- ■　　Maintaining harmony

7　Role of Individuals' Aspirations
- ■　　The group is more important than the individual

8　Bases of Trust
- ■　　Established slowly on the basis of appropriate behavior

9　Risk-Taking Propensity
- ■　　Avoid risk, and maintain face and harmony

10　Value of Time
- ■　　Adhere to norms of punctuality

11　Decision-Making System
- ■　　Decisions made at the highest levels

12　Form of Satisfactory Agreement
- ■　　Written contracts with clauses to allow flexibility

Framework applied to German negotiators

1　Basic Concept of the Negotiation Process
- ■　　Direct, explicit, analytical, and logical

2　Negotiator Selection Criteria
- ■　　Excellent technical knowledge and strong educational background

3　Significance of Type of Issue
- ■　　Get right down to business
- ■　　Honest and straightforward

4　Concern with Protocol
- ■　　Serious, controlled, and disciplined

5　Complexity of Language
- ■　　Low context – frank and realistic

6　Nature of Persuasive Arguments
- ■　　Careful research, orderly and persuasive presentation

7   Role of Individuals' Aspirations
   ■   Strong sense of duty and company loyalty
8   Bases of Trust
   ■   Convince with competence and performance, facts, and actions
9   Risk-Taking Propensity
   ■   Avoid risk by sticking to what is known
10 Value of Time
   ■   Being "on time" is always important
11 Decision-Making System
   ■   Top down
12 Form of Satisfactory Agreement
   ■   Written and binding documents

Framework applied to Russian negotiators

1   Basic Concept of the Negotiation Process
   ■   A competitive process where one side "wins"
2   Negotiator Selection Criteria
   ■   Professional, negotiators are selected on the basis of specialization
3   Significance of Type of Issue
   ■   Hard bargaining, personal relationships play only a small role
4   Concern with Protocol
   ■   Rules and protocol should be known and followed
5   Complexity of Language
   ■   Low context and direct
6   Nature of Persuasive Arguments
   ■   Delaying negotiations and wearing down their counterparts is often a style
7   Role of Individuals' Aspirations
   ■   Individualistic in contrast with the recent past
8   Bases of Trust
   ■   "Caution" is important
9   Risk-Taking Propensity
   ■   High risk-takers
   ■   Corruption endemic
10 Value of Time
   ■   Long and demanding
11 Decision-Making System
   ■   Very hierarchical
12 Form of Satisfactory Agreement
   ■   Contracts are cleverly written, and details are often omitted

Face-to-face with Japanese negotiators[13]

Most gaijin or outsiders find Japanese negotiating behavior, at least on occasion, puzzling. The following statements about aspects of Japanese culture are, for the most part, accurate, but the statements do not apply to all Japanese. In understanding Japanese negotiating behavior, as was covered in Chapter 1, it is necessary to take into account the culture, personality of the individual, and the context in order to interpret accurately observed behavior.

The Japanese culture, as all cultures, changes. However, deeper aspects of culture change slowly. Aspects of Japanese culture that change slowly include the tendency to conceal in a public setting emotions, especially negative emotions. In negotiating situations, negative feelings about progress, people, and direction of the negotiations are often repressed and are difficult for outsiders to detect, and differences are resolved so that no party "loses face."

Decision-making in Japan is based on consensus. A formalized proposal is sent upward and horizontal in the hierarchical structure, and various departments note their approval if that is the case. All contribute to the decision.

The first cartoon (Figure 3.1) expresses a frustration experienced by many outsiders during a negotiation.

Figure 3.1

Number of negotiators

When the negotiations take place in Japan, Japanese representatives almost always outnumber foreign negotiators. When the discussion takes place in other countries, this is not always the case. During the discussions, Japanese are not often direct and to the point, which adds frustration to the feelings of persons not accustomed to such indirectness and the lack of getting to the point quickly. The artist expressed it in the Figure 3.2 cartoon.

Even when words may seem to have the same meaning, they often have different connotations, as the Figure 3.3 cartoon illustrates.

Figure 3.2

Figure 3.3

Silence

Many negotiators become anxious and frustrated when the other side is silent. For Japanese, silence is not empty but a time to reflect and consider. For a Japanese, silence can mean respect for their counterparts and a time for all to review the previously discussed main points. During a negotiation with Japanese, often there are periods of silence which are typically broken by outsiders by repeating, elaborating, or making concessions. Learning to tolerate and then look forward to and enjoy silences is a skill for non-Japanese to learn (Figure 3.4).

Negotiating and entertainment

When being invited for dinner by one's Japanese hosts, they almost invariably ask, "Do you prefer Western or Japanese cooking?" If one chooses Western, there won't be many surprises, but an excellent opportunity to show interest in the Japanese culture will have

Figure 3.4

Figure 3.5

been lost. Almost all Japanese prefer Japanese cooking, as more than one has said, "Japanese food tastes better." The next cartoon (Figure 3.5) expresses what could be the reason for the choice of Western by an outsider.

Contract disputes

In Japan, after the signing of a contract, if the circumstances change for the Japanese, they will try to resolve it by mutual agreement. For outsiders, contingencies should be covered in the contract and arbitration by appropriate authorities clearly identified, but this is not always the case, as is seen in the last cartoon (Figure 3.6).

Professor Dean Barnlund,[14] a long-time professor in Japanese and well knowledgeable of all things Japanese, said it this way, which should be encouraging for all outsiders

Figure 3.6

who have the opportunity to work in Japan, "if we are 'truly ourselves' (honest), and are of 'goodwill' (well intentioned), or 'try hard enough' (persistent), whatever differences divide us will disappear."

CONFLICT RESOLUTION AND NEGOTIATIONS

By definition, all successful negotiations involve at least some resolution of conflicts. Unsuccessful negotiation involves at least one conflict, large or small, that has not been resolved.

Like leadership and power, conflict is a fascinating subject for research and discussion in organizations. Traditionally, the social scientists who have studied conflict have been keenly aware of its destructive element, which is observed in wars, strikes, family disruption, and disharmony. We will identify some themes reflecting the U.S. viewpoint with regard to conflict, and suggest ways that other cultures resolve disputes. As Rensis Likert stated many years ago, "The strategies and principles used by a society and all its institutions for dealing with disagreements reflect the basic values and philosophy in that society."[15]

What is conflict? Like the word culture, there is no single agreed-upon definition. Thomas[16] states, "Conflict is the process that begins when one party perceives that the other has frustrated, or is about to frustrate, some concern of his." This frustration may result from actions that range from intellectual disagreement to physical violence. Another definition of "conflict" holds that it results when two or more persons or things attempt to occupy the same space at the same time. The management of conflict is a major issue at the personal and organizational levels, and all negotiations involve a resolution of conflicting interests and needs.

Most U.S. negotiators view conflict as a healthy, natural, and inevitable part of relationships and negotiations. This constructive approach to conflict views the positive attributes in any conflict situation. The belief that conflict is constructive requires that problems be addressed directly, and that people can be motivated to search for solutions to these problems. Constructive disagreement may in fact be an integral part of American organizations.

Stewart states, "When faced with a problem, Americans like to get to its source. This means facing the facts, meeting the problem head on, putting the cards on the table, and getting information straight from the horse's mouth. It is also desirable to face people directly, to confront them intentionally."[17]

However, conflict in organizations is perceived to have disadvantages when there are wide differences in viewpoints or perspectives and these are carried to the extreme. In this case, conflict is perceived as destructive, as the conflict creates a high level of stress for the individuals involved, which in turn affects their ability to perform. This undermines the cooperative dimension necessary in work groups, and results in time and energy being devoted to finding resolutions which could have been spent on organizational objectives. Such a situation also thwarts the decision-making process. Conflict resolution should be viewed as a win-win situation.

With the change in emphasis from the elimination of conflict to the management of conflict, Thomas[18] identified two models of conflict between social units. The process model appears as follows:

$$\text{Frustration} \to \text{Conceptualization} \to \text{Behavior} \to \text{Outcome} \to \text{Frustration}$$
$$\uparrow \qquad\qquad\qquad \uparrow$$
$$\text{Others' reactions}$$

The frustration of one party leads to a conceptualization of the situation, to some behavior, to the reaction of the other party, and then to agreement or the lack of agreement. In the latter case, the conflict episode is continued with further frustration, a new conceptualization, etc. The process model is concerned with the influence of an event (e.g., the conceptualization of the problems, etc.). The structural model attempts to understand conflict by studying how underlying conditions shape events. "The structural model is concerned with identifying the pressures and constraints which bear upon the parties' behavior; for example, social pressures, personal predispositions, established negotiation procedures and rules, incentives and so on."[19] The structural model attempts to predict the effect of these conditions on the behavior of the individuals involved in conflict. Thomas maintains that the two models complement each other.

Thomas and Kilmann suggest a two-dimensional scheme, with one dimension being the cooperative–uncooperative striving to satisfy the other's concern, and the second being the degree to which one assertively pursues one's own concerns.[20] In Exhibit 3.2, the assertive style (4) is competitive and represents a desire to satisfy one's concern at the expense of the other. The cooperative style (2) attempts to satisfy the other but not one's own concern. A compromising style (3) is a preference for moderate but incomplete satisfaction of both parties. Labor-management disputes in the United States characterize this style. A collaborative style (5) attempts to fully satisfy the concerns of both parties and is most synergistic. The avoidance style (1) is an indifference to the concerns of either party. The cooperative style as opposed to uncooperative is an Eastern mode of resolving conflict, and the assertive mode is more Western.

EXHIBIT 3.2 A TWO-DIMENSIONAL SCHEMATIC SHOWING VARIOUS STYLES OF CONFLICT RESOLUTION

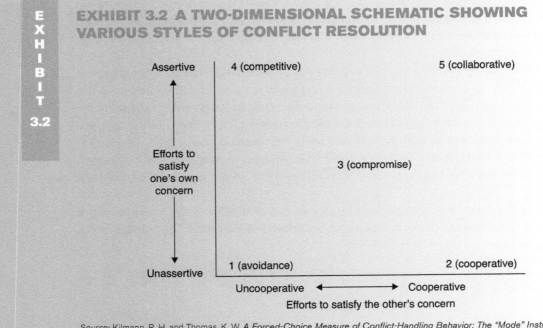

Source: Kilmann, R. H. and Thomas, K. W. *A Forced-Choice Measure of Conflict-Handling Behavior: The "Mode" Instrument.* Los Angeles Graduate School of Management, Working Paper, 1973, p.7.

The effective global manager must achieve a synergistic solution, diagnosing conflict accurately and determining a strategy for managing the conflict.

Conflict management in the Arab world

In the Arab world, the role of the mediator is important in resolving conflict. Thus, "the greater the prestige of the mediator, and the deeper the respect he commands, the better the chances that his efforts at mediating a dispute will be successful."[21] Some highly regarded families and groups carry ascribed status as mediators. The mediator must be impartial and beyond pressures, including monetary ones, from either side in the dispute. The mediator will often promote compromise by appealing to the wishes of other respected parties; for example, "Do it for the sake of . . . your father/brother." The ethical force of such an argument ("for the sake of") has three underlying assumptions, all of which remain unspoken but nonetheless understood by the disputants.

1   Each individual is obligated by ties of kinship to act in a manner that his kinsmen find gratifying.

2   The kinsmen, especially the older ones, are interested in the settlement of any conflict involving their kin group because every conflict represents a potential danger to the honor of the family.

3   By modifying one's position, the disputant can manifest generosity which, in turn, redounds to the honor of kin and bedouin values.

Conflict management in Japan

"To understand typical behavioral responses to conflict situations in Japan requires a basic understanding of the history and cultural environment of Japan."[22] Accordingly, it is necessary to first ascertain the key psychological and cultural variables that affect Japanese conflict management phenomena, and then to determine how they interrelate with each other to create various deviations within a larger cultural norm. The Japanese conflict management system includes both institutionalized conflict management structures and behavioral conflict management techniques.

Styles of handling conflict in Japan

Five styles of handling conflict are used in Japan: avoiding, compromising, obliging, integrating, and dominating; of these five styles, the Japanese prefer the avoiding style. In numerous examples of Japanese managers' response to the statement, "organizations would be better off if conflict could be eliminated," Japanese agree very strongly.

AVOIDING

On a behavioral level, the Japanese commonly employ a number of techniques to avoid conflict. Many of these techniques are not uncommon in cultures around the world, but they provide particular insight into Japanese conflict management.

One of their most effective techniques is sometimes referred to as triadic management. To avoid confrontation between two people, the Japanese often create a triad with another outside individual to manage the situation. Conflict between the two parties may be communicated through the third party in an indirect manner. The third party may take a more active role as an arbiter in situations where there is an apparent stalemate. In such a situation, the third party, who is respected by both of the other individuals, may provide a breakthrough by presenting her- or himself as the person on whose behalf the other two parties are to resolve the conflict. She or he urges the conflicting parties to relent so that she or he can "save face" (*kao*), with an implicit threat that she or he will take offense if her or his intervention is not heeded. To prevent humiliation to the arbiter, both parties may comply, even though they might prefer to remain in conflict with each other. Although this triadic management technique is by no means unique to Japan, it is utilized extensively, and provides one of the greatest vehicles for conflict management within the culture. Those skilled in global negotiations often use this method in Japan.

COMPROMISING

A variant of triadic management, known as displacement, can often manifest itself in a variety of ways. Usually, the displacement will take place in the form of an offended individual attempting to convey his or her anger or resentment to a third party, who is in a far more favorable position to transfer the feelings of the injured party to the injuring party in a manner that is less conflicting.

OBLIGING

Another technique often utilized to avoid direct confrontation is commonly referred to as conflict acceptance. Instead of rejecting or correcting an undesirable state of affairs, the individual persuades her- or himself or is advised by someone else to accept the situation. This somewhat fatalistic or deterministic approach is rooted in the strong Buddhist influence on the culture throughout the history of Japan.

INTEGRATING

Another, less-utilized technique employed to avoid direct confrontation may be referred to as self-aggression or self-confrontation. In this technique, one party expresses a grievance against another by exaggerated compliance.

DOMINATING

This style of conflict resolution is contrary to the very nature of the Japanese character, and consequently is used only rarely.

Interpreters and translators during negotiations

The importance of an interpreter in business negotiations cannot be overemphasized. It is the interpreter who can assist with the accurate communication of ideas between the two teams. A linguistic interpreter can also be a cultural interpreter, letting the negotiators know of actual or potential cultural misunderstandings. It is advisable to remember the following points concerning the use of interpreters:

- Brief the interpreter in advance about the subject. Select an interpreter knowledgeable about the product or subject.
- Speak clearly and slowly.

- Avoid little-known words.
- Explain the major idea in two or three different ways, as the point may be lost if discussed only once.
- Avoid talking for more than a minute or two without giving the interpreter a chance to speak.
- While talking, allow the interpreter time to make notes about what is being said.
- Do not lose confidence if the interpreter uses a dictionary.
- Permit the interpreter to spend as much time as necessary in clarifying points whose meanings are obscure.
- Do not interrupt the interpreter as he or she translates, to avoid misunderstandings.
- Avoid long sentences, double negatives, or the use of negative wordings when a positive form could be used.
- Avoid superfluous words. Your point may be lost if wrapped up in generalities.
- Try to be expressive, and use gestures to support your verbal messages.
- During meetings, write out the main points discussed. In this way, both parties can double-check their understanding.
- After meetings, confirm in writing what has been agreed.
- Do not expect an interpreter to work for over two hours without a rest.
- Consider using two interpreters if negotiation is to last an entire day or into the evening, so that when one tires, the other can take over.
- Don't be concerned if a speaker talks for five minutes and the interpreter covers it in half a minute.
- Be understanding if the interpreter makes a mistake.
- Ask the interpreter for advice if there are problems.

Successful negotiation procedures

Negotiations bring together two parties, each with an expectation of the outcome. On examination, the two parties evaluate their leverage, authority, and tactics. To close a negotiation that was the best possible deal for both sides means that, most likely, neither side feels cheated or duped and that a spirit of fairness pervaded the negotiation. When international negotiations take place, the cultural differences and implications can spin the negotiation in unanticipated directions. Weiss has established five steps for analyzing and developing a culturally responsive strategy for international negotiations.[23]

- *Study your own culture's negotiation script*. When we are in our home culture, we behave almost automatically. Studying observations about their home culture by outsiders as well as their own self-examinations will enable a negotiator to construct an accurate national profile. What does your side bring to the party?
- *Learn the negotiation script of your counterpart*. A first-time negotiator should build a profile of his or her counterparts from the ground up. An experienced negotiator

should review and research his or her counterparts, adding new information. Beware of cultural biases. What does this party bring to the negotiations?

■ *Consider the relationship and circumstance.* Whether you are the buyer or the seller in a negotiation will affect the relationship, and an adjustment of strategy will have to occur. Any previous negotiating relationship with a counterpart, as well as his or her home culture and its familiarity with yours, will also affect the outcome. What is the context of the relationship?

■ *Predict the counterpart's approach.* If your counterpart's approach is similar to yours, or you perhaps can influence the selection of the approach, these deliberations will preview the possible interactions during preparation for the negotiation. Generally, approaches will be complementary or conflicting.

■ *Choose your strategy.* After completing the first four steps, the selection of the strategy must be feasible given the cross-cultural dimensions of the negotiations and the counterpart's approach, be appropriate to the relationship, and, hopefully, be a win-win for both parties.

The following is a summary of a research project that analyzed actual negotiations.[24] The researchers' methods allowed them to differentiate between skilled negotiators and average negotiators by using behavior analysis techniques as they observed the negotiations and recorded the discussion. They identified "successful" negotiators as those who:

■ Were rated as effective by both sides.
■ Had a "track record" of significant success.
■ Had a low incidence of "implementation" failures.

A total of 48 negotiators who met all three success criteria were studied. They included union representatives (17), management representatives (12), contract negotiators (10), and others (9).

The 48 successful negotiators were studied over a total of 102 separate negotiating sessions. In the following description, the successful negotiators are called the "skilled" group. In comparison, the negotiators who either failed to meet the criteria or about whom no criterion data were available were called the "average" group.

During the planning process

Negotiation training emphasizes the importance of planning.

■ *Planning time.* No significant difference was found between the total planning time of skilled and average negotiators prior to actual negotiation.

■ *Exploration of options.* The skilled negotiator considers a wider range of outcomes or options for action than does the average negotiator.

- *Common ground*. The research showed that the skilled negotiators gave more than three times as much attention to common-ground areas as did average negotiators.
- *Long-term or short-term?* With the average negotiator, approximately one comment in 25 met the criterion of long-term consideration; namely, a comment that involved any factor extending beyond the immediate implementation of the issue under negotiation.
- *Setting limits*. The researchers asked negotiators about their objectives, and recorded whether their replies referred to single-point objectives (e.g., "We aim to settle at 83") or to a defined range (e.g., "We hope to get 85, but we would settle for a minimum of 77"). Skilled negotiators were significantly more likely to set upper and lower limits – to plan in terms of range. Average negotiators, in contrast, were more likely to plan their objectives around a fixed point.
- *Sequence and issue planning*. The term "planning" frequently refers to a process of sequencing – putting a number of events, points, or potential occurrences into a time sequence. Critical path analysis and other forms of network planning are examples.

Typical sequence plan used by average negotiators

A then B then C then D issues are linked.

Typical issue plan used by skilled negotiators

Issues are independent and not linked by sequence.

The clear advantage of issue planning over sequence planning is flexibility.

Face-to-face behavior

Skilled negotiators show marked differences in their face-to-face behavior, compared with average negotiators. They use certain types of behavior significantly more frequently, while they tend to avoid other types.

- *Irritators*. Certain words and phrases that are commonly used during negotiation have negligible value in persuading the other party, but do cause irritation. Probably the most frequent example of these is the term "generous offer" used by a negotiator to describe his or her proposal.
- *Counterproposals*. During negotiation, one party frequently puts forward a proposal, and the other party immediately responds with a counterproposal. Researchers found

that skilled negotiators made immediate counterproposals much less frequently than average negotiators.

- *Argument dilution*. This way of thinking predisposes us to believe that there is some special merit in quantity. Having five reasons for doing something is considered more persuasive than having only one reason. One may feel that the more he or she can put on his or her scale, the more likely it is to tip the balance of an argument in his or her favor. The researchers found that the opposite was true. The skilled negotiator used fewer reasons to back up each of his or her arguments.

- *Reviewing the negotiation*. The researchers asked negotiators how likely they were to spend time reviewing the negotiation afterward. Over two-thirds of the skilled negotiators claimed that they always set aside some time after a negotiation to review it and consider what they had learned. Just under half of average negotiators, in contrast, made the same claim.

This research clearly indicates some of the behaviors of skilled negotiators. Negotiators need to practice these behaviors, and others, to increase their skills.

Wederspahn suggests that human resource development programs within global corporations should include an International Negotiations Workshop with a cultural overview of the counterpart party in negotiations.[25] The model is based on the high/low-context approach to culture discussed elsewhere in our book. *Position-based negotiation* is based on the win-lose paradigm – the more one party receives, the more the other has to give up in the pursuit of self-interest and maximizing advantage. The main focus is on position – advancing, defending, and rationalizing it. Concessions made should be compensated by corresponding gains. Objective and impersonal data should be used to justify one's demands and trade-offs. Tactics include overstating demands, multiple fallback positions, pressure and dramatic displays, hidden agendas, bluffing, and keeping one's opponents off balance. In contrast, *interest-based negotiation* assumes that a mutually advantageous agreement is possible and desirable; expectations are for collaboration that is win-win and that brings benefits to both parties. This approach looks to long-term payoff in the relationship, so that there is mutual openness and information sharing to better understand each other's needs, constraints, and aspirations. Trust building includes visits to each other's facilities, establishing explicit and objective standards of fairness, designing systems to share gain/risk, giving and receiving help from one another, as well as socializing and creating a common strategy and culture.

THE PRICE OF FAILED NEGOTIATIONS

War is a conflict in the extreme, and often results when diplomacy and negotiations have failed. Recent research on Post Traumatic Stress Disorder (PTSD) has suggested that serious conflict, such as war or occupation, can produce years of traumatic experiences, especially for many who have engaged in the extreme conflict. David Berceli, a trauma therapist and expert on Arab/American relations, has written on this in personal communication with Robert Moran (Exhibit 3.3).

EXHIBIT 3.3 WAR FORGES A NEW ERA IN CORPORATE ARAB/ AMERICAN RELATIONSHIPS

In the United States, "Roughly 3.6 days of work impairment per month associated with Post Traumatic Stress Disorder (PTSD)[a] translates into an annual productivity loss in excess of $3 billion."[b] These figures and subsequent loss in productivity increase dramatically in countries throughout the world that have been ravaged by war, political violence, or sectarian armed conflict. As a result of recent events in the Middle East, international corporations operating there need to seriously consider the staggering toll that emotional pain and suffering will have on the functional and productive capacity of their employees. "There is no avoiding the traumatic aftermath of war; it reaches into every segment of society."[c] Work impairment due to secondary comorbid disorders of PTSD such as anxiety, depression, irritability, disturbed sleep, and elevated mood disorders all damage the cognitive and interpersonal skills of employees. This has a staggering impact on the social structure and eventually the economy of any corporation or society. As a result of this reality, whether they want to or not, corporations operating in war-torn countries of the Middle East will be forced to implement programs and procedures to deal with the systemic consequences of the trauma their employees have experienced...

As the average duration of each trauma episode is reported to be more than seven years, "the typical person with PTSD has a duration of active symptoms for more than two decades. The process of healing, therefore, will have to be measured in terms of generations rather than years."[d] Beginning with the rebuilding of Iraq, corporate social responsibility and financial profitability should be seen as inseparable ideologies because of the severe and systemic trauma experienced by the Iraqi people. With some simple but strategic trauma behavior modifications, over time corporations will be able to break down antagonism and build alliances across opposing sides. They will be able to use the trauma of their employees as a common opportunity for gain. If they know what they are doing, they can use these opportunities to "reduce contentious behaviors and increase conciliation."[e]

Notes: [a] Post Traumatic Stress Disorder is the reexperiencing of disrupting emotions or behaviors following the initial trauma.

[b] This report is from the Department of Health Care Policy, Kessler. R. Harvard Medical School, Boston, MA. It can be found in the *Journal of Clinical Psychiatry*, 2000, Vol. 61 (Suppl. 5), pp. 4–12.

[c] Levine, P. *We Are All Neighbors*. Boulder: Foundation for Human Enrichment, 2002, p. 3.

[d] This report is from the Department of Health Care Policy, R. Kessler. Harvard Medical School, Boston, MA. It can be found in the *Journal of Clinical Psychiatry*, 2000, Vol. 61 (Suppl. 5), pp. 4–12.

[e] Baldwin, D. "Innovation, Controversy and Consensus in Traumatology," *The International Electronic Journal of Innovations in the Study of the Traumatization Process and Methods for Reducing or Eliminating Related Human Suffering*, Vol. 3, No. 1, Article 3.

E X H I B I T 3.3

Emotional intelligence and negotiations

Everyone knows the meaning of IQ (Intelligence Quotient) and the importance of technical skills and intelligence to perform many job responsibilities. Some in an organization are referred to as "techies." Many also have personal experience with individuals who are very intelligent and have good technical skills but have failed in a leadership position.

Coleman[26] researched about 200 global companies, and found that the traditional attributes associated with leadership – intelligence, vision, toughness, etc. – are insufficient. He states that effective leaders must have a higher degree of emotional intelligence as well. According to Coleman, there are five components of emotional intelligence:

1   Self-awareness or the ability to recognize and understand one's moods and emotions, as well as their effect on others. This is characterized by self-confidence and a realistic assessment.
2   Self-regulation or the ability to control or redirect disruptive impulses and moods and the propensity to suspend judgment. This is characterized by trustworthiness, integrity, and a comfort with ambiguity.
3   Motivation or the ability to work for reasons that go beyond money or status. This is characterized by a strong drive to achieve, optimism even in the face of failure.
4   Empathy or the ability to understand the emotional makeup of other people. This is characterized by expertise in building and retaining talent.
5   Social skills or proficiency in managing relationships and building networks. This is characterized by skills in leading change and expertise in building and leading teams.

CONCLUSIONS

Roger Fisher,[27] the negotiating guru, in an interview about emotions and negotiations, stated, "I don't have people criticizing me for talking about emotions . . . no one says it's a soft, fuzzy side." In short, keeping your feelings hidden, saying, "don't become emotional" during a heated argument, may become obsolete.

This perspective is supported by Fromm,[28] who wrote, "Emotions provide important information to us and to the other side. If we are able to express our emotions in a constructive way and at an appropriate time in the negotiation, rather than destroying or hurting the negotiation process, it can greatly enhance it."

Emotional intelligence contributes to a skillful negotiator's toolbox. The instruments and questionnaire to measure one's emotional intelligence or emotional competence are easily available and recommended to all global negotiators.

MIND STRETCHING

1 As a negotiator, list your strengths and your weaknesses. Write an action plan to become a more skillful negotiator.

2 Become an astute observer of human behavior. As you observe the behavior of others in different situations, what are the determinants? Culture? Personality? Context?

3 How can you increase your styles of resolving conflicts when negotiating across cultures?

4 Apply the concepts in this chapter to any global dispute. Why are there as many unresolved issues?

5 Do our global business and political leaders have a high degree of observable emotional intelligence?

NOTES

1 Moran, R. Stated in a session to executives on negotiation across cultures, February 2010.
2 *The New York Times*, January 27, 2013.
3 Walch, Karen, "Seize the Sky: Discovering the Secrets of Negotiation Power," *Thunderbird Magazine*, Fall 2012.
4 Graham, J. and Herberger, R. "Negotiating Abroad: Don't Shoot from the Hip," *Harvard Business Review*, July/August 1983.
5 Dierdorff, D. (ed.). *The Sage Handbook of Intercultural Competence*. PO 250. Thousand Oaks, CA: Sage, 2009.
6 Acuff, F. L. *How to Negotiate with Anyone, Anywhere Around the World*. New York: Amacom, 1993.
7 "Assess, Don't Assume, Part 1: Etiquette and Material Culture in Negotiation" and "Assess, Part II: Cross-Border Differences in Decision Making, Governance, and Political Economy." HBR Working Paper 10–048 and Working Paper 10–050, 20.
8 Graham, J. "*Vis-à-Vis*: International Business Negotiations," in P. Ghauri and J. C. Usunier (eds), *International Business Negotiations*. Oxford: Pergamon, 1996.
9 Scheu-Lottgen, U. D. and Hernandez-Campoy, J. M. "An Analysis of Sociocultural Miscommunication: English, Spanish and German," *International Journal of Intercultural Relations*, Vol. 22, No. 4, 1998.
10 Graham, J. "*Vis-à-Vis*: International Business Negotiations."
11 Based on interviews conducted in 2010.
12 Moran, R. T. and Harris, P. R. *Managing Cultural Synergy*. Houston, TX: Gulf Publishing Company, 1982. Material updated in 2006.
13 Originally published by Gulf Publishing Company and revised January 2013 by Robert Moran. Cartoons drawn by Karen Johnson.
14 Barnlund, Dean and Bennett, Janet M. "The Public and Private," *International Journal of Intercultural Relations,* Vol. 36, No. 6, 2012.
15 Likert, R. and Likert, J. G. *New Ways of Managing Conflict*. New York: McGraw-Hill, 1976.
16 Thomas, K. W. *Conflict and Conflict Management*. Los Angeles, CA: University of California. Working Paper, 74, 3, 1974.
17 Stewart, E. C. *American Cultural Patterns: A Cross-Cultural Perspective*. LaGrange Park, IL: Intercultural Network, 1979.

18 Thomas, *Conflict and Conflict Management.*

19 Ibid.

20 Kilmann, R. H. and Thomas, K. W. *A Forced-Choice Measure of Conflict Handling Behavior: The "Mode" Instrument.* Los Angeles Graduate School of Management, Working Paper, 1973, pp. 12–73.

21 Patai, R. *The Arab Mind.* New York: Charles Scribner & Sons, 1976.

22 Moran, R. T., Allen, J., Wichmann, R., Ando, T., and Sasano, M. "Japan," in A. Rahim and A. Blum (eds), *Global Perspectives on Organizational Conflict.* London: Praeger, 1994. Material updated in 2006, pp. 18ff.

23 Weiss, S. E. "Negotiating with 'Romans' – Part 2," *Sloan Management Review,* Massachusetts Institute of Technology, Spring 1994.

24 *Behavior of Successful Negotiators.* Huthwaite Research Group Report, 1976, 1982.

25 Wederspahn, G. M. "The Fine Art of International Negotiation," *HR News/ Society for Human Resource Management,* January 1993, pp. C6, 7.

26 Coleman, D. "Inside the Mind of the Leader," *Harvard Business Review,* January 2006.

27 www.news.harvard.edu/gazette/2005/10.13/03-reason.html.

28 Fromm, D. "Dealing with Your Emotions in Negotiations," *The Negotiation Magazine,* November 2005.

ADDITIONAL FEATURES

Please visit the companion website at: www.routledge.com/cw/Moran where you will find additional case studies, study aides, and instructor resources.

4 GLOBAL LEADERS LEARNING FROM OTHERS AND CHANGE

Businessmen go down with their businesses because they like the old way so well they cannot bring themselves to change. One sees them all about — men who did not know that yesterday is past, and who woke up this morning with their last year's ideas.

Henry Ford[1]

We do not make changes for the sake of making them, but we never fail to make a change when once it is demonstrated that the new way is better than the old way.

Henry Ford[2]

LEARNING OBJECTIVES

This chapter considers both how companies learn and also how individuals learn in the contexts of performance and change. The purpose of a commercial enterprise is to achieve a financial return for its shareholders while providing a variety of benefits for all its stakeholders including suppliers, customers, employees, and even the public at large.

A multinational enterprise (MNE)[3] is a company that seeks these returns by doing business in two or more countries. It uses a system of decision-making in one or more decision-making centers that allows for a strategy that encompasses all its operations. Its operations are linked by ownership or agreements such that it is able to significantly influence its operations in order to share knowledge, resources, authority, and responsibility.

The MNE intends to achieve its performance goals by developing an intended strategy, seeking to identify and take advantage of bases of competitive advantage in its industry or industries versus its competitors. In order for this strategy to succeed, the internal capabilities of the MNE must be organized to support the strategy to the maximum. The process by which companies develop strategies by scanning for environmental opportunities and organizing internal capabilities to support their strategies is the subject for detailed discussion in Chapter 7.

Unfortunately for MNEs, their competitive business environments are constantly changing and MNEs have to learn to adapt. Macroeconomic forces, beyond the abilities of any company or government to control, may entirely alter the basis of global competition. The subprime mortgage debacle of 2008 began in the United States but quickly spread worldwide as banks lost the liquidity and confidence to finance international trade. The Keynesian solution to the worldwide credit problem of national governments borrowing vast amounts to provide liquidity to financial institutions produced a debt crisis. This debt crisis has been particularly acute in some of the largest G8 nations (United States, Japan, Germany, France, Italy, United Kingdom, Russia, Canada), severely limiting economic growth. An industry may collapse temporarily, as did the Internet data storage industry, throwing a company like Nortel into a tailspin. A company may fail to respond to a changing basis for competition in its industry, or to the greater competitiveness of its key competitors as happened to RIM.

At the same time, the capabilities of MNEs are also constantly changing, affecting their ability to enact their intended strategies. New corporate leaders may come with different skill sets, values, and management styles. Alan Mulally, President and CEO of Ford Motor Company, was the first CEO of Ford whose background was not in the auto industry. He had been the president that turned Boeing around and saved it. Mulally was credited with having the fresh perspective to see what was wrong with Ford. He eliminated unprofitable brands (Jaguar, Land Rover, Saab, Hummer), resurrected the Taurus nameplate, and achieved cost cutting initiatives by truly globalizing Ford products across international markets. He is credited with bringing Ford back to profitability from near death because he was not committed to the strategies that had almost ruined Ford.[4]

Internal capabilities needed to support corporate strategies may change over time. Operational resources are added through acquisitions, joint ventures, alliances, or planned development. They may be lost due to divestiture. Key human resources come and go — both Nortel and RIM fired thousands of employees once thought essential in their bids to regain profitability. High potential executives and personnel will often leave a company perceived to be underperforming, moving to companies offering greater chances of personal advancement. New systems, IT for example, are added, or formerly latest technologies fall out of date but no one realizes and the MNE loses capabilities it thought it had.

When organizations learn, or need to do so, we call it *organizational learning*. We define learning as "sense-making." Learning means figuring out how to make use of relevant knowledge that is continuously being revised and updated. We assume that for organizations and individuals struggling to be effective in unfamiliar cultural environments that there is rarely a "right" answer, nor is "the" answer even known. Most cross-national problems that organizations and individuals face are new, and there are no known "for sure" answers.

The key to learning is effective problem-solving. We need to know a process for identifying what the problem really is. We need to be able to figure out what the best solution is, both in terms of what is needed to be competitive, and also what we can actually achieve with the capabilities at our disposal. Finally, we need a plan for executing our solution that includes the best and most cost effective sequencing of actions, and checkpoints to make sure our solution is actually remedying the problem we were trying to solve. Dixon[5] defined organizational learning as: "the intentional use of learning processes at the individual, group, and system level to continuously transform the organization in a direction that is increasingly satisfying to its stakeholders."[6] It assumes that:[7]

1   There are many possible right answers in the sense that there may be many ways to reach the same goal. As long as a solution is competitive in the environment and the organization has, or can get the capabilities to do it, it remains a possibility.
2   People who are concerned about and/or affected by a problem are capable of developing useful knowledge to find a solution.
3   Learning occurs in the context of work, often by adapting existing practices, and results from intentional efforts.

Some have argued that the question of "who" learns is a great myth in organizational learning.[8] Organizations don't really learn. Organizations are comprised of individual people. There is no such thing as an organization. The term is just a short-hand for groups of individuals working together in a division of labor. So from this point-of-view, learning simply refers to the processes of thinking and remembering that take place in any given individual's mind.

The antithetical argument is that, in addition to individual learning, people appear to learn differently when they are learning in groups. "People appear to think in conjunction or partnership with others and with the help of culturally provided tools and implements.... In other words, it is not just the 'person-solo' who learns, but the 'person-plus', the whole system of interrelated factors."[9] Salomon[10] took the view, adopted by this chapter, that "solo" and "plus" represented separate forms of learning but that they should also be viewed as being interdependent and in dynamic interaction. The divisions of labor within organizations produced jointly shared kinds of know-how that an individual could not access on his/her own.[11]

Because organizational and individual learning are so interdependent, it may seem to you that it is not always easy to differentiate between them. If we refer to the mindset of an organization as it sees its international operations, is it the organization that sees itself that way, or a majority of the senior management team, or just one powerful leader who runs the company the way he/she sees fit? Personality research has shown that the character of the organization and the way it functions may stem from the preferences of the leader and/or his/her senior managers.[12] Bridges identifies 16 different organizational personalities that have different strengths and weaknesses, and that are more or less effective depending on the situation.[13]

Seagal and Horne observed that individuals from Euro-North American countries prefer individual learning processes different from those that the majority of Chinese or Japanese prefer, and that this affects their ability to work together.[14] Are these questions about how individual learning should be organized, or comparisons of differences in preferred learning processes in specific national cultures? The best advice is that each one of us has to look after our own individual learning and some of the contents of this chapter may be helpful for you to assess what works for you.

At the same time, we need to be aware of the learning styles of the organizations we work for. Some rely more on the latest theoretical conceptions; others on practical experience. Some are fast to change. Others rely more on traditional approaches and accept change more slowly. And we must be aware that people from other cultures may have learning styles quite different from our own. You should not be critical if their approach to learning differs from your own as long as they are trying their best.

In the year 2000, Nortel (Northern Telecom) was the most successful Canadian company of all time. It accounted for one-third of the total valuation of all the companies listed on the Toronto Stock Exchange. It employed 94,500 worldwide and 25,900 in Canada alone. In the late 1990s, Nortel had been the seventh-largest worldwide telecom company. When the Chinese government selected the top worldwide telecom companies to be allowed to do business in China, Nortel was included. Nortel's own industry analysis, however, indicated that only the top five companies would survive increased global competition in the telecom industry and so Nortel switched its focus to producing data storage for the quickly growing Internet. When the speculative telecom bubble of the late 1990s burst in late 2000, Nortel was the most spectacular casualty. Its buyers estimated that they had installed data storage for as much as the next fifty years. Nortel's market capitalization fell from Cdn$398 billion in September 2000 to Cdn$5 billion in August 2002. It filed for bankruptcy protection in early 2009 and is now under liquidation.[15]

Nortel's plummeting fortunes were a direct result of an inability to adapt to a changing competitive environment by learning to adapt its strategy to changing conditions. It abandoned the telecom industry where it had been a success. It failed to adapt when the high-tech bubble burst.

In August, 2009, *Fortune* named Research in Motion (RIM), the manufacturer of the Blackberry smartphone, the fastest growing company in the world. It had achieved 84 percent profit growth over the previous three years despite the worldwide recession.[16] However, by June, 2011, RIM shareholders lost as much as $70 billion, or 82 percent, as market capitalization fell from $83 billion to $13.6 billion. This was the biggest decline among communications equipment providers during the period.[17] Apple's iPhone, and Samsung, and other smartphones running Google's Android operating system decimated RIM's market share. RIM failed to devote as much of its resources as its competitors to the development of new technology in a fast moving market.[18] By March 2012, RIM shares were worth less than $14, falling from a high of over $140 in 2008.

Now in the summer of 2013, we see that the new and much delayed Blackberry 10 operating system, quite possibly RIM's last chance for survival, is selling at less than touted levels though Blackberry's CEO guarantees that this is as expected and investors should be patient.[19] Turnarounds are a coin flip; 50/50. Heads the company recovers. Tails it goes bust.

RIM (now Blackberry) competes in a smartphone industry dominated by R&D in which technological learning is the main predictor of corporate success and product life cycles are exceedingly short due to competitors' advances. RIM's mistake was not hiring enough software developers or spending enough on R&D to keep up. The VP in charge saw these as important problems but not critical compared with all his other priorities.[20] In 2008, according to industry standards, RIM was spending only 76 percent of what its competitors were spending as a percentage of sales, and in real dollars only 46 percent of Apple, and 5 percent of Microsoft. RIM's position collapsed because it did not learn how to change its strategy when as market leader it was faced with more and faster competition. Confident in its earlier success, Blackberry did not recognize how fast the smartphone industry was changing.

ASPECTS OF ORGANIZATIONAL LEARNING

Effects of change and declining performance

Companies' learning behavior is generally driven by their market performance. Market success is critical. The best managers want to work at the best and most successful companies. If a company's performance starts to go downhill, good personnel may begin to leave in search of better opportunities. Banks and financial institutions either don't want to lend to companies doing poorly, or the rates they charge become higher and higher as the company's credit rating declines. The value of a publicly traded company's stock also reflects investors' perceptions of how successful the company is. And the compensation and incentive packages of senior executives are often tied into the share price. The stock options senior managers receive as incentives will not have value if the share price declines. There are many measures of how a company is performing. Some of these are identified in Exhibit 4.1.

Measures of profitability are made more complex because of the possible effects of inflation or levels of competition within an industry. We are not as used to considering the effects of inflation because G8 interest rates have been so low for so many years and inflation has not been more than 1–3 percent for a long time. If, however, a company's sales and/or profits were rising at 5 percent annually, but inflation was running at 10 percent per annum, then the position of the company would be declining in inflation adjusted dollars by 5 percent per year. Similarly, if a company's sales and/or profits rise at 5 percent annually but the average for its industry is rising at 10 percent, then the company is losing ground to its competitors. It is getting smaller versus its competitors though it appears to be growing.

EXHIBIT 4.1 MEASURES OF FIRM PERFORMANCE

Performance outcomes	Outputs	Inputs
▪ Sales results, profit margins	▪ Financial	▪ People (satisfaction, retention, quality of worklife)
▪ Return on assets (ROA), income (ROI), equity (ROE)	▪ Productivity, efficiency and quality	▪ Technology (information and data, reliability, satisfaction)
▪ Objectives defined in strategic plan	▪ Activity ratios (asset and inventory turnover)	▪ Fixed assets (security, utilization, quality)
▪ Customer results: satisfaction, quality, timeliness	▪ Management effectiveness and innovation	

Source: Adapted from http://en.wikipedia.org/wiki/File:Performance_Reference_Model.jpg.

Change and its learning effects

A company usually becomes an MNE to find greater competitive advantage within more globalized industry environments than it enjoyed in its own national domestic environment. An international market may provide a more *secure supply* of raw materials. For example, Canada has become a larger supplier of oil to the United States than any individual Middle Eastern country, and an attractive location for American oil and gas investment, because it enjoys far greater political stability.

An international market may provide *new markets* for products or services. Most MNEs that enter a new international market do so on the basis of having a technological or R&D advantage over the existing domestic competitors.[21] They have a better, more advanced, or more desirable product or service that can be sold for a premium that more than offsets the increased costs of doing business abroad.

In addition, and especially before the global recession of 2008, MNEs sought *low cost factors of production* to reduce the cost of manufactured products. These were then primarily shipped back to the markets of more developed nations. China, for example, initially began to develop its economy after 1979 by attracting foreign investment that was enticed by low labor costs, inexpensive land, and low taxes. China's domestic consumer market was not attractive to MNEs at that time because most people were so poor and couldn't afford the products they produced for foreign MNEs. With the onset of the 2008 global recession and the debt crisis in many G8 countries, the markets in developed countries have become less able to purchase products produced in what are now called the emerging markets. MNEs have learned that the emerging markets themselves are a better opportunity for the sale of their locally produced products[22] as local standards of living rose. Since the early 2000s, for example, average wages in China have risen fourfold.

According to Crossan et al.,[23] all companies including MNEs face three kinds of change conditions that negatively affect their performance and that require them to learn new ways of doing business. *Crisis change* is a situation where a company's performance has declined substantially either because of poor products and/or services, a poor competitive strategy, or an inability to drive the strategy because of inconsistency between strategy and the company's internal capabilities. There is an imminent threat of bankruptcy. In this situation, the company's strategic capabilities are low but the willingness to change is high because "the writing is on the wall."

In 2013, Blackberry (RIM) is in the midst of crisis change. It is not clear that their new Blackberry 10 operating system will save the company, and it appears to be its last chance. As recently as 2009, RIM stood apparently unchallenged at the top of the business and government segment of the smartphone industry. Within two years they were losing significant market share to Apple and Android. In 2012, big client businesses, part of their installed base, began to discard their Blackberries and switch to Apple, Samsung, or Google. RIM's only market growth was achieved in places like India and Indonesia where the Blackberry brand is still popular and this retains hope for the company.

Companies can learn new "tricks" and survive crisis change situations but their odds of success have been estimated at only 50/50, the same as flipping a coin. When General Motors and Chrysler entered bankruptcy and were sustained by government loans in 2009, both were able to find new ways to compete. In 2012, Chrysler was the top selling automobile brand in Canada. General Motors briefly regained its status as the top selling brand in the world in 2011, when Toyota production was stalled by a major earthquake and tsunami in northeastern Japan. The point, however, is that there are many warnings that change is necessary before the crisis sets in, and companies need to change before it is almost too late.

Reactive change is usually the stage where companies realize that they need to change before a crisis can develop. Products and/or services are beginning to lose competitive advantage. Sales and profits are off former highs. Managers begin to realize that the company is on a downslope and the readiness for change begins to develop.

This was the situation at Ford Motor Company[24] when Bill Ford Jr., Henry Ford's great grandson, took over as CEO in 2001, promising that the money losing Ford would make a $7 billion profit within five years. Ford quality had become so questionable that many former customers refused ever to consider buying another Ford. Meanwhile, the company was stuck with high labor costs because of unions that resisted efforts to achieve wage levels consistent with the Japanese competition, and any efforts to increase factory productivity. Ford had too many inefficient plants for the number of vehicles they could sell, and managers that were not above sabotaging each others' efforts to try to advance their own careers at Ford. And, at the same time, high gasoline costs were scaring customers away from the big pickups and SUVs that generated most of Ford's profits.

For a while, Bill Ford was successful. He strengthened Ford's alliance with the Japanese Mazda, and used Mazda and Swedish Volvo technology as the basis for new Ford cars of higher quality. He began development of a hybrid car. Yet his efforts failed when the fuel crisis of 2006 led to the collapse of Ford's truck and SUV sales. In the third quarter of 2006 alone, Ford posted a nearly $6 billion loss, Ford's worst quarter in 14 years. When Alan Mulally took over as CEO, he inherited a crisis change situation. Given that even iconic companies can fail to respond effectively to the need for reactive change, there must be earlier opportunities to learn to respond to the need for change.

Anticipatory change is the awareness that a company's strategy has reached its potential limits to growth. Performance is still rising but at a slower rate. Resistance to the possibility of change is likely to be higher than in reactive or crisis situations. The general feeling may be that growth has slowed because of macro-economic factors and not because the company's competitive position has eroded. Or senior managers may simply be swept away by their feelings of success and invincibility, and not be watching closely enough.

This seems to have been the situation at RIM. Jim Balsillie, co-CEO, seemed more concerned in 2011 with acquiring a National Hockey League team than whether RIM was managing to release more competitive smartphones. RIM missed the early warning sign that they were not hiring as many R&D development engineers in proportion to their sales growth as their direct competitors. The industry was speeding up while RIM slowed down in its capacity for producing R&D innovation.

By contrast, in 1984, Richmond Engineering,[25] a Vancouver British, Columbia, based telephone and streetlight pole manufacturing SME with annual sales of Cdn$24 million, had reached its limits of growth. Richmond was the market leader in pole manufacturing and sales in western Canada but because of the costs of transportation it was not feasible to sell in either eastern Canada or the western United States. Having hit their maximum growth potential in their home market, the CEO, a very strong woman entrepreneur, began to look for joint venture (JV) opportunities in China. Her goal was to manufacture in China at significantly lower costs than in Canada and to supply the quickly expanding China market.

Richmond employed an agent in Hong Kong between 1984 and 1989. In 1987, a JV agreement was being negotiated to produce Richmond poles with Hong Kong financing in Shenzhen but this deal fell apart after Tiananmen Square in 1989. Between 1989 and 1991, Richmond assessed dozens of offers from China before finding a real possibility in the Beijing area. By 1993, a JV agreement was in place and by 1999 the JV was selling poles in China and Abu Dabi, as well as selling a turnkey manufacturing plant in China.

The lesson here about learning to respond to the need for change is that it is best to do so earlier rather than later. This is true even though there will be greater resistance to change as long as managers can fool themselves into thinking things are still OK. Exhibit 4.2 offers some shorthand comparisons between the three stages of need for change.

EXHIBIT 4.2 COMPARISON OF CRISIS, REACTIVE, AND ANTICIPATORY CHANGE SITUATIONS

	Crisis	Reactive	Anticipatory
Situation			
■ Performance	Critically low	Lower than before	Slower but still growing
■ Time pressure	High	Medium	Low
■ Resistance	Low	Mixed to high	High
Concerns			
■ Strategic	Rapid change to avoid business failure	Temporary glitch or changed conditions?	Plan still works well
■ Classification	Urgent change as-soon-as-possible	Normal change: reassess strategic plan	Standard change: take advantage of opportunities
■ Leadership	Reactive	Reactive	Proactive

EXHIBIT 4.2

Source: Crossan, M. M., Rouse, M. J., Fry, J. N., and Killing, J. P. *Strategic Analysis and Action*, 7th edn. Toronto, ON: Pearson Prentice Hall, 2009, p. 217.

The experience of Richmond Engineering illustrates the point that learning to do business internationally as a solution to a need for strategic change is a relatively slow process. It took Richmond nine years to establish a functional Chinese JV once their course was set. After 15 years, JV profitability had not yet been achieved (Richmond owned 25 percent) though Richmond had made money selling equipment to the JV, and the turnkey plant. International expansion is best undertaken under conditions of anticipatory change when there is less time pressure.

Learning and the theory of internationalization

Learning to enter and successfully build a business presence in a new foreign market can be a very uncertain and time-consuming process for any company, including established MNEs. There are so many potential sources of uncertainty in an unfamiliar foreign market: cultural, social, political, and economic. Companies want to limit their exposure to unknown risks until they have learned to assess all relevant uncertainties. It is very costly for MNEs to find and hire well-informed and experienced local human resources as a means of reducing uncertainty. It is expensive and time-consuming to find potential joint venture partnerships with successful local companies as a way of learning how to do business in a new local market. Greenfields (starting your own subsidiary from scratch) and acquisitions require huge investments and are therefore very risky, especially if you are unfamiliar with local business conditions. The problems small and medium sized enterprises (SMEs) face are magnified by their relative lack of resources.

The Uppsala theory of Internationalization predicts that MNEs will intensify their activities in a foreign market as they learn about the market and reduce their uncertainties about it.[26] Typically, at an initial stage when uncertainty is at its maximum, MNEs *export* their products to a new foreign market using an agent or distributor. An export strategy is preferred because the MNE puts as little of its resources at risk as possible. Usually only a small stock of product is provided to the distributor with more available when sales are made. Even less risky is a direct mail approach where the MNE contacts potential customers by mail or through a website, and product is shipped directly upon order and prepayment.

Export strategies tend not to be particularly profitable because only relatively small numbers of sales are made. The MNE is simply dabbling in the new market, hoping to learn about the buying preferences of customers, whether its products are competitive, and whether the new market could be a profitable source of sales. Distributors provide very little push for individual products since the distributor usually represents many products, usually not competitive with each other. If a customer shows no interest in a particular product, the distributor offers other possibilities. And an exporting company should understand that one of the goals of many distributors is to prevent or retard the ability of the exporters to learn about the foreign market because that knowledge represents the competitive edge of the distributor. Distributors generally do not, for example, provide detailed information about customers to exporters. If the MNE understood its customers and the market, its uncertainty would be reduced and it would be confident about attempting a riskier and potentially more profitable entry strategy.

And distributors can be expensive. Kevin O'Leary,[27] of *The Dragon's Den* fame on Canadian TV, was the CEO of Softkey, which began as a software distributor. Softkey offered to invest money to promote a small software developer's product in the United States. If sales were achieved, Softkey would recover its initial marketing investment and then charge about 25 percent of the value of future sales. Softkey became so successful as a software marketing firm that one CEO of another software company reported that Softkey could charge in fees as much as 70 percent of the value of the sales it generated.

The second stage of internationalization usually involves either *licensing or franchising*. The MNE has learned that there is a market for its product but is either unwilling to take the risk of direct investment, or regards the market as either too small or incidental to its main strategic interests. These strategies are also not the most profitable. The licenser and licensee sign a contractual agreement that allows the licensee to produce the product in the local market to the licenser's specifications. The licenser may supply parts, and technicians, and even train the licensee's workers. The licensee guarantees to pay a percentage either of sales or profits in return, and in some contracts also guarantees that any product improvements will flow back to the licenser. The licenser may also insist on a minimum level of sales, being allowed to cancel the contract if these minimum sales levels are not achieved. Licensers must have the resources to constantly monitor the activities of licensees to ensure that they receive their royalty payments, and that licensees do not begin to produce gray market copies of the products for which they provide no royalties.

Human Dynamics International (cited in Chapter 2), an American firm, has recently had difficulties with licensees in the Netherlands not acknowledging that their products are derived from Human Dynamics and not paying royalties. Human Dynamics is threatening to sue but is an SME with limited resources for a legal battle overseas. The licensees are knowingly taking advantage of Human Dynamics' weakness.

The third stage of internationalization generally involves the establishment of strategic collaborations in the form of *alliances or JVs* with other firms. MNEs considering strategic collaborations have learned quite a lot about the foreign market they are considering and know that they are interested in doing business there. Usually there is some gap in their knowledge that they hope to learn through a joint venture. A typical JV strategy is for an MNE to offer its more advanced technology to a local partner in exchange for learning how to market and sell in the local market.

Depending on the level of goodwill, a race to learn may take place. The danger for the MNE is that the local partner will learn its advanced technology before the MNE learns the local market, thereby creating a potential global competitor. The MNE loses the race when its local partner dissolves the JV. It has lost control of its technology but has not yet learned how to be successful in the local market. The danger for the local partner is that the MNE will learn how to market and sell in its local market, and not need the local partner, before the latter learns the technology.

The Indian joint venture between Honda Motor Company the Hero Group is instructive in this regard.[28] The two combined to produce the Hero-Honda JV, the most successful motorcycle manufacturing and sales company in India in the 1990s. Honda provided the motorcycle technology while Hero provided the local marketing and sales. Eventually after ten years, Honda learned to set up its own sales and distribution system while Hero had simply relied on Honda technology and not set up its own R&D capabilities. Honda continued to support Hero but the latter became extremely dependent on Honda's goodwill.

Selecting a compatible JV partner is the best protection against these kinds of competitive outcomes. The partners must ensure that they have:

1   *Complementarity.* Initially, this was the case for Honda and Hero. Honda had world competitive motorcycle technology while Hero was very successful marketing and selling in India. This changed, however, as Honda learned and Hero didn't.

2   *Convergence of goals.* Initially, this was true for Honda and Hero. Honda was a global MNE and was interested in competing for market share in India only to keep up with its global competitors that already had Indian JVs. Hero was only interested in the India market and did not pose a global threat to Honda.

3   *Commitment.* Both partners must believe that they may trust each other, recognizing that cooperation builds trust, as do reliability, competence, and personal relationship over time. Hero communicated a lack of commitment to Honda over time, by trying to sign agreements with Honda's global competitors.

4   *Compatibility.* This is achieved through asymmetrical skills that produce clear and non-overlapping responsibilities. Choi and Beamish[29] argued that Koreans and Americans were so culturally different that they could not successfully work together in JVs. If, however, their roles were asymmetrical and non-overlapping, then Korean-American JVs could be very successful.

Research has shown that the most profitable foreign market strategies are *wholly owned*,[30] and this supports the need for MNEs to learn how to eventually set up wholly owned operations in foreign markets.[31] MNEs are comfortable implementing wholly owned strategies (greenfield and acquisition) when they have fully learned the cultural, social, political, and economic differences in a local market compared with their home markets. They have developed the marketing and sales expertise for the local market, either because their personnel have developed the required tacit knowledge through JVs and/or alliances, or because experienced local or expatriate personnel have been hired. Generally, though not always, they have a technological advantage over local market products.

There are three wholly owned routes. *Greenfield* is the setting up of a wholly owned operation from the ground up. It may include the whole value chain (R&D, manufacturing, marketing, sales, service), or it may be as simple as a sales and service office staffed by the

MNE's own employees. Dell Computer Corporation has been very successful in Latin America, through its greenfield operations there.[32]

Acquisition is the acquiring of a local firm through which the MNE plans to operate. A warning here is that the acquisition should be a successful local company with a strong market position. Canadian Tire, an iconic Canadian company, failed spectacularly entering the United States when it acquired White's. White's came cheap because it required reactive or even crisis change intervention. Canadian Tire was unable to turn White's around, not having a good understanding itself as to how to do business in the United States. Daimler-Benz faced similar problems when it acquired Chrysler years later.

A *merger* is the third method for achieving a wholly owned position. In mergers and acquisitions, "companies are just beginning to learn what nations have always known: in a complex, uncertain world filled with dangerous opponents, it is best not to go it alone."[33] Some mergers and acquisitions thrive, some survive, and some die. Some are perceived as an act of desperation, and others are more strategic. The following points are relevant to mergers:

- Internal growth possibilities are diminished for many organizations, and mergers or acquisitions are strategies to survive or grow.
- Increasing products, markets, and technology lowers risk.
- Organizational culture clash is a major problem in integrating different companies.
- Making the deal is easy; making it work is difficult.

Ashkenas et al.[34] outline the following lessons learned by GE Capital:

- Acquisition integration begins with the due diligence studies of all aspects of the organization.
- Integrating management is a full-time business function like marketing.
- Decisions on structure, roles, and other important aspects of integration should be announced soon after the merger or acquisition is reported.
- Integration involves not only technologies and products, but cultures also.

These lessons are relevant when the integrated organizations are from the same national culture. When they are from different national cultures, the challenges are more significant, and the skills required to make them succeed are broader, deeper, and more sophisticated. Organizational culture, for example, may be based on national culture. The organizational culture of Chinese and Japanese companies will generally be based on Confucian values resulting in a strong hierarchy that conforms to the expectations of its leadership. This kind of organization culture would be anathema for many American companies that favor flat organizational structures and expect managers at all levels to take personal initiative as a form of empowerment throughout the organization. Merging managers and employees, some of whom expect to conform, and others who expect not to have to conform, will produce much resistance to change on both sides.

Global leaders are required to meet, socialize, and negotiate with foreign business-persons and government officials. The manager must be able to communicate and work with persons who have been socialized in a different cultural environment. Customs, values, lifestyles, beliefs, management practices, and other aspects of their personal and professional life are therefore often very different. For the global leader to be effective, he/she must be aware of the many beliefs and values that underlie his/her country's business practices, management techniques, and strategies. Awareness of such values and assumptions is critical for managers who wish to transfer technology to another culture or who wish to collaborate with those who hold different values and assumptions.

The observations in this section take on added significance when computer networking and the Internet are used to form strategic alliances and partnerships. The connectivity of the Internet enables us to create information partnerships with personnel, customers, suppliers, contractors, and consultants around the world. The key in such electronic endeavors is to treat them as collaborators rather than competitors, and to work with them to establish whether the relationship can include complementarity, convergence of goals, commitment, and compatibility. One must be careful not to blithely assume that the people at the other end of the Internet are just like ourselves, or expect to be treated the same way. Extra formality is often a safer approach until you learn more about who you are dealing with.

Management mindsets, internationalization, and learning

The leaders and management teams of MNEs have mindsets about how they see themselves, their companies, and how business should be done in international markets. These mindsets, or attitudes, strongly influence their MNEs' strategies, the way the internal capabilities of the MNEs are organized, and what kinds of learning the MNEs are likely to achieve related to foreign markets, if any. A mindset becomes the intentional basis for an overall international strategy. The strategy becomes the basis for the kinds of internal capabilities the MNE needs to make the strategy work including the necessary skill sets for managers and personnel, required systems, structures, organization culture, operational and financial resources. The mindset becomes part of the administrative heritage[35] of the MNE and, as such, is very difficult to change because all the managers and personnel have been hired to enact it, and the physical resources and their organization are suited to it. Both N. V. Philips and Matsushita Electric (Panasonic) struggled for decades to change their administrative heritage mindsets with very limited success.[36]

The idea of mindsets seems to have developed from the view in International Strategy that any MNE will be committed to one of two basic strategies − global efficiency or local responsiveness − and that the choice between them depends on the nature of the industry one is competing in. Some industries are understood to compete on the basis of the same criteria on a worldwide basis, and so global efficiency is especially important. Customers around the world buy airplanes, computers, automobiles, smartphones, and so on, with the same purchasing criteria regardless of the nation or culture they are part of. Therefore, any MNE competing in such a global industry should use a *global strategy* because the same value equation for global products works with customers everywhere.

By contrast, some industries are very dependent on local and cultural criteria for whether certain of their products will sell or not, and what value equation must be developed to influence customers to buy. Here local responsiveness becomes critical. These observations would apply to any foodstuffs industry, as well as cosmetics, and lately, green industries. For example, the province of British Columbia in Canada forbids the burning of liquid natural gas (LNG) to produce electricity because it produces too much greenhouse gas (GHG). However, it encourages the production and export of LNG to sell to China where it would displace coal burning, resulting in less GHG. Therefore, MNEs competing in these industries would need to use a *local responsiveness* strategy.

Of course, there are some industries traditionally perceived as requiring either global efficiency or local responsiveness, where combinations of both basic strategies have proven successful. Part of Toyota's success in becoming the top selling automobile company in the world has been its ability to focus its production directly at different segments of the car buying public. Short production runs of many differently equipped cars, rather than on huge runs of less differentiated cars intended for any conceivable customer, allow for both cost efficiency and greater responsiveness.

Perlmutter[37] originated the concept of MNE mindsets, arguing that there were three – *ethnocentric, polycentric*, and *geocentric*. He also argued that MNE mindsets evolved over time from ethnocentric to geocentric, as they learned better ways to be successful in foreign markets. The ethnocentric mindset generally resulted in a global efficiency strategy. The polycentric was always locally responsive. The geocentric tried to achieve both global efficiency and local responsiveness at the same time.

Bartlett and Ghoshal,[38] and Bartlett and Beamish[39] refined the concept, arguing that there were four mentalities (or mindsets) – *international, multinational, global*, and *transnational*. They argued, however, that any movement between mindsets was difficult because each formed a difficult-to-change administrative heritage. Their international and global mentalities were both very similar to Perlmutter's ethnocentric mindset, and based on the idea of global efficiency. The multinational mentality was very similar to Perlmutter's polycentric mindset, as the transnational was to the geocentric. Exhibit 4.3 provides points of comparison between Perlmutter's three mindsets.

EXHIBIT 4.3 COMPARING PERLMUTTER'S THREE MINDSETS

Strategy and organization	Ethnocentric	Polycentric	Geocentric
Overall strategy	Global	Locally responsive	Global and locally responsive
Decision-making authority	High in headquarters	Relatively low in headquarters	Collaborative between headquarters and subsidiaries
Organizational control	Headquarters controls. Home country standards applied to all persons and performance	Subsidiary managers control own operations. Headquarters apply overall financial controls	Headquarters and subsidiaries collaborate to find universal and locally applied standards
Organizational complexity	Headquarters full function and complex. Simple at subsidiary level	Subsidiaries full function and operationally independent	Headquarters and subsidiaries increasingly complex and interdependent
Communication and information flow	High volume to subsidiaries: orders, commands, advice, inspections	Little to and from subsidiaries. Little between subsidiaries	Both ways and between subsidiaries, whose managers are on top management team
Perpetuation (recruiting, staffing, development)	Recruit and develop home country people for positions everywhere	Develop local people for key positions in their own country	Develop local people everywhere for key positions everywhere

Source: Perlmutter, Howard V. "The Tortuous Evolution of Multinational Enterprises," *Columbia Journal of World Business*, Vol. 1, 1969, pp. 9–18.

Ethnocentric mindsets: the absence of learning

Learning would be retarded, if it occurred at all, in an organization and leadership with an ethnocentric mindset. Perlmutter imagines the attitude of home country managers about their subsidiaries in the following way:[40]

> We, the home nationals of X company, are superior to, more trustworthy and more reliable than any foreigners in headquarters or subsidiaries. We will be willing to build facilities in your country if you acknowledge our inherent superiority and accept our methods and conditions for doing the job.

This attitude results in "home-made" task and performance criteria being applied to all subsidiary personnel. As well, home-country managers expect that any strategies and products that have been successful in the home-country will also succeed in any subsidiary located in any other country. These expectations result in a communication process in which subsidiary managers receive a huge volume of advice, counsel, and directives from the home office about how things should be done. There are many inspections to make sure the locals are doing things the "right" way. This does not offend the subsidiary managers because all of them are home-country managers that have been prepared for their role, and who see their career progression as being promoted back to headquarters.

In one study of Canadian software manufacturers doing business in the United States,[41] this attitude was commonly found among the least successful companies with the lowest performance in the U.S. In one very low-performance company based in Vancouver, Canada, the CEO reported that Americans were incapable of understanding an effective selling process, even for selling in the United States. All American salespeople were brought to Vancouver to be taught effective sales techniques, and any that insisted on using non-approved American techniques were disciplined or fired. Meanwhile, in the top performing companies, the attitude was quite different. The best salespeople for selling software to Americans were considered to be experienced American software salespersons. In these top-performing companies, American salespeople were hired and expected to rely on their own experience without interference from their Canadian headquarters managers.

It might seem odd to suggest that this is not an uncommon attitude among American MNEs and their leaders. Yet it is common enough for Americans, among others, to observe that much of the best management literature and textbooks are produced in the United States, along with much of the organizational and management behavior research. And most American business school rating organizations rate American business schools as the world's best.

It is easy for many Americans to have the attitude that the management of international business organizations is based on universal principles developed from American practices. And it is easy to believe that this attitude is shared around the world. Go to any major book-store worldwide and ask the clerk to show you the management section. In China, Hong Kong, Singapore, Kuala Lumpur, Seoul, and so on, it is always the same. There is a huge selection of the latest American books on business and management. If you ask, "Are there any locally produced books?" the answer is either amazement at such a strange question, or one is led to a dark corner in the back where there are a few local books on management on a single shelf.

However, researchers in the United States should not assume that American manage-ment techniques are necessarily the best, even for American managers or for managers of other countries. American management techniques are based on American values and assumptions (for example, that we can influence and control the future to a high degree). Managers from other countries do not necessarily have such values and assumptions – at least they may not place as much emphasis or importance on them. Some Japanese, Chinese, and Malaysian managers and business professors have argued that this expecta-tion of the universality of American business values represents a colonial or imperialistic attitude.[42] The idea is that when the colonial troops went home, control was maintained with the expectation that American ideas and practices were the best. Many in Asia seem to want to be the best American managers they can be. They will never be as effective Americans as Americans themselves, and this will give American managers a competitive edge.

It is generally accepted by managers that improved individual as well as organizational performance is the purpose of most organizational changes. In attempting to implement such change, one strategy that has not been sufficiently employed in the United States is that of studying other nations' management systems and asking what we can learn from them. Many managers feel that there's no need to do this. After all, they ask, "Hasn't the United States developed the most highly sophisticated system of management in the world? Don't the managers of the best foreign companies come to U.S. business schools for MBA degrees and executive management courses?" Yes, it may be true that many foreign managers come to the United States for training, but Americans can still learn from and borrow aspects of foreign management systems.

Exhibit 4.4 identifies many U.S. values related to business practices. The second column suggests examples of how the American cultural values might influence management practices. The third column offers possible alternative values that are often more effective when applied appropriately locally. The fourth column suggests where the alternative values might be more effectively applied than the American ones in the first column.

EXHIBIT 4.4 AMERICAN VALUES AND POSSIBLE ALTERNATIVES

Aspects of U.S. culture[a]	Management functions affected	Alternative aspect in other cultures	Where alternative more effective
The individual can influence the future (where there is a will, there is a way)	Planning and scheduling	Life follows a preordained course, and human action is determined by the will of God or nature	Islam acknowledges the supreme will of God; Indian culture acknowledges predestination
The individual can change and improve the environment	Organizational environment; morale; productivity	People are intended to adjust to the physical environment rather than trying to alter it	First Nations (Canada); Aboriginal populations worldwide
An individual should be realistic in his/her aspirations	Goal setting; career development	Ideals are to be pursued regardless of what is realistic	Entrepreneurs and their organizations in any nation

We must work hard to accomplish our objectives (Puritan and Protestant ethic)	Motivation and reward systems	Hard work is not the only prerequisite for success. Wisdom, luck, time and relationships as well	Common enough attitude among workers outside Northern Europe and North America
Commitments should be honored (people will do what they say and in time)	Negotiating and bargaining; deadlines	A commitment may be superseded by a conflicting request. An agreement may only signify intention	Contracts and MOUs (memorandum of understanding) in China, Japan, for example
One should effectively use one's time (time is money, which can be saved or wasted)	Long- and short-range planning	Schedules are important but only in relation to other priorities	High relationship cultures. Slow messaging, polychromic cultures (see Chapter 4)
A primary obligation of an employee is to the organization	Loyalty; commitment; motivation	The individual employee has a primary obligation to family and friends	China, Taiwan, overseas Chinese
The employer or employee can terminate the relationship	Motivation; company commitment; downsizing; succession planning	Employment is lifetime; the value of seniority	Employment is lifetime; the value of seniority
The best qualified persons should be given the available positions	Ethics; employment; recruiting, selection, promotions, rewards	Family, friendship and other considerations should determine employment practices	China for instance
A person can be removed if he/she does not perform well	Promotion; retention	The removal of a person from a position causes great loss of prestige/face, and will rarely be done	Confucian societies; bureaucracies based on seniority
All levels of management are open to qualified individuals (a clerk can rise to the presidency)	Employment practices; promotion	Education or family ties are primary vehicles for mobility	India (castes); Britain or anywhere else ascriptive values trump achievement values
Decision-making should be based on facts and not intuition	Decision-making; market research	The wisdom of the leadership is essential, and questioning it shows lack of confidence	First Nations (Canada); India (castes)
Data should be accurate	Record keeping; accounting; finance	Accurate data are not always valued or possible by Western standards	Third World

EXHIBIT 4.4

Each person is expected to have and express their opinion; conflicts handled by discussing points of disagreement	Communications; negotiations; handling conflicts	Open conflicts cause loss of face. Discuss areas of agreement. Assume opposites complement	Asia
A decision-maker is expected to consult persons who can contribute relevant information	Decision-making; leadership; management style	Decisions should be made by those in authority. Subordinates do not expect consultation	Russia for instance
Employees will work hard to improve their position in the company	Selection; promotion; management by objectives	Personal ambition is discouraged	Asia (especially females)
Competition stimulates high performance	Career development; marketing	Competition leads to imbalances; disharmony; favoring Western vs. local companies	Government monopolies and marketing boards in Canada; chaebols in Korea
A person is expected to do whatever is necessary to get the job done	Assignment of tasks; performance; deadlines; organizational effectiveness	Kinds of work are accorded high or low status. Some work may be below one's dignity or position	India (castes) for instance
Change is considered an improvement and a dynamic reality	Planning; change management; morale; organizational development	Tradition is revered and the power of the leaders is based on maintenance of a stable structure	Confucian societies in Asia
What works is important	Communication; technology; planning; quality control	Symbols and the process are more important than the end point	First Nations (Canada); Aboriginal societies anywhere
Persons and systems are evaluated	Punishments; Rewards; performance appraisal; accountability	Persons are evaluated in ways that do not embarrass or cause loss of face	China; Britain (anywhere ascription trumps achievement as a value)

Note: ª "Aspect" here refers to a belief, value, attitude, or assumption that is part of culture in that it is shared by a large number of persons in tht culture.

In Bartlett and Beamish,[43] the ethnocentric mindset is divided between the *International* and the *Global* mentalities.

The International mentality regards its international operations as distant outposts whose role is to support the success of the home country operations. Products (or services) are developed for success in the home market, and are subsequently sold in the international markets. It is assumed that strategies and products successful in the home market will also be successful abroad. Therefore, managers are not required to learn how to be successful in foreign markets. RIM had this mentality when it attempted to enter China. The Chinese government was not thrilled that the Blackberry contained security software that would prevent Chinese security from monitoring messages sent from Blackberry to Blackberry since it is Chinese government policy to censure citizens' communications. RIM refused to adapt its product in any way to suit Chinese requirements and was only granted the right to sell to expatriates working in China, about 25,000 potential users. Lululemon demonstrated an international mentality when it initially entered Japan, eschewing market research and providing the same range of yoga clothes that had sold successfully in North America. It discovered to its chagrin that Japanese women were smaller, and that the cloth was too warm for the much hotter Japanese climate.

Similarly, the global mentality assumes that products developed in the home country may be sold without substantial modification in any subsidiary market. This allows the global company to invest in hugely scaled manufacturing facilities that produce huge quantities at the lowest possible price. The goal of the global mentality is to become the price leader in its industry. This has been a typical strategy for the great Japanese electronics companies like Matsushita (Panasonic), Sharp, and Sony. In Matsushita's case, an annual trade fair of potentially available products would be organized and subsidiary marketing personnel would attend with the purpose of finding products they believed they could sell. Minor modifications to the standardized products would be allowed that could be easily accomplished on the factory floor.[44] Recent events at the end of 2012 have demonstrated the failure of this mentality in the cases of Panasonic, Sharp, and Sony. All three companies have lost vast amounts of money in recent years, and Sharp is close to either bankruptcy or acquisition. None of the companies have succeeded in challenging the low price supremacy of Korean companies such as Samsung.

It should be easy to see that having an ethnocentric (international or global) mindset or mentality is not conducive to learning how to be successful in foreign markets. The mindsets are not open to whether their strategies and management practices will be effective. It is simply assumed. When American managers, or American wannabees, hold fast to the aspects enumerated in Exhibit 4.4, assuming them to reflect universal management practices, they become less effective where those aspects do not apply, and the performance of their companies is reduced. The case of Matsushita is especially instructive because a series of CEOs over forty years attempted to change the mentality to make it more locally responsive. Their general failure has shown that an administrative heritage is all but impossible to alter even when it produces poor performance.

Polycentric mindsets: learning but not integrating

An organization that adopted a polycentric mindset would place a high premium on having local managers that know how to do business in other nations. It would, however, fail to integrate learning between subsidiaries, or between its subsidiaries and home market best practices. It would assume that anything learned about one foreign market would not apply to any other foreign market. Learning would be local, but apply only within each subsidiary individually. Perlmutter imagined the attitude of home country managers about their subsidiaries in the following way:[45]

> Let the Romans do it their way. We really don't understand what is going on there, but we have confidence in them. As long as they earn a profit, we want to remain in the background.

The key assumptions with this mindset are that foreign cultures are different, non-natives will have difficulty understanding or being effective, and that local people will know what works best for them. A subsidiary located in a foreign culture should therefore be as local as possible, and as locally responsive as possible. Coordination and control across the MNE is achieved with good overall financial controls, but the home office cannot direct local managers how to be operationally successful.

Similar to Bartlett and Beamish's[46] multinational mentality, while the MNE does learn to adapt its products and activities to local markets, the learning is not integrated into a company-wide competitive advantage. Each subsidiary functions as an independent entity and the knowledge learned in one is assumed to apply only to that one. Also, each subsidiary is run essentially as a quasi-independent company, and subsidiary managers jealously guard their independence, both from headquarters and also from other subsidiaries. Nor is the learning collated and integrated in the home country headquarters because it is assumed not to be useful for other subsidiaries, or for the overall company. Bartlett and Beamish argue that this mentality may be called multinational because the MNE's overall strategy is based on multiple nationalities and locally responsive strategies. Bartlett[47] demonstrated in the case of Philips how a multinational mindset also formed an administrative heritage that was very resistant to change when a series of Philips CEOs unsuccessfully tried to establish greater central control and cross-subsidiary integration over a period of almost fifty years.

Geocentric mindsets: worldwide innovation and learning

The organizations and leaders that adapt a geocentric mindset are the ones that achieve the most effective and performance enhancing learning. The goal of a geocentric mindset is to integrate both headquarters and subsidiary learning in order to find the best practices for each, and also to identify where practices and products developed in one worldwide location can be applied or adapted to other locations. Geocentric MNEs seek to simultaneously achieve global efficiency and local adaptation. Perlmutter[48] suggested that geocentric managers say to themselves the following sorts of things:

> Where in the world shall we raise money, build our plant, conduct R&D, and get and launch new ideas to serve our present and future customers . . . . Where in the world can I get the help to serve my customers best in this country? Where in the world can I export products developed in this country – products which meet worldwide standards as opposed to purely local standards.

And in contradistinction to the multinational mindset, the geocentric leader says:

> We aim not to be just a good local company, but the best local company in terms of the quality of management and the worldwide (not local) standards we establish in domestic and export production. If we were only as good as local companies, we would deserve to be nationalized.

The geocentric mindset seeks the best managers and personnel, regardless of nationality, to deal with the MNE's problems anywhere in its operations. Its ultimate goal is to create an integrated worldwide strategy enacted by the worldwide integrated capabilities of both headquarters and all subsidiaries. The subsidiaries are not considered either colonies (ethnocentric), nor independent city states (polycentric), but parts of a whole that is focused simultaneously on the MNE's worldwide and local objectives. This attitude is intended to produce a collaborative and cooperative effort on the parts of both headquarters and all subsidiaries to establish worldwide standards, and permissible local standards variations. It is applied to key allocation decisions on new products, new plants, and new R&D centers.

One benefit of a geocentric mindset is that subsidiaries do not fight, each hoping to become a fully functional independent business. Allocation decisions for producing different elements of a product value chain (R&D, sourcing, manufacturing, marketing, sales, service) may be made more rationally, locating each in the most cost and/or politically effective location. Microsoft, for example, was able to satisfy Chinese government pressure for local R&D as well as manufacturing, by developing a major high technology R&D center in Beijing in addition to their other worldwide locations.[49] In doing so for political reasons, they discovered that Chinese R&D engineers were well-trained, highly motivated, and cost significantly less than American equivalent personnel. In return, Microsoft received greater access to the Chinese microcomputer market.

By contrast, RIM (ethnocentric mindset) resisted[50] transferring any value chain activities out of Canada, let alone to China despite the Chinese preference to only support MNEs willing to manufacture locally in China. And, of course, RIM's negotiations to enter China in a big way failed. Research has shown that Canadian and American companies have been more successful in China when they were willing to transfer value chain activities directly to China.[51] This was generally only possible with a geocentric mindset. In the same way,

American auto manufacturers have moved manufacturing to Mexico to reduce costs. Honda developed an R&D center for the United States, staffed by American designers. This center envisioned the Honda Element, a success in America but never popular in Japan. And, many airline companies have moved their customer service functions to India to reduce costs.

Bartlett and Beamish[52] call this geocentric mindset the transnational mentality. It is the recognition that the demands on an MNE to be responsive to local markets, local political needs, and pressures to achieve global efficiencies are simultaneous. It represents a strategic and organizational mentality in which well-organized MNEs may achieve both the basic strategies – global efficiency and local responsiveness – at the same time rather than having to choose. Its goal is to achieve the best local products at the lowest cost to the end customer through organization-wide coordination, shared decision-making, and an overall corporate vision that all leaders and employees are committed.

Examples of geocentric learning: Japan and America

A word of caution comes from Hamel and Prahalad,[53] suggesting it is a mistake to take aspects of another culture, such as from Japan, and trying to integrate them into one's business philosophy. They cite a survey in which 80 percent of American managers polled believed that "quality would be a fundamental source of competitive advantage." However, 82 percent of the Japanese believed "the ability to create fundamentally new products and businesses would be the primary source of competitive advantage." It's difficult to achieve quality and speed at the same time.

It is, however, possible for Japanese and American managers to work together and develop shared understandings from their interactions that produce new synergies, or syntheses, from the combination of their cultures in the same organization. Furthermore, management is a dynamic process and is constantly changing. We can learn from the "way it was" by contrasting it with practices current at the beginning of the twenty-first century. For example, the following research was conducted over 25 years ago, but shows how American and Japanese management styles have influenced each other and caused changes in how each organizes itself in business contexts.

Ouchi and Jaeger[54] observed that the typical American (A) organization became combined with the typical Japanese (J) organization to produce what they called a hybrid Type Z. The typical American organization had the following characteristics:

1 short-term employment;
2 individual decision-making;
3 individual responsibility;
4 rapid evaluation and promotion;
5 explicit, formalized control;
6 specialized career path; and,
7 segmented concern.

The typical Japanese organization, by contrast, had different characteristics:

1   lifetime employment;
2   consensual decision-making;
3   collective responsibility;
4   slow evaluation and promotion;
5   implicit, formal control;
6   nonspecialized career path; and,
7   holistic concern.

They then compared these organizational styles and related them to their sociocultural roots. They concluded by presenting a hybrid organizational form (Type Z), which they suggested might be useful in the United States as well as for combined Japanese/American ventures. Each of the two types of organizational structures (American and Japanese) represent a natural outflow and adaptation to the environments to which they belong. Ouchi and Jaeger suggested the following characteristics for the Type Z organization (modified American) would include the following:

1   long-term employment;
2   consensual decision-making;
3   individual responsibility;
4   slow evaluation and promotion;
5   implicit, informal control with explicit formalized measures;
6   moderately specialized career path; and,
7   holistic concern for individuals.

One of the most dramatic cases for East–West synergy lies in the interdependent relationship between Japan and the United States. This relationship has been tested many times, but overall it has been mutually beneficial. Japan's previous success in production, distribution, and marketing has been due to the ability of the Japanese to learn from Western nations and then apply this knowledge to their own business situations. Nowhere is this more evident than in the field of management, where Japanese executives borrowed ideas from the United States and then refined them for increased productivity.

Many American companies have made significant changes in manufacturing techniques, learning from Japanese industry, including Kanban manufacturing, quality control circles, and just-in-time (JIT) purchasing. These have become mainstream processes in both American and Japanese industrial production. These techniques can boost the morale, knowledge, responsibility, and therefore productivity of a corporation's workforce. These Japanese practices could, however, only have been implemented by American firms with geocentric mindsets that were willing to consider management practices originating in a country other than the United States.

Another example of Japanese/American synergies was the development of *Total Quality Management* (TQM). Who originated the quality initiatives that are a fundamental part of most, if not all, organizations? Japan? Germany? The United States? A review of the history of quality initiatives shows that the beginnings were in the United States. Edward Deming was the American management consultant who pioneered the TQM but he could not find any companies in the United States willing to give his ideas a chance. After World War II, Deming took his ideas to Japan where they were implemented as part of Japan's postwar reconstruction. Subsequently, after Japan's great reconstruction success, TQM was reintroduced to the United States. "Total quality management" became a buzzword. Goldman[55] outlines the history of quality initiatives and the present-day quality initiatives used worldwide. These included:

1   *Customer involvement* – customers' requirements are integrated into the product services.
2   *Company cultural change* – everyone's responsibility – labor and management to instill a quality orientation in any organization.
3   *Continuous improvement and statistical measurement* – measuring changes resulting from a quality process that can always be improved.
4   *Employee empowerment* – the mentality of the employee changes, and the quality becomes the most important objective.
5   *Teamwork* – working together on mutual goals.
6   *Benchmarking* – comparing your organization to the best of your competition.
7   *Cycle time reduction* – reducing the time to deliver a product from the beginning to customer satisfaction.

Six Sigma, derived from TQM, and including ISO (International Standards Organization) resulted as a business practice used in many organizations for financial improvement.

Environmental changes requiring organizational learning

In addition to learning (or not learning) from the performance of their international operations, MNE leaders must also learn to adapt to a variety of environmental changes. Global leaders with foresight scan for information about their competitive environment, local and worldwide, that may cause changes in strategies, polices, and technologies. They analyze and anticipate trends that influence their companies' futures. Some positive forces of change drive us to increase or decrease the workforce, or to be more aware or responsive to community needs. In other words, global leaders create adaptive systems! This implies overcoming resistive and negative forces seeking to restrain necessary shifts in production and manufacturing, as well as making necessary alterations in roles, rules, regulations, and even markets.

As a case in point, many corporations, nongovernmental organizations (NGOs), and other institutions go global to survive. Over a decade ago, Moran and Riesenberger[56] described 12 environmental forces impacting organizations and influencing change that are still evident today. Some proactive environmental forces are as follows:

1   *Global sourcing* – organizations are seeking nondomestic sources of raw materials because of cost and quality.
2   *New and evolving market* – are providing unique growth opportunities.
3   *Economies of scale* – today's global marketplace requires different approaches, resulting in competitive advantages in price and quality.
4   Movement toward *homogeneous demand* – globalization is resulting in similar products being required worldwide.
5   *Lowered transportation costs* – world transportation costs of many products have fallen significantly because of innovations.
6   Reduced government *tariffs and taxes* – the protectionist tendencies of many governments are declining, as evidenced by the North American Free Trade Agreement (NAFTA) and the European Union (EU) policies and agreements.
7   *Telecommunications* – falling prices as a result of privatization, and new technologies are impacting globalization. Digital communications, the Internet, and wireless communications have vastly expanded this effect.
8   *Homogeneous technical standards* – the International Organization for Standardization (ISO) has been successful in developing global standards, including ISO 9000 (quality management), ISO 14000 (environmental management), ISO 26000 (social responsibility), and six other ISO standards.

Some reactive forces, present in the global environment, are as follows:

1   *Competition* – new competitive threats are regularly experienced by organizations.
2   *Risk of volatile exchange rates* – the constant fluctuation of exchange rates in many countries impacts profits.
3   *Customers are becoming more global consumers* – globalization is impacting customers in ways that increase "local content" in subsidiary-produced goods.
4   *Global technological change* – technological improvements coming from many areas of the world require organizations to adjust their strategies to survive.

In a knowledge culture, smart global leaders do environmental scans. That is, they employ research methods or consultants to help them to anticipate the future. They try to identify trends that will affect their businesses or organizations in the near- or long-term future. For example, they anticipate developing movements – such as the growth of environmental and ecological awareness and coalitions; the rise of activists organized to protect human or animal rights; and the development of space resources.

Social changes: interpersonal roles

For decades, researchers have studied the changing roles of men and women, discovering that gender differences are mostly in our minds and cultures, rather than biological realities. Limitations in gender roles are largely created and kept in place by social, not biological, forces. As such, they are more readily subject to change. Scholars have demonstrated the resulting harm for persons and organizations when individuals are typecast and culture-bound in their career aspirations. Further, social progress is deterred when such attitudes prevail, as we have seen historically in the caste system of India and the class system of England. Fortunately, within modern societies changes in this regard are rapid, as workers move beyond traditional role concepts while assertively seeking equal opportunity and empowerment. Even in India at the beginning of 2013, there are massed demonstrations protesting the treatment of women in Indian society.

Similar representations may be made of organization roles and their place in society. Because human systems are collections of people, institutions may also suffer identity crises. Caught between a disappearing bureaucracy and an emerging "adhocracy," the institution may experience downturns in sales; poor morale and declining productivity; membership reductions; bankruptcy threats; obsolete product lines and services; and increasing frustration with unresponsive management. Organizations, then, are challenged to go through planned renewal to project new images of their positive roles among both personnel and the public. Simply hiring a public relations firm to redesign the corporate image for the public is insufficient – organization members have to be involved in the process of institutional change!

So too, when national roles conflict with observed conditions. When a country's social fabric unravels or wavers, national identities may experience crises. Examples abound, such as the following:

■ The United States' "loss of face" in Vietnam; the seizure of U.S. diplomats in Iran; the 9/11 double bombings of New York City's World Trade Center and Washington D.C.'s Pentagon; the treatment of prisoners or insurgents in the "war on terrorism"; the lack of leadership in Washington D.C. on the U.S. debt crisis.

■ Great Britain lost its empire and colonies, nearly bankrupting the nation, or the country's inappropriate policies and responses to the influx of immigrants from British Commonwealth nations. Now Spain is demanding the return of Gibralter, and Argentina the return of the Falklands.

■ Japan's economic and technological progress threatens its traditional culture; and its youth reject "feudal" customs and practices. Japan has been locked in stagflation and deflation since the 1990s.

■ The Catholic Church and the pedophilia crisis. The Canadian Protestant churches and the First Nations residential school abuse.

■ The continuing challenges in Afghanistan, Iran, and Israel/Palestine.

■ The global economic crisis. The public debt crisis in the EU.

People of various countries have sought to rediscover their collective selves in this post-nation period. So geographers continuously have to redraw maps to reflect the changes in national borders. In some lands, the struggle for national identity is epitomized in a name change, as from Congo to Zaire, or Rhodesia to Zimbabwe. Elsewhere, as in the former U.S.S.R., states such as Lithuania, Latvia, Estonia, Ukraine, Byelorussia, and so on, have become independent countries. Whereas in the People's Republic of China, turmoil centers around information access, air pollution, public corruption, and the seizing of private land for commercial developments without adequate compensation. Often, the identity struggles within or among nations produce violence based on ancient rivalries, or on tribal, clan, or religious affiliation. Such regressive behavior not only transgresses the UN Declaration on Human Rights, but also acts to reverse changes toward a modern, multicultural society.

INDIVIDUAL LEARNING

It would be wrongheaded to claim that none of the above discussions of organizational learning applied to individual learning as well. For example, it is possible that a person reading about the differences between ethnocentric, polycentric, and geocentric mindsets might learn to prefer the advantages of the geocentric for its improved performance outcomes. This section, however, is intended to outline some of the major differences between the preferences by which individuals from one culture learn that may be different from individuals in another culture.

When we work together in joint ventures, for example, or when headquarters managers are trying to teach new ways of organizing to subsidiary managers, or vice versa, learning may fail because learning styles vary from country to country. For example, in North American business education, it is common to discuss points of disagreement, argue over them, and eventually come to some agreement or consensus. This approach generally fails in China where it is not the custom to discuss points of disagreement in case somebody suffers a loss of face. Once one's face has been lost, one feels disrespected and is unwilling to cooperate further, both immediately and in future with those responsible. Instead, the Chinese prefer to consider all the points they agree on until the areas of potential disagree-ment disappear into the overall agreement. And whereas Euro-North Americans tend to think dualistically such that there is always a preferred alterative and a discredited one, the Chinese tend to believe that opposites are complementary and may be combined in a yin/yang fashion.

We all have a set of highly organized constructs around which we organize our "private" worlds. Literally, we construct a mental system for putting order, as we perceive it, into our life spaces. This intellectual synthesis relates to our images of self, family, role, organization, nation, and universe. Such constructs then become psychological anchors or reference points for our mental functioning and well-being. Our unique construct systems exert a pushing/pulling effect on all other ideas and experiences we encounter. We assign meaning almost automatically to the multiple sensations and perceptions that bombard us daily.

Not only do individuals have such unique filters for their experiencing, but groups, organizations, and even national cultures develop these mental frameworks through which information coming from the environment is interpreted. Intense interactions of various segments within our varied groupings form sets that enable us to achieve collective goals. In this way, a group, organizational, or national "style" or type of behavior emerges. Through their communication, people share themselves, so that individual perceptions converge into a type of "consensus" of what makes sense to them in a particular environment and circumstance. Culture then transmits these commonly shared sets of perceptions and expectations.

But because human interaction is dynamic, pressures for change in such constructs build up in both individuals and institutions. For example, when a manager from Grand Rapids, Michigan, is transferred for three years to Riyadh, Saudi Arabia, or Bangalore, India, that person is challenged to change many of his or her constructs about life and people. The same may be said for the corporate culture when a company attempts to transplant operations from Paris, France, to the Middle East or Asia. These forces for change can be avoided, resisted, or incorporated into the person's perceptual field. If the latter happens, then change becomes a catalyst for restructuring our constructs, giving us an opportunity for growth. In other words, individuals and institutions can adapt and develop.

When leaders do not prepare their people for necessary and inevitable change, the consequences can be disastrous. For example, many national, educational, political, and religious systems suffer from "culture lag." That is, as the human mainstream has moved ahead to a new stage of development, this particular community is locked into a past mindset. In the twenty-first century, many countries are burdened with obsolete and archaic religious, political, educational, and economic systems.

In Asia, for instance, inadequate banking and lending practices hold back prosperity for their citizens. In the Middle East, ultra-traditional religious views and practices diminish the role of women, deterring development of female potential and positive contributions. In Europe, centuries-old educational systems are badly in need of reform and updating. In Africa, the tribal ruling system has broken down, and the instability has led to a series of military coups and local despots, along with social chaos and ethnic killings. In North America, open door policies for visitors, foreigners and immigrants are being undermined by fears of terrorism, forcing modernization of immigration and travel regulations, as well as security practices.

When a society or a system is imprisoned by its past traditions, attitudes, and beliefs, it may produce unsavory results. Terrorists or anarchists, for example, often come from countries where the needs of people, especially the young, are so frustrated that violence erupts. The sense of despair or righteousness may turn naive youth into suicide bombers who destroy property and take human life. The subculture of global terrorism recruits young men and even women who are alienated and conditioned to an ideology of violence.

At the same time, many perceive themselves as oppressed, and so they resort to rioting, fire bombings of property, and even the taking of innocent lives – witness tensions in the United States about illegal immigration, the continuing Protestant–Catholic tensions in Northern Ireland, and the Idle-No-More First Nations movement in Canada demanding an immediate end to historic grievances. In Europe, there have been riots by immigrants in the United Kingdom, Islamic hijab clothing has been banned in France, not to mention at universities in Istanbul – an Islamic country. In Hindu India, Muslim mosques have been burned. In China, there have been battles between native Tibetans and Chinese settlers in Tibet. All these events, and many more worldwide, provide further insight into negative results when societies resist change and do not satisfy human needs.

In today's changing culture, people are also challenged to alter the way they perceive or think about their work and how it is to be performed. The shifting context of the work environment has been described as the new work culture.[57] The driving forces behind these social and technological changes are given below:

1   Globalization of markets, consumerism, and workforces.
2   Transformation of traditional organizational hierarchy into a more participative, multi-national, or global network.
3   Fragmentation of work, and creation of a global job market.
4   Ascendancy of knowledge and information services as primary global products.

One outcome of such trends is the reshaping of views of our various roles in the family, community, or workplace.

LEARNING PROCESS DIFFERENCES: UNITED STATES, CHINA, JAPAN

In Chapter 2, we introduced the idea that there were basic personality differences between Asians (Chinese versus Japanese) and Euro-North Americans that had an apparent effect on national culture.[58] We say "apparent" because even though the personality literature describes the effects of personality and culture as independent,[59] if the preponderance of a cultural population is of the same personality type, it will appear to have a cultural effect. Seagal and Horne[60] observed that as many as 70 to 80 percent of Euro-North Americans were of what they called the Emotional Dynamic (Emotional mental 20 percent; Emotional physical 60 percent). By contrast, the Chinese were predominantly Physical emotional, and the Japanese predominantly Physical mental.

These strong personality differences, characteristic of Euro-North American, Chinese, and Japanese cultures have been predicted to have significant effects on how people learn. The basic differences are detailed in Exhibit 4.5.

EXHIBIT 4.5 BASIC DIFFERENCES IN LEARNING STYLES

	Euro-North American Emotional mental	Euro-North American Emotional physical	Chinese Physical emotional	Japanese Physical mental
Learning conditions	■ Structured presentation ■ Forward without repetition ■ Purpose made clear ■ Discussion and debate ■ Independent or small group work plus discussion ■ Experimentation ■ Exchange and mutual respect with instructor ■ Open-ended problem-solving	■ Personal comfort ■ Discussion and personal exchange ■ Personal connection with instructor ■ Discuss and learn with others ■ Schedule ■ Creative expression ■ Identify and process feelings	■ Utility explicit ■ Considerable context provided ■ Hands-on learning ■ Open ended schedule to allow assimilation ■ One topic at a time ■ Lots of data ■ Individuals not singled out ■ Relaxed atmosphere	■ Purpose explicit ■ Structured outline ■ Systematic presentation ■ Learn by doing ■ Careful pacing with sufficient time ■ Reflection and solitary work ■ Work with others after assimilation ■ Models, diagrams, charts
Basic learning process	■ Dialogue ■ Interaction ■ Idea exchange	■ Dialogue ■ Interaction ■ Affectivity	■ Interactive with task ■ Detailed data ■ Hands-on	■ Interactive with task ■ Detailed data ■ Hands-on

Source: Seagal, S. and Horne, D. *Human Dynamics: A New Framework for Understanding People and Realizing the Potential in Our Organizations.* Waltham, CA: Pegasus Communications, 1997.

What is evident from Exhibit 4.5 is that Euro-North Americans have considerably higher expectations of interactive learning. They expect to discuss, debate, and interact with others as a means of processing information. The majority (60 percent Emotional physical) want clear time limits placed on individual learning activities.

By contrast, the Chinese and Japanese prefer to work with the data and the task rather than with the other learners. Both want sufficient time to process the material without artificially imposed time limits. The Chinese seem to expect even more data and context than the Japanese, whereas there is no mention of those needs for the Euro-North Americans.

The lesson here is simply that what Euro-North Americans regard as a normal learning process is not regarded as normal for the majority of Chinese and Japanese. The latter could feel uncomfortable with the Euro-North American expectation to discuss and debate the points. This could cause resistance to learning at an individual level, especially if one is regarded as a slow learner because one's learning process is different. Seagal and Horne[61] observed that the small minority of children in North American schools having either Physical emotional (5 percent–10 percent) or Physical mental (5–10 percent) dynamics were often classified as slow learners by the school system. When allowed to learn using their own learning processes, they proved to be as capable as other children.

In the context of MNEs doing business in China or Japan, it would be important to understand that learning situations should be constructed that suited the learning preferences of one's Chinese or Japanese employees, associates, or conceivably one's JV partners, or superiors. A Chinese or Japanese associate, treated as if he/she was a "slow learner," who suffers loss of face, feels disrespected, is perhaps unwilling to fully cooperate in the building of the effective relationships needed for a joint venture to prosper.

CONCLUSIONS

Global leaders should not only be sources of innovation, but also be skilled in using change strategies and methods. Agents of change may apply their efforts to alter personal, organizational, and national cultural goals. Operating globally in diverse cultures and circumstances necessitates appropriate adaptation of organizational objectives, management procedures, corporate processes, and technologies. Global leaders must learn to be as knowledgeable as possible wherever they are located, even if it means creative circumvention of local constraints. Innovators may respect the established system while working to bend or beat it to make it more responsive to satisfying human need.

What, then, would be the responsibilities of such persons if employed? Obviously, they would be responsible to bring about planned change in an organization or culture. That would imply examining the prospects for alterations in the status quo within these basic categories:

- structure (the system of authority; communication, roles, and work flow);
- technology (problem-solving mechanisms, tools, and computers);
- mindsets (favoring geocentric over ethnocentric or polycentric);
- tasks (activities accomplished, such as manufacturing, research, service);
- processes (techniques, simulations, methods, scenario-building procedures, such as management information systems);
- environment (internal or external atmosphere); and,
- people (personnel or human resources involved).

Having decided on which category or combinations will be the focus of one's energy for change, the leader might follow these additional steps:

- identify specific changes that appear desirable to improve effectiveness;
- create a readiness in the system for such change;
- facilitate the internalization of the innovation; and
- reinforce the new equilibrium established through the change.

The leader could plan his/her changes using *force field analysis* – a systematic way to analyze the driving and resisting forces for change within individual or group life space as well as institutional or national space. One creates two columns – one a list of forces supporting a change, and one a list of forces opposing a change. One rates the strength of all the forces, say on a five point scale. Then you pick out forces resisting the change and try to turn them around one by one until the forces supporting the change are much stronger.

The skilled change maker is also aware that any change introduced in one element of the previous chain affects the other factors. The parts of complex systems are interdependent, so the innovator attempts to forecast the ripple effect. Successful change agents take a multidimensional approach, considering legal, economic, and technological aspects of the change without ignoring its social, political, and personal implications. They also operate on certain assumptions, including:

1 People are capable of planning and controlling their own destinies within their own life space.
2 Behavioral change, knowledge, and technology should be incorporated into the planning process.
3 Human beings are continually in the midst of cultural change or evolution.

The implication of the latter statement is that the people involved in the change process may be suspicious of simplistic solutions as a result of the information/media blitz to which they have been exposed. They may already be suffering from information overload, experiencing a sense of powerlessness and loss of individuality. Essentially, the effective change maker may employ three change models to bring about a shift in the status quo:

1 *Power* – political or legal, physical or psychological, influence or coercion, to bring about change, which may be legitimate or illegitimate. It depends on the purpose of change, its ingredients, and the method of application. For example, legislative power may be used to promote equal employment opportunity or to prevent a disease epidemic, while role or competence authority may be called upon to overcome resistance to change.
2 *Rationale* – the appeal to reason and the common good. This approach must recognize that people are not always altruistic and that self-interest may block acceptance of the proposed change, no matter how noble or worthwhile for the majority.
3 *Re-educative* – conditioning by training, education, and positive rewards becomes the means to not only create readiness for the change, but to also provide the information and skills to implement it.

Each approach has its strengths and weaknesses, so a combination of the models may be most effective. Young proposes examination of business drivers on strategy, structure, system, and personnel requirements in terms of new skills, styles, and the need for renewal.[62] To maximize commitment to change, ten competencies are developed among one's personnel.

1   Mobilize people behind a shared vision, strategy, and structure – especially by involvement.
2   Empower people by defining job directions/boundaries, as well as by providing autonomy and support.
3   Recognize individual and team contributions by clarifying requirements, expectations, motivators, and rewards.
4   Build capacity by developing people, especially by attending to health needs (physical, emotional, intellectual, and spiritual).
5   Create a learning organization by using a systems approach that seeks input, knowledge, and partnerships.
6   Realign the culture through review of stated values and operating principles, as well as by translating norms and expected behaviors.
7   Create a cultural revolution by diagnosis, training, and targets.
8   Promote understanding by describing events and identifying feelings.
9   Facilitate acceptance by moving ahead on commitment and putting the past behind.
10 Enable the change to happen, moving to the new, demonstrating the benefits, and providing transitional steps for implementation.

There are a variety of methods and techniques to facilitate planned change. An approach can be as simple as "imagineering" at a staff meeting about changes likely to become realities in a decade, on the basis of present trend indicators. Or it may be using the more elaborate *Delphi technique*, in which a questionnaire is developed with about a dozen situations likely to occur in the future of a company or a culture. Members or experts may then be asked to rate on a percentage basis the probability of the event's happening. Results are then tabulated and median percentages for each item determined. A report of results is circulated among participants, and they are asked to again rate the alternative possibilities after studying peer responses.

Today, the words "reengineering" or "reinventing" the organization are used to describe planned system-wide change. One consultant maintains that reengineering is not about downsizing, reorganizing, or restructuring. It is about thinking outside of the box, rethinking your work and company. It is a fundamental and radical redesigning of all the processes of business to obtain improvements in critical measures of performance (cost, quality, capital, service, and speed). It is throwing away what is and replacing it with something innovative. For instance, if IBM, Merck, Boeing, etc., did not already exist today, how would they be created and structured?

In this chapter, we have presented the idea that all global leaders must be, first and foremost, learners. The geocentric mindset is particularly open to learning from every direction and encourages others to have the same attitude. By contrast, the ethnocentric mindset is not open to learning, and the polycentric mindset does not assimilate collate and integrate learning to find additional uses for it.

Culture is a dynamic concept that changes, as does the way we communicate it. Those with the mindset and skills of a geocentric or transnational manager exercise proactive leadership in altering both the macro- and micro-levels of culture. To cope effectively with today's accelerating change, effective leaders continuously revise their images of self, role, and organization, and assist their personnel to do the same. Thus, attitudes and behavior are modified to become more relevant.

Although our outlooks on change and leadership are conditioned by culture and personality, we must realize that we must be open to change. We best meet human needs by creating new technologies, markets, processes, products, and services.

Successful leadership styles are dependent to a degree on the people and their cultures at a given point in time. Generally, the contemporary work environment calls for more participative, team-oriented management that responds rapidly and synergistically to changing situations. In the emerging knowledge culture, leadership opportunities are shared with competent knowledge workers, regardless of gender, race, religion, or nationality. The aim is to empower people, so that they will, in turn, develop their own as well as the organization's potential. To meet that challenge, the underlying assumption of this chapter is that global leaders should be planned change makers, beginning with themselves.

MIND STRETCHING

1   Is the "Westernization of the World" happening as a function of globalization?
2   Have we lost our "curiosity" about other people and nations? Curiosity has been demonstrated to be an important trait of skillful global leaders.
3   Do less-developed countries always desire industrialization?
4   If you could be a person from a culture other than your own, what culture would that be? Why?
5   If you were working as an expatriate in another culture, do you think you would have an ethnocentric, polycentric, or geocentric mindset? Offer evidence from the way you behave in the present with people you that you know, to support your view.
6   If you are working in a group, discuss with the other members how each of you prefer to learn. Some prefer reading theoretical material while others prefer hands-on experience. Some like to work together with others, while some prefer to work alone. Do you think that people are "slow learners" if they seem to need more time than yourself to learn something? Why, or why not?

NOTES

1 Hoffman, B. G. *American Icon: Alan Mulally and the Fight to Save Ford Motor Company*. Kindle Edition: Crown Business, 2012.
2 Ibid.
3 Salomon, G. *Distributed Cognitions: Psychological and Educational Considerations*. Cambridge, UK: Cambridge University Press, 1993, p. xiii.
4 Ibid, p. xvi.
5 Salomon, G. and Perkins, D. N. "Individual and Social Aspects of Learning," *Review of Research in Education*, No. 23, 1998.
6 Bridges, W. *The Character of Organizations: Using Jungian Type in Organizational Development*. Boston, MA: Nicholas Brealey Publishing, 2000.
7 Ibid.
8 Seagal, S. and Horne, D. *Human Dynamics: A New Framework for Understanding People and Realizing the Potential in Our Organizations*. Waltham, CA: Pegasus Communications, 1997.
9 Silver, S. "Nortel Will Liquidate Assets," *The Wall Street Journal*, June 20, 2009.
10 Sturgeon, J. "RIM World's Fastest-Growing Company," *Fortune*, August 18, 2009.
11 "Analysts Say RIM Ripe for Takeover," *Ottawacitizen.com*, June 21, 2011.
12 White, R. and Beamish, P.W., "Research in Motion: Managing Explosive Growth," in C. A. Bartlett, and P. W. Beamish (eds), *Transnational Management: Text, Cases, and Readings in Cross-Border Management,* 6th edn. New York, NY: McGraw Hill Irwin, 2011, pp. 68–82.
13 Hartley, M. "Blackberry Urges Patience During Turnaround Effort: CEO Confident Company is on the Right Track but Some Investors Aren't Convinced," *The Vancouver Sun*, July 10, 2013, C1.
14 White and Beamish, "Research in Motion."
15 Moore, K. and Lewis, D. *The Origins of Globalization*. New York: Routledge, 2009.
16 Hoffman, *American Icon*.
17 Dixon, N. *The Organizational Learning Cycle: How We Can Learn Collectively*. London: McGraw-Hill, 1994.
18 Ibid, p. 5.
19 Ibid, p. 2.
20 Prange, C. "Organizational Learning: Desperately Seeking Theory," in M. Easterby-Smith, L. Araujo, and J. Burgoyne (eds), *Organizational Learning and the Learning Organization*. London: Sage, 1999.
21 Root, F. R. *Entry Strategies for International Markets*. San Francisco, CA: Josssey-Bass, 1998.
22 Smick, D. *The World Is Curved: Hidden Dangers to the Global Economy*. Google Books, 2009.
23 Crossan, M. M., Rouse, M. J., Fry, J. N., and Killing, J. P. *Strategic Analysis and Action*, 7th edn. Toronto, ON: Pearson Prentice Hall, 2009.
24 Hoffman, *American Icon*.
25 Abramson, N. R. "Building Effective Business Relationships in China: The Case of Richmond Engineering," in A. E. Safarian and P. W. Beamish (eds), *North American Firms in East Asia*. Toronto, ON: University of Toronto Press, 1999, pp. 119–145. The name of the company is disguised at the request of the company.
26 Blomstermo, A. and Sharma, D. D. *Learning in the Internationalization Process of Firms*. Northampton, MA: Edward Elgar, 2003.
27 O'Leary, K. *Cold Hard Truth: On Business, Money & Life*. Toronto, ON: Doubleday Canada, 2011.
28 Ramaswamy, K. and Sankhe, R. "Hero Honda Motors (India) Ltd.: Is It Honda that Made It a Hero?" in H. Merchant (ed.), *Competing in Emerging Markets: Cases and Readings*. New York: Routledge, 2008, pp. 72–92.
29 Choi, C. B. and Beamish, P. W. "Split Management Control and International Joint Venture Performance," *Journal of International Business Studies*, Vol. 35, 2004, pp. 201–215.

30 Abramson, N. R. "Configuration, Coordination, Learning and Foreign Market Entry: A Study of Canadian Software Companies Entering the United States." University of Western Ontario doctoral thesis, 1992.

31 Root, *Entry Strategies*.

32 Nelson, R. "Dell's Dilemma in Brazil: Negotiating at the State Level," in H. Merchant (ed.), *Competing in Emerging Markets: Cases and Readings*. New York: Routledge, 2008, pp. 1–17.

33 Ohmae, K. "The Global Logic of Strategic Alliances," *Harvard Business Review*, March/April, 1989.

34 Ashkenas, R. N., DeMonaco, L. J., and Francis, S. C. "Making the Deal Real: How GE Capital Integrates Acquisitions," *Harvard Business Review*, January/February, 1998.

35 Bartlett, C. A. and Ghoshal, S. *Managing Across Borders: The Transnational Solution*. Boston, MA: Harvard Business School, 1991.

36 Bartlett, C. A. "Philips versus Matsushita: Competing Strategic and Organizational Choices," in C. A. Bartlett and P. W. Beamish, *Transnational Management: Text, Cases, and Readings in Cross-Border Management,* 6th edn. New York: McGraw-Hill Irwin, 2011, pp. 331–347.

37 Perlmutter, Howard V. "The Tortuous Evolution of Multinational Enterprises," *Columbia Journal of World Business*, Vol. 1, 1969, pp. 9–18.

38 Bartlett and Ghoshal, *Managing Across Borders*.

39 Bartlett and Beamish, *Transnational Management*.

40 Perlmutter, "The Tortuous Evolution."

41 Abramson, "Configuration."

42 See for example, Panitch, L. *American Empire and the Political Economy of Global Finance*. Basingstoke: Palgrave Macmillan, 2009.

43 Bartlett and Beamish, *Transnational Management*.

44 Bartlett, "Philips Versus Matsushita."

45 Perlmutter, "The Tortuous Evolution."

46 Bartlett and Beamish, *Transnational Management*.

47 Bartlett, "Philips Versus Matsushita."

48 Perlmutter, "The Tortuous Evolution."

49 Buderi, R. and Huang, G. T. *Guanxi: Microsoft and Bill Gates' Plan to Win the Road Ahead*. London: Random House, 2007.

50 White and Beamish, "Research in Motion."

51 Abramson, N. R. and Ai, J. X. "Canadian Companies Doing Business in China: Key Success Factors," *Management International Review*, Vol. 39, No. 1, 1999, pp. 7–35.

52 Bartlett and Beamish, *Transnational Management*.

53 Hamel, G. and Prahalad, C. K. *Competing for the Future*. Boston, MA: Harvard Business School, 1994.

54 Ouchi, W. G. and Jaeger, A. M. "Made in America under Japanese Management," *Harvard Business Review*, Vol. 52, No. 5, 1974, pp. 61–69. See also Funakawa, A., *The Transcultural Solution*. San Francisco, CA: Jossey-Bass, 2007.

55 Goldman, H. H. "The Origins and Development of Quality Initiatives in American Business," *TQM Magazine*, Vol. 17, No. 3, 2005, pp. 217–225.

56 Moran, R. T. and Riesenberger, J. R. *The Global Challenge: Building New Worldwide Enterprises*. London: McGraw-Hill, 1994; Harris, P. R. *Managing the Knowledge Culture*. Amherst, MA: HRD Press, 2005.

57 Harris, P. R. *The Work Culture Handbook*. Mumbai: Jaico Publishing, 2003, www.jaicobooks.com.

58 Seagal and Horne, *Human Dynamics*.

59 The argument is summarized in Abramson, N. R. "Measuring the Independent Effects of Culture and Personality on Marketing Behavior: A Canadian–Korean Comparison Using the Cognitive Theory of Strategy," *Journal of Current Research in Global Business*, Vol. 9, No. 14, pp. 1–19.

60 Seagal and Horne, *Human Dynamics*.

61 Ibid.
62 Young, S. "Micro-Inequities: The Power of Small," *Workforce Diversity Reader*, Vol. 1, No. 1, 2003, pp. 88–93. See also Kirton, G. and Greene, A.-M. *The Dynamics of Managing Diversity*. Burlington, MA: Elsevier/Butterworth-Heinemann, 2004.

ADDITIONAL FEATURES

Please visit the companion website at: www.routledge.com/cw/Moran where you will find additional case studies, study aides, and instructor resources.

5 WOMEN LEADERS IN GLOBAL BUSINESS

"Dear Ms. Moran:
Thank you for your email.
We do not carry women's pilot shirts.
I did check online and found a website that lists this item: www.mypilot-store.com.
Please let me know if I can be of further assistance.
Sincerely,
Customer Service"

"Dear Customer Service,
Thanks for your response; it is appreciated. I was able to do a search and was initially excited to find "girls are pilots, too" websites, only to be disappointed in finding they sell pink tank tops with "I love my pilot" written on them, with a link to "dogs are pilots, too" (selling stuffed animals).

After further searching, I was able to find one that sells proper professional women's pilot shirts. The search was a bit of a disappointment (in more ways than one), but if I ever need aviation cookware, I know where to find it online now. I guess one has to have a sense of humor. . . .

May I suggest you (being one of the most popular pilot supply websites) sell women's pilot shirts?

Thank you,
Rebecca,
Pilot in Tanzania, East Africa"

About 6 percent of pilots worldwide are women.

THE "FEMALE" PILOT

"A lady pilot! You go, girl!" is the reaction that I mostly get. But it hasn't always been so complimentary. "Are you a pilot? You're way too young to be a pilot. I'd have to see your license". Actually, I think that was meant as a compliment as well.

Apparently, I am not a pilot. I'm a "female pilot," just as a man isn't a nurse but a "male nurse." Despite being in a profession with mostly male colleagues, many of my passengers are very happy to see a "female pilot." I suppose those Westerners who may have an issue with my gender are aware of their bias and keep it to themselves.

But not everyone hides it. The advantage of being an American, is that most people think that we don't speak any other language and therefore they are at liberty to speak about us within earshot. Being of slightly playful character, I do not always initially reveal the languages I speak.

I had just joined a new company and was on a training flight with another pilot. The Captain, Sarah, and I stood at the foot of the aircraft stairs and greeted the five young and boisterous French passengers. Sarah, several years younger than I, is a highly qualified, very experienced beautiful, blond American pilot. As Sarah and I introduced ourselves and gave the security briefing from the cockpit, one of the French men said nervously and sarcastically to his friends: "Deux jeunes filles pilotes — j'ai confiance."

"Everything is ok back there?" I asked in English to the man. "Yes" he said.

Sarah landed at our destination. Not able to feel the moment of touch-down, it was what we call a greaser — a perfectly smooth landing. I turned around to the passengers and said in French, "Deux jeunes filles pilotes — pas trop mal, eh?"

As the young Frenchman's face went white, his friends burst into laughter.

Source: Rebecca Moran, Tanzania, 2012.

In April 2010, it is estimated that the world's population is about 7 billion, with about half female and half male.[1] The five largest countries in the world by population are: China (1,354,040,000), India (1,210,000,000), United States (314,573,000), Indonesia (238,000,000), and Brazil (194,000,000). The proportion of women relative to men, both working in employed positions, varies globally, and ranges from 20 percent in Arab countries like Bahrain, Iraq, Qatar, Oman, Saudi Arabia, and the United Arab Emirates, to 50 percent in countries like Cambodia, Ghana, and Latvia, to much higher in the United States, Canada, and many European counries.[2] Worldwide, more men than women are found in the upper echelons of government and business, and it is these leaders who hold the greatest influence in shaping their country's policies and corporate HR management structures and behaviors.[3]

Historically and currently, there remains a significant gap in women representation, compensation in the upper echelons of the global workforce, as well as having the same rights as men in all aspects.

The following from recent books or widely respected newspapers in the United States are examples that show that women have a long way to go before they can be considered equal with men in the law or in society. The reason they are not equal is because men have the power.

■ From the book *On Saudi Arabia* by Karen Elliott House:[4] According to Wahabi Islam, men must obey Allah and women must obey men. "Fortunately for men, Allah is distant, but unfortunately for women, men are omnipresent," writes House.

■ Hans Kung, a well-known Catholic priest and long-time colleague and friend of the pope emeritus, wrote the following under the title "A Vatican Spring" in *The New York Times*:[5] "A recent poll in Germany show 85 percent of Catholics in favor of letting priests marry and 75 percent in favor of ordaining women."

■ In *The Economist*:[6] "In India, rape has long been depressingly common. . . . The UN's human-rights chief calls rape in India a national problem . . . sexual violence in villages, though little reported, keeps girls and women indoors after dark."

■ Nicholas Kristof wrote in *The New York Times*:[7] "Gender violence is one of the world's most common human rights abuses. Women worldwide ages 15 through 44 are more likely to die or be maimed by male violence than because of cancer, malaria, and traffic accidents combined."

■ Sohrab Ahmari in *The Wall Street Journal*[8] wrote about a Saudi woman who was driving a car: "A member of the Committee for the Promotion of Virtue and the Prevention of Vice, the Saudi morality police, surrounded the car. 'Girl,' screamed one. 'Get out, we don't allow women to drive.' She asked, 'Sir, what law did I break?' 'You didn't break any laws,' they said. 'You violated our . . . custom.'"

■ Alissa Rubin in *The New York* Times[9] wrote: "A father who borrowed $2,500.00 to pay for hospital expenses for his wife and cannot repay the loan will be forced to have their 6-year-old daughter leave her family home forever to be married to the lender's 17-year-old son."

■ The National Partnership for Women and Families analysis of census data showed the pay gap between men and women in the United States is still significant. Women earn 77 cents for every 1 dollar paid to full-time working men.[10]

And on, and on, and on. Similar examples can be found in the newspapers of any society if the press is free.

We believe that culture counts. Culture provides guidance and some cultures have rigid rules for expected female and male roles, and, as such, provides the values and the subsequent expected behavioral norms for men and women within each culture.[11] Gender norms vary across cultures, and can influence how women combine the expected roles of a female leader with the general role expectations of their culture.[12] Culture sets the expected norms and values of gender-related behaviors, and there are many differences within nations and cultures with how these play out.[13]

While culture can set the standard for expected behaviors, this does not mean that all men, and all women, will automatically respond to these cultural norms accordingly. For example, Egyptian women collectively stood up for their rights and were not required to wear a veil in the 1920s and to vote in 1956; however, in 2009, a survey done in Egypt of 15,000 youth revealed that 67 percent of female respondents still believed that a woman deserves to be beaten by her husband if she speaks to another man.[14] In another example, a global study of 62 women with families and prominent leadership work-related positions found that "the American women leaders pride themselves on never missing their children's school play or soccer games; mothers in Hong Kong put more emphasis in helping their children with their school work; the Chinese mothers across the different societies emphasize family dinners, describing how they eat with their children before they go to their business dinners or go back to work in the office at night."[15]

From an organizational perspective, we contend that companies that use and build on an increasingly diverse workforce that includes women will have the competitive advantage. While the number of international businesswomen has grown over the years, this number has not increased at a rate consistent with the number of women in the workforce of their respective countries. Globalization has transformed worldwide organizational culture and the workforce, and this has created an increased need for enhanced workforce collaboration and support. Since national corporations have expanded to global corporations, companies have had to respond to an increasingly diverse workplace of varying ethnicities, nationalities, and languages.

Over the last 50 years, an increasing number of professional women have entered and remain in the global workforce. For all workforce professionals to perform to their potential, they need support, training, and mentoring. Often, for women and minorities, the challenge can go well beyond this. If women are less than 20 percent of the directors in highly developed countries, progress for women is still far from accomplished.

In this chapter, we address some of the opportunities and challenges faced by women as global businesspeople. Our first objective is to raise awareness about the status and challenges and opportunities of women in global organizations. The second objective is to suggest some ideas about women as global leaders and specific issues women may be confronted with in managing cultural differences.

CURRENT STATUS OF GLOBAL WOMEN MANAGERS

Although globally women have considerably increased their presence in all industries, Exhibits 5.1–5.2 are researched examples illustrating that progress is yet to be made.

Meyerson and Fletcher[16] wrote of an outdated, but prevalent, practice of women still tending to be responsible for the "softer" aspects of work, while corporate culture is predisposed to highly value the traits of toughness, aggressiveness, and decisiveness – all stereotypically associated with men. Nevertheless, this isn't to say that men are to blame and that all men benefit because corporate culture is primarily male dominated.

Many organizations are working hard to leverage workforce diversity and gender equality so that all people can succeed. The key to making concrete changes in organizations is their leadership, which must have a keen interest in recruiting and *retaining* a diverse workforce while promoting qualified women. Unfortunately, statistics demonstrate that companies are falling short of the goal of gender equity in the workplace. Meyerson and Fletcher stated that, "Women at the highest levels of business are still rare. They comprise only 10 percent of senior managers in *Fortune* 500 companies; less than 4 percent of the uppermost ranks of CEO, president, vice president, and COO; and less than 3 percent of top corporate earners."[17] Likewise, tied to the challenge of leveraging a diverse workforce with equal opportunity and compensation, the statistics for women of minority ethnicities are even worse: "Although women of color make up 23 percent of the U.S. women's workforce, they account for only 14 percent of women in managerial roles. African-American women comprise only 6 percent of the women in managerial roles."[18]

EXHIBIT 5.1 STATUS OF GLOBAL WOMEN EXECUTIVE OFFICERS, 2012

Facts	Women	Men
2012 proportion of board positions with FTSE held by women	17.3%	82.7%
Less than 1/5 of companies were found to have three or more women executive officers		
About 1/3 of all companies have no women executive officers		

Source: *Financial Times*, December 31, 2012.

EXHIBIT 5.2 SELECT SURVEY RESULTS OF THE CORPORATE GENDER GAP REPORT, 2010

A select group of over 3,000 companies responded to this survey of about 25 questions in each of the 30 member countries of the OECD (Organization for Economic Cooperation and Development) and Brazil, China, Russia, and India. In each economy, a minimum of 20 completed surveys of 100 companies were completed. The following are some selected results:

Female employees (%)	India	23	Female employees were found to be
	Japan	24	concentrated in entry level to middle
	Turkey	26	level positions.
	Austria	29	
	Finland	44	
	Canada	46	
	Spain	48	
	United States	52	
Average number of women holding the CEO position (%)	Italy	11	Among the following survey respondents —
	Brazil	11	Belgium, Canada, Czech Republic, France,
	Norway	12	India, Greece, Mexico, Netherlands, Switzerland,
	Turkey	12	United States, and United Kingdom —
	Finland	13	there were no female CEOs.
Corporate measurement and target setting	Of the sample, 64% of the companies surveyed did not set any specific targets, quotas, or affirmative goals.		72% of the companies surveyed did not monitor salary gaps between women and men or implement counteractive procedures.
Maternity leave practices	13% of surveyed companies offered no maternity leave.		India, Mexico, and the United States offered the minimum leave time, and 33% of companies in Mexico offered less than the minimum leave time.

Source: Tesfachew, T., Zahidi, S., and Ibarra, H. "Measuring the Corporate Gender Gap," in S. Zahidi and H. Ibarra (eds), *The Corporate Gender Gap Report 2010*. World Economic Forum, Geneva, Switzerland, 2010. Retrieved April 27, 2010 from http://www.weforum.org/pdf/gendergap/corporate2010.pdf.

In 2005, *The Economist* [19] reported the following:

■ In Japan, in the 1980s and 1990s, it was unacceptable for a woman to stay in the office past 5 p.m. There has been some progress since, with two women being appointed in 2005 as the head of two big Japanese companies:
  - Fumiko Hayashi is now the chairman and CEO of Daiei.
  - Tomoyo Nonaka has been appointed CEO of Sanyo Electric.

- In France, Corinne Maier, an economist at EDF, a French energy group, said that 5 percent of French executives are women and that "Equality in the French workplace . . . is a far-off dream."
- In Britain, a large research sample of British companies found that 65 percent had no women on their board at all in 2003. Though 44 percent of the British workforce is female, no British woman has ever been the head of a large British company.

Five years later, in 2010, *The Economist*[20] published an article discussing the position of women in the workplace. While this is not intended to be compared to their article published in 2005, the purpose is to look at working women relative to men worldwide:

- There is an increase in the number of women in the workplace, women in the United States and in Spain now make up 49.9 percent of all workers, and in the United States, women earn almost 60 percent of all university degrees.
- The unemployment rates for men in Japan and in Italy are more than 20 percent higher than for women, and even though women's employment has risen in the last decade significantly, it is still 50 percent below that of men, and more than 20 percent below that of Denmark and Sweden.
- Women, on average, still earn significantly less than men, and are underrepresented at the top of organizations.
- Women are often still forced to choose between motherhood and careers, and, as a response, in Switzerland, more than 40 percent of women are childless or delay having children for so long that they are prime candidates for fertility treatment.

However:

- Finland and Hungary provide up to three years of paid leave for women, and Germany has introduced a parent salary to encourage mothers to stay home for a time while keeping their careers.
- And more than 90 percent of organizations in Germany and Sweden allow for flexible working, dividing the work week in new ways to allow for improved work–family balance.
- In paid family leave, the United States trails most of the globe.[21]

According to a report by the BBC, 75 percent of women work in the five lowest paid sectors; women hold less than 10 percent of top positions in FTSE 100 companies, the police, the judiciary, and trade unions.[22] Retired women have on average a little over half the income of retired men. Barriers to women's entry into senior management, otherwise known as the "glass ceiling," exist across the globe, and it is worse in some areas of the world than in others. An article on the most influential women in business highlighted that it is easier to find ethnic British and Chinese women in positions of power, but much more difficult to find

Korean or German women at the same level.[23] And although women represent 43 percent of the European workforce, they are still largely underrepresented in top management – in the U.K., women represent slightly over 30 percent of managers and senior executives.[24]

One of the best examples of a society that promotes gender equality is Norway.[25] Here, 80 percent of Norwegian women work outside of the home, and half of the current government ministers are women. Scandinavian countries have the highest level of female employment in the world, and the fewest social problems, as the state has been closely involved in promoting gender equality. For example, Norway has used quota threats to increase female representation – and the result is that about 40 percent of the legislators are now women.[26] In 2002, a law was instated requiring that 40 percent of all company board members be women, and gave time until 2006 for companies to comply.[27]

Yet, while representation has increased, the expected link between women and performance in the board room was found to still be questionable. This is possibly because of the fact that the boards chiefly supervise and give advice to executives and top managers who are mostly men. Global representation in the board room and among executives and top managers still has a long way to go: "In the United States, roughly 15 percent of the board members of the *Fortune* 500 companies are women, while at the top of Asian companies, women remain scarce: in China and India, they hold roughly 5 percent of board seats, and in Japan, just 1.4 percent." While "women represent 27–32 percent of managers in Nordic countries, against 34 percent to 43 percent in Australia, Britain, Canada, and the United States, where maternity leave is more limited."[28]

Creating opportunities for female representation in the global workplace is only part of the matter. Biases or stereotypes are beliefs that influence behavior, and, often, these beliefs can lead to unequal treatment and representation. Stereotypes often hinder – although women and men are equal in their managerial abilities and overall ability to succeed – the promotion of women to senior positions.

GLOBAL CULTURAL STEREOTYPES ABOUT WOMEN LEADERS

Psychological research has found that there are two types of sexist ideologies: one, benevolent sexism, is rooted in the belief that the gender differences are complementary and that women should be protected and taken care of; the other, hostile sexism, is rooted in the belief that women are inferior to men.[29] These sexist ideologies are rooted in each culture's stereotypic views about how women "should" behave. When women behave differently from prescribed stereotypes, often there are penalties that are administered.[30] "For example, women who are viewed as self-promoting or as 'acting like men' . . . are judged as deficient in social skills, are less liked and socially accepted, and receive fewer recommendations for employment."[31]

From Asia to the Americas to Europe, some of the unfortunate and disturbing *global stereotypes* include, but are not limited to the following:

Women's behavior at work

■ Women are fundamentally different and too "soft" to handle hardnosed managerial decisions. Women cannot be aggressive enough, and will therefore lose business or do not have the competitive edge needed to win.

■ Contrary to the stereotype that women are too "soft," when women behave in accordance with the behaviors expected of their male counterparts, then the stereotype changes to the following: women overcompensate when in male environments, and become too masculine when managing, alienating employees and often alarming clients.

■ Yet in China, especially after the Cultural Revolution, women are expected to behave more aggressively.

■ Women lack quantitative skills, and therefore cannot hold technical positions or understand the numbers required in a profit-and-loss environment. Women possess "soft" skills such as communication and team building.

Women and mothers

■ Women are not as dedicated or as committed as their male counterparts, and therefore are not "executive material."

■ Once a woman becomes a mother, her priorities change completely, and she can no longer be counted on as before. Women often opt to quit working and become full-time mothers. How can a company promote someone who they know will ultimately leave? Companies cannot afford to have women coming and going whenever they wish.

Women in an international context

■ Women are not interested in an international career, and therefore should not be considered for international positions. In addition, women can't handle the cultural differences that occur outside their home country.

■ When companies send women abroad, their image will be less credible in male-dominated societies.

Women interacting within their working environment

■ Other men won't take the woman manager seriously. Interestingly, many Japanese managers tell us they see "foreign" first and being a woman next.

■ Because of current sexual harassment laws, nothing can be said to women without it getting blown out of proportion, and the result is that all interaction becomes suspect.

- Women cause problems by looking for love in the workplace, and this will disrupt the workplace and ultimately lead to greater problems.
- There aren't enough qualified women to promote. No matter how hard the company has tried, there just aren't any women with the exact qualifications they are looking for.

Such stereotypes are extremely counterproductive in the workplace. Blind stereotypes inhibit women and men from working effectively together, and inhibit women from working to their potential because they are active in keeping women "in their place." Overall, whether they are benevolent forms of sexism, or hostile, they inhibit the advancement of women in business around the world, and obscure women's skills.[32]

Stereotypes can hinder the advancement of women

Quite often, these stereotypes go unnoticed by both men and women, as they are so deeply rooted within a culture. Other times, even when aware of these stereotypes, some women might choose to behave according to the stereotype in order to avoid dealing with strong attitudinal obstructions while at work. There are a variety of global issues that confront women in the workplace. A few are highlighted to gain a greater understanding of the obstacles women must still overcome.

- *Women are more likely to be pigeonholed into less challenging positions than men.* Women are often tracked into separate, and less promising, career paths. As upper management positions require broad and varied experience among other skills and talents, as well as a sense of responsibility, many potential male executives are "pipe-lined" through certain high-visibility and high-responsibility areas such as marketing, finance, and production.[33] These are often referred to as "line" positions, in preparation for upper-management promotion. Women "tend to be in supporting, 'staff' function areas – personnel/human resources, communications, public relations, and customer relations. Movement between these positions and 'line' positions is rare in most major companies. Furthermore, career ladders in staff functions are generally shorter than those in line functions, offering fewer possibilities to gain varied experience."[34]

  This is a stereotype that can be found across the globe; women are seen as more "human" and therefore better suited for a specific type of job, such as human resources, communications, public relations, and marketing. Management, especially in the areas of finance and information services, continues to often be seen as a job better suited for men.

  This stereotype could be linked to the global expectation of a woman's role as mother or primary caretaker in the family. This common stereotype is as follows: if a woman's focus is on bearing children, she would subsequently be taking time off, and could not be considered an effective front-line executive. In Chile, a woman's marital status can be an important consideration during the hiring process; it is generally featured at the top of a resume with other essentials such as name, address, and phone number, along with a photograph. A young, married woman with no children can be considered a "risky investment" because the perception is that she will soon have children, leave her job, and the company will have to pay for pregnancy expenses. Although times may be changing in Chile, it is still generally expected that women will relinquish their career aspirations and stay at home when children arrive. For some women, this can begin immediately after marriage.

During the 1980s, in the United States, the "mommy track" was designed to facilitate having children and maintaining a professional life. Nevertheless, many women who choose to have children still maintain high career aspirations and get stuck in less-challenging or demanding jobs. While this stereotype tends to be focused upon the role of women, it is also evolving into a parental stereotype, as a number of male partners and husbands of working women are staying home to care for children.[35]

■ *Significant pay gaps exist between women and men in the same position.* Despite considerable progress and a variety of laws designed to prevent wage discrimination, women are still earning less than their male counterparts for the same job.[36] The BBC reported that, according to the Equal Opportunities Commission (EOC), there is a 19 percent pay gap between men and women in the U.K.[37]

■ *Exclusive corporate cultures.* One influential factor still affecting women's advancement in business, and this is true in many areas across the globe, is that most of today's existing work environments were designed by men. Women, functioning in sometimes a more male-oriented corporate culture, are often under pressure to adapt or transform their styles of working. This, however, is slowly changing. In Japan, for example, women face a challenge to adapt to the expectation that management requires mixing work and play, often by drinking and bar-hopping until late hours. Women colleagues are nowadays invited to join in with such social activities, although a married woman with a family might find it very difficult to meet, on a consistent basis, such a time commitment. In some South American countries, strong, unspoken norms exist about what is appropriate or inappropriate for a woman to do, regardless of career position; as such, higher-level female executives can be excluded from after-work activities and/or can exclude themselves in fear of the backlash in breaching these norms.

In some American corporate environments, younger generations of women have almost eradicated the "male only" designated corporate culture by joining in, and instigating, happy hours, golf games, and softball tournaments. In some cases, these women have even redefined the culture itself by adding new twists like cultural outings or joining in on the "male only" outings.

■ *Limited access to information, contacts, and high-level networking opportunities.* While the term "old boys' network" was coined long ago, in many companies the institution itself is thriving. The "old boys' network" refers primarily to a group of white male executives who have an informal yet somewhat exclusive club that manifests itself in the upper echelons of management. Women and people of color are generally not included. Communication within these exclusive informal networks can perpetuate gender stereotyping and bias through jokes, stories, and slurs. Whether it is on the golf course, hunting, having late night drinks, or in the men's room, women can often be excluded from this high-level interaction, when it is often these informal networks that can improve chances of promotion and success.

According to *The Economist*, few women are able to reach the higher management levels because of exclusion from informal networks, which across the globe can include late-night boozing and a common tradition for sales teams to take potential clients to strip clubs.[38] Executives and upper-level managers like to hire who they know, and the more contact with an individual the better. Unfortunately for women, many of the "bonding" experiences take place in venues that are not necessarily women-friendly. In Israel, women are almost completely excluded from the senior ranks of the military. This exclusion from what is considered by many in the corporate world as an invaluable learning experience for managing large organizations limits women as choices for future senior executives.[39]

As a result, women often are not informed of advancement opportunities, are not as visible as male colleagues, and are not given additional opportunities to prove their credibility for promotion. According to Wernick,[40] "Managers and executives look for 'signals' from those they will select to advance. Those signals found to be most significant indicate credibility and provide increased access to visibility to decision-makers. Access to information, which is critical to advancement, is often limited to selected groups or individuals within the managerial ranks or workplace." This can be exacerbated when the company does not have a formal executive development program or tracking program that explicitly monitors promotions and pay increases for employees.

■ *Fewer women participate in executive development programs, employer-sponsored training programs, or "fast-track" programs.* As evidenced through a variety of studies, women are often not given as many opportunities as their male colleagues for education, training, or special high-profile programs. This could emanate from the stereotype that women will eventually leave their jobs to have children, so why invest the money in enhancing their skills when a man would be a better "investment" opportunity? Without proper corporate intervention to increase women's participation in such programs and opportunities, the result would be that women remain in their positions with little to no overall growth.

■ *Fewer women are asked to take on risky positions.* One area where this is particularly evident is in expatriate work, where the position and results tend to be highly visible. Fewer women are asked to fill expatriate positions, although just as many women as men request these positions abroad. A prominent researcher on the role of women in global business, Adler interviewed many people to determine whether MBAs from seven management schools in the United States, Canada, and Europe would like to pursue an international assignment during their career.[41] The overall response was 84 percent favorable, with little difference between male and female responses. Adler conducted another survey of 686 Canadian and American firms to determine the number of women sent abroad.[42]

Of 13,338 expatriates, only 3 percent were women, when women actually accounted for 37 percent of domestic management positions. One other obstacle exists for women who would like to hold international assignments: the cultural biases in certain countries against women, both native and foreign, are such that it is very difficult for women to work, to live, and overall to succeed in that particular country.

BALANCING WORK AND FAMILY

THE PLIGHT OF A WORKING MOTHER

Two years ago, while at our summer cottage in northern Ontario, Canada, I took some old, what we call junk, to the local dump. While there, I scrounged around and found some good "junk" that I brought back to our cottage.

I was thrilled with a couple of my new treasures, and sent this email to our five adult children:

"Tell us about an interesting day this week. I just returned from the dump with some treasures that were interesting to me."

Ben emailed: "I woke up in a sleeping bag on the sand in the Sinai, after a night under the stars. Had tea made by a Bedouin, then drove to Mt. Sinai, visited St. Catherine's monastery and saw the burning bush — still alive. After many Army checkpoints, made it to the airport, when I had a Greek salad and checked by email before (now) boarding a flight to Istanbul."

Rebecca's email came next: "I woke up at 5 a.m., pressed my snooze button once, made a take-away breakfast of tea and oatmeal, and headed to the airport when I flew with a trainee pilot of over eight hours, at the end of which our flaps failed (no problem), then the standby backup flap motor failed (also really no problem, but it was interesting) then came home to a yummy home-made pizza and Eli fell asleep without crying, the biggest 'wow' of the day."

Finally, Molly, our daughter with three young children, sent this email: "I picked the kids up from daycare and Martha fell on the way to the car. She skinned her knee a little and started to cry and yell and scream at the top of her lungs … 'Mommy, mommy, I can't walk, my blood, my blood, scream, scream, I don't like this … scream, scream' as if she was about to die. Then I picked up Henry and put him in the car. Then he started to cry because he wanted to get in the car by himself. Then Charlotte started to cry and I don't know why … maybe because her brother and sister were crying. So all three were crying at the top of their lungs. It lasted the entire way home, which was only five minutes, thank goodness, but at that moment I wish I was either at the dump, in the Sinai, or on a plane with failed flaps … anywhere but in the car with three screaming children."

A WORKING MOM

I am 38 years old, work full time, and have three children under 6 years old. I knew once I started to have children that I wanted to continue to work, but I did not know if it would be possible after the second. I have found that working for a company that is supportive of working mothers made all the difference. The company I work for has an on-site daycare, run by Bright Horizons. After my second child was born, I went back to work when he was 12 weeks old. I was able to visit and nurse him during the day. I now have a third child, and again, went back to work when she was 12 weeks old and was also able to make daily visits. While some companies might think this is not being productive, I found that not having to worry during the day and do a few personal feedings helped me be extremely efficient at work.

I know a lot of women do not want to make the choice between family and career. Unfortunately, sometimes you need to if the company you work for is not supportive. A change I would want to make for working moms in the United States is additional time for maternity leave. While the current FMLA entitlement is 12 workweeks of leave in a 12-month period for the birth of a child, I think adding four more weeks for a total of 16 weeks would encourage more moms to go back to work, should that be their choice.

Source: Molly Hyland, New Hampshire, United States, 2013.

Balancing life outside of work and life at work is a major concern of most working professionals. It is also a major concern for working couples who, when working equally together, balance work and family to the benefit of both partners. Here we define balancing work and family "as the degree to which an individual is able to simultaneously balance the temporal, emotional, and behavioral demands of both paid work and family responsibilities."[43] Though in the past, women were required to make a clear choice as to whether they wanted to have a career or a family, today a professional career and motherhood are no longer considered mutually exclusive, as the concept of fatherhood has also evolved.

Nevertheless, working mothers who are not married to men who partake equally in the family responsibilities tend to have to juggle two full-time jobs. When national cultural norms still promote a more traditional model of "parenthood," the work–family balance debate is relegated as an issue that women face. Even though in some cases, this can conceal a male belief that household and child-related work are primarily women's responsibilities,[44] it is also an issue that men face in an effort to find work–family balance.

A series of women were interviewed who were either middle or senior managers and who had recently become new mothers,[45] and all of the women interviewed stated that motherhood had given them a new perspective on their work, and that this was, in general, very positive. They also felt that motherhood had given them a new sense of confidence, enabling them to let their personalities become apparent in the workplace. Planning was critical to juggle the daily demands of family and work.

Nevertheless, many women, particularly in Europe and Asia, choose to take a break from professional work once they begin a family. Furthermore, more research should be done to look at how men balance work and family as well, for as long as the stereotype that caring for children and the home is an expected female role is encouraged worldwide, and relevant research tends to focus on women's attitudes toward work–family balance, this stereotype is reinforced.

Challenges faced with trying to balance work and family

It is certainly a strain to balance one's personal and professional responsibilities. In the United States, for example, there is still a lingering belief that it is the woman's responsibility to take care of children. Separating work and family into two different domains tends to be found in current Western thinking, and it supports a popular myth that women can choose one or the other, but having both is extremely difficult – when, in reality, women have almost always worked and had families, and only the context has shifted and changed over the years.[46] In the United States, many American businesses are addressing the bottom-line implications of employees' need for affordable and high-quality child and elder care. Wiley Harris of GE Capital Services states that, "Every employee is important to our company's health, and when employees are distracted by family issues, we lose productivity."[47] The Family and Medical Leave Act of 1993 in the United States was a response to concerns from men and women about being able to care for family members at critical life stages without the risk of job loss. Even with its enactment, the United States continues to compare poorly with other developed countries such as France, Sweden, Canada, and Finland, where family care is institutionalized.

Research on work–family balance

Lately, research on work–family started to include things like "positive spillover, balance, interface, mutual facilitation," and can incorporate an international perspective.[48] For example, in Chinese society, where work and family are seen as interdependent,[49] and roles tend to be more nebulous, work is seen as having a long-term benefit for the family. Furthermore, the Maoist ideology of gender equality and the one-child-per-family *policy* have greatly contributed to women's promotion and motivation in the workplace with them no longer having to focus on finding day care.[50] However, Chinese Confucian principles of governance and morality still results in women being seen by some as less than men.[51] That being said, however, this study[52] found that Chinese women's work motivation was just as high as that of Chinese men, and managerial motivation was found to be positively related to the hierarchical job level. Among their findings was that intrinsic motivation, standing out from the group, and exercising power might be factors that enable women to supersede negative work-related prejudices about work–family dynamics that could hamper job advancement.

In Europe, a study[53] of managers from 20 different EU countries analyzed the intersection of, and among, the following three variables: (1) the degree of each country's national gender equality, (2) the degree of organizational support for family–work balance, and (3) individual qualities, such as individual manager's work–family balance characteristics. This study noted correctly that a country's national gender equality and context are very relevant. Work–family balance can be supported by national government regulations and programs, such as Sweden's policy on subsidized childcare programs and required parental leave.

Furthermore, it was found that organizations are more likely to follow through if their external environment enforces compliance, thus reflecting the relationship between national context and organizational practice. This study underscored how important national context is to gender equality in the areas of parents being able to have work–life balance; and women's life expectancy, education, and standard of living. Overall, parents who have positive work–family balance tend to be more satisfied with their job, are more committed to their organization, and are more satisfied with their family dynamics as well.[54]

In many European countries, states provide childcare support and have national programs to facilitate work–family balance; in the United States, the individual employers are expected to be the principal purveyor of family assistance, even though they often feel that it is not their responsibility but the family's.[55] However, these programs of the employers are successful only if top management is committed to their implementation.[56] A very recent study[57] of U.S. personnel analyzed supervisors' perceptions of family–work conflict and the ability to balance expectations of both, through investigating two aspects of promotability: (1) the manager's perceptions of the promotability of their employees, and (2) employee statements of whether they had been nominated for promotion or not. They[58] found that managers had the propensity to pigeonhole women as the gender that experienced more work–family conflict, even after the researchers controlled for family responsibilities and the women's own perceptions of work–family balance. The main contribution of this study is the finding that even though women's work–family conflict may impact their career progress, the perceptions of their work–family conflict that their superiors may have also can influence their career advancement, and these perceptions can unwittingly create the "glass ceiling" effect.

THE GLASS CEILING

The "glass ceiling" refers to barriers to reaching the upper echelons of organizations. These barriers to the advancement of women and minorities are often very subtle. For example, a very interesting study[59] in 2008 looked at HR personnel records of a *Fortune* 500 company from 1967 to 1993, drawing a random sample of more than 5,000 managers of both genders. After dividing the sample into four work levels (entry, middle, upper middle, and upper), the analysis revealed that women tended to be hired at lower levels and lower salaries than their male complement, and were more likely to be located in support positions. The result was that women were less likely to be on the path to the top of the organization, and even by 1993, while 40 percent of the women hired were in entry-level positions, in the higher echelons, they were only 20 percent of the middle managers, and 10 percent of the upper middle and upper levels.

Other research[60] has found that there are subtleties that influence the "glass ceiling" barriers, and consist of gender stereotypes, a deficiency of opportunities for women to acquire the necessary work experience and knowledge to excel, a scarcity of top management dedication to initiatives for gender equality and equal opportunity, and a male wealth stereotype that men deserve greater salaries than women.[61]

Exhibit 5.3 presents the findings of research about women and wages worldwide.[62] It provides us with one way to understand the impact of female worker wage proportion relative to men, with *special attention to* merit pay and strikes, on payment within and across organizations and occupations. This interesting study concluded that many employees are underpaid relative to their country's level of wealth, and points toward socio-psychological forces that impact economic compensation.

EXHIBIT 5.3

EXHIBIT 5.3 A STUDY OF WOMEN AND WAGES WORLDWIDE

■ 59 countries which had estimates for wages from a World Economic Forum Global Competitive Report were included in the study. The survey measured the perceptions of 3,934 government officials and senior business leaders working in these 59 countries.

■ The factors used to determine the objective size of the gender contrast (the national proportion of working women) included the country's:
  - Overall male/female ratio (0.52 in Qatar $< x <$ 1.19 in Latvia)
  - Fertility rate (1.2 in Italy $< x <$ 7.6 in Yemen)
  - Economic growth rate (-0.09 in Georgia $< x <$ 0.09 in China)
  - Socioeconomic necessity of families having a dual income
  - War and emigration.

Findings

1   Workers in countries with larger proportions of working women *were found to be underpaid*.

2   Neither payroll taxes, merit pay, nor strikes could substitute working women as the main predictor of underpayment, *however*, they did appear to account partially, in a curvilinear fashion, for *this* underpayment.

3   Both previous results appeared to be driven by the following economic and socio-psychological forces:

    a.   The proportion of working women is a demographic and socio-psychological factor.

    b.   Underpayment across countries with little merit pay or strikes can be tied to men's higher status relative to women.

    c.   Underpayment across countries where merit pay or strikes are more common can be better tied to the absence of salient gender contrasts.

Source: Van de Vliert, E. and Van der Vegt, G. "Women and Wages Worldwide: How the National Proportion of Working Women Brings Underpayment into the Organization," *Organization Studies*, Vol. 25, No. 6, 2004, pp. 969–986.

COMPANY INITIATIVES TO BREAK THE GLASS CEILING

Most companies have put into place specific programs to assist in breaking down barriers impeding a woman's progression. Many include a combination of flexible work arrangements, mentoring, women's support groups, and leadership development. Various companies have also developed support and structures designed to advance women.

Quality management models: audits

Even though a lot of research, conferences, meetings, and workshops have been conducted in the area of gender and diversity, and there are an increasing number of qualified and career-oriented women in industry, there appears to still be limited progress within industry in Europe. This is because, in Europe, resistance is found through low commitment by top managers, weak gender or diversity marketing campaigns, and no incentives or systemic planned methods to improve the diversity and gender policy.[63] In order to improve processes such that women in corporations become a source of productivity and high performance, audits help to provide documented, systemic examination of this topic and can assist industry to improve its gender-related policies. Rather than looking simply at the number of men or women involved in an industry, audits help to examine the contributions of different areas and groups within that industry. Audits help to provide instruments to verify management and information on the efficiency of a company's performance, and provide mechanisms to display how strategic decisions play out, as well as a benchmark to compare with other companies.[64]

A tracking system

Accenture was the winner of the "2003 Catalyst Award for Innovative Programs to Help Women Advance in the Workplace." Accenture developed a global "Great Place to Work for Women" initiative, and uses a variety of innovative processes such as geographic score-cards, global surveys, and performance appraisals to guarantee that company leadership remains accountable for the initiative's results. Joe Forehand, Accenture's chairman and CEO, states that, "Empowerment without opportunity is useless. At Accenture, we've focused on fostering a more inclusive work environment. Our Great Place to Work for Women program is one way we're enabling women to take charge of their careers and move into broader leadership roles."[65]

A support structure: mentoring programs

IBM, 3M, and many other companies have women's networks in place to help promote women's careers. Apparently, one-third of all *Fortune* 100 companies have such networks aimed at developing skills, building careers, and supporting women. Research has demonstrated that mentoring is a critical part of career success. Mentoring is defined as "a cooperative and nurturing relationship between a more experienced businessperson and a less-experienced person who wants to learn about a particular business and gain valuable insight into some of the unspoken subtleties of doing business."[66] Many experts claim that it is beneficial to have more than one mentor present within an organization, and that these mentors should be at different levels. Mentoring comes into play at crucial points in an individual's career and can be an effective source of advice and encouragement.

Burke and McKeen found, however, that men and women view mentoring in different ways.[67] It is often more difficult for women than men to find appropriate mentors. Many Internet sites have popped up in the past few years offering women the opportunity to network with each other in a nontraditional setting. The U.S. Small Business Administration has set up a specific program, open to all women, specifically focused on helping women entrepreneurs and those considering becoming entrepreneurs.

Work still to be done

Although women have achieved significant advances since entering the workplace, much remains to be done for women to be considered as qualified and talented as men. Companies need to take more responsibilities and initiatives to fully integrate women into their environments at all levels of the corporate hierarchy. Companies that champion diversity champion women. Some issues to consider include the following:

- *Increasing the flow of information and educating women about current issues.* It is only with concrete facts and information about women's position in the workplace that any calibration of gains can be measured. Catalyst,[68] a nonprofit organization focused on women's issues in the workplace, has taken a wonderful role in initiating this process. When women appreciate where they have been and understand the issues that confront them, they can see and decide where the future lies.
- *Demonstrating CEO commitment.* As the corporate leader, the CEO has the most significant influence on the direction and vision of the firm. It is through her or his direction that a "persistent campaign of incremental changes that discover and destroy the deeply embedded roots of discrimination" will occur.[69]
- *Closing the pay gap.* A true merit system distinguishes individuals on the basis of their effort and skills, and rewards each person for his or her work regardless of gender. Men and women work equally hard in the same positions; their pay should reflect this equality.
- *Increasing recruitment, providing training opportunities, and placing women in high-profile positions.* Companies should step up their efforts to recruit and train qualified women, and ensure that more women get access to "line" positions versus being immediately segmented into "staff" positions. "Recruiting the right potential very much depends on the individual employer attractiveness. Besides challenging projects and job security, equality and family-friendly policy belong to the most important motivation factors. This means that . . . for a company, it is a must to implement gender mainstreaming activities within the concept of high-qualified diversity management."[70]

WOMEN AND OVERSEAS, EXPATRIATE ASSIGNMENTS

Women's representation in the global arena has grown (albeit slowly) to 17 percent of the expatriate population, though in some industry sections, the percentage is considerably higher.[71] Although the percentage of women expatriates is rising, many companies fail to send women overseas, in particular to areas of the world where the demarcation between male and female roles is clearly defined. Global women managers often talk about the "double-take" or stares they receive in Asia, South America, or the Middle East when they are first introduced. For example, in Latin America, women report having been mistaken for the wife or the secretary during important high-level business meetings and social events. However, most women who were sent abroad say that the first reaction of surprise is quickly replaced by professionalism and respect.

The expatriate glass ceiling (the glass border)

In multinational companies, a foreign assignment is often the stepping stone into a higher-level management position. A recent study[72] found that employees who exhibited greater personal agency and had less family obligations were more willing to go on expatriate assignments, search for expatriate jobs, and leave their home countries. This same study found that women with partners and/or children were most restrained in their willingness to expatriate. Even with willingness to expatriate, there is still a strong disparity between the number of male and female managers, not only in home country operations, but also in expatriate assignments.[73] This expatriate "glass ceiling" has three implications: (1) there is a greater challenge to filling expatriate assignments, as nowadays, men are often opting out because of family and dual-career concerns, (2) a lack of diversity of the top management group can lead to homogeneity, and thus weaker leadership decision-making, and (3) if lower-level women feel that the opportunity is limited, they may be less motivated to compete for higher-level jobs.[74]

Breaking the glass border to succeed in an expatriate assignment

From 2000 on, women's participation in international assignments has been on the rise, as data from Europe, Australia, and the United States have found a rise of 16.5 percent of women in expatriate assignments in 2005.[75] Nevertheless, there is an underrepresentation of women on international assignments. "These barriers are informed, predicated, and reinforced by organizational and societal conventions, including the lack of women mentors and role models, the weakness of female organizational networking, and lack of social support that influence promotion to, and acceptance at, the top."[76] Breaking this ceiling requires concerted corporate programs, as well as determined efforts by women, to actively engage in self-promotion and networking.

Three strategies are recommended[77] to assist women to advance toward top-level positions and into foreign assignments. One, *preassignment strategies*: it is recommended that women be proactive agents of change in their own career, and recognize their cultural values that might influence their behavior. Companies should reevaluate and change policies and procedures related to selection, training, and repatriation of female expatriates. They should improve the training of the selection's decision-makers as well, to avoid anti-women bias, while assisting couples who have dual careers to collectively manage both their careers so that a woman can take an international assignment. Two, *on-assignment strategies*: it is recommended for women to proactively find a mentor and take advantage of reverse learning and hindsight. Companies should match assignments to assist with the expatriate adjustment, and continue training and mentoring programs. Three, *post-assignment strategies*: it is recommended for women to volunteer to be a mentor. Doing so, they also take responsibility to manage their own career. Companies should have women, who were on assignments internationally, become mentors for future female expatriates.

When many women have been nominated for an international business assignment in what the company thought would be a hostile culture, most of these women have succeeded with flying colors. Why? This is because expatriate women are not expected to behave according to the same social guidelines as natives of that particular culture, and women can be "especially adept at cross-cultural management skills because they use behavior patterns emphasizing sensitivity, communication skills, community, and relationships. This personal orientation is valuable in globalization."[78] Women are often seen as foreigners first, and thus can be beholden to different rules of conduct than the local women. Here are some words of advice for women to help lay the groundwork:[79]

1   *Establish credibility.* Have strong support from senior management in the organization, and make sure that your expertise is communicated to the destination location.
2   *Have a higher-ranking person* who knows the people in the culture with whom you will be working, and talk openly about your credentials.
3   *Present yourself* as sincere, professional, and confident.
4   *Act reserved* with male colleagues (and formal).
5   *Wear tasteful conservative clothing*, especially in male hierarchical cultures.
6   *Express your opinions* politely, diplomatically, and tactfully.

The difficulties that women may encounter when working on a foreign assignment depend to a certain extent on the social and economic context of the country in which they are conducting business, and on the individuals with whom they come into contact. Both the woman international manager and the company she represents can take steps to minimize any negative aspects.

■   *Companies and managers should lay the groundwork.* Do not surprise a client. While this recommendation is not only specific to a foreign assignment, before any meeting, regardless of the gender of the participants, it is important to provide adequate information about the agenda and who will be present.
■   *Practice what is preached.* If a corporation empowers women managers and treats them equally and seriously in business dealings abroad, it should ensure that women are also treated equally and fairly in the organization. Success begins at home.
■   *Consider both women and men for international positions.* Do not rely on the assumption that women will not want to accept the position.
■   *Provide proper cross-cultural training and preparation courses.* Training is vital to all managers to be successful abroad. Specific assistance should also include what to expect from male superiors, peers, clients, and subordinates, and how to handle uncomfortable situations, such as discrimination.
■   *Be realistic.* Women managers abroad suffer from the same culture shock as men. It is important to keep expectations reasonable, build trust, and create professional relationships.

HOW HAVE SEVERAL SPECIFIC WOMEN SUCCEEDED? ARE THEY GOING ABOUT BUSINESS DIFFERENTLY?

Selected women managers' views

The August 5, 1996, edition of *Fortune* ran an article titled "Women, Sex, and Power." Contrary to what the title might suggest, the article focused on seven women who are the best of the best in their fields of business. Among these were Charlotte Beers (Ogilvy & Mather) and Jill Barad (Mattel). These women are part of the new female elite who are changing the way women reach the top. The following recommendations are still relevant today:

- *Have confidence in yourself.* In the past, many women felt obliged to hide their femininity so as to be seen as managers first and women second. Many women in today's business world no longer view their sexuality as a hindrance. Despite the fact that the office is often still male dominated, they are no longer attempting to become more male-like or androgynous in order to be promoted.

- *Survive and overcome difficult working conditions.* Most women, especially of older generations, have had to face discrimination from men and women alike. Charlotte Beers remembers, "Early in my career, during my first week at J. Walter Thomson in Chicago, I had a secretary who asked the company for a transfer. She told me, 'No offense, but I want to work for a man who's going to move ahead.'" The story goes that two years later, the secretary, impressed by Beers' stellar career path, asked to come back, and Beers, who liked her honesty, accepted.[80] Many successful businesswomen have had to overcome adverse working conditions and have been able to build their careers during these tough moments.

- *Do things differently.* Many women are successful by incorporating aspects of their personality into their work or by daring to do things differently. In the end, many of them drastically change the way business in their field is done. Linda Marcelli, of Merrill Lynch, started selling stocks by setting up personal meetings instead of cold calling. Anita Roddick was an international hit with her "Body Shop" that brought environmental consciousness to a new level.

- *Have your own leadership style – neither "feminine" nor "masculine."* Women are often described as having a more "open" approach to management, relying on consensus building as opposed to the old style of command and control. Recent research demonstrates that women and men executives in similar positions demonstrate more similar behaviors than dissimilar. This research has shown that, "women who have made it into senior positions are in most respects indistinguishable from the men in equivalent positions. In fact, the similarities between women and men far outweigh the differences between women and men as groups."[81]

Many women are concerned that the debate as to whether men and women exhibit different leadership styles continues to perpetuate typical stereotypes of women as "soft" managers. As Adler and Izraeli point out, managers (male and female) in the United States have tended to identify stereotypically "masculine" (aggressive) characteristics as managerial and stereotypically "feminine" (cooperative and communicative) characteristics as "unmanagerial."[82]

More and more companies are assertively trying to advance women's issues. "Woman-friendly" companies have been proven to provide a more beneficial environment to both *men* and *women*.[83]

THE FUTURE OF WOMEN IN LEADERSHIP POSITIONS

The obvious long-term goal is gender equality in the workplace: equal job opportunity, equal pay, and equal advancement. Once gender parity and equality are achieved, management can redirect its additional time and energy to further enhance corporate objectives.

■ *Increased emphasis on strategic alliances between women.* The May 10, 1999, issue of *The Wall Street Journal* reported on a new conference, "Women & Co.," designed for high-level, high-powered women executives from across the nation. The conference not only facilitated female-specific networking and alliance-building opportunities, but also educated the women on current hot topics such as crisis management, the media, dealing with investors, risk management, and selecting CEOs and directors.[84] With the steady increase of women in management, woman-to-woman mentoring systems, extended support networks and associations will gain significant power in lobbying for change and making significant inroads in the boardroom.

■ *More women and men working out of the home.* Advances in technology, combined with more family-friendly businesses, will allow women and men to easily work out of the home and spend quality time with their children or elder relatives. Email, fax, and tele-and video-conferencing capabilities are just a few of the high-tech conveniences that enable all workers to create an office and work productively for their firm at home. New advances are surely in the pipeline to further facilitate working out of the home. As a result, both the mother and father will have more time to devote to raising the children and sharing family duties.

■ *More women-owned businesses.* Often, women who get discouraged with the traditional workplace create their own businesses. If companies are slow to respond to women's needs, we can expect more women-owned businesses that will change the fabric of today's workplace. Women-owned businesses have already doubled as women are recognizing the value of creating one's own work environment, calling the shots, making the hours, and reaping the monetary rewards. Furthermore, with their comprehensive workplace knowledge, these women will design a workplace that is woman-friendly.

- *Changed roles within the home.* With more and more couples working full time, duties in the home should become equally divided. Equality at home will be a fundamental factor that can assist in opening the doors fully to equality in the workplace. Couples can distribute tasks equally, including chores, child rearing, and elder care, and in the process this might mean paying more for services such as house cleaning, shopping, laundry, prepared meals, etc. As women continue to make more money, it will be more acceptable and common to see a "househusband" as the couple together decides the payoff with one breadwinner in the family.

- *Heightened development of family-friendly policies.* As companies value their human capital more, policies could include allowing for two-year "sabbaticals" for either parent to raise children, with computerized "update" training and a guaranteed job upon return. "A few employers, including Eli Lilly and IBM, guarantee a job after a three-year leave. Such policies take the heat off parents."[85] Via Internet education, companies could update these employees on current corporate issues or the latest technology in order to ensure that the employee transitions effectively back into the company.

- *Acceptance of paid paternity leave designed for new fathers.* When companies offer paid paternity leave, they are further encouraging the active role of the father in the family unit. While many women get paid time off after the birth of a child, most fathers are left out of the loop, with only evenings and weekends to help out with the child rearing. While some companies offer time off for the new parent, paid paternity leave is rare. Nevertheless, in France, the government recently offered two weeks of paid paternity leave to all new fathers.

- *Growth of part-time, contract, temporary, or freelance career paths.* If companies do not adequately respond to working parents' needs, the part-time, contract, temporary, and freelance career options will boom. These types of careers give parents the flexibility to combine work and family life, yet without the responsibility of a full-fledged, self-owned business. Many intelligent and educated women choose to stay home with their families because they are forced to choose between work and a family; these types of careers can offer a lucrative middle ground. *The Wall Street Journal* reported an increase in the profitable temporary executive business, where an individual is hired to do high-powered work for a short period of time.[86]

- *New markets will emerge to support the career woman's work–life balance.* Changes in the workforce and consumer demographics inevitably lead to increased opportunity for new markets. This could translate into increased opportunities in the service industry, retail, food, healthcare, childcare, and elder care to meet the needs of working women. Convenience, portability, and ease of use will become more vital as people have less and less time for complicated items.

Women who choose to be full-time mothers and homemakers should be respected for their choice. However, we recognize and believe that the role of nurturer within the home is increasingly being seen and acknowledged as a role both men and women fulfill.

CONCLUSIONS

Careful observation reveals a rapidly increasing number of countries and companies moving away, for the first time, from their historical men-only pattern of senior leadership. The question is no longer "is the pattern changing?" but rather "which companies will take advantage of the trend, and which will fall behind?" Which companies and countries will lead in recognizing and understanding the talents that women bring to leadership, and which will limit their potential by clinging to historic men-only patterns . . .[87]

Depending on the country, different societal forces have contributed to increasing female presence in high-level positions within corporations. Women in the United States have benefited from affirmative action and equal opportunity laws that hold employers accountable for promoting women. In Germany, women are becoming increasingly present in the political arena. Nevertheless, despite recent progress in most countries, women's advancement in the business arena has been steady but slow. As we move further into the twenty-first century, companies will need to increasingly reflect this diversity in all levels of their workforce.

The problem of how to get women in those positions of great importance throughout the enterprise still remains. Numerous barriers still exist for women across the globe. Women have made incredible advances, yet one of their next great challenges will be to assure proportional representation in senior management positions. A strong business imperative can be made that companies who do not address the needs of their women employees (as well as employees of minority cultures) in terms of recruiting, promotion, and career development will suffer the following long-term consequences:

- Not being viewed as an employer of choice.
- Undervaluing top performers; therefore, not using employees' full potential.
- Losing a competitive edge.

In today's competitive world, ignoring the potential of the greatest (in number and in potential) group of your workforce is more than just an oversight — it is extremely costly.

We end this chapter with a recommendation to read *Lean In* by Sheryl Sandberg.[88] She has, in her book, both valuable information on the place of women in the political and business world and the challenges for both women and men in the roles of men and women today and in the future.

She states:

"Of the 195 independent countries in the world, only 17 are led by women."

"Of the *Fortune* 500 CEOs, only 21 are women."

"A truly equal world would be one where women ran half our countries and companies and men ran half our homes."

MIND STRETCHING

"The most important determinant of a country's competitiveness is its human talent — the skills, education, and productivity of its workforce. Women account for one-half of the potential talent base throughout the world and, therefore, over time, a nation's competitiveness depends significantly on whether and how it educates and utilizes its female talent."[89]

1   What are the expectations of the role of women in your culture?
2   What are the stereotypes about women that are believed and communicated in your culture?
3   What is your personal view of men and women's role:
   ■   In relationships?
   ■   In family?
   ■   In business?
   ■   In politics?
4   How do your personal views of men and your personal views of women influence how you relate to, communicate with, and interact with men and women in each of the above contexts?
5   What are the specific issues women may experience in business in specific countries in North America, Central America, South America, Europe, Asia, the Middle East, and Africa?
6   What are some methods to address negative gender stereotypes, and redefine them such that they are changed into positives?
7   How does religion influence the expected role of men and women?

NOTES

1   http://www.cia.gov/library/publications/the-world-factbook/geos/xx.html# People, Retrieved, February 4, 2010.
2   Van de Vliert, E. and Van der Vegt, G. "Women and Wages Worldwide: How the National Proportion of Working Women Brings Underpayment into the Organization," *Organization Studies*, Vol. 25, No. 6, 2004, pp. 969–986.
3   Ibid.
4   House, Karen Elliot. *On Saudi Arabia*. New York: Alfred A. Knox, 2012.
5   Kung, Hans, "A Vatican Spring," *The New York Times*, February 28, 2013.

6 "Rape and Murder in Delhi," *The Economist*, January 5, 2013.

7 Kristof, Nicholas D. "Is Delhi So Different from Steubenville?" *The New York Times*, January 13, 2013.

8 Ahamari, Sohrab, "The Woman Who Dared to Drive," *The Wall Street Journal*, March 2, 2013.

9 Rubin, Alissa, "Painful Payment for Afghan Debt of 'Alissa Rubin,' " *The New York Times*, April 1, 2013.

10 *USA Today*, April 30, 2013.

11 Halpern, D. and Cheung, F. *Women at the Top; Powerful Leaders Tell Us How to Combine Work and Family*, Malden, MA: Wiley-Blackwell, 2008.

12 Ibid.

13 Ibid.

14 "Arab Women Rights, Some Say They Don't Want Them," *The Economist*, March 27, 2010, p. 53.

15 Ibid, p. 171.

16 Meyerson, D. E. and Fletcher, J. K. "A Modest Manifesto for Shattering the Glass Ceiling," in Sylvia Ann Hewlett and Carolyn Buck Luce (eds), *Harvard Business Review on Women in Business*. Boston, MA: Harvard Business School Press, 2005, pp. 69–94.

17 Ibid., p. 70.

18 Ibid., p. 94.

19 "The Conundrum of the 'Glass Ceiling,'" *The Economist*, July 23, 2005, pp. 63–65.

20 "Female Power," *The Economist*, January, 2, 2010, pp. 49–51.

21 "Renard, Tara Siegel," *The New York Times*, February 23, 2013.

22 "Britons 'Accept' Pay Sexism," *BBC NEWS*, February 28, 2006, www.newsvote. bbc.co.uk/1/hi/business/3038394.stm.

23 "Most Powerful Women in Business, the Power 50: Why Are Some Women More Successful in Some Countries Than in Others?" *Fortune*, September 27, 2002.

24 www.AdvancingWomen2003.org.

25 Clark, N. "Getting Women into Boardrooms, by Law," *The International Herald Tribune*, Thursday, January 28, 2010, p. 1.

26 "We Did It!" *The Economist*, January 2, 2010, p. 7.

27 Clark, "Getting Women into Boardrooms."

28 Ibid., p. 9.

29 Halpern, D. and Cheung, F. *Women at the Top: Powerful Leaders Tell Us How to Combine Work and Family*. Malden, MA: Wiley-Blackwell, 2008.

30 Tyler, J. and McCullough, J. "Violating Prescriptive Stereotypes on Job Resumes: A Self-Presentational Perspective," *Management Communication Quarterly*, Vol. 23, No. 2, 2009, pp. 272–287.

31 Ibid., p. 273.

32 Mihail, D. "Gender-Based Stereotypes in the Workplace: The Case of Greece," *Equal Opportunities International*, Vol. 25, No. 5, 2006, pp. 373–388.

33 Glanton, E. "Pay Gap Endures at Highest Levels," *AP News*, womenconnect.com, November 10, 1998.

34 Glass Ceiling Commission. The Glass Ceiling Fact-Finding Report. "Good Business: Making Full Use of the Nation's Human Capital," 1995.

35 "She Works, He Doesn't," *Newsweek*, May 12, 2003.

36 Catalyst 2002 Census of Women Corporate Officers and Top Earners of the *Fortune* 500.

37 "Britons 'Accept' Pay Sexism," *BBC NEWS*, February 28, 2006, www.newsvote. bbc.co.uk/1/hi/business/3038394.stm.

38 "The Conundrum of the 'Glass Ceiling,'" *The Economist*, July 23, 2005, pp. 63–65.

39 Adler, N. and Izraeli, D. "Where in the World Are the Women Executives?" *Business Quarterly*, London, 1994.

40 Wernick, E. "Preparedness, Career Advancement, and the 'Glass Ceiling,' " *Glass Ceiling Commission*, May 1994.

41 Adler, N. J. and Izraeli, D. (eds). *Competitive Frontiers: Women Managing Across Border*. Cambridge, MA: Blackwell Publishers, 1994, p. 28.

42 Ibid., p. 27.
43 Lyness, K. and Kropf, M. "The Relationships of National Gender Equality and Organizational Support with Work–Family Balance: A Study of European Managers," *Human Relations*, Vol. 58, No. 1, 2005, pp. 33–60.
44 Yegisu, C. "Can Men Stomach Marrying Wealthier Women?" *Daily News and Economic Review*, Istanbul, January 23–24, 2010, p. 10.
45 Tanton, M. *Women in Management: A Developing Presence*, London: Routledge, 1994, p. 82.
46 Halpern, D. and Cheung, F. *Women at the Top: Powerful Leaders Tell Us How to Combine Work and Family*. Malden, MA: Wiley-Blackwell, 2008.
47 http://www.pathfinder.com/ParentTime/workfamily/workcare.html.
48 Halpern and Cheung, *Women at the Top*, p. 176.
49 Ibid.
50 Chen, Yu, and Miner, "Motivation to Manage."
51 Ibid.
52 Ibid.
53 Lyness and Kropf, "The Relationships of National Gender Equality."
54 Carlson, D., Grzywacz, J., and Zivnuska, S. "Is Work–Family Balance More than Conflict and Enrichment," *Human Relations*, Vol. 62, No. 10, 2009, pp. 1459–1486.
55 Halpern and Cheung, *Women at the Top*.
56 Ibid.
57 Hoobler, J., Wayne, S., and Lemmon, G. "Bosses' Perceptions of Family–Work Conflict and Women's Promotability: 'Glass Ceiling' Effects," *Academy of Management Journal*, Vol. 52, No. 5, 2009, pp. 939–957.
58 Ibid.
59 Wyld, D. "How Do Women Fare When the Promotion Rules Change?" *Academy of Management Perspectives*, Vol. 22, No. 4, 2008, pp. 83–85.
60 Bell, M., McLaughlin, M., and Sequeira, J. "Discrimination, Harassment, and the 'Glass Ceiling': Women Executives as Change Agents," *Journal of Business Ethics*, Vol. 37, 2002, pp. 65–76.
61 Williams, M., Paluck, E., and Spencer-Rodgers, J. "The Masculinity of Money: Automatic Stereotypes Predict Gender Differences in Estimated Salaries," *Psychology of Women Quarterly*, Vol. 34, 2010, pp. 7–20.
62 Van de Vliert, E. and Van der Vegt, G. "Women and Wages Worldwide: How the National Proportion of Working Women Brings Underpayment into the Organization," *Organization Studies*, Vol. 25, No. 6, 2004, pp. 969–986.
63 Domsch, M. "Quality Management in Gender and Diversity: The Role of Auditing." *European Commission, Women in Science and Technology: The Business Perspective*, Belgium: European Communities, 2006, pp. 37–47.
64 Ibid.
65 Catalyst 2002 Census of Women Corporate Officers and Top Earners of the *Fortune* 500.
66 www.advancingwomen.com.
67 Karsten, M. F. *Management and Gender: Issues and Attitudes*. Westport, CT: Praeger Publishers, 1994.
68 Catalyst 2002 Census of Women Corporate Officers and Top Earners of the *Fortune* 500.
69 Meyerson, D. E. and Fletcher, J. K. "A Modest Manifesto for Shattering, the 'Glass Ceiling'," *Harvard Business Review on Women in Business*, Harvard Business School Press, 2005, p. 70.
70 Domsch, "Quality Management in Gender and Diversity, p. 38.
71 Solomon, C. M. *Women Managers in the Global Workplace: Success through Intercultural Understanding*. Arlington, Virginia: Mobility, January 2006.
72 Tharenou, P. "Disruptive Decisions to Leave Home: Gender and Family Differences in Expatriation Choices," *Organizational Behavior and Human Decision Processes*, Vol. 105, 2008, pp. 183–200.

73 Inch, G., McIntyre, N., and Napier, N. "The Expatriate 'Glass Ceiling': The Second Layer of Glass," *Journal of Business Ethics*, Vol. 83, 2008, pp. 19–28.

74 Ibid.

75 Altman, Y. and Shortland, S. "Women and International Assignments: Taking Stock – A 25-Year Review," *Human Resource Management*, Vol. 47, No. 2, 2008, pp. 199–216.

76 Ibid, p. 207.

77 Inch, McIntyre, and Napier, "The Expatriate 'Glass Ceiling.'"

78 Adler, N. J. *Organizational Behavior*, 3rd edn. Cincinnati, OH: South-Western Publishing, 1997, pp. 308–309.

79 Adler, N. J. *International Dimensions of Organizational Behavior*, 4th edn. New York: Southwestern/ Thomson Learning, 2002.

80 "Women, Sex and Power," *Fortune*, August 5, 1996.

81 Wajcman, J. *Managing Like a Man*. University Park, PA: Pennsylvania State University Press, 1998.

82 Adler, N. J. and Izraeli, D. J. (eds). *Women in Management Worldwide*. London: M.E. Sharpe, 1988, pp. 20–24.

83 Wilkof, M. V. "Is Your Company and Its Culture Women-Friendly?" *Journal for Quality and Participation*, June 1995.

84 Beatty, S. "A Power Confab for Exclusive Businesswomen," *The Wall Street Journal*, May 10, 1999.

85 Shellenberger, A. "Work & Family: The New Pace of Work Makes Taking a Break for Child Care Scarier," *The Wall Street Journal*, May 19, 1999.

86 "Work Week," *The Wall Street Journal*, May 11, 1999.

87 Adler, *International Dimensions of Organizational Behavior*, pp. 173–174.

88 Sandberg, S. *Lean In: Women, Work, and the Will to Lead*. New York: Knopf Publishing Group, 2013.

89 Tesfachew, T., Zahidi, S., and Ibarra, H. "Measuring the Corporate Gender Gap," in S. Zahidi and H. Ibarra (eds), *The Corporate Gender Gap Report 2010*. Geneva, Switzerland: World Economic Forum, 2010. Retrieved April 27, 2010, from http://www.weforum.org/pdf/gendergap/ corporate2010.pdf.

ADDITIONAL FEATURES

Please visit the companion website at: www.routledge.com/cw/Moran where you will find additional case studies, study aides, and instructor resources.

6 MOTIVATING THE GLOBAL WORKFORCE
The case for diversity and inclusion

Diversity in the world is a basic characteristic of human society, and also the key condition for a lively and dynamic world as we see today.

Hu Jintao[1]

We need to give each other the space to grow, to be ourselves, to exercise our diversity. We need to give each other space so that we may both give and receive such beautiful things as ideas, openness, dignity, joy, healing, and inclusion.

Max de Pree[2]

Most executives state that the effective utilization of the talents of all employees is the organization's greatest asset. This has been viewed as more challenging for multinational enterprises (MNEs) with an increasing multicultural workforce. "In recent years, diversity management has been considered both an issue of employment relations and an issue for all sections of the organization, from financing and accounting to customer relations and from strategy to marketing."[3] To unleash the talent and potential of this changing workforce, companies and governments are assessing their organizational systems to capitalize on the benefits of a diverse workforce and clientele.

In the field of knowledge management, it has been widely acknowledged that having greater relevant problem-solving and decision-making differentiation, or diversity, is a competitive advantage. This is especially the case for highly complex and uncertain international business competitive environments.[4] Diversity in the forms of culture, age, gender, racio-ethnicity, nationality, personality, values, and attitudes[5] provided greater awareness of, and openness to, potentially relevant information. This additional information generally produces better decisions in complex environments than those achieved by more homogeneous decision-makers.[6]

The main issue for achieving these problem-solving advantages is that diversity must be strongly integrated within work groups. Diversity increases the forces of divergence and disagreement, potentially resulting in greater levels of conflict and lower social integration. People tend to be more attracted to working with others who share similar values and attitudes, and tend to be less attracted to those they regard as outsiders, that is, different from themselves in important ways.[7] Bartlett and Beamish argued that the task of integrating diverse capabilities across an MNE was a more important task than developing a corporate strategy based on taking advantage of that diversity.[8]

The purpose of this chapter is threefold. First, it makes the case for why cultural diversity is an important competitive advantage for business organizations. Second, it reviews the potential sources of useful diversity. Third, it discusses the critical question of how to integrate cultural diversity so as to achieve diversity's benefits, because without effective integration, homogeneity may result in better outcomes. The evidence supports the management adage: "Differentiation + Integration = Performance (D + I = P)."

In this context, global leadership itself is considered as a powerful integrator of differentiation and diversity. Ethical, visionary, and even situational leadership are all processes intended to facilitate the greatest expression of the maximum potential of each employee. Leadership, integrates human resources into a common purpose despite their differences.

CULTURAL DIVERSITY COMPETITIVE ADVANTAGES

Knowledge management has been considered a potential source of competitive advantage in international business and comparative management since the times of Lawrence and Lorsch.[9] They observed that increasing amounts of problem-solving and decision-making differentiation helped MNEs to "bridge unavoidable differences among cultures."

Later, Lawrence and Dyer[10] argued that the environmental uncertainty characteristic in international markets produced high levels of information complexity so that it was more difficult to plan an effective course of action than in domestic markets. As information complexity increased, the amount of information needed to make informed decisions also increased. The most effective response that an MNE could make was to increase its problem-solving and decision-making diversity, thereby increasing the capacity to learn (see Chapter 4).

MNEs could increase diversity by including, in its decision-making, managers tasked with global, regional, local, product, and functional roles. Headquarters' managers would have the global perspective of the entire company. Subsidiary managers could be counted on for regional and local views, and might also represent differing cross-cultural perspectives depending on their nationality. Product managers would represent their product-related perspectives. Bringing together the often-antithetical functional views of marketers and operations managers, for example, could provide more creative corporate decisions. Marketing is usually focused on customer needs and is usually organized as a profit center. Operations is usually focused on operational efficiency and is usually organized as a cost center.

Greater cultural diversity could be obtained by including local country managers, especially those who were themselves citizens of those localities who would be familiar with local cultural, social, political, and economic conditions. In American MNEs especially, it is common even for headquarters' managers to represent cultural diversity because the top jobs go to the most competent employees regardless of nationality. By contrast, in Japanese MNEs, Japanese managers almost always hold the top jobs at headquarters.

The more that these various kinds of diversity were allowed to participate in problem-solving, the more differentiated the information available to influence the eventual decision, and the less the uncertainty. The goal of maximizing diversity of perspectives within decision-making teams was to ensure that the best and most comprehensive information was used to set the corporate strategies intended to maximize MNE performance.

Bartlett and Ghoshal[11] observed that increased decision-making diversity would only become a competitive advantage for MNEs if the diversity could be integrated into the MNE's decision-making processes. "The ability to link and leverage knowledge is increasingly the factor that differentiates the winners from the losers," they said.

Bartlett and Ghoshal argued, however, that the key problem was not obtaining greater decision-making diversity but ensuring that it received a hearing and was included in the problem-solving process. Newly included diversity was usually a minority perspective intentionally added to pre-existing decision-making groups that were already used to dominating decision outcomes themselves.

It was not enough that minority perspectives existed on a management team because these perspectives could be excluded from the decision-making process by an organization's dominant perspectives, and the rule of the majority. Derrida,[12] the French existential philosopher, noted that there was generally a democratic principle in play that could predict the probable impact of different perspectives on decision-making outcomes. Perspectives that constituted a democratic majority would dominate decisions because the majority's more similar views would discount the discordant views of minorities.

If no single perspective formed a democratic majority, then compromises were more likely among the bigger pluralities. Even here, a small minority was likely to be ignored or excluded unless it was sufficiently large to form a majority with a large plurality. An organization could only ensure that minority cultural diversity usefully participated in decision-making if special integrative efforts were made to ensure their inclusion.

Buckley and Carter[13] defined knowledge as the antithesis of uncertainty. Uncertainty makes decision-makers unsure about which actions to undertake to achieve desired outcomes. Greater knowledge in advance of decision-making should lead to reduced uncertainty about which actions will be effective. The problem with knowledge, however, is that it is not clear whether an assertion is really knowledge or only belief until after it has been applied and an outcome achieved. At the time the decision is being made, knowledge appears to be just someone's belief based on incomplete information – a prediction – rather than a demonstrably true belief.[14] According to Buckley and Carter, the key factor affecting performance was the quality of judgment of those responsible for choosing which beliefs the firm would act on and which not.

Kogut and Zander[15] divided knowledge into what they called "explicit," and "tacit." *Explicit* knowledge was defined as easy to write down and therefore easy to teach because it was not complex and was easy to state in the form of general principles. It would include the kinds of theories and action principles commonly taught in business education.

By contrast, *tacit* or implicit knowledge was based on having relevant experience and understanding what would, or would not work in practice. This tacit knowledge is difficult to write down or teach because it is complex and often situational. Its value is often contingent on the ability of decision-makers to see its value and make it work in new applications. Kogut and Zander argued that it was this tacit knowledge that most positively affected MNE performance if it could be successfully transferred into the decision process. And because it was difficult to state and teach, the individuals with the tactic knowledge needed to be included in the decision process. Li and Shenkar[16] later added to the definition of tacit knowledge that it was experiential, idiosyncratic, and rooted in action – therefore difficult to communicate, or learn except through direct experience. However, it was also of great value strategically because it was unique and difficult for competitors to acquire.[17]

For example,[18] global marketers generally believe that there are a number of global marketing practices that are effective in any global marketplace. These practices are taught as explicit knowledge to all marketers. In a study of Canadian SMEs doing business in Malaysia and Singapore, it was found that some of these practices were useful for building high performance relationships, but others were useless. And there were two local relationship-building practices that were even more important. A Western marketer would never know about these two local practices until he/she observed them in action, and they became part of his/her tacit understanding about how to market in this region. The only way to obtain this tacit knowledge expertise would be to include experienced Southeast Asian marketers in one's planning, but most Western companies did not because they believed in the universal principles (see Chapter 12).

Diversity and work team performance

It has been for many years an aphorism in Organizational Behavior that higher differentiation or diversity, combined with strong integration, led to higher performance for any MNE. This aphorism is expressed as a formula; $D + I = P$. Current research, however, does not entirely support the view that cultural diversity necessarily results in higher performance.

Some studies have reported performance gains attributed to cultural diversity in work teams, while others have reported the opposite finding. Earley and Moskowski,[19] for example, reported that homogeneous (low diversity) and highly heterogeneous (high diversity) work teams achieved approximately the same levels of performance over time, and both substantially outperformed moderately heterogeneous teams.

Attempting to resolve the question definitively, Stahl et al.[20] conducted a major meta-analysis of 108 previous empirical studies, including 10,632 work teams. They concluded that there was no significant relationship between greater cultural diversity and higher performance. However, the reasons why the culturally diverse work teams generally did not achieve higher performance was because their integration was not sufficient, as predicted by theory. This led to greater levels of conflict and lower social integration than in the more homogeneous groups. Exhibit 6.1 provides monitoring activities that global organizational leaders can utilize to effectively assist the improvement of performance for all employees.

Exhibit 6.2 provides a list of the knowledge, skills, and abilities that all individuals can learn to help improve their own performance when working with individuals who are of a different culture than themselves.

Work groups with higher levels of cultural diversity did, however, achieve significantly higher creativity in their problem-solving. Group members generally felt significantly higher levels of satisfaction that their personal needs had been adequately fulfilled. Creativity could be considered potentially a competitive advantage in itself since standard solutions would also be more predictable and easier for competitors to counter.

There was also no difference between culturally diverse and culturally homogeneous groups in terms of the effectiveness with which they succeeded in communicating. Including

EXHIBIT 6.1 EXAMPLES OF INDICATORS THAT COMPANIES CAN USE TO MONITOR EMPLOYEE PERFORMANCE

- The implementation of employee surveys to evaluate employee attitudes and degrees of satisfaction, and identify areas in need of improvement.
- Ongoing discussions with employee networks and their resource groups.
- The use of workforce profiling to summarize nationalities, religions, gender, languages, and age to understand demographics and understand where there might be an under-representation.
- Setting up a database of employee skills to monitor employee development and progression.
- Providing for diverse perspectives in standard business performance reviews, and provisions for equal pay evaluations.
- Examining the complaints registered with regard to bullying, harassment, and the nature with which, the speed by which, and how solutions are found.
- Examining business costs due to absenteeism, lateness, and illness.
- Monitoring employee responses in exit interviews and organizing comments by gender and ethnicity to determine if there are patterns.

Source: Adapted from European Commission, "The Business Case for Diversity: Good Practices in the Workplace." Luxemburg Office for Official Publications of the European Communities, 2005. Retrieved April 14, 2010 from http://ec.europa.eu/social/Blob Servlet?docID=1428&langID=en.

greater cultural diversity did not, therefore, reduce the ability to communicate effectively within work teams.

We know that diversity management is directly linked to team functioning, and can either improve or upset team performance.[21] As organizations rely on teams to accomplish a vast number of tasks, the question of how teams should be composed and managed has come under greater scrutiny.[22] The composition of teams should take into account the salience of diversity in a team, and the levels of interdependence and longevity that a team will have to deal with,[23] along with the reward structure associated with team output.

For example, Homan et al.[24] reported that a high degree of diversity in both high-performing and low-performing teams influenced performance. The reward structure greatly influenced the highest performing teams, while the teams in which diversity was most salient and had the lowest level of openness also were the lowest performing teams.

Furthermore, the degree to which work teams provide cognitive stimulation to team members impacts team performance. In a recent study,[25] team members' need for cognition was considered in a study of 83 teams from eight organizations. Two types of diversity — age and education — had greater needs for cognitive stimulation. Team performance

EXHIBIT 6.2 SOME KEY INDIVIDUAL COMPETENCIES RELATED TO PERFORMANCE

Barrett encourages individuals and teams who are working within the global arena to cultivate the following competencies. Some of these are tacit and learned through experience. Others are explicitly learned through education and training. Most can be developed with effort.

Knowledge to cultivate

- Learn about other nations' histories, cultures, national systems, values, customs, and the many ethnic groups that live within these nations.
- Learn how different systems, organizations, groups, and individuals discover how to work together through understanding change, management practices, and philosophies.
- Learn about group development and group dynamics to understand how groups interact.
- Learn to understand how the macrolevel (nation, organization) and microlevels (group, individual) of interaction are co-created.

Abilities to cultivate

- Learn how to be at ease with the unfamiliar.
- Learn how to think like people who are remarkably different from yourself. This helps discourage ethnocentrism.
- Learn how to *learn*, and be open to continuous learning and to rapidly adapting to new situations.
- Learn how to cultivate meaningful relationships with people very different from yourself both culturally and personally, based upon respect, cooperation, trust, shared goals, and constructive ways of handling conflict.
- Learn how to manage your stress, and learn to see difficulties as opportunities to *learn*.
- Learn to be aware of yourself; learn to accept feedback, both positive and negative.
- Learn to focus on improving yourself; learn to take personal responsibility rather than blaming others for your own limitations or difficulties.

Source: Adapted from Barrett, G. "Cultivating Global Teams: Diversity Management Square (DM2)," in C. Mann and K. Gotz (eds), *Borderless Business: Managing the Far-Flung Enterprise*. Westport, CN: Praeger, 2006, pp. 275–294.

increased when this need was higher and was satisfied. The implications of this research were that the "need for cognition . . . is a more specific variable that can be more easily linked to the demands entailed by diverse teams performing knowledge-based tasks, but also lends itself well to drawing managerial implications. Need for cognition represents a staple, but not invariant, intrinsic motivation to process a wide range of information."[26]

In another study of cross-national cognitive diversity differences,[27] it was found that American management samples had higher cognitive diversity than Chinese samples, and much higher diversity than Thai samples. The study argued that perhaps this greater cognitive diversity was one reason why Americans and Chinese were more successful as international traders than Thai. They would be better able to handle a greater range of potentially relevant information, and find more creative and innovative strategies and practices.

Globalization is shaping our world today. Globalization has the effect of bringing cultural diversity into direct contact, magnifying the need for tacit understandings of how to proceed in a greater number of cultural contexts. Advances in telecommunications, mass transportation, technology, and changes in the global political arena have led to the emergence of a global, information-oriented culture. With the expansion of globalization, awareness of the global complexities involved in cross-cultural interactions has become more necessary. Globalization has greatly increased interaction at the macro-level, as exemplified by the expansion of technology through business. At the micro-level, it is exemplified by the individual use of laptops, cellular phones, and the Internet to communicate anywhere at any time. While it can be said that at the macro-level there is a form of global culture around the use of technology, communication advances, and the practice of business, at the micro-level, the experiences, values, perceptions, and behaviors of individuals vary within and across national and ethnic cultures. We need to include those with local knowledge in our decision-making to make sure our decisions make sense in local contexts.

Capitalizing on human diversity

As a concept, diversity has different meanings and applications, depending on where you are in the world. Within our information society, it is important to recognize that increasing globalism enormously impacts the workforce worldwide. For leading-edge organizations, this denotes the creation of an organizational cultural norm to embrace diversity to maximize the potential of personnel, especially through cohesive work teams.[28]

Research[29] has demonstrated that as the length of time increases when diverse group members work together, the negative effects of *surface-level diversity* (i.e., age, sex, and ethnicity) decrease. In other words, as you get to know your teammates, you relate to them more as they are, and less as they might appear to be as stereotypes. Furthermore, in this research, the effects of *deep-level diversity* (attitudes, beliefs, values) were positive because they led through discussion to increased information about each group member. These deep-level diversity characteristics at the group level meant that, over time, the richness of information exchange was augmented. This produced a more profound mutual understanding and greater satisfaction among members.

For global managers, the challenge is to find innovative ways to improve human commitment and performance at work. Since so many people aim to achieve their full potential through their work and career, the new work culture fosters values such as empowerment and character development. Success is gauged not so much in terms of organizational status but in the quality of work life. There is very strong empirical confirmation that successful diversity management and a resulting improvement in organizational performance are positively correlated.[30] Furthermore, for meta-industrial workers, Nair[31] suggests that the quest for personal/professional excellence and meaningful business relationships takes precedence over climbing the corporate ladder and the pursuit of external rewards.

A global illustration: European Union diversity and e-Europe

An excellent example of working together for a common good is the European Union (EU). In business today, people are the most important source of sustainable competitive advantage. Every person brings a unique combination of background, heritage, gender, religion, education, and experience to the workplace. This diversity represents a noteworthy source of new ideas and vitality. The phenomenon of growing diversity in the work environment is worldwide. Europe today is a prime example as 27 national cultures now work together to integrate as members of the EU. What began as a small economic community seeking a greater share of the global market has evolved into a grand plan of socio-political association with its own unique constitution. Simons[32] has articulated the challenge of diversity and globalization:

> Our present diversity challenges are being determined by forces shaping the economy and business world generally and cannot be discussed in isolation from them. Diversity is about globalization, organizational learning, and the growing importance of knowledge management, just as much as it is about recruitment, equal opportunity, workforce demographics, and social integration. It concerns the information technology that is almost daily revolutionizing communication. It affects interactive networking and transport. It is perhaps the critical issue in many mergers and acquisitions – and often the least attended to! It is at the root of how organizations transform themselves. . . .
> Historically, Europe, or the "Old World," is different from the lands in which European emigrants settled and made their own. Europe has always been very diverse, and Europeans have always been conscious of their diversity. They differ from North Americans in what they do about it. In the best of times, Europeans believe that "good fences make good neighbors." In the worst of times, those who attempt to shape or create or reshape those borders are painted in blood. . . .
> Diverse by nature, the European Union got its start in the search for peace and prosperity after history's most devastating war (World War II, 1939–1945). . . . In Europe, economic cooperation among its diverse peoples was the starting point. Only later did this cooperative enterprise begin to take responsibility for a social and cultural integration whose necessity, utility, and desirability continue to be questioned every step of the way.

The Cultural Diversity Market Study reported that the European Committee for Standardization (CEN) has been focusing its activities on cultural diversity and e-business.[33]

E-Europe feels that global issues increasingly demand global response, and that is the reason that there is a strong need for a collective European approach. Globalization, enlargement, and internationalization are keywords in e-Europe. This requires consideration of the cultural and linguistic diversity of Europe, thereby giving equal chances to all businesses and citizens in Europe to benefit from the Information Society.[34]

This study had three main conclusions:

1   An identified lack of awareness regarding the importance of cultural diversity was apparent. Diversity was not a high priority of EU industry or its consumers. However, there were many activities handled in a multicultural manner.

2   Issues surrounding cultural diversity are addressed primarily from a technical perspective, with little or no quantitative look at the costs and benefits.

3   The study recognizes the need for cooperation within the international environment and within each industry.

The EU has had to overcome periodic conflicts in the past by working together across cultural differences to build a multinational, multicultural, multilingual powerhouse. In 2013, Germany continued to guarantee bailout funding for the Greek economy despite strong expressions of anti-German feelings by Greek protesters. At the same time, Germany and France worked together at the governmental level to help stave off financial crises in Spain and Italy.

SOURCES OF GLOBAL DIVERSITY

All in all, diversity is related to the vast range of differences that requires attention to facilitate living and working together effectively. Human diversity has been popularly understood to refer to differences of color, ethnic origin, gender, sexual or religious preferences, age, and disabilities. In academic research, diversity has been characterized as either surface-level or deep-level diversity.[35] Surface-level includes demographic characteristics such as gender, age, racio-ethnicity, and nationality. Deep-level refers to differences between individuals' psychological characteristics such as personality types, cognitive preferences, values, and attitudes. Personality preferences, distributions have been found to vary by culture,[36] as have work related values.[37]

Stated definitions of organizational diversity recognize a wider range of characteristics. According to American Express Financial Advisors,[38] they include: race, gender, age, physical ability, physical appearance, nationality, cultural heritage, personal background, functional experience, position in the organization, mental and physical challenges, family responsibilities, sexual orientation, military experience, educational background, style differences, economic status, thinking patterns, political backgrounds, city/state/region of residence, IQ level, smoking preference, weight, marital status, nontraditional job, religion, white collar, language, blue collar, and height.

Migration/immigration as a source of diversity

Historically and currently, the movement of people from one locale to another has encouraged the formation of our diversity. In the late 1990s, Allan Wilson and his colleagues used mtDNA to determine human ancestry. By comparing mtDNA and Y chromosomes from people of diverse populations, they were able to map human migration originating in Africa many years ago.[39] "Migration has helped to create humans, drove us to conquer a planet, shaped our societies, and promises to reshape them again. . . . If they [people] had not moved and intermingled as they did, they probably would have evolved into a different species."[40]

In addition to business and government global travelers, and tourists, there are also four other major categories of people on the move:[41]

Refugees: People living outside their country of nationality, afraid to return for reasons of race, religion, social affiliation, or political opinion.

Internally displaced persons: People forced to flee their homes because of armed conflict, but who have not yet crossed international boundaries. Like refugees, they have generally lost all they own and are not protected by their national governments. Today, we estimate that there are 41.9 million refugees and internally displaced persons, many of whom seek asylum from some kind of persecution or discrimination.[42]

Migrant workers: People, both skilled and unskilled, who work outside their home country, including employed migrants without legal permission to work, and undocumented immigrants. It is estimated that there are about 214 million international migrant workers and their families worldwide, and an estimated 20–30 million of them are unauthorized.[43]

Economic refugees: People who legally immigrate, or attempt to illegally enter developed countries hoping to improve the lifestyle of themselves and their families. In Canada, there is a special class of expedited immigrants consisting of people bringing assets of at least Cdn$500,000, willing to invest Cdn$160,000 in a five-year bond intended to create jobs in Canada. In the United States, refugees from Cuba and Haiti attempt to cross the Caribbean sea to find better economic and social prospects in Florida.

The social fabric in host countries is often reconfigured and strained by massive waves of immigrants, legal or illegal, who migrate to live and work permanently or temporarily in another country. The demographic changes may transform a nation from developing economy to industrialized nation. These mass migrations are usually in pursuit of a better way of life. However, this movement of people from different cultures and backgrounds has frequently caused costly, complex social and financial problems for the host culture struggling to absorb the new arrivals.[44] Canada, for example, accepts approximately 350,000 immigrants of all types every year, though its total population is only approximately 30 million.

Exhibit 6.3 summarizes the dual impact of the ongoing push and pull of immigration. When people leave their homes, generally there is a "push" factor from the country of origin, and a "pull" factor from the destination country. Of course, individual, religious, political, and/or economic reasons play a critical role.

EXHIBIT 6.3 ROOT CAUSES OF IMMIGRATION

Principal "push" factors	Principal "pull" factors
War and civil strife including religious conflicts	Substantial immigration markets and channels opened up to the West
Economic decline and rising poverty	Family reunion
Rising unemployment	Safety
Population pressures; burgeoning numbers of unemployed young people	Freedom from fear of violence, persecution, hunger, and/or poverty
Political instability	Political freedom
Large-scale natural disasters and ecological degradation	Economic opportunity
Human rights violations	Education
Denial of education and healthcare for selected minorities including women; other persecutions	Maintaining ethnic identity
Government resettlement policies threatening ethnic integrity	Access to advances in communication and technology
Resurgent nationalism	Hope

Source: Adapted from Stalker, P. "The Work of Strangers: A Survey of International Migration," in W. R. Bohning and M. L. Schloeter (eds), *Aids in Place of Migration*. Geneva: International Labour Office, 1994.

Recent immigrants can bring new energy, talent, and enthusiasm to their new homes, communities, and new workplaces, while adding both human and financial capital. The mix of citizenry, ethnicity, and tribal backgrounds is like a mosaic. We believe that the global work culture is best characterized by two words: change and diversity. It is best to remind ourselves that, as in nature, diversity makes for adaptation.

Three additional global trends

As the twenty-first century progresses, global leaders who understand what is happening to societies and work places should also be aware of two other trends impacting world development.

Resurgence of the world's attention to peoples' interest in their ethnic identities, religious roots, and ancient affiliations are related to conflict. "One-sixth, at most, of the world's population identifies with politically active cultural groups. More precisely a survey. . . has identified 268 politically significant national and minority peoples in the larger countries of the world. The outer bound of potential supporters for these ethno-political movements is slightly more than one billion, or 17.7 percent of the global population."[45]

An emergence of transnational ethnic groups or global tribes who have a major influence on international trade and the economy. The latter, whatever their origin, are frequently venture capitalists, financiers, arbitrageurs, and entrepreneurs who benefit by the discipline of their traditions.

A third trend to recognize is the desire of peoples everywhere for the protection of their human rights both political and/or economic, including at work. This means that leadership should always be committed to resolving any conflicts that arise, with full respect toward the rights of all individuals involved. The United Nations has best articulated their aspirations in its Declaration of Human Rights. Those who would be competent and nondiscriminatory global leaders recognize that both society and the corporate work environment must follow the declaration's guidance.

Global diversity and conflict

Longstanding conflicts between cultural groups can have an effect on how well employees work together in international organizations.

In the real world, relations between most groups have a history; they are often influenced by complex socio-cultural factors that extend their influence over long periods of time. The history of slavery in the United States is likely to be relevant to the present relations in that country. The history of European colonialism is likely to be relevant to the present relations between newly arrived Third World immigrants and indigenous European populations. The past history of English domination in Canada is likely to influence the present state of relations between English and French Canadians.[46]

Because of technological and human advancement, our world is deeply interconnected, and we are in constant contact with our differences, characterized by varying cultures, ethnicities, religions, fundamental beliefs, and values. When in conflict with each other, it is difficult for individuals to perform to their potential. Human discord results from many factors and, throughout history, there are examples of forced assimilation of minority cultures into the dominant culture, in both nations and organizations. However, consistently, history has shown that few cultures can be completely assimilated into another. There are many current and historical global examples of the differential treatment of various ethnic groups in political, social, and economic areas.

Currently in Canada, the federal government and a number of mainline Christian churches have apologized and offered compensation for the attempted cultural assimilation of First Nations' Aboriginal children through the twentieth-century residential schools' program. These apologies were required after Canada's Supreme Court ruled that residential schools violated First Nations' rights under Canadian law.

"Disadvantages" means socially derived inequalities in material well-being or political access in comparison with other social groups. In chaos theory, or "the butterfly effect," events in one part of the world can significantly affect events on the other side of the world. Likewise, events in the political arena spill into the business arena, and political oppression is linked to social and economic oppression. "Traditional concepts, like the balance of power or ideology, are. . . not as useful as they once were in explaining the sources of. . . conflict, particularly when conflicts are rooted in a complex and rich brew of ethno nationalism, religion, socio-economic grievances. . . globalized markets, and geopolitical shifts."[47]

We must learn to appreciate the fact that our common survival and the satisfaction of our universal needs and concerns are interdependently linked. All must work toward our common survival through multilateral action that reflects appreciation and acceptance of differences, with mutual respect for each other. In order to do so effectively, learning conflict analysis and resolution skills are necessary in today's world.

Bartos and Wehr[48] define conflict as something that occurs when actors utilize conflict behavior against each other to achieve incompatible goals. While this is defined in the more extreme sense, they believe that determining the operational causes for conflict should help us in understanding the conflict, as this is the first step toward finding ways to resolve it. Understanding why individuals or groups are engaged in conflict behavior requires us to learn what these individual grievances, goals, and motivations are with regard to the conflict, and then determining ways to find an equitable solution. One of the greatest causes of conflict is when one group, or all groups, involved in the dispute remain inflexible and see only their own perspective as valid. Through refusing to comprehend, acknowledge, and appreciate the perspective of another, while holding on to stereotypical assumptions of the other party, conflict behavior is almost an assured outcome.

An example of one organization that seeks to address this need is Stirling University. This school has recently developed a course for leaders, students, writers, and politicians to learn skills in conflict resolution, management, and prevention. Course director Vassilis Fouskas states:[49]

Although we would all wish otherwise, there is little likelihood that the world in the twenty-first century will be a better place to live in, or that it will be without conflict, war, dictatorship, terrorism, genocide, or poverty. The least we can do as academics and teachers is to try to produce serious-minded, prospective leaders able to understand the past, intervene in the present, and shape a more just, fair, and equitable world.

INTEGRATING DIVERSITY

The benefits of diversity in terms of greater collective access to relevant information, more creative solutions, and reduced conflict, can only be achieved when problem-solving and decision-making groups are tightly integrated. There is a general human "similarity-attraction" tendency[50] for people to prefer to work with, and cooperate with, others whom they perceive as similar to themselves in values, beliefs, and attitudes. Less similar individuals tend to be perceived as outsiders.[51] As a result, there is a naturally greater tendency for more diverse decision-making groups to have greater levels of intra-group controversy and conflict.

In addition, MNE decision-making groups are under considerable external stress and time pressure because they are tasked with understanding a complex and relatively unfamiliar international environment. Usually strategic planning is undertaken because the firm's performance is less than expected, or worse, has begun to decline due to changes in the competitive environment. Decisions are needed quickly to reverse the performance declines.

Lau and Murnighan[52] observed the tendency under external pressures for diverse groups to fracture along the fault-lines of their diversity into opposing sub-groups. Their analogy was that of an "earthquake" where the "fault-lines" were split apart. If the disagreements or conflicts are too great, the members of the sub-groups believe that the differences are irreconcilable.[53]

Bartlett and Ghoshal[54] argued that three coordination mechanisms could be used to integrate diverse teams effectively enough to prevent these kinds of internal conflicts and divisions. First, diverse perspectives had to be *legitimized* by creating a balance between multiple perspectives. *Legitimizing diversity* required three steps:[55]

Building legitimacy: An under-represented group could be given more legitimacy in the eyes of other more influential groups by transferring into it high-status personnel. Bringing in new people was necessary because the status and credibility of those already in the under-represented group had already been well-established in others' minds.

Providing access: Managers representing the under-represented perspectives and/or capabilities needed to be seen as supporting, and be supported by the MNE's objectives, interests, and priorities. The emergent group needed to be plugged into the company's information system, and the information system modified to facilitate the group's particular needs for receiving and transmitting information. This encouraged the development of new channels of communication. It created information linkages across management groups, and encouraged information sharing and joint decision-making based on access to the same information.

Ensuring influence: The managers in the under-represented group needed organizational clout to ensure their ability to influence decisions. The group needed to receive an allocation of resources: financial (budget), operational (authority over, and responsibility for physical sites, locations, or other operational resources), and/or human (groups of personnel). Control over resources empowered the emergent group in its negotiations with established management groups. Established groups needed to win the cooperation and support of the emergent group to achieve their own ends. They could no longer afford to ignore or alienate the emergent group.

This latter step of insuring influence is the most important step. It requires that senior management support the re-allocation of resources and influence, and deal with any resistance to the change. Bartlett[56] provides an interesting example where the manager of global brands and the United Kingdom country manager compete for influence in an Australian wine company. The former wants to create brands to be sold worldwide, while the latter wants to produce local brands that would be especially appealing in the United Kingdom and Western Europe. The MNE's CEO legitimates both managers and refuses to settle their conflict because he believes that the conflict of perspectives will produce a better overall global outcome for the company – a transnational solution (see Chapter 4) that integrates headquarters and subsidiary expertise.

Bartlett and Ghoshal's[57] second coordination mechanism, *information coordination*, is intended to manage information complexity by developing flexible informal coordination. Highly diverse management teams will be better able to collect relevant information for their decision-making through the use informal and group information coordination mechanisms. Teams that rely only on formal information coordination are likely to obtain less information and be less effective.

Informal information coordination is based on the creation of relationships between managers representing diverse perspectives that are outside the boundaries of formal working relationships. Group information coordination is based on the use of task forces, joint problem-solving teams, and committees. Formal information coordination is based on policies, procedures, and information systems that define what information is required and should be collected.

MNEs may use training and development workshops as a means of building informal coordination. Managers gather, apparently to learn a new technique or process. They have, however, been carefully selected as individuals who should be able to call on each other to solve commonly faced problems or situations. The real hope of such programs is that the participants will build informal relationships both during the training, and during the downtime between training sessions. Later, these individuals may be assigned to committees and/or task forces to further develop and strengthen their informal relationships.[58]

Informal and group coordination mechanisms are more likely to improve information gathering and decision-making because the important information needed is likely to be geographically dispersed and situation specific. It is likely to be tacit (based on personal experience), and not explicit (written down somewhere). Senior management generally does not know exactly what information is, or will become critical for its planning processes. If it did know, the information could be collected formally through reporting procedures, and no company would ever suffer from declining performance because every company would always be ahead of all its competition.

Bartlett and Ghoshal's[59] third coordination mechanism, *shared vision*, was intended to motivate all MNE managers to cooperate, share information, listen to others' contributions, and use all available information in decision-making. Shared vision consisted of a process for uniting the entire organization with "a common understanding of, identification with, and commitment to the organization's objectives, priorities, and values."[60] All individuals and units in the organization must be inculcated with a common vision of organizational goals.

Genuine commitment to these goals is achieved by creating genuine interdependence between managers at headquarters, subsidiaries, functions, line, staff, etc. This interdependence ensures that managers must cooperate to achieve their individual and collective goals. Integration, collaboration, and cooperation become self-enforcing processes because each organizational unit is connected to other units by shared goals and rewards. Each has to cooperate with those it is connected with so that all linked units may achieve their jointly held performance goals.

Rewards are similarly linked so that units cannot achieve performance rewards if other associated units do not achieve their requisite performance. Without cooperation, no unit can achieve the jointly held performance goals, and then all units are held accountable for their failure.

An interesting example of shared vision is found in the story of how Alan Mulally saved the Ford Motor Company.[61] By creating a shared vision of Ford as a transnational and geocentric company ("One Ford" – see Chapter 4), Ford was transformed. In just five years, Ford went from a perennial money loser with a history of poor automobile quality, to become the top American car company in the eyes of American car buyers.

The research on cultural diversity seems to support the view that tight integration of diversity could produce better decision-making outcomes. While Watson et al.[62] and Earley and Mosakowski[63] both reported that the performance of homogeneous and heterogeneous teams were equal, this may have been due to inadequate experimental design. Both reported that the performance of homogeneous teams was initially higher and did not improve over time. Both reported that the performance of heterogeneous teams improved continuously over time and had achieved equality by the end of their experiments. Both speculated that had the experiments been of longer duration (Watson et al.'s was 17 weeks long), the hetero-geneous teams would have bested the homogeneous teams. In Stahl et al.'s[64] meta-analysis, the reasons given for the culturally diverse work teams not achieving higher performance were intra-group conflict and lower social integration, both symptoms of weak integration. At the same time, Stahl et al.'s study did show higher levels of creativity, and satisfaction among group members, and no increased difficulties in intra-group communications.

Leadership as an integrator

Global leadership has two main purposes. The first is to set the strategy for an MNE to compete in both the global business environment as well as in each local environment the MNE competes. The subject of strategic planning will be discussed in detail in Chapter 7.

The second purpose of global leadership is to integrate the worldwide internal capa-bilities of the MNE so that it may effectively pursue and implement its strategy. Style of leadership is a function of senior management's preferences. It affects organizational systems and structure, organizational culture, as well as the selection and management of the MNE's human resources.

Over the years, there have been many approaches to understanding what leadership is and how it functions.[65] In the first half of the twentieth century, *trait* theories were devel-oped in an attempt to find the intellectual, psychological, social, or physical characteristics that were consistent with leadership success. Even today, Jungian psychologists categorize leadership styles in terms of their underlying personality preferences for information processing.

Keirsey,[66] for example, identified four basic leadership styles, each with characteristic strengths and weaknesses that leaders might not even be aware because the preferences were pre-intentional and possibly genetically based. People simply behaved in these ways habitually and without reflection.

The *logistical* leader (Sensing/Judging, or SJ) is particularly skilled at building complex formal organizations and is often a valued manager in MNEs.

The *strategic* leader (Intuiting/Thinking, or NT) is particularly skilled at developing innovative and efficient organizations, and is especially valued in senior management.

The *diplomatic* leader (Intuiting/Feeling, or NF) is particularly skilled at building interpersonal relationships based on cooperation, trust, and shared goals.

The *tactical* leader (Sensing/Perceiving, or SP) is particularly skillful at identifying opportunities and finding the means to grasp them quickly, but uncomfortable with formal organization. These leaders are often entrepreneurs.

Freudian psychologists also developed trait theories about how leadership was impacted by personal psychological characteristics.[67]

In the latter half of the twentieth century, *behavioral* theories of leadership emerged. Leaders were understood to manage between two principle variables in their efforts to motivate staff to get work done in an efficient or an effective fashion. *Task orientation* (TO) was the focus on getting tasks done, and organizing workers efficiently. TO involved initiating and structuring the roles, tasks, goals, supervision, and checkpoints intended to facilitate task achievement. *Relationship orientation* (RO) was building positive and personal relationships with one's staff that would influence and motivate them to get the tasks done. RO involved demonstrating consideration for staff by being cooperative, building trust, and mutual respect, showing understanding for others' feelings, and building personal relationships.

Blake and Mouton[68] used these two dimensions to create a *situational* leadership grid containing five leadership styles including: (1) High TO/Low RO; (2) High TO/High RO; (3) Low TO/High RO; (4) Low TO/Low RO; and Medium TO and RO. Reddin[69] used the task and relationship dimensions to created a leadership grid containing four leadership styles. Reddin's grid is illustrated in Exhibit 6.4.

EXHIBIT 6.4 REDDIN'S LEADERSHIP GRID

Related leader	Integrated leader
Low TO High RO	High TO High RO
Separated leader	**Dedicated leader**
Low TO Low RO	High TO Low RO

Source: Adapted from Reddin, W. J. *Managerial Effectiveness*. London: McGraw-Hill, 1970.

187 ■ ■ ■

Dedicated leaders dominated their staff by giving many verbal instructions, evaluating performance, and assigning rewards and punishments, all without feeling the need to build personal relationships with their staff. *Integrated* leaders negotiated goals and organized work while providing high levels of socio-emotional support for their staff. *Related* leaders built personal relationships with staff and counted on their staff to be motivated by the positive relationships to get the work done. *Separated* leaders relied on policies, procedures, and rules to define how work should be done, and offered little task guidance or relational support.

Blake and Mouton[70] argued that the integrated leadership style was the best one because leaders had to achieve requisite task performance, and also build and maintain good working relationships with their staff. By contrast, Reddin,[71] Fiedler,[72] and Hersey and Blanchard[73] all agreed that all four leadership styles could be effective or ineffective depending on whether they were applied in the correct situation or not.

This idea of *situational leadership* has become a standard for understanding leadership effectiveness. It has been suggested that situational leadership is the ideal pattern, or archetype, for Western conceptions of leadership effectiveness. Even in Judaic and Christian bible stories, dating back thousands of years, God led Abraham using what could be considered situational leadership.[74]

Hersey and Blanchard observed that the most appropriate leadership style depended on the *maturity* level of the staff persons being led and managed. Maturity was defined as a function of level of motivation, willingness/ability to set goals and accept responsibility, relevant education level, and relevant experience. A follower with low maturity should be led with a Dedicated style. Relatively unmotivated, uneducated employees with little relevant experience would fit this bill.

Business students, in contrast, are motivated or they wouldn't be in class or in school. Most all of them are quite able to set goals and generally take responsibility for completing assignments. On the other hand, they are in the middle of their relevant education, and many have limited relevant business experience. It would be appropriate to assume them to have medium maturity and use an Integrated leadership style. A professor using an Integrated leadership style would set work goals, negotiate what constituted good output and goal achievement, and build positive relationships hoping to encourage motivation and commitment.

Professional employees — senior managers, and experienced lawyers, accountants, and professors, for example, would be considered to have high maturity. They know the tasks they are responsible for, have an established track record for doing them, and are well trained to achieve them. It is appropriate to expect to manage them with a low TO leadership style. The question is whether you need to build positive relationships (RO) with them or not. This would depend on your personal style — whether you were happier building relationships with staff or not. However, highly skilled professional workers should function well with either a Related or a Separated leadership style. If they do not, you should reevaluate your assessment of their maturity level and alter your leadership style as needed.

In the context of International Business, it is also evident that some styles of situational leadership better fit certain MNE mindsets. In Chapter 4, we discussed *ethnocentric, polycentric*, and *geocentric* mindsets,[75] and how Bartlett and Beamish[76] had adapted them into what they called *International, Multinational, Global*, and *Transnational* MNE mentalities. These mindsets or mentalities governed how MNEs organized their worldwide operations, defining appropriate relationships between headquarters and subsidiaries.

The hallmark of the ethnocentric mindset (and the very similar international and global mentalities) was that headquarters controlled all the operations of its subsidiaries, requiring the subsidiaries to conform to the MNE's home country standards. Headquarters provided a steady stream of instructions, and inspections by headquarters personnel. Subsidiary personnel were not valued for their expertise or experience in a local market. Under these conditions, a Dedicated leadership style might be considered the most situationally appropriate. High TO is required to ensure that a subsidiary is always on track with headquarters' expectations. High RO is not required, and perhaps not even advisable, because the leaders from the headquarters do not value the expertise or experience of local employees except insofar as they conform to expectations. Since no highly educated, experienced, and motivated local personnel would want to work in such a repressive organizational culture, the maturity of these local employees may not be very high. Anyone local with good prospects based on their education or experience would look for opportunities elsewhere.

Now in Chapter 4, we argued that this ethnocentric mindset was not an effective way to manage an MNE. The point here, however, is that it creates an internal organization culture in which the leadership style most likely to be perceived as effective would be the Dedicated. A subsidiary leader who adopted a high RO leadership style would be seen at headquarters as behaving inappropriately, and might well disappoint the local staff with whom he/she had built personal relationships with.

The hallmark of the polycentric mindset (and the very similar multinational mentality) is that local personnel best understand local market conditions and should be allowed to function without headquarters interference. Here the most appropriate situational leadership is quite different. Headquarters values the ability of its subsidiaries to achieve effective task performance without significant headquarters intervention. Headquarters only imposes overall financial controls and leaves active management to the subsidiaries. Therefore, the situationally appropriate leadership style would appear to be either Related if good relationships with the subsidiaries are desired, or Separated if the financial controls are deemed sufficient. Of course, subsidiary leaders in this situation would require a high TO style, either Integrated or Dedicated depending on the qualities of their employees, and applied on an individual employee basis.

The hallmark of the geocentric mindset (and the transnational mentality) is to integrate the cultural and functional diversity that exists within all headquarters and subsidiaries units, to produce the best possible performance outcomes. Headquarters and subsidiaries collaborate at all levels so that any innovations discovered in any location may be adapted or applied to any other location where such a product or service could add to the performance of the overall company. And ultimately the senior managers at headquarters will be the most competent leaders whether they originally came from the home country or any local country that the MNE does business. Here, both high TO and high RO are appropriate – an integrated leadership style. This would foster the greatest commitment to the overarching vision of the MNE, and the strongest relationships to facilitate informal coordination of information, and strong relationships to integrate the diversity. Of course, even if the overall leadership style was Integrated, relatively immature individual employees would be managed in a Dedicated style. And very mature professional staff would be best motivated with either Related or Separated leadership.

Other forms of integration: diversity training

While the leadership must also approach diversity from a macro-systemic perspective, all employees must be made aware of company-wide efforts to leverage employee potential. This may be accomplished through *diversity training*. Pedagogically well-rounded training programs should include the following components:[77]

- A cultural general section.
- A section that emphasizes mastering cross-cultural communication.
- A section that teaches cultural self-awareness.
- A section that teaches specifics related to relevant other cultures.
- A section that teaches how to resolve conflict in culturally appropriate ways.
- A section that focuses on developing cross-cultural skills.
- A section that addresses specific (and current) employee-requested concerns, such as "I have a meeting with a manager from Russia, how do I market our product in their culture?" or "How do I improve my customer service skills when interacting with customers from Brazil?"

It would be a mistake to consider cross-cultural diversity training to be merely "lip service." If the same employees are experiencing at the same time negative micro-messages that insinuate subtle discrimination in the workplace, then all training efforts are in vain.[78] When negative micro-messages are focused on employees who are of specific ethnic backgrounds, and are not addressed by management, the end result is a workplace where certain employees cannot work to their full potential.

Young wrote about the impact of "small" communicated messages on the entire organization.[79] From 10-minute conversations, he estimated that two people can send from 40 to 120 micro-messages, verbal and especially nonverbal, to each other. Though small isolated messages might not have a significant effect, continuously repeated micro-messages do.

Negative micro-messages, "micro-inequities," erode organizations. They are a cumulative pattern of subtle, semiconscious, devaluing messages, which discourage and impair performance, possibly leading to damaged self-esteem and withdrawal. For example, micro-inequities can occur within a team when a manager or a colleague communicates different messages to team members, often linked to differences between them.[80]

Within the organization, one challenge that companies face is encouraging peak performance from every employee. This means that every employee must feel valued by the organization.

Other forms of integration: empowerment

The concept of empowerment refers to altering management style and transforming organizational arrangements from hierarchical to more participatory – sharing authority and responsibility with workers in a variety of ways. It is often a hallmark of the geocentric mindset. It is expressed through an Integrated leadership style that works to include all potentially relevant diversity in an MNE, and integrate it to achieve the best possible result both globally and locally.

To *empower* means that leaders give individual members more freedom to act, thereby allowing them to demonstrate their capabilities. Inclusion, rather than exclusion, particularly with regard to women and minorities, becomes the organizational norm, based on the competence of the individual. This approach is more open and decentralized.

This form of team management is spreading across Asia and Europe. The Japanese, who are culturally group-oriented, use consensus decision-making that sacrifices implementation speed in favor of giving all relevant employees input. Meanwhile, in some countries in Asia and Eastern Europe, empowerment is manifesting itself in political restructuring from authoritarianism to democracy and free enterprise. Managers are freed from government or party controls and are able to involve their coworkers in the process of reshaping factories, cooperatives, and businesses. As globalization bridges the gap between national economies and peoples, empowerment does the same between management and labor. Kouzes and Posner[81] state that there is one clear and consistent message about empowerment: "feeling powerful – literally feeling 'able' – comes from a deep sense of being in control of our own lives."

When we feel we can determine our own destiny, and we have the assurance that the resources and individuals needed to support us are available, we can persist in our efforts. Conversely, when others control an individual, he/she may comply, or passively resist, but not excel. Leadership through empowerment enhances the individual's self-confidence and personal effectiveness. Kouzes and Posner[82] have identified five fundamental strategies for empowering others.

Ensure self-leadership by putting people in control of their lives. When leaders share power and control with others, they demonstrate trust and respect in others' abilities. They, in essence, make a covenant with them that is reciprocal and mutually beneficial. Individuals who can influence their leaders are more attached to them and committed to the organization. In the Integrated style of leadership, negotiating goals is an example of both high TO and empowerment. For lower maturity employees, some freedom may be granted and frequent checks made to ensure responsibility is being taken. This is a means of incrementally developing greater maturity in employees.

Provide choice. Providing individuals with options and discretion in the day-to-day operation of their jobs increases creativity and flexibility as one is freed from the standard set of rules and procedures. Jobs that are broadly designed and defined encourage this. However, this is not an option that may be provided to low maturity employees who do not have the experience or commitment to warranty the trust.

Develop competence. Leaders must invest in developing individuals' skills and competencies — maturity[83] in other words. Giving employees opportunities to grow in their area of expertise, as well as in general business knowledge, enables them to act in the best interest of the corporation and the customer.

Assign critical tasks. Usually, those with the most power or authority address the most critical organizational problems. However, in innovative corporations like Chaparral Steel, research and development, for example, is brought to the factory floor. Empowerment encourages involvement and responsibility regarding tasks that employees can own and make excellent critical judgments about.

Offer visible support. Leaders who want to empower are highly visible and make conscientious efforts to have employees gain recognition and validation. Making connections and building strong networks and relationships is empowering. A leader should also introduce employees to others in the corporation or community who may help them along their career path. Individuals take responsibility for their own career development, while leaders create a work environment that encourages others to achieve their human potential.

Employees who feel powerless often hoard whatever shreds of power or authority they possess, reinforcing organizational cultures that are often hierarchical and bureaucratic. Leaders who share power help to build profound trust and shared responsibility. Employees view improvements and communication as a two-way street, with the leader being as influenced by his or her workforce as the workforce is by management. Each is committed to effectively doing their part.

With a multicultural workforce and customer base, leadership must provide the vision, motivation, and reasons for commitment. For contemporary organizations and their workers, knowledge and innovation lead to global marketplace power.

CONCLUSIONS

Cultural diversity, as well as diversity in its other forms, is one of the most vital assets any MNE possesses in its efforts to solve problems and make decisions that promise high performance worldwide. The jury is still out as to whether diversity plus integration always leads to higher performance. However, it has been established that high diversity work groups do achieve more creative and innovative solutions on the basis of having greater amounts of potentially relevant information at their disposal. And the members of these teams are more motivated because they experience greater satisfaction working together than those in less diverse groups.

The key to making diversity a competitive advantage is strong and tight integration. The research suggesting that greater diversity did not achieve higher performance was characterized by problems that generally only become serious when integration levels are not sufficiently strong. Underrepresented diversity must be empowered by being recognized by senior management. They must be given authority over budget and operational resources so that other groups must engage with them, and cooperate in order to achieve jointly shared goals. Information must be coordinated informally to ensure that as much information as possible will be available when it is needed. All the elements of diversity must be united by a common corporate vision, usually represented by a geocentric mindset, organized by leaders who adopt situationally appropriate Integrated leadership styles. And facilitating the value of diversity is not just a task for the leadership of an MNE. Employees may need diversity training so that they do not discourage culturally diverse employees by micro-messages of intolerance or belittlement.

The following statements, from Bassi and Russ-Eft,[84] are helpful in considering the value of diversity and how to achieve its maximal benefit for organizational decision-making.

1   People who are part of the minority culture do not want to be tolerated. Neither do other employees. They want to be valued. If they are valued, they can be more effective.

2   Few will admit to feelings or expressions of racism or cultural intolerance in any organization or society, but we all need to learn how to work with one another more effectively and sensitively.

3   When power is shared, people are able to devote tremendous energy to the work at hand.

4   Human beings are the most important asset of any organization. They are the only sustainable competitive advantage for the future.

5   There is no simple model for effective cross-cultural and diversity training. However, it should address the specific needs of the organization's employees. Prewritten generic training programs are generally ineffective.

6   Diversity initiatives should be system-wide but with enough flexibility to adjust to specific regional needs. If effective, they impact positively on an organization's productivity.

7   Diversity initiatives should focus on information, management, processes, and results.

8   Diversity initiatives are not a replacement for Equal Employment Opportunity (EEO) or Affirmative Action (AA).

9   Diversity is to be cherished, for it enriches life and advances the actualization of human potential.

MIND STRETCHING

1   In what ways does a multicultural workforce impact an organization's productivity?

2   Why is it important to take a systems approach to improve employee performance within global organizations?

3   Provide an example of a cross-cultural organizational experience that you were involved in that was difficult for you. How was it difficult? How would you improve the situation?

4   What kinds of diversity are you aware of in your classroom? Does everyone seem to have the right and the willingness to be able to speak his/her mind? Is there anything, or any micro-messages, that discourage this ability on anyone's part? How could the expression of diversity be improved?

5   When you work in a small group, which integrators do you use to ensure team effectiveness? Which could you use that you do not currently?

6   Do you believe your organization or educational institution values diversity? Explain why or why not, and give specific examples.

NOTES

1   Quoted at www.brainyquote.com/quotes/keywords/diversity.html. Retrieved January 13, 2013.

2   Ibid.

3   Ozbilgin, M. "Global Diversity Management," in P. Smith, M. Peterson, and D. Thomas (eds), *The Handbook of Cross-Cultural Management Research*. Los Angeles, CA: Sage, 2008, pp. 379–380. Quote taken from pp. 395–396.

4   Bartlett, C. A. and Ghoshal, S. *Managing Across Borders: The Transnational Solution*. Boston, MA: Harvard Business School.

5   Stahl, G. K., Maznevski, M. L., Voigt, A., and Jonsen, K. "Unraveling the Effects of Cultural Diversity in Teams: A Meta-Analysis of Research on Multicultural Work Groups," *Journal of International Business Studies*, Vol. 41, No. 4, 2010, pp. 690–709.

6   Lawrence, P. R. and Dyer, D. *Renewing American Industry*. New York: Free Press, 1983.

7   Stahl, G. K. et al., "Unraveling the Effects."

8   Bartlett, C. A. and Beamish, P. W. *Transnational Management: Text, Cases, and Readings in Cross-Border Management*, 6th edn. New York: McGraw-Hill Irwin, 2011.

9   Lawrence, P. R. and Lorsch, J. W. *Organization and Environment*. Boston, MA: Harvard Business School, 1967.

10 Lawrence and Dyer, *Renewing American Industry*.

11 Bartlett and Ghoshal, *Managing Across Borders*.

12 Derrida, J. *The Other Heading: Reflections on Today's Europe*. Indianapolis, IN: Indiana University, 1990.

13 Buckley, P. J. and Carter, M. J. "A Formal Analysis of Knowledge Combination in Multinational Enterprises," *Journal of International Business Studies*, Vol. 35, 2004, pp. 371–384.

14 Fransman, M. "Information, Knowledge, Vision, and Theories of the Firm," in G. Dosi, D. J. Teece, and J. Chytry (eds), *Technology, Organization and Competitiveness: Perspectives on Industrial and Corporate Change*. Oxford: Oxford University, 1998.

15 Kogut, B. and Zander, U. "Knowledge of the Firm and the Evolutionary Theory of the Multinational Corporation," *Journal of International Business Studies*, Vol. 24, 1993, pp. 625–645.

16 Li, J. and Shenkar, O. "Knowledge Search and Governance Choice: International Joint Ventures in the People's Republic of China," *Management International Review*, Vol. 43, 2003, pp. 91–109.

17 Barney, J. "Firm Resources and Sustained Competitive Advantage," *Journal of Management*, Vol. 12, 1991, pp. 99–120.

18 Abramson, N.R., "Building Business Relationships Using Western Marketing Practices in East Asia," in M. A. Abdullah and M. I. B. Bakar (eds), *Small and Medium Enterprises in Asian Pacific Countries*. Huntington, NY: NOVA, 2000, pp. 3–27.

19 Earley, P. C. and Moskowski, E. "Creating Hybrid Team Cultures: An Empirical Test of Transnational Team Functioning," *Academy of Management Journal*, Vol. 43, No. 1, 2000, pp. 26–49.

20 Stahl et al. "Unraveling the Effects."

21 Homan, A., Hollenbeck, J., Humphrey, S., Knippenberg, D., Ilgen, D., and Van Kleef, G. "Facing Differences with an Open Mind: Openness to Experience, Salience of Intragroup Differences, and Performance of Diverse Workgroups," *Academy of Management Journal*, Vol. 51, No. 6, 2008, pp. 1204–1222.

22 Kearney, E., Gebert, D., and Voehpel, S., "When and How Diversity Benefits Teams: The Importance of Team Members' Need for Cognition," *Academy of Management Journal*, Vol. 52, No. 3, 2009, pp. 581–598.

23 Joshi, A. and Roh, H. "The Role of Context in Work Team Diversity Research: A Meta-Analytic Review," *Academy of Management Journal*, Vol. 52, No. 3, 2009, pp. 533–627.

24 Homan et al., "Facing Differences."

25 Kearney et al., "When and How."

26 Ibid., p. 595.

27 Abramson, N. R. and Keating, R. J. "Knowledge Management Through the Lens of the Cognitive Theory of Strategy: American, Chinese, and Thai Decision-Making Capabilities," *Journal of Global Business*, Vol. 17, No. 34, pp. 27–42.

28 Gardenswartz, L. and Rowe, A. *Managing Diversity: A Complete Desk Reference*. San Diego, CA: 1993.

29 Harrison, D., Price, K., and Bell, M. "Beyond Relational Demography: Time and the Effects of Surface- and Deep-Level Diversity on Work Group Cohesion," *Academy of Management Journal*, Vol. 41, No. 1, 1998, pp. 96–107.

30 Ozbilgin, M. "Global Diversity Management," in P. Smith, M. Peterson, and D. Thomas (eds), *The Handbook of Cross-Cultural Research*. Los Angeles, CA: Sage, 2008, pp. 379–396.

31 Nair, K. A. *Higher Standard of Leadership: Lessons from the Life of Gandhi*. San Francisco, CA: Berrett-Koehler, 1994.

32 Simons, G. *EuroDiversity: A Business Guide to Managing Differences*. Burlington, MA: Butterworth-Heinemann/Elsevier, 2002, pp. xviii, 1, 2.

33 "Cultural Diversity Market Study," *Luxembourg: Pricewaterhouse Coopers*, Draft Final Report, February 14, 2001.

34 Ibid.

35 Stahl et al., "Unraveling the Effects."

36 Abramson and Keating, "Knowledge Management," for example.

37 House, R. J., Hanges, P. W., Javidan, M., Dorfman, P., and Gupta, V. (eds). *Culture, Leadership, and Organizations: The GLOBE Study of 62 Societies*. Beverley Hills, CA: Sage, 2004.

38 American Express Financial Advisors. "Diversity: Report to Benchmark Partners," in B. Abramms and G. F. Simons (eds), *Cultural Diversity Sourcebook*. Amherst, MA: ODT, 1996.

39 Parfit, M. "Human Migration," *National Geographic*, October, 1998, pp. 11–14.

40 Ibid.

41 World Report, "A Global Pursuit of Happiness," *Los Angeles Times*, October 1, 1991, p. H13.

42 http://www.refugeesinternational.org/who-we-are.

43 http://www.iom.int/jahia/global-estimates-and-trends.

44 Stalker, P. "The Work of Strangers: A Survey of International Migration," in W. R. Bohning and M. L. Schloeter (eds), *Aids in Place of Migration*. Geneva, Switzerland: International Labor Organization, 1994.

45 Gurr, T. R., "Minorities, Nationalists, and Ethnopolitical Conflict," in C. A. Cocker, F. O. Hampson, and P. Aall (eds), *Managing Global Chaos: Sources of and Responses to International Conflict*. Washington, DC: International Institute of Peace, 1999.

46 Taylor, D. M. and Moghaddam, F. M. *Theories of Intergroup Relations: International Social Psychological Perspectives*, 2nd edn. Westport, CN: Praeger, 1994, pp. 197–198.

47 Crocker, C. A., Hampson, F. O., and Aall, P. (eds). *Managing Global Chaos: Sources of and Responses to International Conflict*. Washington, DC: International Institute of Peace, 1999.

48 Bartos, O. and Wehr, P. *Using Conflict Theory*. Cambridge, UK: Cambridge University Press, 2002.

49 "Course Teaches Conflict Solving." Published April 4, 2006, http://news.bbc.co.uk/2/hi/uk_news/scotland/4876028.stm.

50 Stahl et al., "Unraveling the Effects."

51 Tajfel, H. "Social Psychology of Intergroup Relations," *Annual Review of Psychology*, Vol. 33, 1982, pp. 1–39.

52 Lau, D. C. and Murnighan, J. K. "Interactions within Groups and Subgroups: The Effects of Demographic Faultlines," *Academy of Management Journal*, Vol. 48, No. 4, 2005, pp. 645–659.

53 Dyck, B. and Starke, F. A. "The Formation of Breakaway Organizations: Observations and a Process Model," *Administrative Science Quarterly*, Vol. 44, 1999, pp. 792–822.

54 Bartlett, C. A. and Ghoshal, S. "Managing Across Borders: New Organizational Responses," *Sloan Management Review*, Fall, 1987, 43–54.

55 Bartlett and Ghoshal, *Managing Across Borders*.

56 Bartlett, C. A. "BRL Hardy: Globalizing an Australian Wine Company," in C. A. Bartlett and P. W. Beamish (eds), *Transnational Management: Text, Cases, and Readings in Cross-Border Management*, 6th edn. New York: McGraw-Hill Irwin, 2011, pp. 612–628.

57 Bartlett and Ghoshal, 1987, op cit.

58 Abramson, N. R. *Configuration, Coordination, Learning and Foreign Market Entry: A Study of Canadian Software Companies Entering the United States*. London, ON: University of Western Ontario, 1992.

59 Bartlett and Ghoshal, "Managing Across Borders."

60 Ibid.

61 Hoffman, B. G. *American Icon: Alan Mulally and the Fight to Save Ford Motor Company*. Kindle Edition: Crown Business, 2013.

62 Watson, W. E., Kumar, K., and Michaelson, L. K. "Cultural Diversity's Impact on Interaction Process and Performance: Comparing Homogeneous and Diverse Task Groups," *Academy of Management Journal*, Vol. 36, No. 3, 1993, pp. 590–612.

63 Earley, P. C. and Mosakowski, E., "Creating Hybrid Team Cultures."

64 Stahl et al., "Unraveling the Effects."

65 Abramson, N. R. "The Leadership Archetype: A Jungian Analysis of Similarities between Modern Leadership Theory and the Abraham Myth in the Judaic-Christian Tradition," *Journal of Business Ethics*, Vol. 72, 2007, pp. 115–129.

66 Keirsey, D. *Please Understand Me II: Temperament, Character, Intelligence*. Del Mar, CA: Prometheus Nemesis, 1998.

67 See Zaleznik, A. *Executive's Guide to Motivating People: How Freudian Theory Can Turn Good Executives into Better Leaders*. Chicago, IL: Bonus Books, 1990. Also see Kets de Vries, M. *The Leadership Mystique: A User's Manual for the Human Enterprise*. London: Prentice Hall, 2001.

68 Blake, R. R. and Mouton, J. S. *The Managerial Grid: Key Orientations for Achieving Production*. Houston, TX: Gulf Publishing, 1964.

69 Reddin, W. J. *Managerial Effectiveness*. London: McGraw-Hill, 1970.

70 Blake and Mouton, *The Managerial Grid*.

71 Reddin, *Managerial Effectiveness*.

72 Fiedler, F. E. *Leadership Experience and Leadership Performance*. Alexandria, VA: US Army Research Institute for the Behavioral and Social Sciences, 1994.

73 Hersey, P. and Blanchard, K. H. *Management of Organizational Behavior: Utilizing Human Resources*. Englewood Cliffs, NJ: Prentice-Hall.

74 Abramson, "The Leadership Archetype."

75 Perlmutter, H. V. "The Tortuous Evolution of Multinational Enterprises," *Columbia Journal of World Business*, Vol. 1, 1969, pp. 9–18.

76 Bartlett, C. A. and Beamish, P. W. *Transnational Management: Text, Cases, and Readings in Cross-Border Management*, 6th edn. New York: McGraw-Hill Irwin, 2011.

77 Barrett, G. "Cultivating Global Teams: Diversity Management Square," in C. Mann and K. Gotz (eds), *Borderless Business, Managing the Far-Flung Enterprise*. Westport, CN: Praeger, 2006, pp. 275–294.

78 Moran, S. "Comprehensive Evaluation of a Diversity Training Initiative in a Global Company." Arizona State Universite master's thesis, 2000.

79 Young, S. "Micro-Inequities: The Power of Small," *Workforce Diversity Reader*, Vol. 1, No. 1, 2003, pp. 88–93.

80 Moran, S., "Comprehensive Evaluation."

81 Kouzes, J. M. and Posner, B. Z. *The Leadership Challenge*. San Francisco, CA: Jossey-Bass, 1995.

82 Ibid.

83 Hersey and Blanchard, *Management of Organizational Behavior*.

84 Bassi, L. J. and Russ-Eft, D. (eds). *What Works: Assessment, Development, and Measurement*. Alexandria, VA: American Society for Training and Development, 1997.

ADDITIONAL FEATURES

Please visit the companion website at: www.routledge.com/cw/Moran where you will find additional case studies, study aides, and instructor resources.

7 GLOBAL LEADERS SET STRATEGIES FOR EMERGING MARKETS

You've got to trust the process . . . Do you have a point of view about the future? Check. Is it still the right vision today? Check. Do you have a comprehensive plan to deliver that? Check. If you get skilled and motivated people working together through this process, you're going to figure it out. But you've got to trust it. The leader's job is to remind people of that vision, make sure they stick to the process, and keep them working together. Working together *always* works.

Alan Mulally[1]

If you know the enemy and you know yourself, you need not fear the result of a hundred battles.

Sun Tzu[2]

With the onset of the global recession in 2008–2009, and the resultant debt crises in the United States, European Union countries, and Japan, the major First World national economic growth engines of the world economy stalled. While economic growth languished, or even declined in the United States and Western Europe, growth accelerated in the Emerging Markets. In the first half of 2009 when the American economy was in crisis, the FTSE International Emerging Markets Index was up 41.1 percent, compared with the FTSE All World Developed Markets Index growth of only 7.2 percent.[3] Anecdotal reports suggested that the economy of Brazil, for example, was booming and entirely untouched by First World economic crises.

Prior to these economic crises, the primary role of Emerging Markets was to supply inexpensive factor costs (labor, production facilities, tax regimes) for the production of less expensive goods and services. These were then exported primarily to the United States, the European Union, and Japan.[4] When the purchasing power of these First World nations dried up, MNEs saw as their best chance for growth developing markets in the Emerging Markets themselves.[5]

There is little consensus as to exactly which nations constitute the Emerging Markets. The most important four – the BRIC as they are often called – include Brazil, Russia, India, and China.[6] The World Bank has added South Korea and Indonesia to the BRIC and has predicted that half of all world economic growth will come from these six nations by 2025.[7]

The largest seven, by either GDP (gross domestic product) or PPP (purchasing power parity) are, in order, China, Brazil, Russia, India, Mexico, Indonesia, and Turkey.[8] Columbia University's list includes 16 countries, while the IMF (International Monetary Fund) includes 24.[9] The FTSE list includes ten advanced Emerging Market nations plus 12 more secondary ones.[10] This FTSE list is a bit curious because China is included as a secondary Emerging Market even though it is the world's second-largest economy, predicted to surpass the United States in size between 2016[11] and 2020.[12] India is also secondary even though it is predicted to pass China (and the United States) in gross size by 2050.[13] The most reliable list is derived from the membership of the G20 including those countries not recognized as traditional economic powerhouses during the twentieth century. See Exhibit 7.1.

With the exception of Saudi Arabia, these ten Emerging Market nations have been acknowledged by the world's established economic powers to be very important to the world's economy through their G20 membership. The G20 nations together account for two-thirds of the world's population, 84 percent of the world's nominal GDP, 82 percent of PPP, and 80 percent of world trade.

The subject of this chapter is strategy. Particularly, we are concerned with how global leaders identify strategies intended to achieve competitive results in international markets, and especially these high growth potential Emerging Markets. An *intended strategy* is understood to be the basis for a concrete *plan* through which an organization intends to achieve competitive advantage within its business environment. The goal of an intended strategy is to achieve strong positive financial performance results, either along with its competitors in a growing market, or at its competitors' expense in a mature and stable market.

There is also *emergent strategy*.[14] If the purpose of the intended strategy is to produce an action plan going forward in time, the emergent strategy becomes apparent when we look back at the actions of the managers working to implement their plans. Managers have systematic cognitive biases, often the result of their personalities, habitually predisposing them in favor of certain kinds of actions, and against certain other kinds of action.[15] These cognitive biases represent both strengths and weaknesses depending on the intended strategy. The important point, however, is that managers are often generally unaware of these unintentional emergent effects,[16] negatively but unintentionally impacting the implementation of their intended strategies.

A strategic plan is useless if it cannot be implemented. The strategy must result in a concrete plan that is consistent with the internal capabilities of an organization, or the organization must realistically be able to acquire the required capabilities.[17]

The plan must be aligned with the *leadership* (L) capabilities and values of senior management, and the leader and his/her top management team must have the skills, experience, and inclination to make implementation work. The *organization* (O) must have the required *structure*, *systems*, and *organization culture*. The organization must have any required *human*, *operational*, and *financial resources* (R). Any L, O, or R gaps that would cause strategy implementation to fail must be filled, or a proposed plan will fail and must be abandoned, and replaced with a workable plan.

EXHIBIT 7.1 G20 MEMBERSHIP

EXHIBIT 7.1

First World economic powers	Emerging Markets
Australia	Argentina
Canada	Brazil
European Union	China
France	India
Germany	Indonesia
Italy	Mexico
Japan	Russia
United Kingdom	Saudi Arabia
United States	South Africa
	South Korea
	Turkey

Source: This represents our own thinking on Emerging Markets membership.

The purpose of strategic planning is to reduce the uncertainty about what the organization must achieve, and how, in terms of performance required to succeed in its competitive environment. The competitive environment is carefully analyzed in order to understand what are the bases of competitive advantage which we will call *key success factors* (KSFs).[18] The organization is compared against its key competitors. An opportunity exists where the organization is stronger on a KSF than its competitors. A threat exists where one or more competitors are stronger. Strategic proposals are made on the basis of taking advantage of opportunities and ameliorating threats. And then a plan must be developed for the implementation of the strategic proposal that details the internal capabilities required to make it work. Ongoing performance checkpoints ensure that the plan is achieving its targets. If the plan underperforms expectations, or if the competitive environment changes producing reduced or negative results, then global leaders need to reanalyze and adjust their plan. This is the standard process for doing strategic planning as generally applied by companies in their business environments.

In Emergent Markets, however, there are complications. MNEs have generally assumed that the strategic planning and implementation process that worked for Western companies in Western markets will also work in Emerging Markets. Bartlett and Beamish,[19] for example, do not distinguish between First World and Emergent Markets in the applications of their strategic planning frameworks. Khanna and Palepu[20] argued that this was not the case — Emergent Markets were different and required different approaches to strategic planning and implementation. And individual Emerging Markets were different from each other for cultural, economic, social, and political reasons. So, a planning process that worked in China, for example, might not be an effective approach in Russia or India.

Our own view is intermediate between Khanna and Palepu on the one hand, and the standard one-size-fits-all approach on the other hand. We adopt Courtney et al.'s[21] view that it is the level of perceived environmental uncertainty that varies between Emerging Markets. Some Emerging Markets may have no greater levels of uncertainty than Western markets and in these cases the standard Western strategic planning process is fully applicable.

Some Emerging Markets may be much more uncertain for a foreign expatriate, but if an MNE hires competent local managers, these locals will experience no greater uncertainty than is usual in Western markets. An MNE with an ethnocentric mindset (see Chapter 4),[22] that staffed all senior local market management positions with home country managers, would experience greater uncertainty. However, those MNEs with polycentric or geocentric mindsets, allowing local senior management responsibility, would experience less.

Brazil or Mexico would be examples of Emerging Markets with not much greater uncertainty than Western markets where the standard strategic planning process would work. China would be an example where apparently greater uncertainty could be reduced to more comfortable levels by hiring competent local Chinese managers.

There are, however, Emerging Markets where there are far greater levels of cultural, social, political, and economic uncertainty than is usual for Western markets regardless of whether Westerners or local managers are in charge of the planning process. At the time of writing, India seems to have greater and more unpredictable levels of political uncertainty. It is not clear that the government, or a newly elected alternative government, will remain committed to the process of globalization that has been successfully implemented since the 1990s.

A country like Iran could be considered to have the highest levels of conceivable uncertainty due to political, social, cultural, and religious factors. There are, however, Western oil-producing companies that face these uncertainties and manage to conduct some form of strategic planning. However, planning itself becomes uncertain under these conditions, and this uncertainty means that the standard planning process cannot be applied, and an MNE's willingness to commit its resources is severely constrained.

The learning objectives for this chapter include the following:

1   An overview model of the strategic planning process.
2   How to identify the bases of competitive advantage, or KSFs, at the industry level, using Porter's Five Forces model.[23]
3   How to identify opportunities and threats at the MNE level, based on competitive analysis of the MNE and its direct competitors on the identified KSFs.
4   Basic types of strategies, and how an MNE derives strategic options by intending to exploit strategic opportunities and ameliorate strategic threats.
5   Evaluating the ability of the MNE to implement strategic proposals by ensuring that its internal capabilities are consistent with, or can be made consistent with a proposed strategy.[24]
6   Proposing how a four-stage model of increasing levels of uncertainty in Emerging Markets affects the ability of MNEs to use this strategic planning process, and limits its ability to implement strategic actions.[25]
7   Considering how the personality-based habitual behaviors of leaders create an emergent strategy that supports or detracted from the intended strategy.

THE STRATEGIC PLANNING PROCESS

The *Double Diamond* model of strategy provides a useful overview of all the elements involved in strategic planning and how they interact. See Exhibit 7.2.

On the left diamond of the Double Diamond model, we have *planning* functions. Global leadership has a *vision* for what the MNE intends to accomplish, and how it is to be accomplished. The competitive industry *environment* that the MNE competes in must be analyzed in order to determine the sources of competitive advantage, or KSFs. This includes both industry analysis and competitive analysis.

EXHIBIT 7.2 DOUBLE DIAMOND STRATEGY MODEL

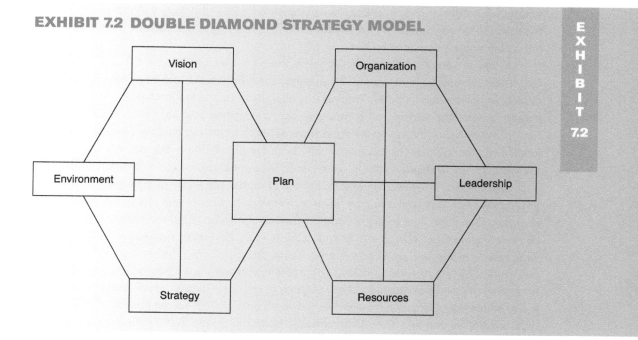

Industry analysis[26] analyzes the industry environment, including all the factors that affect all companies providing competitive products or services, to identify KSFs. KSFs are product/service or organizational characteristics that provide significant competitive advantage for any company possessing them. *Competitive analysis* compares one's own company against its direct competitors to determine which companies are stronger on which KSFs. If your company is stronger on a KSF, that is an opportunity to take advantage of in your planning. If your company is weaker on a KSF, that is a threat you must make allowance for.

A *strategy* is formulated that is intended to take advantage of specific opportunities and ameliorate specific threats. The strategy must be formulated into an operational *plan* that details what actions and what resources are needed to make the strategy work. A plan includes checkpoints to monitor progress of implementation and results achieved.

On the right diamond of the Double Diamond model, we have *implementation* issues. Bossidy and Charan[27] observe that implementation is a critical weakness in many companies' strategic plans because its importance is not emphasized in business education. *Leadership* will implement the plan by organizing the MNE's human, operational, and financial *resources. Organization* entails having an effective structure, required systems, and organization culture that keeps people motivated and on track. Does the leadership have the required competencies, capabilities, values, and experience? Do we have the right structure, systems, and organization culture needed to support the plan. Do we have the necessary human, operational, and financial resources? If there is a gap – a key piece needed, but not currently in place, for successful implementation – can it be filled? If not, the plan will fail so you better find a better plan. The strategy and the plan are both worthless if the plan cannot be implemented.

In the middle of the Double Diamond is the *plan* itself. On the one hand, it is based on opportunities existing in the competitive environment right now, and it satisfies the decision criteria, or performance goals, imposed by the vision of the leadership. It should work. It should achieve the anticipated competitive positioning and lead to improved performance. On the other hand, the company must have all the internal capabilities needed to make it work. The strategy must be *consistent* with both the conditions in the external environment, the vision of leadership, and the internal capabilities either existing or realistically obtainable.

We should, however, remember that the plan may not work as expected, or that over time it may work less well. We may have inadvertently blown our analysis of the environment like when Canadian Tire, a very successful Canadian retailer, failed to recognize Walmart as its direct competitor when it entered the U.S. market. Canadian Tire was quickly forced to withdraw from the United States in an ensuing sea of red ink. The environment may have changed, slowly and incrementally, or suddenly, requiring anticipatory, reactive, or crisis change of the plan (see the discussion of types of change, Chapter 4). Walmart has become a very successful Canadian retailer over the years but in 2013, Target entered the Canadian retail market for the first time. Walmart was forced to spend $350 million to update and modernize its Canadian stores. The improvements were not necessary to compete with Canadian retailers, but the U.S. retail market is more competitive, and Target was upgrading the stores acquired from its takeover of the Canadian retailer Zellers. Global leaders learn how to improve their planning from the performance achieved by their existing plans. Walmart knew what they needed to improve in their Canadian operations from its ongoing competition with Target in the United States.

Planning functions

A strategic plan is constructed based on the interaction between management's vision of what their company should achieve, and the bases of competitive advantage in each industry that the company competes. The *vision* is important because it is the guiding philosophy and the performance expectations. The *competitive environment* is important because it is real – real competitors are doing their best to develop better products, services, and organizations to gain market share and profitability at each other's expense.

Even the biggest and apparently most successful companies in the world may be driven to the wall or into bankruptcy because they failed to maintain their competitive positions. Think of General Motors in the auto industry, Research in Motion in the smartphone industry, or Lehman Brothers in the financial industry. Ideals like *values* are important because the ethics of your company may motivate people and encourage them bring out their best efforts and commitment. Values must, however, be applied effectively in real situations where the other guy may mean you harm.

Vision

The vision is the guiding philosophy of the organization. This vision is usually expressed as one or more overarching goals that encompass the intentionality of the leadership for what they want to achieve. It determines whether a company will behave ethically or opportunistically. *Ben and Jerry*, the quality ice-cream company, has always been known to place a high premium on ethicality because this was the value of its founders. By contrast, the *Budget Rent a Car* franchise in Vancouver, Canada, is being sued by a class action lawsuit of former customers. The suit alleges that the franchise falsely charged customers for damage to cars. Disaffected former employees claimed that they had been ordered to engage in this behavior.

The vision may define senior management's expectations for market share, sales growth, and/or level of profitability. All these values and goal expectations become aspects of the leadership's *decision criteria* for evaluating proposed strategic plans. If a plan does not conform to management's values, or performance expectations, it will be modified or discarded.

The vision may be expressed as a *mission statement* made available to all employees so they have a quick reference – like the wallet cards provided at Ford Motor Company – to what the company expects of itself and them. The Ford Motor Company vision of *One Ford, One Team, One Plan, One Goal* provides an excellent example of a mission statement including values, performance expectations, and even the way personnel will be organized into cooperative teams. "One Ford" referred to the resolve of Ford leadership to focus solely on the Ford marquee and to eliminate the previous leadership's acquisitions of Jaguar, Land Rover, Volvo, Mazda, and even Mercury. These related brands were diluting the financial and technological ability of the company to stay abreast of its competition.

"One team" referred to the fact that Ford had been previously organized with a polycentric mindset so that the team in Europe designed and built for Europe, the team in North America, for North America, and so on. Under the previous leadership, a best-selling car in Europe would not be introduced to North America without substantial modifications that often meant that its character was substantially changed. These days, Ford's best sellers in North America are European models introduced with very few alterations. "One plan" referred to a value of teamwork. Ford had had the reputation of a management organization culture that was fratricidal and intra-group competitive. The "one goal" was that Ford would have "exciting" products that would deliver profitable growth to "all" – shareholders, management, workers, unions, and customers.

IKEA's vision statement, while far less comprehensive, had interesting consequences for the company. In the 1980s, IKEA furniture was found to produce formaldehyde gases that made people sick. Later in the 1990s, when IKEA was accused of selling Indian rugs made with child labor, IKEA's vision had simply stated, "*To create a better everyday life for the many people.*" IKEA's founder, Ingvar Kamprad, had originally understood this mission to apply only to IKEA's customers. IKEA's strategy, derived from this mission, was "*selling affordable, good-quality furniture to the mass-market consumers around the world.*"

When the formaldehyde scandal hit – the gases came from the glue that held the wood veneer in place – and IKEA sales dropped 20 percent, IKEA realized its customers were concerned with environmental issues. When IKEA was accused of selling rugs made with child labor, IKEA already knew that their customers were motivated by social conscience as well as the desire for low-cost products. As IKEA came to understand that its customers were motivated by environmental and social values, the mission to serve "*the many people*" expanded from customers to shareholders, even including the workers of independent suppliers manufacturing products for IKEA in Emerging Markets.

Environmental analysis

Environmental analysis ensures a systematic relationship between a company's external conditions and its strategies.[28] Companies compete with each other within industries that share common characteristics not necessarily shared with other industries. The smartphone industry, and other high technology industries for example, generally compete on the basis of the ability of research and development (R&D) to develop new and more advanced products (or services) quickly because products have short lifecycles. That is, 2012's most desirable new smartphone product, say the iPhone 4s, is replaced before the end of 2012 with the iPhone 5 because Samsung's new Galaxy makes the 4s look dated. By 2013, *Consumer Reports* is already rating the new iPhone 5 as less advanced than the latest Galaxy 4S.[29] And Apple's share prices tumbled as a result. No doubt the Apple 5s or 6 is already on the drawing board, being readied for production.

By contrast, the beer industry is a mature market in which there is relatively little product innovation – craft beer is not that different for many. The main KSFs are branding and marketing product value equations (product, price, place you can get it, and promotion).

Industry analysis

Porter[30] observed that the competitive dynamics any industry could be analyzed in terms of five forces that determined the bases of competitive advantage. A KSF would be any characteristic way in which any company could reduce the power of any of these forces as limiting factors for a company's success. These KSFs would be true for any company that competed in that industry. Porter's Five Force model for industry analysis included:

1   *Barriers to Entry*, or conversely the *Threat of New Entrants*. New entrants bring new capacity, new resources, and the desire to gain market share at others' expense. The threat of new entrants depends on the barriers to entry that are present or that companies can develop to defend their positions. If barriers are high, the threat of new

entrants will be low. In the smartphone industry, a KSF could be the ability to manufacture in an Emerging Market to achieve high product quality at a low price – iPhones are manufactured in China; Galaxies in Korea.

2   *Buyer Power.* Customers have product and service expectations. If companies in an industry face a small number of concentrated buyers that purchase in large volumes, or even if many individual customers are psychologically organized to expect the same product values, then buyers may have considerable power. When Honda introduced its new iteration of the Civic car in 2012, *Consumer Reports* (CR) magazine panned it as less good than the previous model and refused to recommend it. Honda Civic had been CR's top compact for more than a decade, and the kind of customers who bought Civics read CR. Honda rushed out a revised model by 2013 even though normally a new iteration would have taken five years. CR now recommends the 2013 Civic. KSFs for reducing customer power usually entail having just what most, or segments of customers want. Because of the cache of Apple products, Apple can charge more and customers have so far not minded. If a company does not have the most desirable product characteristics, charging a lower price may be a compensating KSF.

3   *Supplier Power.* A supplier may exert power over an industry if it controls supply, and can raise prices without the fear of backward integration by its customers. Backward integration means the customers set up their own supplier or acquire the existing supplier. In the 1990s, Intel was the only leading edge chip-maker for personal computers because of its technological edge over competitors, and had tremendous pricing power. Sun, one of its customers, secretly spearheaded the drive to develop a competing chip-maker and now Intel's supplier power is somewhat reduced. A KSF would be having multiple suppliers each able to replace the others. Then, the power of individual suppliers is reduced.

4   *Substitutes' Power.* Substitutes are products or services from other industries that may be used for the same, or a similar function as those in the industry being analyzed. They place a ceiling on the prices that can be charged, and may even eventually result in an older industry being replaced by a newer one. In the 1990s, the cellphone industry was in its heyday, and a substitute product with greater capabilities was the PDA (personal digital assistant), the forerunner of the smartphone. In the 2000s, the smartphone was a substitute for PDAs and cellphones. Now smartphones are the predominant product, cellphones a niche product for older customers and Third World countries, and PDAs have disappeared. A substitute for the smartphone may be the tablet computer. The KSF here in the consumer electronics industries is having better features at a competitive price. Substitutes may, however, cost considerably less, have only critical features, and act as *disruptive technologies* because they demonstrate that customers are willing to settle for less if the price is right. Since tablets were released, sales of personal computers have declined worldwide for the first time. Most consumers don't need the writing and analytical capabilities built into personal computers.

5   *Rivalry*. Rivalry occurs either because some competitors feel the pressure of competition, or see opportunities to improve their position, or have the size, scope, and/or reach to take advance of other companies' lesser capabilities. "Firms are mutually dependent"[31] so a rise in the fortunes of one may come at the expense of others unless the whole market is growing rapidly. The competitive dynamics in the other four forces feed into rivalry, so for example, KSFs that satisfy customers may represent rivalry opportunities if one company can achieve them, and other companies cannot. Size, however, is often a KSF here. Larger automobile companies like Toyota and GM are able to produce different cars in a full range of prices, sizes, and capabilities. A small company like Subaru has the capabilities to compete only in the small automobile and SUV all-wheel drive segments.

Porter[32] proposed a number a number of criteria that analysts could use to gauge whether these five forces exerted power in any industry. In order to do an industry analysis, one would consider whether these criteria existed in the industry, and whether they had the effect of making a force *strong* or *weak* (if you aren't sure, you would say the strength was *medium*). If a force was strong, then it would exert a strong effect on competitive dynamics within the industry, and the criteria identified as making that force strong would be considered as likely to be KSFs.

Most industries would have between 3 and 15 KSFs identified as bases of important competitive advantage. Too few and it would be hard to identify specific opportunities for individual companies that were not shared by all companies. Too many, and it would be hard to develop a cohesive plan for taking advantage of so many opportunities, or ameliorating so many threats.

And we could gauge the relative importance, or ranking, of the KSFs by how many times the same KSF was identified in different forces. For example, *low price* is undoubtedly a KSF in the consumer products industry and Walmart has been a champion in that worldwide industry. Walmart's customers value the low prices for reasonably good quality that they get at Walmart (customer power). Having such low prices makes it hard for small, medium, and even large companies to compete (barriers to entry). Walmart sources many products from small Chinese and other Asian suppliers whose prices are low, and who are easily replaced so Walmart can demand low prices from them (supplier power). Walmart's size as a giant MNE means that it can compete on price against smaller competitors, and even sell some products at a loss to gain or keep market share (rivalry). The same KSF appears in four of five forces and is therefore very important in this industry – for Walmart and all its competitors.

For *Barriers to Entry*, Porter[33] proposed a list of criteria, some or all of which could apply depending on the industry. These are reported in Exhibit 7.3. For *Buyer Power*, Porter[34] proposed the list of criteria found in Exhibit 7.4. For *Supplier Power*, Porter[35] proposed the criteria found in Exhibit 7.5. For *Substitutes' Power*, Porter[36] proposed the criteria listed in Exhibit 7.6. For *Rivalry*, Porter[37] proposed the criteria listed in Exhibit 7.7.

EXHIBIT 7.3 ENTRY BARRIER CRITERIA

Economies of scale or scope
Proprietary product (or service) differences
Brand identity
Switching costs
Capital requirements
Access to distribution
Absolute cost advantages
- Proprietary learning curve
- Access to necessary inputs
- Proprietary low-cost product design
Government policy
- Home base government (ex: tax policy, anti-corruption, etc.)
- Local government
Nongovernmental organization policy
Expected retaliation.

Source: Porter, M. *Competitive Strategy: Techniques for Analyzing Industries and Competitors.* New York: Free Press, 1980.

EXHIBIT 7.4 BUYER POWER CRITERIA

Bargaining severage
- Buyer concentration versus firm concentration
- Buyer volume
- Buyer switching costs relative to firm switching costs
- Buyer information
- Ability to backward integrate
- Substitute products.
Price sensitivity
- Price divided by total purchases
- Product differences
- Brand identity
- Impact on quality and/or performance
- Buyer profitability
- Incentives for purchase.

Source: Porter, M. *Competitive Strategy: Techniques for Analyzing Industries and Competitors.* New York: Free Press, 1980.

EXHIBIT 7.5 SUPPLIER POWER CRITERIA

Differentiation of inputs
Switching costs of suppliers, and firms being supplied
Potential substitute inputs
Supplier concentration
Importance of volume to the supplier
Cost relative to total customer purchases
Impacts of cost on price leader or differentiation strategies
Threat of forward or backward integration.

Source: Porter, M. *Competitive Strategy: Techniques for Analyzing Industries and Competitors.* New York: Free Press, 1980.

EXHIBIT 7.6 SUBSTITUTES' POWER CRITERIA

Relative price performance of substitutes
Relative product or service performance of substitutes
Switching costs
Buyer propensity to substitute
Disruptive technology potential: a simpler product eliminating unnecessary features.

Source: Porter, M. *Competitive Strategy: Techniques for Analyzing Industries and Competitors.* New York: Free Press, 1980.

EXHIBIT 7.7 RIVALRY CRITERIA

Company size
Industry growth (more rivalry in slower growth industries)
Fixed costs versus value added
Cyclicality or intermittent over-capacity
Product differences
Brand identity
Switching costs
Information complexity
Diversity of competitors
Mindset (ethnocentric, polycentric, geocentric)
Exit barriers.

Source: Porter, M. *Competitive Strategy: Techniques for Analyzing Industries and Competitors.* New York: Free Press, 1980.

An analyst would consider which of these criteria applied in the industry being analyzed, and would discuss only those that did apply. The analyst would be concerned with which forces exerted a strong or weak power over the industry's competitive dynamics. For forces exerting a strong power, then the most important criteria for that effect would be considered KSFs.

It should also be noted that in some cases different aspects of a force might have strong and weak effects at the same time. For example, in high technology industries R&D capability and/or technological innovation are often KSFs. For supplier power, R&D technologists or other groups of innovation-producing employees could be disproportionately important as suppliers. By contrast, suppliers of physical components might have relatively little power because there were many potential suppliers. It would be more appropriate to say that the R&D personnel had high power and the other suppliers low power, than to argue that because there was a range from high to low, the force should be evaluated as having medium power.

In addition, it is often appropriate to segment different classes of customers under buyer power. High-, medium-, and low-end customers may be moved by different purchase criteria and have more or less power as buyer groups. Low-end customers are more often compelled to seek price leader lower priced options. High-end customers are more likely to find differentiated products with more features and higher cost more appealing and be willing and able to pay. And higher end customers are more likely to be early adopters of new and innovative products, and therefore have more power in newly emerging high technology industries.

Competitive analysis

The industry analysis is successfully completed when we have identified the KSFs that would be the sources of competitive advantage for any company in that particular industry. Now the analysis shifts from the industry to the company level. We want to know for each KSF whether our company is doing better or worse than our direct competitors. If our company has an advantage on a KSF, it is an opportunity we might be able to take advantage of when we select our strategy and build our plan. If our competitors have an advantage on a KSF, it is a threat we need to find means to counter. We know the competitor will be looking for ways to take advantage of their opportunity at our expense. The process of competitive analysis is best explained with an example.

AC[38] was a small to medium size (SME) MNE located in central Canada that manufactured specialty carpet. Its main markets were in Canada and the United States with a smaller presence just being developed in Western Europe.

The industry analysis indicated that AC's customers could be segmented into commercial and residential segments. In the largest segment of the specialty carpet industry, commercial, the most important KSF was *low price*, followed by *reliable delivery*. In the second most important segment, residential, the most important KSF was *quality reputation*, followed by *reliable delivery*.

In the competitive analysis, we found that AC was unable to compete on low price in the commercial segment. A Chinese company, whose Chinese manufacturing costs were much lower than AC's, dominated segment sales. AC relied on carpet manufactured in its high-cost Canadian plant. It was only able to hold onto a small share of the commercial segment because it had relatively speedy delivery, compared with Chinese carpet coming by ship.

AC was also unable to compete on quality reputation in the residential segment because it was the reincarnation of an earlier carpet manufacturing company known for poor quality. By contrast, other competitors in the residential segment had extremely high quality but very slow delivery. AC held onto a small share of the residential segment only because its faster and more reliable delivery.

Going forward, AC needed to improve its competitive position in either the larger commercial segment or the smaller residential segment. It needed a strategic plan to either produce products of acceptable quality for the commercial segment at a lower price, or it needed to achieve a higher quality reputation. We considered that, because of AC's administrative heritage – its name was associated with poor quality through its predecessor – it could never achieve a reliable reputation for quality.

We recommended that it pursue a proffered opportunity to produce low-cost specialty carpets through contract manufacturing in Southeast Asia. The designs could be transmitted electronically, and local Asian AC employees, supervised from AC, could ensure the design and quality at the contract factory.

This would give AC both KSFs required for the commercial segment. A customer could choose between the same low price as provided by the Chinese market leader, or much faster delivery for a higher price.

Mechanically, the process of doing competitive analysis is not hard. You can arrange the KSFs in order of their importance on the vertical axis of a table, and your company and its competitors on the horizontal axis. Following along with the AC example and the commercial segment, we have charted the competitive analysis in Exhibit 7.8. Ratings may reflect either quantitative or more subjective evidence. We have rated AC and its competitors based on our own interpretation of the evidence on a scale of 1 (lowest) to 3 (highest). Objective evidence could be obtained from one's sales force, for example. Salespeople hear about their customers' assessments of the competition in relation to themselves. Product/service characteristics and pricing are often available on competitors' websites.

We rated *low cost* as the most important KSF because it was the only KSF the market leader excelled at. We rated speedy *delivery* second most important because AC was able to compete despite its poor quality reputation. Quality was not picked as a KSF in commercial segment but we included it because the two residential competitors were very strong on quality.

What we have is a numerical statement as to why commercial customers would vastly prefer the Chinese market leader. DCC's position is at best slightly better than the top

EXHIBIT 7.8 COMPETITIVE ANALYSIS, COMMERCIAL SEGMENT

KSFs	DCC	Chinese market leader	Residential quality competitor #1	Residential quality competitor #2
Low cost (×3)	1	3	1	1
Delivery (×2)	2	1	1	0.5
Quality (×1)	1	1	3	3
Total score	8	12	8	7

EXHIBIT 7.8

residential competitor. If, however, DCC had low-price carpets available from Southeast Asia, their competitive position would become higher (14 instead of 8) than the market leader. DCC would have a comparably priced carpet available, but also be able to offer a faster delivery on a more expensive carpet.

Strategy

Porter[39] argued that there were only three strategies (see Exhibit 7.9). A company could seek to be the *price leader* in its industry by achieving the lowest costs and prices to its customers. In fact, most MNEs used to enter Emerging Markets to obtain low factor costs. American and Canadian companies set up their production facilities, for example, in the Maquiladora region of northern Mexico after the North American Free Trade Agreement (NAFTA) was signed because of the lower Mexican wage rates. Thanks to NAFTA, the products could be transferred back to the United States and Canada duty free. When China began its industrialization with its "Open Door" policy in 1979, all it had to offer were

EXHIBIT 7.9 THREE GENERIC STRATEGIES

	Uniqueness perceived by customer	Low-cost position
Industry-wide target	Differentiation Strategy	Overall cost Leadership
Segment target only	Focus Strategy	Focus Strategy

EXHIBIT 7.9

Source: Porter, M. E. *Competitive Strategy*. New York: Free Press, 1998, p. 39.

low wages, free land to set up production, and low tax regimes in the Special Economic Zones where foreign companies were invited.

The goal of the *cost leadership* strategy is to produce a competitive product at the lowest cost to customers. It is important to note that only one company can be the absolute cost leader and it is likely to be the company with the lowest factor, selling, and administrative costs.

By contrast, a *differentiation* strategy is intended to offer additional features that customers want, and are willing to pay more for. Customers pay more because they perceive the product or service either as unique or better fitting their needs. For example, BMW produces relatively expensive cars for a well-heeled segment that values driving dynamics, the latest technology, and the image of being seen to be successful. By contrast, a poorer man's or woman's BMW could be a Mazda ("zoom zoom") or VW. These cars have similarly impressive driving dynamics but are cheaper and lack the BMW cache. When a company uses a differentiation strategy to target a particular buyer segment then it is called a *focus* strategy, which may rely on a low-cost position, or on differentiation aimed at the specific needs or desires of that segment. Subaru's all-wheel drive focus concentrates on customers facing difficult weather or terrain.

In the AC example given above, we recommended that AC employ a low-cost focus strategy aimed at buyers in the commercial segment of the specialty carpet industry. AC's administrative heritage as a low quality carpet manufacturer seemed to preclude achieving a reputation for high quality and so AC could not effectively compete in the residential segment. It has been shown to be very difficult for companies to shake off historical perceptions of their quality. In the 1980s, Hyundai exported the Pony car from Korea to North America. It was a very poor quality, unreliable, and biodegradable (rusty) car. Today, Consumer Reports acknowledges that Hyundai cars are as good or better than most North American brands but many buyers still regard them with suspicion so that resale values are lower than average.

We should, however, regard Porter's three strategies with some skepticism. According to Bartlett and Beamish,[40] MNEs with geocentric mindsets or transnational mentalities are able to achieve cost leadership and differentiation simultaneously. By locating each activity related to the development, manufacture, marketing, sale, and service of their products, they are able to achieve the lowest costs for each. At the same time, they are able to pool their worldwide learning (see Chapter 4) to provide a vast array of product or service differentiations developed throughout their global operations, and at the lowest possible cost. Hyundai has become legendary in the automobile industry for having lower prices and higher levels of features than its North American, Japanese, or European competitors. Its *Genesis* luxury sedan is rated higher in 2013 in quality and equal in reliability to Cadillac's *CTS*, and Mercedes *E350* while costing $7,000 less than the former and $11,500 less than the latter.

We should also be aware that the Chinese teach their business students using both Sun Tzu,[41] and the 36 stratagems of Ancient China (see Chapter 13).[42] The Japanese teach their business students the *Book of Five Rings*[43] containing five additional strategies. The point is that these Chinese and Japanese business students are being equipped with strategic ideas that Western students do not hear about. If you are going to do business with Asians, you should make the effort to read what they are studying to prepare to deal with you.

The plan from the planning side of the Double Diamond

From the planning side of the Double Diamond model (the left diamond), the plan is relatively straightforward. We know the vision so we know the values and performance expectations of senior management. We have analyzed the competitive industry environment, bearing in mind that many MNEs compete across the globe, often in many industries. It's important to remember that the competitive environment for the same industry may be different in different countries or regions. We have identified KSFs, and opportunities and threats in relation to our direct competitors.

The plan is where we say how we think we can take advantage of selected opportunities based on the weaknesses of our competitors. And we have identified what we think are the advantages of our competitors, so our plan should include what we are planning so as not to be taken advantage of by them.

Plans are very specific to corporate and environmental circumstances. For example, in Aboriginal Tourism projects, the vision is generally to allow tourists to experience Aboriginal life as the Aboriginals themselves do. The goal is for global tourists to participate in First Nation lifestyle rather than as tourists being bused here and there to see sites, eat, and watch staged cultural events. The First Nations' bands are an internal-to-Canada Emerging Market. Tourists would experience and participate in Aboriginal arts and culture, enjoy unique cuisine and accommodations, and participate in a variety of wildlife viewing adventures.

Accommodation, however, usually provides the greatest challenge because of the limited financial resources (the right side of the Double Diamond) of the First Nations' communities developing these projects. In one project, the original plan was to accommodate the eco-tourists in tipis, a traditional form of mobile Native dwelling, providing an experience rather like camping.

The problem was that market research found that the tourists most likely to respond to this kind of adventure were Germans and other Western Europeans. These tourists expected first-class facilities when they paid high-end prices, and would not be willing to endure primitive camping facilities. A relatively luxurious (for an Aboriginal reserve) hotel or guesthouse would be required, with indoor plumbing and the usual amenities. It was fine to expect these Euro tourists to rough it during their daily adventures, but they also needed to be comfortable. These strategic requirements put a severe strain on the band's limited resources, and their ability to implement it became considerably more challenging.

Implementation issues

On the right hand side of the Double Diamond model (see Exhibit 7.2), the concern is whether the internal capabilities of the company are capable, or could be made capable, of implementing the strategic plan. A plan is worthless if it cannot be executed.[44]

Usually the question of how to organize the company's capabilities to execute the proposed strategy is more challenging that finding an appropriate strategic plan.[45]

We must consider three categories of internal capabilities. Available or obtainable *resources* are critical, including *human*, *operational*, and *financial* resources. Often, these resource capabilities interact with each other. For example, a large Canadian public accounting firm wanted to attract business from Chinese companies investing in Canada. It had extensive financial and operational resources but the Chinese companies wanted to do business with capable and senior Chinese personnel with whom long-term relationships could be built. This accounting firm had relatively few Chinese personnel and none in senior positions. Although Chinese personnel had been hired, retention was a problem because its Canadian partners and managers had not been sensitized as to how to manage Chinese personnel. As a result, when the firm opened a branch in Hong Kong to expedite its strategy, Chinese customers were not attracted and the branch failed.

Organization structure, *systems*, and *organization culture* are also critical for implementation. For example, a company competing for overall cost leadership will (or should) reduce costs by implementing a more authoritarian structure with tight reporting and approval systems that limit decision-making freedom for managers at lower levels. Its organization culture should be one of dependency on the leadership to set policy on spending decisions.

These structure, systems, and culture are consistent with ensuring lower spending authority, and lower costs. However, they also discourage high quality human resources who are looking for opportunities to demonstrate personal competence in order to advance their careers. They have the effect of lowering the quality of human resources. This suits the company since human resource costs will be lower as well.

Under these conditions, however, it would be difficult for the company to change to a differentiation strategy, or delegate additional decision-making authority because of a new strategic plan. And you should note that there are interaction effects between organizational and resource capabilities.

Ford Motor Company had these sorts of difficulties when Bill Ford II was CEO. Senior managers, both functional and geographic, pursued their own strategic plans and refused to cooperate with each other, even sabotaging each other's efforts to make their own chances of promotion better. The control structure was weak. Bill Ford recognized he was not strong enough as a leader to force a more cooperative culture. He recruited Alan Mulally and stepped away from the CEO role and active leadership.

Leadership is the third critical element in managing a company's internal capabilities (see Chapter 6). It interacts with resources and organization to produce results. A more authoritarian leader will prefer a tighter and more authoritarian structure, more systems to control outcomes, and a culture that discourages delegation of decision-making authority. It could be argued that authoritarian leadership may be more effective for MNEs pursuing cost leadership strategies.

A more democratic leader will be more likely to institute a more democratic structure, and fewer systems to control subordinates' behaviors, hoping to empower them. Delegation of decision-making authority and responsibility will be the order of the day. We could argue that more democratic leadership could be more suited to companies pursuing differentiation or focus strategies. The production of differentiating product or service innovations often come from bright ideas originating among employees and/or managers at lower levels of the organization – in R&D, production, marketing, or sales. Greater freedom to participate in decision-making is more likely to allow these ideas to surface and be adopted in product and service designs. Personal empowerment tends to attract more capable employees looking for opportunities to show off what they believe they can do.

In addition, we should consider that leaders may be habitually influenced – even unconsciously – to behave in certain ways because of their personality preferences. This is because these personality preferences influence what kinds of information they are predisposed to regard as important, and how they judge its relevance. We must consider how these kinds of cognitive biases may influence the implementation of the plan in the form of an unintentional *emergent* strategy, either supporting or detracting from the intended plan.

Resources and implementation

Resources include human, operational, and financial resources. The basic idea for ensuring that resources are, or can be made, consistent with the strategic plan is simple enough. We consider *not* the entire scope of resources existing in the MNE, but only those that we anticipate will be directly required to make this particular strategic plan work. We identify those resources that we will need that do exist within the company and cost them in relation to the implementation of this plan. When we see that a particular resource is inadequate for the required tasks, we are identifying a critical resource *gap*. We ask ourselves, or our colleagues who are responsible for that resource, how we could obtain it in the form needed, and how much it would cost. If we believe that the gap can be filled in a cost-effective manner, our analysis proceeds. If the gap cannot be filled in a cost-effective manner, then the strategic plan cannot be successfully implemented, and the plan must be altered in a way that makes it feasible. There are many kinds of resources that must be considered. Exhibit 7.10 offers a list of possibilities that should not be considered complete.

As when lists of criteria were given for the Five Forces analysis, the analyst should consider only those resource capabilities that are relevant to the strategic plan being considered for implementation.

In considering whether resource gaps exist in relation to the proposed plan, a tabular approach is recommended. This is illustrated in Exhibit 7.11. The same approach could be usefully applied to gap analysis for organizational, or leadership gaps.

E
X
H
I
B
I
T

7.10

EXHIBIT 7.10 POTENTIALLY NECESSARY RESOURCES

Human

- Potential; depth, experience; skills; flexibility of management, professional staff and workforce
- Commitment, loyalty, morale
- Union and association relationships.

Operational

- Facilities; locations; geographical coverage
- Access to low-cost inputs/factors of production; distribution of product value chain (R&D, sourcing, manufacturing, marketing, sales, service) to low-cost locations
- Supplier relationships
- Plant costs, capacity, efficiency, and flexibility
- Proprietary processes, information technology, and knowhow
- Expertise in relevant product and process development
- Scalability of facilities, personnel efforts
- Technology/marketing partnerships and agreements
- Logistics reliability and efficiency
- Quality or cost reputation; customer relationships
- Marketing sales force and distribution capabilities.

Financial

- Performance, scale, cash flow, assets, cash
- Capacity to raise capital; cost of capital
- Shareholder expectations; market assessments
- Banking and investor relations
- Resilience to cyclical or unanticipated market downturns.

Source: Adapted from Crossan, M. M. et al. *Strategic Analysis and Action*, 7th edn. Toronto, ON: Pearson Prentice-Hall, 2009, p. 108.

Organization and implementation

Organization includes structure, systems, and organization culture. The basic ideas for assessing whether organizational capabilities are consistent with a proposed strategic plan are the same as for resources as described above. Exhibit 7.12 offers a list of potential organization-related capabilities to consider.

EXHIBIT 7.11 GAP ANALYSIS PROTOCOL

Resource category	Required resources	Available resources	Major gaps	Gap-closing solution and cost
Human Operational Financial Other				

Source: Adapted from Crossan, M. M. et al. *Strategic Analysis and Action*, 7th edn. Toronto, ON: Pearson Prentice-Hall, 2009, p. 118.

EXHIBIT 7.12 POTENTIALLY NECESSARY ORGANIZATION CAPABILITIES

Structural

- Authoritarian versus democratic decision-making
- Ethnocentric (HQ dominates subsidiaries); polycentric (portfolio of subsidiaries independent of HQ except financial controls); geocentric (HQ and subsidiaries pool authority and learning)
- Geographic divisions versus functional areas versus matrix management.

Systems

- Control; reporting; decision-making; information technology (IT); recruitment; hiring; performance appraisal; compensation; inventory — there are many.

Organizational culture

- Authoritarian versus democratic; flexibility; resistance to change; bureaucratic; entrepreneurial
- Innovative: capacity to support strategies based on new ideas — through new markets, products/services, processes, technologies
- Productivity: capacity to support strategies based on cost efficiency and price.
- Speed: capacity to support speed to market, speed of R&D, speed to satisfy new or existing customer needs
- Cross-cultural effectiveness: ability to support cooperation between employees from different cultures; ability to attract and retain local market employees in subsidiaries and at headquarters. Cultural diversity as a competitive advantage
- Interdependence and cooperation (or not) between functional areas (marketing (and operations) or geographical units (headquarters and subsidiaries).

Source: Adapted from Bartlett, C. A. and Beamish, P. W. *Transnational Management*, 6th edn. New York: McGraw-Hill Irwin, 2011. Also Crossan, M. M., et al. *Strategic Analysis and Action*, 7th edn. Toronto, ON: Pearson Prentice-Hall, 2009, p. 159.

EXHIBIT 7.11

EXHIBIT 7.12

Leadership and implementation

The leadership of the company influences both the planning process through their vision, and also the implementation through its actions. In addition to the leaders or senior management team, middle-level managers and lower level supervisors may facilitate or retard the achievement of the strategic plan. They may actively support the plan, offer only lip service in support, or even resist its implementation. Leadership influences the implementation in a number of ways through:

1   Management preferences.
2   Ethical orientation.
3   The unintended effects of leaders' personalities may support or hinder the achievement of the plan through emergent strategies.

Management preferences

Management preferences are based on personal attributes, education and learning, and experience derived from job contexts. These characteristics influence how leaders and managers perceive business situations, evaluate options, and select actions. While management preferences influence the strategic planning process through the vision of company leaders, here we are concerned with the preferences of all levels of management as they affect actions intended to achieve implementation.

The question related to management preferences is similar to the one posed for resources and organization. Will management preferences support the proposed plan, or are there preference gaps that will need to be filled if the plan is to succeed? And as before, if management preferences cannot be made consistent with the proposed plan, then the plan will fail and will have to be revised. Exhibit 7.13 lists a number of critical management preferences that must be satisfied for successful implementation.

Managerial ethics

Worldwide issues of character[46] and honesty in human exchanges are critical. Witness what has happened recently in the political, business, religious, and virtually every center of power. One observes lying, cover-ups, lack of integrity, accountability, and stewardship together with unfocused, narrow, and self-serving visions of the future. Cases abound in the newspapers and in business journals.

In 2012, HSBC was described by Carl Levin of the United States Senate as being "pervasively polluted for a long time," having been found to have laundered more than US$15 billion in cash for "Mexican and Russian drug gangs, terrorists and rogue regimes such as Iran." HSBC chief Stewart Gulliver said the bank had put aside US$700 million to cover the cost of the "shameful and embarrassing scandal," but admitted the number could

EXHIBIT 7.13 MANAGEMENT PREFERENCES CRITICAL TO PLAN IMPLEMENTATION

Goals

A strategic plan will state measureable goals indicating what it is intended to achieve both absolutely and in relation to the competition. *Hard* goals may be related to profitability, market position, growth, and willingness to accept risk. *Soft* goals may be related to outcomes for a variety of stakeholders including managers, employees, customers, and communities.

■ Are there observed gaps between these goals and the observed preferences of managers at any level? Are there risks and/or consequences if these gaps cannot be filled?

Product market focus

A strategic plan indicates the specific products/services to be offered, and the characteristics of the market where these products/services will compete. This information will be derived from the KSFs, opportunities, and threats determined by the industry and competitive analysis.

■ Are there observed gaps between these requirements and the observed preferences of managers at any level? Are there risks and/or consequences if these gaps cannot be filled?

Value proposition

A strategic plan will indicate whether a cost leadership, differentiation, or focus strategy will be used to achieve competitive advantage in the defined marketplace.

■ Are there any observable gaps between the expertise and/or experience of key managers responsible for implementing the strategy? Will managers prefer, and be able to complete any core activities related to implementation? Can observed gaps be filled by recruiting managers with relevant experience and where need they be placed for effective implementation?

Source: Crossan, M. M. et al. *Strategic Analysis and Action*, 7th edn. Toronto, ON: Pearson Prentice-Hall, 2009.

EXHIBIT 7.13

be "significantly larger."[47] At the same time, HSBC was warning that banking businesses could leave the United Kingdom "if London's reputation is not restored" after some British financial institutions were found to have rigged Libor interest rates, and money-laundered for rogue regimes.[48] It was an interesting ethical juxtaposition that the same bank that was paying fines in the United States was threatening to exit the U.K. because other banks had engaged in apparently similar practices.

Corruption and bribery are present in most, if not all, societies; more so in some cultures than others. Truth and honesty are noble ideals, but they are also relative. As managers operate globally, they must be aware of the relativism in each culture regarding acceptance of a tip, bribe, incentive, etc. Different criteria and values between Eastern and Western cultures, for example, determine what is acceptable or appropriate. In developing countries where people struggle to survive, bribes and corruption, especially in the public sector, are endemic to the system. In industrialized countries, the practice is often more sophisticated, less visible, but prevalent. In 2012–2013, two mayors of Montreal, Canada's second largest city, have been forced to resign amidst allegations from a public inquiry that they accepted bribes in the form of political contributions to award public construction projects.[49]

In China, small gifts and favors associated with guanxi relationships are considered normal business practice (see Chapter 13). For American businesspeople, these gifts and favors represent corrupt practices,[50] though it may be that individual instances may or may not represent corrupt intentions.[51] It is, however, possible that we Westerners apply different standards to the Chinese than ourselves. It is a common practice for North American businesses to buy season tickets for boxes at professional football or baseball stadiums. The tickets are available so that a company's more favored clients or customers may attend with company representatives. In China, this would be considered a gift or favor.

Ethical relativism

The perception of bribery is culturally relative and one's conscience is "culturally conditioned." In some countries, the same action condemned as bribery might be considered a tip (to ensure promptness or service), especially when dealing with the bureaucracy. Among government officials in many lands, the ethical dilemma has also been labeled "influence peddling." Here, there is a fine line between legal and illegal, or even moral and immoral behavior. Government officials in Beijing are allowed to accept small gifts up to a certain value because gift-giving is customary in Chinese culture. A $10 package of Canadian ginseng is acceptable according to department policies, but a gift valued over $20 would be questionable. If you offered the same gift to a Canadian or American official, it would raise his/her eyebrows in disbelief and suspicion.

The spread of questionable and inappropriate behavior in both business and government within the so-called advanced countries has led to a demand by the public for more character education in schools. Business schools are now under pressure to offer business ethics as a required class. What is ethical or standard in one culture may not be so in another.[52] Hooker[53] makes three distinctions regarding perspectives we could have about cross-cultural ethics.

First, Contextualism allows for different obligations in different cultural contexts, though they may flow from the same universal principles. Cronyism and nepotism may be unacceptable if one's culture is built on transparency and merit, but acceptable in a culture that is relationship-based. People tend to support the cultural system from which they come, or on which they rely.

Second, Ethical Relativism claims that fundamentally incompatible ethical principles rule in different cultures. Western individualism leads to ideas such as equality and human rights, while Hindu pantheism recognizes the connectedness of all beings, and permits a stratified society based on karma (fate or destiny). On the other hand, Ethical Universalism holds that world cultures ultimately agree on basic values.

Third, Meta-ethical Relativism argues that value statements are inherently relative – judgments based on prevailing conditions. Thus, in this analysis, ethical assertions, as opposed to normative ethics, mean investigating the circumstances in which decisions or behavior occur. For example, corruption in Western societies is criminal behavior because this is a rule-of-law-based culture that perceives rules as fair and justly enforced; people are generally expected to play by those rules. In Chinese culture, guanxi, or the giving of favors to build relationship, contributes to stable and trusting relationships important in their trade and negotiations.

Our view is that the need to choose between ethical universalism and ethical relativism in its three varieties represents a Western cultural propensity for dualistic thinking. Dualism is essentially the need to choose between apparent opposites because if one is right, the others must be wrong. Insisting on choosing is actually the imposition of a Western cultural value that may be foreign to particular societies' alternate cultural beliefs. By contrast, the Chinese view of opposites is that they are complementary in the same way that the principle of passivity (yin) and activity (yang) complement because each may be appropriately applied depending on the situation and one's position in it. Situations require mixtures of yin and yang behavior.

There are ethical values that seem to us to be approximately universal; for example, the golden rule of treating others as you would hope to be treated. We think that most people, worldwide, would not disagree with the compassionate values, "To proclaim release for prisoners, and recovery of sight for the blind, to let the broken victims go free."[54] Christians, Muslims, Buddhists, Communists, Democrats, and Republicans would likely agree though the specific implementations might well differ.

If opposites complement, then we do not have to choose between ethical relativism and ethical universalism. There are ethical values that are clearly relative to one's culture like the appropriateness of hiring one's relatives or friends particularly without an open competition. And there are values that seem to have universal validity across a variety of cultures. The Christian "Golden Rule" of "so, in everything, do to others what you would have them do to you," attributed to Jesus Christ,[55] was independently expressed almost five centuries before by Confucius as "do not impose on others what you do not wish for yourself."[56] One finds expressions of this principle in most world religions.

Surprisingly, there are remarkable similarities even between the Chinese Confucian views of Xunzi on individual moral development, and those of the Western European philosopher Kierkegaard, even though there is no evidence that Xunzi (circa fourth century BC) was known to Kierkegaard (circa nineteenth century AD).[57] Both argued that there were three main stages of ethical orientation and development, and their descriptions of these stages were remarkably similar. Both argued that education and life experience were bases for moving to higher stages of ethicality.

In Kierkegaardian terms, almost all humans related to ethics in one of these three orientations, and through education and life experience a person could advance to a higher stage, or regress to a lower one. These stages are, from lower to higher, as follows:[58]

- *Pre-ethical.* Individuals at this stage have no commitment to any personal ethics. Their primary motivation is to belong and be accepted by their reference groups. Consequently, they repress their own individual desires and are unaware of what they might really want. In a sense, they might appear as chameleons. If their reference group is ethical, they will appear ethical. If their reference group is not ethical, then they are not.
- *Aesthetic.* Individuals at this stage are committed only to the ethic of self-interest. They seek to exploit the malleability of the Pre-ethical, and the predictability of the Ethical for their own advantage. They recognize, however, that others will be predisposed against them if they appear to be unconcerned with public goods, so they attempt to appear overtly ethical. At the same time, they pursue their self-interest covertly as necessary. A good practical example might be derived from the two news releases about HSBC that began this section on ethics. On the one hand, HSBC was apparently caught money laundering in the United States and was putting money aside to pay the fines. On the other hand, the same bank was decrying the behavior of other banks in the United Kingdom that had been caught engaging in similar behavior. HSBC wants to be seen as an advocate of ethics, but at the same time is apprehended for putting its self-interest first.
- *Ethical.* Individuals at this stage are committed to publicly held ethics and willingly sacrifice their own self-interest to support it. They regard ethical principles as universal and their duty to enforce their observance. They may regress to the aesthetic level if they realize that ethics are often relative to a historical time, and a cultural location, and therefore are not absolute.

Both Kierkegaard and Xunzi postulated a very similar fourth stage but both regarded it as unlikely that more than a very few would achieve it. Xunzi (and Confucius) called this stage the sage, who had achieved moral enlightenment. Kierkegaard called it the religious – a person who had discovered truly universal values nested in the universal deity.

In today's global marketplace, there is a positive trend toward good corporate citizenship and business ethics. Thus, global leaders at all levels of management are concerned that neither the organization nor its personnel engage in behavior that harms society. The proper goal of business is still maximizing shareholder value, but within the constraints of appropriate ethical conduct. That means global leaders recognize that some actions may be legal, but unethical; also, that many things required by ethics are not required by law. Shareholder value, however, implies respect of others' property rights, especially "intellectual property." Edith Sternberg, a business philosopher, maintains that "ordinary decency" excludes behavior in commerce such as lying, cheating, coercion, violence, spying, stealing, and killing. Normally, honesty and fairness are good for business, and crime does not pay. Corruption and intimidation, as well as the subversion of politics and law enforcement, not only undermine business, but also society.

Distributive justice, on the other hand, implies that performance and promotion are based on merit, not influence; benefits are distributed in return for helping the organization achieve its goals. In too many corporate scandals, managers acted as if they were accountable to nobody. Procedural justice means that the processes through which decisions are made are both fair and transparent. Interpersonal justice means that people are treated with politeness, dignity, and respect by authorities implementing procedures and making decisions. Informational justice means that explanations are given, and information conveyed about why procedures were implemented in certain ways, or why outcomes were distributed in certain ways. All of these forms of justice are considered goals to be achieved by business ethics.

Thus, the movement toward corporate social responsibility (CSR) – that is, good management and accountability for the benefit of stakeholders and society – is a positive. It means that ethical behavior, like ordinary decency and distributed justice, are adhered to by organizational leaders[59] even in Emerging Markets where employees are hired, and factories set up to take advantage of low cost factors. When a clothing factory, or sweatshop, collapsed in Dhaka in April, 2013, killing 1,100 workers, the corporate response was swift. The factory had been producing Joe Fresh brand clothes for Loblaw Inc. Loblaw senior officials immediately flew to Dhaka promising compensation for the workers' families, and pledged never to accept suppliers unless their worksites were inspected for safety. However, not all MNEs are as committed to ethics as Loblaw was. A number of U.S. companies declined to endorse the new worksite safety protocols.[60] Therefore, it is up to governments to be guardians of the public interest by reasonable legislation and enforcement, mediating among diverse interests, collecting taxes to provide public goods and services, and, when necessary, organizing resources in cases of disaster.

Unintended emergent strategies

The idea that managers could be influenced in their strategic implementation by unintended, habitual patterns of behavior based on personality is an argument based on an evolutionary psychology (EP) perspective. EP research has established that humans have evolved (or been blessed with) competitive self-interested, and cooperative altruistic behavioral sequences as means of coping with and adapting to recurrent situations in their external environments.[61] And these adaptive responses, differentially distributed, are understood to influence cultural strategic adaptations.[62]

Keirsey[63] has provided an interesting analysis concerned with how heritable personality temperament preferences[64] affect leadership style at a level below leaders' conscious awareness. Mintzberg et al.[65] make the same arguments as the basis for what they call the "Cognitive School" of strategic management. Jungian personality theory,[66] upon which Keirsey's work was based, argued that there were two essential and competing preferences for selecting relevant information from the external environment. These two were characteristic of all humans, and individual humans were predisposed in favor of one or the other.

- Sensing (S): Concrete, realistic, practical, experiential, and favoring traditional interpretations. Strong preference for sensory data – observing what is actually happening.
- Intuiting (N): Abstract, imaginative, conceptual, theoretical, and preferring the original and creative over traditional solutions. Strong preference for reading between the lines to understand underlying causes.

Keirsey argued that all people were either Sensing or Intuiting in their predominant approach to selecting what they considered relevant information, and many studies have demonstrated this to be true across cultures.[67] If a person's predominant preference for information gathering was Sensing, Keirsey argued that his/her predominant preference for information sorting would be one of two inherent and competing preferences:

- *Judging (J)*. Systematic, planful, early starting, scheduled, and methodical. Judgers were fast decision-makers because they were organized and knew when they had enough information to make a decision and begin implementation.
- *Perceiving (P)*. Casual, open-ended, pressure-prompted, spontaneous, and emergent. Perceivers were slow decision-makers because they were not organized and always hoping for additional information for a better solution.

If a person's predominant preference for information gathering was Intuiting, however, then Keirsey argued that his/her predominant preference for information sorting would be quite different. Again, these choices represented inherent and competing preferences:

- *Thinking (T)*. Logical, reasonable, questioning, critical, and tough-minded. Thinkers were impersonal in their analysis and favored efficiency or effectiveness ahead of interpersonal values.
- *Feeling (F)*. Empathetic, compassionate, accommodating, accepting, and tender-minded. Feelers were committed to using interpersonal values and existing or hoped-for relationships as a basis for decision-making.

On the basis of this analysis, Keirsey identified four personality temperaments and observed four styles of leadership, each characteristic of a particular temperament. Individuals of a specific temperament would lead in ways that were characteristic of the associated leadership style. They would lead in these systematic directions without being aware that there was a specific cognitive bias[68] underlying their perceptions and judgments. See Exhibit 7.14 for the four leadership styles and some of their associated characteristics.

We take the position that if a leader, or potential future leader, becomes aware of these unintended cognitive biases and their implications for habitual leadership behavior, they may be corrected. At least the leader becomes aware of his/her potential strengths and weaknesses and can attempt to correct the latter.

EXHIBIT 7.14 FOUR TEMPERAMENT-BASED EMERGENT LEADERSHIP STYLES

Leadership style	Logistical leadership	Tactical leadership	Diplomatic leadership	Strategic leadership
Personality temperaments	SJ (Sensing and Judging)	SP (Sensing and Perceiving)	NF (Intuiting and Feeling)	NT (Intuiting and Thinking)
Strategic bias Biased in favor	Altruistic Concrete strategy. Organizational approach to task achievement	Self-interested Concrete strategy. Utilitarian personal approach to task achievement	Altruistic Abstract strategy. Cooperative interpersonal approach to task	Self-interested Abstract strategy. Efficient utilitarian approach to task achievement
Usual focus	Formal organization: stabilize and consolidate organizations with schedules, routines, rules, procedures. See themselves doing their duty	Tactical adaptability. Everything is negotiable. The art of give and take. Eschew formal organizations, rules and procedures	Natural aptitude with people. Builds trust, cooperation, shared goals, friendships. Helps others. Wants harmonious people-oriented workplace	Systems thinkers. Schedules human and material resources efficiently to achieve well-defined goals. Eliminates inefficient bureaucracy
Strengths	Quick decisions based on facts and not theory. Lots of data. Orderly and expects others to be so. On time and on schedule	Flexible, patient, open-minded, risk-taking. Shifts position easily with new information. Doesn't search for hidden meanings	Empathetic. Appreciative. Strong builders of relationships. Intuitive insights on social consequences	Visionary. Statistical analysis and flowcharting. Contingency planning. Committed to effective change
Weaknesses	Bureaucratic. Resists changing rules and procedure. Formal, critical and impersonal. Forgets to give credit. Impatient. Angry if tired	Doesn't like to be told how to work. Impatient with bureaucracy. Forgets to follow through. May initiate without necessary approvals	Sensitive to criticism. Takes it personally. Avoids problems to avoid disharmony and unpleasantness	Too technical approach makes communicating vision difficult. Hates to repeat. No positive feedback — unaware of others' feelings

Source: Adapted from Keirsey, D. *Please Understand Me II: Temperament, Character, Intelligence.* Del Mar, CA: Prometheus Nemesis, 1998, pp. 286–330.

A useful exercise is for students to complete the KTS II (Keirsey Temperament Sorter) online at "Keirsey.com." Students are divided into homogeneous groups; all SJ, SP, NF, or NT. Each group discusses the percentage of temperament descriptors true for all members of their group (usually between 45 percent and 95 percent). Then, the groups are redistributed to get as many temperaments as possible in each group. The new groups are asked to identify areas of potential conflict between members based on the temperament descriptors. For example, the SJ propensity for bureaucracy and formal organization can alienate both the SP who is impatient with procedures, and the NT who seeks to eliminate inefficient bureaucratic procedures. The SJ may also alienate the NF through impersonal criticism that the NF takes personally. The point is that students, and managers, are generally unaware that their social and leadership behavior is so affected by habitual behaviors they are unaware of. And they do not realize that many of these unintended behaviors may cause negative reactions on others' parts.

One interesting trend has been the increase in altruism-oriented business students in both the United States and Canada since the 1990s.[69] Abramson[70] argued that the NF and SJ temperaments were more altruistic, and the NT and SP temperaments more self-interested. In the 1990s, approximately half of business students in both countries were NT and we could assume that American and Canadian businesses were habitually biased in favor of self-interested strategies. Nowadays, three-quarters or more of business students are either SJ or NF, and the numbers of NT's had become less than 5 to 10 percent. This suggests a more altruistic bias for future business organizations and their strategies. These findings offered hope that in the future, international relations between MNEs, and between MNEs and their stakeholders may be characterized more by helping and less by obtaining the best outcomes at the expense of others.

Strategic planning and emerging market uncertainty

Courtney et al.[71] argued that some Emerging Markets may exhibit levels of uncertainty such that the strategic planning process described in this chapter would not apply. They proposed that there were four levels of uncertainty in Emerging Markets (see Exhibit 7.15). The "traditional" strategic planning toolkit described in this chapter had been developed for level 1 uncertainty, and would work for level 2 or level 3 uncertainty through multiple analyses. It would, however, be inadequate for level 4 uncertainty because the nature of the probable external environment could not be accurately predicted.

In level 1, it is possible to develop a single forecast precise enough to identify KSFs, opportunities and threats versus direct competitors, and the organization, resources and leadership needed to make the plan work. While this "traditional" strategic planning model was originally developed for companies and MNEs competing in First World markets, it also applies to Emerging Markets when MNEs adopt polycentric, or geocentric mindsets that value local expertise.

Locally experienced managers will experience local business environments as having level 1 uncertainty, even when an MNE's headquarters leadership may experience the same environment as having level 2 or even level 3 uncertainty. As long as local country managers are allowed to manager local subsidiary operations (polycentric mindset), or are able to be integrated fully into the MNE decision-making process (geocentric mindset), the level of perceived uncertainty will be considerably less.

There are, however, situations of level 2 uncertainty even for competent local managers. The case of Dell's wholly owned greenfield entry to manufacture computers in Brazil is a case in point.[72] Dell negotiated the deal for its entry with a centrist pro-capitalist state government. Before it began to build its local factory, a socialist administration was elected on a platform that included renegotiating deals with MNEs based on extracting better benefits for "the people." It was not clear whether the new administration would, in fact, honor the original agreement or not. It was no longer clear that this state government would be supportive of Dell's entry.

However, strategic planning could still proceed. Two strategic plans would be required for comparison because the new state government and its possible new legislation would affect barriers to entry (the Five Force), possibly adding KSFs, as well as opportunities or threats, and require additional internal capabilities.

EXHIBIT 7.15 STRATEGIC PLANNING IN FOUR LEVELS OF UNCERTAINTY

	Level 1: A clear future	Level 2: Alternate futures	Level 3: A range of futures	Level 4: True ambiguity
What can be known?	Forecasting is certain enough for a strategic plan	Two equally possible outcomes that will define the future	A range of unpredictable but possible outcomes	No reliable basis for predicting future direction
Analytic tools	"Traditional" strategic planning toolkit	"Traditional" approach done for both. Prepared either way	Scenario planning	Qualitative cataloguing what is known or could be known. Find a subset of more predictable variables
Examples	First World: USA, EU, Japan	Uncertain politics: elections could go to left or right	Entering Emerging Markets without competent local leadership	The Russian market in 1992. The Egyptian, Libyan, or Iranian markets in 2013

Source: Courtney, H., Kirkland, J., and Viguerie, P. "Strategy Under Uncertainty," in H. Merchant (ed.), *Competing in Emerging Markets: Cases and Readings.* New York: Routledge, 2008, pp. 168–184.

Courtney et al.[73] argued that typically entering an Emerging Market represented level 3 uncertainty. We disagree unless the MNE has an ethnocentric mindset and believes that the local subsidiary strategic plan should be defined by how things are done at headquarters and in the home market. Companies with ethnocentric mindsets often find China to exhibit level 3 uncertainty. They experience the Chinese cultural practice of building guanxi-based business relationships as opaque because they do not understand which relationships will be critical. They also question the legality and ethics of offering small gifts and favors as a means to build relational reliability and long-term trust. However, these questions are often easily resolved for companies employing local managers or consultants who understand the Chinese system, and which gifts/favors are considered normal versus those that even the Chinese regard as illegal or unethical.

We do, however, agree with Courtney et al. that there are Emerging Market situations where there are more than the two competing possible futures defined as level 3 uncertainty. Strategic planning as described in this chapter still works but becomes considerably more complex and difficult when there are multiple scenarios to consider. Since the whole purpose of strategic planning is to reduce uncertainty and find a clear plan, companies would tend to find level 3 uncertainty an impediment to market entry. They would probably choose to export (see Chapter 4) to that market until they felt they had learned the ropes.

It is at level 4 that traditional strategic planning completely breaks down. The external environment is so potentially changeable, and for unpredictable reasons, that even multiple scenarios become uncertain. If the external environment cannot even be guessed, then an MNE cannot say what internal capabilities could be required. Most MNEs avoid this kind of situation. Kevin O'Leary[74] of the Canadian venture capital television series *Dragon's Den* was asked his opinion of investing in Russia, under the current conditions of political, insurgent, and criminal uncertainties. He said he expected it would be a good move in about fifty years when things would perhaps have settled down. Equally, an MNE would have to be very brave to invest in Egypt, Libya, Iran, or Syria in 2013, as those countries wrest with questions of insurgency, revolution, and internal conflict.

Courtney et al.[75] also argued that the strategic moves MNEs would be willing to undertake in Emerging Markets would depend on the level of perceived uncertainty. A *big bet* is a large commitment like a major capital investment or acquisition. Its purpose is to attempt to achieve a large payoff, and is often intended to re-structure an industry environment in an intended direction favorable to the big bettor. But big bets are inherently risky because they could result in big losses if they do not work out.

By contrast, *options* are designed to achieve big payoffs if everything works out while minimizing losses in the worst-case scenarios. Options often involve making modest investments that would allow a company to expand if it was desirable without putting too many resources at risk. A company could open a local sales and service office that could be expanded to subsequently to include manufacturing. A joint venture or licensing one's technology to a local company could also be limited risk options to facilitate future expansion.

EXHIBIT 7.16 STRATEGIC PLANS UNDER INCREASING UNCERTAINTY

Uncertainty	Big bets	Options	No regrets
Level 1	Yes	Yes	Yes
Level 2	Yes	Yes	Yes
Level 3	No	Yes	Yes
Level 4	No	?	Yes

Source: Courtney, H., Kirkland, J., and Viguerie, P. "Strategy Under Uncertainty," in H. Merchant (ed.), *Competing in Emerging Markets: Cases and Readings*. New York,: Routledge, 2008, pp. 168–184.

No regrets' moves are limited actions that are likely to payoff no matter what happens. Finding the means to reduce costs, or gathering local environment information, or hiring and training employees with local market experience could all be no regrets' moves. Exhibit 7.16 is intended to show how these three kinds of strategic plans could be applied in the four levels of uncertainty.

Options receive a question mark under level 4 uncertainty because European oil companies have made limited investments in level 4 nations such as Iran, and Canadian oil companies in Sudan, in recent years. These companies believed they were reserving the right to expand their presences over time. It is difficult when the environment is entirely unpredictable to know whether you are simply reserving the right to lose. In Iran, oil companies have been forced by the regime to pay to develop their oil fields but then have been granted a limited number of years of ownership before the property reverts to state ownership. Meanwhile, international embargoes of Iran have made it difficult to export the oil. In Sudan, Canadian companies found it politically correct to abandon their investments during the Sudanese civil war because of well-documented atrocities by the (northern) government against its southern population. SNC-Lavalin, another Canadian company, came under investigation after the Gadhafi regime in Libya was deposed, for paying out $160 million in alleged bribes to secure business deals. The Canadian police, the RCMP reported that, "It is alleged that these sums of money were paid as compensation for having influenced the granting of major contracts to SNC-Lavalin Inc."[76] It is unlikely this information would have become public had the Gadhafi regime not fallen.

CONCLUSIONS

Bourgeois et al.[77] offers some handy rules of thumb for how to generally decide what your plan should be after you have analyzed the external environment and considered the internal capabilities that are either available or obtainable. These are summarized in Exhibit 7.17.

EXHIBIT 7.17

EXHIBIT 7.17 RULES OF THUMB FOR STRATEGIC PLANNING

	Weak internal capabilities	Strong internal capabilities
Good external opportunities	Address/fix capabilities, weaknesses	Grow
Major external threats	Divestiture	Diversification

Source: Bourgeois, L.J. III, Duhaime, I.M., and Stimpert, J.L. *Strategic Management Concise: A Managerial Perspective*. Fort Worth, TX: Harcourt College, 2000.

An MNE with strong opportunities in its external environment and the internal capabilities needed to make its plan succeed should be pursuing a *growth* strategy. If the same company has internal capability gaps that prevent its plan from succeeding, it should address those weaknesses before attempting to take advantage of its identified opportunities in its business environment.

If an MNE has strong internal capabilities but its industry is not attractive and there are threats to its current levels of performance, then it should consider diversification into a related industry where its prospects may be better and its capabilities are still relevant. On the other hand, if an MNE is faced with both serious external threats and weak internal capabilities, it should consider divestiture. While such a simple rule of thumb does not tell you exactly what the plan should be, it does help to inform you whether your plan seems to be on the right track. Below we invite you to stretch your mind around some of the ideas in this chapter.

MIND STRETCHING

1   Porter would argue that every strategic decision-maker facing the same industry and competitive analysis, and internal capabilities, would produce the same strategy. We argue that because managers are logistical (SJ), tactical (SP), diplomatic (NF), or strategic (NT) that this would not be true. What do you think?

2   Consider what you know about the top 11 Emerging Markets (see Exhibit 7.1). What levels of uncertainty (1, 2, 3, or 4) would you predict each one had?

3   Go to Keirsey.com and do his free KTS-II temperament test. What do you think your emergent managerial biases might be? What would your strengths be?

NOTES

1   Hoffman, B. G. *American Icon: Alan Mulally and the Fight to Save Ford Motor Company*. Kindle Edition: Crown Business, 2012.

2 Sun Tzu. *The Art of War*. New York: Dover, 2002.

3 Oakley, D. "Emerging Market Equities Outperform West," *Financial Times* (FT.com), June 7, 2009.

4 Merchant, H. *Competing in Emerging Markets: Cases and Readings*. New York: Routledge, 2008.

5 Khanna, T. and Palepu, K. G. *Winning in Emerging Markets: A Road Map for Strategy and Execution*. Boston, MA: Harvard Business Press, 2010.

6 Ibid.

7 http://www.thejakartapost.com/news/2011/05/18/ri-may-become-one-six-major-economies.html.

8 http://www.wikipedia.org/wiki/Emerging_markets#section_2.

9 http://www.imf.org/external/pubs/ft/weo/2012/update/02/index.htm.

10 http://www.ftse.com/research_and_publications/FTSE_Glossary.jsp.

11 Cooper, R. "China 'To Overtake America by 2016," *The Telegraph*, July 13, 2013, http://www.telegraph.co.uk/finance/china.

12 Rodriguez, P. *China, India, and the United States: The Future of Economic Supremacy: Course Guidebook & Transcript*. Chantilly, VA: Teaching Company, 2011.

13 Ibid.

14 Mintzberg, H. and Waters, J. A. "Of Strategies, Deliberate and Emergent," *Strategic Management Journal*, Vol. 6, 1985, pp. 257–272. Also see Abramson, N. R. "From Self-Interest to Altruism: A Longitudinal Analysis of Anticipated Change and Convergence of the Emergent Consensus Strategies of American and Canadian Managers," unpublished working paper.

15 Mintzberg, H., Ahlstrand, B., and Lampel, J. *Strategy Safari: A Guided Tour through the Wilds of Strategic Management*. New York: Free Press, 1999.

16 Chia, R. and Holt, R. "Strategy as Practical Coping: A Heideggerian Perspective," *Organization Studies*, Vol. 27, 2006, pp. 635–655.

17 Crossan, M. M., Rouse, M. J., Fry, J. N., and Killing, J. P. *Strategic Analysis and Action*, 7th edn. Toronto, ON: Pearson Prentice Hall, 2009.

18 Abramson, N. R. and Ai, J. X. "Canadian Companies Doing Business in China: Key Success Factors," *Management International Review*, Vol. 39, No. 1, 1999, pp. 7–35.

19 Bartlett, C. A. and Beamish, P. W. *Transnational Management: Text, Cases, and Readings in Cross-Border Management*, 6th edn. New York: McGraw-Hill Irwin, 2011.

20 Khanna and Palepu, *Winning in Emerging Markets*.

21 Courtney, H., Kirkland, J., and Viguerie, P. "Strategy Under Uncertainty," in H. Merchant (ed.), *Competing in Emerging Markets: Cases and Readings*. New York: Routledge, 2008, pp. 168–184.

22 Perlmutter, H. V. "The Tortuous Evolution of Multinational Enterprises," *Columbia Journal of World Business*, Vol. 1, No. 1, 1969, pp. 9–18.

23 Porter, M. E. *Competitive Advantage: Creating and Sustaining Superior Performance*. New York: Free Press, 1980.

24 Crossan et al., *Strategic Analysis*.

25 Courtney et al., "Strategy Under Certainty."

26 Porter, M. E. "Strategy and the Internet," *Harvard Business Review*, March, 2001, pp. 1–18.

27 Bossidy, L. and Charan, R. *Execution: The Discipline of Getting Things Done*. New York: Crown Publishing, 2002.

28 Mintzberg et al., *Strategy Safari*.

29 "Ratings & Recommendations: Smart Phones," *Consumer Reports*, August, 2013, p. 22.

30 Porter, *Competitive Advantage*.

31 Ibid, p. 17.

32 Ibid.

33 Ibid.

34 Ibid.

35 Ibid.

36 Ibid.

37 Ibid.

38 The name has been disguised to protect the company's privacy.

39 Ibid.

40 Bartlett and Beamish, *Transnational Management*.

41 Sun Tzu, *The Art of War*.

42 Yuan Gao. *Lure the Tiger Out of the Mountains: How to Apply the 36 Strategems of Ancient China to the Modern World*. New York: Touchstone Books, 1992.

43 Musashi, M. *The Book of Five Rings*. Kindle Edition: Shambhala, 2005.

44 Crossan et al., *Strategic Analysis*.

45 Bartlett and Beamish, *Transnational Management*.

46 Badaracco, J. L. Jr. *Questions of Character: Illuminating the Heart of Leadership Through Literature*. Boston, MA: Harvard Business School, 2006.

47 "HSBC in Talks to Settle US Money Laundering Claims," *The Telegraph*, January 27, 2013.

48 Wilson, H. "Businesses Could Leave UK After Banking Scandals, Warns HSBC," *The Telegraph*, January 27, 2013.

49 Austen, I. "Montreal Mayor Resigns After Bribery Arrest," *The New York Times*, June 18, 2013, http://www.nytimes.com/2013/06/10/world.

50 Su, C., Singy, M. J., and Littlefield, J. E. "Is Guanxi Orientation Bad, Ethically Speaking? A Study of Chinese Enterprises," *Journal of Business Ethics*, Vol. 44, 2003, pp. 303–312.

51 Dunfee, T. W. and Warren, D. E. "Is Guanxi Ethical? A Normative Analysis of Doing Business in China," *Journal of Business Ethics*, Vol. 32, 2001, pp. 191–204.

52 Daly, M. "The Ethical Implications of Globalization of the Legal Profession," *Fordham International Law School Journal*. New York: Fordham University, 1998.

53 Hooker, J. *Working Across Cultures*. Stanford, CA: Stanford University Press, 2003, pp. 314–330.

54 Suggs, M. J., Sakenfield, K. D., and Mueller, J. K. (eds). *The Oxford Study Bible: Revised English Bible with the Apocrypha*. New York: Oxford University Press, 1992, p. 1333. This is traditionally known as Luke 4:18.

55 Matthew 7:12.

56 Freedman, R. *Confucius: The Golden Rule*. New York: Arthur A. Levine, 2002.

57 Remington Abramson, N. "Reappraising the Confucian Foundations of Chinese Business Ethics in the Light of the Xunzi," unpublished working paper.

58 Remington Abramson, N. "Kierkegaardian Confessions: The Relationship Between Moral Reasoning and Failure to be Promoted," *Journal of Business Ethics*, Vol. 98, No. 2, 2011, 199–216.

59 Beniff, M. and Southwick, K. *Compassionate Capitalism: Can Corporations Make Doing Good an Integral Part of Doing Well?* London: Career Press, 2004.

60 Fox, E. J., "U.S. Companies Drag Their Feet on Bangladesh Factory Safety," *CNN Money*, May 14, 2013, http://money.cnn.com/2013/05/14/news/companies/.

61 Buss, D. M. *Evolutionary Psychology: The New Science of the Mind*, 3rd edn. Boston, MA: Pearson, 2008.

62 Barkow, J. H., Cosmides, L., and Tooby, J. *The Adapted Mind: Evolutionary Psychology and the Generation of Culture*. New York: Oxford University Press, 1992.

63 Keirsey, D. *Please Understand Me II: Temperament, Character, Intelligence*. Del Mar, CA: Prometheus Nemesis, 1998.

64 Bayne, R. *Ideas and Evidence: Critical Reflections on MBTI Theory and Practice*. Gainesville, FL: CAPT, 2004.

65 Mintzberg et al., *Strategy Safari*.

66 Jung, C. G. *Psychological Types*. Princeton, NJ: Princeton University Bollingen Series XX, 1976.

67 See for example Abramson, N. R. "Internal Reliability of the Keirsey Temperament Sorter II: Cross-National Application to American, Canadian, and Korean Samples," *Journal of Psychological Type*, Vol. 70, No. 2, 2010, pp. 19–30.

68 Bazerman, M. *Judgment in Managerial Decision Making*, 4th edn. New York: John Wiley & Sons, 1998.

69 Abramson, N. R. "From Self-Interest to Altruism: A Longitudinal Analysis of Anticipated Change and Convergence of the Emergent Consensus Strategies of American and Canadian Managers," unpublished working paper.

70 Ibid.

71 Courtney et al., "Strategy Under Uncertainty."

72 Nelson, R. "Dell's Dilemma in Brazil: Negotiating at the State Level," in H. Merchant (ed.), *Competing in Emerging Markets: Cases and Readings.* New York: Routledge, 2008, pp. 1–17.

73 Courtney et al., "Strategy Under Uncertainty."

74 O'Leary, K. *Cold Hard Truth: On Business, Money and Life.* Toronto, ON: Doubleday Canada, 2011.

75 Courtney et al., "Strategy Under Uncertainty."

76 Barnes, R. "RCMP Alleges SNC-Lavalin Made Bribes for Libyan Deals," *Construction News*, January 28, 2013.

77 Bourgeois, L. J. III, Duhaime, I. M., and Stimpert, J. L. *Strategic Management Concise: A Managerial Perspective.* Fort Worth, TX: Harcourt College.

ADDITIONAL FEATURES

Please visit the companion website at: www.routledge.com/cw/Moran where you will find additional case studies, study aides, and instructor resources.

8 MANAGING GLOBAL TRANSITIONS AND RELOCATIONS

We need to throw our hats far away to make retrieving them interesting.

French saying

A tourist is someone who travels to see things that are different and then complains when they are not the same.

Anonymous

The number of leisure travelers and passport-holders for most countries has increased over the past five years, as has the number of business travelers from many countries.

This chapter has several objectives: first, to understand the challenges inherent in transitional experiences and relocations; second, to examine ways for fostering acculturation when abroad, especially through training in business etiquette and protocols for living and working skillfully in a different environment. We will begin with four examples.

SAGA OF MY BRAZILIAN ADVENTURE

The adventure was finally started. The airplane landed smoothly in Guarulhos Airport in São Paulo, Brazil, early in the morning on January 2, 2004. This was to be about the last smooth experience I would have for a long while.

Many times, I wondered how I was so lucky to have found my way into the position that I was in. Here I was, a person from the rural Midwestern United States, being charged with upgrading the breadth and depth of a major multinational company's corn-breeding organization in Brazil. I was to do this from a base in central Brazil, right on the frontier of the Cerrados, the vast Brazilian savannah. This must have been what it was like when my grandfather emigrated from Europe to southwest Minnesota about a hundred years ago. He was moving to the land of Crazy Horse, the famous Sioux Indian Chief, big sky, and horse races by the pool hall. I was moving to the land of Rondon, Amazonia, big-time agricultural entrepreneurs, and the best football (soccer) in the world.

At customs, I immediately noticed things were different. People from the United States were being segregated into a separate line. This had never happened before. Fortunately, I was at the head of the line, since there were only a few people on the flight from the United States, and only a very small group of them were U.S. citizens. As I walked up to the tables, I noticed they were manned by the Federal Police, and the tables were in addition to the customary immigration booths that one passes through to enter the country. It all seemed rather haphazard but very police-like.

As I handed the tall, brasiliera in a Federal Police uniform my passport, I inquired:

"What is going on?"
"What do you think of your president?" she growled.
"What is the right response?"

She gave me an attractive smile and eased off. She then explained "that some judge in Mato Grosso," had ordered her to come to the airport and provide the same scrutiny to the incoming people from the United States as the United States was giving to the brasilieros. This was done at the last minute, and this guy was doing this only for political reasons.

She then proceeded to fingerprint me, all ten fingers dipped into ink and pressed onto a card. I then had numbers somehow arranged onto a card, maybe it was my passport number, and held this against my chest while the other policeman "photographed" me. Both were a source of amusement, as I was the first one for them, and they were somewhat shocked at the process once they actually did it, especially for an *ianqui* who, they learned, enjoyed their country.

Finally, I was appropriately documented, and allowed to go to the other line for the normal immigration and behind all the other foreigners on my flight and another much fuller flight. Eventually, I passed through immigration and went to retrieve my luggage.

I was coming into the country with only what I was carrying, so I was traveling heavy. After filling my luggage cart with the four bags I was carrying, two quite large and heavy, plus my carry-on bag and briefcase, I headed out the door, finally!

No sooner had I passed through the door than a very smartly dressed man with a perfect haircut and smile came up to me and asked me if I was an American. I indicated I was, and only then noticed the person with the television camera coming up. He introduced himself as working for a television station in São Paulo, and he asked if he could interview me regarding my thoughts on the revised immigration procedure for U.S. citizens.

My immediate thought was, "This is trouble." I had some experience with the press in the past and had an inherent distrust of their appetite for controversy. I politely responded, "No, but I am sure there are others that would be happy to respond to your questions."

With that I turned away and began to make my way through the crowded airport. Guarulhos is one of the few airports that I travel to that can be crowded on January 2.

I must have looked like a beleaguered American with lots of heavy baggage, tired from 18 hours of traveling, needing to change clothes, wanting to brush my teeth, needing a cup of coffee, and working my way through the crowd. Before I went 20 feet, the television reporter again asked for an interview, only this time the man with the camera appeared to have it running. Again, I politely declined.

By the time I reached the center of the main hallway in the airport, the crowd thinned, but once again, my shadow, the television news personality, was there to ask for an interview. This time, I reconsidered. I decided he was not going to go away, and I did not want to be cast as the ugly American. The best approach was to give him a brief interview, and then I would be able to have some peace.

"How did you feel about the new immigration procedures, fingerprinting and photographing of everyone from the United States?"

"I like Brazil so much that it is worth the effort."

A noticeably perplexed look began to appear on his face.

"Was the line long, and did you have to wait a long time?"

"Yes, the line was long, but so was the other line."

By this time, the interviewer realized this would be a rather boring interview, so he stopped asking questions and thanked me for my time.

I was sure I had escaped unscathed and went on to my destination, Brasilia, which required another six hours of travel time.

Two weeks later, I traveled back to São Paulo to participate in a weeklong Portuguese immersion course. No sooner had I been introduced to my first professor than she recognized me from television. She was shocked.

Apparently, the news program had found a U.S. citizen who was sufficiently angry that they obtained the desired emotion. They ran my interview along with the other one as a measure of the range in response.

About this time, widely publicized reports began to appear of an incident involving a pilot of a U.S. commercial airline. Apparently, the pilot became angry with the delays on entering the country; flight crews normally do not have to stand in line with all the passengers and get preferential treatment at immigrations. So he very publicly insulted the federal police. He was arrested and fined quite a considerable amount of money.[1]

MY FIRST TRULY GLOBAL EXPERIENCE

I was the Learning and Development Program Manager for a global executive development course with modules taking place in Brazil, China, India, United States, and the United Kingdom over an 18-month period. The modules became mini projects with temporary virtual work teams established, working together for short, intensive periods of time, and then disbanding. My goal was to quickly establish trust and rapport, an environment where you can individually give your best and speak up with your ideas or concerns.

I have undertaken the role of program manager on significant but predominately UK/European-based change programs. I felt confident in terms of the development process; however, I soon learnt the complexities and significance of working across cultures.

Our first overseas module in São Paulo, Brazil, was a challenge – first, I had difficulty in understanding the spoken English of our Brazilian team members and, more importantly, their way of working. I had to check myself when I started the telephone calls – I wanted to get straight into the tasks, updates, and issues, and I quickly learnt that our colleagues would prefer an informal start with general chat over how we are doing, the weather, our family, etc. A crucial step in building relationships and a good lesson learnt.

Our second overseas module took place in Georgia, United States, supported by a very focused, dynamic, and experienced events team. Our calls would start, "Hi, how are you? Great, thanks. Right, where are we up to?" Our working was efficient and we established some very strong working relationships. During a lessons-learnt conference call I chaired at the end of the hugely successful module, I was provided with a list of items which had not gone well and should be put right next time. This was a significant difference from our Brazilian colleagues and meant I needed to shift my style to be more direct, clear, concise, and resilient to ensure we maintained rapport.

Our third module took place in Shanghai, China. I was taken aback by a lack of challenge, discussion, or ideas which were offered to counter my suggestions. I actually found it unnerving to not receive any obvious feedback such as I had experienced with the United States. I wanted a "sense of certainty," and I wasn't able to achieve this to the extent I required. I learnt that our Chinese colleagues are not direct in their communication style and that I should look for more subtle messages.

Our fourth and final overseas module took place in India. I started this module in a similar way as the others, working collaboratively, and happy to lead as and when required. I did notice early on that some decisions were made without my involvement. Having learnt more about the Indian culture, attitudes towards women, and respect for seniority, I took an opportunity to share my background with our Indian colleagues, and adapt my style to become more assertive and decisive in our discussions. However, I knew there was a line – to try too hard would flip from collaboration to compliance – and I didn't want that. The contrast from my colleagues was dramatic; I was now referred to for decisions, with greater involvement and transparency.

This global experience has had a profound effect on me personally and professionally. The opportunity to travel and learn from our overseas colleagues and delegates has left a lasting effect on me, which I am truly grateful for.[2]

BEING NORMAL IN MY "PERSONAL" CULTURE

I was raised in a big family that had elements of individual freedom "to be a kid" while following a tight scheme of family discipline. The freedom included being released, unsupervised, with my seven brothers, almost on a daily basis to explore the desert surroundings. This is where I learned the double life of (1) being curious and having fun with a bundle of kids, as well as (2) listening to my elders and "follow the crowd/conform."

I went happily along in my childhood and young adult life collecting my "normal labels," like a nicely decorated Girl Scout sash. When I tried real hard, I got good grades and I was able to attend "the best schools." I performed well and did what was "expected" of me. I was normal. My personal culture (value, ideals, etc.) were a mix of what I experienced myself and what was taught to me.

Getting older, the expectations people had for me started to feel uncomfortable. It started when I needed to defend my choice of undergraduate degree: biology. Why was I studying biology and NOT becoming a doctor? I was in no way interested in medicine, but had a CURIOSITY as to why clouds formed and how fish guts worked. I wanted to understand the natural science part of the world. This was what seemed to be the beginning of picking and choosing what parts of my culture fit me best and what parts just weren't "me." Choosing for myself, it was perceived by others that I was not following the path that was expected of me.

After graduating, I continued in the NORMAL expected trajectory of getting a "good and promising job." After three years, by "applying myself," I competed for and was offered a prestigious job that included work in environmental law. This new job would be comfortable, it would advance me, and it would keep me in the world of "making it/being normal," and . . . I panicked. This was not entirely "me." I saw my life flash in front of me, with me as the passenger and not the driver.

SO, I pushed the eject button and jettisoned myself out of that world, out of the watchful eye of the culture that was comfortable. I made it a bit easier by physically removing myself far away.

I moved to Africa.

There, I could challenge myself, disown the labels that did not suit me, and attempt to discover what IT was that forms me. What was left that I valued once removed from the "normal" life? It became easier to understand my personal culture/identity by experiencing/encountering it in another culture, outside my own culture. This is where my curiosity and need to engage with others worked nicely. I could pick, choose, reject, and/or adapt ideas and values, and connect with other people and their ideals and values. I didn't need to change; I just needed to understand myself better.

I could see my culture from the outside while fully submerged/surrounded by an entirely different culture. I found many similarities, many conflicting ideas, and some new and interesting twists about how other people thought and acted.

Nowadays, I continue to be surprised and find comfort in the uncomfortable; and I have a normal life. I have learned to not be threatened by another culture nor mesmerized by it. I didn't "go native" and abandon the values and ideals I felt were mine. I found that people were curious about my culture, and I about theirs. By being open, intrigued, and curious, both parties enjoyed finding the silly idiosyncrasies of each other's culture. I have found the possibilities in the impossibilities.[3]

CURIOSITY, REFLECTION, TOLERANCE, ATTITUDE, FLEXIBILITY

Constraints: Labels, identities, external culture (nonpersonal culture) expectations that do not fit with your personal culture.

Liberations: Curiosity, exploration, interest, engagement, selecting values from the other cultures (including the culture you were raised in.) that fit with your personal culture.

UPROOTED CHILDHOODS

In a wonderful book of memories of growing up global, *Uprooted Childhoods*,[4] the memories of several well-known authors who were born in one country and grew up in different countries were chronicled. They were, in many ways, nomadic children. The following quotations seem relevant to the subject in this chapter.

■ From Isabel Allende, author, who experienced a nomadic childhood: "The contrast between the puritanism of my school, where work was exalted and neither bodily impurities nor lightning flash of imagination allowed, and the creative idleness and enveloping sensuality of those both branded my soul."

■ From Pat Conroy, author and son of a Marine Corps fighter pilot: "Our lives were desperate and sad. . . ." "I moved more than 20 times, and I attended 11 schools in 12 years. . . ." "Home is a foreign word in my vocabulary."

■ From Faith Eidse, author: "During my first 18 years, I moved 18 times. . . ." "I grew up not knowing what I would be. . . . I felt pressure to fit in . . . but there was a constant tearing inside . . . of not belonging."

■ From Nina Sichel, author: "For them, home is a real place, and for me, it is a shifting definition."

■ From Peter Ruppert, author: "History and language also shape us."

■ From Carlos Fuentes, author: "The shock of alienation and the shock of recognition are sometimes one and the same."

In December 2012, the UN World Tourism Barometer stated that someone became the one billionth (1,000,000,000) tourist setting a new record for world travel.[5]

Culture impacts identity: "culture shock"

One reason the transitional experience is so significant is that it may alter our sense of identity. Fearn[6] writing on the subject of philosophy makes the point that all humans are faced with three critical questions: (1) *who am I?* (mind and body); (2) *what do I know?* (language and knowledge); (3) *what should I do?* (morals and meaning of life). Major turning points in our lives often force us to rethink our answers to these inquiries which affect our self-perception, and the image we project to others.

All transitions influence one's sense of identity – some strengthen this sense of self, while others may threaten that identity or even change it. That is why we should deal with this matter before departure overseas. When we go outside our home culture into a foreign culture, we may, for example, experience an identity crisis abroad. As a result, personal development occurs when we redefine our answers to the above questions, thereby expanding our perceptual field.

Perhaps the most important lesson for the cross-cultural sojourner is to understand one's cultural baggage.

RELOCATION CHALLENGES

When we relocate within our own country or abroad, we may be subject to culture shock. Although scholars have only researched this phenomenon since the 1960s or so, its impact on people has been written about in works of fiction as early as 1862, including Tolstoy in his book *The Cossacks*. Again, Jack London, in a 1900 story, described what it felt like to be a "foreigner," but in a literary, not scientific, way. London describes what a sojourner should expect:

> He must be prepared to forget many of the things he learned, and to acquire such customs as are inherent with existence in the new land; he must abandon the old ideals and the old gods, and oftentimes he must reverse the very code by which his conduct has hitherto been shaped. . . . The pressures of the altered environment are almost unbearable, and they chafe in body and spirit under the new restrictions which are not understood. This chafing is bound to act and react, producing diverse evils and leading to various misfortunes.[7]

Essentially, culture shock, as described by London, is our psychological reaction to a totally unfamiliar or alien environment, which often occurs with any major transitional experience.[8] Culture shock is neither good nor bad, necessary nor unnecessary. It is a reality that many people face when in strange and unexpected situations that makes it difficult for automatic coping, as we do in our home culture. Oberg referred to culture shock as a generalized trauma one experiences in a new and different culture because of having to learn and cope with a vast array of new cultural cues and expectations, while discovering that your old ones probably do not fit or work. More precisely, he notes:

> Culture shock is precipitated by the anxiety that results from losing all our familiar signs and symbols of social intercourse. These signs or cues include the thousand and one ways in which we orient ourselves to the situations of daily life – how to give orders, how to make purchases, when and when not to respond. Now these cues, which may be words, gestures, facial expressions, customs, or norms, are acquired by all of us in the course of growing up, and are as much a part of our culture as the language we speak, or the beliefs we accept. All of us depend for our peace of mind and efficiency on hundreds of these cues, most of which we are not consciously aware of.[9]

Myriad forms of culture shock

A new form of this trauma, growing exponentially throughout the world, is *future shock*, of which Alvin Toffler warned in his 1970 book by that title and again in a 1980 volume, *The Third Wave*. Essentially, this mass culture shock is being experienced by whole groups and nations because of the inability to transition rapidly from a previous stage of human development (e.g., agricultural or industrial) into our present Information Society, or knowledge culture. The technological, scientific, and knowledge advances have been so large and so accelerated that many people cannot cope with the pace of these changes. They opt out or are bypassed by the mainstream of civilizations; many end up in an underclass position in modern society. Furthermore, today, countries and institutions – such as religious, educational, and political systems – are resisting modernization, suffering from culture lag, and living in the past, unable to cope with present and future challenges. For institutions, the same phenomenon is referred to as *organization shock*.

According to Klopf,[10] there are six stages of culture shock resulting from relocation.

1   The *preliminary stage* involves preparation for the experience. During this stage, anticipation and excitement build as one packs, makes reservations, and plans for departure with many unrealistic expectations.

2   Arrival at the destination marks the *spectator stage*, during which there are many strange sights and different people. All of this newness produces fascination with the culture. This honeymoon stage may last from a few days to six months.

3   The *participation stage* occurs when the individual must do the hard work of living in the culture and learning about it, especially its language – the honeymoon has ended. The sights have been visited and, now, coping with everyday life must occur.

4   When problems begin to arise that are difficult to handle, usually the *shock stage* sets in. Irritability, lethargy, depression, and loneliness are symptoms. One must find ways to confront and adjust to the differences in culture.

5   If the individual reaches the *adjustment stage*, identification with the host culture has progressed satisfactorily. Relationships with locals develop, along with a sense of belonging and acceptance.

6   For individuals living permanently in a culture, the adjustment stage finishes the transition period – one may assimilate or become bicultural in mindset. For those who are temporarily living in a host culture, the return to the home culture introduces the *reentry stage*. Culture shock in reverse may set in, with individuals again going through the above five stages, but this time in their native land. A sense of discomfort, disorientation, and even frustration may be experienced, often up to six or more months.

The pace at which one advances through these stages is different for each individual. For those who are experienced in international travel, it may quicken and perhaps lessen the trauma.

However, for the *long-term expatriate* exposed to a very different culture from one's own, physical and psychological concerns may be real or imagined. Those experiencing culture shock manifest the obvious symptoms, such as excessive anxiety over cleanliness and sanitary conditions, feeling that what is new and strange may be "dirty." This may be seen with reference to water, food, dishes, and bedding, or evident in unreasonable fear of servants and shopkeepers because of disease they might bear. Other indications of such traumatic behavior are feelings of helplessness and confusion, growing dependence on long-term residents of one's own nationality, constant irritations over delays and minor frustrations, and undue worry about being cheated, robbed, or injured. Some may exhibit symptoms of mild hypochondria, expressing apprehension about minor pains, skin eruptions, and other ailments, real or imagined – it may even get to the point of actual psychosomatic illnesses. Often, individuals experiencing culture shock postpone learning the local language and customs, dwelling instead on their loneliness and longing for back home, to be with one's own, and to talk to people who "make sense." However, persons who seek international assignments as a means of escaping "back-home problems" with career, marriage, or substance abuse will probably only exacerbate personal problems that would be better resolved in their home culture.

Osland[11] uses the concept of "learning to live with paradox" instead of emphasizing the shock that may come from experiences in an alien society. Such paradox occurs when we have to hold ideas in mind that are seemingly opposite to the home perspectives. Osland calls this the "road of trials" when we are confronted with obstacles and tests on our way to "normally" perceiving and functioning. To deal with such paradoxes more effectively, she proposes we learn from expatriates who have gone before us, which can begin before departure and continue on-site.

To facilitate acculturation, organizations responsible for sending others abroad should be careful in their recruitment and selection of individuals for international assignments. Surveys have shown that those who adjust and work well outside their own culture are usually well-integrated personalities, with qualities such as *flexibility*, *personal stability*, *social maturity*, and *social inventiveness*. Such candidates for overseas work are not given to unrealistic expectations, irrational concepts of self or others, nor do they have tendencies toward excessive depression, discouragement, criticism, or hostility. Global corporations, government agencies, and international organizations that sponsor people abroad have a responsibility to prevent or reduce culture shock among their representatives. It is not only necessary for individual acculturation, but is more cost effective, while promoting out-of-country productivity and improving client or customer relations with host nationals. This will be discussed further in the section on deployment systems.

One should also be realistic about the difficulties that may be experienced when living abroad. Intestinal disorders and exotic diseases are real, and may not always be avoided by inoculations or new antibiotics. In some countries, water, power, transportation, and housing shortages are facts, and one's physical comfort may be seriously inconvenienced.

Political instability, ethnic feuds, and social breakdown may make an assignment unacceptable. Adjustment may also be slowed because of not knowing the local language, or in trying to cope with strange climates and customs. But we are born with the ability to learn, to adapt, to survive, to enjoy. After all, human beings do create culture, so the shocks caused by such differences are not unbearable or without value. The intercultural experience can be more satisfying, contributing much to personal and professional satisfaction. One can discover friends everywhere. The expatriate experience has always meant accepting risk implicit in living and traveling beyond your own borders.

As nongovernmental organizations (NGOs) increase in number and influence, *global humanitarians* are more prevalent. But today, their service abroad on behalf of others may often place them in "harm's way." Civil strife may cause them to shut down operations, or they may face kidnapping, bodily harm, and even death.

Role shock

The phenomenon and process of culture shock have applications to other life crises. For instance, there is also role shock. Each of us chooses, or is assigned, or is conditioned to a variety of roles in society and its institutions – man or woman, family member, son or daughter, parent or child, husband or wife (single/married/divorced), teacher or engineer, manager or union organizer, amateur or professional. In these positions, people have expectations of us, as we do of their varied positions. These role opportunities or constraints often differ in another culture. A woman, for instance, may do in one culture what is forbidden in another. In some societies, senior citizens are revered, and in others ignored. In some cultures, the youth regard teachers with awe, while others treat them as inferiors or "buddies."

Role perception is subject to change according to time, place, and circumstances. But since the mid-twentieth century, our defined roles have changed at an accelerating rate. In the past, our roles were fairly stable, clear, and predictable. Today, our roles are fuzzy, more unpredictable, and fluid. The person who has a particular understanding of what a manager is and does may be upset when he or she finally achieves that role, only to discover it to be altered considerably! Our traditional views of such functions are suddenly obsolete. All this role uncertainty can be very disconcerting; the resulting shock to our psyche may be severe and long lasting. Role shock can lead to an identity crisis, especially if one's sense of self and life are tightly linked to a career or work role. Consider the trauma an older person experiences when suddenly there is a reduction in the workforce, and unemployment lines are long, while jobs are scarce. Furthermore, a cross-cultural assignment can accentuate role shock. Many individuals sent abroad find themselves adjusting to totally different role requirements than back home.

Role shock may be apparent as a result of organizational mergers or acquisition, or of reorganization or redesign of a system. The outcome may cause a person's position to be combined with others, downsized, or even lost. In the past decade, many middle managers were simply eliminated in corporations trying to cope with new economic conditions. Even when one retains his or her post within a newly acquired company, the organization and its culture may perceive "your role" in an entirely different way. Role transformation or elimination may come from new technologies, new research, new markets, or new crises.

Reentry shock

When expatriates return from foreign deployment, they face another form of reverse culture shock. Reentry research and its impact on the individual and the organization has been largely neglected.[12]

Having objectively perceived his or her culture from abroad, one can have a more severe and sustained jolt through reentry into a home culture. The intercultural experience widens perceptions and broadens constructs, so the person is less myopic in the homeland and more cosmopolitan. Some returning "expats," or those returning from long service over-seas, feel a subtle downgrading and loss of prestige and benefits. Others bemoan the loss of household help and social contacts, as well as other "perks." This is especially evident with members of the military who come home after a lengthy deployment in other parts of the world. Many feel uncomfortable for six months or more in their native land, frustrated with their organization and bored with their "narrow-minded" colleagues who never left home. Some returnees seem out of touch with what has happened in their country or corpo-ration during their absence, and no longer seem to fit into the domestic organization.

The coming home phenomenon described here can be temporary and less intense if the expatriate is helped by a professional reorientation program. For some, culture and reentry shocks may be the catalysts for major choices and transitions, such as a new locale and new relationships, pursuit of additional education or training, a change in job or career, and generally an improved lifestyle. While some expatriates never make the necessary readjustments, living as strangers in their home cultures, for the majority, the intercultural experience is very positive, a turning point toward an enriched quality of life.

CROSS-BORDER GLOBAL TRAVEL

Today, global travel for short or long periods is common. Such travel may be for pleasure, professional development, and education, or for business and military service. Humans have the capacity to move their bodies and/ or their brains. The latter is evident in unmanned, automated space missions to the far corners of the universe. Electronic travel may range from telephone, radio, and television, to computer exchanges via the Internet in the form of email, websites, chat rooms, podcasts, blogs, and wikis. In all cases, cross-cultural sensi-tivity and skills can facilitate global communications.

In today's global village, the number of people living in another country for lengthy periods is increasing. Virtually everyone comes in contact with individuals who speak a different language or who were reared in another culture. In this twenty-first century, cultural homogeneity and isolation exist in very few places – heterogeneity, or diversity, is the reality everywhere. Within our shrinking world, everyone, from executives to entertainers, soldiers to humanitarian volunteers, needs skills in managing both cultural differences and synergy.[13] Furthermore, we are transitioning into an emerging *knowledge culture* that offers new applications for such competencies. Richard Lewis suggests that it is a risk-taking, electronic culture that: (1) encourages entrepreneurialism, Western-style individualism, and rapid decision cycles; (2) responds quickly and flexibly to end-user needs; (3) allows for greater customization of brands and services; and (4) communicates interactively for "communities of families and friends."[14]

Embarking on a "hero's journey" is the way the late anthropologist Joseph Campbell describes the challenge of living outside one's culture, while Osland reports on adventures abroad as "hero's tales."[15]

Furthermore, we have not even to risk the adventure alone, for the heroes of all time have gone before us. The labyrinth is thoroughly known. We have only to follow the thread of the hero path, and where we have thought to find an abomination, we shall find a god. And where we have thought to slay another, we shall slay ourselves. Where we had thought to travel outward, we will come to the center of our own existence. And where we had thought to be alone, we will be one with the world.

COPING WITH TRANSITIONAL CHALLENGES

Early researchers in cross-cultural studies were concerned primarily with what happened when a person transitioned from home culture to a host culture. Today, interdependence between nations has facilitated the cross-border flow of people, ideas, and information. But we have a broader view of *transition trauma* associated with life's turning points, be they relocation or other personal and professional challenges. The trauma may simply be triggered by multiple career assignments or opportunities, whether experienced domestically or internationally. In addition to the ordinary lifestyle transitions that everyone faces, contemporaries must cope with rapid alterations in their work, environments, and cultures.

Increasingly, we interact with people who are very different from us, or in situations that are unfamiliar. Even when we share a common nationality, we may have to deal with citizens who are indeed "foreign" to us in their thinking, attitudes, vocabulary, and background. Individuals may face challenges within their environment due to their upbringing or local cultural conditioning. These challenges present opportunities either for growth or disruption. Such life-turning points may range from married couples who divorce; to families who move from one geographic area to another, whether at home or abroad; to those who have major alterations in careers, jobs, or roles; to personally confronting issues of serious illness or even death. To get a sense of transitional experiences that can cause culture shock, consider the scenarios shown in Exhibit 8.1.

All of the incidents in Exhibit 8.1 are *real, transitional experiences*. Each is an example of a life challenge that can be perceived as either devastating or a new chance. Having in-depth, intercultural encounters can be stimulating or psychologically disturbing, depending on your preparation and approach to them. Acculturation, or the process of adjustment to new experiences or living environment, takes time, possibly months and even

EXHIBIT 8.1 UN STUDY CITES VALUE OF GLOBAL MIGRATION

A recent United Nations study reports a surge in global migration at the turn of this century that is keeping populations from declining in Europe, as well as stimulating economic growth in North America by increased foreign income and workers.

Majority to minority culture

Your company transfers you and your family to a section of your country where you feel like an alien. From the Northeast, you come to this Sunbelt state that is so different and unique. Your boss suggests you enroll at the local university to take a course entitled "Living Texas" to introduce you to the myths and mannerisms of Texans.

Transitions in the global marketplace

You are a North American marketing consultant for a high technology company worldwide. Because of your expertise, you are much in demand, traveling beyond your home culture on short assignments. Your professional activities take you to a variety of host cultures. Typically, you are there for one to two weeks, consulting with local executives, many of whom are quite different in their approach to you as a woman. Most of your clients are men from cultures as diverse as Indonesia, Malaysia, Mexico, India, Hungary, and Russia.

Technology transfer

You are an engineer from a highly industrialized nation. Your overseas assignments are mainly to less-developed countries. You realize that the indigenous population is not ready for sophisticated technologies. To help them in their transition to modern economies, and rather than sell them expensive equipment that they cannot afford or maintain, you prefer to design appropriate machines that pump water, cook food, and meet their real and practical needs.

Adjusting to new immigrants

You live in east San Diego near a local Somali community and have been a leader, helping new arrivals to acculturate. You have been notified that some 10,000 more Somali Bantu refugees are being relocated to the United States with your government's assistance. Two hundred of these tribal people, descendants of slaves, are coming to "America's Finest City."

Immigration or movement from one area to another has been part of the human story for thousands of years. Eugene Tartakovsky's book entitled *Immigration and Policies, Challenges and Impact* gives viewpoints on key issues of immigration and studies using a variety of methodologies on many topics, such as the psychological theories of premigration motivating immigration policies of selected countries towards immigrants and the challenging adjustment issues of immigrants.

E X H I B I T 8.1

Deployment for war and peacekeeping

As a U.S. Marine sergeant, you are a veteran of the Iraq War. You were one of those marines who went off to fight in the last decade and returned forever changed by your brief, intense experience with death and privation. You came back a driven and changed man, worrying if your marriage would also become a casualty.

Source: Tartakovsky, Eugene (ed.). *Immigration and Policies, Challenges and Impact.* Hauppauge: Novo Science Publishers, 2013.

years, while one learns new skills for responding and adapting to the unfamiliar. The extent of the trauma depends on the situation, such as whether one lives abroad among the native population or in a protected compound, be it a military, diplomatic, corporate, or religious enclave. The experience of coping with global diversity can be renewing or debilitating. When we are strangers in a place where the traditions and customs are foreign and unexpected, we may lose our balance and become unsure of ourselves. The same thing can happen within our own society when change happens so rapidly that the old traditions, the cues we live by, are suddenly undermined and irrelevant, threatening our sense of self.

Transitional experiences offer two alternatives – to cope or to "cop out." One can learn to comprehend, survive in, and grow through immersion in a different culture. The positive result can be increased self-development. Whenever we leave home for the unfamiliar, it involves basic changes in habits, relationships, and sources of satisfaction. Inherent in cultural change is the opportunity to leave behind, perhaps temporarily, one set of relationships and living patterns and to enrich one's life by experimenting with new ones. Implicit in the personal conflict and discontinuity produced by such experiences is the possible transcendence from environment or family support to self-support. Intercultural situations of psychological, social, or cultural stress also stimulate us to review and redefine our lives – to see our own country and people in a new perspective. Or, we may reject the changes or new culture and lose a possible growth opportunity.[16]

FOSTERING ACCULTURIST STRATEGIES

After the initial phases of culture shock pass, with hope, acculturation begins. Anyone who has gone from home to live, work, or study in a foreign country must learn about and adapt to another quite distinct cultural environment. As early as the 1930s, *acculturation* was being formally researched by scholars. The definition developed then is just as valid today – when groups of individuals having different cultures come into continuous firsthand contact with subsequent changes in the original cultural patterns of either or both groups.[17]

Most obviously, one must assimilate to fulfill practical needs for survival and accommodation in strange situations, like finding grocery stores, doctors, schools, banks, etc. Integration into a different society produces more personal changes, as one moves beyond the familiar patterns and institutions of the old, while attempting to absorb and understand the new. Value systems and attitudes also undergo alteration in this process. Furthermore, there may be biological changes as one adjusts to a different climate, bacteria and viruses, or unknown food and plant life. Also, social changes occur as the visitor seeks to find and form new relationships and friendships. All of these happenings may result in stress or tension.

Sociologists point out that stable, healthy family relationships can make the difference between success and failure in the foreign assignment. Families who interact in mutually supportive ways can be their own resource for acculturation into another environment. As ambassadors of your native culture, do endeavor to establish wholesome intercultural relations with the local people. Such behavior not only contributes to creating a favorable image of your own country, but facilitates your adjustment as well. Extending culture shock can be a hindrance to forming friendships and effective business relations abroad. Travelers abroad have to reach out and create a friendly, positive impression, lest we be perceived as arrogant and imperious.

The following ten recommendations will help to deflate the stress and tension overseas, while advancing successful acculturation:

- *Be culturally prepared.* Forewarned is forearmed. Individual or group study and training are necessary to understand cultural factors and cultural specifics. Public libraries and the Internet provide a variety of resource material. Also, the public health service will advise about required inoculations, dietary choices, and other sanitary data. Before departure, the person scheduled for overseas service can experiment with the food in restaurants representative of the second culture. Furthermore, one might establish contact in his or her homeland with foreign émigrés, students, or visitors from the area to which he or she is going. A helpful approach is to seek out your own *cultural mentor* – a wise friend or counselor who has lived in the host country, or who is there upon arrival. The expatriate's mentor is capable of guidance, encouragement, and help in mastering the intricacies of a new culture. Sometimes your organizational sponsor abroad may link you to such a resource or even provide a *cultural coach.*
- *Learn local communication complexities.* Study the language of the place to which one is assigned. At least, learn some of the basics that will help in exchanging greetings and shopping. In addition, to advance your communication skills in the host culture, published guides can be helpful in learning expected courtesies and customs.

- *Interact with the host nationals.* Meeting with people from the country you are going to is helpful. There are many such foreign nationals within your own organization or local community who may provide introductions to relatives and friends abroad, as well as useful information regarding their native culture and its unique customs. If one lives overseas within a corporate or military colony, avoid the "compound mentality." Immerse oneself in the host culture. Whenever feasible, join in on the artistic and community functions, the carnivals and rites, the international fraternal or professional associations. Offer to teach students or businesspeople one's language in exchange for knowledge of their language; share skills from skiing to tennis, from the performing to intellectual arts – all means for making friends worldwide.

- *Be creative and experimental.* Innovating abroad may mean taking risks to get around barriers of bureaucracy and communication to lessen social distance. This principle extends from experimenting with the local food to keeping a diary as an escape to record one's adventures and frustrations. Tours, hobbies, and a variety of cultural pursuits can produce positive results. One needs to be existential and open to the daily opportunities that will be presented. Consider preparing a newsletter for the "folks back home" in which you share your cross-cultural adventures and insights, either by regular or electronic mail.

- *Be culturally sensitive.* Be aware of the special customs and traditions that, if followed by a visitor, will make one more acceptable. Recognize that in some cultures, such as in Asia and the Middle East, saving face and not giving offense is considered quite important. Certainly, avoid stereotyping the natives and criticizing their local practices and procedures, while using the standard of one's own country for comparison. Americans are dynamic and pragmatic, generally liking to organize things "better," so it may be a challenge for them to relax and adjust to a different rhythm of the place and people they are visiting.

- *Recognize complexities in host cultures.* Counteract the tendency to make quick, simplistic assessments of situations. Most complex societies comprise different ethnic or religious groups, stratified into social classes or castes, differentiated by regions or geographical factors, separated into rural and urban settlements. Each of these may have distinct subcultural characteristics over which is superimposed an official language, national institutions, and peculiar customs or history that tie a people together. Avoid pat generalizations and quick assumptions. Instead, be tentative when drawing conclusions, realizing one's point of contact is a limited sample within a multifaceted society.

- *Understand oneself as a culture bearer.* When going abroad, each person takes his or her own culture, conditioning, and distortions. Thus, one views everything in the host culture through the unique filter of his or her own cultural background. For example, if one is raised in democratic traditions, it may be unsettling to live in a society that values the authority of the head male in the family and extends this reverence to national leaders. But with locals, quiet conversations and behavior may persuade others to appreciate your cultural perspectives.

■ *Be patient, understanding, and accepting of self and hosts.* In an unfamiliar environment, one must be more tolerant and flexible. An attitude of healthy curiosity, a willingness to bear inconveniences, and patience when answers or solutions are not forthcoming or difficult to obtain are valuable ways to maintain mental balance. Such patience may also extend to other compatriots who struggle with cultural adjustment.

■ *Be realistic in expectations.* Avoid overestimating oneself, your hosts, or the cross-cultural experience. Disappointments can be lessened if one scales down expectations. This applies to everything from airline schedules to renting rooms. Global managers, especially, must be careful in new cultures not to set unreasonable work expectations for themselves or others until both are acclimated.

■ *Accept the challenge of intercultural experiences.* Anticipate, savor, and confront the psychological challenge of adapting and changing as a result of a new cross-cultural opportunity. Be prepared to alter one's habits, attitudes, values, tastes, relationships, or sources of satisfaction. Such flexibility can become a means for personal growth, and the transnational experience can be more fulfilling. Of course, a deep interest and commitment to your work – professionalism – can be marvelous therapy in intercultural situations, counteracting isolation and strangeness when living outside your home culture.

Deployment systems

When an organization is sending people out of the country as its representatives, it has an obligation to ensure that such persons are adequately selected, prepared, and supported, as well as assisted when they return to the homeland. The sponsors need to have a *system* for relocating their personnel or members. Behavioral scientists have been investigating the whole phenomenon of people exchanges, especially for those who live and work in isolated and confined environments (ICE).[18] The latter experience may range from offshore oil rigs and polar research stations to undersea submarines, orbiting space stations, or a lunar base. The following describes the four major components in a relocation or deployment system, whether terrestrial or in space. The extent to which these guidelines are followed depends on the length of the assignment.

The *Sage Handbook of Intercultural Competence*[19] has many chapters that are especially relevant for anyone who wishes to explore this topic in more detail (especially Chapters 1, 3, 6, 14, 28, and 29).

STAGE 1: PERSONNEL AND PROGRAM ASSESSMENT

The first major component in a relocation or foreign deployment system involves assessing individual candidates for service abroad or in ICE, and later evaluating their on-site performance. In addition, the sponsor should periodically and objectively evaluate its relocation services and training, including transfer and reentry process.

- *Predeparture assessment* – From the perspective of the sponsoring organization's responsibilities, a complete foreign deployment evaluation system needs to:
  - Ascertain the adaptability of key personnel for foreign service, including their ability to deal with the host nationals effectively.
  - Develop a psychological profile for the candidate – summarize a psychological evaluation of the candidate's skills in human relations within an intercultural context, as well as determine the candidate's ability to cope with changes and differences, and the candidate's susceptibility to severe culture shock.
  - Identify specific physical and intellectual barriers to successful adjustment in the foreign environment, if possible, to correct any deficiencies before departure.
  - Highlight any specific technical or management factors that need strengthening before the cross-cultural assignment.
  - Seek out any personal or family problems that would undermine employee effectiveness abroad.
  - Develop a performance review plan for the individual when abroad, as well as assessment of the support services to be rendered.
  - Adapt the above evaluation process to foreign nationals brought on assignment into domestic operations.
  - Involve expatriate employees who have returned from foreign sites or host country nationals in predeparture training of émigrés.
  - Provide instruments for data gathering about the candidates' attitudes and competencies regarding change, intercultural knowledge and relations, and communication skills. These may involve commercial or homemade questionnaires, inventories, checklists, and culture shock tests.
  - Use, assessment and training, simulations, case studies, and critical incidents that approximate life abroad.
  - Employ a reality check on individual expectations regarding the foreign post, as to living conditions, job requirements, opportunities, and incongruities.
- *On-site assessment* – When the individual is sent overseas, the continuing performance review might further investigate:
  - The actual tasks or activities the expatriate engages in, and the person's ability to accomplish them.
  - The people with whom the individual interacts – his or her ability to deal with the indigenous or local population.
  - The extent to which the official posting requires social interactions with host and third-country nationals, as well as expatriates from other organizations – capacity of the sojourner to deal with such variety of human relationships.

- The work duties required, whether by an individual or team collaboration, especially with persons outside the company.
- The language skills required (English or a foreign language), and the capacity of that employee to meet them.
- The individual's outlook abroad, whether provincial or cosmopolitan. Has that person demonstrated interest in the local culture and its manifestations? Has the organization's representative made satisfactory progress in the foreign culture?
- The expatriate's self-reporting – his or her sense of how the international experience is affecting personal and family life, including impact of absence from the homeland while on foreign assignment (i.e., influence on personal life and that of dependents, as well as on career development and life plans).
- The overall rating of the individual's performance and adjustment in the foreign assignment and its society.

■ *Continuing system improvements* – Findings and insights obtained from both the predeparture and on-site assessment programs should be viewed as feedback to further improve the relocation system with the next group of candidates. For example, a survey of employees on foreign assignment or of expatriates who have returned may reveal special needs and problems that the organization's foreign deployment system is, or is not, addressing satisfactorily.

The selection systems of organizations vary, but some use the following techniques:

- Within the HRD division or department, establish an assessment center that has the responsibility for recruitment and selection of overseas personnel.
- Outsource for services by contracting an external relocation resource, such as intercultural consultants and/or an international executive/management/technical search firm.
- Set up a selection review board made up of an organization's own employees or members, qualified volunteers who have served abroad, especially in the target culture; include company specialists in corporate health and personnel services.
- Limit selection for overseas assignments to expatriates who have previously demonstrated their effectiveness abroad, whether within the organization or hired from outside.

■ *Selection criteria* – Overall, seek candidates for overseas service who are capable of empathy, openness, persistence, sensitivity to intercultural factors, respect for others, role flexibility, tolerance for ambiguity, and who possess two-way communication skills. Research indicates that possession of these characteristics is correlated to adaptation and effectiveness outside an individual's home culture.

STAGE 2: PERSONNEL ORIENTATION AND TRAINING

The second component in a foreign deployment system is some type of self- or group-learning experience or training about culture generally, as well as specifics about the target area's culture. This can be accomplished electronically or in live sessions with *PowerPoint* briefings. The general content can include learning modules on cross-cultural communications and change, understanding culture and its influence on behavior, culture shock and cross-cultural relations, improving organizational relations, and inter-cultural effectiveness. To increase cultural awareness and skills, several alternative methods are possible.

An increasingly popular means of cross-cultural learning is electronic, especially by means of the computer and television. To supplement or replace formal group instruction, individualized learning packages can be provided for the employee and his or her family. Such programmed learning and media systems can educate on cultural differences in general, as well as on the specific country to be visited. This type of learning can occur in a company learning center or at home with one's family. It might also serve as preparation for classroom instruction.

Culture-specific briefing programs can be developed for a particular geographical region or country, such as those provided in Chapters 10–16 of this volume. For example, the Middle East could be a subject of study, with particular emphasis on Egypt, Saudi Arabia, and Turkey, or even Israel/Palestine, Iraq, and Iran. A learning program of 12 or more hours can be designed with a self-instruction manual for individual study, or the materials used for group training. Obviously, no relocation orientation is complete without adequate language and technical training. However, the focus here is on cultural training and preparation.

Current thinking on this second stage of foreign deployment leads us to these recommendations for dividing the preparation for service abroad into four phases. In other words, the predeparture program would involve the following components. The time and scope of each activity would again depend on whether it was a long- or short-term assignment out of country:

Phase 1: general culture/area orientation

1   Become aware of the factors that make a culture unique and the characteristics of the home culture that most influence employee behavior abroad.
2   Seek local cross-cultural experience, and engage in intercultural communication with minority cultures within the homeland so as to sensitize oneself to cultural differences.
3   Foster more global attitudes and tolerance within the candidate family, while counter-acting prejudice and ethnocentrism. For example, cook national dishes of other countries, attend cultural weeks or exhibits of foreign or ethnic groups, or invite a foreigner to your home.

Phase 2: language orientation

1   Undertake formal training in the language of the host country.
2   Supplement classroom experience with self-learning in the language, by listening to the foreign tongue via audio/videocassettes or radio; by watching television and films or using the Internet; by reading newspapers, magazines, or books in the new language; by speaking to others who have this language proficiency.
3   Build a 500-word survival vocabulary in the target language.
4   Develop specialized vocabularies for the job, marketplace, etc.
5   Practice the language at every opportunity, especially with family members.
6   Seek further education in the language upon arrival in the host country.

Phase 3: culture-specific orientation

1   Learn and gather data about culture specifics of the host country.
2   Understand and prepare to counteract "culture shock."
3   Check out specific company policies about the assigned country.
    These policies are related to allowances for transportation, housing, education, expense accounts, and provisions for salaries, taxes, and other fringe benefits, including medical service and emergency leave.
4   Obtain necessary transfer documents (passports, visas, etc.), and learn customs, policies, and regulations, as well as currency restrictions, for entry and exit to host country.
5   Interview, in person or electronically, fellow employees who have returned from the host country. Get practical information about banking, shopping, currency, climate, mail, and law enforcement.
6   Read travel books and other information about the country and culture.

Phase 4: job environment/organization orientation

1   Obtain information about the overseas job environment and organization.
2   Be aware of the government's customs, restrictions, and attitudes regarding business, and your local corporation or project.
3   Arrange for necessary technical training to assure high performance abroad; seek a local mentor or coach.

Relocation strategies should encompass the staff engaged in recruiting, selecting, and training; the employee and dependents assigned abroad; as well as the host culture managers who are responsible for expatriate personnel in the new environment. The focus should be on the opportunities afforded by the international assignment for personal growth, professional exchange and development, and the effective representation of country and corporation.

STAGE 3: SUPPORT SERVICE: ON-SITE SUPPORT AND MONITORING

Once employees have been recruited, selected, trained, and transported abroad, the organizational responsibility to personnel should be to:

1   Facilitate their integration into a different work environment and host culture.
2   Evaluate their needs and performance abroad.
3   Encourage morale and career development, especially through homeland communications.

As a follow-up to the predeparture training and after the employee or family arrives in the host country, some type of on-site orientation and briefing should be arranged. Back home, there might have been a lack of readiness to listen to details about the job and new community. Now that the expatriates are faced with the daily realities of life abroad, they may have many questions. Periodically, the newcomers should be provided opportunities to come together socially and share as a group.

The in-country orientation should be pragmatic and meet the needs of the expatriate family. It should demonstrate that the organization cares about its people. It should aid the employee and his or her family to resolve immediate living problems; to meet the challenge of the host culture and the opportunities it offers for travel, personal growth, and intercultural exchange; to reduce the culture shock and to grow from that experience; and to provide communication links to the local community and the home organization. Much of this can be accomplished in a systematic, informal, friendly group setting, or even electronically.

STAGE 4: REACCULTURATION: REENTRY PROGRAM

The last component in the foreign deployment system involves reintegrating the expatriate into the home society and domestic organization. The person or family who has been abroad for some time will discover when they return that the homeland and the organizational cultures will have changed. The reentry process begins overseas with the psychological withdrawal the expatriate faces with returning home. Upon return, reentry shock may occur for six months or more, as the person struggles to readjust to the lifestyle and tempo of the changed home and organizational cultures. Apart from the challenge of reestablishing home and family life is the issue of reassignment in the parent company or agency.

For many expatriates, the last stage of the culture shock process is a time of crises and trauma. Such personnel may experience mild or severe *reentry shock*. The experience abroad for those who are sensitive and who become involved in the host culture is profound. It causes many people to reexamine their lives, values, attitudes, to assess how they became what they are. It is a turning point, prompting lifestyle changes when they get back. The reentry process becomes the opportunity to carry out these aspirations. Individuals may not be satisfied to return to old neighborhoods, old friends, or the same job or company affiliation. Many wish to apply their new self-insights and to seek new ways of personal growth. The organization that sent them abroad in the first place should be empathetic to this reality and be prepared to deal with it, including by providing severance benefit packages or even outplacement services. The relocation system is incomplete unless it helps returning employees to fit comfortably into their home culture and organization. Closing the deployment loop may involve group counseling with personnel specialists, psychologists, and former expatriates. Always consider expatriates coming back from an overseas assignment as a valuable resource. The corporation can learn much from their cross-cultural experience.

An example of the reentry complexity is described by Chang,[20] demonstrating how the interaction between mothers and their children changed when the student returned. The research demonstrated that the mothers' confusion about their children's cultural identity resulted in a confusion about their motherhood identity. One of the coauthors of this book remembers overhearing his mother on the telephone with one of her friends after he returned from working overseas for five years. "I don't know what happened to Bob when he was in China." However, he wasn't in China; he was in Japan.

BUSINESS ETIQUETTE AND PROTOCOL ABROAD

Cooperation in world trade and commerce is considered by many to be humanity's best chance to maintain global peace and prosperity. Training in managing change, interpersonal skills, cultural difference, and creating synergy can improve not only human relations, but the "bottom line."

Webster's Dictionary defines protocol as *a code prescribing adherence to correct etiquette and procedures.* While modern management, the Internet, and mass communications are forming new protocols for the global marketplace, we still cannot ignore the local expectations for business and professional activities. Nelson[21] advises these basic protocols be observed:

1   Remembering and pronouncing people's names correctly.
2   Using appropriate rank and titles when required.
3   Knowing the local variables of time and punctuality.
4   Creating the right impression with suitable dress.
5   Practicing behavior that demonstrates concern for others, tact and discretion, and knowledge of what constitutes good manners and ethics locally.
6   Communicating with intercultural sensitivity, verbally and nonverbally, whether in person, electronically, or in writing or printing.
7   Giving and receiving gifts and favors appropriate to local traditions.

8   Enjoying social events while conscious of local customs relative to food and drink, such as regarding prohibitions, the use of utensils, dining out and entertaining, and seating arrangements.

According to Lewis,[22] a *psychological contract* is forged between the individual and the institution which employs that person. This represents unwritten, unexpressed needs and expectations on the part of both parties. For an employee or member, it is a highly subjective perspective, and is the glue that binds that person to the organization. In the disappearing industrial work culture, the psychological contract focused on job security in return for loyalty and hard work. Currently, the emphasis is for employees to give their organizational support in return for compensations, plus opportunities to learn and acquire new skills. Employability, rather than stability, is the centerpiece of the contract. And the contract varies somewhat when personnel are posted outside their homelands.

For expatriate workers, the employer has more influence in terms of provisions for housing, education, welfare, recreation, and social events. Because of this, perceived contractual violations may provoke intense reactions from employees overseas. This dissatisfaction may be expressed in a variety of ways from negative communications and damage to company reputation, to misconduct, hostility, and even sabotage. Continued exposure abroad to a stressful environment may cause alterations in sleeping patterns, high anxiety, neurotic defense mechanisms, and other manifestations of culture shock.

ASSESSMENT INSTRUMENTS[23]

Most global leaders have received feedback from completing a variety of questionnaires and instruments designed to measure skills and attitudes, such as linguistic ability, which is easy to access, and global mindset attitudes,[24] which are very difficult to measure.

Over the years, we have found the following instruments to be valuable from the list of Fantini in *The Sage Handbook of Intercultural Competence*.[25]

■   Assessment of Intercultural Competence (AIC)
      Measures: Intercultural competence, including language proficiency
      Description: This questionnaire, designed in a YOGA format ("Your Objectives, Guidelines, and Assessment") is used for self-assessment and assessment by peers and teachers. The tool monitors the development of the intercultural competence of sojourners (and hosts) over time, providing valid and reliable indicators.

■   Cross-Cultural Adaptability Inventory (CCAI)
      Measures: Individual potential for cross-cultural adaptability
      Description: A culture-general instrument designed to assess individual potential for cross-cultural adaptability.

- Cross-Cultural Assessor (CCA)
  Measures: Individual understanding of self and others
  Description: This tool is designed to improve people's understanding of themselves and others, as well as to promote positive attitudes to cultural difference.
- Cultural Orientations Indicator® (COI®)
  Measures: Cultural preferences
  Description: A web-based cross-cultural assessment tool that allows individuals to assess their personal cultural preferences and compare them with generalized profiles of other cultures.
- Global Literacy Survey
  Measures: World knowledge
  Description: A self-test used to measure the degree of knowledge young Americans have about the world.
- Global Team Process Questionnaire™ (GTPQ)
  Measures: Effectiveness of global teams
  Description: A proprietary instrument designed to help global teams improve their effectiveness and productivity.
- GlobeSmart
  Measures: Effectiveness of global teams
  Description: A web-based tool that investigates how to conduct business effectively in 35 countries.

CONCLUSIONS

Life is filled with changes and challenges, some of which can be turned into opportunities for personal and professional growth.[26] Some happen by going abroad into another culture, or even in making the passage from an industrial to a knowledge work environment. The trauma experienced in this adjustment process can take a many forms, whether it is called culture or reentry shock, role or organization shock, or even future shock. Essentially, cross-cultural transitions threaten our sense of identity. Such transitions force us to rethink and reevaluate the way we read meaning into our private worlds. They are opportunities to learn and develop, causing a transformation in our behavior and lifestyle, as well as in our management or leadership.

Organizations can reduce such shocks to their personnel by coaching, counseling, and training. The stress and anxiety that may result need not lead to severe disorientation, depression, and unhealthy behavior. These can be countered by increasing awareness and information that provides more enjoyable intercultural experiences.

When considered in the context of sending employees overseas on assignment, the return on organizational investment in cross-cultural preparation and continuing support services can be considerable. We recommend that sponsoring multinational corporations or agencies institute a foreign deployment *system*. This approach to relocation activities will not only reduce premature return costs and much unhappiness among expatriates and overseas customers, but it can improve performance, productivity, and profitability in the world market. Furthermore, observing and practicing both national and international protocol facilitates human performance and cooperation, especially in development projects. Such counsel becomes even more meaningful in the context of technology transfer, whether within a nation or across borders.

MIND STRETCHING

1 Explain the concept of the transitional experience and its many manifestations. Apply these insights to the university graduate going into the world of work, or civilian and military personnel assigned overseas.

2 Why are so many workers leaving their culture of origin to work abroad, despite the many difficulties encountered? What are the responsibilities of communities and organizations in facilitating the acculturation of foreign newcomers?

3 Why does a relocation assignment pose a challenge to one's sense of identity? What are culture and reentry shock? How can these phenomena be avoided or delimited?

4 What is your understanding of being "global"?

5 Why should world-class corporations have a foreign deployment system? Overall, what does such a system entail?

NOTES

1 Shoper, J. April 18, 2006, email to Robert Moran. Used with permission.
2 Green, K. March 28, 2013, email to Robert Moran. Used with permission.
3 Terhell, P. McCauley, February 1, 2013, email to Robert Moran. Used with permission.
4 Sichel, E. F. and Sichel, N. (eds). *Uprooted Childhoods: Memories of Growing Up Global*. Boston, MA: Nicholas Brealey/Intercultural Press, 2001, 2004.
5 *Hemispheres Magazine*, April 2013.
6 Fearn, N. *Philosophy: The Latest Answers to the Oldest Questions*. New York: Atlanta Books, 2005.
7 Quoted from Lewis, T. and Jungman, R. (eds). *On Being Foreign: Culture Shock in Short Fiction*. Yarmouth: Intercultural Press, 1986.
8 Furnham, A. and Bochner, S. *Culture Shock: Psychological Reactions to an Unfamiliar Environment*. New York: Methuen, 1986.
9 Oberg, K. *Culture Shock and the Problem of Adjustment to New Cultural Environments*. Washington, DC: Foreign Service Institute, 1958; Storti, C. *The Art of Crossing Cultures*, 2nd edn. Sichel and Sichel, *Uprooted Childhoods*. London: Nicholas Brealey 2001.
10 Klopf, D. W. *Intercultural Encounters*, 3rd edn. Englewood, CO: Morton Publishing Company, 1995. Also refer to Gundling, E. *Working Global Smart: 12 People Skills for Doing Business Across Borders*. Palo Alto, CA: Nicholas Brealey, 2010; Ember, C. R. (ed.). *Cultures of the World*. New York: Macmillan, 1999.

11 Osland, J. S. "The Hero's Adventure: The Overseas Experience of Expatriate Business People," unpublished doctoral dissertation, Case Western University, 1990. Available through University Microfilms International, 300 N. Zeeb Road, Ann Arbor, MI 48106. Also refer to Dr. Eileen Sheridan (Wibbeke), more recent doctoral dissertation on this subject in 2005 at the University of Phoenix Online (email: docwibbeke@ gmail.com).

12 Szkudlarek, B. "Reentry: A Review of the Literature," *International Journal of Intercultural Relations*, No. 34, 2010.

13 Peterson, B. *Cultural Intelligence: A Guide to Working with People from Other Cultures*. Palo Alto: Nicholas Brealey, 2004; Storti, C. *Figuring Foreigners Out*. Boston, MA: Nicholas Brealey/Intercultural Press, 1999.

14 Lewis, R. D. *The Cultural Imperative: Global Trends in the 21st Century*. Boston, MA: Nicholas Brealey, 2002, p. 228. See also Lewis, R. D. *When Cultures Collide: Managing Successfully Across Cultures*. Boston, MA: Nicholas Brealey, 2000.

15 Campbell, J. *Hero with a Thousand Faces*. Princeton, NJ: Princeton University Press, 1968; Osland, J. S. *The Adventure of Working Abroad: Hero Tales from the Global Frontier*. San Francisco, CA: Jossey-Bass, 1995; Hofstede, G. J., Peterson, P. B., and Hofstede, G. *Exploring Culture: Exercises, Stories, and Synthetic Cultures*. Boston, MA: Nicholas Brealey/Intercultural Press, 2002.

16 Spencer, S. A. and Adams, J. D. *Life Changes: Growing Through Personal Transition*; Bridges, W. *Transitions: Make Sense of Life's Changes*; Biracress, T. and Biracress, N. *Over Fifty: Resource Book for the Better Half of Your Life*; Cort-VanArsdale, D. *Transitions: A Woman's Guide to Successful Retirement*. These books on lifestyle transitions are available from Knowledge Systems, Inc., 7777 W. Morris St., Indianapolis, IN 46231.

17 Berry, J. W. "Psychology of Acculturation," in R. W. Brislin (ed.), *Applied Cross-Cultural Psychology*. Newbury Park, CA: Sage, 1990; Laroche, L. *Managing Cultural Diversity in Technical Professions*. Burlington, MA: Elsevier/Butterworth-Heinemann, 2002.

18 Relative to *deployment systems*, refer to Haines, S. G. *The Manager's Pocket Guide to Systems Thinking and Learning*. Amherst, MA: HRD Press, 2004. Also contact the Society for Human Performance in Extreme Environments for information and publications (email: Society@HPPE. org or Website www. hpee.org). Relative to a *space deployment system*, Harrison, A. A. *Spacefaring: The Human Dimension*. Berkeley, CA: University of California Press, 2001; Harris, P. R. *Launch Out: A Science-Based Novel about Lunar Industrialization*. Infinity Publishing, 2003; Freeman, M., *Second Edition Challenges of Human Space Exploration*. Chichester, UK: Springer Praxis, 2000; Harris, P. R. *Living and Working in Space: Human Behavior, Culture, and Organization*. Oxford: Wiley-Blackwell, 2000. These space books are available from Univelt Inc., Escondido, CA (www.univelt.com or EM: roberthjacobs@compuserve.com).

19 Deardorff, D. K. (ed.). *The Sage Handbook of Intercultural Competence*. Newbury Park, CA: Sage, 2009.

20 Chang, Y. "A Qualitative Study of Temporary Reentry from Significant Others' Perspective," *International Journal of Intercultural Relations*, Vol. 33, 2009, pp. 259–263.

21 Nelson, C. A. *Protocol for Profit: A Manager's Guide to Competing Worldwide*. London: International Thomas Business Press, 1998; Olafsson, G. *When in Rome or Rio or Riyadh: Cultural Q&A's for Successful Business Behavior Around the World*. Palo Alto: Nicholas Brealey, 2004; Mole, J. *Mind Your Manners: Managing Business Cultures in the New Global Europe*. Boston, MA: Nicholas Brealey/Intercultural Press, 2004.

22 Lewis, K. G. "Breakdown: A Psychological Contract for Expatriates," *European Business Review*, Vol. 97, No. 6, 1997, pp. 279–293. Also refer to Rampersad, H. K. *Total Performance Scorecard: Redefining Management to Achieve Performance with Integrity*. Burlington, MA: Elsevier/Butterworth-Heinemann, 2003.

23 Deardorff, D. K. (ed.). *The Sage Handbook of Intercultural Competence*. Newbury Park, CA: Sage Publications, Inc., 2009.

24 Javidan, M., Teagarden, M., and Bowen, D. "Making It Overseas: Developing the Skills You Need to Succeed as an International Leader," *Harvard Business Review*, April 2010.

25 Deardorff, D. K. (ed.). *The Sage Handbook of Intercultural Competence*. Thousand Oaks, CA: Sage, 2009.
26 Sheehy, G. *New Passages, Mapping Your Life across Time*. New York: Random House, 1995.

ADDITIONAL FEATURES

Please visit the companion website at: www.routledge.com/cw/Moran where you will find additional case studies, study aides, and instructor resources.

9 GLOBAL TEAMS AND GLOBAL LEADERSHIP

Multinational organizations have a special role not only in building cross-cultural bridges, but in innovating synergies through their practical knowledge of putting together human and natural resources with the knowhow of managing both in the most effective ways.[1]

Linda Zhou, Alice Wei Zhao, Lori Ying, Angela Yu-Yun Yeung, Lynnelle Lin Ye, Kevin Young Xu, Benjamin Chang Sun, Jane Yoonhae Suh, Katheryn Cheng Shi, Sunanda Sharma, Sarine Gayaneh Shahmirian, Arjun Ranganath Puranik, Raman Venkat Nelakant, Akhil Mathew, Paul Masih Das, David Chienyun Liu, Elisa Bisi Lin, Yifan Li, Lanair Amaad Lett, Ruoyi Jiang, Otana Agape Jakpor, Peter Danming Hu, Yale Wang Fan, Yuval Yaacov Calev, Levent Alpoge, John Vincenzo Capodilupo, and Namrata Anand.[2]

I have been a participant or a leader of many global teams. The biggest challenge is to create alignment and commitment among members.

A senior scientist working for a major global European pharmaceutical company

Synergy is a difficult word to understand, and even more challenging to implement. It implies a belief that we can learn from others and others can learn from us. On global teams, it implies every member has the potential to contribute. On global teams, it means the collective contribution of the team far exceeds the adding up of the individual contribution of each team member.

Fareed Zakaria said it well: "If, on the one hand, we come together and work on common problems of humanity, imagine the opportunities it would create for everyone."[3]

Cultural synergy is a dynamic approach to managing cultural diversity in a variety of contexts.

Cultural synergy builds on common ground, transcending mere awareness of difference, to form multifaceted strategic alliances and partnerships. In this manner, people who represent disparate perspectives and needs find ways through working together to seek a solution where all parties are content with the outcome and therefore together succeed.

Synergy comes from the Greek word meaning *working together*. This powerful concept:

1   Represents a dynamic process.
2   Involves adapting and learning.
3   Involves joint action in which the total effect is greater than the sum of effects when acting independently.
4   Creates an integrated solution.
5   Does not signify compromise, yet in true synergy nothing is given up or lost.
6   Develops the potential of members by facilitating the release of team energies.

Synergy is a cooperative or combined action, and occurs when diverse or disparate individuals or groups collaborate for a common cause. The objective is to increase effectiveness by sharing perceptions and experiences, insights, and knowledge.

Synergy begins between colleagues, then extends to their organizations, and finally involves countries. The differences in the world's people can lead to mutual growth and accomplishment that is more than the single contribution of each party. As people, we can go beyond awareness of our own cultural heritage to produce something greater through synergistic actions. The sharing of dissimilar perceptions and cultural backgrounds can be used to enhance problem-solving and improve decision-making. Using information and technology to promote cooperation among disparate elements in human systems creates something better than existed by separate endeavors.

Some cultures are synergistic and inclined toward cooperation, while other cultures tend toward individualism and competition. The late anthropologist Ruth Benedict studied this phenomenon. Her research was amplified by groundbreaking humanistic psychologist Abraham Maslow. A summary of their characterizations of high-synergy and low-synergy societies is presented in Exhibit 9.1.

EXHIBIT 9.1 CHARACTERIZATIONS OF HIGH-SYNERGY AND LOW-SYNERGY SOCIETIES

High-synergy society	Low-synergy society
■ Emphasis is on cooperation for mutual advantage.	■ Uncooperative, very competitive culture; enhances rugged individualistic and "dog-eat-dog" attitudes.
■ Conspicuous for a nonaggressive social order.	■ Aggressive and antagonistic behavior toward one another, leading to either psychological or physical violence toward the other.
■ Social institutions promote individual and group development.	■ Social arrangements self-centered; collaboration is not reinforced as desired behavior.
■ Society idealizes win-win situation.	■ Society adheres to win-lose approach.
■ Leadership fosters sharing wealth and advantage for the common good. Cooperatives are encouraged, and poverty is fought.	■ Leadership encourages private or individual gain and advantage, especially by the power elite; poverty is tolerated, even ignored.
■ Society seeks to use community resources and talents for the commonwealth, and encourages development of human potential of all citizenry.	■ Society permits exploitation of poor and minorities, and tolerates the siphoning of its wealth by the privileged few; develops power elites and leaves the powerless undeveloped.
■ Open system of secure people who tend to be benevolent, helpful, friendly, and generous; its heroes are altruistic and philanthropic.	■ Closed system with insecure people who tend toward suspiciousness, ruthlessness, and clannishness; idealizes the "strong man" concerned with greed and acquisition.
■ Belief system, religion, or philosophy is comforting and life is consoling; emphasis is on the god of love; power is to be used for benefit of the whole community; individuals/groups are helped to work out hurt and humiliations.	■ Belief system is frightening, punishing, terrifying; members are psychologically beaten or humiliated by the strong; power is for personal profit; emphasis is on the god of vengeance; hatreds go deep and "blood feuds" abound; violence is the means for compensation for hurt and humiliation.
■ Generally, the citizenry is psychologically healthy, and mutual reciprocity is evident in relationships; open to change; low rate of crime and mental illness.	■ Generally, the citizenry tend to be defensive, jealous; mass paranoia and hostility; fears change and advocates status quo; high rate of crime and mental illness.

Source: Ruth Benedict, Anthropologist; Abraham Maslow, Psychologist.

E X H I B I T 9.1

GLOBAL TEAMS

High-performing teams

Virtually every working person is on some team or group who agree on a goal or task and are assigned or volunteer to work with others to accomplish successfully the task. Most agree all teams go through the four states of forming, storming, norming, and performing. Exhibit 9.2 is a useful way of linking the performance of a team along the path of becoming a high-performing team over time.

EXHIBIT 9.2 TYPICAL PHASES ON THE PATH TO BECOMING A HIGH-PERFORMING TEAM[3]

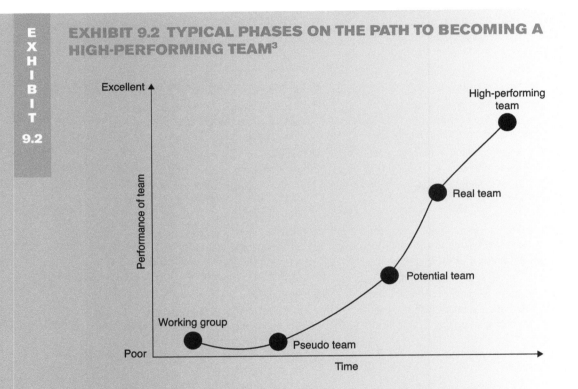

Working group: A working group is a collection of individuals each doing his or her best.
Pseudo team: They call themselves a team but they are really still a collection of individuals.
Potential team: They are at the beginning of committing to a common purpose and holding one another accountable.
Real team: A real team consists of people with skills who are committed to a shared purpose, goals, and work practices.
High-performing team: These teams go beyond real teams in the level of commitment members have to the organization, to each other, and to the tasks of the team.

Rating the performance of your global teams

In seminars and workshops the authors have conducted since the 1990s, we often ask participants to rate the performance of teams they participate on using the scale in Exhibit 9.3.

We have found there are very few ratings of 1 or 2 and very few of 9 or 10. When the average ratings of 30 or more participants is calculated, the score is almost never above 7, indicating clearly that most teams never reach the high-performing team of Exhibit 9.2. What follows suggests some of the reasons.

Understanding team strategy

The dictionary defines a *team* as a number of persons associated in some joint action, while *teamwork* is described as a cooperative or coordinated effort by persons working together. Teams are collections of people who must rely on group collaboration if each member is to experience the optimum of success and goal achievement.

Changing technology and markets have stimulated the team approach to management, because temporary groups can function across organizational divisions and better cope with diversity of membership. Multicultural and multifunctional teams are becoming commonplace. Furthermore, the complexity of society and the human systems devised to meet new and continuing needs require a pooling of resources and talents. Inflation, resource scarcity, reduced personnel levels, budget cuts, and similar constraints have underscored the demands for better coordination and synergy in the use of "brainpower."

In effect, the team management model alters organizational culture. The term used currently is *self-managed teams*, which contribute to employee empowerment and problem-solving. Such work units evolve their own unique *team culture*. As noted previously, high-technology corporations excel with project teams consisting of a variety of skilled specialists from management information systems, accounting, and new technologies. With the team approach, obsolete business separations give way to synergistic, functional arrangements among those employed in manufacturing, marketing, and administration; line and staff activities overlap and often merge.

EXHIBIT 9.3 TEAM PERFORMANCE

Poor performance									Excellent performance
1	2	3	4	5	6	7	8	9	10

E X H I B I T 9.3

Team building for success and synergy

Many executives make provisions for team building or training within their organizations by qualified internal or external consultants. In such human-relations training, leaders seek to cultivate a *team environment* that facilitates the group's performance. However, these guidelines might be questioned in whole or in part by readers from other national or cultural backgrounds. In essence, in team building, members learn:

■ Tolerance of ambiguity, uncertainty, and seeming lack of structure.

■ To take interest in each member's achievement, as well as the group's.

■ The ability to give and accept feedback in a nondefensive manner.

■ Openness to change, innovation, group consensus, team decision-making, and creative problem-solving.

■ To create a team atmosphere that is informal, relaxed, comfortable, and nonjudgmental.

■ The capacity to establish intense, short-term member relations, and to disconnect for the next project.

■ To keep group communication on target and schedule, while permitting disagreement and valuing effective listening.

■ To urge a spirit of constructive criticism, and authentic, nonevaluative feedback.

■ To encourage members to express feelings and to be concerned about group morale/ maintenance.

■ To clarify roles, relationships, assignments, and responsibilities.

■ To share leadership functions within a group and to use total member resources.

■ To pause periodically from task pursuits to reexamine and reevaluate team progress and communications.

■ To foster trust, confidence, and commitment within the group.

■ Sensitivity to the team's linking function with other work units.

■ To foster a norm that members will be supportive and respectful of one another, and realistic in their expectations of each other.

■ To promote an approach that is goal-directed, seeks group participation, divides the labor fairly, and synchronizes effort.

■ To set high performance standards for the group.

■ To cultivate listening skills.

Since each team experience is different, uniqueness and flexibility should be encouraged. Yet, at the same time, coordination and integration of team effort with other units and the whole enterprise are essential if the sum is to be greater than its parts. When team cultures contain the elements previously outlined and are reflective of the whole organizational environment, then they become closely knit and productive. The more team participation is provided and employees are included in team decision-making, the healthier and more relevant is that human system.

Improving performance through team culture

Just like the organization in general, we might have an image of the team as a smaller "energy exchange system." When the group functions well, human psychic and physical energy is used effectively. Team interaction is an energy exchange. As the group seeks to achieve its goals, members energize or motivate themselves and one another by example. Team planning and changes become projections on energy use and its alteration. Every aspect of the group process can be analyzed in terms of this human energy paradigm. The key issue, then, is how the team manages its energies most productively and avoids underutilizing or even wasting the group energies. There are ways that members can analyze their functions and performance in projects, task forces, or product teams.

Team behavior can be examined from the viewpoint of task functions, which initiate, give, or seek information, clarify or elaborate on member ideas, and summarize or synthesize. It can also be seen from the angle of group maintenance or morale building, such as encouraging, expressing group feeling, harmonizing, and compromising. It is the last element that builds group cohesion and camaraderie.

Such periodic behavioral review and data gathering can be useful to improve the group's effectiveness. Not only can the information help a member to change his or her team behavior, but when such findings are combined into a visual profile, they offer a diagnosis of team health from time to time. It is recommended that teams pause on occasion for such self-examination. Sometimes a third-person facilitator, such as an internal or external consultant, can be most helpful in this analysis of team culture and progress. When the group's assessment is summarized, the team can then view its implications for more effective use of member energies.

Team participation is an intensive learning experience. When members voluntarily involve themselves and fully participate, personal and professional growth is fostered. The team is like a laboratory of the larger organizational world in which it operates. Although a temporary experience, it is an opportunity for individual and team development. Each participant shares self and insights from the basis of unique life and organizational experiences. Synergy occurs when the members listen to each other and enter into the private worlds of the others. Total team perception and wisdom then become more than the sum of the parts.

If the organization's culture emphasizes employee participation through team management, the group microcultures are likely to reflect that system's macroculture. Thus, collaborative management should be evident not only within an individual team, but in intergroup relations. There is an implicit assumption that the team culture exerts a significant influence on an individual member's behavior. As a team member, one functions beyond the individual level, becoming representative of the group "persona." Those who serve in two or more interlocking groups are expected to act as linking pins in the accomplishment of the organizational mission through these separate but interdependent entities.

Everything that anthropologists would examine in the culture of people in a national or organizational group can be analyzed in the miniature environment of the team. These can range from the group's beliefs and attitudes, to procedures and practices, to priorities and technologies. The team atmosphere, task orientation or processes, communication patterns, role clarification or negotiation, conflict resolution, decision-making, action planning, intragroup and intergroup relations, all can be scrutinized for better diagnosis of the group's dynamics. When a global manager or consultant engages in such analysis, the team can become more effective in the use of its energies.

Global teams

Social scientists are conducting research on what people can do in small multinational groups to facilitate a meaningful experience and productive outcome. One exciting example of this occurred at the East–West Center in Honolulu, Hawaii.

At its Culture Learning Institute, Dr. Kathleen K. Wilson spearheaded an investigation with 15 other distinguished colleagues on the factors influencing the management of International Cooperative Research and Development (ICRD) projects. Their ICRD findings have implications for any professional seeking to improve human performance and collaboration. Although the researchers examined project team effectiveness among internationals, their insights can be extrapolated to other forms of inter- and intragroup behavior, whether it is a matrix organization, product team, taskforce, or any work unit.

The contexts in which international cooperative groups operate may vary, but there are similar factors present that affect performance. These external factors affect the environment within the project itself, and include such diverse elements as political, organizational, and cultural aspects, the size and scope of the endeavor, the disciplinary background of team members, and their individual characteristics, research, and development policies and problems. A summary of factors that foster or hinder professional synergy follows in Exhibit 9.4. Certainly, the exhaustive list of situations that influence a project's effectiveness points up the need for strategies to manage the many cultural differences existing between and among professionals attempting to work together. One can apply these observations to real-time group situations, such as teams functioning:

■   within the United Nations or UNESCO, the World Health Organization, World Bank, or International Monetary Fund;

■   within a global corporation that spans many countries and includes multinational membership;

■   within the International Space Station, both on the ground and in orbit, with its sponsorship of some 16 nations; and

■   within the European Union as it moves from 15 members to include 10 more from Central and Eastern Europe.

EXHIBIT 9.4 HUMAN FACTORS THAT FOSTER OR HINDER PROFESSIONAL SYNERGY WITHIN A PROJECT

- How project business is planned
- Consideration of other problem-solving viewpoints
- How the work should be organized
- Approach to R&D tasks
- Definition of R&D problems
- Ambiguity resolution and problem formulation
- Methods and procedures
- Decision-making relative to recurring problems
- Allocation of resources to team members
- Accountability procedures relative to resource use
- Timing and sequencing approaches
- Determining objectives for an R&D effort
- Affiliation and liaison with external groups and degree of formality in their work relations
- Quantity and type of project human resources
- Qualifications, recruitment, and selection of new members
- New member orientation and training on the project
- Management of responsibilities
- Underutilization of workers relative to skill competencies
- Motivating behavior and reward expectations
- Coordination of long-/short-term members
- Agreement on degree of innovation required
- Experience with cooperation especially relative to international R&D tasks
- Official language(s) to use on projects
- Method of reporting everyone's involvement in the project
- Coping with internal demands and visitors
- Meeting face-to-face or having to resort to other forms of more impersonal communication
- Involvement in making viewpoints known
- Power differences because of institution resources brought to the project
- Prestige, risk-taking, tolerance of uncertainty, and perceptions
- Project leadership and/or organizational policies changing unexpectedly
- Quality of work presented in evaluation methods
- What constituted success in project work, and what to do when members fail to meet group expectations
- Clarification of roles on the relationships

The East–West Center's research on international cooperation projects offers some criteria that can be used in recruiting, selecting, and assessing professionals. *Team member characteristics* that foster group synergy are also implied in Exhibit 9.2. Such benchmarks can be helpful in interviewing potential team members, choosing collaborators, and setting goals for self-improvement in organizational relations.

Finally, these ICRD researchers offered some indications for ensuring synergy within global teams. First, they established these criteria for evaluating international project effectiveness and management competence:

1   Individual team member satisfaction.
2   Group satisfaction and morale.
3   Work progress relative to intended goal statements.
4   Social and cultural impact of the endeavor on people.

Second, the East–West Center's researchers also identified interpersonal skills that influence a professional group's situation and accomplishments. These international team competencies and capacities are summarized in Exhibit 9.5.

EXHIBIT 9.5 SELF-MANAGEMENT COMPETENCIES AND EFFECTIVE TEAM MEMBERS

Self-management competencies permit the project member to:

- Recognize other members' participation in ways they find rewarding.
- Avoid unnecessary conflicts among other team members, as well as resolve unavoidable ones to mutual satisfaction.
- Integrate different team members' skills to achieve project goals.
- Negotiate acceptable working arrangements with other team members and their organizations.
- Regard others' feelings and exercise tactfulness.
- Develop equitable benefits for other team members.
- Accept suggestions/feedback to improve his or her participation.
- Provide useful specific suggestions and appropriate feedback.
- Facilitate positive interaction among culturally different members, whether in terms of macrodifferences (national/political), or microdifferences (discipline or training).
- Gain acceptance because of empathy expressed and sensitivity to end users.
- Encourage dissemination of project outcomes throughout its life.
- Recognize national/international differences in problem statements and procedures, so as to create appropriate project organizational responses.

- Anticipate and plan for probable difficulties in project implementation.
- Recognize discrete functions, coordinating discrete tasks with overall project goals.
- Coordinate transitions among different kinds of activities within the project.

The effective team member has the capacity for:

- Flexibility and openness to change and others' viewpoints.
- Exercising patience, perseverance, and professional security.
- Thinking in multidimensional terms and considering different sides of issues.
- Dealing with ambiguity, role shifts, and differences in personal and professional styles or social and political systems.
- Managing stress and tension well, while scheduling tasks systematically.
- Cross-cultural communication and demonstrating sensitivity to language problems among colleagues.
- Anticipating consequences of one's own behavior.
- Dealing with unfamiliar situations and lifestyle changes.
- Dealing well with different organizational structures and policies.
- Gathering useful information related to future projects.

Meeting when teams are virtual

In today's global world, it is not unusual to have important meetings of team members when two are located in Switzerland, two in the United States (one on the East Coast and one on the West Coast), one in Brazil, one in China, and one in Japan. They work for a pharmaceutical company and all have a Ph.D. in chemistry or biology.

Just setting up the meeting is a major task, as time zone differences are many. A good list of learnings and suggestions is provided by David Mittleman, Robert Briggs, and Jay Nunamaker.[4]

Meetings with virtual (geographically distributed) teams

Lesson 1: It is hard to follow what is happening during a virtual meeting.
- Distribute an explicit pre-meeting plan including specific times for involvement (takes into account multitasking and focuses attention when needed).
- Clearly communicate the transition from one meeting stage to the next.

Lesson 2: People don't get feedback when working over a distance.
- Seek feedback from, and give feedback to, different team members. Engage the quiet ones.

Lesson 3: People forget who is attending the meeting.

- Develop a practice of feeding back participants' names when communicating. "Brigitte, I understand your concern. . . ."
- Do a periodic poll to see who is still part of the meeting.

Lesson 4: It is harder to build a team when we are not face-to-face.

- Develop and communicate an unambiguous vision and set of goals for the team.
- Have face-to-face kick-off meetings, when possible.

Lesson 5: It is tough to sort out email communications.

- Develop a set of email rules and hold the team accountable for following them. For example:
  - Answer requests within 24 hours.
  - Send group mail only when all recipients need it.
  - Reread before sending emails from the recipients' perspective.

Lesson 6: It is harder to reach agreement over a distance.

- Agree on structured decision-making processes up front. Who will be responsible for what decisions, and how will differences in opinion be resolved?

Lesson 7: Small empathetic gestures go a long way with those who usually suffer the most with time-zone differences.

- Gestures such as switching the late-night or very early morning burden periodically builds significant appreciation among distributed team members.

GLOBAL LEADERSHIP

We all have the capacity to inspire and empower others. But we must first be willing to devote ourselves to our personal growth and development as leaders.[5]

Read the example of when one person with leadership responsibilities "worked" on his personal growth and development.

PERSONAL GROWTH AND DEVELOPMENT

The first example I can think of was when I was in Japan as a young man. I arrived in Japan by ship in 1964 as a Catholic priest. It didn't take a long time to meet missionaries and others who didn't like being in Japan, who didn't speak Japanese at all or not well, and who were counting the days till they could go home to North America or Europe.

I also met and worked with people who loved Japan, spoke Japanese well, and considered Japan their home. I engaged regularly with them and observed their behavior and positiveness. I never worked harder in my life than I did in Japan to learn a difficult language well. And I almost always associated with others who loved being in Japan.

My mom and dad were chemically dependent — my father on alcohol and my mother on prescription drugs. As a graduate student with two young children in the mid-70s, I learned that I "was a child of parents who were chemically dependent." I also read research that demonstrated persuasively that I had to understand how being a child of an alcoholic could influence how I was parenting my two children then and three other children within the next four years. All seven of us spent time attending courses, workshops with professionals.

When I finished my graduate studies, I was employed by a university. I wanted to be a professor who influenced his students. To do this, I attended lectures of the best professors rated by students and watched how they conducted their classes. They were my models and in time I asked them to come to a class when I was teaching and they gave me feedback. Sometimes it was positive, sometimes it wasn't.

Towards the end of my professional career, I was elected by my peers to be chairman of the department. I watched the behavior of the teachers in our academic institution. I tried to behave as the best of them by speaking clearly, being transparent, understanding strategy, listening to all, judging fairly, but mostly by being committed to students.

Source: Moran, Robert. Notes of a talk given in London, England, March 2013.

Since the 1960s, leadership scholars have conducted more than a thousand studies in an attempt to determine the definitive styles, characteristics, or personality traits of great leaders. None of the studies have produced a clear profile of an ideal leader.[6]

Leadership remains a hot topic among bestselling business books. Some world leaders share their insight into leadership and performance in a political context.

Jimmy Carter, 39th president of the United States, commented about leadership in conflict resolution: "All too often, conflicts and wars arise when we fail to consider the views of others or to communicate with them about differences between us."[7] The Carter Center Principles (see www.cartercenter.org/peace) for Peacemakers amplifies their vision of what a global leader should do, which provides useful guidance for corporate executives:

- Strive to have the international community and all sides in any conflict agree to the basic premise that military force should be used only as a last resort.
- Study the history and causes of the dispute thoroughly.
- Seek help from other mediators, especially those who know the region and are known and respected there.
- Be prepared to go back and forth between adversaries who cannot or will not confront each other.

■ Be willing to deal with the key people in any dispute, even if they have been isolated or condemned by other parties or organizations.

■ Insist that human rights be protected, that international law be honored.

■ Tell the truth, even when it may not contribute to a quick agreement.

■ Never despair, even when the situation seems hopeless.

Mikhail Gorbachev, former President of the Soviet Union, observed this on leadership: "The world is becoming ever more integrated. . . . The real leaders of today are capable of integrating the interests of their countries and peoples into the interests of the entire world community. . . . [A] leader combines a political and a moral authority."[8]

Desmond Tutu, the South African Archbishop who received the Nobel Peace Prize in 1984, writes: "The authentic leader has a solidarity with those he or she is leading. . . . The good leader is one who is affirming of others, nurturing their best selves, coaxing them to become the best they are capable of becoming . . . [has] the capacity to read the signs of the times . . . knows when to make concessions."[9]

L. D. Schaeffer, when CEO of Blue Cross of California, described leadership not as a "state, but as a journey, requiring different styles that are determined in part by the demands of the marketplace."[10]

Meena Surie Wilson[11] in her book on corporate India states clearly, "Aspiring leaders must learn continuously, which is why there is so much power in learning to learn from experience," which applies to political and business leaders.

The challenge of measuring effectiveness and predicting global performance

In an earlier survey[12] of over 100 executives of global organizations, we found that along a continuum of 0–100 percent, over 60 percent agreed that "global managers are made, not born" and 72 percent agreed "in global organizations, a new kind of leader is required."

Many business school professors and executives of global organizations know what the key positions are in organizations, but most are less successful in predicting who will be a star performer in that position. And when star performers are identified, they find it difficult to articulate what makes them the best.

Wilson Learning Corporation[13] has developed a global competency model based on an examination of the literature and interviews with organizations in the airline, high-tech, telecommunications, and consumer goods' industries. They have identified the following themes related to global leadership:

■ Understanding the business from a global perspective.

■ Assimilating and acting on large amounts of complex or ambiguous information.

■ Driving change based on global strategy.

- ■ Commitment to learning.
- ■ Effective cross-cultural communication.
- ■ Establishing personal connections readily across cultural boundaries.

Moran and Riesenberger[14] developed a straightforward model of globalization related to performance based on research and experience. The framework is presented in Exhibit 9.6. External factors such as the economies of scale, global sourcing opportunities, exchange rate exposure risks, and other factors are presenting increasing opportunities for organizations to become global.

EXHIBIT 9.6 MORAN/RIESENBERGER FRAMEWORK

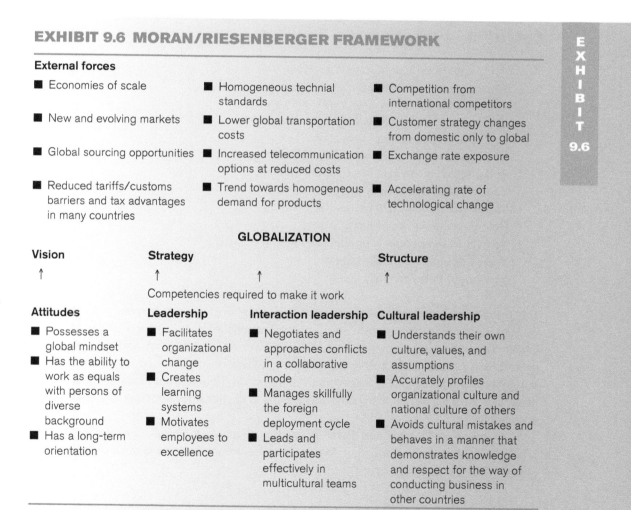

External forces

■ Economies of scale	■ Homogeneous technial standards	■ Competition from international competitors
■ New and evolving markets	■ Lower global transportation costs	■ Customer strategy changes from domestic only to global
■ Global sourcing opportunities	■ Increased telecommunication options at reduced costs	■ Exchange rate exposure
■ Reduced tariffs/customs barriers and tax advantages in many countries	■ Trend towards homogeneous demand for products	■ Accelerating rate of technological change

GLOBALIZATION

Vision ↑   Strategy ↑   ↑   Structure ↑

Competencies required to make it work

Attitudes	Leadership	Interaction leadership	Cultural leadership
■ Possesses a global mindset ■ Has the ability to work as equals with persons of diverse background ■ Has a long-term orientation	■ Facilitates organizational change ■ Creates learning systems ■ Motivates employees to excellence	■ Negotiates and approaches conflicts in a collaborative mode ■ Manages skillfully the foreign deployment cycle ■ Leads and participates effectively in multicultural teams	■ Understands their own culture, values, and assumptions ■ Accurately profiles organizational culture and national culture of others ■ Avoids cultural mistakes and behaves in a manner that demonstrates knowledge and respect for the way of conducting business in other countries

Source: Moran, R. T. and Riesenberger, J. R. *The Global Challenge: Building the New Worldwide Enterprise*. New York: McGraw-Hill, 1994.

As a result, the vision, mission, and structure of the organization change. However, to benefit from organizations becoming "global," new and different leadership competencies are required. When the competencies possessed by the leaders are marginal, the benefits are minimal. When leaders possess these competencies to a high degree, the benefits are significant. "Making It Overseas," a recent *Harvard Business Review* article,[15] suggests similar skills continue to be required today.

DESCRIPTION OF COMPETENCIES

Leadership attitudes

Possess a global mindset. In the play *South Pacific*, Rogers and Hammerstein wrote:[16]

> You've got to be taught to hate and fear
> You've got to be taught from year to year,
> It's got to be drummed in your dear little ear,
> You've got to be carefully taught.
> You've got to be taught to be afraid
> Of peoples whose eyes are oddly made,
> And people whose skin is a different shade,
> You've got to be carefully taught.
> You've got to be taught before it's too late,
> Before you are six or seven or eight,
> To hate all the people your relatives hate,
> You've got to be carefully taught.
> You've got to be carefully taught.

The lyrics state eloquently what we have known for a long time: namely, a fundamental vehicle for learning has always been, and will continue to be, other humans. At birth, infants are completely dependent on others for survival. In maturing and throughout the socialization process, children learn that the gratification of needs is, to a large extent, dependent on demonstrating "appropriate" behavior. In groups, whether family, business, or other, individual social needs become suggestible to the influence of others, especially those in authority.

Attitudes are learned, and therefore can be unlearned. A *global mindset* is an attitude; it is not knowledge or information. We learn to be ethnocentric, and we can learn to be global in our perspective.

Global mindset

Stephen Rhinesmith postulates that a "global mindset" is a requirement of a global leader who will guide institutions and organizations into the future. He defines a mindset as:

> a predisposition to see the world in a particular way that sets boundaries and provides explanations for why things are the way they are, while at the same time establishing guidance for ways in which we should behave. In other words, a mindset is a filter through which we look at the world.[17]

Rhinesmith states that people with global mindsets approach the world in a number of particular ways. Specifically, they:

1   Look for the "big picture"; that is, they look for multiple possibilities for any event or occurrence – they aren't satisfied with the obvious.
2   Understand that the rapidly changing, interdependent world in which we are living is indeed complex, and that working in these environments where conflicts need to be managed skillfully is the norm rather than the exception.
3   Are "process"-oriented; in our experience, this is the most important dimension, and the one that is most lacking in individuals who are not globally oriented. Many individuals are unable to understand or are unwilling to learn to "process"; namely, to reflect on the "how" as opposed to the "what."
4   Consider diversity as a resource and know how to work effectively in multicultural teams; an ability to collaborate instead of competing is also integral to the person with a global mindset.
5   Are not uncomfortable with change or ambiguity.
6   Are open to new experiences.

With globalization, contact between persons from different cultures increases. What happens when this occurs? Do individuals become more global or more ethnocentric?

Following a review of the literature on intergroup contact, Amir concluded that the direction of attitude change, following contact with people who are different, depends largely on the conditions under which the contact has taken place.[18] He indicates that there are "favorable" conditions, which reduce prejudice, and "unfavorable" ones, which may increase prejudice.

The favorable condition of "equal status" as a factor in reducing prejudice was reported by Allport.[19] He pointed out that, for contact between groups to be an element in reducing prejudice, it must be based on equal status contact between majority and minority groups in the pursuit of common goals. Organizations that are globalizing must have common goals.

Works as an equal with persons from diverse backgrounds

The ascendance of people from minority groups to leadership positions offers the organization an opportunity to explore new ideas and approaches. Companies that find new, innovative approaches are the ones that are experiencing success today — not the ones that have maintained the status quo. Tom Peters, coauthor of *In Search of Excellence*, declares: "Gone are the days of women succeeding by learning to play men's games. Instead, the time has come for men on the move to learn to play women's games."[20]

Has a long-term orientation

There are many reasons why companies have not been successful in competing in the global marketplace. One of these reasons is "short-termism." Dick Ferry, president and cofounder of Korn/Ferry, addresses this issue:

> Corporate America may talk, on an intellectual level, about what it'll take to succeed in the twenty-first century, but when it gets right down to decision-making, all that matters is the next quarterly earnings report.
>
> That's what's driving much of the system. With that mindset, everything else becomes secondary to the ability to deliver the next quarterly earnings push-up. We're on a treadmill. The reward system in this country is geared to the short term."[21]

Why do our foreign competitors take a long view? In Germany and Japan, "cross-ownership" is the norm. *Stakeholders* (customers, suppliers, and banks) are closely involved in the operations of the business.

The short-term view also has other implications. For total quality management to work, organizations must take a long-term view and exercise patience. Few dispute the importance of total quality. However, several recent studies on total quality management have questioned the short-term "quick-fix" mentality of individuals who do not recognize the need for long-term approaches in the implementation of total quality management.

The orientation to short-termism is almost an addiction, and is present in most corporations. Long-term orientation is a critical competency to make globalization work.

The global leader facilitating change

Most global leaders believe managing organization change is a serious challenge. This was true in the 1990s when the *Harvard Business Review* World Leadership Survey of approximately 12,000 global managers from 25 countries[22] concluded that change is a part of corporate life.

Percy Barnevik, the former CEO of Asea Brown Boveri (ABB) Ltd., puts it this way:

I try to make people accept that change is a way of life. I often got the question from Swiss and Germans: "Mr. Barnevik, aren't you happy now? Can't we relax a bit?" They see new targets as a threat or an inconvenience. But I say, you must get used to the idea that we are changing all the time.[23]

Why do most change initiatives fail to reach their full potential? Steve Gambrell and Craig Stevens suggest there are three phases of organizational change: what occurs before, during, and after changes.[24] They believe that for the change process to be successful, an organized plan is necessary throughout each phase of the change process. Part of this action plan includes understanding motivations for resistance, differences in employee/ management perceptions, and the importance of ongoing communication.

Gambrell and Stevens state that to maximize the chances of positive outcome, it is important that the following skills of leaders are developed:

■   Unbiased open-mindedness.
■   Good strategic planning abilities.
■   Good team-building skills.
■   Effective communications skills.

Global leaders need these skills to effectively facilitate and lead organizational change.

Creates learning systems

Peter Senge said it best in his book, *The Fifth Discipline*: "The organizations that will truly excel in the future will be the organizations that discover how to tap people's commitment and capacity to learn at *all* levels in an organization."[25] The case study is an example of a nonlearning organization in a global context.[26]

CASE STUDY

Several long conversations I've had recently with a European executive have made me acutely aware of two major cross-cultural organizational problems. The first is the inability of many companies to make use of new expertise developed by individuals in the firm. The second is the rather serious reentry problems experienced by many expatriates following a successful international experience.

My friend is 51 years old. He has worked for one of the largest chemical companies in Europe for more than 25 years. He joined the company as a young chemical engineer, completed his apprenticeship, and accepted a position as a sales representative in Australia. He lived there until his return to Europe five years ago.

After his first five years in Australia, he was appointed president of a small subsidiary. Though the European parent company has a policy of job rotation every three years, no replacements were available, so he was happy to stay on in Australia working for various subsidiary companies.

By the end of his Australian stint, he was a member of many of the most important boards in the country. By all obvious measures, he was a success. The companies he managed flourished, and several of them were sold at considerable profit. Yet during his long spell in Australia, he never once had a performance appraisal, and never knew clearly how his work was viewed by his superiors in Europe.

When he was eventually replaced in Australia by another European, he was brought home and given a job that he has found to be neither satisfying nor challenging. He has specific responsibilities related to overseas assignments in one country. Ironically, his immediate boss has never lived outside his native country.

The executive's case highlights the tragic inability of many large organizations to handle their people well, and to integrate their individual learning into the organization. What is most surprising to me is the executive's claim that since his return, he has never been consulted about Australia by anyone in his company.

He knows the country well — his company has large investments there, not all of them going so well today. He believes that his replacement is not doing well, and that two or three of the Europeans assigned there should be reassigned. The trouble is that all are "being propped up," he says, by someone in the European headquarters.

But the real problem, as this case illustrates, is what to do with these people when they eventually return to Europe or their home country.

In creating learning systems, the leader must be the teacher. Senge believes that "leaders of learning organizations must do more than just formulate strategies to exploit emerging trends. They must be able to help people understand the systemic forces that shape change. It is not enough to intuitively grasp these forces." Leaders must help others see the bigger picture, and cannot just impose their strategies and vision. Concurrently, and perhaps most importantly, leaders must "foster learning" continually for all employees.

Source: Senge, P. M. *The Fifth Discipline*, New York: Doubleday Currency, 1990.

Motivates employees to excellence

George Land and Beth Jarman address the challenge of getting a large organization to pull its employees together to work toward a common goal.[27] They recommend following the principles of "Future Pull." The task will then become easier, and should result in greater trust and loyalty of the employees. Future Pull has several components:

1   *Know your purpose and vision.* A vision is the bigger picture. In other words, what is the company's ultimate goal and purpose for its employees? This should relate to the employees and not to the product.
2   *Commit to achieve your vision and purpose.* "Actions speak louder than words." The leader and members of top management must be committed to the vision, and must reinforce it on a daily basis with their actions.
3   *Abundance is nature's natural state.* When the vision is embraced and the employees have been empowered, it follows that the rewards will also be there.
4   *Make the world a better place by living according to shared values.* Team building is almost always a key component. Expand the vision externally to customers – not just employees.

In global companies, the complexity of motivating employees to excellence is increased. To whom do they give their allegiance? Robert Reich asks, "Who is them?"[28] He defines "them" as the growing group of global managers. Their allegiance is not to any particular nation or culture, but to the success of their company. Motivating employees to excellence is a task of the leaders of global organizations.

Negotiates and approaches conflicts in a collaborative mode

To make globalization work, we need to negotiate and approach conflicts collaboratively. Skillful international business negotiators *know* more than, and *behave* (act) differently from, nonskillful negotiators.

This leadership skill is covered in detail in Chapter 3.

Manages skillfully the foreign deployment cycle

The necessity to prepare for global assignments and a successful global deployment process is demonstrated by research on Canadian technical advisors by the Canadian International Development Agency. The book, *Cross-Cultural Effectiveness,*[29] found an important interaction between overseas effectiveness and overseas satisfaction.

In terms of overseas effectiveness, the study found that 65 percent of the technical advisors were neither effective nor ineffective, 20 percent were highly effective, and

10 percent were very ineffective. However, no matter how effective or ineffective they were, 75 percent were satisfied, 10 percent were neutral, and 15 percent were highly dissatisfied with their assignments.

This competency is covered in detail in Chapter 8.

Leads and participates effectively in multicultural teams

My worst experiences at Thunderbird were the project teams I had to participate in.

Recent Master of International Management Graduate

The teams I was a member of were the best learning experiences I've ever had.

Another Recent Master of International Management Graduate

Every morning in Africa, when a gazelle wakes up, it knows that it must run faster than the fastest lion or it will be killed. Every morning when a lion wakes up, it knows that it must run faster than the slowest gazelle or it will starve.

Moral: It doesn't matter whether you are a lion or a gazelle. When the sun comes up, you had better be running.

"High performance teams," "teamwork," "worldwide global product teams," and other words expressing similar ideas are commonplace in management literature today. Stories of teams producing remarkable accomplishments are well known. Well-functioning teams can increase productivity and creativity.

However, functioning skillfully on a team is a learned skill. We have covered aspects of effective teams in the first part of this chapter.

Understands their own culture, values, and assumptions

Know thyself.

Socrates

Global managers from one country have to work and negotiate with their global counterparts regularly. A common requirement is that they must each be able to communicate effectively and work with individuals who have been socialized in a different cultural environment, and whose customs, values, lifestyles, beliefs, management practices, and other important aspects of their personal and professional lives are different.

A European executive during a personal conversation said, "I can't think of any situation in my 25 years of international experience when international business was made easier because people from more than one country were participating." A global manager must be aware of the many beliefs and values that underlie his or her own country's business practices, management techniques, and strategies.

"The journey to authentic leadership begins with understanding the story of your life."[30] When the 75 members of the Stanford Graduate School of Business Advisory Council were asked to recommend the most important capability for leaders to develop, their answer was nearly unanimous: self-awareness. Meena Wilson[31] wrote, "Self-awareness is sensing our impact on others, which is trickier to grasp."

Accurately profiles the organizational culture and national culture of others

Corporate culture is the way of life of an organization. The best recent book on the subject is John Kotter and James Heskett's *Corporate Culture and Performance*. From their studies of many large organizations, they conclude that:[32]

1   Corporate culture can have a significant impact on a firm's long-term economic performance.
2   Corporate culture will probably be an even more important factor in determining the success or failure of firms in the next decade.
3   Corporate cultures that inhibit strong long-term financial performance are not rare; they develop easily, even in firms that are full of reasonable and intelligent people.
4   Although tough to change, corporate cultures can be made more performance-enhancing.

Hofstede's research on aspects of national culture is covered in Chapter 1.

Avoids cultural mistakes and behaves in a manner that demonstrates knowledge of and respect for other countries

Many years ago Jack Condon and Fathi Yousef wrote:

> Many people believe that the language of gestures is universal. Many people believe that one picture is worth a thousand words, the implication being that what we see is ever so much clearer than what is said. Many people believe that communication means speaking, and that misunderstandings only occur with speaking. Many people believe that smiling and frowning and clapping are purely natural expressions. Many people believe that the world is flat.[33]

Mark Dankberg[34] summarized a quality every global business leader should possess: "empathy – the ability to understand whoever it is you are dealing with."

It is important to state loudly and clearly that it is our experience, supported by long discerions with many global managers, as well as research, that *not only American globals make mistakes; Japanese, French, German, Swedes, Chinese, Mexicans, and globals from all other countries also make cultural errors.*

GLOBAL LEADERS AS INFLUENCERS

A challenge global leaders experience today is how to influence across cultures and functions the individuals with whom they work and their global partners. Aware of the cultural influences on the personalities, motivations, and values of their counterparts, skillful leaders are able to influence others, whether it is by giving orders and directions to individuals under their authority or by "influencing with authority." Leaders know what they want to accomplish but how to achieve it and who are the key people they need to influence to succeed are routine unknowns.

According to Cohen and Bradford,[35] the following points are key in successfully influencing others:

■ Assume any individual, even an adversary, can be an ally.
■ Be clear what you want.
■ Understand the "cultures" of all those to be influenced.
■ Identify your own and others' currencies.
■ Build the relationships and develop partners.
■ Use formal and informal influencing skills.

Exhibit 9.7 shows a model of influence without authority.

EXHIBIT 9.7

EXHIBIT 9.7 COHEN/BRADFORD MODEL OF INFLUENCE WITHOUT AUTHORITY

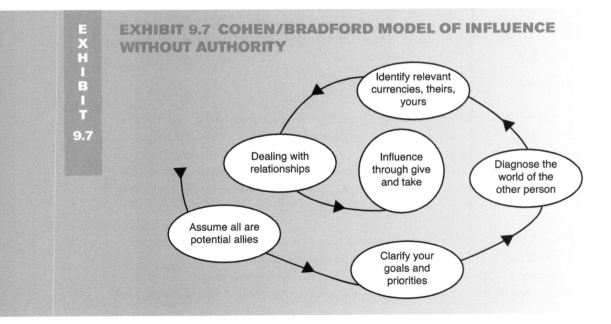

All leaders have some power, which is the ability to influence others, inside or outside of an organization or enterprise whether it is a business, government agency, or a nation, to do what you want them to do when you want them to do it. The total power of any individual is a combination of formal power or power associated with position plus informal power, which is personal and a function of one's skills, expertise, and credibility.

Verma[36] states that there are eight sources of power:

- *Legitimate power* – derives from position or status.
- *Persuasive* – derives from personal skills and ability in winning others' cooperation.
- *Contact/network* – derives from who we know and our connections.
- *Information* – derives from the information we have and knowledge of how organizations work.
- *Expertise* – derives from knowledge.
- *Referent* – derives from our reputation in an organization.
- *Coercive* – derives from our ability to punish.
- *Reward* – derives from our ability to reward.

High-performing global leadership

To ensure top performance, the global leader continually updates and broadens his or her understanding of culture and its impact on our lives. Although there may be few management theories that can be universally applied across all cultures, there are many principles and practices of leadership that can be adapted to various countries. Despite the cultural differences in managerial approaches, it is possible to produce cultural synergy in the pragmatic operations of management.

Elashmawi and Harris,[37] in their research into global joint ventures, focused on clashes within multicultural work environments, such as establishing a plant overseas. These offshore enterprises require the hiring, training, and management of local in-country personnel of differing cultural and technical backgrounds. Elashmawi identified cultural clashes arising from language and nonverbal communication, time and space orientation, decision-making and information systems, conduct of meetings and training, as well as motivation. On the other hand, Hampden-Turner and Trompenaars[38] urge transforming conflicting values into complementary values.

Technology transfer in the twenty-first century has seen accelerated growth in *outsourcing/insourcing/nearsourcing*, especially in the fields of information technology and services.

A project story: a team and a great leader[39]

One of the greatest leadership stories of the last century is the story of the great Antarctic explorer Ernest Shackleton. He is credited as one of the "best leaders ever" for saving the lives of his 27-member crew who were stranded on an ice floe in the Antarctic for almost two years. The original scope of his project was to be the first to walk across Antarctica. A few years earlier, Shackleton attempted to be the first to reach the South Pole. He did not succeed. His ship was named *Endurance*, which brought him to Antartica.

In the best leadership book we have ever read, *Shackleton's Way: Leadership Lessons from the Great Antarctic Explorer*, the authors Morrell and Capparell analyze the diaries of Shackleton and the crew and asked: how did Shackleton lead, what did he do? Leadership is not theoretical – leadership is behavior.

The following are some behaviors Morrell and Capparell identified that we believe are particularly relevant to leaders of global projects.

Shackleton's way of developing leadership skills

- Broaden your cultural and social horizons beyond your usual experiences.
- Find a way to turn setbacks and failures to advantage.
- Be bold in vision and careful in planning.

Shackleton's way of selecting and organizing a crew

- Start with a solid core of talent you know from past experience.
- Your No. 2 is your most important person.
- Work with those who share your vision.
- Surround yourself with cheerful, optimistic people.
- Hire those with the talents and expertise you lack.

Shackleton's way of forging a united and loyal team

- Always keep the door open to all.
- Be fair and impartial.
- Lead by example.
- Have regular meetings to build *esprit de corps* (group loyalty).

Shackleton's way of developing individual talent

- Make sure each person has challenging and important work.
- Give consistent feedback on performance.
- Reward the individual as well as the group.

Shackleton's way of getting the group through a crisis

- Get rid of unnecessary middle layers of authority.

- Keep your malcontents close to you.
- Ask for advice and information from a variety of sources.

Shackleton's way of forming groups for the toughest tasks

- Make sure you have some highly skilled individuals who can handle tough challenges.
- Empower the team leaders so they have the authority to handle their own team.
- Do not be afraid to change your mind when you see your plan is not working.

Shackleton's way of finding the determination to move forward

- Go-for-broke risks become more acceptable as options narrow.
- Let your team inspire you.

CONCLUSIONS

After explaining the concept of cultural synergy, this chapter provided a contrast of societies that could be characterized as having high or low synergy, as well as organizational culture that reflects high and low synergy.

Within organizations, the research insights reported here centered on behaviors and practices that contribute to synergy and success among teams, particularly in terms of international projects. Global leaders actively create a better future through synergistic efforts with fellow professionals. Global leaders seek to be effective bridge builders between the cultural realities or worlds of both past and future.

MIND STRETCHING

1   Synergy is a goal but why is it so difficult for global teams to become a highly performing team?
2   Give examples of teams you have been on that are poor or excellent? What did the role of the leader play?
3   Are leaders made?
4   Rate your leader's skills/attitudes/knowledge along the dimension of Moran and Riesenberger.
5   Shackleton's leadership behaviors: do they apply today?

NOTES

1 Freeman, O. L. " 'Foreword' by Former President of Business International Corporation, Governor of Minnesota, and U.S. Secretary of Agriculture," in R. T. Moran and P. R. Harris (eds), *Managing Cultural Synergy*, Houston, TX: Gulf Publishing, 1982.

2 Friedman, T. "America's Real Dream Team," *The New York Times*, March 22, 2010, listing the majority of high school finalists in the 2010 Intel Science Talent Search.

3 Katzenback, J. R. and Smith, D. K., *Wisdom of Teams*. New York: Harper Business, 2003.

4 Mittleman, D. D., Briggs, R. O., and Nunamaker, J. F. *Best Practices in Facilitating Virtual Meetings: Some Notes from Initial Experiences*. Internal Association of Facilitators, No. 2, Winter 2000.

5 George, B., Sims, P., McLean, A. N. and Mayer, D. "Discovering Your Authentic Leadership," *Harvard Business Review*, February 2007.

6 George, Sims, McLean, and Mauyer, "Discovering Your Authentic Leadership."

7 Carter, J. "Searching for Peace," *Essays on Leadership*. Washington, DC: Carnegie Commission on Preventing Deadly Conflict, 1998, pp. 26, 36–36.

8 Gorbachev, M. "On Non-Violent Leadership," *Essays on Leadership*. Washington, DC: Carnegie Commission on Preventing Deadly Conflict, 1998, pp. 64–65.

9 Tutu, D. "Leadership," *Essays on Leadership*. Washington, DC: Carnegie Commission on Preventing Deadly Conflict, 1998, pp. 70–71.

10 Schaeffer, L. D. "The Leadership Journey," *Harvard Business Review*, October 2002.

11 Wilson, Meena Surie. *Developing Tomorrow's Leaders Today*. New Delhi: Jossey-Bass, 2010.

12 Moran, R. T. and Riesenberger, J. R. *The Global Challenge: Building the New World Enterprise*. New York: McGraw-Hill, 1994. And more strongly supported in interviews by Robert Moran in 2009 and 2010.

13 Leimbach, M. and Muller, A. *Winning the War for Talent: Global Leadership Competencies*. Minneapolis, Minnesota: Wilson Learning Corporation, Version 1.0, 2001.

14 Moran, R. T. and Riesenberger, J. R. *The Global Challenge: Building the New World Enterprise*. New York: McGraw-Hill, 1994. And more strongly supported in interviews by Robert Moran in 2009 and 2010.

15 Javidan, M., Teagarden, M., and Bowen, D. "Making It Overseas: Developing the Skills You Need to Succeed as an International Leader," *Harvard Business Review*, April 2010.

16 Song "You've Got to Be Taught," in the play *South Pacific*, music by Richard Rogers, lyrics by Oscar Hammerstein II, 1949.

17 Rhinesmith, S. *A Manager's Guide to Globalization*. Homewood, IL: Business One Irwin, 1993.

18 Amir, Y. "Contact Hypotheses in Ethnic Relation," *Psychological Bulletin*, Vol. 71, 1969, pp. 319–342.

19 Allport, G. *The Nature of Prejudice*. Reading, MA: Addison-Wesley, 1954.

20 Peters, T. and Waterman, R. *In Search of Excellence*. New York: Harper Row, 1982.

21 Quoted by Bennis, W. *On Becoming a Leader*. Reading, MA: AddisonWesley, 1989, p. 23.

22 Kantor, R. "Transcending Business Boundaries: 12,000 World Managers View Change," *Harvard Business Review*, May/June 1991.

23 Barnevik, P. "Mr. Barnevik, Aren't You Happy Now?" *Business Week*, September 27, 1993, p. 128.

24 Gambrell, S. W. and Stevens, C. A. "Moving through the Three Phases of Organizational Change," *International Management*, July/August 1992, pp. 4–6.

25 Senge, P. M. *The Fifth Discipline*, New York: Doubleday Currency, 1990.

26 Moran, R. T. "Cross-Cultural Contact," *International Management*, January 1988, modified 2010.

27 Land, G. and Jarman, B. "Future Pull," *The Futurist*, July/August 1992, pp. 25–27.

28 Reich, R. B. "Who Is Them?" *Harvard Business Review*, March/April 1991, pp. 77–88.

29 Kealy, D. J. *Cross-Cultural Effectiveness: A Study of Canadian Technical Advisors Overseas*. Quebec: Canadian International Development Agency, 1990.

30 George, Sims, McLean, and Mauyer, "Discovering Your Authentic Leadership."

31 Wilson, *Developing Tomorrow's Leaders Today*.

32 Kotter, J. P. and Heskett, J. L. *Corporate Culture and Performance*. New York: Free Press, 1992.

33 Condon, J. and Yousef, F. *An Introduction to Intercultural Communication*. Indianapolis, IN: Bobbs-Merrill, 1988.

34 Wibbeke, E. S. and McArthur, S. *Global Business Leadership*, 2nd edn. Abingdon: Routledge, 2013.

35 Cohen, A. R. and Bradford, D. L. *Influence without Authority*. Hoboken, NJ: John Wiley, 2005.

36 Verma, V. K. *Managing the Project Team*. Newton Square, PA: PMI Publications, 1997.

37 Elashmawi, F. and Harris, P. R. *Multicultural Management 2000: Essential Skills for Global Business Success*. Burlington, Mass: Elsevier, 1998. Also refer to Elashmawi, F. (ed.). *Competing Globally: Mastering Multicultural Management and Negotiations*. Burlington, MA: Elsevier/Butterworth-Heinemann, 2001.

38 Hampden-Turner, C. M. and Trompenaars, F. *Building Cross-Cultural Competence: How to Create Wealth from Conflicting Values*. New Haven, CT: Yale University Press, 2002.

39 Originally published in Moran, R. T. and Youngdahl, W. E. *Leading Global Projects*. Burlington: Elsevier, 2008, revised 2013.

ADDITIONAL FEATURES

Please visit the companion website at: www.routledge.com/cw/Moran where you will find additional case studies, study aides, and instructor resources.

10 DOING BUSINESS IN THE MIDDLE EAST
Turkey, Egypt, Saudi Arabia, Iraq, and Israel

The Orient and Islam have a kind of extra-real, phenomenologically reduced status that puts them out of reach of everyone except the Western expert. From the beginning of Western speculation about the Orient, the one thing the Orient could not do was to represent itself. Evidence of the Orient was credible only after it had passed through and been made firm by the refining fire of the Orientalist's work.

E. W. Said[1]

This is about the revival of the spirit of doing business the Islam way . . . Muslims must start thinking globally . . . (to) prevent a total "westernization" of the globe . . . Islam is the only faith that has an economic system that is well defined and that has proven its efficacy and strength. We have to go back to this system . . . in order to give strength to the Islamic world.

K. Mahmood[2]

This chapter is dedicated to a better understanding of the cultures and complexities of that region of the world known to geographers as the Middle East. Specifics will be shared on the Arab culture, plus in-depth contrasts on the cultures of Turkey, Egypt, and Saudi Arabia. In addition, cultural reviews of other nations in the area including Iraq, and Israel, will offer a more comprehensive overview of the region's peoples.

The Middle East commonly refers to the lands from the eastern shores of the Mediterranean and Aegean Seas up to but not including Pakistan. Geographically, it encompasses areas of the eastern Mediterranean and central Asia. Many know it as the Arab homeland. Most countries in the Middle East are predominately Islamic, a religion with strong expectations about how business should be conducted. An exception is Israel, the Jewish homeland since Biblical times, and there are large minorities of other religious faiths such as the 10 percent of Egypt's population that is Coptic Christian.

The Middle East is where three continents meet — Europe, Africa, and Asia. In ancient times, it was known as the Fertile Crescent. It was the birthplace of two of the four most ancient human civilizations, Egypt and Sumer. It was the heartland of ancient Babylonia and Assyria; the breadbasket of the Persian Empire. It was the biggest prize sought by Alexander the Great, and later the Romans, the Ottoman Turks, and the French and British Empires. Three religions were birthed there — Judaism, Christianity, and Islam. Four of the seven wonders of the ancient world were built in the Middle East including the Great Pyramids in Egypt (circa twenty-sixth century BC), the Hanging Gardens of Babylon (circa 600 BC), the Mausoleum of Halicarnassus in present day Turkey (circa 351 BC), and the Great Lighthouse of Alexandria (circa 280 BC). Before them all, the first stone temple ever built by humanity was constructed at Gobekli Tepe in present day Turkey. It has been dated to approximately 9,600 BC, 6,600 years before Stonehenge.[3]

Today, according to the Global Intelligence Monitor,[4] four of the world's most promising Emerging Markets for the period 2012–2017 are located in the Middle East. Turkey is number 9. Saudi Arabia is number 18. The U.A.E. is number 21. Egypt is number 22. According to Bloomberg,[5] Turkey is an even more promising number 7 with an estimated growth in GDP between 2013 and 2017 of 21.2 percent. All four of these Emerging Market nations are predominantly Islamic in religion. All, but Turkey, are Arab countries. This chapter's learning objectives include the following:

1   The religion of Islam has strong expectations about how business should be done, and what kinds of business should not be done. Perhaps this is because the Prophet Muhammad was a businessman before he was called to be a prophet. In any event, Islam has defined how businesspeople should behave in doing

business, and some everyday Western business practices are considered inappropriate or worse. It is a goal to acquaint readers with Islamic views about appropriate business behavior.

2   All the nations considered in this chapter are predominantly Muslim except Israel. A review of Israel is provided with the goal of indicating how Israeli business culture is different.

3   Three countries considered in this chapter represent Arab culture including Egypt, and Saudi Arabia in some detail. It is a goal to familiarize readers with Arab cultural expectations about business. A review is also included for Iraq.

4   Extensive portraits are presented for Turkey, Egypt, and Saudi Arabia. These are considered the economic powerhouses of the region. As Emerging Markets, they will have greater influence in world business affairs in future years. It is a goal that readers understand cultural conditions related to business in these countries.

MIDDLE EAST OVERVIEW

The modern Middle East

The word *caldron* describes this region because, for a very long time, the Middle East has been embroiled in different forms of conflict and violence. The seeds of contemporary turmoil there were largely sown in the past, so one should analyze current events in the region within that larger context.

From the sixteenth to nineteenth century AD, the Muslims of the Middle East were under the domination of the Ottoman Turks. In the twentieth century alone, we witnessed a series of external wars extending to the region, resulting in European colonial occupiers with League of Nations' mandates, taking countries over as "protectors." New nations were created after World War I, with land divided without respect for tribal differences, nor promises fulfilled that were made to Arabs for their aid during that war. This has resulted to this day in unresolved issues.

The re-creation of the nation of Israel in 1948 has led to several wars between Israel, Egypt, Syria, Jordan, and Palestinians, many of whom became refugees in neighboring countries. This conflict has continued since the mid-twentieth century. It shows no sign of ending as Palestinian governments (Hezbollah in Lebanon; Hamas in Palestinian Gaza) refuse to acknowledge Israel's right to exist, and Israeli settlements continue to be built on land the Palestinians believe to be theirs. People of goodwill on both sides still struggle for peaceful co-existence.

Late in the twentieth century, American and Allied invasions triggered by Iraq's invasion of Kuwait led to the first Gulf War and United Nations' sanctions against Iraq. In the twenty-first century, the United States and its coalition partners fought the second Gulf War, supposedly to topple the dictator of Iraq while searching for weapons of mass destruction that were never found.

Sometimes the conflicts are within countries as Muslim and Arab populations oppose dictatorial governments. In what has been known as the Arab Spring,[6] totalitarian rulers were forced from power in Tunisia, Egypt, Libya, and Yemen. The newly democratically elected leader of Egypt was forced from office for being too autocratic. There have been major civil uprisings in Bahrain and Syria. While the hope of Western nations has been that these revolutions have moved away from totalitarianism and towards democracy, and elections have been held in Egypt and Tunisia, and promised in Libya, the democratic will of the majority has seemed to favor Islamic states run by Islamic law. Even in Turkey where the armed forces have guaranteed a secular state for almost a century, democratic elections have produced the first openly devout Muslim president in recent Turkish history.

A watershed event occurred on September 11, 2001, rudely bringing the problems of the Middle East into global consciousness. On that day, a terrorist network under the leadership of Osama bin Laden crashed four hijacked airliners into New York's World Trade Center, Washington, D.C.'s Pentagon buildings, and a Pennsylvania field, killing over 3,000 people. Fifty-six Muslim states immediately condemned the attack, pointing out that such behavior was against the basic tenets of Islam. These atrocities against humanity generated a global war against terrorism, accompanied by Western invasions, occupations, and reforms in both Afghanistan and Iraq. Though Osama bin Laden died at the hands of American commandos in Pakistan in 2011, in 2013, his Al Qaeda terrorist organization was battling for control of northern Mali in North Africa against a French-led international coalition. The death of bin Laden has not ended the global terrorist threat.

In a Discovery Channel television broadcast on the root causes of the 9/11 catastrophes, commentator Thomas L. Friedman[7] summarized the problems of the contemporary Arab world that might prompt individuals to commit such terrorist acts (March 26, 2006). Primarily, they seemingly result from frustration of people's needs because of the challenges faced within contemporary Arab societies. These include:

- Corruption of their often totalitarian leaders.
- Poverty and economic powerlessness of the majority, despite some oil riches.
- Male oppression of women by exclusion and underdevelopment of their potential.
- Radicalization of their youth in *mosquesdia* by fundamentalists and extremists.
- Double standards used by the West in supporting Israel over Palestinian human rights and welfare.

Friedman emphasized that the younger Arab generation, including those educated abroad, often had a sense of being oppressed and humiliated by Westerners. Some of these disillusioned young people have been recruited into militant, terrorist networks. Economic factors almost beyond their control are sweeping the Muslim nations and peoples into the global marketplace. In general, the Middle East today can be described as a region in the midst of profound cultural, social, political, and economic transition![8]

While some in the Muslim world[9] are evidently hostile to the West, and believe the West is hostile to them, R. D. Lewis, a Western Islamic expert reminds us that this attitude may be overstated. He reminds us that:[10]

- A persistent historical characteristic of the Muslim religion has been open tolerance for other faiths. . . .
- Western civilization is indebted to Arabic translations, in the Middle Ages, of Hellenistic knowledge and tradition, especially in science and medicine. . . .
- Mutually enriching co-existence of Muslims and Westerners has been the rule, rather than the exception, over the centuries. . . .
- Islamic scholars maintain they are not against the West, but fear its power and influence within their own societies, particularly with reference to materialism and cultural imperialism. . . .
- More than half of the one billion Muslims are not Arab, and most Muslims are moderates who admire piety and devoutness. . . .
- Muslims are divided among themselves with a multiplicity of interests and agendas, especially in their Sunni and Shi'ite communities. . . .

THE INFLUENCE OF ISLAM

Historical influences

Since the seventh century, Islam has been the principal binder among the peoples of the Middle East – it is a *way of life*, not just a religion. *Islam* is an Arabic word that means surrender or submission to Allah or God. A person who follows the teachings of Islam and follows its prescribed behaviors is called a Muslim. Non-Arabs, such as the Turks and Iraqis are linked to their Muslim brothers and sisters throughout the world through their religion of Islam.[11]

The Middle East is the same area from which the religions of Judaism and Christianity arose. All three faiths revere the prophet Abraham. Jews and Christians traditionally understand themselves to be descended from Abraham's second son Isaac. Muslims believe themselves descended from Abraham's first son Ishmael.

Islam began in AD 570, with the birth of Muhammad the Prophet in Mecca. In the century following the Prophet's death in 632, zealous Bedouin forces swept out of the Arabian peninsula to impose Islam on vast areas stretching from Spain to the borders of China. They were inspired by this great prophet leader; a combination of general, statesman, social reformer, and visionary. As both a religion and a philosophy, Islam owes its origin to Muhammad's teachings, which he encapsulated in the *Qur'an* (Koran), the sacred book of Muslims. This book is as precious to Muslims as is the Torah to Jews, and the Bible to Christians.

The Qur'an contains the discourses Allah revealed to his prophet Muhammad. Yet, as a religion, Islam is diverse in terms of having different interpretations of its teachings. The main divisions include the Sunni Muslims in Algeria, Turkey and Saudi Arabia, and the Shia Muslims in Iran and Iraq. So visitor, busines, or military person traveling to the Middle East can hope to comprehend its peoples without understanding the powerful religious and cultural force of Islam. Its primary tenets are summarized in Exhibit 10.1.

At its height, Islam's empire was larger than that of Rome at its zenith. Islam produced great civilizations that made enormous contributions to art, architecture, astronomy, literature, mathematics, medicine, and other intellectual pursuits which we still benefit from today.[12] Islam preserved the learning from the classical period of Western history – Plato, Aristotle, and so on – after it was lost in the West during the medieval period.

EXHIBIT 10.1 PILLARS OF ISLAMIC BELIEF

Profession of Faith (Shahadah) – open proclamation of submission that "there is no God but Allah and Muhammad is the messenger of God" – at mosques this is chanted five times a day.

Prayer (Salah) – at prescribed hours, worship or ritual prayer five times daily, individually if not preferably in groups – the bowing or kneeling for this is toward Mecca; the Muslim doing this must be pure, hence newly washed and not dirty. Friday is the traditional day of rest, when the congregational prayers of men at midday should ordinarily be performed in the mosque.

Almsgiving (Zakah) – the Koran teaches that all believers must give to the needy, and today this is normally a personal act ranging from 2 to 10 percent of one's yearly income.

Fasting (Sawm) – throughout the 30-day lunar month of Ramadan, a Muslim abstains from food and drink, while practicing continence in other respects, from dawn to sunset; in some Muslim countries, such as Saudi Arabia, the obligation is legally enforced.

Pilgrimage (Haj) – at least once in a lifetime, if one is able, a Muslim is expected to perform this act of piety by going to Mecca as a pilgrim during the month of Haj; merit is great for those who go there and perform the rites and ceremonies for 8–13 days.

Note: Some Muslims believe in a sixth pillar, *Holy War* or *Al-Jihad*, which offers the reward of salvation. This effort to promote Islamic doctrine among nonbelievers is not necessarily done through actual war as occurred in past ages. All observant Muslims are expected to practice hospitality toward strangers, even "infidels," as well as to enhance family relationships.

E X H I B I T 10.1

To appreciate Islam's origins in the Middle East, consider the many other countries outside the region to which it spread. For example, the Muslim culture and way of life is global in scope. Parts of Europe have large Muslim populations, including Albania, Bosnia, France, Spain, and Russia. In North America, there are large Muslim communities in both the United States and Canada. But in Asia (e.g., Bangladesh, Pakistan, Malaysia, and Indonesia) as well as in Africa (e.g., Gambia, Morocco, and Nigeria), entire nations are predominantly Muslim. In the twenty-first century, Indonesia is the largest Muslim nation, and Malaysia the model Islamic economic state.[13] Throughout the world, there are 42 Muslim majority nations, and Iran, Sudan, and Mauritania are officially Islamic states ruled by Islamic law. There is evidence that the democratic majority in Egypt appear to favor this outcome despite the resistance of Christian and secular minorities, and the same may be the case in Libya. There are currently approximately 1.5 billion Muslims worldwide.

Islamic business versus Western business[14]

Islam views different aspects of the worldly life as interrelated parts that should be integrated into a person's spiritual life. It offers guidance on family, social and political issues, economics, and education. Islam acknowledges the importance of business and/or trade. In fact, the Prophet Muhammad was a merchant involved in international trade prior to his divine duty. When the Qur'an was revealed to the Prophet Muhammad, he made trips to major trade centers around Mecca in order to spread the message of Islam.[15]

"*Divine guidance*" is a fundamental component of the Islamic economic system. While Western business isolates any divine principles from guiding economic activity, Islam establishes a certain set of divine rules on the economic activities of its adherents in an attempt to create a control mechanism over individuals. This is intended to maintain balance, distributive justice, and equality of opportunities. The divinity aspect of economic activity of a Muslim businessperson sets him/her apart from a Western businessperson whose main criterion in his/her involvement in business is to maximize benefit and self-interest.

Islam does not hold a primarily materialist perspective to business. Furthermore, business activities can be part of worship and obedience to Allah if they are performed in accordance with the Islamic code of conduct. According to Islam, persons are considered to occupy the center of the Universe because humankind was created to be the viceregent of God on earth.[16] Humans are God's agents, and their relationship with the environment and society is embedded in their relationship with God. Therefore, a person will implement his/her responsibility to the environment and society in order to please God. Pleasing God serves as a motivating factor for a devout Muslim to be in compliance with the Islamic principles when conducting business.

One of the well-known differences between the Western and Islamic systems lies in the financing sphere of economics. Like contemporary economics, the Islamic economic system recognizes both debt and equity financing. Unlike contemporary economics, the Islamic economics' system forbids a lender to charge a predetermined rate of interest irrespective of the economic circumstances of the borrowers of money. Thus, "interest" is prohibited.

Islam offers profit-loss sharing transactions that are alternatives to interest-based transactions for devout Muslims to make profit on their capital. Through these partnerships, Islam seeks to foster "brotherhood" among people, which is thought to be destroyed by interest-based transactions. Musharakah and Mudarabah are the two profit-loss sharing arrangements preferred by Islamic economics.

Musharakah

In Musharakah contracts, both the entrepreneur and the investor supply capital to the joint venture. Therefore, profits and losses are borne by both partners based on a pre-determined ratio, but the ratio does not necessarily coincide with the relative input in financing.[17] Thus, the proportion of profit and loss is left to the mutual consent of the partners. Additionally, all the parties play a role in managerial decisions.

Mudarabah

Mudarabah is a partnership agreement where a partner (the investor) allocates money to the other party (the entrepreneur) who is in charge of business activities and management. The investor may determine a particular business for the entrepreneur in which case the entrepreneur is allowed to invest the money only in those specified directions. For a Mudarabah partnership, it is necessary to determine a definite proportion of actual profit to which each party is entitled.

Mudarabah is similar to angel investment where the entrepreneur funds his economic initiatives through the investments by the angel investors. In this type of business partnership, the entrepreneur realizes his/her business opportunity with the contribution of the investor. The latter seeks to utilize his/her capital through entrepreneurship initiated by the borrower and in turn makes profit.

Islamic finance is growing at the rate of 15–20 percent annually and has growth prospects not only in Muslim majority countries but also in Western countries. The U.K. is the leading Western country where government policies fully support Islamic products in the banking sector. There are five financial institutions that are fully Sharia compliant, more than in any other Western country. Also, Malaysia, Singapore, and China recently have made significant investments in the Islamic finance industry. However, there is still a considerable growth potential even in Muslim majority countries including Turkey and Egypt where Islamic banking accounts for only 4 percent to 5 percent of the total banking assets. Exhibit 10.2 indicates the amount of financing, worldwide, that follow these Islamic practices.

EXHIBIT 10.2 ISLAMIC FINANCE BY COUNTRY, US$ BILLIONS, 2010[a]

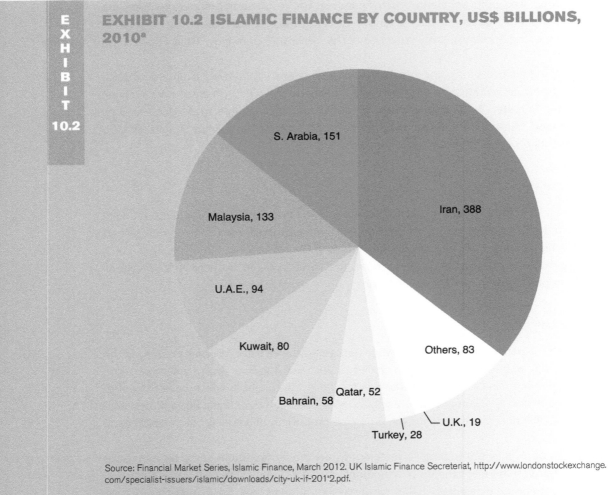

S. Arabia, 151

Iran, 388

Malaysia, 133

U.A.E., 94

Kuwait, 80

Others, 83

Bahrain, 58

Qatar, 52

U.K., 19

Turkey, 28

Source: Financial Market Series, Islamic Finance, March 2012. UK Islamic Finance Secreteriat, http://www.londonstockexchange.com/specialist-issuers/islamic/downloads/city-uk-if-201'2.pdf.

Note: [a]Banking, takaful, and fund assets.

"Brotherhood" versus "self-interest"

The concept of "Economic Man" has been universally accepted as underlying conventional economics. According to the utility theory that has been considered the cornerstone of conventional economics for a hundred years, economic man seeks to maximize his/her utility and acts in his/her own best interest to achieve his/her goal. It is fair to say that the economic systems established in Western societies have been largely influenced by this utility theory.

In contrast, Islam promotes "brotherhood" and "benevolence" amongst people, instead of the "self-interest" principle of conventional economics. The obligation of *zakah* plays a facilitating role to create the concept of brotherhood in Muslim societies. It decrees that practicing Muslims pay, depending on the amount of wealth and the type of assets the individual possesses, to support the poor and the needy in society. In some Islamic countries, the *zakah* institutions facilitate the distribution of the alms to the poor and the needy individuals in the society.

Utility maximizing behavior is also constrained in Islamic philosophy by two primary notions: *halal* and *haram*, which represent the very fundamental classification of prohibited and permitted acts. *Halal* designates any object or action that is permissible to use or engage in. *Haram* designates any object or action that is prohibited to use or engage in. Muslims are prohibited to be involved in any "haram" business areas, or any activities related to "haram" business, or to trade "haram" goods. Alcohol, illegal drugs, and pork are described as "haram" goods. A Muslim businessperson would consider any involvement in activities related to "haram" business inappropriate on an ethical basis.

Islam prohibits its adherents from being involved in interest-based transactions as "haram," on the basis that interest-related transactions do not contribute productively to the economy. Instead, Islam makes it easier for capital owners to acquire wealth without actively participating in commerce. Exhibit 10.3 indicates activities generally considered either legitimately "halal" or illegitimately "haram."

Egyptian hotel entrepreneur Teymour Adham maintained that most of his fellow believers were "Spiritual Muslims" who identified themselves by their faith. It was a personal and spiritual thing, so they did not talk or preach about their religion, but just lived it. Unfortunately, some people develop Muslim stereotypes, particularly because of the Islamic terrorist fringe, conveniently forgetting the great diversity within this global religious culture. Like their counterparts in other religions, Muslims have their inflexible ultra conservatives, as well as tolerant, open-minded progressives. Islam is a vast mosaic.

EXHIBIT 10.3 ISLAMIC TENETS OF BUSINESS TRANSACTIONS

Halal business transactions	*Haram* business transactions
Earning legitimate (*halal*) earnings	Dealing in prohibited (*haram*) items (alcohol, pork, drugs, gambling, prostitution)
Profit-loss partnerships	Interest (riba)
Justice and fairness	Cheating, fraud, bribery
Fulfilling obligations	Hoarding of foodstuff

Source: http://www.jamiaislamia.org/halalharaam.html.

E X H I B I T 10.3

Islamic management practices

Ahmad and Gazdar[18] maintain that the Qur'an, and Islamic commentaries related to it, define a set of management practices that have been recommended for application in Islamic business and management for over a thousand years. They provide guidance on economics, education, politics, social organization, and management. Islamic management experts believe that modern Western management practices are slowly converging with these established Islamic principles.

These Qur'an-based principles of management are understood in Muslim cultures to be divine revelations, and entirely free from any practical shortcomings. This is as opposed to Western practices that are open to constant revision on the basis of new research, and where there may be little agreement as to what the "ideal" practices should be.

Ahmad and Gazdar[19] argue that Islam has encouraged all those who engage in business to adopt 40 management principles as a set of consistent guidelines to be applied within all Islamic countries. They observe that Western businesses that have been successful in Islamic countries – Citigroup, Deutsche Bank, HSBC, and Lloyds TSB in the financial sector, for example – have adopted these principles.

Islam focuses its attention more on the individual people who manage or are managed, and less on the methodologies and processes of management. This is because Islam believes that it is the individual people that guide and apply these management methodologies and practices through their motivations, enthusiasm, desires, and emotions. Sixteen of the principles are related to the qualities of a good manager (see Exhibit 10.4). Another six principles are related to best management practices, and the final 18 principles are related to leading teams (see Exhibit 10.5).

EXHIBIT 10.4 QUALITIES OF A GOOD MANAGER AS DEFINED BY ISLAM

Qualities	Operationalization
Work as an act of worship	Islam defines taking care of one's family a duty. Working is therefore an act of worship of God, and must be done in a spirit of commitment and sincerity.
Fulfill all contracts	Islam requires contractual obligations to be fulfilled. Not doing so, or subsequently arguing about terms is sinful and unlawful. This will ensure justice and fair dealings.
Keeping promises	This is mentioned many times in the Qur'an ("Fulfill promises because you will be held accountable for promises" – Chapter 17, Verse 34).

Loyalty to employer	The manager is always loyal to the employer because he/she is under contract. Company secrets are protected from competitors, or ex-employees with grudges.
No kickbacks	A manager neither offers nor receives kickbacks, including gifts or business expenses. Islamic practice is to avoid gray areas between clearly lawful or unlawful.
Do not fight for leadership	People who fight or maneuver to be appointed leaders are disqualified as unsuitable. One registers interest through one's career plan, but must be recognized by others simply from the quality of his/her work.
Build trust	Honesty, integrity, reliability, safeguarding confidences, and commitment to justice are required behaviors so that a manager will be clearly trustworthy.
Always be truthful	"There is no charity more beloved to God than speaking the truth" (Bayhagi, www.almoltaga.ps/english/archive/index.php/t-1182.html). It is acknowledged that this is a challenge for salespeople.
Be optimistic	Even if a manager violates an Islamic principle, he/she should be optimistic because sins will be erased if they are sincerely repented and followed up with good deeds.
Admit mistakes; learn from them	Not admitting mistakes is to defy humankind's imperfect nature. Acknowledge at once. Inform superiors so correction is possible. Show sensitivity to those injured. Apologize. Accept responsibility. Develop a superior-reviewed plan of action.
Avoid pride	Pride is defined as "disdaining what is true, and despising people" (Sunan Abu Dawud, Book 27, Hadith 4081). Never conceal the truth, or look down on others. Pride results in discrimination against others.
Time management	Control Internet time wastage. It leads to a 40 percent productivity loss according to Gartner. Avoid using office time for non-business activities.
Seek and share knowledge	This increases personal and team effectiveness.
Manage anger	Islam advises managers not to become angry, and never to make judgments while angry.
Aim for excellence	Since work is an act of worship, it should be a worthy gift to God.
Be just	Justice and fair dealing is an obligation (Qur'an, Chapter 16, Verse 90). This includes distributive and procedural justice. Subordinates will be angry if treated unjustly.

Source: Ahmad, S., and Gazdar, M. *40 Islamic Principles for Successful Management.* Kindle Edition: HotHive Publications, 2009.

E
X
H
I
B
I
T

10.5

EXHIBIT 10.5 BEST MANAGEMENT PRACTICES ACCORDING TO ISLAM

Best management practices	Practices for leading teams
Remove ambiguity	Use teamwork
Establish written agreements	Appoint on merit
Pay full wages	Use good communication styles
Settle debts on time	Give clear instructions
Do not be wasteful	Show respect
Plan and action well	Recruit great people
Think outside the box	Smile — it's a charity
	Confront evil
	Decisiveness
	Offer leniency for errors
	Be compassionate and merciful
	Consult
	Call to account
	Do not discriminate
	Preserve dignity and honor of women
	Be aware — God watches you always

Source: Ahmad, S. and Gazdar, M. *40 Islamic Principles for Successful Management.* Kindle Edition: HotHive Publications, 2009.

In the context of managing cultural differences, it is important for non-Muslims to recognize that some typical and everyday Western business practices contravene these 40 Islamic principles of management. Work is not an act of worship for most secular Westerners. Lawyers may be employed, and court battles fought, subsequent to the signing of contracts in an attempt to avoid some contractual obligations as interpreted by the other side. Promises are more likely to be kept if they are written into contracts. Western managers maneuver for leadership positions, perhaps "shamelessly" in the eyes of Islamic counterparts. Truth is not always spoken so as to maintain an advantage. Pride is often evident in the clothes, jewelry, and automobiles managers prefer to be seen with. The point is that Westerners may offend Islamic counterparts unintentionally through their normal everyday management and behavioral styles. Westerners doing business with devout Muslims must be sensitive to Muslim management expectations. And it is not clear who is devout, or not, when Islam may simply be a way of life.

These principles are reasonably self-explanatory and not unlike many Western practices. Confronting evil may need some explanation. A manager who deviated from any of these management principles could be accused of "evil" and censured. The prophet Muhammad stated that the best response to evil was to confront it and take steps to establish justice in its place. Second best, if one did not have the power or authority to confront, was to speak out against evil. Third best was to silently condemn and resist, passively or actively.

Islamic leadership

Islamic leadership[20] is similar to Western leadership in resting on either personal power or positional authority. Where it begins to differ is in its definition of the two primary roles that a leader may fulfill in his/her organization. The *servant-leader* sees him/herself as the servant of his/her followers, seeking the welfare of followers and guiding them toward the good.[21] As Greenleaf[22] put it:

> The servant-leader is a servant first . . . it begins with the natural feeling that one wants to serve, to serve *first* . . . . The best test, and the most difficult to administer, is: Do those served grow as persons? Do they, *while being served*, become healthier, wiser, freer, more autonomous, more likely themselves to become servants? *And*, what is the effect on the least privileged in society; will they benefit, or, at least, not be further deprived?

The second legitimate primary role of an Islamic leader is as *guardian-leader*. The prophet Muhammad defined this sense of leadership as the one who protected his/her community against tyranny and oppression. He/she encouraged awareness of the requirements of Allah and Islam, protecting him/herself against sin (*taqwa*), and promoting justice. Abu Hurairah,[23] an Islamic commentator, wrote:

> The Prophet of Allah (peace be upon him) said: "A commander (of the Muslims) is a shield for them. They fight behind him and they are protected by him (from tyrants and aggressors). If he enjoins fear of Allah, the Exalted and Glorious, and dispenses justice, there will be a (great) reward for him; and if he enjoins otherwise, it rebounds on him."

The point to note about both Muslim leadership roles is that they require the leader to set aside his/her self-interest in favor of social goods. This is a major difference between Western and Islamic leadership values. The basis of modern Western economic theory, derived from the philosopher Adam Smith, has been that it was possible to derive the best economic benefits for everyone in a society when individuals consistently acted in their own self-interest.[24] The self-interests of all the people in an organization or society created a self-regulating mechanism in the marketplace, or "invisible hand," ensuring an equitable distribution of social benefits. By contrast, the Islamic view is that self-interest is a social evil that must be confronted and discarded in favor of social values as defined by the Qur'an and its commentators. The Chinese Confucian philosophers Mencius[25] and Xunzi[26] also held this view that self-interest was evil (see Chapter 13).

The evident conflicts between Islamic and Western business values and practices may result in Islamic businesspersons feeling uncomfortable doing business with Westerners or even refusing to be recruited as managers in Western enterprises doing business in the Middle East. Exhibit 10.6 describes the case[27] of a devoutly Islamic Turkish MBA student who decided after completing her MBA in Canada that she could never practice as a Western manager because of value conflicts between her Islamic faith and what she had been taught in her Western MBA program.

One Islamic, but non-Arab Middle Eastern, nation is discussed as part of our survey. From the point-of-view of the West, Turkey is the most interesting and significant Islamic,

EXHIBIT 10.6 EFFECTS OF VALUE CONFLICTS BETWEEN WESTERN BUSINESS AND ISLAM

A case study of a Muslim MBA business student

It was my first week at the university, as a first-year business student, and I was looking forward to the first lecture with the professor of Microeconomics. I remember that I was puzzled by his answer, referring to conventional Economics theory, to his own question with regard to the definition of an "Economic Man." He said that "Economic Man" is described as a rational individual who intends to maximize his utility. Based on the "self-interest" principle of Economics, if every individual acts in the best interest of him/herself, total and equitable welfare will be maintained in the society. I thought that it would not be possible to maintain welfare in a society where everyone acted in the best interest of him/herself and concluded that the self-interest principle was completely in contrast to the brotherhood concept of Islam which enjoins every Muslim to look after his/her Muslim brothers and sisters.

Furthermore, even someone with a basic knowledge of the Islamic principles would know that we, Muslims, are prohibited to become involved in "haram" business areas, or trade "haram" goods, or earn our living through "haram" means. I would be considered "irrational" in the eyes of a Western businessperson in a situation where I did not take advantage of an opportunity to make a large profit by declining to get involved in haram professions such as contributing to the production or consumption of alcoholic beverages.

Having a business career was a meaningful profession in my eyes because the Prophet Muhammad was involved in trade and he acquired fame as honest merchant in his society at the time when the Qur'an was being revealed to him. Given that the fundamental principles underlying conventional Western Economic theory are in conflict with my religious values, I lost my motivation to function as a businesswoman.

Source: Produced by Zeynep Arslan Kara.

but non-Arab, economy in the Middle East because of its status as an important Emerging Market. It has been considered a bridge between Europe and Asia because of its location encompassing territories on both sides of the Bosphorus, or Istanbul Strait, that divides the two continents. Over the past several decades, Turkey has unsuccessfully sought membership in the European Union a number of times. More recently, it has begun to assert membership in, and influence over, the Middle Eastern regions that were part of the Turkish Ottoman Empire until after World War I. These include present-day Syria, Jordan, Lebanon, Israel, and Iraq.

CULTURAL ASPECTS OF DOING BUSINESS IN TURKEY[28]

Turkey is located at the crossroads of Europe and Asia. Western Turkey is located in Europe and borders several Balkan countries. Eastern Turkey, comprising the far larger Anatolian peninsula, borders on Middle Eastern countries. Due to its strategic location at the junction of Europe and Asia, Turkey has played a significant role in bridging Western countries into the Middle East in its history.

The Republic of Turkey was established in 1923 after the last sultan of the Ottoman Empire was overthrown. Mustafa Kemal Ataturk became the first president of the Republic, moving the capital to Ankara, and introducing fundamental reforms including the Turkish alphabet derived from the Latin alphabet, and the dress laws. The reforms of Ataturk were intended to lead the country out of its "dark" past into a more Western and secular future. Contrary to other Middle Eastern countries, Turkey adapted a secular constitution and turned its face to the West.

The people and their homeland

The Turkish population is approximately 76 million. The majority is of Turkish ethnicity although Kurdish and Arab minorities are dominant across the eastern parts of the country. The government's official language and major spoken language is Turkish. Turkish is the mandatory language in schools even in Kurdish dominant regions where there are a number of people whose first language is Kurdish.

There has been a long history of tension between Turks and Kurds since the early years of the Republic and there is long-lasting argument between Turks and Kurds as to which are the original inhabitants of Turkey. The Kurdistan Workers Party (PKK), a terrorist organization committed to establishing a free Kurdistan, launched a guerrilla campaign in 1984 for an ethnic homeland in the Kurdish heartland in the southeast. Thousands of civilians and soldiers have been killed since the 1980s as the result of guerrilla attacks. In the early years of the Republic, Turkish governments insisted that Kurds were ethnic Turks, and banned the Kurdish language until 1991, backed by Articles 3 and 42 of the Constitution. These articles stated that the official language of the state was Turkish and that no other language other than Turkish could be taught to Turkish citizens in any educational institution.

Urged by the European Union to deal with the Kurdish issue, the Turkish government started in 2008 to address some of the issues dividing Turks and Kurds. In 2013, the prohibition against the use of the Kurdish language in schools was lifted. There are now also Kurdish-language radio and TV channels.[29]

Political and social conditions

In the 1940s, there was only one political party allowed in Turkish politics. Currently, due to reforms, there are multiple political parties as in any democratic state. Politics are part of the daily lives of Turks. You will find that many people from many age ranges will have a lot to say about politics.

The ruling party, the Justice and Development Party (AKP), was elected with a majority of the vote in 2002. The AKP is a rather conservative party but still advocates a free market economy and European Union membership. However, in 2007, millions of Turks held demonstrations against the government for electing the country's first Islamist president, putting the secular identity of the country under threat. In many Turks' minds, secularism is identified with following Ataturk's principles, and Ataturk is still considered with reverence as the Father of modern Turkey. For this reason, many protestors marched to Ataturk's Mausoleum in Ankara holding posters asking "Are you aware of the danger?" and shouting "We are the children of Ataturk."[30] Perception of a threat in the minds of secular Turks arose from the fact that an Islamist president was taking the office, while the power of the army, the guarantor of secularism, was declining. It was feared that an Islamic President could lead the country to becoming an Islamic state ruled by "*shariah rules*" similar to Iran.

Hence, politics is a controversial issue between secular and religiously conservative Turks. There is a significant separation between the social life of regular citizens and their political orientations. Therefore, it is important not to bring up any politics if you are unfamiliar with another's political orientations because of the possibility it may cause distortion of relationships. However, politics can easily be a part of a regular conversation and may turn into a heated debate even in business meetings.

The AKP government has conducted serious diplomatic campaigns to gain influence and power in international politics since taking the office. Part of Turkey's diplomatic endeavors are related to the government's desire to obtain European Union membership. Turkey was elected to provisional membership in the United Nations Security Council in 2008. This provisional membership certainly helped the Turkish government become more influential in international politics. Although the Turkish government has worked hard to gain permanent EU membership, the AKP's policy of "*Zero problems with Neighbor countries*" may have negatively affected EU prospects. Berdal Aral claims that "the posture and voting preferences which Turkey adopts in the Security Council will have immediate repercussions for the overall context of Turkish foreign policy."[31]

Religion

Turkey, known as *Anatolia* in the past, has been the cradle of monotheistic religions over the centuries. The country, historical home of both Christian and Jewish shrines, attracts thousands of Christian and Jewish pilgrims every year. Although Christianity and Judaism have significant numbers of followers, Islam is the majority religion in the country where a synthesis of Islamic traditions and Western thought is prevalent in society. Almost 99 percent of Turks are registered as Muslim but this information holds true only for identification purposes. It is required for Turkish citizens to declare their religious orientation on their national identity cards even though they may not practice that religion in their daily lives.

Turkey is a secular country with no state official religion, unlike many other Islamic countries in the same region. Secularism is a fundamental pillar of the Turkish Constitution. Ironically, the Turkish government, with the support from the army, has sought to remove religion from the public sphere since the inception of the Republic. The Islamic headscarf was banned in universities by dress regulations put into effect in 1984 by the High Education Council (YOK). This edict was canceled in 2008.

In many Turks' minds, being secular is viewed as being patriotic to the Republic. Thus, it is highly likely that you find people with very secular beliefs who do not practice Islam. This is especially likely in metropolitan cities such as Istanbul, Izmir, and Ankara. Alcoholic beverages are readily available across the country, despite being banned by Islam, and are commonly consumed among secular and Westernized circles in social life. Still, Turkey is a dominantly Muslim country and Turkish culture is largely affected by Islamic traditions. Turks, even those not practicing the religion at all, respect the Islamic roots of the Turkish culture. They may even fast at least one day in the holy month of Ramadan and not drink alcohol on particularly holy days of Ramadan.

Conservative Turks have achieved a remarkable influence in the economic and social spheres. This is largely because the AKP's political power has increased in recent consecutive elections.

Society

Turks are proud of their history and their pride is expressed in a famous Turkish phrase "How happy is she/he who can say I'm Turkish." Article 301 of the Turkish Penal Code prohibits insulting Turkey, the ethnicity of Turkey, and Ataturk. Nobel award winning Turkish author Orhan Pamuk is amongst people who have allegedly claimed to have dared to contravene Article 301.

Depending on where you are and whom you are dealing with, your experiences in Turkish society may vary. Eastern regions of the country contain greater overtones of Middle Eastern culture partly because of geographic proximity and historical ties. In eastern regions of the country, people are usually more traditional. Islamic rituals and traditions play a significant role in social life. By contrast, Western cities such as Istanbul, Izmir, and Ankara are modernized and people less conservative and more Westernized. Both women and men wear Western looking clothes and can socialize in mixed gender social gatherings. Family is a very important phenomenon in all parts of the country; but, levels of family relationships may vary.

Social customs

Turkish culture is a blend of traditional and modern values, sharing stronger ties with the East through traditions and religious values, and connecting to the West through the inspiration of modernity. Turks adhering to Islamic values have more similarities with people from the Middle East with respect to particular aspects of their daily lives than secular Turks do. Still, Turkey may be viewed as a model for outward-looking Islam because even many conservative Turks may embrace modern values.

Turks are known for their hospitality. They like to invite people to their houses for dinners, breakfasts, lunches, and even make their guests welcome to stay at their homes if they are traveling from another city. It is important for Turks to make their guests feel as comfortable as in their own home. A famous Turkish expression about visitors as "*God's guest*" means that a visitor must be taken as if she/he has been sent as an envoy from God.[32]

The following gestures should be noted when in the company of the Turkish:

■   Formal forms of address should be used unless you become a close friend to a Turk. Avoid addressing an elderly person by his/her first name. It is regarded as disrespectful to her/his age and life experiences. Add " Bey (Mr.)" or "Hanim (Miss)."

■   Shoes are not allowed in the majority of houses because they may be dirty. Slippers will be provided to guests at the entrance.

■   People greet each other with a kiss on both cheeks, man to man, woman to woman. An appropriate greeting from man to woman is either a nod or a "dead fish" handshake with as little contact as possible. Avoid offering a handshake to a conservative Muslim women who may be identified with a headscarf or a conservative outfit. As a sign of respect to the elderly, younger people kiss their hand and press it to their forehead.

■   "Saving face" is very important both in social life and business interactions. Turks are sensitive to criticism and it is rude to criticize someone in public as criticism may be seen as hostility. There is a significant emphasis on core values such as shame, honor, loyalty, and unity in the society.

The economy and business

Turkey has been a member of the World Trade Organization (WTO) since 1995 and signed Free Trade Agreements with a number of countries in Europe, Asia, and Middle East. With a rapidly rising growth rate in its economy, Turkey has been the fastest-growing economy in Europe and one of the fastest growing economies in the world in 2010 and 2011, following China and India (see Exhibit 10.7). Between 2002 and 2011, GDP increased by 234 percent, reaching US$772 billion. During that period, annual average real GDP growth was 5.2 percent.[33]

Foreign investors have been attracted to Turkey because its labor force (27 million) has a higher level of average education than many EU countries. Turkey's population is also, on average, younger (29.7 years) than is commonly the case in EU countries. Aggressive privatization programs and economic reforms instituted in the drive for EU membership have been major growth factors for the Turkish economy. EU countries have been a major export market for Turkish products. See Exhibit 10.8 for Turkish trade statistics.

EXHIBIT 10.7 A COMPARISON OF FAST-GROWING NATIONAL GDPS

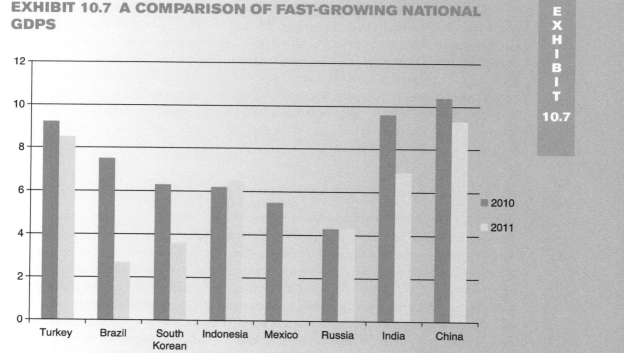

Source: The World Bank, World Development Indicators (http://data.worldbank.org/indicator). Retrieved March 3, 2013.

EXHIBIT 10.8 FOREIGN TRADE STATISTICS, IN US$

	2005	2006	2007	2008	2009	2010	2011
Exports (FOB)	73,476	85,535	107,272	132,002	102,143	118,883	134,969
Imports (CIF)	116,774	139,576	170,063	201,961	140,929	184,544	240,838
Trade	190,251	225,111	277,334	333,963	243,072	299,428	375,807
Trade balance	−43,298	−54,041	−62,791	−69,959	−38,786	−71,661	−105,869

Source: Macroeconomic Indicators, Invest In Turkey (http://www.invest.gov.tr). Retrieved March 2, 2012.

Family owned businesses are of significant importance to the Turkish economy. Of all Turkish enterprises, 90 percent are family owned.[34] Three Turkish family-owned conglomerates are ranked in the Europe's top 100 family businesses. Of these, Koc Holding, 16th in the list, generated a corporate revenue of €32.35 billion. The 52nd ranked Sabanci Holding generated a corporate revenue of €9.57 billion, followed by the 95th ranked Dogus Group with €3.69 billion in 2011.[35]

The life of the majority of family owned businesses is usually limited to the life duration of the founder. The main issue challenging the Turkish family owned businesses is lack of institutionalism and a long-term corporate vision. Relatively small family owned enterprises are usually run in traditional ways by their founders. Fifty percent of family businesses are reluctant to accept any outsider involvement and, moreover, they consider outsourced consulting services unnecessary. Succession struggles are common and generally not well managed, resulting in bankruptcy or the wind-up of 65 percent of family businesses. A well-known cultural factor in succession struggles for Turkish family owned businesses is competition between co-sister-in-laws.

Work values and business relationships

Turks are mostly relationship oriented in their business dealings. It may take some time for you to close a deal with Turks if you have just started building a relationship, or if you have not been referred by a mutual friend. Turks usually prefer to do business only with those they know and like. Third party introductions are key to creating new contacts and widening business networks. Turks would like to establish long-term relationships so it is essential for outsiders to build trust and show willingness to maintain a long-term relationship.

Turkish women are increasing in the workforce, especially in the business environment and in governmental organizations across the country. Especially in metropolitan cities, large domestic and/or international firms employ many young Turkish women. These highly educated Westernized Turkish women are so career oriented that they are willing to postpone marrying to their late twenties and thirties. It is critical for Western investors to research their Turkish counterparts to determine whether they are religiously conservative or secular managers because attitudes vary greatly.

Comparing American and Turkish work values

Turkey scored high on Hofstede's *power distance*, suggesting that Turks "expect and accept that the power is distributed unequally."[36] The parent–child inequality is perpetuated by a subordinate–boss inequality. Parents expect their children to respect and obey the rules laid down respectfully by the parents. Similarly, subordinates are expected to do what they are told by their superiors. Subordinates are afraid of disagreeing with their superiors and there is a little consultation between subordinates and superiors. The superior generally has ultimate decision-making authority over his/her subordinates, and the latter are generally comfortable with the superior's authority.

In contrast, Americans generally scored much lower than Turks in power distance. This creates the possibility that Americans will behave in ways that may make Turks feel uncomfortable. Rank and status will likely be much more important to Turks than Americans, and Americans will be well advised to pay more attention to formalities than they would at home in the United States. Americans, and other foreigners, that did not visibly respect rank, status, and formalities would seem disrespectful to Turks, and possibly not be seen, themselves, as high status. Exhibit 10.9 details differences related to power distance.

EXHIBIT 10.9 BEHAVIORAL DIFFERENCES BASED ON POWER DISTANCE

Low power distance (Americans)	High power distance (Turks)
People value independence over conformity	People value conformity over independence
Managers accept support of subordinates	Managers reject assistance from subordinates
Consultative decision-making with subordinates is the norm	Superiors consult with peers but not with subordinates
Subordinates are relatively unthreatened by disagreement with superiors	Subordinates fear authority and avoid disagreements
Subordinates cooperate rather than compete	Subordinates compete for the attention and favor of the superior
Education signals accomplishment	Education signals greater social status
Social policies are intended to reduce inequalities	Social policies support and reinforce inequalities
Being seen as average means acceptance and inclusion	Being seen as average means lack of power

E X H I B I T 10.9

Source: Drake, B. *Cultural Dimensions of Expatriate Life: Turkey.* Kindle Edition: Cultural Dimensions Press, 2010.

The *individualism–collectivism* scale measured the extent to which persons see themselves as individuals whose identity is separate from their various work, or as members of a social groups. Turkish culture scored high on *collectivism* – as high as China and other Asian cultures. By contrast, the United States was the second most *individualist* nation after Australia. Turks could be expected to exhibit and expect respectful and loyal behavior between people in the same groups. In more conservative parts of Turkey, group orientation is still so strong that it may be regarded as rude to express your individual opinion.

However, this strong difference between Americans, and other similar foreigners, and Turks means that many American assumptions about managing, motivating, and training personnel must be carefully scrutinized before implementation. Collectivist Turks may feel uncomfortable, or be unmotivated, or even resist management practices based on individualist assumptions. Exhibit 10.10 details some key practical differences.

Masculinity–femininity, or what has been called *task/relationship* orientation, is the extent to which goal attainment is achieved either by nurturing and supporting people

EXHIBIT 10.10 BEHAVIORAL DIFFERENCES BASED ON INDIVIDUALISM VS. COLLECTIVISM

Individualism (Americans)	Collectivism (Turks)
Individual achievement and earned merit are the basis of social standing	Birth circumstances, ethnicity, and gender confer social standing
Strong social and legal support for individual rights	Legal structures protect group and community standards
People are expected to act on their own behalf	Individuals defer to group interests
Individuals can hold and express unpopular opinions	Individuals cannot express unpopular opinions without threat of sanction
Individual decision-making is admired	Consensus decision-making is preferred Individual decision-making is dangerous
Philosophies favor universal principles, not social particulars	Philosophies support privileges and prerogatives
Loyalty to the company not expected; pay for performance is expected	Loyalty to company and superiors is more valued than performance
Individuals work better alone	Individuals perform better in groups
Efficiency and productivity is valued above participation and attitude	Participation and attitude are valued more than efficiency and productivity

Source: Drake, B. *Cultural Dimensions of Expatriate Life: Turkey.* Kindle Edition: Cultural Dimensions Press, 2010.

(femininity or relationship), or by controlling and dominating people (masculinity or task). In *task* cultures like the United States, individuals are valued because of what they can do. They demonstrate their capabilities through having skills or knowledge, and accumulating power and/or wealth. In *relationship* cultures like Turkey, people are valued for who they are. Their personality, character, appearance, behavior, and family are all part of the equation.

Americans with a strong task orientation want to get the job done quickly and right the first time. They may experience resistance in Turkey where time is usually taken to get everyone involved in agreement. Exhibit 10.11 suggests some key American–Turkish differences on task versus relationship.

Turkish culture scored very high on *uncertainty avoidance* – one of the highest scores of any country. Turks minimize uncertainty and ambiguity by adhering to social norms and rules. "Strictness of the rules" is found to be an important factor of the Uncertainty Avoidance construct.[37] This means that Turkish business people have an emotional need for rules, formalization, and structures. Turkish employees face very strong organizational pressures to contain deviant thoughts and behaviors, and they are used to this situation, and comfortable with it. This translates into resistance to change, structured learning and training situations, and lesser flexibility in meetings. It also suggests that you need to be patient with your Turkish business partner as it will take some time for him to trust you for a long-term business relationship, or to make a decision. By contrast, Americans scored low on uncertainty avoidance. Exhibit 10.12 indicates some likely differences between Americans and Turks due to this work value.

EXHIBIT 10.11 BEHAVIORAL DIFFERENCES BASED ON TASK VS. RELATIONSHIP

High task (Americans)	High relationship (Turks)
Work relationships more important than social relationships	Social relationships take priority over work relationships
Family commitments less important than work commitments	Family commitments take precedence over work commitments
Achievement measured by accomplishment, possessions, power	Achievement measured by friendships, peer recognition, respect
Demonstrated expertise determines professional recognition	Peer recognition determines professional recognition
Criticism may be constructive or destructive	Criticism is usually interpreted as negative

Source: Drake, B. *Cultural Dimensions of Expatriate Life: Turkey.* Kindle Edition: Cultural Dimensions Press, 2010.

E
X
H
I
B
I
T
10.11

EXHIBIT 10.12

EXHIBIT 10.12 BEHAVIORAL DIFFERENCES DUE TO UNCERTAINTY AVOIDANCE

Low uncertainty avoidance (Americans)	High uncertainty avoidance (Turks)
The future is welcomed with anticipation	The future is uncertain and threatening
Readiness to accept and take risks	Strong reluctance to take risks
Emotional resistance to change is low	Change is resisted emotionally
Young people can lead organizations	Young people cannot be trusted
Loyalty to boss only concerns personal relations	Loyalty to boss determines personal success or failure
Conflict accepted as normal. Losing a round is OK	Conflict is a threat because you could lose
Compromise is an acceptable outcome from conflict	Compromise is a sign of weakness and the same as losing
Formal rules can be broken with sufficient reason	Only the highest in authority can break rules
Job security is less important than job satisfaction	Job security is more important than satisfaction
Career changes are growth opportunities	Career changes are evidence of failure or inability
Managers expect to give direction and offer support	Managers are expected to give and enforce orders
Subordinate initiative is valued and supported	Subordinate initiative is feared and discouraged

Source: Drake, B. *Cultural Dimensions of Expatriate Life: Turkey.* Kindle Edition: Cultural Dimensions Press, 2010.

CHARACTERISTICS OF ARAB CULTURE

For Westerners, another key to a better understanding of the contemporary Middle East is Arab culture. Over twenty Arab countries may be identified as members of the League of Arab States. Arab countries include: Algeria, Bahrain, Comoros Islands, Djibouti, Egypt, Iraq, Jordan, Kuwait, Lebanon, Libya, Mauritania, Morocco, Oman, Palestine, Qatar, Saudi Arabia, Somalia, Sudan, Syria, Tunisia, United Arab Emirates Arab, and Yemen.

To say that member countries have similar cultural attitudes, behaviors, and communication is very misleading. For example, in the Muslim countries of Sudan, Somalia, and Mauritania, tribal languages, rather than Arabic, are spoken, and there are cultural practices that favor their African heritage. Not all Arabs believe in Islam, as Christian Arabs will confirm. But Arab peoples have a Muslim majority in the Middle East – outside the region, they represent only 20 percent of the Muslim population. As a rule, *Arab* is an ethnic reference to a Semite, whereas *Muslim* signifies religious belief and grouping.

Here are five key distinguishing characteristics of Arab culture:

1   *Arab language.* For Arabs, their language is sacred because it was the means by which God revealed the Koran to Muhammad. Classical Arabic is used not only by religious scholars, but also the educated and the media. There are many forms of colloquial Arabic and these days radio, television, computers, and mobile telephones are spreading these other dialects. The Bedouins excel in oral verse, filled with emotion and an evocative form of poetry that are used to express strong feelings. Literature is most prized in this culture, contributing to group solidarity.

2   *Arab values.* In traditional societies, the paramount virtues are considered to be dignity, honor, and reputation. A shared honor code frequently dictates certain behaviors, especially to preserve the family's reputation. Gender roles differ substantially from the West in Arab societies which may be ultra-conservative. Foreigners at all costs should avoid causing an Arab to lose face or to be shamed. Loyalty to family, as well as courteous and harmonious communications, is emphasized. Arabs are noted for their love of family and its privacy, as well as for their hospitality. In tribal and traditional communities, Arab priorities are first to one's self, then kinsman, townsman, or tribesman, and those who share the same religion and country.

3   *Arab personal distance.* Arabs seek close personal relationships, preferably without great distance or intermediaries. Thus, olfaction is prominent in Arab life. For many Arabs, smells are necessary and a way to be involved with each other. Body and food odors are used to enhance human relationships; the former is even important in the choice of a mate. This cultural difference also extends to an Arab facing or not facing another person; to view another peripherally is impolite, so to sit or stand back to back is rude. Although Arabs may be very involved when interacting with friends, they may not seek a close distance in conversations with strangers or casual acquaintances. On such social occasions, they may sit on opposite sides of a room and talk across to one another. Yet, they are generally a warm and expressive people, both verbally and nonverbally.

4   *Arab sociability and equality.* Cordiality is at the core of this culture, and is evident from such occasions as feasting at a lamb banquet to drinking strong black coffee. It extends also to business meetings when the first session is devoted to getting acquainted with little regard for schedule or appointments. The traditional greeting is to place one's right hand on the chest near the heart as an indication of sincerity and warmth, though modern Arabs may precede this with a long, limp handshake. The custom is for men to kiss one another on both cheeks. For those Arabs who are Muslims, there are Islamic teachings that affect social relations, such as taboos against eating pork, drinking alcohol, gambling, and prostitution.

5   *Arab women.* The Arab patriarchal culture places the male in the dominant role, while protecting and respecting the female. In an Arab household, for example, the man is overtly the head with a strong role and influence. The mother is often the authority, "behind the scenes," on family matters. Honorable female behavior implies being

loving mothers and daughters, acting in modest and respectful ways, including running efficient and generous households. Publicly, the woman defers to her husband, but privately she may be more assertive. Paradoxically, Islam does not advance the notion of women's inherent inferiority, only her difference. It does not perceive biological inferiority and affirms potential equality between the sexes. During an interview, Dr. Fatima Mernissi stated: "The whole Muslim system is based on the assumption that the woman is a powerful and dangerous being."[38]

In some Arab countries, women enjoy equality with men, while in others there are limitations on their role. In more traditional Arab communities, where mullahs control marriage laws, men are allowed to marry more than one woman, including foreigners. Women may marry only one husband, excluding foreigners. Husbands may divorce without stating a cause, whereas a wife must specify grounds to the satisfaction of the court, and in a courtroom, it takes the testimony of two females to equal one male.

The Koran does not say that women must be veiled, only that they must be modest in appearance by covering their arms and hair, which are considered sensual. Scholars see the use of the veil as having sociological symbolism. The veil's use depends on circumstances. Some Arab countries are without dress restrictions for women, so they may wear the latest fashion. In more socially conservative countries, women may be expected to wear a long cloak of black gauze or chiffon *abaya* to cover themselves from head to ankle.

The cultural contrasts within Arab societies on this matter are considerable. In some Arab countries, most females are illiterate, whereas in others they are well educated. In some, they are not allowed outside their homes alone nor permitted to drive an automobile, whereas in other states, women may hold jobs and drive cars. In many Arab states, women are not allowed to vote, whereas in others they do.

In most Arab societies, marriages are arranged, whereas in a growing number, freedom of marital choice is respected. Within an Arab world in turmoil and change, one may observe both resurgent Islamic fundamentalism and an emerging feminist movement. In the traditional societies, a Committee to Prevent Vice and Promote Virtue – the *matawa*, or religious police – enforce required codes of behavior. In more conservative Arab communities, when a woman disobeys these rulings, she may be flogged or caned by these religious police.[39]

Yet, there is great diversity within the Arab world on the status of women. Contrast a women's role in Saudi Arabia with that in the Muslim country of Brunei, Southeast Asia. There, women outnumber men at the university, drive automobiles, hold senior offices in both the public and private sectors, and can even serve as ambassadors and airline pilots. Some Muslim women are protesting and working toward greater emancipation for their gender against stifling morality.[40] However, foreign females visiting Arab countries must exercise great sensitivity to what is acceptable or unacceptable in the local situation.

CULTURAL ASPECTS OF EGYPT AND SAUDI ARABIA

By focusing on two similar but distinctly different cultural targets, one may gain insight into the cultural dimensions of these and other remarkable peoples in the region. Both Egypt and Saudi Arabia are part of the Arab world, but Egypt originates from an ancient civilization and is more liberal, whereas Saudi Arabia is a traditional nation created in the twentieth century, propeled by vast oil discoveries. Geographically, Saudi Arabia is located on the Arabian Peninsula. Egypt lies on the continent of North Africa, but is traditionally and historically a part of the Middle East.

EGYPT

Ancient Egypt was one of the five cradles of human civilization along with ancient Anatolia, Sumer, the Indus Valley in India, and China. Its earliest settlements, found by archaeologists, date to 3500 BC. The great pyramids at Giza were built between 2600 BC and 2500 BC. Later, Egypt was a rich and prized possession for many empires including the Assyrians, Babylonians, Persians, Greeks, Romans, and even the French under Napoleon, and the British in the twentieth century AD. Egypt gained its independence from the British in 1953.[41]

The people and their homeland

Most of Egypt is high dry plains, rugged hills, and mountains, stretching along the Red Sea Coast to the valley of the Nile with desert beyond to the west. The population of the Old Kingdom was less than two million, while today's Egypt has more than 85 million, who are 90 percent Sunni Muslim (9 percent Coptic Christian). The official language is Arabic but English and French are widely understood because of the colonial past. The population is very young as compared with many Western nations with an average age of 24.6 years. This most populous of Arab states has one of the highest population densities in the world. Cairo, the capital, has approximately 17 million people, and is the largest city in Africa and the Arab world.

Political and social conditions

Since the late President Sadat signed a Peace Treaty with Israel (March 25, 1979), Egypt was for many years both the target of Arab economic reprisals and the recipient of significant foreign aid from the United States. To curb attacks of Islamic militants in the area, President Mubarak hosted a summit in Cairo at the beginning of Ramadan in 1995. Prime Minister Yitzhak Rabin of Israel, PLO leader Yasser Arafat, and King Hussein of Jordan joined him in the elusive pursuit of peace and prosperity for the Middle East. In a collective communiqué, "The four parties condemned all outbreaks of bloodshed, terror, and violence in the region and reaffirmed their intentions to stand staunchly against and put an end to all such acts." Ironically, Rabin was assassinated that same year by a Jewish fundamentalist who opposed this reconciliation. But Egypt has continued to cooperate as a peace-broker in a region where nations have more to gain by peaceful collaboration than from continuing conflict.

The governance and political system have undergone some liberalization in recent times. The constitution provides for a strong president, vice presidents, prime minister, cabinet, and governors for 26 provinces. The single legislature is the People's Assembly with 444 elected delegates and 10 appointed by the president. Fifty percent are reserved for farmers and workers. The *Shura* is a consultative council for advising on public policy that has little legislative power. The governing National Democratic Party (NDP) dominates politics. Today, Egyptians are intensely nationalistic and Arab sensitive. Although a secular state and somewhat Westernized, especially with reference to international business, traditional Arab patterns are also present.

In 2011, as the "Arab Spring" movement for democracy swept through the Middle East, the Mubarak government was overthrown by a non-violent peoples' uprising that the army did not attempt to quell. Mohammed Morsi, the candidate of the conservative Muslim Brotherhood, won in a democratic election despite the active protests of the secular minority. He was deposed by the army within a year, due to mass demonstrations and the fear that he was attempting to impose conservative Muslim values as part of a re-writing of Egypt's constitution. There are also reports that Egypt's Coptic Christian minority may not have the same guarantees of religious freedom under the Morsi regime compared with the previous Mubarak regime.

The economy and business[42]

Egypt is a relatively poor country with a GNP (PPP) of only approximately US$538 billion in 2012, and a per capita GDP (PPP) of US$6,700, and 20 percent of the population below the poverty line. Its workforce of 27.3 million currently suffers from 12.5 percent unemployment.

In 2012, Egypt exported only US$8.4 billion; mainly petroleum products, cotton, textiles, metal products, chemicals, and processed foods. These were primarily received by Italy (8.7 percent), India (7.3 percent), Saudi Arabia (6.1 percent), the United States (5.2 percent), and Turkey (4.9 percent). Egypt imported US$58.8 billion; mainly machinery and equipment, food products, chemicals, wood products, and fuels. These came primarily from the United States (10.7 percent), China (9.1 percent), Germany (6.3 percent), Italy (5.1 percent), Kuwait (4.7 percent), and Turkey (4.4 percent). Egypt's trade balance is a concern given that in 2012 its reserves of foreign exchange were only US$15.3 billion.

Social life

This is oriented toward extended families and public gatherings, with a close sense of distance. Prepare for a slower way of life, including decision-making, and a lack of punctuality in keeping appointments. People follow the Islamic calendar. Five national holiday dates are fixed, whereas Ramadan and Islamic New Year are variable since they follow the lunar calendar. The workweek is from Saturday through Wednesday, with no business conducted on Thursday and Friday (Muslim Holy Day). Business hours vary, but typically in summer are 8 a.m. to 2 p.m.; in winter, 9 a.m. to 1 p.m.; and 5 to 7 p.m. all year.

SAUDI ARABIA

The Arabian Peninsula is the heartland of Islamic culture. After hundreds of years of subsistence living, a nomadic, patriarchal, and impoverished society has been transformed suddenly into a more prosperous, educated, and internationally oriented one. Within this whirlwind clash between tradition and modernization, the affluent kingdom founded on Islamic principles has experienced cataclysmic change. Popular magazines have described the nation as a desert super-state – a rich, vulnerable, feudal monarchy being hurdled into the space age.[43]

The people and their homeland[44]

Approximately 90 percent of the Saudi people are Arabs, with a 10 percent minority of Afro-Asians. The kingdom's population has risen rapidly to almost 27 million, with an average age of 25.7. The population is 100 percent Muslim, and Arabic is the official language, though English is widely used for commercial activities. The country occupies four-fifths of the Arabian Peninsula, a landmass of 850,000 square miles, making it geographically one of the largest countries in the region. Geographically, it is a harsh, rugged, desert plateau. Saudi Arabia is reputed to have the greatest oil reserves of any nation at 261.8 billion barrels.

Approximately one million immigrants and technicians are in Saudi Arabia to help build the infrastructure and defense, as well as to provide new technologies and services. This influx includes Americans, Europeans, Japanese, and Third World laborers and servants, such as Filipinos, Africans, and other people from the Middle East. Thus, one of every five workers in the kingdom is foreign born. The kingdom follows a form of strict Islamic conservatism called *Hanabalism* (or *Wahhabism* by detractors). It is among the most restrictive of Sunni Muslim states.

Riyadh, the royal capital of some 3.5 million, is a modern desert city with new freeways, hospitals, schools, shopping malls, and one of the largest airports in the world. The Red Sea port city of Jeddah is the nation's leading commercial center and hub of the country's 8,000-mile highway system. Jeddah's huge $10 billion airport handles the two million Muslim guests annually en route to Saudi holy places such as Mecca.

Political and social conditions

Abdullah bin Abdul Aziz, the sixth king of the Saud dynasty, rules today with assistance from a royal family of some 30,000, of whom 7,000 are "princes". About 500 princes are in government service, but only around 60 are thought to be involved in decision-making. Tribal connections are maintained through the Saudi National Guard. The combined wealth of the Al Saud family is estimated to be in the hundreds of billions of dollars.

In Saudi Arabia, Islam permeates Saudi life – Allah is always present, controls everything, and is frequently referred to in conversation. Islamic *Sharia* law governs national life and behavior. A judiciary interprets and advises the king on this law and in other matters. Seven hundred judges preside over the *Sharia* courts, the backbone of the legal system, but the bane of reformers. The *Majlis al-Shura* is a consultative council of 100 appointed members, broadly representative of the kingdom's diversity, except it excludes women. Although there are no elections or legislature, the king and his provincial governors of provinces, govern by consensus but with absolute authority. It is a system based on trust. Any citizen may receive an audience to make requests, or lodge complaints. Internationally, the king opposes Western democracy and its institutions, while gently nudging his country forward on social matters without unduly offending conservatives.

The role of women

Islam limits the number of wives a man may have by imposing restrictions on divorce, and ensuring a woman's rights to property and inheritance from husband or father. Men may divorce their wives with a simple oath, while women must plead before an all-male, extremist Wahhabist judiciary, and mothers have no right to custody of the children. Husbands may deny wives the right to travel, work, or study at university. Following the impact of the first Gulf War with Iraq, women began a quiet revolution.

With advanced education, Saudi women have begun to enter the business world and the professions, especially teaching, along with social and public services. Though women today make up over half of university enrollment, they number only a fraction of the workforce. The so-called invisible women are said now to control as much as 40 percent of private wealth, much of it inherited under the law. Despite social limitations on women, as well as bans on their driving, travel, and political activity – all enforced by the *mutawa* or religious police – cosmopolitan female Saudis slowly forge ahead.

The economy and international trade[45]

The Saudi economy is oil based, and the government exercises strong controls over major economic activities. In 2012, the GDP was US$740.5 billion, with a growth rate of 6 percent, a GDP per capita of US$25,700, and a 10.7 percent unemployment rate.

The country exported a value of US$381.5 billion, mainly petroleum products, to Japan (13.9 percent), China (13.6 percent), the United States (13.4 percent), South Korea (10.2 percent), India (7.8 percent), and Singapore (4.8 percent). It imported US$136.8 billion, primarily machinery, foodstuffs, chemicals, vehicles, and textiles, from China (12.8 percent), the United States (11.9 percent), Germany (7.1 percent), South Korea (6.0 percent), Japan (5.6 percent), and India (4.9 percent).

International political issues

In the political caldron of the Middle East, Saudi Arabia is the main Sunni banker and powerbroker that confronts Shiite Iran with the help of its staunch ally, the United States. Saudi Arabia supported the Allied consortium that dislodged Iraq from its occupation of Kuwait in the First Gulf War, and again in the Second Gulf War when Saddam Husain was overthrown. The Saudi position on Israel has been relatively moderate though it supports the movement for a Palestinian homeland. American troops have protected Saudi Arabia from its regional enemies. While many American troops have been removed, the country is criticized by fellow Muslim nations because of its close ties for eight decades to the United States. Osama bin Laden, the former leader of Al Qaeda, was originally a Saudi dissident.

IRAQ REVIEW

Iraq is another Islamic Arab state. It is the land of ancient Mesopotamia, between the Tigris and Euphrates rivers. The ancient city of Babylon was located here, with a population reputed to have been as high as 500,000 in its heyday 2,400 years ago under King Nebuchadnezzar.[46] Ancient Sumer was also located in what is now Iraq.

In 1921, the British established Iraq as a monarchy with a figurehead king. The new political entity was created out of three Ottoman, ethnically diverse provinces – Shiite, Sunni, and Kurd. An army coup installed dictator Saddam Hussein, a Sunni, in 1979. He fought a war with the Iranians, practiced genocide on his own citizens, and invaded Kuwait in 1990. This provoked United Nation sanctions, and two invasions by the United States and its coalition partners – first the Gulf War in 1991 and again in 2005 – in which the regime and its large armed forces were quickly defeated both times.

The occupation of Iraq by American and coalition troops triggered a serious insurgency by locals and foreign terrorists. While the majority of the population was Shiite, much of the subsequent terrorism was Sunni in origin, trying to maintain some semblance of its former influence under Saddam Hussein, a Sunni. Saddam Hussein was eventually captured, put on trial, and executed by the new democratically elected government. Iraq's majority are Shiite Muslims who share power with the minority Kurdish Islamic parties and some Sunnis who together govern along ethnic and sectarian lines.

Iraq's population of approximately 32 million is 97 percent Muslim (Shia 65 percent, Sunni 32-37 percent). Ethnically, the population is 75 to 80 percent Arab, with a Kurdish minority of approximately 15 to 20 percent. Both Arabic and Kurdish are official languages.

The Kurds in Iraq have gained a measure of autonomy and peace for their mountainous northern region, and are currently cooperating with the central government in Baghdad. Their goal is to control some nine billion barrels of crude oil in Iraqi Kurdistan, and eventually gain independence to form a new state with the Kurds living within the borders of Syria, Turkey, and Iran – something vehemently opposed by those three nations.

In 2012, Iraq exported a value of US$88.3 billion, mainly petroleum, to India (22.5 percent), the United States (22.3 percent), China (13.4 percent), South Korea (11.7 percent), and Japan (4.8 percent). It imported US$ 56.9 billion, mainly food, medicines and manufactures, from Turkey (25.3 percent), Syria (18.3 percent), China (11.7 percent), and the United States (7.4 percent).

ISRAEL REVIEW

Israel is the only predominantly non-Muslim state in the Middle East. It was founded in 1948, by United Nations' resolution, as a Jewish homeland for Jews that had survived the Nazi holocaust during World War II. This represented the re-establishment of a Jewish state that had existed from the time of King David (1000 BC?) to the Roman expulsion in the first century AD.

The Arab states surrounding Israel launched wars to eradicate the Jewish state in 1948, 1956, 1967, and 1973. Israel won these wars but peace has never been fully achieved because Israel has continued to occupy territories that the Palestinian refugees – the descendants of Palestinians who fled Israel during the 1948 war – claim for themselves for a Palestinian homeland. Currently, there are two territories – Gaza and the West Bank – with limited Palestinian self-rule under the authority of the Israeli government. The establishment of a full peace has defied solution because, on the one hand, Israel has claimed territories on the West Bank to protect its security from Palestinian terrorists that see themselves as freedom fighters. On the other hand, these Palestinian terrorists and their allies in Iran, Syria, and other nations, have refused to declare Israel's right to exist as an independent Jewish state.

President Jimmy Carter of the United States came the closest to achieving peace among the parties in 1978. Israel offered 98 percent of the Palestinian claimed territories but refused to cede Old Jerusalem where Jewish worshippers had been denied access to the most sacred Jewish religious site, the Wailing Wall, when it had been under Jordanian control. The leader of the Palestinian Liberation Organization, Yasser Arafat, refused the deal because of this, but peace was signed as a result between Israel and Egypt in 1979. Since that time, there have been a number of limited and inconclusive wars between Israel and Palestinians located in southern Lebanon, and Gaza.

In 2013, Israel's population of 7.7 million was 76.4 percent ethnic Jewish, the remainder being mostly Arab. Hebrew is the official language, though Arabic is officially recognized for the Arab minority, and English is common. The main religions are Jewish (75.6 percent), and Muslim (16.9 percent).

Economy and international trade[47]

Israel has a First World technologically advanced economy. Recent natural gas finds off its Mediterranean coast have offered it energy security despite Arab hostility. In 2012, its GDP was US$247.9 billion, with a per capita GDP of US$32,200, and a 2.9 percent growth rate. However, 23.6 percent of the population was under a poverty line of US$7.30 per day. In 2012, exports of US$64.7 billion were recorded, primarily machinery and equipment, software, cut diamonds, agricultural products, chemicals, textiles, and apparel. These exports went primarily to the United States (28.8 percent), Hong Kong (7.9 percent), Belgium (5.6 percent), the United Kingdom (5.0 percent), India (4.5 percent), and China (4.0 percent). Israel imported US$77.6 billion including raw materials, military equipment, investments, rough diamonds, fuels, grain, and consumer goods. These came from the United States (11.8 percent), China (7.4 percent), Germany (6.2 percent), Belgium (6.1 percent), Switzerland (5.4 percent), and Italy (4.2 percent).

Doing business in Israel

Israel's economy is primarily secular. While the suggestions about Islamic and Arab culture made in this chapter would apply to the Arab minority, most Israeli business is conducted on a different basis. It's interesting to see what the Israelis say about themselves. The Israeli Economic and Cultural Office in Taipei offers the following observations for Chinese considering doing business in Israel:[48]

> The Israeli, who is often perceived as being arrogant, aggressive, and pushy, is actually being direct and honest. And the American, European, or Asian, who are seen by the Israeli as being artificial, phony and weak – are actually displaying politeness and respect. If both sides are to go into a commercial venture, without taking the time to understand each other's cultural traits – they are heading for disaster. . . .
>
> Israeli society is what is referred to as a polyphonic culture (relationship-oriented), in contrast to American, Taiwanese, British, or German culture, which are monochromic (rule-oriented). In the relationship-oriented Israeli culture, feelings and emotions are primary, while intuition and objective facts are secondary! Israeli culture can be viewed as witnessing one large family. In a family, one can dismiss formality and act in a direct, immediate and honest fashion. What can be excused in a "family" as being direct – is often interpreted outside of the family or Israel's borders as being rude or impolite.

Recommendations for dealing with Israelis include the following:

- *Greetings.* Israel is a very touchy and feely society. However, they do not usually shake hands. Physical contact is made with a smile and direct eye contact. Israelis may stand closer to you than you feel comfortable with. If you step back, however, communications will not be as smooth.

- *Gestures.* Israelis signal readiness for immediate action by sitting, leaning forward, ready to stand. If they lean back, hands crossed behind their heads, this is a sign of greater informality and improved relationship. If they place their hand up, palm toward their body, and shake it, they are signing "Please wait a moment."

- *Time.* Israelis are impatient. Meetings can be spontaneous. Punctuality is relaxed and you should allow 15–20 minutes in case a contact is late. Israelis will not "do" breakfast or lunch. They may prefer to eat in their offices while meeting. During a meeting, an Israeli may take phone calls, and speak to others about other matters. This is not intended as rude, impolite, or arrogant. Israeli society is very informal and Israelis normally multitask.

- *Social occasions.* Find out if your Israeli counterpart is religious or "observant." If so, respect their values and go to a "kosher" restaurant. Israelis are not big drinkers but it is OK to invite your counterpart out for "a beer." In informal get-togethers, do not speak about the Israeli government, politics, or religious issues. If they do, be a good listener.

- *Negotiations.* Be prepared for tough but friendly negotiations. Israelis love to bargain and their first offer may be ridiculously low. Having a professional translator is useful since you would know what your Israeli counterparts were saying to each other in Hebrew, and also have a more accurate understanding of their points. Get agreements in writing. A handshake is not enough.

- *Gift giving.* If you are invited to an Israeli home, it is appropriate to bring flowers, chocolates, or wine. Framed pictures of yourself with your Israeli counterparts are an excellent gift and wall decoration, reminding the Israeli of the personal ties he/she shares with you.

MIDDLE EAST BUSINESS CUSTOMS AND PROTOCOL

Consider this case in point:

> A Midwestern banker is invited by an Arab sheik to meet him at the Dorchester Hotel in London. A friend of both arranges the get-together, and facilitates the introduction. Dark sweet coffee is served. No business of consequence is discussed, but there is a sociable exchange. . . . Subsequently, the American is invited to a series of meetings in Riyadh. The Saudi greets the banker with, "There is no God but Allah, and Muhammad is his messenger." More strong coffee is served, and sometimes others are present in the meeting room. . . . In time, a mutually beneficial business relationship is established.[49]

This short episode encapsulates several important points for succeeding in Middle Eastern business ventures. First, nothing happens quickly and patience is a virtue. Second, trust is paramount, and it is cultivated over a period of time, often with the assistance of a third-party acquaintances. Although business customs will vary somewhat in the region, by trying to understand Islam and Arab culture, an individual is in a better position to be effective. In this section, insights from the write-up on Saudi Arabia may be adapted and selectively applied elsewhere in the Middle East, but are subject to change.

Among the modern institutions of higher education recently established within Saudi Arabia, King Fahd University of Petroleum and Minerals is among the best. There, Dr. Mohammed I. Al-Twaijri has conducted and published studies comparing Saudi and American managers, purchasing agents, and negotiators. Some of his research findings and comments are:

■ There is a trend toward "Westernization" of Middle East managers, and Saudi managers are becoming less paternalistic.
■ There are significant differences in the way Arab managers respond to questionnaire items in their native Arabic language, as opposed to the English version of the same instrument.
■ In negotiations, the Saudis have two dominant styles, competitive and collaborative, both of which are expressed within the Arab cultural context.
■ In joint ventures under way with Saudi Arabia, foreigners are required to build exten- sive training programs for the locals into their project management, increasingly the trend in most Middle Eastern countries.

Apart from what has already been described about Middle Eastern peoples and their cultures, Arabs are a people of great emotion and sentimentality – and sometimes of excess and extremes. They hold in high regard friendship, loyalty, and justice. When events and behavior go against that sense of justice, Arabs will likely be morally outraged and indignant. Generally, Arabs tend to be warm, hospitable, generous, and courteous.

Furthermore, Arab society places great emphasis on honor. Its concept of shame is somewhat alien to Western mindsets. Shame must be feared, avoided, or hidden, so one prays to Allah for protection from others (public exposure). Thus, foreigners should avoid embarrassing Arabs. Because of the society's powerful identification between the individual and the group, shame means a loss of power and influence, particularly for the family. In addition, the tribal heritage influences and values a high degree of deference and conformity, often expressed in a somewhat authoritarian tone. In return, the individual has a strong sense of place, and shares in the group's social prestige. That is why Arabs typically worry about how their decisions, acts, and behavior reflect on their family, clan, tribe, and then country.

In a traditional society, honor is important, and to admit "I don't know" may be difficult. Constructive criticism can be taken for an insult. For an Arab, the "self" is buried deep within the individual. This relates, then, to the previously explained sense of distance – because the "self" is personal and private, in public touching and jostling among males is quite acceptable.

Business tips

To an Arab, commerce is a most blessed career – the prophet Muhammad, after all, was a businessman married to a businesswoman. Thus, business and trade are highly respected, and one is expected to be sound, shrewd, and knowledgeable. Some Middle Eastern business practices to observe are noted below:

■ *Business relationships* are facilitated by establishing personal rapport, mutual respect, and trust – business is done between people, not merely with a company or contract.

■ *Connections* and *networking* are most important – vital to gaining access to both private and public decision-makers, so maintain good relations with people of influence.

■ *Negotiating* and *bargaining* are somewhat of an art, so expect some old-fashioned "haggling."

■ *Decision-making* is traditionally done in person, thus requiring an organization's representative to be of suitable rank. Decisions are usually made by the top person in the government agency or corporation, and normally are not accomplished by correspondence, fax, or telephone.

■ *Time is flexible*, according to the concept of "tomorrow if God wills," an expression of the cultural pattern of fatalism. Arabs may be prompt, or not, and appointments will likely not be exact or may start late. Their day is divided into five prayer times, and meetings are scheduled accordingly.

■ *Socialization* in business is traditional, and social gestures, courtesies, and invitations are commonplace, but deals are not usually concluded under such circumstances.

■ *Communication* is especially complex in the Middle East, and outsiders should show harmony and agreement, following the host's lead. Arabic as a language is high context, manifested with raised voices and much nonverbal body language (wide gestures, animated facial expressions, eyebrow raising, tongue clicking, standing close, eye contact, and, except with strangers on first meeting, a side nod of the head is often given as affirmation). Hyperbole is normal, and a *yes* may really mean *maybe* or even, *probably not*.

Middle Eastern reactions to Westerners

Peoples from ancient civilizations, like Egypt, Persia, Turkey, and Arabia, are proud of their past – its history, art, poetry, literature, and cultural accomplishments. Unfortunately, many Westerners and Asians carry distorted cultural images or stereotypes about people from the Middle East and their contributions to human development. North American and European media have been particularly inept, slanted, and at times false in their presentations about the Middle East and Arabs.

There is deep underlying suspicion in the Middle East against former European colonial powers, especially the British and French, who once ruled much of the area. But insensitive American behavior toward Middle Eastern peoples and their religion explain, in part, reactive "anti-American" campaigns abroad that undermine both political and business relationships. Currently, resentment centers on America as the only superpower capable of military intervention in the region, especially the U.S. coalitions that went to war against terrorism twice in Iraq, support of Israel against Palestinians, as well as against the Taliban in Afghanistan. Both Arabs and Westerners are given to distorting each others' actions, behavior, and beliefs, thus promoting mutual xenophobia. The global terrorist movement among Islamic militants rose partially out of fear for Western culture and values destroying or undermining traditional Arab culture.

As they see us

Seventy percent of the world's oil reserves are in the Middle East. This results in an influx of Europeans, Americans, and even Asians into the region. Here is a summary of the feedback about foreigners from the Arab perspective:

■ Many foreigners express superiority and arrogance. They know the answers to everything.

■ Many do not want to share the credit for what is accomplished by joint efforts.

■ Many are frequently unable or unwilling to respect and adjust to local customs and culture.

■ Some fail to innovate to meet the needs of local culture, preferring to seek easy solutions based on the situation in their own homeland.

■ Some individuals refuse to work through the normal administrative channels of the country, and do not respect local legal and contractual procedures.

■ Some tend to lose their democratic ways when on foreign assignments, becoming instead more autocratic and managing by instilling fear in subordinates.

■ Westerners are often too imposing, aggressive, pushy, and rude.

■ There is frustration over American and European imbalance in support and aid for Israel, in contrast to the Palestinian cause and human rights.

SYNERGY: MIDDLE EAST HOPE

To realize the economic potential of their region, more people from the Middle East of all types are beginning to prefer collaboration with one another, even former enemies. Since they are only a short jet hop away from Europe, the interchange with peoples on both continents has increased. Arabs fly regularly to EU countries for study, investment, commerce, medical assistance, vacations, or even to reside. Europeans in greater numbers go to the Middle East seeking new markets and as tourists. In place of former colonial dominance, the present and future offer opportunities for more synergistic relationships if Arabs, Europeans, as well as Americans, Asians, and Africans appreciate each other's cultural heritages and differences, while seeking mutual benefits from interchanges. Practicing synergy is the key to peace and prosperity in the twenty-first century, both for that region and the world.

Efforts promoting cultural synergy need to be widely extended at all levels of education, as well as through churches and community forums. Indeed, knowledge of foreign languages and culture are keys to successful interaction and security in today's globally interconnected world – cultural skills are necessary to help peoples comprehend what is actually meant when they communicate with or about one another. If bridges are to be built across cultural divides, all must reach out to learn about other religions and countries. Only in such peaceful cooperation can the world community, especially through the United Nations, contribute to solutions of current Middle Eastern challenges.

CONCLUSIONS

The Middle East is critical for world peace and prosperity, so global organizations will continue to seek commercial opportunities and relationships there. Particular attention has been devoted to increasing understanding of both Islam and Arab culture, the dominant factors for the vast majority of population in the area.

While each country in the Middle East is unique and different, we have provided an overview mainly of business customs and protocols. We concluded with a call for cultural synergy, not only within the region, but also between the Middle East and Europe, Africa, America, and Asia, because so many of its former inhabitants now live and work in these other areas.

MIND STRETCHING

1 Have you ever read the Qur'an, eaten Middle Eastern foods, or made friends with an Arab, whether a Muslim or Christian?

2 What do you know about the Islamic contributions in the Middle Ages and thereafter to advancement in science and medicine, art and architecture, trade and travel?

3 What major differences do you perceive between Turkey and Saudi Arabia?

4 How could the implementation of synergistic relationship benefit Iran, Iraq, Lebanon, Syria, Palestine, and Israel?

5 What are your reactions to the following quotation?

Some Western commentators go to great length to portray Arab societies as backward or feeble.... But the West's inability to deal productively with the allegedly simplistic Arab culture actually highlights the weakness of the West's own condescending logic. In reality, there is no naiveté in the Arab world about its centrality in future success or failure of globalization, both geographically and geologically. It will not be, as some commentators claim, left behind.[50]

NOTES

1   Said, E. W. *Orientalism*. New York: Vintage, 1979.
2   Mahmood, K. *Islam Inc.: Rebuilding Islamic Business*. Kindle Edition: worldfutureonline, 2012.
3   Mann, C. C. "The Birth of Religion," *National Geographic*, June 2011, http://ngm.nationalgeographic. com/2011/06/gobekli-tepe/mann-text.
4   www.globalintelligence.com/insights-analysis/emerging-markets/.
5   www.bloomberg.com/slideshow/2013-01-30/the-top-20-emerging-markets/.
6   Wikipedia. *Arab Spring*, http://en.wikipedia.org/wiki/Arab_Spring.
7   See Friedman, T. L. *Longitudes and Attitudes: Exploring the World After September 11*. New York: Farrar, Straus & Giroux, 2002.
8   Devji, F. *Landscapes of Jihad: Militancy, Morality, Modernity*. Ithaca: Cornell University Press, 2005; Little, D. *American Orientalism: The United States and the Middle East Since 1945*. Chapel Hill, NC: University of North Carolina Press, 2002; Reeves, M. *Muhammad in Europe: A Thousand Tears in Western Myth-Making*. New York: New York University Press, 2000; Lewis, B. *The Crisis of Islam: Holy War and Unholy Terror*. New York: Modern Library, 2003; Lewis, R. D. *When Cultures Collide: Managing Successfully Across Cultures*. Boston, MA: Nicolas Brealey Publishing, 2000.
9   Mahmood, *Islam Inc.*
10 Lewis, R. D. "Epilogue: After September 11," in *The Cultural Imperative: Global Trends of the 21st Century*. Boston, MA: Nicholas Brealey/Intercultural Press, 2003.
11 Esposito, J. L. *The Oxford History of Islam*. Oxford: Oxford University Press, 2000; Armstrong, K. *Islam: A Short History*. New York: Modern Library, 2000; Lunde, P. *Islam: Faith, Culture, and History*. Fremont, CA: DK Publishing/Rumi Bookstore, 2002; Aslan, R., *No God But God: The Origins, Evolution, and Future of Islam*. New York: Random House, 2005; Brown, B. A. *Noah's Other Son: Bridging the Gap Between the Bible and the Quar'an*. London: Continuum International, 2005.
12 Kennedy, H. *The Great Arab Conquests: How the Spread of Islam Changed the World We Live In*. London, UK: Weidenfeld & Nicolson, 2007; Roy, O. *Secularism Confronts Islam*. New York: Columbia University Press, 2007; Roy, O. *Globalized Islam: The Search for a New Umah*. New York: Columbia University Press, 2005; Kepel, G. *The War for Muslim Minds: Islam and the West*. London: Belnap Press, 2005; Zaytuna Institute and Al-Qalam Institute. *Islam in the Balance: Toward a Better Understanding of Islam and Its Followers*. Fremont, CA: Rumi Bookstore, 2001. For further information, visit these websites: www.rumibookstore.com. www. islaminthebalance.org.
13 Mahmood, *Islam Inc.*
14 This section was written by Zeynep Arslan, an accounting executive at KPMG, Vancouver, Canada branch.
15 Khan, M. Z. *Islam: Its Meaning for Modern Man*. Suffolk: Richard Clay, 1962.
16 Rice, G. "Islamic Ethics and Implications for Business," *Journal of Business Ethics*, 1999, 345–358.
17 Usmani, M. T. *An Introduction to Islamic Finance*. New York: Springer, 2001.
18 Ahmad, S. and Gazdar, M. *40 Islamic Principles for Successful Management*. Kindle Edition: HotHive Books, 2009.
19 Ibid.
20 Beekun, R. I. and Badawi, J. *Leadership: An Islamic Perspective*. Beltsville, MD: Amana Publications, 1999. See also Beekun, R. I. *Islamic Business Ethics*. Herndon, VA: International Institute of Islamic Thought, 2006.
21 Kasule Sr., O. H. "Leadership Module, General Theme: Leadership Workshop 1," in *Muslim Leaders' Forum 98 Handbook*. Kuala Lumpur: Tarbiyyah and Training Center, International Islamic University Malaysia, 1998, p. 3.
22 Greenleaf, R. *The Servant as Leader*. Indianapolis, IN: Greenleaf Center for Servant Leadership, 1970, p. 7.

23 Abu Hurairah, in *Sahih Muslim*, hadith no. 4542.

24 http://en.wikipedia.org/wiki/invisible_hand.

25 Mencius, *Mencius*, revised edition. London: Penguin Books, 2003.

26 Xunzi, *Xunzi: Basic Writings*. New York: Columbia University Press, 2003.

27 This case was written by Zeynep Arslan Kara, formerly an accounting executive at KPMG, and currently a sessional lecturer at Simon Fraser University in Vancouver, Canada. Zeynep was a very competent MBA student and likely would have been a capable business manager had she not rejected such a role because of the conflicts she perceived between her faith and Western practices. She has now been encouraged to seek a career as a business professor, researching value differences between Islam and Western business in international business contexts.

28 The Turkey country review was written by Zeynep Arslan, currently a sessional lecturer in the Beedie School of Business, Simon Fraser University, Vancouver, Canada.

29 Education in Kurdish seems unlikely as major parties oppose demands, *Today's Zaman*, 2011, http://www.todayszaman.com/newsDetail_getNewsById.action?newsId=237841.

30 Kaplan, H. *Turkiye'nin Olmeyen Babasi (Immortal Father of Turks)*. Istanbul: Timas, 2011.

31 Aral, B. "Turkey in the UN Security Council: Its Election and Performance," *Insight Turkey*, 2009, pp. 151–168.

32 McPherson, C. *Turkey: Culture Smart! The Essential Guide to Customs & Culture*. Kindle Edition: Kuporard, 2005.

33 Macroeconomic Indicators, Invest In Turkey (http://www.invest.gov.tr). Retrieved March 2, 2012.

34 Caliskan, S. *Overview of Family Business Relevant Issues*. Brussels: European Commission, 2008.

35 Campden FD. Top 100 Family Businesses in Europe (http://www.campdenfb.com/article/top-100-family-businesses-europe-1).

36 G. Hofstede, G. J. Hofstede, and Minkov, M. *Cultures and Organizations: Software of the Mind*. New York: McGraw-Hill, 2010.

37 Altuncu, Y., ÖzAktepe, Ş., and İslamoğlu, G. "Preliminary Study for the Development of Uncertainty Avoidance Instrument in Turkey," *Journal of Business, Economics & Finance*, 2012.

38 Mernissi, F. *Los Angeles Times*, June 8, 1990, p. VII/25.

39 These authorities may also enforce codes related to men. In Afghanistan under the Taliban, men were required to wear full beards and could be beaten on the street if they did not comply.

40 Ali, A. H. *The Caged Virgin: An Emancipation Proclamation Women and Islam*. New York: Free Press, 2006; AlMunajjed, M. *Saudi Women Speak: 24 Remarkable Women Tell Their Success Stories*. Riyadh: Institute for Research and Publishing, 2007.

41 Goldsmith, A. *Brief History of Egypt*. New York: Checkmate Books, 2008; Bradley, J. R. *Inside Egypt: The Land of the Pharaohs on the Eve of a Revolution*. New York: Palgrave Macmillan, 2008; Sayyid-Marsot, A. L. *A History of Egypt: From Arab Conquest to the Present*. Cambridge, UK: Cambridge University Press, 2007; Brewer, D. J. *Egypt and the Egyptians*. Cambridge, UK: Cambridge University Press, 2007.

42 CIA, *CIA World Factbook 2013*, www.cia.gov/library/publications/the-world-factbook/.

43 Bowen, W. H. *The History of Saudi Arabia*. Westport, CT: Greenwood Press, 2007; Vivano, F. "Saudi Arabia on the Edger," *National Geographic*, October 2003, pp. 22–23, www.ngs.com; Al-Rasheed, M. *Contesting the Saudi State: Islamic Voices from a New Generation*. Cambridge, UK: Cambridge University Press, 2006; Rodenbeck, M. "A Long Walk: A Survey of Saudi Arabia," January 7, 2006, 12 page insert, www.economist.com/surveys.

44 CIA, *World Factbook*.

45 Ibid.

46 http://truthmagazine.com/archives/voulume44/V44021708.htm.

47 CIA, *World Factbook*.

48 www.moital.gov.il/NR/exeres/3614E1A7-2D84-4F27-A4DC-3585A6F6450E.htm.

49 Elashmawi, F. and Harris, P. R. "Managing Intercultural Business Negotiations," in *Multicultural Management*. New York: Simon & Schuster, 1993; Elashmawi, F. *Competing Globally-Mastering Multicultural Management and Negotiations*. Burlington, MA: Elsevier/Butterworth-Heineman, 2001.

50 Parag Khanna, *The Second World: Empires and Influence in the Global Order*. New York: Random House, 2008.

ADDITIONAL FEATURES

Please visit the companion website at: www.routledge.com/cw/Moran where you will find additional case studies, study aides, and instructor resources.

11 LATIN AMERICA

The debate over the causes of Latin America's economic failures relative to the success of Canada and the United States has been a recurrent focus of Latin American intellectuals, and there are enough explanations to suit everyone. At the beginning of the nineteenth century, they blamed their Iberian and Catholic roots. Around the middle of that century, the shortcomings were attributed to the demographic weight of a native population that was supposedly opposed to progress. At the beginning of the twentieth century, and particularly around the time of the Mexican Revolution in 1910, it was said that poverty and underdevelopment were caused by an unfair distribution of wealth, above all by the peasants' lack of access to land. Starting in the 1920s and accelerating thereafter, "exploitative imperialism" was blamed.

During the 1930s and 1940s, the view was espoused that Latin America's weakness was a consequence of the weakness of its governments. Experience demonstrated in the 1980s that all these arguments were false. So who, in fact, is responsible? One possible, although partial, answer is "the elites," the groups that lead and manage the principal sectors of a society – those who act in the name of certain values, attitudes, and ideologies that, in the Latin American case, do not favor collective progress.[1] Now, in the twenty-first century, there has been no serious conflict between any two South American countries, aside from stand-offs like the 2008 Andean diplomatic crisis. At the same time, almost every Latin American country is constantly at war with itself over its raison d'être, leadership, resources, and social stability.[2]

LATIN AMERICAN OVERVIEW

Latin America extends from Mexico in the north to the southernmost regions of Argentina and Chile that approach Antarctica in the south; it includes both North and South America. It is, furthermore, a region of the world in which Romance languages (principally Portuguese and Spanish) are spoken as official languages. Many countries in this part of the world differ widely in terms of their history, socioeconomic status, education, governance, and society. Regardless, there are commonalties and overlapping cultural themes in Latin American countries, such as the influence of the Catholic Church and shared linguistic heritages: for many, family values and established gender roles are also part of the Latin American experience.

The Americas have been inhabited for thousands of years. However, archaeologists do not know the origins of the region's earliest inhabitants.

We will begin our examination of the diverse cultures in the southern parts of the Americas with their Aboriginal descendants, the so-called "Amerindians." Many are descendants of ancient, highly developed people and civilizations, such as Aztecs, Inca, and Maya. Many countries in the region today, including Mexico and Bolivia, have large indigenous populations.

Global and local developers frequently impinge upon the rights and lands of such native people in the name of economic development. Agencies like the World Bank are now demanding the inclusion of programs that protect the rights of Aborigines before they fund economic development projects in the Amazon. Indigenous peoples are struggling to survive civil and guerrilla warfare.

This chapter presents an overview of Latin America, including specifics principally about Brazil and Argentina. In addition, information will be presented on the principal cultural themes and conditions that affect doing business in or visiting this part of the global market. Finally, we examine some of the challenges for Pan-American cooperation in the decades ahead. In previous editions of this book, we included a section on Mexico, which is geographically in North America. The material on Mexico is now available on the *Managing Cultural Differences* website.

Sometimes the rebels seek haven or recruits among the Indians, while the government troops destroy the native villages. The Amerindians are often caught in the middle of various socio-political revolutionary struggles currently taking place regionally, as in Venezuela. As the original European colonies of the last six centuries were gradually replaced by the contemporary nation-states, these southern countries of the Americas have failed to keep up with their rich neighbors to the north, the United States and Canada. Despite their natural beauty and resources, the Latin countries have been plagued by poverty, despotic governments, bloody revolutions, and profound social unrest. Part of this has been caused by the financial mismanagement of their enormous natural and human resources, and partly by the unequal distribution of wealth

LEARNING OBJECTIVES

and power that is concentrated among less than 5 percent of the total population – the upper-class educated "elites." In the twentieth century, some progress was made in the growth of a middle class, the adoption of democracy, and free enterprise, the latter especially because of NAFTA (North Atlantic Free Trade Association), the Organization of American States (OAS), and MERCOSUR (Mercado Común del Sur).[3] Today, smaller Latin countries can attract the attention of other players in the global marketplace.

In the past, a convenient way to designate economic development in countries throughout the planet was to associate them with the First, Second, or Third Worlds. The First World was composed of the rich nations, such as those that attended the G8 meetings. The Third World was simply the poor, somewhat unstable nations. The Second World was composed of the Eastern Bloc countries formerly under Soviet domination. With the demise of the Soviet Union, many of these post-communist states are transitioning into the "First World" category, especially those who have become members of the European Union. In the geopolitical marketplace, Paraga Khanna suggests a redefinition of the label Second World, as the undeveloped swing states that are determining global order. [4] He sees such nations as the tipping point that will determine the twenty-first century balance of power. There is a shift of influence from the North–South to the East–West. Many of these new Second World states are found in Latin America. They include resource-rich nations like Bolivia, Brazil, Colombia, and Venezuela, as well as the Andean bloc of countries. The big power investors in these states are now China, Japan, and the European Union, in addition to the United States.[5] We end this opening section with a profile of Latin America (Exhibit 11.1) with its diverse people and culture.

E X H I B I T 11.1

EXHIBIT 11.1 LATIN AMERICA: PROFILE

Population landmass

- Approximately 8,134,980 square miles (depending on the definition used)

National cultures

- Nineteen countries
- One commonwealth (Puerto Rico)
- 13 sovereign states in the Caribbean
- Many indigenous cultures

Major cultural inputs

- Native Indians – descended from ancient, highly developed civilizations that flourished prior to European arrival (e.g. Mayan, Incas, Aztecs)

- European — in most countries, largely Spanish with lesser influences of Germans and Italians; except in Brazil where dominant influence was Portuguese
- African
- Asian — ancient Polynesian influence and some Japanese influence

Socio-political developments

- Napoleonic Code of Laws
- Feudalistic societies of Spain/Portugal imposed by conquerors on developed Indian civilizations
- French/Austrian Empire imposed on Mexico, the latter being the center of revolutions in 1821, 1824, and 1838, which impacted South America
- Family-oriented with authority centered in the father and often extended to the "father of the nation"
- Universities and republics from the nineteenth century, with great dependence on military institution controls
- Problems of social class integration — although there was much intermarriage of the races, the powerful elites from an economic/social/political standpoint control and dominate the poor, often peasants of Indian heritage. The disenfranchised have moved beyond political/military protest for social justice to terrorism as a means of changing the status quo
- Economically and technically developing, and in the process of moving from the agricultural through the industrial stage of development; energy discoveries and development in Mexico can dramatically forge a new relationship with its neighbors
- Despite significant growth in spiritualism and Protestantism, the Roman Catholic tradition is still dominant, but undergoing a profound role change — instead of traditional support for the oligarchy, many clergy provide some leadership in a revolution for social justice

In summary, the Latin American people are transitioning in this twenty-first century, caught between their pasts and possible futures. They are in the process of modernizing their economies, social institutions, and infrastructures. Because of their cultural heritage, many of these countries are popular as tourist destinations, where visitors may appreciate a wide spectrum of human development — from ancient cities like Machu Picchu in the Peruvian Andes, to the Galapagos Islands off the coast of Ecuador, to nascent space programs in Mexico and Brazil.

CENTRAL AMERICAN COUNTRIES

On the western side of the Caribbean Sea is a land bridge between the northern and southern continents of the Americas that also borders the Pacific Ocean in the west. The seven nations located between Mexico and Colombia are usually referred to as Central America. The future of these countries depends on whether they can capitalize on their geographical position in order to become a corridor of intercontinental globalization!

If ever there was a need and case for synergy, it is in these Central American states, with some 41.7 million people. The nineteenth-century federation called the Federal Republic of Central America may have been premature, but it provided a cooperative model for the future – if not politically, at least economically. Only by collaboration can this bloc of countries overcome their chronic poverty, illiteracy, and internal strife. Perhaps local business leaders and global managers may succeed in raising the standards and quality of living for the populace. Sandwiched between North and South America, this strategic area cries out for new solutions and contributions from its neighboring nations with their Anglo and Latin cultures.[6] Adjoining to the east are the many small island nations scattered across the Caribbean Sea, the largest of which is Cuba.

A hopeful Central American trend is toward greater integration of the nation-states. The region is finally moving toward some form of federal get-together, as the dream of Simon Bolivar. The isthmus' five current free market governments have a Central American Free Trade Agreement (CAFTA) they include Costa Rica, Nicaragua, Honduras, El Salvador, and possibly Panama, with the United States and Canada as participants to lower their tariffs on CAFTA exports. For many years, the isthmus' seven small countries have been trying to become more unified. What is different at this time is the unstoppable trend toward economic integration from the bottom up, along with regional business consolidation. The area's growth in financial services and tourism is stimulating modernization of infrastructure, such as joint national projects, like the new container port of La Union in El Salvador. Regional law enforcement is improving in its battle against the *maras* – dangerous, well-organized regional gangs. (See "Together Again, After All These Years?" *The Economist*, May 14, 2005, p. 41.)

Education

Colegios are numerous and offer the equivalent of junior college in the United States. Upper classes tend to send their offspring to private schools and universities, often conducted by the orders of the Catholic Church. Although literacy is increasing, many in the overall population do not receive more than a very few years of primary education; notable exceptions are found in the larger countries that provide more education. There is rigorous examination competition for university entrance. Technical education also is on the increase, as well as the use of mass media.

Panama, which has never considered itself a part of Central America, has been spared from regional strife and might become a laboratory, along with Costa Rica, for the creation of models that would influence the other states to join in a regional entity for self-improvement. Application of new techniques to promote social peace and reduce internal political violence, as in El Salvador and Guatemala, should become the concern of Pan-American social scientists. Simplistic, anticommunist, and military approaches will not solve the region's problems or tap its vast, undeveloped human and natural resources. China appreciates such resources, so is very active in the region with investment, trade, and building factories.

Other Latin American trends

Apart from Puerto Rico, which is a U.S. commonwealth, there are two other Latin American states in the Greater Antilles. Both are island nations in the Caribbean Sea that share the Spanish language and culture. Cuba is 110,860 square kilometers with a population of 10,219,630 (July 2013 est.), and has a communist dictatorship, despite the influence of Roman Catholicism. It has a literacy rate of 96 percent, a life expectancy of 76 years, and a GDP per capita of $1,700. The Dominican Republic shares with strife-torn Haiti the island of Hispaniola, which consists of 48,670 square kilometers. This country, largely Roman Catholic, has a literacy rate of 87 percent, a 78-year life expectancy, and a $5,700 annual per capita income. Although Latin in culture, its neighbor Haiti has been influenced by French culture and language, as well as African. Presently, the presence of UN peace-keepers from China, Chile, and Brazil are keeping this country from relapsing into anarchy.

SOUTH AMERICAN CULTURAL DEVELOPMENT

As the global manager flies over the 12 countries that compose the southern continent of the Americas, he or she is struck by the immensity of this land mass and the potential resources down below, especially in Brazil and Argentina. Among the 387 million people living on this continent, nine countries have, in addition to their ancient native heritages, descendants from Africa and Asia, and a European cultural base (e.g. Spanish, French, British, Italian, and Dutch). One nation, Brazil, enjoys both Portuguese and African languages and cultural influences. Centered between the Atlantic and Pacific Oceans, South America is shaped like an elongated triangle of some seven million square miles that extends down to the apex of Cape Horn.

South America is a place where we can simultaneously be amazed at the beauty of the pre-Colombian artifacts and civilization, or the very modern and colorful artworks and high-rise architecture. Yet, visitors are also appalled by the poverty of the masses and the great wealth of the few, by the violence and terrorism, and by the dominance of a powerful military or dictators. But outsiders are also encouraged by the progress in democratic institutions, education and literacy, health services and population control, changing the images and aspirations of South Americans.

Despite the great diversity in Latin America, there are common themes and patterns. After the development of fairly sophisticated Amerindian civilizations, there was a period of European colonization and exploitation from the fifteenth through eighteenth centuries, followed by wars of independence and attempts at federation during the nineteenth century. Since the early twentieth century, Latin American nations have been engaged in internal and external conflicts. But the last half of that century saw relative peace and significant economic progress among many nations of Central and South America.

With the exception of Suriname in South America's northeast, these countries also share another factor – a Roman Catholic cultural tradition that pervades not only their history but also their way of life and thinking. At first, the clergy protected and educated the indigenous people. Their network of Franciscan, Dominican, and Jesuit missions became agricultural and trading centers and, eventually, the great cities of South, Central, and North America's southwest. With the passage of time and increase in wealth, the Church became part of the establishment, despite the notable successes of priest revolutionaries, like Father Miguel Hidalgo, who espoused the causes of nationalism and freedom for the peasants. As a major landowner itself, the Church has not only supported the oligarchy but also opposed population control, divorce, and social change. The growth of the militant theology and activities in the Latin American Church caused the late Pope John Paul during his visits to the southwestern hemisphere to protest social inequities, while warning the clergy to concentrate on their spiritual mission. In any event, no modern manager operating in Latin America can afford to ignore the Catholic Church as a cultural force. Cooperation and collaboration for social improvement in Latin America will be significantly advanced when business cooperates with all institutions for human development. The new brand of Christianity on the rise there is "Evangelico," principally Pentecostal, with a fundamentalist view of scriptural teachings. In the twenty-first century, Protestants have now risen to 50 million on that continent. With a conversion rate of 400 per hour, demographers predict Latin American will be newly evangelical before the end of this century.

The "born again" movement matches the transition toward industrialization and urbanization. The religious cultural shift is toward self-reform, spiritual empowerment, and responsibility for improving your own life now, not just in the hereafter. A powerful tool for this religious revolution is satellite television beamed southward from what is left of Protestant America's "Bible Belt." Four hundred years of authoritarian Christianity may be overturned in a single generation, and Latin American people will never quite be the same again.

A positive development within South America has been the creation of a partial common market, called MERCOSUR. It originated in 1985 when Argentina and Brazil signed an economic integration agreement. This trade bloc was expanded in 1991 by the Treaty of Asunción, which added Paraguay and Uruguay. In 2006, Venezuela became a full member, while Chile, Bolivia, Colombia, Ecuador, and Peru are associate members without full access and voting rights. This restriction is because these nations are also members of

CAN, the Andean Community of Nations, which is a smaller trade bloc. Presently, some 250 million people benefit from this trading security, which has a collective output of $1.1 trillion. Ultimately, it is hoped that all the nations in South America will become associated with this trade and business network.[7] Whether this common market will ever evolve as the European Union did is an open question.

The former president of Mexico, Felipe Calderdón, stated the continental challenge well: "Latin America faces a critical choice between the past and the future, between returning to authoritarian rule or strengthening democratic systems, between protectionism and more open markets, between the wastefulness of populist measures and a responsible balance in public finances."[8] There is also a growing global interest in the Latin American market, both for exports and imports. Exhibit 11.2 provides one indicator of this trend.

EXHIBIT 11.2 CHINA'S ROLE IN LATIN AMERICA

While the United States is losing its influence in Latin America, former outsiders, such as China, are assuming a greater role in hemispheric affairs. Their economies have been growing at a reasonably healthy rate. In 2005, the U.S. Presidential Administration, opposed by Venezuela and Bolivia, failed again to get a majority for its candidates in the Organization of American States, a 35-country entity. While Washington did succeed in signing a free trade deal with Central America and the Dominican Republic at the Mar del Plata Summit, the presidents of both Argentina and Venezuela made speeches against the United States, blaming it for the region's ills. Although the region's forecasts are for modest economic growth, Brazil and other Latin countries are becoming successful players in the global economy, thereby reducing the region's poverty somewhat.

Meantime, China is emerging as one of the largest trading partners of South American countries. Press reports claim that PRC has already invested some $50 billion and plans a $100 billion trade exchange by 2010 in Pan-America. China is developing a commercial and strategic presence in the region. It seeks Latin American resources — raw materials, like iron ore, minerals, oil, soy beans — which have significantly impacted the economic growth of Brazil and Argentina. A Chinese firm now operates port facilities at both ends of the Panama Canal and essentially controls that waterway relinquished by the United States. Further, to accommodate its huge tankers, it signed an agreement with Panama to expand the canal. China has also renovated Central American ports and factories to expedite delivery of its goods to the United States. It assists Latin states with infrastructure improvements and export revenues, so that the local government can improve social safety nets and empowerment provisions. This Asian superpower is offering Latin countries a new way of doing business without a ticket of codes and regulations. Imperialistic *El Norte* no longer rules the hemisphere.

Source: Adapted from Parag Khanna's *The Second World*, New York: Random House, 2008; Andres Oppenheimer, "China Topping U.S. in Latin America," *Miami Herald*, reproduced in the *San Diego Union-Tribune*, December 30, 2005, p. B8.

BRAZIL

Since it is impossible to cover all countries in South America, we have first selected Brazil for a detailed cultural analysis because it is the largest in terms of population, land mass, and economy.

Historical, political, and economic overview

Brazil is a federated republic of more than three million square miles. First inhabited by nomads from Asia millennia ago, the indigenous people evolved into tribal groups, which today are called Amerindians. The civilizations they developed included empires, such as the Inca, which stretched from Colombia to Argentina. The first Europeans to discover Brazil may have been Jean Cousins in 1488 or Christopher Colombus in 1498. But Portuguese claimed the land in 1500 when their fleet of some dozen ships under the command of Pedro Alvarez Cabral arrived mistakenly in what is called today the state of Bahia! For almost four centuries, Portugal maintained control of Brazil, exploiting many of its resources. Gold, gems, rubber, cocoa, cattle, and other products were shipped to the homeland or abroad. Portuguese noblemen ruled in 12 areas of the colony, and established a plantation economy. This led to the import of some four million African slaves to work in the land. In 1615, Brazil became the seat of the entire Portuguese empire. When the emperor returned to Portugal, his son Pedro II declared Brazil an independent nation in 1822. In 1865–1870, the country engaged in a ruinous war with Paraguay. His 49-year reign transformed the country into a modern state, including the freeing of the African slaves in 1888.

When the military overthrew his monarchy, they declared Brazil a republic in 1889. By the twentieth century, the nation had experimented with various forms of governance – from military rule to dictator to democracy, which prevails today. Between 1955 and 1960, the president, Jucelino Kubitcheck, undertook major construction projects, including building a new capital, Brazilia, in the middle of this vast country. From 1945 to 1964, a military coup took over the government and produced the "Brazilian Miracle," when the economy grew by as much as 11 percent a year. The sinister side was that this regime arrested, imprisoned, and killed its supposed opponents, forcing many into exile, especially artists and academics. Finally, the military dictatorship was replaced by the election of Fernando Collor de Mello as president in 1990. After he was later impeached, Fernando Cardoso, a sociologist and former minister of the economy, was chosen as head of state. During his term from 1995 to 2001, many economic and social reforms were undertaken, some of which still benefit the society and its citizens.

The material on Brazil was originally written by Kristine Elaine Menn. She has lived in Sao Paulo, Brazil, since 1992, where she works as a consultant and teacher of cross-cultural communication and English. Subsequently, the authors have updated and added material to this section.

Today's federated republic has a bicameral National Congress with a Federal Senate and Chamber of Deputies. The latter's 513 members are elected by proportional represent-ation and serve four-year terms. Besides this legislative branch, the judiciary consists of the Supreme Federal Tribunal with 11 members appointed by the president for life and confirmed by vote of the Senate. There are many political parties, and passing reforms is difficult; governance is by coalitions and concessions. The country has formal relationships with many international organizations, such as the United Nations, World Trade Organization, World Bank, and economic partnership with its neighbors through MERCOSUR, a regional trade group.

The Brazilian presidential election on October 27, 2002, was a milestone. For the first time, a simple man from a poor family was successfully elected to the highest position in Brazilian politics. Luiz Ignácio Lula da Silva, known as "Lula," was one of the founders and foremost leader of the metallurgical union and the Workers' Party (PT). Historically, Brazilian presidents have come from the elite class. Because of his origins, and because a significant percentage of the population lives below the official poverty level, former president Lula chose to focus his administration upon the "Zero Hunger" program, while seeking solutions to critical social problems: improving education; century-long land reform problems; cleaning up rampant corruption and crime; reducing unemployment, and reformulating the pension and benefit system; curbing inflation, and national debt problems; jump-starting a stagnant economy. His first term enjoyed many accomplishments, but was hampered by corruption scandals within the Workers' Party. As a result, changes are occurring now, which have never before been seen in the country's long history. The battle is between progress and inertia, especially in a stifling government bureaucracy and regulations. The country is in the midst of a slow economic metamorphosis from unequal and hierarchical to more universal and equalitarian conditions. Brazil will host the 2014 FIFA World Cup and the 2016 Summer Olympic Games in Rio de Janeiro.

In the twenty-first century, Brazil is a large democratic and stable society, rich in resources, with a strong economy. Yet, having won a second term until 2010, former presi-dent Lula was trying to expand upon the stability and predictability his administration had established. Two economic programs have been successful. The consolidation of sugar and ethanol production has alleviated energy needs and powers automobiles, while creating a new export business. Biofuels and flex-fuel cars, operating on both ethanol and gasoline, are now big businesses. Biotech laboratories are springing up everywhere, and researchers are studying new possibilities ranging from drought-resistant soya to new energy sources. Brazil is learning to capitalize on nature's sun, water, and soil, and its corporations are becoming multinationals. The other success story is *Bolsa Familia* – a benefit program that gives federal cash (95 reais a month) to poor parents who ensure that their children stay in school and take them to clinics for health tests. This conditional cash plan now reaches 46 million people. In 2008, Petrobas, the state oil giant, announced the development of a new field containing 5–8 billion barrels of light, sweet crude oil. Known as *tupi*, this offshore rich resource is located under a layer of salt deep beneath the floor of the Atlantic Ocean.

Since it sits up to 7 km below sea level, with some fields 350 km off the coast, pumping this oil will be a complex technological challenge. In the waning days of his administration, President Lula seeks to have income from this new enterprise devoted to education.

Protecting the Amazon

Brazil's 3.3 million square miles of Amazon rain forest, 40 percent of its national territory, is a world resource in need of careful management. Unregulated agriculture, mining, and logging threaten this green belt – destruction in the Amazon forests contributes to pollution and three-quarters of the country's carbon emissions. So those who would preserve this rich environment and its indigenous people are contributing to the government's new Amazon Fund. Size and accomplishments make Brazil the continent's natural leader, but it could lead the environmental movement by preserving the earth's largest ecosystem in the Amazon Basin.[9] This could be the capstone in the energy leadership Brazil already demonstrates!

The Amazon forests are shared with several of Brazil's neighbors, including Peru and Colombia. Here, as elsewhere in Latin America, the government owns the subsoil and any oil, gas, and minerals found there. All these Amazon nations are attempting to use the rain-forest for oil and gas exploration. In all cases, an improved policy is needed to reconcile national interests with those of the environment and local inhabitants, usually Amerindians. NGOs are urging industries to watch over the jungle as they would the ocean, to use heli-copters and aero imaging, instead of building logging roads or pouring waste into the rivers.

The people

SOCIAL STRUCTURE, RACE, VALUES, AND RELIGION

Brazil is a spectacular country in both social contrasts and geographical size. First-World living conditions are seen in upper-class neighborhoods; across the street from the massive electronically operated skyscrapers, people live in *favelas* (shantytowns), sometimes with not even the most basic of services. An estimated four million people live in these shantytowns in the cities of Rio de Janeiro and São Paulo alone. Another contrast is in the people's skin tone – a complete spectrum of skin colors, from black to white, and all hues in between. Although 47 percent of the people consider themselves to be "white" (primarily descendants of Portuguese, German, Italian, Spanish, and Polish, as well as Lebanese and Japanese), only 7 percent consider themselves to be "black"; it is estimated that about 45 percent of the population has some degree of African ancestry. With 50 percent of its total population under 20 years of age, Brazil is a very "young" and diversified country. Here, segregation is more class based than race based.

A prevalent cultural generalization concerning the people of Brazil is that they are a warm, friendly, and emotionally sensitive people who are generous and receptive to foreigners. The Brazilian class structure is based on economics. While the highest 10 percent of the population enjoys 47 percent of the country's consumption share, the lowest 10 percent only has 1 percent. The rich in Brazil consists of both the old wealthy class and a new affluent class made up of mainly the descendants of poor immigrants from Europe who built up empires of riches. Perhaps more important in Brazil than in any other Latin American country, the family has been the single most significant institution in the formation of Brazilian society. The meaning of family in Brazil is not limited to the immediate family, but instead includes the entire *parentela*, or extended family, from both the mother and father's side. This group can consist of hundreds of people, and it provides the foundation of the individual's social structure. It is not unusual to see many generations living together under one roof, or at least in the same town or city. It is customary for children to live with their parents until they marry, although this has been changing, especially in the big cities. Loyalty to one's family is the individual's highest ranking obligation. Although the traditional family is usually male dominated, for economic reasons many women work outside the home, and single-parent families are common. Other traditional dominant values in the Brazilian society include community, collectivism, procreation, and a hierarchical society. And in a hierarchical society, it is always important to know who one is talking with.

A traditional value that has its basis in the Catholic Church is one of fatalism. Evidence of this can be found in expressions that are very common in everyday conversations, such as "*se Deus quiser*" ("the Lord willing"). The Brazilian attitude is the result of a history full of unpredictable changes and circumstances over which the individual has had little control. Some examples of more recent circumstances of this type include electricity and water shortages that have resulted in periods of blackouts and lack of water supplies. Even though the Catholic Church has had a profound effect in the formation of the dominant values found in Brazil, a large percentage of Brazilians are only nominally Catholic. Brazilians are very accepting of different religions, and some even practice more than one type of religion. Additionally, though they profess to have at least some alliance to the Catholic Church, Brazilian Catholics have adopted many traditions of Afro-Brazilian religions as well, with offerings made at intersections, even on the busiest of streets in the largest of cities. Brazilians' religious tolerance is evident in the rapid growth of Protestant evangelism.

Cultural characteristics of business

Brazil is rich in both natural and human resources. However, doing business in Brazil can be a challenging experience due to economic uncertainties involving inflation, currency exchange, and interest rates, among other things. At the same time, working in Brazil can be enjoyable and exciting because of the immense economic opportunities that the country offers. Brazil's diverse economy produces everything from automobiles and airplanes to shoes and orange juice. The service and high-tech industries are rapidly growing. By trying to understand this culture better, it is easier to avoid committing blunders that could potentially lead to negative results in business situations. One of the biggest mistakes that can be made is to consider Brazil to be just another country in Latin America, and to assume that what works in Chile or Mexico or Panama will also work in Brazil. One of the most blatant differences is that it is the only country in Latin America in which Portuguese is the official language. In addition to this example, there are innumerable subtler cultural differences.

GREETINGS

Handshakes are the appropriate form of greeting between men and women in a business setting. However, because Brazilians are warm and friendly people who feel free to show their affection in public, one or two kisses on the cheeks are common between a man and a woman as well as between two women. Women sometimes will kiss three times if one of the women is not married. This is said to bring good luck in finding a husband. Men do not kiss, but it is normal for acquaintances to pat each other on the back or on the arm while shaking hands. It is usual for men and women who are friends to hug each other when they meet. Brazilians touch each other more and for longer periods of time than is acceptable in some other cultures. Upon arriving and before leaving, it is important to greet and say goodbye to each individual, while refraining from use of impersonal statements, like "Hi/Bye, everyone!"

NAMES AND TITLES

Most Brazilians are less formal than people in the other Latin American countries; consequently, titles are not always used. First names are used routinely, but it is a good idea to let the Brazilian ask you to call him by his or her first name before doing so. Often, a title is used with a first name, such as *Dona* (Lady) Maria or *Senhor* (Mister) John. *Doutor* or *Doutora* (Doctor) is commonly used to express respect even if the person is not a doctor or Ph.D. (especially with older folks). First and last names may be made up of two or more names. Take the example, *Luis Henrique Meirelles Reis.* In this case, it appears that *Henrique* is the middle name, but friends and family will call him *Luis Henrique.* Furthermore, a first name may be a combination of the mother and father's first names. An example of this is *Carlene*, which is a combination of *Carlos* and *Marlene.* A person's compound last name may be a combination of the mother's maiden name followed by the father's last name. This order is different from the order used in Spanish-speaking countries. It is not uncommon for a person's full name to be made up of five or six individual names! Another interesting point is that in the Portuguese language, there are two words for the English word *you.* The use of *o senhor* or *a senhora* denotes more respect than the use of the casual *você.*

HOSPITALITY AND ENTERTAINING

Brazilians are well known for being courteous and hospitable. They endeavor to make visitors feel welcomed and comfortable. Expect to be offered limitless cups of very small, but very strong, coffee, both in the office and while visiting someone's home. It is polite to accept the coffee, but it is not considered rude to politely refuse it. Brazilians will often keep offering even if they think that you don't want any more. Do not feel that it is necessary to keep accepting more food or drinks just because your host continues offering! It is just a way of being polite. It is also usual for a person who is about to begin eating to offer some of his food to others. This is only done to show consideration to those around him, and the person offering the food probably has no intention of sharing, but instead expects a polite "No, thank you" in return. Although Brazilians do entertain in their home, among coworkers it is more common to go out for lunch, drinks, or dinner. It is normal for the person who invites to pay, but it is just as normal for the bill to be split equally among all present, regardless of who ate what. Toasts are common in Brazil, but they are not an elaborate ceremony as they are in some cultures. To make a toast, simply lift your glass and say, "*Saúde!*" ("Health!"). Never tap your glass with a piece of silverware to get your group's attention before making a toast. Another form of behavior that is not considered polite is to snap your fingers or hiss to get a waiter's attention. Even though this action might be seen in some restaurants, it is not typical behavior.

APPEARANCE, HYGIENE, AND DRESS

Considered by many to be very beautiful people, Brazilians in general are extremely concerned about their appearance. They go to great pains to keep in good physical condition by working out in health clubs, running in parks or along the beaches, and undergoing plastic surgery. It is usual for both women and men to keep their fingernails and toenails neatly manicured, and a visitor doing business in Brazil should do the same. Due to the typically hot weather, it is not uncommon for Brazilians to take two showers a day, one in the morning and another before going to sleep at night. Brazilians also like to brush their teeth after every meal, so it is not unusual to see people brushing their teeth in the restrooms of restaurants or companies.

Dressing for work in Brazil depends on the employer codes, but the standard dress for men is a dark- or light-colored two-piece suit, shirt, and tie. Many companies have adopted the casual Friday concept, and some have casual day every day. While men in the Brazilian workplace dress in much the same way as their American counterparts do in general, the same may not be true for Brazilian women. While many Brazilian businesswomen do wear suits, they also dress in a variety of other ways. For example, it is not unusual to see women dressed in low-cut, tight, transparent tops, even with spaghetti straps (or no straps) in the office. Sundresses are also common. Often, women will wear sandals without pantyhose. One important point is that a woman's purse and shoes should always match. Brazilian women in general prefer a more natural look, and little if any make-up is worn. It is also not uncommon to see a woman come to work without drying her hair. Usually, visiting businesswomen from abroad dress more conservatively than that described above. Outside the workplace, dressing is usually casual. During the weekends, even at some fine restaurants in São Paulo and Rio de Janeiro, men wear khaki shorts, slacks, or jeans, and either a button-down or polo-type shirt. Keep in mind when traveling to Brazil that the seasons are opposite, and when it is freezing cold in the northern hemisphere, it is quite hot in Brazil.

GIFTS AND BRIBES

Doing business in Brazil does not require gift giving, but since Brazilians regard business relationships as personal relationships, they value all acts of generosity, including receiving presents from their visitors. It's a good idea to try to personalize the gift as much as possible, due to the fact that Brazilians appreciate the attention and thought that goes into selecting the right present. Some appropriate gifts include calendars, chocolate, wine, top-quality scotch whiskey, name-brand perfume, or anything unique from the visitor's country that may not be available in Brazil.

When does a "gift" become a "bribe"? This is a difficult line to determine, so it is best for a visitor to err on the safe side and not participate in this practice. Although it is traditionally true that bribes are sometimes given in Brazil, things are changing. If you are not familiar with the culture's subtleties, you could get into trouble either by offending someone by offering the bribe or by not offering the right thing. For this reason, it may be beneficial to hire a *despachante* to help you. *Despachantes* are specialists in knowing what is appropriate and cutting through the endless bureaucracy that can be found at any level of government. A tactic that is very useful in Brazil is *jeitinho*, which is a term that means "getting around obstacles in order to obtain what you want." Another Brazilian tradition is the *cafezinho*, literally meaning "little coffee." This is a small tip that you give someone when they help you out. If you offer to pay someone for doing a favor for you and he tells you that a *cafezinho* would be fine, he really is not asking for coffee!

TIME

Brazilians' idea of time is more flexible than it is in some cultures. Although in the workplace punctuality is considered important in theory, in reality it is common for meetings to start 5–20 minutes late (or more). One reason for this (or maybe more of an excuse) is the unpredictable traffic found in the big cities. Once the meeting does start, it is important to spend some time with small talk. Some topics appropriate for small talk include family (only if you have met the family previously), current events, the weather, any positive topic, and sometimes soccer, depending on the person you are talking to. In general, negative and controversial subjects should be avoided because they could lead to feelings of embarrassment and an uncomfortable situation. Expect to spend a long time in meetings before any results are produced. Brazilians are not always very direct; in their opinion, it is important to establish personal relationships and a sense of trust before doing business with someone. Time in social situations is seen in a different way. Parties always start later than the time shown on the invitation. If you receive an invitation for dinner at someone's home, you should arrive no more than 15 minutes late; do not come early or exactly on time because the host may not be ready to receive you.

COMMUNICATION: VERBAL AND NONVERBAL

While Portuguese is the official language, many distinct dialects exist in different parts of the country. Accents and even the meaning given to words vary from region to region. Moreover, there are many subcultures in Brazil who still use the language of their ancestors. It is common to hear German and Polish spoken in the South, Italian and Japanese spoken in São Paulo, and Spanish spoken along the borders of neighboring countries. Among the members of the "international business subculture," English is definitely the official language. Individuals in managerial positions at global companies often have some degree of proficiency in English.

Brazilian communication style is very expressive and animated. The norm is to speak fast, without much time between words. Due to variations in the pitch and volume of the voices, a dialogue may resemble more a song than a conversation. Depending on the topic, it may even appear that a fight is about to break out, but, more often than not, it is just an emotionally friendly discourse. Furthermore, Brazilians like to say one thing, give examples or details, and then rephrase the sentences many times, repeating the same idea over and over again. Foreigners may find this style of communication to be confusing, unorganized, or misleading.

The Brazilian writing style shares many characteristics with their oral communication style. Comma splices and run-on sentences, considered incorrect in English, are common in Portuguese writing. Brazilians also use the indirect style of digression more than other cultures do. This sometimes can make it difficult to understand the writer's line of thought.

The concept of low- and high-context communication styles involves both verbal and nonverbal communication aspects. While Brazilians generally are more low context than the Eastern and Middle Eastern countries, they are usually more high context than the United States and northern European countries. Although Brazilians use words profusely, at times they can be very indirect in expressing their feelings. Therefore, it is imperative that the visitor be aware of the possible underlying meanings in communicative exchanges in order to avoid serious misunderstandings.

While it has been said that nonverbal communication accounts for about 70 percent of all communication, this percentage can be even higher when members of different cultures try to exchange information, especially if one does not speak the local language. At times, the nonverbal forms of communication carry more weight in a conversation than the actual words do. One form of nonverbal communication is eye contact. Brazilians in general, and especially among individuals who hold the same status level, look each other in the eye when speaking. However, it is also common for a person from a lower class to look down when speaking to someone he considers his superior. This is a form of showing respect, and should not be looked on with suspicion.

In public places, it is not unusual for people to stare at others for lengths of time that may make members of different cultures uncomfortable.

Silence during conversations has no room whatsoever in Brazilian communication, and the use of interruptions in discussions is common in Brazil. While this may be considered rude in some cultures, there are situations when a person might use interruptions to show enthusiasm and interest in the conversations. In this country, close physical contact is the norm. An individual's personal distance is short, and touching during a conversation is considered normal. It is common for pedestrians walking on crowded city streets to brush or even run into each other without apologizing. Brazilians like to talk with their hands; it is almost impossible for them to have a conversation without moving their hands to help express themselves. Consequently, the use of hand gestures is widespread. The following is a description of some of the most commonly seen gestures in Brazil:

- The "OK" sign used in the United States is considered extremely vulgar, especially when the three extended fingers are held parallel to the ground, close to the chest, with the palm up.
- Extending the middle finger upward is also vulgar.
- Hitting an open palm into a clenched fist sends the same message as the two examples above.
- Extending the index and little finger upward while making a fist with the other fingers means, "Your wife/girlfriend is cheating on you."
- Opening and closing all fingers together many times with the palm up means that a place is crowded or full.
- Pulling the lower eyelid down with the index finger means "pay attention!"; "watch out!"; or "I am watching and paying attention."
- Brushing the fingertips of one hand under the chin and continuing to move the hand out in an outward direction, palm facing inward, means "I don't know."
- Snapping all fingers on each other while moving the hand up and down quickly adds emphasis to what is being said.
- Snapping the thumb and middle finger, pointing the fingers inward while moving the hand from the chest to the shoulder at ear height means "a long time ago."
- Wiping the fingers of one hand with the fingers of the other hand, in a downward direction in front of the chest with palms facing upward, means "it doesn't matter."

WOMEN'S ROLE IN BUSINESS

Though traditionally Brazil shares the *machismo* characteristic that is common throughout Latin America, the reality in Brazil today is very different. In many situations, women need to work outside the home to help support the family. This is especially common in big cities. More and more, women are achieving upper-management positions, and even directorships. However, it is still rare to see women presidents in large companies, both domestic and international. Women are also gaining greater roles in political areas, such as obtaining the position of city mayor or state governor. Women also are serving at the national level of government as cabinet and Supreme Court members.

NEGOTIATING IN BRAZIL

Although a sense of fatalism exists in Brazil due to a feeling of lack of control over one's own future, and the "get rich quick and get out quick" philosophy can still be found, the general attitude while doing business and negotiating in Brazil is more along the lines of "take your time." Negotiations cannot be rushed in this country. Business is done with friends, and friendships take a long time to build. Because personal relationships form the basis of trust in business deals, nepotism and giving preference to friends is common in both companies and government. The following are some characteristics of negotiating styles in Brazil:

- *Particular over universal.* When making decisions, Brazilians like to look at the details involved in each particular situation, instead of applying universal rules or patterns of behavior to all situations.
- *Relationship over task.* Brazilians feel that a good relationship must be in place before anything can be accomplished, and it is never a good idea to damage a relationship that is intact, even if it means not completing a task.
- *Polychronic over monochronic.* Brazilians tend to view the concept of time in a polychronic way, often discussing the details of a proposal in a random order instead of in a sequential manner.
- *Indirect over direct.* Seemingly a contradiction, Brazilians are a very emotional and affective people, but their style in both personal and business affairs is very indirect. Brazilians are usually nonconfrontational and believe in face saving.
- *Group over individual.* Although this depends on the circumstances, Brazilians feel the group and relationships within the group are more important than individual aspirations. This has implications concerning methods of motivation. Sometimes an individual manager would prefer to share a bonus with his subordinates or coworkers instead of keeping it all for himself.
- *Flexible over inflexible.* Due to constant changes in Brazilian laws, as well as the uncertainty brought by fluctuations in exchange rates, interest rates, and inflation rates, Brazilians have become very adept at "rolling with the flow." They consider people who always follow standard procedures to be unimaginative and lacking intelligence.

ARGENTINA

The second-largest nation on the continent of South America is Argentina, in terms of population, landmass, and economy. Geographically, it is bounded by five other Latin countries – Bolivia and Paraguay to the north, Uruguay and Brazil to the east, and Chile to the west. This most southern country extends with its neighbor Chile to the tip of Cape Horn, where the Atlantic and Pacific Oceans converge. It is the eighth largest national state in the world; its people dance to the *tango* and the tune of free market enterprise. It is a founding member of a South American trading group known as MERCOSUR, previously discussed. Buenos Aires in the northeast is its beautiful capital city. Beside this federal city, the country is divided into 26 provinces.

Cultural influences

■   *Inhabitants.* About 3 percent of the population descends from the original "Amerindian" people, who now live largely in remote areas. This percentage includes *mestizo* (mixed) and other nonwhite groups. The remaining 97 percent are of European stock, largely Spanish and Italian ancestry. Argentina's cosmopolitan and progressive citizens express intensive opinions about world affairs, their government, its police, politics, and taxes, but usually avoid personal public criticism, except among trusted friends. Gregarious by nature, Argentineans are noted for their respect of the individual, acceptance of failure, and lack of punctuality.

■   *Geography.* Argentina, over a million square miles, has a large plain that rises above the Atlantic Ocean and extends to the towering Andes Mountains to the west. The northwest is home to *chaco,* or swamp land, and the great rivers of the *Plata* system. The rolling *pampas,* or prairies, are in the central part, featuring ranches, cowboys, and famous for wheat growing and cattle raising. Sheep raising occurs in the southern tableland of Patagonia. Although its climate is generally temperate, the *Chicao* region is subtropical, while in southern Patagonia, the winters are quite cold. The country's expansive capital is the largest in Latin America, with the world's largest boulevard, elegant retail shops, and 150 parks!

■   *History and governance.* After the Amerindian civilizations flourished, the Europeans entered this land's Rio de la Plata area by way of the Spanish influx in 1516. By 1580, they had established Buenos Aires as the center of their government on the central east coast, adjoining Uruguay on the Atlantic Ocean. In 1810, a tradition of revolutionary revolts and military *juntas* began as a continuing struggle for governmental control. By 1816, Argentina gained independence from Spanish colonial rule under the leadership of its national hero, General José de San Martin. The economy prospered because of rubber plantations and beef production until the end of World War II, when Argentina's unique position of neutrality ended. After decades of instability, Colonel Juan Peron became president in 1946. Under his dictatorship, and with the help of his wife, Evita, the poor supposedly benefited, while the unions, military, and the economy declined. So much so that Peron was forced into exile in 1955. When a provisional military government fared no better, he managed to return to rule with the assistance of the Peronist party, which still has influence there – Peron was elected president along with his second wife, Maria, as vice president. Within a year, he was dead from natural causes, and his widow became the first woman to head a national government in the Western hemisphere. In 1976, her administration ended with a bloodless coup and the establishment of martial law.

Then the ruling military *juntas* were responsible for a campaign supposedly against terrorism, which itself resulted in thousands of kidnappings, arrests, assassinations, and executions. The military's loss of the war against the British over possession of the Falkland Islands brought a return to civilian rule and democracy in 1983 with the election of President Carlos Menem. Sweeping economic reforms and various international agreements brought a measure of prosperity. But in 2001, defaults on $95 billion in bonds led the subsequent administration of President Nestor Kirchner into conflict with the International Monetary Fund over international loans and repayment of a $14.8 billion debt with the IMF. As industrial production shrunk in 2003, Argentina was forced to restructure debt and promote economic reforms, despite $12.3 billion in foreign reserves. In 2007, Kirchner's wife, Cristina Fernandez de Kirchner, was elected chief of state for four years. Presently, a bicameral National Congress consists of the Senate – 72 members elected by direct vote to serve a six-year term – and a Chamber of Deputies elected by popular vote for four-year terms. The Supreme Court includes nine justices appointed by the President and elected by the Senate. The nation also is a member of numerous international and regional associations, including the World Trade Organization. Argentina continues to claim Islas Mavinas off its southeast coast, which the United Kingdom continues to administer under the name of the Falkland Islands.

RELIGIOUS AND SOCIAL LIFE

The observations made elsewhere in this chapter on Latin America also apply, for the most part, to spiritual and social life most evident in Argentina. For example, 95 percent of the people are nominally Roman Catholic, but only 25 percent are regular practitioners, while the remaining limit their participation to special occasions. Pope Francis is Argentinian. Foreigners and minorities are free to practice their preferred religions. Again, Latin social customs are prevalent here, such as those described in the next section. The *Señores* (men), *Señoritas* (unmarried, usually younger women), and the *Señoras* (married, usually older females) typically shake hands while nodding to show respect. Close friends among males may embrace, while females will kiss one another on the cheeks and shake with both hands. First names are only used with close acquaintances. Ordinarily, females do not speak to strange males without an introduction. Normally, Argentineans do not yell at one another from a distance, but simply raise a hand and smile.

Upper-class Argentineans are proper, with reserved manners, yet friendly. Social etiquette in this country requires one not to open a conversation with a question, but to start with a greeting. Wait for an invitation to be seated in an office or home. The locals appreciate compliments about their children, décor, and gardens. They also eat in the European style, with knife in the right hand and fork in the left. It is considered bad manners at the dinner table to place your hands in the lap, to use a toothpick, to clear your throat, or blow your nose – rather, you should excuse yourself and go outside the dining area for such purposes. Beef is a favorite dish. Waiters will respond if you raise your hand and index finger. Dress is elegant but conservative – men's hats are removed when in buildings, elevators, or the presence of women. In families, the elderly are respected, the wife is the household manager, and deference is shown to the father as the head of the family. When meeting an Argentinean, it is advisable not to question the person as to his/her career or how he or she earns a living; their occupation will be revealed when they are ready. Generally, in Argentina, business hours are 8 a.m. until noon; then 3–9 p.m. Retail stores usually are closed on Sundays. Soccer is a favorite sport, followed by racing, boating, basketball, and horseback riding.

SOCIAL CHALLENGES

Like other countries in both North and South America, Argentina has its social inequities and difficulties. Approximately 23 percent of the population lives below the poverty line, and there is no strategy to reduce that percentage. It is also a transshipment center for illegal drugs to Europe, along with money laundering in the Tri-Border Area. There is also a lack of vigorous confrontation with law enforcement corruption. Argentina is also a source, transit, and destination country for trafficking of people in forced labor and sexual exploitation. However, their Congress enacted new federal antitraffic legislation aimed at protecting human rights. Despite its advantageous climate and resources, Peter Khana views Argentina as a new second world entity.[10]

However, this nation, so rich in natural resources, is a world leader in environmental protection, especially in the setting of voluntary greenhouse targets. It is also an active participant in numerous international conservation programs. Argentina now has much to gain in emulating and cooperating more with Chile, its neighbor, with a Pacific coastline of some 3000 miles that is a gateway to oversees markets. Today, Chile consistently demonstrates 5 percent annual economic growth. It was governed by a successful center-led coalition and a progressive female president, Michelle Bachelet. In the twenty-first century, Argentina continues to be a land of promise with enormous potential!

LATIN AMERICAN CULTURAL THEMES

Central and South America are made up of many nations and cultures. In addition to the Amerindians' cultures and languages, the Spanish heritage and language dominate, except for Brazil, where the Portuguese language and culture are prevalent. Across the Americas, other European cultural inputs are German, Irish, Italian, as well as African and some Asian influences. Some countries, such as Mexico, Bolivia, Colombia, and Brazil, have strong manifestations of ancient cultures of indigenous tribes. The latter people are growing in influence with improved education and economic opportunities. For example, in 2005, the newly elected president of Bolivia, Evo Morales, had a powerful mandate because of his indigenous origins. He gained political support from the poor, the Andean Indians, and the *mestizos* (mixed race). Global managers realize that all the countries and people south of the U.S. border are not basically the same. Communication and business practice have to be adapted to local circumstances. Generalizations regarding Latin America are dangerous. Many of the countries differ greatly in socioeconomic status, educational levels, governance, and composition of the population. However, the following observations from the late Alison Lanier's classic, *Living in Latin America,* and others may prove helpful.[11,12]

Social customs

- *Shaking hands.* This is the same as in Europe. If there are several people in the room, with a little bow, go around to each person and shake hands. The "Hi, everybody" is considered rude and brash. "So long; see you tomorrow" is equally poor. The *abrazo* (embrace) is a greeting used with individuals one knows well.
- *Pleasantries.* Nobody rushes into business. As a foreign businessperson, take your time and ask about your colleague's family's health, the weather, or perhaps the local sports team.
- *Expressing gratitude.* Send "thank you" notes promptly after any courtesy. Flowers are often presented as an expression of appreciation.
- *Time.* Latin Americans may appear often to be late for appointments, according to North American standards, but they expect North Americans to be on time. Business hours normally begin about 8 or 9 a.m., depending on local custom. A lunch break or *siesta* may extend from 12 to 3 p.m. Their offices and stores usually close about 6–8 p.m. Dinner may begin at 8–9 p.m. As a guest, it is appropriate to arrive a little late rather than on time.
- *Party traditions.* Traditionally, women congregate on one side of the room and men on the other, but that is changing. For large formal affairs, invitations are written by hand. Flowers are often sent before a large affair. At a smaller party, you should take them to your host or hostess.
- *Privacy.* There are often closed doors, fences, and high walls around homes, especially of the more affluent. Knock, and wait to be invited in. Do not drop in on neighbors, for

this is not customary. Personal security is very important, so the more affluent may have bodyguards and a security system.

■ *Questioning.* Some North Americans get to know people by asking questions. However, in Latin America, it is safer to talk about local issues of interest. Personal questions are often interpreted as prying.

■ *Space.* Latin-speaking distance is closer than North American speaking distance. Instead of handshakes, men often embrace.

■ *Class and status.* People may not be served on a first-come, first-served basis. Their place in society may determine the order of preference as to serving and seating.

■ *Business practices.* The pace in Latin America is traditionally slow, relaxed, and less frenetic, especially when negotiations are under way. Normally, decisions are made at the top. Brazilians, for example, do not like quick, infrequent visits. They like relationships that continue. This implies a long-term commitment in Brazil. Deals are usually concluded in person, not finalized over the telephone or by letter or electronic mail. Again, do not call anyone by his or her first name unless the person has invited you to do so. When in doubt, be formal. Dress conservatively, and use business cards of good quality and in the local language.

Cultural themes and patterns

Themes are basic orientations that are shared by many or most of the people in the region. They are beginning points for understanding, and they sometimes form a pattern of behavior.

Personalismo. For the most part, a Latin's concerns are family, personal friends, hobbies, political party, and possibly sport, such as the local bullfight. But transcending all these is the concern for oneself. So, to reach a Latin, relate everything to him or her in personalized terms.

Machismo. It means "maleness" and is an attitude that men have toward women. The macho is aggressive and sometimes insensitive; machismo represents power. Machismo is made up of virility, zest for action, daring, competitiveness, and the will to conquer. How is it translated into daily business life? A man must demonstrate forcefulness, self-confidence, visible courage, and leadership with a flourish. The machismo concept is implanted early in childhood and varies from country to country. Saving face and honor are important concepts for Latin males. Never criticize family or friends.

Femaleness. Traditionally, women were "up on a pedestal" to be carefully protected by the male who was in charge. Yet, the female may actually control the home, children, and husband. As women in Latin America become better educated and pursue careers, their historical role in the family and society as wife and mother is changing. For example, in 2005, Michelle Bachelet was elected President of Chile, only the third woman to be so elected to national office in Latin America – the first who was not the widow of an illustrious husband. Instead, this moderate socialist was a twice-separated mother of three children. In her socially conservative country, she previously served in the national government as

Minister of Health and Defense. Realize that in some countries, like Venezuela, there is the "public" wife who runs the home and its finances, as well as raises the children, and the "private" wife, or mistress, who is for male pleasure.

Desires to get rich quick – fatalism. There is instability in many Latin American economies, and, as a result, there is a boom-or-bust attitude. Many desire to make it rich by speculation, manipulation, or gambling. As a result, some Latin businesspeople are less interested in stable growth than U.S. businesspersons. Related to this is the Latin American tendency to let chance guide their destiny. Most are convinced that outside forces govern their lives. They are willing to "accept the inevitable." Don Quixote, who followed his quest whether or not it appeared hopeless, seems like a foolish man to many foreigners. To most Latin Americans, he is heroic. He was "bowing to fate," "taking what comes," and "resigned to the inevitable." Their attitude is, "what will be, will be, God willing."

Good manners, dignity, and hospitality. Latin Americans are much like Europeans in this respect. They are more formal and more elaborate. They shake hands on meeting and departing. In Latin America, the work one does is directly related to the social class one is in, "high" or "low." Latin Americans are, by and large, stratified societies. Latin Americans are born with a sense of place, but the two classes of very rich and very poor is giving way to a growing and more affluent middle class. Latin people have enriched cultures because of their skills in music, art, and architecture. At the same time, Latin Americans are warm, friendly, and hospitable. They like to talk and want to know about a visitor's family and interests.

Human resources. Aristocratic values, late industrialization, and strong central governments have combined to create an imbalance in human resource needs of South America and the supply. Large numbers of South American workers have no industrial skills, but there is an oversupply of professional and white-collar workers, especially an acute shortage of trained managers. Part of the problem lies in a centuries-old university curriculum with an overemphasis on lawyers and engineers, which is very much in need of modernization. The global market, foreign investments, and increase in high technologies are facilitating the emergence of a knowledge culture in Pan-America.

Authoritarianism and egalitarianism. Signs of respect can be determined in both tone of voice and manner that denote grades of inferiority and superiority in a hierarchical society. The *patron* is the man of power or wealth who sustains loyalty from those of lesser status. He can be the employer, the politico, the landowner, and in other cases, the money lender or merchant. Authoritarianism does not allow for questioning. The *patron* knows everything and is all powerful. To play these roles, one has to be respectful in a subservient position. However, as the middle class continues to grow in size and strength, authoritarianism is less prevalent. Latin America is going through a social revolution in which agricultural and traditional societies are giving way to modern industrial and technological economies. The impact of Roman Catholicism is strong in the Latin cultures, but lessening as a force in the daily lives of people, especially in the urban areas. The profound social, economic, and political changes under way are altering many of the above customs and influences, especially among the younger generation. Democratization, worldwide communications, international exchanges, and contemporary realities are transforming Latin America. Its global managers are sophisticated in the ways of international business, and may not illustrate, at least on the surface, the typical social or cultural characteristics of the region.

Latin cross-cultural communications

Gordon has done extensive research to improve cross-cultural communications throughout the Americas, as the following excerpt emphasizes:

> The real difficulties in cross-cultural communications may be occurring because value systems are in conflict. While North and South Americans at a Pan-American conference, for instance, may be in agreement on general goals, the conflict might be anticipated in the means to achieve such goals; that is, the time, place, division of labor, sequence of actions, and other factors. When one is not open to consideration of the other's values, then emotions may rise and disagreements increase.[13]

For successful Pan-American exchanges and collaboration, Gordon's research indicates that each party in the cross-cultural encounter must learn (a) to recognize symptoms of miscommunication in oneself and the other; (b) to separate fact, interpretation, and conclusion; (c) to derive silent assumptions about major premises in the interpretive process from the foreigner's minor premises and conclusions; and (d) to request information from the host country citizen in such a way as not to bias or inhibit the response.

CHALLENGES FOR PAN-AMERICAN COOPERATION[14]

The prospects for Pan-American synergy in the twenty-first century are encouraging. Inflation is still a major problem, coordination of economic policies is distant, but barriers to trade are being reduced, and governments are committed to cutting fiscal deficits. There has also been relative peace between the nations of the Western hemisphere, despite internal upheavals within various Latin American states. Yet, political factions do often block hemispheric efforts toward shared energy and trade exchanges.

There have also been some noble efforts toward economic cooperation that lay the groundwork for real collaboration in the future. It takes time for such diverse cultures to learn the value and skills of joint endeavors. But the ground for synergy has been broken in such undertakings as the Organization of American States, the former Alliance for Progress, the Central American Common Market, the Andean Pact, the North American Free Trade Agreement, and MERCOSUR. All such cooperative arrangements seek to collaborate in common economic and trade policies that are more market friendly, while reducing protectionism. Another hopeful sign is the shift away from unilateral foreign aid to sharing of resources through multilateral institutions, such as the World Bank and the Inter-American Development Bank. Lately, the concerns of the various Latin American nations have shifted more to the social arena with the establishment of such entities as the Inter-American Commission on Human Rights. Another reason for optimism about the future of relationships is the Pan-American Development Foundation (PADF). Its objective is to help the lowest income people in Latin America and the Caribbean to participate productively in the socioeconomic and cultural development of their societies. PADF activates the involvement of the local private sector, especially the business community, through the formation of national development foundations in the various countries.

Underlying all of Latin America's difficulties is the need for integral development in the areas of education, healthcare, and opportunities for self-development. The interdependence of North and Latin America and the need for the other are obvious. Economic development is now more horizontal in the Americas, and not just vertical. Those with vision will set goals to close the Pan-American poverty gap within by around the middle of the twenty-first century.

Achieving synergy within Latin America requires leaders able to:

- Better manage the national resources of all states in the hemisphere by more effective collaboration of public and private sectors in each country, and between north/south regional relations.
- Manage the transfer of technology and information for mutual development of North and Latin American people.
- Contribute to economic and social development of Latin America through the exercise of corporate social responsibility by multinational enterprises on both continents.

Meeting the challengers of globalization has increased support for the proposed South American Community of Nations (SACN), perhaps as a replacement for the less-effective Organization of American States (OAS).

The Organization of American States (OAS) is a regional organization that has all of the 35 independent states of North and South America as members.[15] The charter of the OAS was signed in Bogotá, Colombia, on April 30, 1948, which is the founding date of the Organization. Operating out of its headquarters in Washington, D.C., the Organization promotes the values described in Article 2 of its Charter, which include but are not limited to security, representative democracy, conflict resolution, and interregional collaboration.[16] The OAS is in a unique position to affect politics and economics across the Americas.

A number of the Organization's online resources are notably pro-business. In the field of intellectual property, the Directory of National Authorities on Intellectual Property helps to promote the image of the Americas as a safe place in which to invest, in addition to providing essential contact information. The Foreign Trade Information System publishes the texts of trade agreements, in addition to detailed information regarding intellectual property.[17] The Organization's efforts to promote sustainable development and to root out corruption are also worthy of careful analysis by those interested in investing in the region.

CONCLUSIONS

Chapter 11 provided global managers with an overview of doing business in Brazil and Argentina. To improve the quality of life for all the America's inhabitants, effective and ecologically controlled utilization of resources on these twin continents is a major management challenge. Trained and experienced managers in transnational enterprises throughout Pan-America may be able to accomplish in the decades ahead what politicians, dictators, revolutionaries, and soldiers have failed to accomplish in the past centuries – cooperation and collaboration for the common good. The potential of Latin America is finally beginning to be actualized.

MIND STRETCHING

1   What is most striking to you in the contemporary development of Mexico? (See Mexico section on website.)
2   Why do the Central American states need to implement their negotiations for regional economic trade and development?
3   What is the significance of Portuguese culture and language in Brazil, in contrast to Spanish culture and language elsewhere in Latin America?
4   How do you envision the future of indigenous people or Amerindians in Latin America?
5   Why are North America, Europe, China, and Japan so interested in Latin America?
6   What are the implications of so many Latin Americans migrating to the United States and Canada?
7   Why does Latin America have to act as a trading bloc with Asia, Europe, and North America?
8   How can Latin Americans expand their business relationships with Africa, the Middle East, and Russia?

NOTES

1   Montaner, C. A. "Culture and the Behavior of Elites in Latin America," in L. E. Harrison and S. P. Huntington (eds), *Culture Matters*. New York: Basic Books, 2000, pp. 57–58. Also refer to Chong, N. and Baez, F. *Latino Culture: A Dynamic Force in the Changing American Workplace*. Boston, MA: Nicholas Brealey/Intercultural Press, 2005.
2   Khanna, P. *The Second World: Empires and Influence in the New World Order*. New York: Random House, 2008.
3   Abbott, J. and Moran, R. T. *Uniting North American Business: NAFTA Best Practice*. Burlington, MA: Elsevier/Butterworth-Heinemann, 2002.
4   Khanna, *The Second World*.
5   Cardoso, F. and Bell, P. *A Break in the Clouds: Latin America and the Caribbean in 2005*. Washington, DC: Inter-American Dialogue, 2006; Fay, M. (ed.). *The Urban Poor in Latin America*. Washington, DC:

World Bank; D. de Ferrantid et al. (eds), *Inequality in Latin America and the Caribbean*. Washington, DC: IBRD, World Bank, 2005; Paige, J. *Democracy in Central America*. Cambridge, MA: Harvard University Press, 1998.

6 Cardoso and Bell, *A Break in the Clouds*; Fay, *The Urban Poor in Latin America*; de Ferranti et al., *Inequality in Latin America and the Caribbean*; Paige, *Democracy in Central America*.

7 Klonsky, J. and Hanson, S. *Mercosur: South America's Fractious Trading Bloc*. Washington, DC: Council on Foreign Relations, 2008, www.cfr.org/publications/12752/mercosur.html.

8 Calderón, F. "Mexico's Road," *The World in 2008, The Economist*, 2008, www.economist.com or www.theworldin.com.

9 Unger, B. "Dreaming of Glory: A Special Report on Brazil," *The Economist*, April 14, 2007, p. 16, www.economist.com/specialreports.

10 Khanna, *The Second World*.

11 Council on Foreign Relations, Barshefsky, C. et al. (eds). *U.S.–Latin American Relations: A New Direction for a New Reality*. Washington, DC: CFR Publication, 2008, (Task Force Report #60) www.dfr.org/publication/16279; Morrison, T., Conway, W. A., and Douress, J. J. *Dun & Bradstreet Guide to Doing Business around the World*. Paramus, NJ: Prentice Hall Press, 2008; Axtell, R. E. *Gestures: The Do's and Taboo's of Body Language Around the World*. White Plains: John Wiley & Sons, Inc., 2008; Stephenson, S. *Understanding Spanish-Speaking South Americans*. Boston, MA: Nicholas Brealey/Intercultural Press, 2003.

12 Lanier, A. *Living in Latin America*. Boston, MA: Nicholas Brealey/Intercultural Press, 1988; Gordon, R. *Living in Latin America*. Skokie, IL: National Textbook, 1976; Stephenson, *Understanding Spanish-Speaking South Americans*.

13 Gordon, *Living in Latin America*.

14 Skidmore, T. E. and Smith, P. H. *Modern Latin America*. New York: Oxford University Press, 2005; Burns, E. B. and Charlip, J. A. *A Concise Interpretive History of Latin America*, 8th edn. Upper Saddle River, NJ: Prentice Hall, 2006; Goodwin, P. B. *Global Studies: Latin America*, 13th edn. New York: Dushkin, 2008.

15 OAS, "OAS: Member States," http://www.oas.org/en/member_states/default.asp.

16 OAS, "Charter of the Organization of American States," http://www.oas.org/dil/treaties_A-41_Charter_of_the_Organization_of_American_States.pdf.

17 OAS, "OAS: Intellectual Property," http://www.oas.org/en/topics/intellectual_property.asp.

ADDITIONAL FEATURES

Please visit the companion website at: www.routledge.com/cw/Moran where you will find additional case studies, study aides, and instructor resources.

12 DOING BUSINESS WITH SOUTH AND SOUTHEAST ASIANS, AND AUSTRALIANS

He who is unconcerned about the future will soon have cause to regret the present.

Confucius[1]

In past editions of *Managing Cultural Differences*, doing business in Asia was a single chapter, the same as all the other major world regions. Now, however, we have entered what has been called "The Century of Asia,"[2] as the twentieth century was that of America, and the nineteenth century that of Great Britain. Two Asian economic giants are poised to become the economic superpowers of the twenty-first century. China is poised to pass the United States in economic might by either 2016 or 2020. India is predicted to pass both China and the United States by 2050. In future years, the Asian Development Bank has predicted that Asians will enjoy the same standards of living as will exist in the European Union.[3]

We have chosen, therefore, to expand our coverage of Asia into two chapters. This chapter now considers South Asia (India), as well as Southeast Asia (Singapore, Malaysia, Thailand, Vietnam), and Australia. These are the strongest and most vibrant economies in the areas — the ones most interesting for international trade. Chapter 13 concerns East Asia — China, Japan, and South Korea.

In the coming years, Western economic prosperity will rely, more and more, on successful trading relations with Asia. Some countries are already leading the way. Japan's total economic trade with China is greater than Japanese–American trade. Canada is working to reduce its trade reliance on the United States, seeking to expand its trade in Asia. Canada's trade with the United States has fallen since the 1990s from 85 percent to about 70 percent of its total foreign trade. As the United States becomes self-sufficient in the production of oil in the next decade, this percentage will fall further.[4]

The purpose of this chapter is to acquaint you with economic, social, and cultural conditions in these South and Southeast Asian countries. Several, including India and Thailand, are throwing off traditional forms of social organization to achieve free market economies. Others, like Vietnam, have abandoned their centrally controlled economy for the quickly expanding benefits of free enterprise.

Our central purpose, however, is to offer criteria for achieving successful and profitable business opportunities in these nations. We have tried to identify the key success factors (KSFs) for doing business, and the ways that these may be achieved. For most of these nations, the most important factor is building trusting and cooperative business relationships with local business counterparts.

GENERAL CONSIDERATIONS

South and Southeast Asia require careful consideration for those intending to do business there. The regions contain countries where it is relatively easy to do business, but also countries where business conditions are very challenging. Exhibit 12.1 provides country rankings for ease of doing business for each year from 2009 through 2013. There were a total of 185 countries, worldwide, included in this analysis, so the rankings are out of 185.

EXHIBIT 12.1 EASE OF DOING BUSINESS (WORLD RANKINGS)

Country	2009	2010	2011	2012	2013 (estimate)	5-year average
Singapore	1	1	1	1	1	1.0
Australia	9	9	10	15	10	10.6
Thailand	12	12	19	17	18	15.6
Malaysia	21	23	21	18	12	19.0
Vietnam	91	93	78	98	99	91.8
India	132	133	134	132	132	132.6

Source: "Economy Rankings," Doingbusiness.org, October 23, 2012.

Singapore was consistently judged to be the easiest country in the entire world to do business. Australia also seemed to be a promising location to do business. India, despite its economic promise over the next decades, was judged to be a very difficult business environment, as was the rapidly expanding Vietnam. Conditions were becoming easier in Malaysia and more difficult in Thailand.

Ease of doing business is generally understood to be a function of how much uncertainty MNEs face when they enter a new business environment. There is usually uncertainty related to differing political, economic, social, cultural, and demographic factors. Uncertainty is reduced over time as MNEs and their staff become familiar with local conditions (see Chapter 4). Exhibit 12.2 is helpful in highlighting the effects of local business regulations on ease of doing business. Again, the rankings are out of the 185 worldwide countries included in the survey.

EXHIBIT 12.2 MEASURING BUSINESS REGULATIONS (WORLD RANKINGS)

Country	Ease of doing business (2013 est.)	Starting a business	Protecting investors	Exporting products	Enforcing contracts	Average of the five indicators
Singapore	#1	#4	#2	#1	#12	4.0
Malaysia	#12	#54	#4	#11	#33	22.8
Australia	#10	#2	#70	#44	#15	28.2
Thailand	#18	#85	#13	#20	#23	31.8
Vietnam	#99	#108	#169	#74	#44	98.8
India	#132	#173	#49	#127	#184	133.0

Source: International Finance Corporation, The World Bank. "Doing Business: Measuring Business Regulations, Economy Rankings," www.doingbusiness.org/rankings. Benchmarked to June, 2012. Retrieved February 6, 2013.

It is relatively easy to do business in Singapore because it is relatively easy to start a business, investors are well protected by law, and products or services are easily exported without bureaucratic "red-tape." Contracts are more enforceable in Singapore than in any of the other countries we are considering in these regions. Malaysia surpasses Australia in terms of the indicators we are considering because investors are far better protected, and products/services far easier to export. Even Thailand is better than Australia on these two indicators. By contrast, India now looks even more challenging because it is very difficult to start up a business, difficult to export, and almost impossible to legally enforce a contract (184th of 185 countries).

A rationale was needed for deciding in what order we would arrange our discussions of these nations. We presumed that nations with larger GDPs, that exported and/or imported more goods/services, and that MNEs made more direct investments (FDI = foreign direct investment), would be more important. Certainly, international businesspersons would be more likely to do business with companies from these countries in this order. These rankings are found in Exhibit 12.3.

We start with India even though MNEs have made considerably greater direct investments in both Australia and Singapore and, in the short term, MNE staff might be more likely to find themselves assigned there. India is the country in the region with the greatest predicted potential. Already its combined exports and imports are greater than even Singapore, a legendarily successful trading country. Over the course of their lifetimes, our student readers are likely to find themselves doing business either in India, or with Indian companies trading in their own home countries.

EXHIBIT 12.3 INTERNATIONAL BUSINESS COUNTRY COMPARISONS BY IMPORTANCE, 2012

Country	Exports (US$ billion) and country rank	Imports (US$ billion) and country rank	FDI in country (US$ billion) and country rank	GDP (PPP in US$ billions) and country rank	Average country ranking for the four indicators
India	309.1 (#18)	1500.3 (#9)	1256.6 (#21)	14,735.0 (#4)	13.0
Australia	263.9 (#23)	258.1 (#21)	598.3 (#12)	960.7 (#19)	18.8
Singapore	430.6 (#14)	390.4 (#14)	522.1 (#15)	326.7 (#40)	20.8
Thailand	218.1 (#26)	213.7 (#25)	158.7 (#27)	646.1 (#25)	25.8
Malaysia	239.8 (#25)	197.2 (#27)	123.0 (#33)	492.0 (#30)	28.8
Vietnam	109.4 (#37)	109.6 (#33)	75.5 (#47)	320.5 (#42)	39.6

Source: International Finance Corporation, The World Bank. "Doing Business: Measuring Business Regulations, Economy Rankings," www.doingbusiness.org/rankings. Benchmarked to June, 2012. Retrieved February 6, 2013.

E
X
H
I
B
I
T

12.3

Australia will be the second country we consider. While it is not the international business powerhouse that Singapore is, its GDP is much larger and it has more future potential. We will then consider Singapore and Malaysia together as a unit. Singapore is a city-state at the southern end of the Malay peninsula. The key success factors (KSFs) for doing business successfully in Singapore are not different from those in Malaysia.[5] Then we will consider Thailand, and Vietnam.

INDIA

You'll likely be dealing with people who speak the Queen's English, and who graduated from top Western universities. You can get lulled into a false sense of security – but for people dressing a little different and talking a little different, they are just like me. That's a completely false premise. There are all kinds of nuances in the culture; implicit cultural norms that we don't know about until we run afoul of them.

Jitendra Singh[6]

The Indian economy is sometimes likened to an elephant, which is not capable of running as swiftly as some of the smaller "tiger-like" Asian countries, but has the advantage of being stable and less affected by shocks and disturbances. These elephantine qualities were severely tested during the recent years when political and economic problems were aplenty. These included the global economic slowdown (exacerbated by the terrorist attacks of September 11, 2001), increased political tension with neighboring Pakistan (especially after the terrorist attack on the Indian Parliament), a poorly performing industrial sector, stagnant exports, and a capital market that remained in the doldrums. . . . But today, India is suddenly an emerging superpower.

Arvind Panagariya[7]

India[8] is in process of developing from an autarkic to an open-market economy. The recent growth has stemmed from economic liberalization including industrial deregulation, privatization of state-owned enterprises, and reduced controls on foreign investment and international trade. This process began in the early 1990s and since 1997 India's GDP has grown at an average 7 percent per year. Slightly more than half of India's workforce is still engaged in agricultural production but services, especially related to information technology, are the major growth engine accounting for nearly two-thirds of India's economic output. India has capitalized on its large educated English-speaking workforce to become a major exporter of information technology services, and software development workers. Although affected by the global recession of 2008–2009, India's economy rebounded with 10.1 percent growth in 2010, due to strong domestic demand. Recent growth rates have been 6.8 percent in 2011, and 5.4 percent in 2012. Part of this slowdown has been political uncertainty and the fear that a new governing party would view internationalization less favorably.

The majority of Indian exports in 2011 went to the U.A.E. (12.7 percent), United States (10.8 percent), China (6.2 percent), Singapore (5.3 percent), and Hong Kong (4.1 percent). The primary categories of exports were petroleum products, gemstones, machinery, iron and steel, chemicals, vehicles, and clothing. The majority of India's imports came from China (11.9 percent), U.A.E. (7.7 percent), Switzerland (6.8 percent), Saudi Arabia (6.1 percent), and the United States (4.9 percent). Major import categories included crude oil, gemstones, machinery, fertilizer, iron and steel, and chemicals.

Historical perspective

As in East Asia, the sixteenth century saw the Western European nations establishing trading posts in India. The Portuguese efforts were focused upon Goa/Cochin on the west coast, and the French in Pondicherry on the east coast. However, the British were the most successful and expanded their influence and power throughout the subcontinent. They built a colonial infrastructure that remains today in large part, including the heritage of English in a *land of many tongues*. After World War I, nationalism grew in India. Mahatma Gandhi organized a series of passive-resistance campaigns and civil disobedience to British rule. The British reign ended on August 15, 1947. On January 26, 1950, the Indian constitution was promulgated, and the country became a sovereign republic and the world's largest democracy.

Hinduism, believing birth is destiny, perpetuates the caste system, separating the social classes by occupations, so that privileges or disadvantages are transmitted by inheritance. For over 5,000 years, the caste system with its thousands of subsystems has divided people into four divisions – priests, warriors, traders, and workers. Then there are the untouchables, or *dalits,* excluded because of the nature of their crafts, such as working with leather, and waste disposal.

When industrialization began in twentieth-century India, many untouchables were recruited by foreign investors to learn new skills for factory work. An example of how this injustice is breaking down for some 200 million so classified is the late K. R. Narayanan. Born of a poor southern Indian family and educated by Christian missionaries, he won scholarships to the London School of Economics and proved to be a very talented student. Upon his return, India's first prime minister, Jawaharial Nehru, found Narayanan a job in the diplomatic service where he ended up an ambassador to Thailand, Turkey, China, and the U.S.A. In 1984, he was elected to parliament from his native Kerala. To the surprise of the elite, he subsequently was elected vice president and then president, saying: "My life encapsulates the ability of the democratic system to accommodate and empower marginalized sections of society." Today, discrimination on the grounds of caste is illegal, and affirmative action programs are under way.

Business insights on India

GOVERNANCE

The government of India is based on the British parliamentary system with a bicameral legislature and executive and judicial branches. India is governed by a council of ministers led by the prime minister (appointed by the president). The ministers and prime minister are responsible to the House of People, the Lok Sabha, elected by universal adult franchise. There is an upper house called the Rajya Sabha, i.e., legislation submitted by the prime minister has to be passed by both the Lok Sabha and the Rajya Sabha before being signed by the president. The bills only become law on the president's signature. The president may return the bills to the legislature for changes that he/she may suggest. The powers of the government are, in fact, vested in the prime minister, who is generally the leader of the majority party in Parliament and usually the lower house, Lok Sabha. Nevertheless, the president is the commander-in-chief of the armed forces, and also has the right to fire the prime minister in cases of national emergency or because of lack of confidence. The president has very little executive power.

ECONOMICS

The Reserve Bank of India, India's central bank, manages money supply. The unit of currency is the rupee. The Reserve Bank acts as banker for the government, the commercial banks, and other financial institutions. The banking system is deeply involved in the industrialization of the country through financing of both fixed assets and working capital. The State Bank of India is the largest commercial bank in the country, and it also carries out some of the functions of the Reserve Bank of India.

The industrial economy of India has a public sector and a private sector. The public sector companies are government-run industrial and commercial undertakings, while the private sector is composed of profit-oriented business organizations run increasingly by professional managers. The country has achieved rapid industrial growth in recent years, with capabilities increasing in almost every sphere of industry, especially information technologies. Exhibit 12.4 is an indication of why India is becoming an "economic tiger."

EXHIBIT 12.4 THE HIGH-TECH REVOLUTION

E X H I B I T 12.4

Bangalore is the center of India's booming information technology (IT) industry. Yet, it is something of a paradox — inside its modern industrial parks, business and living conditions operate at a higher level. Outside, its surrounding urban area suffers from deteriorating infrastructure and attempts at renewal. This city is a global and national hub of sophisticated software and remote services, such as business processing outsourcing (BPOs or call centers). The old city and local government, however, strains to keep up with the demands of its economic drivers, companies like Wipro and Infosys. These high-tech endeavors employ some 260,000 employees, and leading firms are hiring 1,000 new staff per month. Foreign firms are arriving to set up businesses at a rate of three per week. No wonder the economic forecasts for this dynamic ecosystem are 25 percent or more annually. However, this city, known for its beauty, lush parks, greenery, and mild climate, struggles to cope with a population that has grown from 800,000 in 1951 to more than 8.6 million in 2012.

This municipality has also become a knowledge center that attracts technical and scientific institutes. Their leaders are the Indian Institution of Science, a world-class university known for its excellence, plus Karnataka, whose 77 engineering colleges alone produce 29,000 graduates per year and spearhead India's space program. A few miles out of town is "Electronics City," a cosmopolitan oasis with amenities to suit the needs of these knowledge workers. These range from "state-of-the-art" remote network management systems and cappuccino bars to lively nightlife.

Urban chaos and commuter nightmares in major cities like Bangalore, Delhi, and Mumbai, make second-tier cities very attractive. They are growing fast as postindustrial corporations are attracted to Gurgaib and Noida on the edges of New Delhi; Mumbai's new town; Chennai, formerly Madras; Hyderabad in the south; Pune in the west; Molhali in the north. Even old Calcutta, now called Kolkata, is trying to woo investments for its IT and BPO firms. As successful companies expand aggressively, many move out to less congested areas.

Within attractive IT and BPO campuses, the R&D is either outsourced or extended to new global market niches — for example, processing insurance claims, desktop publishing, remote management and maintenance, backup navigation systems, compiling audits and completing tax forms, transcribing medical records, and financial records and analysis. Predictions are that in a few years many MNEs will have up to 25 percent of their staff in India. Also, security and data protection at these advanced facilities are tight! In 2008, IT and its enabling services employed over 4 million people who earned up to US$65 billion from exports, accounting for 7 percent of India's GDP.

Part of this success is attributed to keeping government out of this new business. Also, India has a big competitive edge in its annual production of 2 million English-speaking graduates, many of whom benefit from a quality education.

Source: Adapted from "Special Report on Outsourcing and IT in India:The Bangalore Paradox," *The Economist*, April 23, 2005, pp. 67–69. (Report updated.)

HUMAN AND CAPITAL RESOURCES

There are large pools of managerial, skilled, and semiskilled labor. There is also a good and developed capital market and a large domestic market. Since the early 2000s, Bangalore, a beautiful city in south central India, has emerged as the Silicon Valley of India. In fact, two-thirds of all custom software programming for the United States is done in India.

COMMUNICATIONS

India has a great variety of languages, customs, beliefs, and cultures. There are 15 official languages including English, plus more than 1,400 dialects. Language reflects regional differences, and is a problem in achieving national unity. Most languages find their origin in an ancient Indian language called Sanskrit. Radio, television, mobile telephones, and the computer, especially the Internet, are advancing internal communications within India and with the outside world.

RELIGIONS

India is a land of gods – over 230,000 such deities – though some Hindus maintain these are manifestations of a single god. The subcontinent reflects great spirituality, most evident in ashrams, meditation, swamis, and gurus. Over millennia, it has suffered numerous invasions and assimilated the invaders' beliefs. It is also a place of great religious discord, even in modern times.

Hinduism is the majority religion in India (80.5 percent), followed by Islam (13.4 percent), Christianity (2.3 percent), and Sikhism (1.8 percent).[9] Hinduism is not only the principal religion of India, but its philosophy dominates the entire culture and relationships. It can also be a source of serious ethnic conflict with Muslims, Sikhs, and Christians. It determines a woman's role in society. Although the Hindu woman's legal position has greatly improved over the years, she is still bound by ancient traditions of behavior that emphasize her dedication, submission, and obedience to her husband and his wishes. This may not be so strictly adhered to in the big cities and Westernized circles where Indian women are increasing in the workforce, especially in the professions (doctors, engineers, lawyers) and in government.

CORRUPTION AND ETHICS

While honesty is esteemed in this vast and poor country, corruption and fraud are endemic in all levels of society. Corruption, bribes, or payments for "fixing" exist in everyday life and are something that must be dealt with, even accepted, to get things accomplished. While bribery is a crime punishable by suspension and jail time if convicted, corrupt officials rarely encounter resistance. Lately, the "Zero Rupee" note has been used by those resisting corrupt practices to condemn bribery. A person who has been asked by an official to present a bribe may offer a zero rupee note, indicating a willingness to ask for a disciplinary hearing that could cause the official to lose his/her job.[10] In India, business is based on personal contacts, and it is crucial to know the right person in order to get contracts. As India's global corporations become more integrated with a more universal approach to organization behavior worldwide, expect ethical standards to rise.

Eileen S. Wibbeke examined the issue of ethics from a cross-cultural perspective, urging managers abroad to look beyond Western traditions.[11] For example, her analysis of

Hindu ethics pointed out its complexity due to historical and cultural tradition. There are a number of ways a believer may seek spiritual liberation, and there are many Hindu scriptures from which to choose. This religion is flexible, tolerant, and socially important. Some Hindu philosophers teach that an act is *amoral* only if it is not based on informed choices that are freely made. Hindus live by two principles:

1   *Karma,* or by acting morally and you affect your future reincarnated life for the good or bad.
2   *Dharma,* or the path of learning to choose right and appropriate actions, including moral ones.

The virtues of dharma include honesty, patience, temperance, hospitality, and kindness. Other religious traditions in India express their attitudes toward ethics in different ways, adding to the country's diversity.

To appreciate the new business environment in India, consider the implications of Exhibit 12.5.

EXHIBIT 12.5 INDIA'S TATA ENTERPRISES

One of India's most successful global corporations originated in 1958 with a Parsi family named "Tata." Now, this diversified enterprise operates in 85 countries, and is continually acquiring high-profile businesses. In 2000, it acquired the London-based iconic tea company Tetley. In 2007, it acquired Corus, a European steel-maker. The same year, it acquired for US$2.3 billion the legendary automobile marques Jaguar and Land Rover, and their British manufacturing plants, from Ford. Tata Industries reflects great financial strength from both domestic and foreign markets and looks upon these acquisitions as long-term investments. Alan Rosling, the company's chief British strategist, believes that Tata will reap the benefits of Ford's previous efforts with these prestigious automobiles. Due to its Indian origins, he is optimistic about Tata's increasing global research because of its sensitivity to cultural differences, and because it seeks to imitate some of the world's best corporations.

The Tata Group is an Indian conglomerate that spans countries and products, such as automobile and steel manufacturing, software and tea production. An example of its innovation in emerging markets is Tata's Consulting Services. specializing in the outsourcing of business processes of higher value. Perhaps one of Tata's most exciting ventures is the building of a small, inexpensive automobile called the Nano. This car, selling for about US$2,500, is intended not only for the massive Indian market but also for emerging markets everywhere. The Nano is to be the "people's car" yet its manufacture uses state-of-the-art virtual design technology. Mr. Tata sees these endeavors as safe and less-expensive alternatives for consumers in both developing and mature economies.

Source: Adapted from "A Bigger World: A Special Report on Globalization," *The Economist*, September 20, 2008, 26 page insert.

EXHIBIT 12.5

The manufacturing and industrial sector, however, has not grown in India to the same extent as in China, and this continues to be a problem. Most of the growth in Indian GDP has been in the services sector, now contributing approximately 59 percent in 2012 and still growing rapidly, especially in information technology and outsourcing. By contrast, the industry and manufacturing sector has remained a relatively constant 20 percent of GDP since the early 1990s. This means that India has not been able to match China's growth which has been driven by export of manufactures. Exhibit 12.6 provides additional current insights on the subcontinent of India.

More than services or agriculture, India's entrenched bureaucracy and poor infrastructure negatively impact industry. Indian labor costs are high by emerging market standards

E X H I B I T 12.6

EXHIBIT 12.6 INDIAN GROWTH RATES SLOWING?

On a 4,200 km train ride through 615 stations, one traveler reported that she/he never lost a usable mobile-phone signal. Ten years ago, no one would have cared because only 5 percent of Indians had a mobile phone. Now, according to Ericsson, 75 percent of Indians have access to one. In addition, of India's 247 million households, two-thirds have electricity, half have television and bicycles, though as yet only 5 percent have cars.

PriceWaterhouseCoopers reports that in 2010, 470 million Indians had incomes between $1,000 and $4,000 per year. This is expected to rise to 570 million within 10 years, creating a $1 trillion market for goods and services. Yet, this forecast was made when the economy was booming when it seemed that in a decade or two India would become a very prosperous country. Now, much slower expansion seems likely.

Growth should be maintained at a higher level than the 3 percent that was normal before the market reforms of the 1990s. Recent years, however, have brought high inflation (8.6 percent in 2011), especially for food. Roads, ports, and railways are overwhelmed. Electricity blackouts are common. Labor has become as expensive as in China even though the Chinese have, on average, three times the wealth.

The Transport Corporation of India reported in 2012 that every one of India's major road networks was clogged with traffic. Roads are being expanded at 4 percent per year but vehicle traffic is expanding at 11 percent. Driving from Delhi to Mumbai, 1,380 km, takes three days at an average speed of 21km per hour. The railways are no better. It is a political necessity to keep passenger fares level but these subsidies are paid for with rising freight rates. The result is that goods are sent by truck on the very overcrowded highways.

Given that the infrastructure seems to have reached its limits, a slowdown in economic growth to 5 percent would be very welcome. It was 7.2 percent in 2011. Cyrus Guzder, a Mumbai businessman commented, "We should not try to get back to the highest growth path. India hurts when it is growing at 8.5 percent."

Source: Adapted from *The Economist* Special Report on India; "The Economy: Express or Stopping," September 25–October 5, 2012, pp. 8–10.

and legal regulations are restrictive. As Chinese wages have risen, "busy-fingers" labor-intensive industry has fled to places like Bangladesh but not to India. Indian car manufacturers have been an exception. After the Chinese riots against Japan in 2012, Nissan was the only Japanese car company whose profits rose significantly and this was because it immediately chose to expand in India and to put a temporary halt to expansion plans in China. Tata's Nano (see Exhibit 12.5), however, has not yet achieved the wide-ranging success it was billed for in 2008. And there seems no expectation that there will be any large increase in the Indian manufacturing sector in the near future.[12]

Cultural guidelines for business in India

The people of India are very friendly, hard-working, and diverse. Extended family living is the norm and somewhat hierarchical. A friend's role is to "sense" a person's need and to do something about it. Young, educated urban youth have more modern clothing and attitudes that are far different from their counterparts in rural villages.

SOCIAL CUSTOMS

Social amenities and practices vary in this huge country, depending on location. Those of the Brahman elite living in urban areas differ from those of village peasants, or Christian communities in Goa or Kerala. There are, however, some guidelines that may prove generally helpful in India:

- Social freedom between the sexes is not appreciated, except within more progressive communities. Normally among traditionalists, a stranger should not speak to a woman if he is not acquainted with her or her family. For a young woman to take the hand of a man who is not her husband is usually objectionable. Bold, emancipated women may dare to indulge in dancing with their husbands, but for her to dance with anyone not her husband would be improper.
- Use of first names in addressing others should be avoided. It is customary to add to the names of the Hindus the affix "ji" as a mark of respect. For instance, Ravi in polite speech becomes Raviji. Here, Ravi is the first name, but by adding the affix "ji," you are treating the person with respect and, in this instance, use of the first name will not be improper. In Bengal, "Mister" is replaced by "Babu." Thus, Ravi Babu means Mr. Ravi. In much of India, in correspondence or invitation cards, the classic Sanskrit prefixes "Shriman" for men and "Shrimati" for women are used.
- The method of greeting depends on the social status of the persons meeting. A son usually greets his father by bowing down and touching his feet. A foreign businessperson will be considered an equal. Among equals the usual method used will be to press one's palms together in front of one's chest and say *namaste*, meaning, "greetings to you." Among the other classes of people, educated in

Western style, shaking hands is acceptable. Educated Hindu women usually would not mind shaking hands with men when introduced. However, it is safer not to extend one's hand to a Hindu woman until she takes the initiative and extends her's first. It is safer to stick with "namaste." This actually is the universal form of greeting in India.

▪ For the businessperson visiting India, shirt, trousers, tie, and suit will be proper attire, but lightweight in fabric and white or light tan color. The Indian climate is hot. Therefore, a very light suit is recommended even in winter. If a person is in the north during winter, he or she will find it a little cooler and, again, a light sweater and/or a jacket will be sufficient. In public places, women visitors avoid wearing shorts or revealing dresses, as it draws unwanted attention. Though Western business dress is common-place, in this climate coats are often eliminated and hats worn to protect from the sun. Indian businessmen, in many situations, wear "dhotis" – a single piece of white cloth about five yards long and three to four feet broad. It is passed round the waist up to half its length, and the other half is drawn between the legs and tucked at the waist. For the upper part of the body, they wear long shirts. Sikhs from Punjab wear turbans, which have a religious significance. Well-to-do Hindus who wish to appear aristocratic wear long coats like the Rajahs. The long coat, known as *sher-wani*, has been standardized and is the dress recognized by the government of India for official and ceremonial wear. Many modernized Hindu males have adopted European costume in their outdoor life and Indian dress at home. The Hindu lady is extremely loyal to her *sari*, while female dress may vary in ethnic communities (e.g., Punjabi women may feature scarfs and shawls, with loose-fitting blouse and billowing pants). The modern sari compares favorably with fashionable clothes of Western women.

▪ The noble teachings of Mahatma Gandhi on nonviolence and tolerance are frequently ignored today. Hindu nationalism dominates the government, often to the exclusion of Muslims.

Work values and business relationships

The Indian business community is very focused on the importance of relationship. Jitendra Singh, a management professor at the Wharton School of Business commented:

> The United States is a much more transaction-oriented society. When you're doing business, you're there to talk about a particular transaction, and you either do it or you don't. But Indian business is still very much relationship-based. Sometimes being too transactional can be not a smart way to go. Do a lot of homework and figure out who might be the right people to deal with. There's a very tight network at the top of Indian business, and you need to get access to that network in order to succeed. Finding the right partners can be key, but you need to be diligent.[13]

Pawean Budhwar, Associate Dean of Research at Aston Business School, agreed, saying that the key to success doing business in India was tapping into networks and resources that could provide useful information related to your business interests. "Have persistence," he said, "And don't give up. The mileage to get into India is great. Don't expect it to be a smooth ride. Expect it to be irritating. But once you're there, you'll enjoy it – and you'll make a great deal of money."[14] Exhibit 12.7 offers ten "top tips" for successfully doing business in India.

EXHIBIT 12.7 TOP TIPS FOR DOING BUSINESS IN INDIA

Tip 1: India is as culturally diverse a country as any on earth. All generalizations, including our own, about Indian culture should be treated with caution. Research each client thoroughly before any negotiation. Are you dealing with a more traditionally minded family business, or a more modern corporation used to Western business practices?

Tip 2: Indian culture places a much higher value on the quality of interpersonal relationships than found in Western business. Do not push your agenda too hard in the opening phases of discussion. Take the time to let relationships develop.

Tip 3: Indian society and business is hierarchically structured. Many Indians find it difficult and uncomfortable working in a non-hierarchical structure, or a consulting culture where expectations are not clearly stated.

Tip 4: Attempting to introduce a flatter and more egalitarian structure or organization culture will be difficult and painful both for Indian employees and those initiating these changes.

Tip 5: Most decisions are made at senior levels of management. It is a waste of time to negotiate at middle levels if top level approval has not already been given.

Tip 6: The boss is "the boss" and is expected to play the part. Senior managers are not expected to do work that could be delegated to someone at a lower level.

Tip 7: Managers are expected to give clear and specific instructions to subordinates. Subordinates are expected to carry out instructions without question.

Tip 8: Subordinates, contractors, etc., will not take the initiative. Plan in detail, and be prepared to explain exactly what is required.

Tip 9: Meetings can be very informal. It is not uncommon for one person to conduct several meetings at the same time and in the same room. It is inappropriate to express irritation at this approach.

Tip 10: Time is flexible. Be prepared for meetings to start and end late. Interruptions are common.

Source: "Top Tips on Indian Business Attitudes and Doing Business in India," *WorldBusinessCulture* (http://worldbusinessculture. com/Doing-Business-in-India.html). Retrieved February 10, 2013.

A useful way to consider the dynamics of relationship building in India is to look at how Indian business culture rated on Hofstede's five work-related values.[15] See Chapter 1 for a discussion of Hofstede's work-related values.

Hofstede identified India as a *collectivist* rather than an *individualist* culture. It had a clearly defined hierarchical structure such that most Indians were sensitive to others' rank or status in relation to their own. This resulted in meetings and discussions being led by senior managers, and work being carefully monitored by supervisors. Interpersonal relationships may be governed by collectivist values. Individuals prefer to work in teams, and team members tend to participate in activities together.

The abilities to compromise, and to avoid conflict are valued. This results in an *indirect* approach to communication. You should learn to interpret non-verbal signals and cues. Harmony is especially valued in all business negotiations so you should focus on expanding areas of agreement to reduce areas of disagreement, rather than directly confronting areas of disagreement.

India scored high on Hofstede's *power distance*. Status in India is often on the basis of ascription (born to it) rather than achievement because there is not much upward mobility. High status individuals are usually both respected and obeyed. It is difficult to build personal relationships with Indians who are either higher in rank than yourself, or Indian subordinates. The strongest relationships can be built between colleagues.

Indian culture scored higher on *masculinity* than is usual in many cultures. The gap between men's and women's values is higher than average. Generally, Indian culture values masculine assertiveness and traditionally consigns women into homemaker roles. Educated Indian women are now commonly found in business careers because of the cultural value placed on education, but are still expected to maintain traditional female roles. Foreigners should be careful of this ambiguity. Public displays of physical affection should be avoided since in some locales they are even illegal. You should initiate the shaking of hands, if you are female especially, since Indian businessmen consider it inappropriate to initiate a greeting to a woman.

Indian culture scored low on *uncertainty avoidance*. This means that Indian business-people are relatively open to unexpected situations, and more willing to take risks. This translates into greater flexibility in meetings including willingness to accept new ideas or options, and the valuing of innovation. However, one should remember that Indian culture takes a flexible view of time. Negotiations will likely take longer than expected, and much of that time is consumed with getting to know your business partner and building a relationship. It is likely that meetings will not start on time, and some attendees will likely arrive late. Indian businesspeople will expect a foreigner to display flexibility. If the foreigner's presentations appear too rigid and structured, credibility may be diminished. You should not expect to receive a decision even after a number of meetings because your Indian business associates may require a considerable period of time to consider your proposals.

AUSTRALIA

Australia's substantial and diversified natural resources have attracted substantial foreign investment (see Exhibit 12.3).[16] There are large commercial deposits of coal, iron ore, copper, gold, natural gas, and uranium. Australia is currently a major exporter of natural resources, energy, food, and wine. Investments are currently being made through the Gorgon Project to produce liquefied natural gas (LNG) for export to China and/or Japan. Australia also has an extensive service sector.

The Australian economy grew for 17 consecutive years before the onset of the global financial recession in 2008. Demand from China – especially for natural resources – limited contraction to a single quarter. The economy grew by 1.4 percent in 2009, 2.5 percent in 2010, 2.1 percent in 2011, and 3.3 percent in 2012. Unemployment peaked at 5.7 percent in 2009, and fell to 5.2 percent in 2012. Because of its rapid recovery from the global recession, Australia was one of the first developed countries to raise interest rates in October 2009, and again in November 2010.

Australia is currently engaged in Trans-Pacific Partnership trade talks, and also is negotiating free trade agreements with China, Japan, and Korea. The majority of its exports in 2011 went to China (27.4 percent), Japan (19.2 percent), South Korea (8.9 percent), and India (5.8 percent). Its major national sources for imports in 2011 were China (18.5 percent), the United States (11.4 percent), Japan (7.9 percent), Singapore (6.2 percent), and Germany (4.7 percent).

Cultural guidelines for doing business

Although originally founded as a British colony in 1778, and with 92 percent of its population of about 22 million being European, Australia has become a multicultural nation. Asians consist of 7 percent of the population, and Aboriginals 1 percent. As of 2005, Australia was admitting 120,000 immigrants a year, a third from Asian countries, to relieve labor shortages. Melbourne has become a showcase for multiculturalism with John So, a Hong Kong immigrant, having been Lord Mayor between 2001 and 2008.

Australians are generally easygoing, friendly, and relatively informal. Most greet each other either with a firm handshake, or a "G'day." More formal greetings may include a simple "Hello, how are you?" style of greeting, but without the formal British reserve of most of their ancestors. It is customary for men to shake hands both at the beginning and the end of meetings. Handshaking is not required for women who may instead give each other a kiss on the cheek both in greeting and leaving. It is entirely acceptable for newcomers to introduce themselves in social situations rather than waiting to be introduced.

In business settings, it is appropriate to offer your business card but do not be surprised if you are not offered one in turn. Many Australian businesspersons do not carry cards. When introduced initially, Australians may address you with your full name, or say "sir" as a sign of respect. However, they are quick to switch to an informal first-name basis, and visitors are welcome to imitate if an Australian initiates.

Basic rules of etiquette include the following:

- Men should not wink at women even if they are friends. This is considered inappropriate behavior.
- Yawning in public is considered rude.
- Men should not express physical affection as this may be considered unmanly.
- The American expression for "2," forming a "V" with the index and middle fingers of one hand, is considered a vulgar gesture.
- Other gestures considered rude are the "OK" (thumb and forefinger touching with other fingers raised), and hitchhiking (hand raised in fist with thumb extended), signs common in North America.
- You should avoid using the terms "stuffed" or "rooting" (for your team) which have vulgar connotations.
- Lines of waiting people are to be respected. You should not cut into a line, but take your place at the end and wait your turn.
- Sportsmanlike gestures of any kind are appreciated because sportsmanship is a respected characteristic.
- Guests of honor should sit at the right side of the host.
- When addressing audiences, one should stand erect and use modest restrained body language.

Australians prefer to speak frankly and directly, and may use humor even in tense situations. They dislike pretension and will not shy away from disagreements. They generally dislike class distinctions. They are, however, generally a warm and friendly people, who enjoy life and prefer to "work to live," rather than to "live to work." They highly value close friendships.

There is a close Australian–American relationship, perhaps derived from the two countries being close geopolitical allies since the Vietnam War. This relationship covers the spectrum from commercial and cultural contacts, to political and defense cooperation. Euro-American companies wishing to do business in Australia will find relatively few obstacles though legal regulations are less helpful in protecting investors' interests, and there is "red tape" to overcome before products may be exported (see Exhibit 12.2).

It is important, however, to remember that while Australians speak English as their first language, and seem to behave much as do Americans, there are differences in language and culture. These should be respected and even appreciated. This respect will cement relationships already predisposed towards friendship, and lead to success in business.

Negotiating with Australians

Keating and Abramson[17] reported in a cross-national negotiation study about the comparative strengths and weaknesses of Australian negotiators in relation to their Japanese and Thai counterparts. They used the Keirsey[18] model of four personality temperaments to predict Australian negotiating behavior. This model is discussed in Chapter 7 in the context of leadership. These four temperaments included:

1   *Guardians (SJ)*. Guardians' core needs are for group membership and taking responsibility. Guardians hunger for responsibility, accountability, and predictability. They trust hierarchy and authority, and may be surprised if others are not equally respectful. Guardians prefer traditional solutions. They are effective working within formal organizations, bound by rules, procedures and protocol. They admire those having commonsense, and those in authority. Guardians represented a common Australian negotiating stance since 45.8 percent of the Australian managers were Guardians.

2   *Rationalists (NT)*. Rationalists' core needs were for efficiency, and mastery of contents, knowledge, and competencies. Rationalists want to know how things work and they have theories for everything. They value expertise, logical consistency, and ideas. They seek progress. They are planful, analyzing situations and finding creative theoretical alternatives. They are skillful at long-range planning, invention, design, and finding patterns between discrete concepts. Rationalist represented a common Australian negotiation stance since 39.6 percent of the Australian managers were Rationalists.

3   *Artisans (SP)*. Artisans' core needs were to have freedom to act without restraint, and ability to see a tangible result from that action. Artisans are predisposed to seek adventure and stimulation. They trust their intuition for finding solutions to problems. They are natural tacticians and negotiators, focused on skillful performance. They are especially good at seeing opportunities and swiftly moving to achieve them. Artisanship represented *an Australian negotiation weakness* because only 8.3 percent of the Australian managers were Artisans. In a negotiation team, their potential contribution might be lost, overwhelmed democratically by the 85.4 percent who were either Guardians or Rationalists.[19]

4   *Idealists (NF)*. Idealists' core needs were for trust-based relationships, cooperation, and achievement of ethically minded results. Idealists valued interpersonal unity, self-actualization, and personal authenticity. Idealists were especially gifted at unifying diversity, and helping people achieve their maximum potential. They built bridges between others with empathy, and clarification of deeper-than-surface issues. Idealism also represented *an Australian negotiation weakness* because only 6.3 percent of Australian managers were Idealists.

Following this study, we may conclude that in your negotiations with Australians, you are more likely to encounter Guardians and Rationalists, and considerably less likely to be dealing with Artisans or Idealists. Australians would be methodical and careful negotiators who followed an established and set pattern (Guardian). They would be relatively efficient, and relatively creative, at least at a theoretical level (Rationalist). They would not, however, be fast and decisive decision-makers (not Artisan), and would be satisfied with relatively shallow businesslike relationships (not Idealist).

SINGAPORE AND MALAYSIA

We have chosen to consider Singapore and Malaysia together because the two countries are tightly interlinked geographically, socially, and in terms of business practices. Singapore is a small city-state only 697 square kilometers in area – approximately 3.5 times the size of Washington, D.C. It occupies several islands at the south end of the Malay Peninsula, the main part of Malaysia. Malaysia is approximately the same size as New Mexico in the United States.

During the British colonial period, ending after World War II, Singapore and Malaysia were part of the same administrative unit, and they were united as a single nation between 1957 and 1965. They also mirror each other in ethnic composition. Singapore is 76.8 percent Chinese, 13.9 percent Malay, and 7.9 percent Indian. Malaysia is 50.4 percent Malay, 23.7 percent Chinese, and 7.1 percent Indian. In terms of similarity of business practices, Abramson and Ai[20] reported that Canadian companies doing business in Singapore and Malaysia encountered no country-specific factors – differences between the two – that significantly affected their performance.

Singapore[21] is a highly developed First World free market economy. It has intentionally created a relatively bureaucracy-free, and corruption-free business environment, achieving a per capita GDP higher than most developed countries. Singapore's economy depends on export and re-export (transshipping), especially consumer electronics, information technology products, pharmaceuticals, and financial services. Singapore has in recent years attracted major investments in the pharmaceutical and medical technology sectors, and is regarded by many as Southeast Asia's financial and high-tech hub. While GDP growth fell 1 percent in 2009 with the impact of the global financial recessions, it rebounded to 14.8 percent growth in 2010 due to renewed growth of exports. In 2011 and 2012, growth slowed to 4.9 and 2.1 percent due to the second European recession in that period.

The majority of Singapore's exports in 2011 were bound for Malaysia (12.2 percent), Hong Kong (11 percent), Indonesia (10.4 percent), China (10.4%), United States (5.5 percent), and Japan (4.5 percent). The majority of Singapore's imports in 2011 came from the United States (10.8 percent), Malaysia (10.7 percent), China (10.4 percent), Japan (7.2 percent), South Korea (5.9 percent), Indonesia (5.3 percent), and Saudi Arabia (4.8 percent).

Malaysia[22] has transformed its economy, since the 1970s, from a producer of raw materials to a middle-income country with a multi-sector economy. Malaysia is currently attempting to achieve high-income status by 2020 by attracting investments in Islamic finance, high technology industries, biotechnology, and services. Nevertheless, the export of electronics, oil and gas, palm oil, and rubber remain major economic drivers of current prosperity levels. The oil and gas sector currently produces 40 percent of Malaysian government revenues so that Malaysian prosperity has hinged heavily of rising and falling energy prices. The majority of Malaysian exports in 2011 were bound for China (13.1 percent), Singapore (12.7 percent), Japan (11.5 percent), United States (8.3 percent), Thailand (5.1 percent), Hong Kong (4.5 percent), and India (4.1 percent). The majority of Malaysia's imports in 2011 came from China (13.2 percent), Singapore (12.8 percent), Japan (11.4 percent), United States (9.7 percent), Indonesia (6.1 percent), Thailand (6.0 percent), and South Korea (4.0 percent). Malaysia is widely regarded as the ideal Islamic economic state – the one other Islamic countries hope to emulate.

Global efficiency versus local responsiveness

Abramson[23] reported a study of Canadian small and medium sized enterprises (SMEs) doing business in Singapore and Malaysia. The purpose of the study was to determine whether companies created better performance enhancing buyer–seller relationships using Western marketing strategies or local practices.

The backstory here is that the argument has raged in international business circles whether Western marketing practices represented universally acceptable and effective practices that could be applied anywhere in the world (see Chapter 4). The argument was based on the idea that widely divergent national cultures were slowly converging towards a set of universally accepted business practices. The counter-argument was raised by Chen.[24] He argued that these "universal" practices were Western practices and their imposition on local conditions represented a neo-colonial attitude. And former Malaysian Prime Minister Mahathir[25] echoed these sentiments, arguing that Malaysia's Vision 2020 economic development plan required development to be in harmony with Malaysian culture. Malaysians should feel "psychologically subservient to none."[26] At the same time, the Singapore government promoted the expectation that Singaporean core cultural values should be the basis for business behavior.[27]

It was well known that the most important key success factor for doing business in Singapore and Malaysia was building effective relationships between buyers and sellers.[28] The same was true in China (see Chapter 13).[29] However, it was also well known that the basis for interpersonal relationships was different in Southeast (and East) Asia than in the West. Malay and Chinese cultures placed a great emphasis on friendship, good relations, and cooperation between business associates. There was a strong expectation that business associates would understand, tolerate, and respect each other while working out compromise or consensus solutions that satisfied both sides. Malaysians expected that their personal dignity, or "face," would be preserved in interactions characterized by honesty, generosity, sincerity, and caring. If these qualities were not evident, there would be loss of face on both sides, and no effective relationship.[30]

In Singapore, the expectation of personal financial gain was moderated by interpersonal tolerance and respect for differences. Singaporeans preferred cooperative bargaining strategies such as collaborating, compromising, and accommodating, over competitive strategies.[31] By contrast, Westerners emphasized individualism and confrontation over differences in negotiation goals. There was a continuing sense that Western trade with Singapore and Malaysia had long been retarded by North American ignorance over Southeast Asian business practices.[32]

By contrast, Leong and Tan[33] ably stated the Western view. There were two paradigms defining sets of marketing practices that had proven themselves effective in a wide variety of cultural contexts. These would again be demonstrated to be effective in the Asia Pacific as well.

One paradigm considered universal was the "4P marketing mix:"[34] (1) product (R&D development and/or product or service features); (2) price (higher or lower to communicate quality); (3) promotion (advertising and incentives); and (4) place (where it should be sold). Together, these four decisions created a value equation for a product or service that would be irresistible to targeted customers. The second paradigm was "relationship marketing" in which sellers built close relationships characterized by trust, cooperation, and constructive ways of handling disagreements with their best customers.[35]

Abramson[36] proposed to test whether the marketing mix and relationship marketing paradigms were universally applicable for producing effective performance outcomes for Canadian SMEs in Singapore and Malaysia. He added some traditional Southeast Asian marketing practices to the mix to compare their efficacy with the "universal" Western practices. These local practices included the exchange of gifts and favors between buyers and sellers,[37] and the building of networks of relationships intended to provide introductions for sellers to ever more senior and influential contacts.

The exchange of gifts and favors was considered ritual behavior, signifying commitment to the principle of mutual benefit, and giving "face" or respect back and forth. Westerners generally feel uncomfortable with this "questionable" practice and question its ethicality. Their fear is gifts may actually be bribes, illegal in the United States for example, especially when large amounts of cash are involved. Or, gifts may be given coercively in the expectation that a buyer's or seller's mind will be changed. Malaysians counter these criticisms, saying that Westerners only began to object when the Malaysian economy became an international force.[38] Singaporeans argue that gifts and favors are exchanged in politeness instead of "thank yous" which is regarded as insincere expression of appreciation.[39]

Networks of influential relationships are the Southeast Asian expression of what is called guanxi in China (see Chapter 13). In a sense, it is the practice of relationship marketing, in a *LinkedIn* fashion, with all the business associations an individual has. It differs from the Western approach to relationship marketing in that it is applied to all relationships, and not just to the best ones.

These relationships tend to be characterized by a developing sense of trust based personal friendship, competence, and long-term reliability. Relationship partners find ways

to achieve mutual benefits through cooperation, and to resolve disagreements constructively for both sides.[40] Foreign buyers who achieve these kinds of relationships experience
less environmental uncertainty about what's going on in Singapore and Malaysia and how
these changing conditions will affect their business. Their friends keep them informed. And
they achieve higher performance outcomes than foreigners without these relationships.[41]

The results of this study[42] were interesting. The best predictors of relationship quality
and effective performance outcomes were the willingness to give and receive gifts and
favors, and the development of relationship networks. It was also evident that SMEs that
had made greater local investments were also the most willing to provide gifts and favors to
their buyers. Either they had learned the best ways to operate using local practices, or were
doing their best to protect their investments.

Some Western practices were successful in developing effective relations and performance outcomes but others were not. Promotion of products, and the selection of places
where products should be sold, were significantly and positively related to relationship
quality and performance outcomes. Product development (R&D) and pricing did not
contribute significantly to either positive outcome. Repackaging products and their features,
presumably to suit local market conditions, actually resulted in weaker relationships and
lower performance outcomes.

The lesson here is that an MNE or SME that mindlessly applied "universal" marketing
practices to their business development in Singapore and/or Malaysia would be doing
themselves some good, and some harm, and wasting some of their efforts on activities
having no effect. At the same time, if they eschewed local practices, they would be depriving
their efforts of the best tactics for success.

Abramson proposed four main principles for doing business successfully in Singapore
and Malaysia:[43]

1   Use persuasion to convince local buyers of the value of products and/or services.
    Persuading means maintaining one's position while identifying sources of disagree-
    ment and addressing these potential concerns in a convincing non-confrontational
    manner before any confrontation develops.
2   Address the buyer's agenda. Find out what the buyer needs and how specific prod-
    ucts/services may satisfy these needs. Find out what the buyer's goals are and attempt
    to address them. Attempt to make the interaction satisfying for the buyer.
3   Express willingness out of politeness to repackage products/services to meet buyers'
    needs. Existing packaging seemed to be satisfactory for local buyers and product
    redevelopment seemed unnecessary.
4   Consider the possibility of opening a local representative office or a sales office in
    either Malaysia or Singapore. Companies that did so, and staffed them with local
    managers and employees, tended to be more successful. Note, however, that this
    recommendation is more expensive, and that it was less important for relationship
    quality and performance outcomes than the others.

Hamzah-Sendut, Madsen, and Thong[44] offered more general guidelines for building effective business relationships in addition to the ones above.

1   Circle the outside before penetrating to the center. Direct approaches are not normally appreciated especially when outsiders are seeking business opportunities for the first time. Westerners tend to be linear thinkers and go straight to the point once initial small talk is done. Asians employ spiral logic, making a series of discussions that triangulate their goals without necessarily stating them. Your Asian counterpart will get the drift. He/she is used to connecting the dots and will anticipate where the discussions are leading.

2   The initial contact is very important. First impressions are seldom forgotten. A letter written in English asking for a meeting is considered cold. It is better to receive a telephone call from someone seeking to introduce you. Never send a junior person to make the first contact. It may be seen as disrespectful – a loss of "face."

3   Forbearance will achieve more than directness. Be prepared to suggest "trial balloons." Be prepared to achieve nothing unless friendly alliances have been cemented. Accept failure without bitterness. Asians are more adept than Westerners at reading negative body language, interpreted as lost of "face" for the recipient.

4   Building friendship takes a long time by Western standards. Friendship is built through repeated social engagements, as well as demonstrating competence and long-term reliability. Civil servants should be handled with care to help preserve their professional neutrality.

5   Time is handled differently and you should not be surprised to be kept waiting. You should respond with politeness, flexibility, and generosity.

6   Surprises should be avoided in your dealings with others. Sudden shifts in thinking or action may be perceived as wily or tricky. Tactical maneuvers and bluffing are not considered appropriate. The mood should be conciliatory and not confrontational. From the Asian side, the question is whether a marriage of interests will be appropriate.

7   Meeting agendas should not be rigidly fixed. There should be no artificial boundaries to the development of trust.

8   When doing business with Muslims (Singapore = 14.9 percent; Malaysia = 60.4 percent), remember that Islam is more conservative about the separation of genders and appropriate interactions with females.

9   Negotiations should not be considered as competitive zero-sum engagements. You should not strive to win at the expense of your friend. The objective is agreement. Both sides must sincerely believe they will benefit.

Local Singaporean and Malaysian values

The organizational culture of an MNE could be considered a KSF for successfully doing business in Singapore and Malaysia. Both national cultures emphasize the importance of cooperative and harmonious relationship building. All local business personnel are engaged in building networks of relationships so the way a company is run internally quickly becomes public knowledge. One cannot present a public face to one's customers that is different from one's true attitudes and values as expressed in one's management of internal company affairs. Hamzah-Sendut, Madsen, and Thong[45] offered their suggestions about what an MNEs or SMEs organizational culture should look like in order to be a KSF:

1   *Basic norms and values for the company.* Honesty, loyalty, work ethic, positive and mutual respect.
2   *Specific norms and values at managerial and supervisory levels.* Staff are the company's most valuable asset. Practice delegation, coaching, assessment, appreciation, innovation.
3   *Specific norms and values at the staff level.* Dedication, participation, cooperation, and development.
4   *Specific norms and values towards customers.* Customers are one's *Bosses*. All personnel must strive all the time for the highest possible levels of quality and service.
5   *Basic company philosophy.* Fair but Firm. The attitude must be right.
6   *Company norms and values.* Aimed at creating satisfied customers – all of them – as well as efficient, effective, reliable and contented staff.
7   The better you understand the effective implementation of the norms and values, the more profitable the company will be.
8   Profit is a subordinate goal to the norms, values, and basic philosophy. These must include business principles safeguarding integrity.

THAILAND

Thailand[46] is characterized by a free market economy, pro-investment policies, strong export industries, and a well-developed economic infrastructure. It has achieved steady economic growth largely due to a mix of industrial and agricultural exports, including electronics, agricultural commodities, and processed foods. Thailand has an extraordinarily low unemployment rate – less than 1 percent – resulting in an upward pressure on wages, and the importation of approximately 2.5 million migrant workers. Thai economic policy has been to attempt to stimulate domestic consumption, resulting in a nation-wide minimum wage, and attempts to reform the tax code to reduce taxes for the middle class.

Thailand suffered a double digit drop in GDP in the 2008 global recession. In 2009, GDP dropped an additional 2.3 percent. In 2010, the recovery was on and the economy expanded at 7.8 percent. Flooding in industrial areas in 2011 brought growth down in 2011 to only 0.1 percent, but in 2012 GDP is estimated to have grown a further 5.6 percent.

The majority of Thailand's exports go to China (12.0 percent), Japan (10.5 percent), the United States (9.6 percent), Hong Kong (7.2 percent), Malaysia (5.4 percent), Singapore

(5.0 percent), and Indonesia (4.4 percent). Principal exports include, in order, textiles and shoes, fishery products, rice, rubber, jewelry, automobiles, computers, and electrical appliances. The majority of Thai imports are sourced from Japan (18.4 percent), China (13.4 percent), U.A.E. (6.3 percent), United States (5.9 percent), Malaysia (5.4 percent), and South Korea (4.0 percent). These include, in order, capital goods, intermediary products and raw materials, consumer goods, and fuel.

Thailand's population of approximately 67 million is 75 percent Thai, and 14 percent Chinese by ethnicity. It is 94.6 percent Buddhist, and 4.6 percent Muslim. Thai is the principal language though English is the second language of the economic and social elite.

Thai cultural values

There have been relatively few studies of business practices in Thailand and their underlying values. There is one major discrepancy, viewed through Western eyes. Thais are reported to place a high value on social harmony, and to behave in friendly, cooperative, and even passive ways, and yet to have a strong undercurrent of individualism that may result in revenge-seeking behavior under certain circumstances.[47]

Pornpitakpan[48] observed the same. Thais placed a high value on maintaining harmonious interpersonal relationships, emphasized saving "face," and preferred working interdependently. There was, however, a "dark side." Thais could behave in rough, rude, competitive, and uncooperative ways especially with those who were not members of their relationship networks or in-groups. These negative behaviors could be directed at foreigners, but also on the streets of Bangkok among Thais themselves. Driving practices are aggressive with insults and curses thrown from car to car. People push ahead of others who are waiting in line-ups, or people refuse to line-up at all, mobbing forward seeking to get ahead of the others.

Hofstede's[49] cross-national work values research supported the view that Thais were more orderly, cooperative, and relationship oriented than Americans. The Thais were higher in *power distance*, suggesting a greater willingness to accept unequal power distribution in organizations. They were higher in *uncertainty avoidance* suggesting they felt less comfortable in ambiguous situations and would behave in ways to increase feelings of certainty. Thais were considerably higher on *collectivism* (versus individualism) meaning they preferred to belong in their reference groups where they exchanged loyalty for care. Thais were also much higher on *femininity* (versus masculinity) suggesting greater caring for others; putting quality of life ahead of success, income, and status. Thais were also much higher on *long-term orientation*[50] indicating a higher value placed on the Confucian virtues of persistence and perseverance.

Taken together, these findings suggested that Thais would be more relationship-oriented, and more accepting of structured and orderly relationships, than Americans. Pornpitakan[51] supported the view that Thais were more relationship oriented than Americans. Americans who adapted to Thai ways, building personal relationships ahead of business ones, and accepting social invitations, were more attractive to Thais.

Building buyer–seller relationships

Abramson[52] conducted a study comparing American and Thai preferences for building effective buyer–seller relationships based on the two marketing paradigms of *relationship marketing*, and the *4P Marketing Mix* plus after-sale service. The American sellers believed that they could build effective relationships using relationship marketing by: (1) building trust and satisfaction; (2) engaging in social activities; (3) avoiding negative conflicts; (4) developing a sense of shared goals; and (5) developing a personal relationship.

The American sellers valued all these activities significantly more than the Thai buyers. By contrast, the Thai buyers preferred significantly more than the American sellers to build a personal relationship *in advance* of any business activities. The mistake the Americans seemed to be making was engaging in these relationship-building activities as part of their approach to business with the Thais. In Thailand, the personal relationship did not develop in conjunction with the business relationship.

The study[53] also measured whether marketing mix activities contributed to building better American–Thai business relationships. Here, there were some interesting differences:

1   The Thais believed that *product* related activities were the most important activity in the value equation for building an effective buyer–seller relationship. The Thais expected that products should be modified to meet customer needs. It was most appropriate to offer either to redesign products, or to add or subtract product features to satisfy customers. By contrast, the Americans were considerably less willing to think this was important to the relationship.

2   The Americans and the Thais agreed that *pre-sale service* in the form of demonstrations and product training was critical to the value equation. This was the most important variable for the Americans, and second most important for the Thais.

3   The Americans believed that *promotion*al and advertising activities were very important for building effective sales levels. The Thais were significantly less likely to think so.

4   Both the Americans and the Thais agreed that after-sale service, and pricing, were important to relationship building and sales. Service included better-than-usual delivery, liberal after-sale service, and personal selling contact. Pricing included special discounts, easy credit, lower prices for special customers, and even selling below cost to build initial market share.

These findings suggested that the Thais were moved to develop relationships because of values related to obtaining suitable products, pre-sale service, after-sale service, and pricing advantages. American mistakes included too great an emphasis on promotional activities, and too little emphasis on adapting their products for special Thai needs.

Negotiating with Thais

Abramson and Keating[54] conducted a study intended to discuss the comparative decision-making strengths and weaknesses of America, Chinese, and Thai managers. The purpose was to test Lawrence and Dyer's[55] theory that management teams having a greater useful diversity of information processing would have an advantage problem-solving and decision-making in complex international business environments (see Chapter 4). It was hypothesized that because the United States and China were the greatest and most successful trading nations, their management teams would have access to greater cognitive information processing capability. By contrast, Thailand had not been that successful an international trading country. It had twice the population of Canada (67 vs. 30 million), and had been independent more than 650 years versus Canada's less than 150. However, its international export trade was less than half that of Canada (US$229 billion vs. US$463 billion, in 2012). It was predicted its management would have access to less cognitive diversity, resulting in having less relevant information available for decision-making.

The study[56] used the same Keirsey personality temperament variables described in the Australia section of this chapter: (1) *Guardians* (called Logistical); (2) *Rationalists* (called Strategic); (3) *Artisans* (called Tactical); and (4) *Idealists* (called Diplomatic). Over 69 percent of the Thai managers were Guardians. Artisans (13.6 percent), Rationalists (11.4 percent), and Idealists (9.1 percent) were all very small minorities. Imagine a Thai negotiating team of ten members. The team would include seven Guardians, and possibly only one each of the other three information-processing preferences. Discussions would be dominated by Guardian perceptions and judgments. In the event of a vote, a two-thirds majority was always possible in the direction of Guardian preferences. Therefore, Thai negotiation preferences were heavily predisposed in one direction – Guardian.

This study defined Guardians (Logistical) in the following way:

■ *Task oriented and bureaucratic*: authority centered; values the useful; seeks order; organized; dependable and conservative; seeks stability and security; prefers to follow precedents and traditional solutions; dislikes ambiguity.

By contrast, the American managers were 42.3 percent Rationalists (Strategic), and 36.6 percent Guardians (Logistical), as well as having small minorities of Artisans (16.9 percent) and Idealists (4.2 percent). Imagine an American negotiating team of ten members. It could include four Rationalists, three or four Guardians, one or two Artisans, and zero or one Idealist. This team would understand the Guardian perceptions of the Thai team, but have problem-solving access to the perceptions of the Rationalists, and possibly the Artisans. A majority decision could not be achieved except by combining two of the information-processing preferences. Three majority combinations were possible: (1) Rationalists + Guardians; (2) Rationalists + Artisans; and (3) Guardians + Artisans. This study defined Rationalists (Strategist) in the following way:

■ *Task oriented and efficient*: knowledge centered; values the conceptual; seeks competence; trusts logic and reason; subordinates the human element to organizational efficiency; eliminates unnecessary systems and bureaucracy; logical and ingenious.

While the American negotiators would have access to considerably more information than the Thais, and were likely to find more ingenious alternatives and solutions, they could get in trouble. The Thais might not have access to Rationalist information either because there was no Rationalist on their team, or because that minority viewpoint had been discarded as unreliable. American negotiators that relied on Rationalist solutions (combining viewpoints with the Artisan minority instead of the Guardian minority) could produce bargaining stances the Thais found unacceptable or even inexplicable.

VIETNAM

Vietnam[57] has been transitioning from a centrally planned economy to a free-market one since 1986. The Vietnamese government has affirmed its commitment to economic modernization, joining the World Trade Organization (WTO) in 2007. This has facilitated the development of more competitive and export-driven industries. Vietnam became a negotiating partner in the Trans-Pacific Partnership trade agreement in 2010. Between 2000 and 2010, agriculture as a share of national GDP has shrunk from 25 percent to 22 percent. Industry's share has increased from 36 percent to 41 percent. State-owned enterprises still account for 40 percent of GDP.

The global recession of 2008–2009 hurt Vietnam's export economy. However, between 2009 and 2011, GDP grew by an average 7 percent per annum. In 2012, GDP grew by an impressive 12 percent and government policies brought imports roughly in line with imports (see Exhibit 12.3). Foreign direct investment inflows, however, declined in 2012 by 4.5 percent to US$10.5 billion. Vietnam currently has issues with high inflation (9.2 percent in 2012) and public debt load (48.2 percent of GDP in 2012).

The biggest recipients of Vietnam's exports go to the United States (18.0 percent), China (11 percent), Japan (11 percent), and Germany (3.8 percent). These exports include, in order of value, clothes, shoes, marine products, crude oil, electronics, wooden products, rice, and machinery. The biggest suppliers of Vietnamese imports are China (22 percent), South Korea (13.2 percent), Japan (10.4 percent), Taiwan (8.6 percent), Thailand (6.4 percent), and Singapore (6.4 percent). These imports include, in order of value, machinery, petroleum products, steel products, raw materials for the clothing and shoe industries, electronics, plastics, and automobiles.

Vietnam is 85.7 percent Kinh, or Viet, in ethnic origin. Its official language is Vietnamese, but English is becoming increasingly popular as a second language. Only 9.3 percent of the population is Buddhist, and another 6.7 percent Catholic. No religion is the preference of 80.8 percent.

Socio-political context

Vietnam has an interesting history often connected with that of Western Europe and the United States during the twentieth century. While Europeans first arrived in 166 AD, it was beginning in 1516 that European influence became pronounced with the arrival of the Portuguese, and in 1630, Spanish missionaries. France made Indochina (Vietnam, Cambodia, and Laos) its colony in 1867. Its rule lasted until the Japanese arrived at the beginning of World War II.

After the war, France reasserted its control over South Vietnam. China chose a new emperor for the northern Vietnam, Boa Dai, who stepped down in favor of Ho Chi Minh, the founder of Vietnam's Communist Party. Ho was responsible for initiating wars that led to the 1975 reunification of Vietnam by defeating first France, and later the United States, supporters of an independent South Vietnam.

Since then, Vietnam has focused on internal matters. In 1986, Nguyen Van Linh, Communist Party General Secretary, introduced the concept of *doi moi*, or renovation. This term includes private enterprise and the approval of 100 percent foreign ownership of firms and joint ventures, openness to overseas Vietnamese, an interest in tourism, and greater individual freedoms. It took three years, however, for the South to start implementing these reforms, along with the withdrawal of Vietnamese troops from Cambodia in 1989.

Since then, the government has been fully committed to the idea of *doi moi*, as is evidenced by new investors from Japan, Taiwan, Hong Kong, and Australia. These countries already know they won't have to wait long for the emerging, thriving Vietnamese economy. Australia has targeted Vietnam as its "Asian Business Success Program," while billboards with ads for Minolta and Hitachi dominate intersections in Hanoi and Ho Chi Minh City. For the rest of the non-Asian countries who didn't jump at the early opportunities, competition will be stiffer now.

It was also the 1989 peace treaty with Cambodia that opened up diplomatic talks with the United States and the countries of Western Europe. In fact, the treaty was the turning point for Vietnam. Within months, diplomatic ties had been fully reestablished with China and the above-mentioned countries. Washington opened a diplomatic office in Hanoi in 1991 to coordinate the search for American MIAs (soldiers missing in action).

After cooperation from the Vietnamese in this search, the United States lifted some economic sanctions in 1992 and 1993. President Clinton then lifted the trade and invest-ment embargo in February 1994, and since then the United States has established itself as a significant investor in Vietnam. The Vietnamese people heralded the removal of the trade embargo as the end of the "American War," rejoicing in total independence from foreign invaders for the first time in centuries.

The year 2000 was significant for Vietnam, as it marked 55 years of independence and 25 years since the end of the Vietnam War. The main changes now are more openness than before; founding of the first stock exchange center in Ho Chi Minh City; membership in the World Trade Organization; and reduction of the poverty level to below 10 percent.

Under the administration of technocrats, a top priority of Vietnam is to fix the corruption that has been widespread in government. Inventory in coal, cement, steel, and paper has increased due to foreign competition. Near the end of 2001, the U.S.–Vietnam Bilateral Trade Agreement was launched in an effort to increase Vietnam's exports.

As the world's 13th largest country by population, the government has shown a strong interest in becoming a market economy and opening itself to outsiders. Furthermore, with the reestablishment of diplomatic relations with the United States and other major economic players, business opportunities have increased dramatically over the past years. Those companies who take advantage of conducting business in Vietnam now will be rewarded with a high-growth market of consumers. This economic transformation is described in Exhibit 12.8.

EXHIBIT 12.8 TRANSFORMING VIETNAM

Today, Vietnamese welcome the tourist dollar, even for excursions to their wartime Cu Chi tunnels. Such excursions demonstrate their ingenuity, adaptability, perseverance, and determination to resist foreign invaders down through the centuries.

The period since the 1990s has transformed Vietnam by rapid and relatively equitable development in a free-enterprise environment. You can see this in vibrant Ho Chi Minh City (formerly Saigon), especially downtown at the smart Dong Khoi Street where young, prosperous Vietnamese shop. In what was a poor country, the quality of life has dramatically improved despite choking traffic and constant construction. With the switch from a command economy, gradual financial liberalization and market reforms have been fostering rapid poverty-reducing growth.

The country is still handicapped by legislative and bureaucratic processes, especially with regard to the justice system, and countering Communist Party corruption. Other problems to be confronted are rising inflation, a slumping stock market, need for greater trade, and political liberalization, as well as improvement of corporate governance.

A positive aspect of Vietnamese culture is its flexibility to seek better role models which are then melded into something uniquely Vietnamese. Vietnam is active in the Asia-Pacific Summit, World Trade Organization, and ASEAN, all of which provide insights for social and economic change. This is a syncretistic society with increasing entrepreneurship and booming business. Further, foreign MNEs have been permitted to undertake a huge range of projects throughout the land. Refugees, who left in the 1970s as boat people, are either returning or sending back funds for their families and/or investments.

Nothing reveals Vietnam's remarkable turnaround more than the agricultural sector. The countryside with 70 percent of the population now provides 21 percent of exports. But climate change could imperil this progress in agriculture.

The Communist Party, with 3.7 million members, has a congress policy "to be friends with all the people." And this has contributed to a rise in tourism, along with a lessening of

EXHIBIT 12.8

restrictions against religious groups and ethnic minorities. With the selling of public assets to private enterprise, the state has become less important as employer and provider, and membership in the Party matters less. As Vietnam continues to open its economy to business and strives to meet the United Nations Millennium Development goals in poverty reduction, its youthful population is filled with optimism about its future.

Source: Adapted from Collins, P. "Half-Way from Rags to Riches: A Special Report on Vietnam," *The Economist*, April 25, 2008 (www.economist.com/specialreport/).

Great social and economic change is now taking place in Vietnam, and with it the struggle to get ahead. People in the urban areas have received improved basic services, and a more open political and cultural environment. However, people in the rural areas, which constitute 70 percent of the Vietnamese population, have not been as fortunate. There has been a dearth of cultural opportunities in rural areas, lack of electricity and other basic services, and neglect of the poor. Party officials still take advantage of the peasants, who do not hold much weight in voting matters. For Vietnam to obtain prosperity, the inequalities that exist between urban and rural citizens must disappear.

Customs and courtesies

In Vietnam, people shake hands when greeting and saying goodbye. Also common is the use of both hands, which indicates respect. A slight bow of the head also shows respect. Elderly people in rural areas may also nod their head upon greeting someone, and women are more inclined to bow their head than to shake hands.

Here, names begin with the family name followed by the given name. For example, in the name Nguyen Van Duc, Nguyen is the family name and Van Duc is the given name. Although they address each other by given name, the Vietnamese add titles which show their relationship to the other person. These titles tend to be used more personally, in one's family, than professionally. Among coworkers, the younger of the two might call the other *ahn*, or older brother. To say hello to someone using the given name and title, they would say "Xin chao," or hello. However, "Xin chao" could have one of six other meanings, since Vietnamese is a tonal language. Therefore, it is important to stress the proper syllable. The Vietnamese appreciate international visitors who can properly say "Xin chao." In business settings, business cards may be exchanged in greetings, and should be in both Vietnamese and English.

The following gestures should be noted when in the company of the Vietnamese:

- Do not touch anyone's head, as the head is considered the spiritual center of a person.
- Do not use your index finger to call someone over; it is considered rude.

- When calling someone, wave all four fingers with the palm down.
- Men and women do not show affection in public.
- Members of the same sex may hold hands in public. This is normal.
- Vietnamese use both hands to give an object to another person.

The Vietnamese place a great deal of importance on visiting people. Therefore, one should not just "drop by" someone's house without first being invited. They also show a strong sense of hospitality and prepare well in advance of the guest's arrival. Gifts for the hostess are not required but greatly appreciated. A small gift for the children or elderly parent is also much appreciated. Acceptable gifts include flowers, tea, or incense.

The traditional Vietnamese family is an extended one, including parents, unmarried children, and married sons with their families. The extended family still predominates in rural regions; however, there is a trend toward single-family homes in urban locations. Families maintain strong ties with each other and provide financial and emotional support as needed.

Doing business in Vietnam[58]

Vietnam is a Confucian country. Confucian philosophy emphasizes the importance of hierarchy, relationships, responsibility, and obligation. This philosophy is a vital element in Vietnamese society. It is applied in business culture to maintain interpersonal harmony, and the collective good.

The idea of saving "face" – preserving the dignity of the other – is important. The Vietnamese will do anything to prevent loss of face including avoiding confrontation, or telling others what they seem to want to hear. A foreigner will lose face by criticizing someone in public, or by not fulfilling promises.

Vietnam is a collectivist society in which one is expected to place the needs of the group ahead of those of the individual. Family and community concerns take precedence over those of business or individuals. Ties between families and communities will have a significant effect on individual behavior.

WORKING PRACTICES IN VIETNAM

Business hours are generally between 8 a.m. and 5 p.m., Monday through Friday, with an hour off for lunch. Vietnamese prefer to schedule all meetings as much as several weeks in advance to facilitate preparation. You will be expected to arrive on time and to phone ahead if running late. Business attire tends to be professional and conservative.

STRUCTURE OF VIETNAMESE COMPANIES

Business organizations tend to be hierarchical following the Confucian model. Ideas and decisions are generated at senior levels and often, the oldest manager has the most influence.

Employees are expected to be loyal to the hierarchy, but in return, the boss is expected to guard the welfare of the employees and is responsible for their behavior.

Status is important. Supervisors and coworkers should be treated with respect. Titles are important. Status is earned through education and age. It is very important to your acceptance and success to show respect to senior individuals, based on their education, position, and age. At a meeting, the eldest participant arrives first. Status is also based on gender though this is becoming less pronounced. Most Vietnamese women work in assistant or clerical roles. However, Vietnamese men will treat foreign women in senior roles as equals.

WORKING RELATIONSHIPS

Business relationships are formal and take time to develop. Vietnamese businesspeople prefer to get to know foreign counterparts before serious business talk can begin. You may be treated with suspicion if you try to get right down to business, so several meetings may be required just getting acquainted. It is important to demonstrate competence and reliability at all times.

International business is usually conducted in English though the Vietnamese appreciate efforts to speak some Vietnamese. It is advisable to have all documents translated into Vietnamese. Face issues may inhibit your Vietnamese counterparts from admitting not understanding. Therefore, it is also useful to have your own translator. French language is an asset since English will not be understood often in rural areas.

Negotiations may be lengthy and time-consuming. The Vietnamese will want to examine all details. They will have to consult within their group, and the entire process will be reviewed at senior levels. The Vietnamese are known for bureaucratic procedures, also slowing down the process. Don't be surprised in actual negotiations if there are long periods of silence. The Vietnamese may think and consider before responding. They may also remain silent in the face of a potential disagreement in order to save their face, and yours. Maintain a soft voice when speaking. Loud voices and extensive hand gestures are considered rude and make Vietnamese uncomfortable. Always accept any tea or food offered by your negotiation partners since not doing so is considered rude.

Introductions are formal. It is helpful to be introduced by a mutual acquaintance, suggesting the value of building relationship networks. Gift-giving is a common practice. Gifts need not be expensive – they simply show appreciation. Fruit and flowers are common gifts, to be wrapped in colorful paper.

CONCLUSIONS

South and Southeast Asia are demonstration models of the complexity and multidimensional aspects of culture. Although we have provided cultural specifics on only a few countries, it is enough, perhaps, to convince global managers of the important distinctions that exist. South and Southeast Asians are very different culturally from Westerners. These differences include language, religion, family, and social attitudes, that influence business practice, and building effective relationships.

The new market opportunities and diversity in the Pacific Basin alone should motivate us to seek further cultural information, whether we are dealing with Australians who are seemingly Western in outlook, or with Vietnamese who are so obviously different. South and Southeast Asian economies will become more and more important players in the global economy as the twenty-first century progresses.

The social situation in Asia is normally peaceful, but also very dynamic, often volatile. Traditional societies are in transition to a technological and knowledge culture. In these ancient lands and cultures, peaceful exchange and trade have always been the way to promote well-being, commerce, and prosperity. International trade is already transforming Asian societies, such as in the emerging superpowers of China and India.

The area also benefits from the global cooperation of nations to curb negative behaviors endangering the world community. The nations have a history of working together to cope with natural disasters, limit drug trafficking, as well as contain infectious disease. Joint efforts are being made to address the unequal distribution of wealth and opportunity for the planet's inhabitants! Two examples of synergistic relationships in this region are South Asian Free Trade Alliance and the Asian Development Bank. Their leaders are in agreement that by 2020, the "new Asia," as well as their own organizations, will need radically different strategies with a global focus.

MIND STRETCHING

1   What seemingly is involved as traditional Asian societies transition into modern ones (e.g., India, Malaysia, Thailand, Vietnam)?
2   What are the commonalities in building effective business relationships in India, Singapore/Malaysia, Thailand, and Vietnam? What are the differences?
3   What cross-border commonalities have you observed in this study of Asian cultures?
4   Why is it important for you to increase your knowledge and skill in Asian cultures, languages, negotiation styles, and business practices?
5   With the expansion of global terrorism and insurgencies in Asia, what cautions should you observe in travel to the region?

NOTES

1   Confucius. *The Analects*. New York: Alfred A. Knopf, 2000.
2   http/en.wikipedia.org/Asian_Century/.

3   "Asia 2050: Realizing the Asian Century," Asian Development Bank. Adb.org. March 26, 2012. Retrieved February 13, 2013.

4   "US Shale Oil Supply Shock Shifts Global Power Balance," *BBC News*, http://www.bbc.co.uk/news/business–22524597.

5   Abramson, N. R. and Ai, J. X. "Practicing Relationship Marketing in Southeast Asia: Reducing Uncertainty and Improving Performance," *Management International Review*, Vol. 38, Special issue 1, 1999, pp. 113–143.

6   Hume, T. "The Secrets of Doing Business in India," *CNN: International Edition*, February 3, 2012, http://edition.cnn.com/2012/02/03/business/. Retrieved February 9, 2013.

7   Panagariya, A. *India: The Emerging Giant*. Oxford: Oxford University Press, 2010.

8   CIA. *The World Factbook*, 2013, www.cia.gov/library/publications/the-world-factbook/geos/as.html.

9   Ibid.

10 India.5thpillar.org/ZRN.

11 Wibbeke, E. S. *Global Business Leadership*. Burlington, MA: Elsevier/Butterworth-Heinemann, 2009, pp. 55–71. See also Moran, R. T. and Youngdahl, W. E. *Leading Global Projects: For Professional and Accidental Project Leaders*. Burlington, MA: Elsevier/Butterworth-Heinemann, 2008.

12 This paragraph is derived in part from *The Economist*, "Special Report India," 12 page insert, September 29, 2012, p. 10.

13 Hume, T. "The Secrets of Doing Business in India," *CNN: International Edition*, February 3, 2012, http://edition.cnn.com/2012/02/03/business/. Retrieved February 9, 2013.

14 Ibid.

15 Hofstede, G. *Culture's Consequences: International Differences in Work-Related Values*. Beverley Hills, CA: Sage, 1984. See Hofstede, G. *Uncommon Sense about Organizations: Cases, Studies, and Field Observations*. Thousand Oaks, CA: Sage, 1994. See also "Building Successful Business Relationships: India," *WorldSpeaking: A Berlitz Company,* 2011, http://news.telelangue.com/en/2011/09/etiquette-india. Retrieved February 9, 2013.

16 CIA. *The World Factbook*, 2013, www.cia.gov/library/publications/the-world-factbook/geos/as.html.

17 Keating, R. J. and Abramson, N. R. "A New Framework in the Quest for Cultural Understanding Using Australia, Thailand, and Japan as an Example," *International Journal of Business Studies*, Vol. 17, No. 1, 2009, pp. 45–59.

18 Keirsey, D. *Please Understand Me II: Temperament, Character, Intelligence*. Del Mar, CA: Prometheus Nemesis, 1998.

19 Derrida, J. *The Other Heading: Reflections on Today's Europe*. Bloomington, IN: Indiana University, 1992. Derrida argued that diverse viewpoints would only be included in decision-making if they represented a democratic majority, or were a plurality sufficient in size to combine with others into a democratic majority. While the Artisan temperament was sufficiently large to combine with the Guardians to form a majority, these two temperaments were opposites. Guardians voluntarily bound themselves with rules and procedures while Artisans sought freedom of action and struggled against artificial bindings.

20 Abramson and Ai, "Practicing Relationship Marketing."

21 CIA. *The World Factbook*, 2013, www.cia.gov/library/publications/the-world-factbook/geos/as.html.

22 Ibid.

23 Abramson, N. R. "Building Business Relationships Using Western Marketing Practices in East Asia," in M. A. Abdullah and M. I. B. Baker (eds), *Small and Medium Enterprises in Asian Pacific Countries*. Huntington, NJ: Nova Science Publishers, 2000, pp. 3–27.

24 Chen, K.- H. "Introduction: The Decolonization Question," in K.- H. Chen (ed.), *Trajectories: Inter-Asia Cultural Studies*. London: Routledge, 1995, pp. 1–56.

25 Mahathir, M. *A New Deal for Asia*. Selanger Darul Ehsan, Malaysia: Pelanduk Publications, 1999.

26 Ibid, p. 42.

27 Chi-Ching, E. Y. "Socio-Cultural Context of Perceptions and Approaches to Conflict: The Case of Singapore," in H. Leong and D. Tjosvold (eds), *Conflict Management in the Asia Pacific: Assumptions and Approaches in Diverse Cultures*. Singapore: John Wiley, 1998, pp. 123–145.

28 Hamzah-Sendut, Madsen, J. and Thong, G. *Managing in a Plural Society*. Singapore: Longman, 1990.

29 Abramson, N. R. and Ai, J. X. "Canadian Companies Doing Business in China: Key Success Factors," *Management International Review*, Vol. 39, No. 1, 1999, pp. 7–35.

30 Mansor, N. "Managing Conflict in Malaysia: Cultural and Economic Influences," in H. Leong and D. Tjosvold (eds), *Conflict Management in the Asia Pacific: Assumptions and Approaches in Diverse Cultures*. Singapore: John Wiley, 1998, pp. 49–57.

31 Chi-Ching, "Soclio-Cultural Context."

32 Gibney, F. "Hot Economies and Changing Politics," *International Business*, Vol. 7, No. 9, 1994, pp. 66–70.

33 Leong, S. M. and Tang, C. T. "Marketing in the Year 2000: An International Perspective," in S. M. Leong, S. H. Ang, and C. T. Tan (eds), *Marketing Insights for the Asia Pacific*. Singapore: Asia Pacific Marketing Association and Heinemann, 1998, pp. 33–54.

34 Waterschoot, W. van, and Bulte, C. van den. "The 4P Classification of the Marketing Mix Revisited," *Journal of Marketing*, Vol. 56, No. 10, 1992, pp. 83–93.

35 Kotler, P., Cunningham, P. H. and Turner, R. E. *Marketing Management: Analysis, Planning and Control*, 10th edn. Toronto, ON: Pearson Education Canada, 2000.

36 Abramson, "Building Business Relationships."

37 Hamzah-Sendut, Madsen, and Thong, *Managing in a Plural Society*.

38 Mahathir, *A New Deal for Asia*.

39 De Mente, B. *Chinese Etiquette and Ethics in Vusiness*. Lincoln, NE: NTC Business Books, 1990.

40 Abramson and Ai, "Practicing Relationship Marketing."

41 Ibid.

42 Abramson, N. R. "Building Business Relationships Using Western Marketing Practices in East Asia," in M. A. Abdullah and I. S. B. Mohd (eds), *Small and Medium Enterprises in Asian Pacific Countries: Volume II, Linkages and Policy Support*. Huntingdon, NY: NOVA Science Publishers, 2000, pp. 3–27.

43 Ibid., pp. 20–21.

44 Hamzah-Sendut, Madsen, and Thong, *Managing in a Plural Society*, pp. 152–155.

45 Ibid., pp. 116–117.

46 CIA. *The World Factbook*, 2013, www.cia.gov/library/publications/the-world-factbook/geos/as.html.

47 Roongrengsuke, S. and Chansuthus, D. "Conflict Management in Thailand," in S. M. Leong, S. H. Ang, and C. T. Tan (eds), *Marketing Insights for the Asia Pacific*. Singapore: Asia Pacific Marketing Association and Heinemann, 1998, pp. 167–221.

48 Pornpitakpan, C. "Trade in Thailand: A Three-Way Cultural Comparison," *Business Horizons*, March/April 2000, pp. 61–70.

49 Hofstede, *Culture's Consequences*.

50 Hofstede, G. *Cultures and Organizations: Software for the Mind*. Kindle Edition: McGraw-Hill, 2010.

51 Pornpitakpan, C. "The Effects of Cultural Adaptation on Business Relationships: Americans Selling to Japanese and Thais," *Journal of International Business Studies*, Vol. 30, No. 2, 1999, pp. 317–338.

52 Abramson, N. R. "A Comparative Analysis of Thai and American Marketing Behaviors: Distinguishing Between the Effects of Culture and Personality," *Journal of Current Research in Global Business*, Vol. 6, No. 10, 2004, pp. 43–54.

53 Ibid.

54 Abramson, N. R. and Keating, R. J. "Knowledge Management Through the Lens of the Cognitive Theory of Strategy: American, Chinese, and Thai Decision-Making Capabilities," *Journal of Global Business*, Vol. 17, No. 34, 2006, pp. 27–42.

55 Lawrence, P. R. and Dyer, D. *Renewing American Industry*. New York: Macmillan USA, 1984.

56 Ibid.
57 CIA. *The World Factbook*, 2013, www.cia.gov/library/publications/the-world-factbook/geos/as.html.
58 Adapted from Communicaid, "Doing Business in Vietnam: Vietnamese Social and Business Culture," www.communicaid/access/pdf/library/doing-business-in/.

ADDITIONAL FEATURES

Please visit the companion website at: www.routledge.com/cw/Moran where you will find additional case studies, study aides, and instructor resources.

13 DOING BUSINESS WITH EAST ASIANS
China, Japan, and South Korea

Chinese military strategists learned that the highest principle of all was flexibility. . . . Good strategists, like water on rock, yield to the terrain in order to wear away the most unyielding of obstacles. They don't simply confine themselves to stratagems that ostensibly fit their circumstances, rather they mix and match according to actual conditions. . . . In short, the ultimate rule for applying these stratagems is to follow no rule.

Gao Yuan[1]

The cognitive mind conceives constants in the flux of phenomena and flow of events, but in the context of combat, where instantaneous adaptation to the unexpected is essential, this "freeze-frame" function of cognition, otherwise necessary for ordinary life, becomes a fatal handicap. As a Zen saying describes it, "As soon as you call it thus and so, it has already changed." Therefore the moment-to-moment presence of mind produced by Zen training is valued for overcoming . . . entanglement in conceptualization.

Zen Master Takuan[2]

This chapter is concerned with three of the most successful economic powers and trading nations in the world — China, Japan, and South Korea. The twenty-first century has been called "The Century of the Pacific," led by China.[3] The People's Republic of China (China) has risen from Third World status in 1979 to become the second-largest world economy behind only the United States. At current growth rates, the Chinese economy will surpass the American in size between 2016[4] and 2020.[5] The Japanese economy was the world's second largest for decades until it was surpassed by China in 2010,[6] and it remains comfortably the world's third-largest. After decades of stagflation following the collapse of the Japanese economic boom in the early 1990s, and recent years of deflation, the Japanese government embarked in 2013 on policies intended to devalue the yen and improve global trade competitiveness. South Korea's economy would be considered of impressive size if Korea was part of the European Union rather than positioned between China and Japan. South Korea's economy, 15th largest in the world, is three-quarters as large as Spain, and 44 percent bigger than Turkey's. All three nations are important world trading nations. Exhibit 13.1 (including the United States for comparison purposes) shows that Korea's importance as an exporter and importer is even larger than would be assumed by the size of its economy.

As United States' influence diminishes somewhat in Asia, Europe is playing a larger role there, particularly because the EU represents a large market for imports. Thus, Asia-Euro cultural, trade, business, and scholarly exchange have increased. For example, in the early 2000s, China began to emphasize stronger trade relations with the EU to express its dissatisfaction with U.S. criticisms of human rights issues in China. China has also built significant economic and political influence in Africa, seeking

EXHIBIT 13.1 WORLD TRADE COMPARISONS, 2011–2012

	United States	China	Japan	South Korea
Exports, 2012 (billion)	US$1,612	US$2,050	US$793	US$553
Exporter rank	#2	#1	#4	#7
Imports, 2011 (billion)	US$2,313	US$1,743	US$795	US$525
Importer rank	#1	#2	#4	#8
Total trade (billion)	US$3.926	US$3,793	US$1,588	US$1,078

Source: Export data from CIA, *The World Factbook* (http://en.wikipedia.org/wiki/list_of_countries_by_exports). Import data from World Trade Organization (http://en.wikipedia.org/wiki/list_of_countries_by_imports).

greater access to natural resources and the ability to grow food crops for export back to China. Strong relationships have been developed in Myanmar with the goal of building the terminus of an oil pipeline to China, bypassing the threat of the Indian navy on oil supplies sourced from the Middle East. Military tensions abound between China and India, in part due to territorial border disputes, and in part because both countries rely on oil supply lines from the Middle East. Both are building larger armed forces intended to protect themselves from each other.

These three countries have both great cultural similarities, and significant differences that sharply divide them. Both Japanese and Korean cultures have been significantly influenced by the diffusion of Chinese culture. Japanese history recognizes the profound influence of Chinese cultural forms commencing in the eighth century AD.[7] Even today, Japanese students learn between four and five thousand Chinese characters used in Japanese writing in addition to their own kanji writing. Archaeology has established that Korean forms of fine arts — dance, painting, crafts, and ceramics — were strongly influenced by Chinese forms.

A critical factor distinguishing Asian cultures from that of other peoples is their ancient philosophies and religions. For example, Buddhism, developed originally in India some 2,500 years ago, is still a major influence in the region. Confucianism, a code of conduct developed by its Chinese founder in 551 BC, impacts many East Asian cultures as an ethical system to guide social relations, with special emphasis on meritocracy. To lesser degrees, Christianity from the West also has significant sway on large numbers of Asian peoples.

Confucian philosophy and ethical thinking have profoundly influenced all three cultures though with varying results. For example, a Confucian principle in China is that the subordinate is expected to be absolutely loyal to his/her leader, but the leader is equally responsible to look after the interests of his/her subordinates. In Hong Kong and Taiwan especially, this has meant a more entrepreneurial attitude where subordinates feel free to leave positions where they believe that their superiors have not looked after their needs. In Japan, by contrast, the subordinates are expected to remain loyal regardless of whether their superiors are loyal in return. Japanese employees generally remain even when they are cruelly exploited by their superiors. They suffer intense psychological discomfort thinking of quitting for a more promising situation.

By contrast, Christianity has become a major basis for ethical thinking in both Korea and China, but not Japan. Just over 53 percent of Koreans profess religious affiliation and in 2005, 55 percent of these were Christians, up 11 percent from ten years before. In China, Christianity is reputed to be the fastest growing minority religion. Japan attempted in the seventeenth century AD to eradicate Christianity as a pernicious force supporting Western imperialism, and even today Christians represent less than 1 percent of the population.

At the same time, there are strong feelings of antipathy in China and South Korea against Japan for the treatment of their ancestors at the hands of the Japanese Imperial government and its soldiers during the 1930s and 1940s. China has begun to express its hostility to Japan by disputing Japan's sovereignty over the Sendaku Islands (known as the Diaoyu Islands in China), and even Okinawa (an integral prefecture of Japan). There have been riots in China against the Japanese embassy and consulates, and Japanese factories have even been burned. In response, the Japanese have recently elected a new government (2012) whose prime minister, Shinzo Abe, seeks to reform the Japanese constitution to better allow Japan to defend itself against Chinese (and North Korean) aggression. Koreans have continuously protested and demanded apologies for the wartime Japanese practice of forcing Korean "comfort women" to provide sexual services for Japanese soldiers. And there has been considerable resentment in South Korea against Chinese support for the North Korean regime that has continued to menace South Korea, recently with nuclear weapons.

All these political differences not withstanding, the trade relationship between Japan and China is greater in total value than that of Japanese–American trade, and South Korea has become a major trading partner with China. Korea has remained a major Japanese tourist destination, and Korean arts are very popular on Japanese television.

The purpose of this chapter is to acquaint readers with the cultural contexts of China, Japan, and Korea as they impact the nature of business relationships with Westerners. Topics of special interest include the following:

1 Cultural contexts and guidelines for doing business.
2 Culturally based strategies that affect how Chinese, Japanese, and Koreans do business.
3 East Asian business ethics.
4 Strategies for Westerners to build effective business relationships, and/or reduce the impact of cultural differences.

CHINA

The Chinese miracle is the most amazing story of economic growth in world history, but it is also a uniquely Chinese story that perhaps no other nation could have written . . . . Nothing about a visit to China is quite as striking as their incredible infrastructure, beginning with the airport . . . . Its [Terminal 3 at the Beijing International Airport is] the second largest airport terminal in the world after Dubai, and the third largest building in the world by area. The Chinese completed it all in about 4 years, about 3 times as fast as it would have been completed anywhere else I can think of. How did they do it? Well, they worked 24 hours a day, 7 days a week, 365 days a year. It is a massive, glistening, clean, elegant, and super-friendly place.

Peter Rodriguez, Darden School of Business[8]

Geographic perspective

China is on the western seaboard of the Pacific Ocean, south of Russia, with the Himalayan Mountains separating it in the south from India. It is the largest nation by population in the world (1.27 billion), and the fourth-largest nation by area (9.60 million kilometers square), almost identical in area to the United States. Its largest city, Shanghai, is the fifth-largest city in the world (20.9 million). Beijing, the capital, is 12th largest worldwide (17.3 million), and Guangzhou is 15th (16.8 million). There are ten Chinese cities with populations over 4 million, and 161 more with populations over a million.

To comprehend the vastness of this country, divide it into four quadrants. The southeast contains 60 percent of the population and the major cities of Shanghai, Guangzhou and Hong Kong. The northeast includes Beijing and is known now for impressive industrialization, infrastructure, and air pollution. Its two western quadrants, including interior provinces of Tibet and Xinjiang, are developing economies with immense natural resources.

Offshore, the 11-square-mile outpost of Macau has in ten years eclipsed Las Vegas as the gambling capital of the world. By 2011, seven new mega resorts with 20,000 more hotel rooms had gone up in this city alone, costing some $16 billion. It is the largest development project in Asia and is moving three million cubic meters of sand from the Pearl River to create more land on this island. This former Portuguese colony has become a world-class tourist center for sophisticated travelers. The former British colony of Hong Kong, returned to China in 1997, is also a modern megapolis where English is an informal second language. It retains quasi-independent status, in part, because it retains independent quota for exporting garment trade to the United States tax-free. Many countries recognize Hong Kong as an independent source of Chinese exports.

With modernization and the velocity of economic growth, come problems on a scale much bigger than elsewhere, especially relative to the environment. So, China is now the second largest global polluter behind the United States with air pollution readings in Beijing occasionally "off the scale." At times, the pollution reaches across the China Sea to Japan, more than a thousand miles away. Even in the countryside, the air pollution can be severe at times, such as in Hunan Province, when the stubble from the second rice crop is burned off in the autumn. However, this pollution is not ubiquitous. In the beautiful South China Yangsuo/Guilin tourist destination, the air is pristine.

When it comes to energy, China is the world's green energy leader. China uses more solar power for heating water than the rest of the world, has more hydroelectric and nuclear power projects, as well as natural gas terminals than any other nation. It does, however, still derive the majority of its energy from burning coal though liquid natural gas is to be imported from Australia and Canada to replace the soft dirty coal. Now, clusters of wind farms are appearing in its western provinces near the Kazakh border. These are just some indicators of how China today is transitioning from a Third World to First World economy. The population of 1.3 billion people includes a peasantry of seven hundred million, but also a middle class almost as populous as the entire United States.

Just as the ancient Silk Road was once China's land route to the West, today the South China Sea and the Straits of Malacca are its maritime passageways to the resources and markets of Europe, Latin America, Persian Gulf, and Africa. Another indicator of this new reality is that while China produces a third of the world's steel, it now consumes twice as much as the U.S.A. and EU.

Chinese pride

For millennia, the Chinese have always held themselves in high esteem, often deservedly so. The name of their ancient country translates as "center of the world" – their image of themselves.[9] Chinese have long regarded their country and their culture as the heartland and center of human civilization. For past centuries, they expected that all other peoples and nations would pay tribute to the Chinese and their unique culture so influenced by Confucianism, Taoism, and Buddhism. When the British arrived in the eighteenth century seeking to trade European goods for Chinese tea, the Chinese Qing dynasty insisted on payment in silver because it had no interest in goods from "barbarian" nations. This attitude led to two Opium Wars and the first Chinese humiliations at the hands of Western imperialist powers. Britain sought to addict Chinese to opium, so opium could be traded for Chinese goods. Opium was finally banned when the Communists came to power in 1949.

Throughout the history of this civilization, Chinese agriculture and handicrafts have been renowned for their high level of development. China has produced notable thinkers, scientists, inventors, statesmen, authors, and artists. The art of papermaking was discovered 1,800 years ago. Printing was invented over 1,300 years ago. Tao Zhu Gong, born in 517 BC, is reputed to have invented business, strategic planning, and economic analysis.[10] The Chinese writing system, lasting more than 3,000 years, has helped unify China, its culture, and tradition. Even today, the Mandarin, Shanghainese, and Cantonese dialects of the Chinese language share the same written forms though pronounced very differently. China is one of the oldest civilizations in the world, and has also influenced other cultures, including Japan, Korea, and Vietnam. "Overseas Chinese" live all over the planet. They represent a culture that has often been misrepresented as very collectivistic, perhaps because of the long Communist interlude. In fact,

> despite the stereotype of the collectivist Oriental . . . Chinese are often more individualistic than foreigners. Forced into groups [during the Communist period] all their lives, Chinese actually hated them. Chinese are, on the whole, poor team players. Having had socialist solidarity shoved down their throats for so many years, the idea of team spirit was anathema.[11]

Within this context, foreigners doing business in China simultaneously face both modern realities and ancient traditions. China is a member of the World Trade Organization (WTO), and the G20 organization of the most important First World and Emerging Markets. Progress can be seen in macroprojects like the Three Gorges Dam on the Yangtze River; and the world's largest bridge (36 kilometer), across the Gulf of Hangzhou from Ningbo to Shanghai. There are leading edge modern industrial parks, emblematic of China's commitment to the highest technologies. There are affluent home developments around its major cities.

In 2008, Beijing's Olympic Games redefined the country's international image. In 2010, ambitious Shanghai hosted the World Expo in its futuristic Urban Planning Exhibition Hall. This is a new dynamic urban area which hopes to "become a global mecca of knowl-edge workers" with its nine planned communities for 800,000 residents. In the aftermath of the global recession of 2008, and the continuing lack of dynamic economic growth in the United States, European Union, and Japan, many have hoped for Chinese salvation. Chinese economic growth and Chinese consumer demand has been the panacea many Westerners hoped would lead the way out of global recession.

And the Chinese have adopted a very modern national industrial strategy aimed at continuing to build the nation's economic base. Foreign MNEs are generally required to invest foreign exchange to develop local Chinese R&D and manufacturing, and expected to export these manufactured goods to earn further foreign exchange for China. MNEs that hope only to export their products to Chinese markets have been discouraged, and their products disallowed for sale in China. MNEs that seek to protect their advanced intellectual property by not making it available in China have also been refused entry because the Chinese policy is to only allow entry to the most advanced technologies.

RIM, for example, was unable to sign a deal in the later 2000s to sell its Blackberry smartphones throughout China, in part because RIM refused to manufacture its handsets in China, preferring its existing factories in Canada. Ultimately, as a compromise, RIM was allowed only to sell Blackberries to foreign expatriates stationed in China; about 25,000 a year. The Apple iPhone faced the same issues a few years later, and now manufactures all its iPhones in China. Microsoft was required to develop an R&D center in Beijing as a condi-tion for receiving relatively free access to the China market.[12] At first, Microsoft sought to protect its core technologies from its Chinese R&D staff in Beijing but soon realized the Chinese were at least as capable as its other R&D technologists, and worked for consider-ably lower salaries. When Google sought to enter China, it also established a Chinese R&D center as a condition of entry. Even in the 1990s, Nortel was required by the Chinese government to provide its latest telecom technologies and manufacture them in China as a condition of entry into the national market.

At the same time, Chinese business practices have remained heavily influenced by ancient Chinese philosophies and strategic thinking. The Chinese government has been reviving the ancient Chinese philosophy of Confucianism,[13] describing itself at the opening ceremonies of the 2008 Beijing Olympics as a Confucian rather than a Communist state. It is speculated that the revival of Confucianism has been intended to combat the damage to Chinese values and ethical thinking that resulted from Mao Zedong's Cultural Revolution, 1966–1976. During this period, Chinese intellectuals were forced to betray parents, family, and friends, and learned that values and principles didn't matter when survival was at stake.[14] Certainly, the new Chinese president, Xi Jinping, has sworn to root out the all too common corruption endemic in Chinese society and business.

Yet, the official Chinese Confucianism,[15] likely derived from the Chinese philosopher Xunzi,[16] has interesting implications for foreigners doing business with Chinese. Western business has suffered under the misapprehension that Chinese Confucian philosophy is derived from both Confucius and Mencius. Mencius taught that universal human nature was good and that people (including foreigners) could be trusted to be, at heart, well-intentioned. Unfortunately, Mencius also taught that rulers who lost the "mandate of heaven" by behaving in corrupt and anti-humanitarian ways should be overthrown. There was always much corruption associated with Communist Party rule and during the Cultural Revolution, the works of Confucius and Mencius (but not Xunzi) were banned.

Xunzi taught that universal human nature was evil. Most business counterparts would be unreliable because they were guided primarily by self-interest even if they pretended to have others' interests at heart. Therefore, even ethical Chinese were advised to tempt potential relationship partners with the possibilities of private gains through corrupt practices to test whether the counterparts would be ethically reliable.

Confucius observed that there were three types of good friends that could be very helpful. Straight friends were honest and fair. Loyal friends were sincere and never fake. Well-informed friends could offer useful guidance. On the other hand, there were also three kinds of bad friends: ingratiating flatterers (opposite to straight); two-faced friends who slandered you to others; and fast-talkers who bragged and exaggerated everything.[17] The wise person needed to find ways to distinguish good friends from false friends. It is interesting to note that Yu Dan's[18] book, cited above, began as a series of very popular Chinese television lectures, and his subsequent book was a Chinese bestseller, selling more than ten million copies.

Chinese business thinking has also been traditionally guided by two contrary forces – the need to build reliable relationships through guanxi (or networking) practices, and the use of ancient military strategies to build business success. China has been ruled throughout its long history by strong personalities rather than by rule of law. Every ruler had the power and authority to change the law according to his/her own desires. Mao Zedong, for example, who ruled between 1949 and 1976, abolished private property and indiscriminately persecuted members of the middle and upper classes.

The Chinese traditionally needed to build reliable relationships, called guanxi, to protect their mutual interests because they could not count on the consistent rule of law. Guanxi relationships, considered by some to be a Confucian practice,[19] were initially built through the exchange of gifts and favors, but the fruition of guanxi was in the development of ganqing. This constituted heartfelt feelings of mutual concern and commitment that dictated behaving reliably towards one's true friends.[20] Friends bound by ganqing looked after each other's interests ahead of their own.

If foreign counterparts are not sufficiently responsive to Chinese efforts to build guanxi – and many foreigners regard guanxi as a corrupt practice[21] – then the Chinese may resort to ancient Chinese military strategies adapted for business purposes.[22] These include the precepts of Sun Tzu,[23] and the 36 Stratagems of Ancient China,[24] all taught to Chinese business students in China. When you hear accusations of apparent Chinese spying or industrial espionage through the Internet, you wouldn't be surprised if you knew that the 13th chapter of Sun Tzu is on the deployment of spies.

A complicating factor for foreigners contemplating building guanxi in China is another less ancient strategy called *Thick Black*, or thick face and black heart. This strategy of pretending to build guanxi and ganqing was first written down in the late nineteenth century. To the Chinese credit, *Thick Black*[25] was immediately banned in China and has been ever since. It is the Chinese equivalent of Machiavelli's famous book of deceitful practices for gaining power and influence at others' expense (*The Prince*). The goal is to appear to build ethical and committed relationships while being motivated entirely by hidden self-interest. Useless relationships are thrown aside. *Thick Black* is freely available as a book in Taiwan.

Therefore, Chinese pride is based on two factors. China has created as impressive an economic miracle as any in the history of humankind, and at record speed. At the same time, the Chinese are proud of their cultural heritage, insistent on doing business the Chinese way, and resistant of "global" practices they regard as manifesting American business imperialism.[26]

Historical perspective

The Chinese trace their history back to their legendary Emperor Fu Xi who ruled in the mid-twenty-ninth century BC, and is reputed to have invented writing, fishing, and trapping.[27] The history that followed included feudalism, hindering China's economic and political development. Once a leader in ocean-going exploration and trade, Zheng Ho, a Muslim of Mongolian ancestry, led the largest fleet ever assembled on seven expeditions from 1405 to 1433 throughout the Indian Ocean. With some 317 huge ships with up to 30,000 diplomats and troops, he projected China's power, wealth, and influence for political and trade purposes as far as India. A Chinese fleet is reputed to have reached the Americas.

The emperor Hung-shi, put an end to these voyages. For many years, China generally isolated itself behind the Great Wall, forcing most traders and merchants to remain outside. From the Ming Dynasty (fourteenth century AD) until the 1950s, it sought to close itself to the rest of the world, despite incursions by Western and Japanese imperialism, sources of great humiliation for the Chinese.

In 1949, following the revolution and establishment of the People's Republic of China (P.R.C.), the Communist Party attempted to change basic attitudes, values, and behavior of the Chinese people, including simplifying both verbal and written language. Its chairman, Mao Zedong, and his reformers gave the country a new direction, transforming a traditional feudalistic society into a modern socialistic one. With Mao's death in 1976, China's new leader, Deng Xiaoping, realized that economic progress required infusions of Western capital, technology and skills. His "Open Door" policy, commencing in 1979, opened possibilities for investors that have resulted in China becoming the world's second largest economy in just over 30 years.

On January 1, 1979, full diplomatic relations between the People's Republic of China (P.R.C.) and the United States of America were established. Soon, embassies of the U.S.A. and the P.R.C. opened in Beijing and Washington, respectively. A requirement for full diplomatic relations with China has been Chinese insistence that a foreign nation could not also have formal diplomatic relations with Taiwan. China regards Taiwan as an integral part of China that broke away during the Communist Revolution. Until the 1970s, the Taiwanese government also claimed sovereignty over all China. This "fiction" is still heatedly maintained on both sides, especially in China.

Since 1949, two major events of catastrophic proportion have occurred. Mao initiated The Great Leap Forward in the late 1950s, intending to industrialize China in record time but the result was a famine in which 30 million people are estimated to have died. Mao also initiated the Cultural Revolution, 1966–1976, intending promote continuous social revolution but the result was the persecution of most educated Chinese and the closing of most schools and universities.

During these two periods, economic efficiency and social order were forsaken as the country embarked on major new programs that were designed to eliminate "revisionist" elements and to illustrate to the people the importance of their role in building society. By mid-1985, Deng Xiaoping had inaugurated campaigns for modernization and economic reform, even encouraging entrepreneurialism and replacing senior party leaders with younger officials. By 1989, many students were protesting for democratization and their movement was crushed at Tiananmen Square in Beijing by the People's Liberation Army. Hundreds are reputed to have died and many either fled China or were imprisoned. Since that time, the Communist leadership has been committed to raising the overall Chinese standard of living as an alternative to greater social freedom.

In the twenty-first century, the Chinese leadership is moving quickly towards a market economy where individual enterprise is becoming a norm. Increasingly, state-controlled entities are becoming consumer-driven and market-oriented. Necessary legal supports and financial reforms have occurred more slowly, thus inhibiting economic development and personal initiative. Rodriguez[28] has argued that even after China's economy surpasses that of the United States in sheer size, New York and London will remain the financial capitals of world trade because the Chinese banks and financial system are still controlled by the Chinese government.

Seemingly, the political and military leadership operates by consensus, especially to ensure economic reforms and political stability. In practice, the CCP (Chinese Communist Party) officials make the major decisions. Ministries and/or standing committees of the National People's Congress, the legislature, formulate policy on long-term and daily issues. Some provincial governors, especially in fast-growing coastal regions, may adopt policy variations. Despite a strong new president, Xi Jintao, who is also head of the Party, it appears that the real power in China is concentrated in an oligarchy. A relatively small number of senior officials control policy. In many cases, these officials owe their allegiance to past presidents who raised them to their current status. Mr. Xi is reputed to be a protégé of former president Jiang Zemin (1993–2003), serving as his vice president (1998–2003).

Socio-political insights

Presently, China is governed under a constitution formally adopted in 1982. Under its provisions, the highest order of state power is the National People's Congress (NPC). Deputies are elected from every region in China for five-year terms. The NPC then elects the head of state, the president of China. They also elect the State Council that administers the country. The State Council comprises the premier, two vice premiers, ministers, and heads of various state agencies. The CCP controls all government functions. Recently, the people have been permitted to elect local town officials, but are expected to elect the approved candidates. Although the country's political leaders call themselves communists, they are increasingly acting like capitalists, as Exhibit 13.2 indicates.

EXHIBIT 13.2 LENOVO: A CHINESE GLOBAL CORPORATION

Today, world-class corporations are more globally integrated and oriented toward resource productivity for effective use of energy and water, as well as material and human resources. One such enterprise in an emerging market country is Lenovo, a Chinese company with a global brand. Its personal computer business produces revenues of $16 billion or more annually, and is now listed in the *Fortune 500*! In 2005, it purchased IBM's personal computer division for $1.75 billion, with rights to the IBM logo for five years. Despite being a state-owned company, it enjoys remarkable independence to pursue the developing world's rural markets.

Its chairman, Yang Yuanqing, has been the leader behind Lenovo growth and its unique management style. It hires competent international managers, like chief executive Bill Amelio, with a distinguished career history at IBM and Dell. Although proud of the company's Chinese roots, Yang sought to make it global by having its headquarters worldwide, so senior managers rotate among corporate bases abroad. Its development teams are made up of diverse peoples from these various centers, such as its market department in Bangalore, India, and often working virtually by telecommunications.

To buttress this management philosophy, Yang has sought to integrate its organizational culture and promote cross-cultural teamwork. One corporate policy statement reads: *In all situations, assume good intentions; be international about understanding others, and being understood; respect cultural differences.* To confirm this approach, Yang has moved himself and his family to North Carolina, so as to deepen their understanding of American culture. He himself speaks English well, while encouraging all employees to improve their command of this global business language. Lenovo, for instance, encourages its Chinese employees, who are normally reticent at management meetings, to speak candidly with their American colleagues.

Source: Adapted from "A Bigger World: A Special Report on Globalization," *The Economist,* September 20, 2008, 26-page insert (www.economist.com/specialreports or /rights). See also this London magazine's reports on "The World Economy," October 11, 2008; "Corporate IT," October 25, 2008.

E
X
H
I
B
I
T
13.2

Today, China's priority is to restructure state-owned enterprises (SOEs) established in the 1960s. Many of these entities seek to make a mark on world commerce. One indicator is that senior executives in publicly owned companies earn on average $180,000 annually, plus stock options up to $140,000 in equity stakes that are rarely exercised. Still, the aim is ensure the state's more effective control over the economy, so political, not management, skills are more important in these undertakings.

It is a sign of the exponential growth of the Chinese economy that in the last edition of *Managing Cultural Differences* (8th edition, 2011), only 11 Chinese companies were reported to be on the *Forbes 500* list of top global firms, but now there are 17. Companies on this list are measured in terms of revenues produced. The *Fortune Global 500* list of the largest 500 companies in the world includes 24 Chinese companies, including three of the top ten in 2012.

While the northeast is home to hulking state industries and socialism, the south along the coast is a capitalist heartland, especially Zhejiang where the per capita annual income is the third highest in the country, and its inhabitants earn twice as much as those in the north. Sixty-two of China's wealthiest citizens have homes here. Ninety-one percent of its 240,000 enterprises are privately owned with annual revenues of 700 billion yuan. There, an entrepreneurial trading heritage combines with family-controlled businesses which are taking the global markets by storm. The City of Wenzhou alone is home to 3,000 small firms that club together in flexible production to create real wealth. People here believe in Chairman Deng's exhortation – *to get rich is glorious, and to be a wealth creator is morally uplifting!* No wonder this is a culture that rarely transcends the individual. Exhibit 13.3 tells another story of Chinese entrepreneurs.

There is a wide income disparity between rural and urban areas in China, which the government is trying hard to address. Several coastal cities have a GDP per capita of almost US$5,000 per year, while the interior of China, more underdeveloped, remains below US$400 per year. With the mass migration of peasants to urban areas, their income has risen dramatically, though these peasants are often denied residence permits, find work in "sweatshops", and discover that local labor codes do not apply to them as nonresidents. Now, as a member of the World Trade Organization, the government is also encouraging private companies to compete with state-owned enterprises for markets and resources.

In China, *The Economist* Intelligence Unit ranks Shanghai as the best city in China for doing business, followed by fast-growing Guangzhou, and then Beijing.[29] No wonder that China now attracts more financial investment from outside its borders than any other country, while seeking multinationals that are prepared to provide top-tier technologies to further their mega-economy. Moreover, it has now become the world's most trade-oriented nation, using its $1 trillion foreign currency reserve to invest widely in foreign markets so as to acquire more knowhow. China holds more American debt than any other country.

China's main trading partners in 2011[30] were the European Union (US$567.2 billion total exports + imports), the United States (US$446.7 billion), the ASEAN region (US$362.5 billion), Japan (US$342.9 billion), Hong Kong (US$283.5 billion), and South Korea (US$245.6 billion). It has a healthy trade surplus with Hong Kong (US$252.5 billion),

EXHIBIT 13.3 PIONEERING ENTREPRENEUR AND CAPITALIST

The 2005 obituary of Rong Yiren was a unique account of a Chinese anomaly about the scion of a family commercial empire founded in 1902. His death at 69 raised the question of how this Chinese billionaire, who was not a known member of the Communist Party, ever became vice president of the People's Republic and twice chairman of the National People's Congress. More intriguing is how he managed to regain his wealth after ceding his family's business holdings after the 1949 revolution, and losing the rest during the Cultural Revolution of 1966–1976. Yet, within a decade or so, he arose as one of the 50 most charismatic businessmen in the world, and one of its richest by a 1999 reckoning of *Fortune* magazine. All this despite his family fleeing to Taiwan and the United States, leaving him alone in mid-century to run 24 flour mills, textile, and printing plants employing 80,000.

Mr. Rong presented himself as a "patriotic" capitalist who remained to help China end its poverty by shifting to a market economy. When he gave the Party what it wanted, he subtly asked for a favor in return. The astute and handsome executive not only survived, but along the way became vice-mayor of Shanghai, and in 1959, vice-minister for the textile industry. Through *guanxi,* or personal connections, he positioned himself to creatively help Deng Xiaoping open windows to the capitalist world. Educated under the British system at Shanghai's St. John's University, this graduate became Deng's symbol of the new Chinese entrepreneur.

In 1979, at the Party's behest, he founded CITIC as an investment arm of the state to acquire telecoms, utilities, and highways. When a Special Economic Zone was established in southern China for foreign investments, CITIC was there to exploit the property boom. Rong, roving extensively, found the foreign concerns willing to invest in China, and lured them to the Zone. This handsome, sophisticated executive did well for his country and himself. In 2000, *Forbes* estimated the wealth of Rong and his son, Larry Yung, now head of CITC-Pacific, to be $1.9 billion. Their conglomerate boasts global assets of $6.3 billion, and includes two-hundred affiliated enterprises. And, in the process, China has been moving steadily toward a free enterprise system!

Source: Adapted from "Obituary: Rong Yiren," *The Economist*, November 5, 2005, p. 94.

the United States (US$202.3 billion), and the European Union (US$144.8 billion), and small negative balances with South Korea, Japan, and the ASEAN. A major change since the early 2000s has been that China has become a very influential investor around the world including in First World countries. In the past, MNEs invested in China to achieve lower factor costs for products intended for export. These days, Chinese MNEs are investing in other countries, often to obtain guaranteed access to natural resources or national markets. Exhibit 13.4 details the influence of Chinese MNEs in Canada as an example.

EXHIBIT 13.4 CHINESE INVESTMENT IN CANADA

Canadian natural resources have been a major source of fuel for the rapidly developing Chinese industrial complex. More and more Chinese companies are coming to do business in Canada either through acquisitions of Canadian companies, or starting Canadian subsidiaries. The Leung Maritime Group of Hong Kong acquired Asia Pacific Maritime Container Lines, one of Canada's biggest cargo transportation companies. China Metals Corporation attempted to acquire Noranda and Falconbridge, major Canadian mining companies, in 2005. China Investment Corp. spent US$1.7 billion in 2009 to acquire Teck Resources. Sinopec, the Chinese state-owned petroleum giant, acquired Addax Petroleum, one of Canada's nine Fortune 2000 companies, in 2009. Chinese SOEs were bidding to invest in the Alberta oil sands, including CNOOC acquiring Nexen in 2013. Other Chinese companies were opening mines in northern British Columbia staffed by their own Chinese miners. The large concentration of overseas Chinese in Vancouver and Toronto were a powerful magnet for private Chinese investment.

The Canadian and British Columbian governments realized the tremendous potential Chinese business represented. As early as the 1990s, BC (British Columbia) Trade, a BC government department, had opened a number of trade offices across China to facilitate Canadian companies hoping to do business in China. The government of Canada provided similar services through the commercial wing of External Affairs, and through Industry Canada. By 2012, the Canadian government had established six new Canadian Trade Offices in China to help Chinese companies do business in Canada. The mission of these offices was to provide "services and expertise" to help investors from China successfully expand their business in Canada. They provided services to Chinese companies including preparing for international markets, market potential assessment, qualified contacts, and problem-solving. Canada also provided services for Canadian companies seeking Chinese business, and Chinese companies seeking Canadian business, through its Trade Commissioner Service in China.

In 2013, the Canadian government was negotiating an investment agreement with China – the Canada–China Foreign Investment Protection and Promotion Agreement (FIPPA). This agreement focused on the treatment of investments that had already been made. It offered protection for Chinese investors in Canada against such risks as discrimination, expropriation without compensation, and arbitrary decisions by governments, once their investments in Canada had been made. The FIPPA would make Canada a safer and more attractive place for Chinese investment.

Deloitte estimates that China will invest upwards of US$250 billion into developing its own consumer economy. Typically in the past, Chinese foreign direct investment (FDI) has focused on obtaining access to secure resources for its major industries. The deal to buy Nexen fell into this category. The latest Chinese National Five-Year Development Plan has placed a greater emphasis on building a Chinese consumer economy. Deloitte predicts that

Chinese investors will eye private British Columbian companies as hot targets for investment. For example, the Vancouver based micro-brewery company Russell Breweries Inc. signed a joint venture deal funded by Chinese investors, in 2012, to brew and sell its beer in China. Chinese investors are also interested in the Canadian clean tech and bio-tech sectors, and deals with Ballard Power Systems to build fuel cell powered buses for Beijing.

Source: Abramson, N.R. "James Williams International." Unpublished business case. Penner, D. "B.C. Firms Poised to Dip into Deep Chinese Investment Pool," *Vancouver Sun*, June 6, 2013, p. D1.

EXHIBIT 13.4

Finally achieving economic, though not political liberation after decades of Communist rule, the Chinese people have shown themselves to be among the most entrepreneurial in the world. Even originally poor peasants have been able to achieve great economic success. The "American Dream" that anyone could become successful through his/her own efforts has also become the Chinese Dream. Exhibit 13.5 recounts one such success.

EXHIBIT 13.5 YOUNGER GENERATION OF CHINESE ENTREPRENEURS

EXHIBIT 13.5

Shantou, a once poor district in southern China, is the birthplace of one of the mainland's richest men. As a deprived boy, Wong Kwong Wu recycled bottles after school to supplement his family's income. At 16, he and his elder brother left to seek their fortunes, ending up in Beijing where they opened a clothing store called Gome. At 17, Mr. Wong switched its emphasis to home appliances and consumer electronics. In 1992, the brothers split the business – the elder went into commercial real estate, and the younger kept the retail store. By 2005, they were both rich and jointly owned the skyscraper Eagle Plaza and the block that houses it in North Beijing. Today, Gome is a prosperous electrical appliance retailer with 437 stores in 132 cities with $3 billion in revenues. A clear leader in the 500 billion yuan electrical appliance market, the company now seeks foreign partners for further expansion. At 36, Wong himself was worth some $1.7 billion. Having acquired this wealth within socialist China, the young billionaire has become one of Beijing's biggest residential developers. "*The beauty of property over retailing,*" he smiles, "*Is that you don't have to deal with so many people!*"

Yet Wong lives frugally – he, his wife, and children live in a commonplace apartment. Although he is driven around in a stretch Mercedes for meetings on the move, personally he is a workaholic given to self-denial. Like many young Chinese entrepreneurs, Wong is sensitive to a regime still ambivalent about private property and the rapid rise in private wealth. Conspicuous consumption is still to be indulged in cautiously, especially given President Xi Jintao's promise to root out corruption by identifying those living beyond their means.

Source: Adapted from "Face Value: China's Uneasy Billionaire," *The Economist*, February 4, 2006, p. 60.

Cultural guidelines for business in China

China is a hierarchical society, making it often difficult to practice Western management theories of empowerment and delegation. Chinese tend to think in terms of "role fulfillment": give me a role or title and I will perform the job. This Confucian culture is pragmatic – people prefer to learn by doing, rather than learning the theory and then applying it creatively. However, the Western assumption is "prove that you can do your job well and more responsibility will be added." Western managers can misconstrue this difference as a lack of initiative on the part of the Chinese. The Chinese usually have a "role expectation" for their bosses and maintain a certain distance with them. Confucians expect their leaders to protect their interests, and offer their full allegiance in return. The leadership traits they admire are determination, calmness, strength, intelligence, honor, and reserve.

China is a culture that values harmony in interpersonal interactions. Perceived conflict is easily interpreted as loss of "face," or disrespectful. Chinese are not comfortable making recommendations or suggestions publicly. By using one-on-one communication and understanding nonverbal signals, one can usually determine the true meaning in conversation over time. In the Beijing office of Nortel back in the 1990s, a Chinese vice president observed that his American counterparts insisted that a particular American marketing plan would work. The Chinese executives observed that it would not work in China, and were confronted with demands to explain why not. Confronting areas of disagreement is a normal American problem-solving approach, but direct confrontation is seen as disrespectful in China. The vice president said that the Chinese executives said, "Well, give it a try if you are so sure," to avoid an uncomfortable situation. It didn't work, and later the Americans confronted the Chinese again. "Why didn't you tell us," they said. The Americans were poorly prepared for dealing with Chinese culture. The episode reduced the willingness of the Chinese executives to help Nortel become successful in China.

Yet, personal development and growth, as well as monetary reward, are important motivators for Chinese employees. Good training programs are very attractive to them, and often they are willing to take less pay for educational and career opportunities. In any bonus plan or performance award system, consider both team and individual performance. A detailed and clear reward system is important to such workers.

Experienced China traders advise that when it comes to doing business, *throw away the rulebook, and expect the Chinese to be one step ahead of you!* The local business environment is eccentric and often apparently nonrational, causing managers and negotiators from abroad to make false assessments of the situation. Foreigners are further puzzled by the cultural challenge in the Chinese game to *save face*, so that deception with an opponent is acceptable. Appearance and scoring points often seems more important than substance or making a good deal.

Despite reforms in China, foreign investors and managers are still concerned about inadequate protection of intellectual property and human rights, rapid price inflation, and corruption. They have to act defensively, such as by trying to avoid joint ventures with government entities, and monitoring carefully the local Chinese responsible for hiring staff to avoid nepotism. Some outsiders play the role of the "dumb foreigner" by asking detailed questions, supposedly to better understand the system. The reality is that many Chinese government officials live in fear of being criticized for not upholding the state's interests. Avoid being overanxious and giving up too many concessions, lest an unfair deal is forced upon you in the local expectation that foreigners will give anything in order to operate in China.

Managing in China requires the introduction of effective human resource programs. Too many ordinary workers prefer not to think creatively, and avoid taking responsibility for decisions. The rote education that conditions them needs to be countered by training that increases the power of analysis and leadership. Furthermore, among China's 800 million workers, there is a shortage today of qualified surplus labor. While the shift of workers from agriculture to industry has been significant, there is an acute need to train migrant workers in new factory skills.

To uplift the 800 million poor Chinese, China has a vigorous program under way, including a $40 billion social investment program. The government is also building fifty thousand miles of modern new highways to connect both major cities and remote villages, but many main roads in rural areas are still unacceptably poor by Western standards. Much money is also being spent on fiber-optic cables so as to connect the people of the countryside to the information superhighway.

Furthermore, China's culture values knowledge and education. Nowhere is this more evident than in the Chinese Academy of Social Sciences, the world's largest think tank, where intellectual discussion has increasing impact on global social order. Like the timeless character of its language, Chinese leaders take a long view of current events, while pursuing harmony and economic co-prosperity!

CORRUPTION

China was ranked 61st of 150 nations on a worldwide corruption index conducted by World Audit.org in 2013. New Zealand, Denmark, and Finland were tied for being the least corrupt. Afghanistan, Somalia, and North Korea were tied in 148th and last place. Singapore was 5th; Canada 9th; Japan 13th; the United States 15th; South Korea 32nd; India 74th; Mexico 84th; and Russia was tied with Iran at 110th. So, corruption is a major problem in China but not as bad as India or Mexico.

In 1993, China officially began an anticorruption campaign. Progress has been made. In 1998, the former mayor of Beijing was jailed on graft charges. In 2011, two former vice mayors from eastern China were executed on bribery convictions. However, despite these show trials, fraud is endemic. Jamie Flor Cruz of CNN wrote, "corruption is so entrenched that honest officials are now part of a minority that risks being left behind. It is a system where corruption is the rule rather than the exception."[31] When China's new president, Xi Jintao, took office in 2013, he guaranteed a major battle to reduce corrupt practices, and punish any official that was apprehended. The dining and entertainment industries in Beijing have recently suffered major reverses as officials wait to see if Mr. Xi is serious.

One small to medium sized (SME) Canadian enterprise, intent on finding partners to develop a joint venture manufacturing entity for its telephone and lighting pole business, found that it received as many as ten fraudulent offers for every potentially genuine one.[32] Richmond's vice president of international business reported that fraudulent proposals even included apparently genuine bank statements showing that the fraudsters had the assets they claimed. Richmond found that employees at a Chinese bank had the capability to produce such statements, and were willing to if properly gifted for their efforts.

Corruption, counterfeiting, and even blackmail are also thought to be rampant in China, especially when dealing with import taxes and kickbacks to get contracts. Often, to avoid bribery, many MNCs use creative ways to build relationships. One way is partnering with other local companies, or with top business schools to launch special executive education programs, inviting local businesses to participate. The expatriate executive confronts a culture in which business is about survival – someone has to win or lose! Also, be aware that the Chinese executives today are not only very competent, but increasingly sophisticated as executives. Never underestimate them.

Foreign firms in China are well advised to:

- Investigate carefully and vigilantly supervise the quality and safety of products.
- Avoid bullying suppliers to cut costs, or make complex logical demands.
- Maintain a product review system, especially with brand development.
- Assist in management development.

But in developing economies like China, leaders of would-be world-class corporations would do well to heed these words:

It is true that multinationals shop around for taxes, but in other ways they are usually sticklers for good behavior. Encouragingly, firms from emerging markets are finding that a globally integrated company needs a single culture, and that the best way to foster this is to make the highest ethics anywhere in the firm, the norm for everyone wherever they are working. Anything less tends to corrode the culture.[33]

The cultural practice of guanxi

Guanxi, or social networking, is perhaps the most important Chinese cultural practice affecting the performance and success of foreign businesses in China. Guanxi relationships are characterized by trust and personal relationship between two parties. They are intended to result in a reciprocal flow of transactions and benefits between the parties.[34] Guanxi is variously understood as social networking, a web of interpersonal connections, a pervasive lubricant intended to increase the efficiency and effectiveness of business relations, and an essential informal governance method for ensuring fairness of treatment.[35]

Abramson and Ai[36] reported that successful guanxi relationships with local Chinese counterparts were more important to the success of Canadian firms than willingness to invest in local Chinese operations, or lower levels of perceived environmental uncertainty. A recent meta-analytical study of 53 quantitative studies of guanxi by Luo, Huang, and Wang[37] confirmed that guanxi does enhance MNE organizational performance in China. Guanxi with business associates enhanced operational performance. Guanxi with government officials enhanced economic performance.

Chen, Chen, and Huang[38] reviewed 200 previous studies of guanxi and concluded that the basis for the success of guanxi is personal relationship. They observed that scholars have been debating whether guanxi will remain a key aspect of doing business in China, or whether the development of more impartial legal and regulatory institutions will make reliance on guanxi unnecessary. While this discussion has not been resolved, it seemed evident that guanxi was deeply rooted in Chinese culture.[39] It continued to have a significant role in economic activities despite reforms,[40] and the number of Chinese businesspersons building guanxi connections within China was increasing.[41]

Guanxi[42] takes a somewhat different form in northern China than in the south. The difference is not so large as to be statistically significant, but the tendency is for guanxi in the north (Beijing, Tianjin) to focus on developing heartfelt ganqing, whereas there is more focus in the south on the exchange of reciprocal gifts and favors. However, the development of ganqing is the dominant form throughout China.

In its dominant form, successful guanxi demands the development of trust between partners based on the demonstration of long-term reliability and competence. Both parties must feel that they share common goals, and will receive mutual benefits, and that any disagreements will be resolved through constructive means that will benefit both sides. Gifts and favors are exchanged but they are symbolic of the feelings of personal consideration developing between the parties. Gifts and favors may entail taking someone out for lunch, remembering someone's birthday, and/or attending dinners and/or social events that honor one or the other. Government officials in Beijing are allowed to receive simple and inexpensive gifts, usually in the range of US$10–20, but are required by their regulations to refuse gifts of greater value.

One gives a gift to honor another and to acknowledge his/her value to you. One does a small favor because it shows that one party is concerned with the other's needs or problems. This kind of gift- or favor-giving is no more a corrupt practice than salespersons in Canada offering to take an important client to a professional hockey (or baseball, or football) game, and sitting in the seller's company's box seats. Western companies generally have season's tickets available for such purposes.

As trust develops, so do feelings of ganqing. Individuals joined by heartfelt ganqing tend to put their friend's needs ahead of their own. In such an intersubjective[43] or I/Thou[44] relationship, the buyer would buy generously because s/he knows it would benefit the seller, but the seller will generously not sell unless s/he knows it would truly benefit the buyer.

In the less common form of guanxi found more commonly in the south, the gifts and favors are the central focus of the relationship. Reciprocal altruism governs the relationship so a gift from one party must be matched by a gift from the other. And the rule of reciprocity is that the value of the gifts depends on the power and position of the giver. A less powerful or wealthy individual may give the best gift s/he has at his/her disposal. The receiver must give equally the best gift he/she is able to even if it is of considerably greater value. Not reciprocating in this fashion would lead to loss of face. And in this form of guanxi, a relationship may be cemented by a "big gift" in the form of cash, expensive automobiles, or foreign travel, indistinguishable in practice from bribery. Foreigners are advised to stay away from giving gifts and favors of this sort. Soon, there will be a line of Chinese all coming for their share because big gifts are illegal even in China. The favor the foreigner will receive in return is not being reported to the authorities.

It should be noted, however, that guanxi is regarded in China as a Confucian relational practice and this has implications for the understanding of guanxi. Confucius[45] observed that humans were divided into two groups: "petty" or amoral small-minded people, and "junzi" or great men or women who were motivated by ethical considerations. Confucius argued that wisdom was the art of knowing and understanding others. You needed to be able to distinguish between the petty and the junzi.[46] One could distinguish between the two only through observable behaviors in one's interpersonal interactions because the petty man/woman would try to disguise his/her self-interest by trying to seem only concerned with the public good.

The junzi behaved with modesty and spoke mildly. He/she behaved ethically, was kind and fair with subordinates, and loyal to superiors. He/she was not competitive, but was sincere and trustworthy, and refused to associate with people he/she regarded as bad or unethical. His/her behavior was characterized by benevolence, righteousness, and fidelity. The junzi was entirely reliable, and trustworthy, and a good friend to have.

By contrast, the petty man/woman was cliquish, and proud but not dignified. He/she expected subordinates to offer praise and to work to perfection. He/she would be courteous to superiors but not really respect them. He/she was not reliable in keeping his/her word, did not care for the success of others ahead of him/herself, told untrue stories about his/her associates behind their backs, and was primarily motivated to seek personal profit. The petty man/woman was unreliable, and untrustworthy, and his/her friendship should be avoided.

The question for Confucians is how to determine whether the person you are thinking of doing business with is a trustworthy junzi, or an untrustworthy petty man/woman. The origins of guanxi as a long-term relationship building strategy lie at the heart of the answer to this question.

According to Confucianism, there are three stages in the ethical development of a person. We say stages, but this does not imply that any particular individual inevitably proceeds from one stage to another. It is quite possible to remain at a single stage for one's whole life, and the only path of advancement is moral or ethical education, and practice of virtuous behaviors.

At the first stage, there is no ethical reasoning and individuals simply seek to be like the people around them. They are collectivist in the sense that their desires, goals, and actions mirror the people they associate with.

At the second stage, an individual may realize that some people get ahead while others do not. The first ethical realization is self-interest and results in the petty man/woman. Others may be taken advantage of in order to further one's own individualistic opportunities. If, however, the others realize that they are being taken advantage of, they will protect themselves, so the petty man/woman learns to disguise his/her self-interest under a façade of public mindedness.

It is at the third stage – junzi – that individuals are motivated by values of benevolence, righteousness, and fidelity. These trustworthy values are learned through moral education and practiced until they become second nature.

The relevance of these observations for foreigners seeking to build guanxi is in the assumptions the Chinese make about the morality and ethicality of the foreigners. In Mencian Confucianism, understood in the West to be the dominant form of Chinese Confucianism, it is assumed that human nature is basically good. People are born inclined towards behaving with benevolence, righteousness, and fidelity. Admittedly, they need to practice these inclinations in order to remain good people but the key assumption is that all people including non-Chinese are decent people who will behave in trustworthy and helpful ways if given the opportunity.

In Xunzian Confucianism, however, it is assumed that human nature is basically evil in the sense that humans are naturally predisposed from birth with a fondness for profit at others' expense. This natural desire for profit leads to "wrangling and strife," "envy and hate," "violence and crime," and "license and wantonness."[47] A person is assumed to be petty and untrustworthy until transformed by prior education and sufficient ritualistic opportunities to practice the application of virtue. A foreigner is assumed to be "evil" – self-interested – until proven otherwise. And in the Xunzi,[48] the junzi is advised to offer illicit opportunities and corrupt practices in order to test the morality of one's counterpart.

Twohey,[49] Bell,[50] and others have argued that the Xunzi is the basis for Confucianism in modern China. Yan[51] has acknowledged it as a major influence on Chinese government policy. The Mencius[52] was banned along with Confucius' Analects during the Cultural Revolution as reactionary and supportive of the positions of the feudal overlords the Communist state was intending to eradicate. Mencius also advocated the overthrow of corrupt rulers, making his philosophy unpopular with various Chinese emperors and leaders including the Communists. Twohey has traced the strains of Xunzian thought in Mao Zedong's own thoughts and writings.

Therefore, foreigners seeking to build guanxi in China should understand that even the more ethical Chinese may test their ethicality by offering them corrupt and illicit opportunities. And of course, there will be many petty men or women for whom corrupt practices are a normal expression of their pursuit of self-interest.

Traditional strategic thinking in China

It would be a fair argument that Chinese businesspeople are better prepared for strategic combat than are their Western counterparts. Perhaps that is one reason why Chinese business has been so startlingly successful so quickly. Western strategic planning is generally taught on the basis of ten possible theoretical frameworks[53] but most management education on strategic planning is focused on the ideas of Michael Porter (see Chapter 7) and what Mintzberg et al.[54] call the "Positioning School." Chinese business students learn the Western strategic planning frameworks, but they are also taught ancient Chinese military strategic thinking that has been adapted to business situations. The most common of these Chinese approaches to strategic thinking are Sun Tzu's *The Art of War*,[55] and the *36 Strategems of Ancient China*.[56]

Sun Tzu observed that a general who knew both himself and his enemy would always win the battle. A general that knew only him/herself *or* his/her opponent would only win half the time. A general who knew *neither* him/herself nor his/her opponent would always lose. Chinese businesspeople have a tremendous strategic planning advantage because they know Western strategic thinking, whereas their own Chinese strategic thinking is not generally taught in the West.

Sun Tzu's thinking is the better known in the West. According to McNeilly,[57] Sun Tzu's strategy may be summarized into six principles:

1   How to win wars without fighting battles – capturing markets without destroying them.
2   Avoiding opponents' strong points – attacking opponents' weaknesses unexpectedly.
3   Deception – the use of market information and business intelligence.
4   Preparation and speed – moving quickly to achieve surprise.
5   Shaping the competition – make them respond to your strategy, according to your plan.
6   Moral leadership – inspiring your organization to provide obedience and commitment.

Sun Tzu proceeds similarly to Western strategic planning. The leader scouts out the battlefield terrain (External Environment). He/she assesses the ability of his units (Internal Capabilities) to execute the leader's battle strategy (Strategic Plan). He argues that the leader should be able to answer seven critical questions:

1   Which ruler possesses moral influence?
2   Which commander is more able?
3   Which army has advantage of climate and terrain?
4   Which army carries out regulations and instructions better?
5   Which troops are stronger?
6   Which has better trained officers and soldiers?
7   Which administers rewards and punishments better?

Questions (2) through (6) appear to be covered in Western strategic thinking. Sun Tzu, however, includes consideration of some unusual topics. Western strategic models do not usually cover conquering by strategems, prudence, deception, flanking, and espionage. And strategems includes discussions of strategems both for attack and defense whereas

Western models generally focus on the former. Sun Tzu believed, however, that the defense was inherently a stronger strategic position, and that the attacker weakened him/herself allowing a more successful counter-attack. Regarding question (7), Western theory tends to focus on the use of rewards while ignoring the effectiveness of punishments.[58]

Western strategic theory tends to entirely ignore question (1) about the moral influence of the leader. Most Western models only consider management preferences in the form of performance objectives, or decision criteria related to what management hopes to achieve in a specific situation. Some Western theory considers management experience, or the strengths of the senior management team, or even the cognitive biases of senior management in terms of how biases unconsciously and unintentionally affect implementation of their intended strategies. Sun Tzu, however, argued that good leaders needed to put the needs and expectations of others ahead of their own, and be willing to sacrifice. Moral leadership was based on six principles:[59]

1　Build your character, and not just your image.
2　Lead with actions, not just with words.
3　Share your employees' trials and difficulties, and not just their successes.
4　Motivate emotionally, and not just with material rewards.
5　Assign clear and segmented tasks, avoiding overlap and not allowing confusion.
6　Make your strategy drive your organization, and not vice versa.

The *36 Strategems of Ancient China*[60] is relatively unknown in the West and has even fallen out-of-print. This is unfortunate because these strategems are well-known in China, and part of many Chinese businesspersons' bag of tricks. The strategems include six each for each of six kinds of battleground situations:

1　Strategems for when you are in a position of strength versus your opponent:

  ■　These strategems are the most straightforward and therefore the most easily seen through by one's opponent. Therefore, one must be in a superior position, and even then the strategems may backfire. Deception is usually involved.

2　Strategems for confrontation:

  ■　These strategems are for situations where the opponents are of roughly equivalent strength. Victory requires more deception and therefore more complexity. The goal is to make the opponent underestimate you through trickery and stealth.

3　Strategems for attack:

  ■　Attack is dangerous and most likely to result in casualties. Surveillance, concealment of intent, and luring the opponent to strike first may minimize the dangers.

4　Strategems for confused situations where advantage is not clear;

■   Negotiations and peace overtures mixed with threats may result in short term alliances and the breaking alliances among opponents. Manipulation of third parties and divisive tactics facilitate success.

5   Strategems for gaining ground against a somewhat superior opponent:

■   The intent is to obtain what the opponent controls. Diversionary tactics, misrepresentation, and entrapment are useful in this regard.

6   Strategems for desperate situations where your opponent is in a position of strength:

■   These are last resorts in an emergency. If hitting below the belt, or bluster and bravado fail, you can always try running away.

There are two features common to almost all of these strategems. First, they are deceptive. They seek to disguise from the opponent the strength of one's own forces. Second, they place a strong value on beginning with superior defensive positions and trying to entice the opponent to be the first to attack. These two principles are applied even to the six strategems where one believes oneself to be in a position of commanding superiority to one's opponent. For example, Strategem 1, "Cross the Sea by Fooling the Sky," involves appearing to organize for an attack through extensive maneuvers, but then not attacking, over and over. Eventually, the opponent concludes that you are bluffing and ceases to respond. Then you attack an unprepared enemy. This may well be a universal strategy. Interestingly, it was the strategy Alexander the Great used more than 2,300 years ago crossing the Ganges River to attack an Indian army armed with elephants the Greeks had no experience of. It is also encapsulated in the English fable of the "boy who cried wolf." It is not, however, generally taught in Western business schools.

Ultimately, however, the Chinese manager knows that his/her opponent may also be well versed in the 36 strategems. The opponent may deduce one's own assessment of the situation by observing one's selection of strategems. For example, if you believe that you are weaker than your opponent and use a strategy for gaining ground, then your opponent knows that you believe you are weaker. Gao Yuan[61] recommends, therefore, that the best strategists do not confine themselves to strategems that conform to their assessment of the situation. The ultimate rule is that there is no rule. Using an inappropriate strategem is a means of deceiving the opponent. If one is in a strong position, and uses a desperate stratagem that conveys the fear of terrible weakness, the weaker opponent may be encouraged to strike and be defeated more quickly and with less cost.

Negotiating in China

Chinese negotiators tend to work in teams, and new negotiators may be brought in periodically in an attempt to gain fresh concessions. In meetings, Chinese will examine a counterpart's attitude and speech and apply it to the problem-solving. Technical competence is critical, and some negotiators have requested more seasoned technical people join their negotiating team midway through negotiations.

The Chinese rank among the toughest negotiators in the world, but they are normally reputable and honorable with outsiders. In addition, China is probably one of the most difficult countries to understand and adapt to. Foreigners are advised of the following, regarding Chinese negotiators:

- Emphasis is placed on trust and mutual connections.
- Chinese usually stick to their word. They expect the same from you.
- Long-range benefits are preferred.
- Utilize global consultants who understand the workings of the P.R.C.
- Consider national sensitivities, while being wary of propagandistic slogans and codes.

Initially, a business meeting is devoted to pleasantries (e.g., serving tea, chit-chat), while waiting for the right opening to begin serious discussions. An early key signal of the intensity of Chinese interest in doing business with you is the caliber of the Chinese assigned to the sessions. Chinese posture becomes rigid whenever they feel their goals are seemingly being compromised. So as not to lose face, Chinese often prefer to negotiate through an intermediary. When negotiations are at a standstill, a useful strategy is to send an intermediary either to offer a compromise or sound out the Chinese about their ideas to overcome an impasse. Any compromise agreed to will be announced in the next session of the formal negotiations.

Many outsiders are convinced that the Chinese consciously use slowdown techniques as bargaining ploys (e.g., exploit a natural American tendency for impatience to get things done quickly). During first encounters, the Chinese usually seem to be bound by their traditional nonlegalistic practices. Businesspersons soon appreciate that they operate only at the tolerance of the Chinese. Those of Chinese origin who live and work outside China are more flexible and attuned to global business expectations. It is true that Chinese negotiators may take advantage of Westerners' fixed schedules. Western negotiators do not want to come home empty-handed and may agree to additional concessions in the taxi to the airport, for their homebound flights. On the other hand, Chinese negotiators hope to build initial relationships with their Western counterparts and do not want to discuss business until they take the measure of those they are dealing with. Westerners should allow time for these processes to take place.

Chinese seem to have a compelling need to dwell on the subject of friendship, convincing foreigners that reciprocity in this spirit was a prerequisite for doing business with China. However, once Chinese decide who and what is the best, they show great steadfastness. Curiously, the literature on negotiating with the Chinese is almost evenly divided between studies emphasizing the Chinese desire to build relationship (guanxi), and Chinese attempts to deploy Sun Tzu-like stratagems instead.[62] It is our opinion that there are two factors in play. Ethical Chinese prefer to build guanxi relationships over considerable periods of time, but may want to test whether their foreign counterparts are also ethically minded. They will, however, employ Sun Tzu-like stratagems against foreigners they assess as unethical, or those that are unwilling to take the time to build effective guanxi relationships. Unethical Chinese (see the above discussions of Confucian stages of ethical development, and *Thick Black*) will want to appear as if guanxi relationships are valued, but will be governed by their self-interest to use Sun Tzu-like stratagems that are neither benevolent, righteous, nor having fidelity.

Sometimes the Chinese strategy is to put pressure on visitors when discussing final arrangements for an agreement (e.g., suggesting that the spirit of friendship in which the business relationship was originally established has been undermined or strained). In Chinese negotiations, nothing should be considered final or complete until it has been actually realized in the contract. Chinese language contracts should be translated to ensure they have the same terms as those in the English translations provided. Chinese do not treat the signing of a contract as a completed agreement. They conceive of the relationship in longer and more continuous terms, and will not hesitate to suggest modifications immediately on the heels of an agreement. For this purpose, it is wise not to inform people of your departure date. Recognize China has an inadequate system for dispute resolution. Westerners are unlikely to win in Chinese courts.

Business courtesies

Without a business card, a visitor on business is a nonperson – have an ample supply with information on one side in English, and in simplified P.R.C. Chinese characters on the other side. Remember, when using colors that gold is considered prestigious, while red is considered lucky. Since Confucianism gives ranks to everyone in society, deference to those in higher ranks is expected. At a business conference, the highest in authority leads the delegation. Thus, take time with Chinese people and be patient, anticipating speeches. Despite official disapproval, expect locals to resort to traditional beliefs, even in making a business deal (e.g., astrology, feng shui, geomancy). A knowledge of Chinese astrology can be helpful in understanding how Chinese understand their own characteristics.

When a foreign visitor has an appointment with a Chinese official, one will generally be introduced and offered tea and cigarettes. Prior to your entrance, your Chinese host will be briefed on who you are and why you are there. Polite questions about your trip, your home country, and even your family may be initiated as pleasantries. If your call is merely a courtesy call, it may not go beyond this. If this were more than a courtesy call, your Chinese host will begin with a summary of relevant (and irrelevant) considerations. Then, it would be appropriate to begin discussion of a business nature. The Chinese host will generally indicate when it is time for a person to leave.

Seating arrangements during formal meetings are a critical issue. Guests are seated according to their business or social status. The head of the meeting will be seated at the "master table," or the "master seat." The most important counterparts will be seated to the right and left of the head. Generally, there will be a key Chinese member at each table to facilitate discussion.

It is also important to reciprocate invitations when they are given in China, especially with a government representative. For example, if a banquet is given in the honor of the foreign team, they should reciprocate by giving a banquet for the Chinese team. Small company souvenirs, picture books, or ginseng make good presents and are expected. Expensive gifts should not be given.

Business cautions

The Chinese are sensitive about foreigners' comments on Chinese politics. Even a joke about the late Chairman Mao, or any of their other political leaders, is extremely *inappropriate*. It is best to listen, ask questions related to your particular business reason for being in the P.R.C., and leave it at that.

The Chinese are punctual, and you should arrive promptly on time for each meeting. Being stuck in heavy urban traffic is not an adequate excuse.

Chinese people do not like to be touched or slapped on the back, or at times even shake hands. A slight bow and a brief limp handshake are more appropriate. The traditional Chinese greeting is to clasp one's hands and bow slightly.

In business meetings, the Chinese expect businesspeople to dress formally. In addressing another, the family name is always mentioned first. For example, Teng Hsiao-ping should be addressed as Mr. Teng.

During one's stay in China, a visitor may be invited to a dinner in a restaurant by the organization that is sponsoring the visit. The guest should arrive on time, or even perhaps a little early. The host would normally toast the guest at an early stage of the meal, with the guest reciprocating after a short interval. During the meal, alcoholic beverages should not be consumed until a toast has been made. It is a custom to toast other persons at the table throughout the meal. If the Chinese initiate a series of toasts, it is poor judgment to allow oneself to become inebriated. The Chinese may be testing your self-control. At the end of the dinner, the guest of honor makes the initial move to depart. The usual procedure is to leave shortly after the meal is finished. Most dinner parties usually end by 8.30 or 9.00 in the evening.

The Chinese generally believe that foreign businesspersons will be highly qualified technically in their specific areas of expertise. The Chinese counterpart does not need to show his/her intellectual expertise or to make an impression on the foreign guest. The foreign businessperson will have discreet but lavish attention showered on him/her while in China. Remember, your Chinese counterpart may be well qualified in engineering, science, and mathematics, but less astute in the ways of Western business and management practices.

The Chinese representative traditionally places much emphasis on proper etiquette. It is recommended that the qualities that foreign businesspersons possess going to the P.R.C. are dignity, reserve, patience, persistence, and sensitivity about and respect for Chinese customs and temperament. Cultural and basic language preparation is essential.

The Chinese generally give preference to companies with long-standing relationships with state trading companies, or large companies with financial strength, and/or political clout. They prefer market leaders. Newcomers and new business organizations have to adjust to the Chinese style of arranging and negotiating contracts. Very often, several visits to the P.R.C. are necessary to consummate any business transaction. Be prepared for long-term follow-up actions. The Chinese may wish to visit your home organization. The purpose is to assess whether it is well established and can be counted on. You should do the same.

Privacy is not highly regarded due to the strong emphasis on personal relationships and living together in extended families. Personal information that Westerners consider private, like salary, is openly discussed in China. In most state-owned companies it is common knowledge what individuals earn. Yet with economic development, the concept of privacy is growing. Modern Chinese are beginning to resent intrusions of nosy employers, data-gathering marketers, ubiquitous security, and officious government inquiries into personal and family life. Generally, better-educated people are taking charge of their own lives as central planning yields to the market system. Although Orwellian controls over politics, news media, religion, and free expression remain in place, and legal protections for privacy are limited, times are changing, and the trends support the concept of personal privacy.

Facilitating cross-cultural communications

Usually,[63] foreigners should not focus on the individual Chinese person, but rather on the group of individuals who are working for a particular goal. If a Chinese individual is singled out as possessing unique qualities, this could very well embarrass the person. People from China have had negative experiences in the past with Western imperialism and superiority. China is unique in being a former victim of Western imperialism that has risen to Great Power status. Generally, in discussions with Chinese, the foreigner should avoid "self-centered" conversation in which "I" is excessively used.

Generally, the Chinese are somewhat more reticent, retiring, reserved, or shy as compared with North Americans and Europeans. They avoid open displays of affection, and the speaking distance between two people in non-intimate relationships is greater than in the West. Smartphones, emails and texting, Internet, and other forms of modern telecommunications are a vital part of Chinese business, but Chinese prefer important business be conducted face-to-face.

The insights shared in this section also largely apply to Chinese living in territories beyond China. These include the de facto independent state of Taiwan (Republic of China), as well as the large communities of overseas Chinese living in Singapore, Malaysia, Canada, and many other parts of the world. They also apply to the former European colonies of Hong Kong and Macao, reacquired by China in the 1990s.

Exhibit 13.6 is a good way to conclude discussions of China. China has become a Great Power fully equally to any other in the world. The Chinese expect to be treated that way, and they have earned it.[64]

EXHIBIT 13.6 OLYMPIC MILESTONE IN TRANSFORMING CHINA'S IMAGE

In August 2008, something happened in China's 5,000-year history that was akin to building the 4,000-mile Great Wall to keep out invaders. This time, the country hosted an international sporting event, the XXIX Summer Olympic Games, welcoming the world to the New China! Its success was a turning point in the global perception of a modern nation and its people, while changing the Chinese image of their place on the planet! It gave the people of this ancient civilization a sense of national pride and identity in modern times. By means of television and computers, an audience of four billion worldwide watched the spectacle. Humanity was awed by the scope of the Chinese preparations and presentations, as well as of their management of this momentous undertaking. It was confirmation of the transformation under way from a backward, communist, Third World nation, to an emerging economic superpower – in one generation, China has pulled 300 million inhabitants out of poverty!

Both visitors and viewers were stunned by changes in the country's infrastructure. To provide facilities and housing for their Olympic guests, some $40 billion was invested by the government and local planners over a seven-year period. Top architects came from across borders to design many of the unique buildings, including the huge stadium dubbed *The Birdsnest*, with 91,000 seats in its concrete bowl; the *Terminal 3* in the new $3.8 billion airport, the world's largest with its 10.6 million square feet; the newest Beijing subway line from the airport to the city center (now the area has 8 such lines with 120 miles of track, and by 2015 plans call for 19 lines and 350 miles of track); the 49-story masterpiece for CCTV headquarters; the National Center for the performing arts, a giant titanium egg surrounded by a moat so visitors can enter through tunnels under water. Then there were the many Olympic venues provided the athletes, including the *Water Cube* for aquatic events.

Eleven thousand athletes from 205 nations, plus 80 heads of state from across the globe attended the spectacular opening or closing ceremonies, which inspired viewers in many nations. Hundreds of drummers greeted guests in a 2,500-year-old performance, while thousands engaged in a musical extravaganza with colorful, oriental dances and acrobatics. For this "coming out party," the Chinese spruced up their *Forbidden City*, even managing to curb pollution and improve the air quality, as well as to cause a little needed rain to fall! And, to top this off, Chinese athletes won the largest number of gold medals for the sporting contest.

The lucky-numbered 8/8/08 Olympic opening and closing ceremonies boosted citizen morale, while the whole feat indicated that China was on its way to having the most influential culture in today's world. All this in a historical context was a turning point to help 1.3 billion Chinese forget the past humiliations of the nineteenth-century colonialist powers who occupied their land; the painful Long March to unite the country; the chaotic and damaging Cultural

EXHIBIT 13.6

Revolution; the traumatic Tiananmen Square crackdown in 1989 on youthful reformers; the destruction of recent earthquakes which killed some 50,000 citizens; and the 8/7/08 rebuke by the U.S. president of their Communist government over repression of human rights and freedoms. Now that their space program has put Chinese astronauts in orbit, no one doubts their ability to accomplish plans to put some of their own on the moon by 2024!

Source: Adapted from Mark Ziegler's "China Emerges from the Chairman's Shadow," *The San Diego-Union Tribune,* August 7, 2008, pp. AI and 8; international television broadcast commentary by NBC, August 7–24, 2008. For further insights, read Professor Susan L. Shirk's *China: Fragile Superpower.* New York: Oxford University Press, 2008.

JAPAN

Contemporary Japanese culture is considerably different from previous, traditional notions of it and from most people's current stereotypes, including those of the Japanese themselves. Japan is commonly and stereotypically known as a land of nobility and chivalry, with values such as honor, pride, and perseverance. These form a moral code of everyday living that has permeated Japanese society for generations, even centuries. Yet contemporary Japanese culture (especially for younger Japanese) seems to operate from different values, attitudes, beliefs, norms, and behaviors. In short, Japan is evolving into a society with a different culture.

D. Matsumoto[65]

No country in modern history has moved so swiftly from worldwide adulation to dismissive contempt as did Japan. In the past twenty-three years, amid crushing stock and property markets, mountains of dud debt, scores of corruption scandals, vast government deficits, and stagnant economic growth, Japan mutated from a giver of lessons to a recipient of lectures, all of which offers recipes for its reform and revival. Now, however, the time for lectures is over. Japan is back. It is being reformed. It is revising. Really?

Bill Emmott[66]

Asia is a potpourri of nations and cultures, so it is difficult to generalize about its diverse peoples and their mindsets. Japanese behavior may seem puzzling and be a source of both confusion and wonderment. For North Americans, perched on the Pacific Rim, Japan is the epitome of the Far East and its enigmas. Because Japan is going through profound economic and social transformation within a generation or so, its cultural specifics must be viewed in that context. Realities of their participation in the global market and media are only two of the driving forces altering cultural preferences in that traditional society, especially among the new generation.

Japanese markets are indeed hard, but not impossible, to penetrate, as McDonald's, Coca-Cola, IBM, and many others have demonstrated. Informal protection, in the form of close linkages between supplier and customer, is a handicap to outsiders.

Historical perspective

Geographically, the Japanese archipelago in located on Asia's east coast, consisting of four large islands (Honshu, Hokkaido, Kyushu, and Shikoku), plus approximately four thousand small islands – they are spread in a 2,000-mile arc in the Western Pacific. If a map of Japan was laid over a map of the United States, Japan would extend from Los Angeles to New York, but only include a land area the size of Montana.

Honshu, the largest island and cultural center, has about 50 percent of the population, including five major cities. These include the capital, Tokyo, as well as Yokohama, Osaka, Nagoya, and Kyoto (its ancient capital). Steep mountains run through the centers of these islands, so that the flat terrain is only along the coasts and valleys. Only about 15 percent of the terrain is suitable for agriculture – the staple local foods are rice, fruit, and vegetables, plus extensive seafood. This relatively small landmass has contributed to a collective mindset of paradox, insularity, and expansionism of a relatively homogeneous population of about 125 million.

Indeed, Japan is an ancient society – myth indicates its founding in 660 BC by Emperor Jimmu, but records on this country do not appear until 3 AD.[67] Seemingly, the majority of its people are descendents of migrating Mongolians from the northeast. Its minority population of *Ainu* inhabitants used to dominate all Japan but have been driven back over the centuries to the northern island of Hokkaido. The Ainu seem to be descended from the same people who migrated across the Bering Sea to become the American Aboriginal peoples.

From the beginning, Japanese culture was intertwined with Chinese and Korean cultures. Its major native religion was Shinto,[68] still entwined with the state. This "way of the gods" details rituals and customs that foreigners perceive as religious ceremonies, though Shinto's main message is "know thyself" and looking at a Shinto altar one sees oneself in the mirror hung there.

From the fifth century AD onward, there is evidence of development of a clan-based society on the Yamato plains. It is here that the myth originated of the clan leaders' divine descent from the sun goddess, continued through the imperial line down the centuries until Emperor Hirohito in 1946 recanted his divinity, a traumatic postwar experience for his subjects.

The clan system of governance gave way in 1192 AD to military overlord rule and establishment of the feudal system. Emperors were relegated to ceremonial roles. Power shifted to powerful noble family control whose leader held the title of *shogun*. This was the period of family lineage and honor. Self-discipline and bravery was epitomized in the warrior retainer or *samurai*. Various shogun dynasties rose to rule.

This agrarian economy changed slowly as a result of encounters with Westerners, starting with the Portuguese in 1542. By the mid-1600s, foreign missionaries were expelled, Japanese Christian converts were persecuted to force them to apostatize, and Japan cut itself off from the world for two hundred years. For most of its modern history, the Japanese were influenced by feudalistic concepts of absolute obedience and loyalty to their superiors. Japanese feudal society lasted until the nineteenth century, when U.S. Navy's Commodore Perry and his fleet forced Japan open to the West. In the 1868, the Tokugawa shogunate was overthrown and the Emperor re-established as the ruler in the Meiji restoration.

Typically, a series of changing images about the Japanese people and culture emerged and can be grouped around stages. Pre-World War II, the Japanese were admired for their ambitious efforts to catch up to European and American industrialization. Japan developed a military and industrial base sufficient to become the first modern Asian nation to defeat a European power, the Russian Empire, in a war (1904–1905). Japan also defeated China in a war, annexing Taiwan, and receiving Korea and parts of southern Manchuria as settlement territories. By 1931, Japan controlled all of Chinese Manchuria. In World War I, Japan was an ally of the Allied side, defeating the Germans at Qingdao, the German "Hong Kong" in northern China.

As Japan sought further modernization, it became a major colonial power, invading China in the early 1930s. Before World War II, the nation aligned itself with Nazi Germany and Fascist Italy. In 1941, President Roosevelt of the United States provoked war with Japan by imposing sanctions related to its invasion of China, and demanding that Japan exit China. State Department documents, classified for 50 years, show that Roosevelt sought to enter the war against Nazi Germany and saw war with Japan, Germany's ally, as the means.[69] The United States and its allies were abashed by the daring and destructive Japanese attack upon Pearl Harbor in 1941, though America knew it was coming, having broken Japanese military communication codes, and moving its aircraft carriers out of harm's way.[70]

During World War II, Japan continued to expand in China, Vietnam, and elsewhere in Asia until the Allied military successfully forced a retreat. Japan surrendered and accepted American occupation after the United States exploded two nuclear devices in Hiroshima and Nagasaki with great civilian loss of life. The victors then proceeded to demilitarize the nation, democratize the government, and reform the Japanese society and economy. The Allied peace terms stripped Japan of all territories acquired since 1894 in East Asia.

During the postwar period, the foundations were laid for today's economic and political society. The occupation ended in 1952 when Japan was declared an independent state. Since then, in the late twentieth century, Japan transformed itself into an industrial superpower. By 1960, it had the third-largest economy in the world. Interestingly, in the early twenty-first century, its old enemy, Russia, is building an oil pipeline passing north of Lake Baikal to the Sea of Japan to supply both the Japanese and Koreans. Today, Japan seeks to be both a world leader in climate change and environmental matters, as well as a cooperator in the international space program.

Although there are eight political parties, the Liberal Democratic Party (LDP) ruled between 1955 and 2009, despite corruption, other scandals, and economic reverses. In 2007, it lost its majority in the upper house of the Diet (parliament), and the opposition Democratic Party (DPJ), which captured the prime ministership, 2009–2012.

The DPJ proved unpopular. It was blamed for the Fukushima Daiichi nuclear disaster caused by a major 2011 earthquake and tsunami. Radioactivity threatened the northern outskirts of Tokyo and the safety of food grown in northern Honshu. The DPJ was also blamed for a relatively weak response to Chinese (Sendaku Islands) and North Korean aggression. In 2012, the LDP was returned to power under Prime Minister Shinzo Abe.

Japan is a strong democracy where human rights are respected and militarization avoided. Under the new constitution, the parliamentary form of government has been retained and the Emperor's role is symbolic. The head of government, the Prime Minister, is elected by the parliament or National Diet. The Upper and Lower Houses are elected by the public.

Despite its economic "miracles" and leadership in the global marketplace, Japan is still a highly insular culture with an entrenched bureaucracy and protectionist trade policies. It suffers today from economic setbacks and political confusion. Yet, the nation has trade agreements throughout the world with various countries, such as Chile, while also investing in other economies, such as India. Like China, it holds over $1 trillion currency reserves in the U.S.A. Also, many people of Japanese heritage are to be found in the United States, Peru, and Brazil.

Cultural guidelines for business in Japan

Japan is a "high-context" culture (see Chapter 2) that thrives on subtlety and consensus. Its people manifest high educational abilities, formidable technological skills, and powerful social coordination.[71] Since 20 percent of the world's earthquakes occur here as a result of three interacting tectonic plates, the citizenry live in a state of perpetual preparedness for 10,000 annual tremors.

With national motives directed to success and status, the acquiring of credentials through education is a high priority. At anything undertaken, most Japanese are usually meticulous and methodical. The following general insights may prove helpful when dealing with the Japanese, whether at home or abroad.

LANGUAGE AND COMMUNICATION

The Japanese language is complex, subtle, and predictable. By the time a native speaker is halfway through a statement, a Japanese will translate simultaneously and likely know how the sentence will end. Whereas that same person interpreting from English will wait until the foreigner has finished before beginning the translation into Japanese. Communications there are usually marked by these characteristics:

- Indirect and vague communications are more acceptable than direct and specific references. Ambiguous terminology is preferred. Sentences frequently are left unfinished so that another may conclude them. Conversation transpires within an ill-defined and shadowy context, never quite definite, so as not to preclude personal interpretation.
- Language is capable of delicate nuances regarding states of mind and relationships. While rich in imagination, it can be clumsy for science and business. There are layers of soft language with various degrees of courtesy and respect. This especially affects females for whom "plain" or "coarse" language is considered improper.
- The listener makes little noises of tentative suggestion, understanding, and encouragement. "*Hai*" may mean more than "yes" and imply, "I'm listening," or, "I understand."
- Nonverbal communications are subtle, and Japanese are disconcerted by the broad expressions and gestures of Americans.

There is a formal politeness for official negotiation and ordinary business communication. A different and more informal approach may be used while socializing. Frequently, while entertaining, the real business and political deals are concluded.

The Japanese require more information about the person with whom they interact, so as to determine which form to use in their complex language. Thus, they are given to asking questions about your job, title, responsibilities, and so on. When a business meeting is scheduled, they prefer advance information in the form of electronic mail, brochures, and even proposals to help them prepare.

Japanese appreciate it when outsiders seek to learn more about their unique culture and language, even if it is only a few phrases or expressions in Japanese.

DRESS AND APPEARANCE

Managers and businesspeople are expected to dress in neat, orderly, and conservative ways usually including dress shirt, tie, and suit. Ordinary workers and students frequently wear distinctive uniforms and even a company pin, which managers also may sport (a holdover from feudal days when a kimono carried a lord's symbol). The ancient, classical dress, the kimono is becoming less common even in the privacy of the home but is retained for ceremonial events, and public bathhouses and traditional hotels. Western formal dress is used for important state occasions. Traditional native dress is sexless, although the shape of the garment is different, and the obi, or belt, is placed and tied differently. The colors are often neutral with women sometimes tending toward flowery patterns.

Japanese youth prefer to wear contemporary clothes and hairstyles. They want to look like teenagers do elsewhere. Also, with changes in diet, the young appear to be physically larger than their parents, and obesity is a growing problem with this affluent generation.

Colors have different significance in Japanese culture (e.g., white for sorrow, black for joy).

FOOD AND EATING HABITS

Eating in Japan is ritualistic, communal, and time consuming. The interaction is considered as important as the food. While the traditional diet emphasizes rice, noodles, and fish, youths tend toward popular Western foods. The alcoholic beverage of *sake* often accompanies the main or ceremonial meal so as to facilitate conversation. Tokyo is said to have a restaurant, bar, or cabaret for every 110 members of the population, with many international foods represented. Fast-food establishments are everywhere and popular.

TIME, AGE, AND REWARDS

Japanese are punctual, and need time for connections to make proper contacts. Yet they expect you to wait for group decisions that also take time because of the expectation to arrive at consensus.

Traditionally, they respect seniority and the elderly. There is a sense of order, propriety, and appropriate behavior between subordinates and superiors.

In the past, young managers, recruited from the universities after stiff examinations, were expected to stay with a company until they were 55 years of age; conforming, doing what was expected of them, and showing respect and deference to senior or older employees. Then, the crucial decision would be made whether the 55-year-old manager would become a company director. If he or she made it, he/she could stay beyond the normal Western retirement age and even work into his/her seventies or eighties. Some of those not so honored could be transferred to become department or subsidiary directors, retiring at 60. Others might be required to retire between 55 and 60, though even then they might be retained in a temporary capacity. These customs are now changing. Lifetime employment is no longer the norm.

There is a tendency to reward and recognize the group or organization rather than the individual in Japanese organizations. One achieves and is recognized through the group in ever-widening circles: family, team, department, division, company, nation.

Great emphasis is placed on security and the social need for "belonging." Notice that when traveling abroad, Japanese stay within their own group, generally avoiding individual contact with the locals. However, Japanese managers, working abroad, may be more engaged with their foreign workers.

RELATIONSHIPS

A nation the size of Montana, Japan is cohesive and crowded, which accounts for its rituals of bowing and politeness in crowded urban areas. Japanese relationships are familial and group oriented, instead of individualistic. Japanese value group relations and harmony. Group leadership is more highly regarded than individual initiative. There is a tendency toward clannishness based on family or group connections. One needs to know one's place and be comfortable with it.

Personal relationships score high with Japanese, and future relationships depend on how you respond in the first encounter. Cut-and-dried relationships with business contacts are inadequate and must be supplemented by a social relationship for maximum effect. This usually means gift giving,[72] entertaining the client with a "night on the town" but not at one's home. Part of the Japanese manager's reward is a generous budget for entertaining. When away from home on business, the Japanese businessperson expects to be entertained lavishly (meals, theater tickets, etc.), but repays this kindness without reservation.

With regard to international relationships, Japan has close emotional and economic ties to the United States, but is suspicious of aggressive Americans. The Japanese fear China, yet they are emotionally allied and identify with the Chinese. China has been an important location for offshoring expensive Japanese manufacturing jobs. China was Japan's leading export market, and leading source of imports in 2009.[73] This may be changing to some degree with the recent upsurge of anti-Japanese feelings in China. Nissan was on the verge of a major manufacturing investment in China. With Nissan sales down 16 to 30 percent in China, expansion of manufacturing capacity was put on hold in China, and Nissan geared up in India where sales were expected to treble in 2013.[74]

In business relationships, there are two Japans – officialdom and intellectuals (e.g., politicians and businesspersons). In both, decision-making tends to be consensus oriented, and slow. Senior people have more influence. There is a symbiotic relationship between government and business – cozy but not constricting.

In context of social relations, Japanese tend to be clean, polite, and disciplined. Sociality and self-control disguise a highly emotional quality of the Japanese character and relationships. While the Japanese are sensitive to what others think or expect of them, and have a sharp sense of right and wrong, they find it difficult to deal with the unexpected and strange, and so may smile or laugh when feeling unsure or uncomfortable.

Again, youth epitomize the culture in transition. They are energetic and productive, yet anxious for change, gaining a new sense of "I/my/me-ness," while the pattern for their elders is "we-ness." The general gap between the generations is very wide. For example, younger university graduates are more open to entrepreneurship, especially in information technologies.

In business organizations, the "bridge" for the young manager is an elder, upper middle manager assigned as a guide or facilitator. This senior person is rarely the direct superior of the young manager. He/she is expected to know him/her, meet regularly, and be available for advice and counsel, and to assist in transfers and discipline, when necessary. This respected elder manager is always consulted on promotions and other personnel matters concerning the young person's career. He/she is the human contact for the organization with the young manager, the listener, guide, and mentor who provides a significant and helpful human relationship.

ATTITUDES AND BELIEFS

The typical Japanese character[75] is diverse with a sense of poetry and of the ephemeral. There is a concern for the transitory, inconclusive qualities of life, for nature, and its observation. It is actively curious, energetic, and quick, with a sense of delicacy and wistfulness. One manifestation is in the art of flower arrangements.

Although many Japanese will not admit to being religious, and the usual attitude is syncretic, there are three religious philosophies of life that are pervasive and that influence their behavior. Confucianism[76] and Buddhism were both introduced from China around the end of the eighth century AD.

Shintoism was native to Japan. It teaches respect for nature and counsels harmony between man and nature. Shinto minor deities are found in shrines (*jinja* distinguished by red wooden archways), and in nature itself (e.g., mountains and rivers). The dominant religious thrust is the syncretic convergence of Shintoism and Buddhism. Individuals are baptized, honored as children, and married in Shinto ceremonies. They are buried in Buddhist ceremonies. Shintoism has become less influential since World War II because the Emperor was and is its symbolic leader, and the Emperor's role has become largely ceremonial.

Buddhism is the largest conventional religion in Japan, while Christianity has made limited impact (except with Christmas celebrations and decorations in retail stores). The crusading Buddhist Soka Gakkai sect is also a political party that fights inequalities of the social structure, while enshrining the idealistic, self-denial, and the espousal of the underdog.

VALUES AND STANDARDS

The dominant Japanese ethos includes familial relationships, loyalty, conformity, and the collective good. Japanese personality is generally self-confident and flexible, demonstrating a sense of order, propriety, and appropriate behavior. There is a tendency toward diligence and thrift, balanced by a fun-loving approach, which, at times, seems almost frivolous and extravagant.

In outlook, the Japanese are cautious and given to stalling tactics. They are also insular, which is manifested by the in-group tendency. The rigid, ossified Japanese class system is disappearing. Most Japanese regard themselves as middle class.

Japanese value peace, harmony, and economic progress, ensured somewhat by the fact that only 1 percent of the nation's gross national product is devoted to defense spending. Japan is precluded by its constitution to have offensive military capability. This culture highly regards new ideas and technologies, swallowing them up until they are Japanized (internalized) after careful, detailed examination. The success of Japanese communications and automotive industries confirm this value. Today, there is a subtle shift in emphasis under way from copying others to creating one's own by innovation.

Japanese society also values training and education, especially of the young. It also values a spirit of intensity and craftsmanship manifested by a quality of deep penetration and pride in work no matter how humble. This has been expressed not only in arts and crafts, but in graphic novels and animation.

Japanese prefer congenial, known surroundings, and seek to create an atmosphere of well-focused energy and disciplined good cheer. A basic standard of Japanese life is work and play hard – work particularly for the good of the family or company family, and maintain controlled competition and cooperation in the process. Then play hard – younger Japanese devote more time to leisure and recreational activities.

Postwar Japanese fear foreign military involvement, but are willing to engage in humanitarian endeavors sponsored by the United Nations. However, because of the pressure from China and North Korea, Prime Minister Shinzo Abe hopes to revise the Japanese Constitution to allow for better military capability and the freedom to use it. A current debate in Japan concerns nuclear weapons. The United States has guaranteed Japan's nuclear security for many years but the question in Japan is whether the United States would go to war with China to defend Japan?

The younger generation seeks more control over their lives. A minority of radical, revolutionary Japanese youth have an entirely different set of values from the majority. These youths can be vicious and violent, yet espouse a spirit of self-denial, self-correction, and self-dedication to what they consider a higher cause. Even criminal gangs will publicly apologize in press conferences to the public when they cause too much violence and disruption in society. Youths are transforming this traditional society, and are more globally attuned because of telecommunications and travel.

Also, a declining birthrate is causing economic concern and distress. Japan's overall population has fallen over the past few years – deaths outnumber births. Japan has the highest percentage of elderly population in the world, and this results in lower economic productivity, and higher needs for government and medical services. Globalization and acquisitions have brought more foreign managers and professionals into this rather closed society where they are politely treated as guests but always as outsiders.

Essentially, in the twenty-first century, this is a society concerned about national economic welfare, market penetration, and humanitarian endeavors. Increasingly, Japanese companies are giving a percentage of profits to promote education, social welfare, culture, and protection of the environment.

Managing in Japan

The old industrial model of management, which initially produced a "Japanese miracle" in the last half of the twentieth century, is undergoing rapid change. It was based on:

1   Lifetime employment within the same organization.
2   Workers spending their entire career working their way up in the same firm to gain seniority-based pay.
3   Company-based unions that promoted cooperation between labor and management.
4   Close relationships between companies and their banks, subsidiaries, and other corporate groups bound together in cross-shareholdings – called a *keiretsu*.

This model once ensured social stability and cohesion, as well as rapid economic growth abroad. To remain globally competitive, a new model is emerging:

1   Effective redeployment of labor, including proper use of women and the elderly. For most companies, the policy of lifetime employment has ended.
2   Encouraging entrepreneurship and innovation.
3   Greater integration in the global economy by accessing fast-growing foreign markets and meeting international competition.

A more hybrid Japanese model of economic enterprise is developing that is closer to Western ways of managing, while still utilizing some of the old ways that work in this culture. Japan is searching for its own capitalistic approach to a market economy, so that both shareholders and stakeholders are protected. Thus, the traditional "salaryman system" is giving way to a more flexible labor market that is performance-based. There is also greater use of part-time, temporary, and contract workers. The challenge is for improvement in the working conditions of "nonregular workers," and women. Rigidity in the Japanese workforce is slowly moving away from cultural factors like group conformity, to creative individualism. Today, young professionals are not afraid of moving between companies, or to work for foreign firms. The "now" generation refuses to make work the center of their lives, and is less willing to accept corporate paternalism.

The Japanese continue to pursue the acquisition of Western management skills, including sophisticated management theory and concepts transferred to the Japanese environment. This is forcing changes in the way of dealing with foreigners. A more competitive climate is developing for foreigners or *gaijin* that permits more direct investment in Japanese enterprises. Furthermore, when expatriate managers return from working in Japanese operations abroad, they introduce some of their new learning from that experience into local management.

In their organizations, the goals are product quality and superiority; team work and consensus; corporate growth and social responsibility. Yet too many Japanese managers avoid saying what they think because it disrupts harmony, and seems immodest. Subordinates are usually reluctant to challenge managers' ideas, lest the boss lose face. Risk-taking and initiative are stifled, and seeking consensus can become an excuse for compromise and avoiding hard decisions. Mental health problems are rising in the workplace, and the country's suicide rate is among the highest in the world. Many Japanese still die each year from "overwork" – a medical condition in Japan. The work environment needs to provide more individual incentives, responsibility, and rewards based on performance, rather than age or seniority.

Here are some observations about this unique but changing business culture:

■   Japanese will try to achieve sales and profits without harming face and harmony or creating a poor standing in the business community.

- Third party or indirect introductions are important for creating trust between individuals who come together through a mutual friend, go-between, or arbitrator. This person may be involved until the conclusion of the negotiation.
- Whomever you approach in the organization, do so at the highest level. The first person contacted is also involved throughout the negotiation.
- Avoid direct communication about money. Leave this to the go-between or lower echelon staff. Money, if passed to a Japanese businessperson, should be in an envelope.
- For social visiting, a guest is frequently given a present or small gift, such as a hand towel beautifully wrapped, or a food article. At the next exchange of visits, you are expected to offer a gift in kind.
- Avoid publicly putting a Japanese in a position where he or she must admit failure.
- Play down self-praise of your product or services. Let your literature or go-between do that. Japanese respect senior managers who are modest in demeanor and expression.
- Use business cards with your titles in both Japanese and English.
- Logical, cognitive, or intellectual approaches are insufficient. The emotional level of communication is considered important (e.g., as in dealing with a known business associate versus a stranger).
- Formality prevails in senior staff meetings with interpreters present. The more important the meeting, the more senior executives are present.
- Wait patiently for meetings to move beyond preliminary tea and sometimes long formalities.

DECISION-MAKING

Again, the Japanese value decision by consensus. Before action is taken, much time is spent on defining the question. The Japanese decide first if there is a need for a decision and what the situation is all about. The focus is on what the decision is really about, not what it should be. Once agreement is reached, the Japanese move with great speed to the action stage.

Referral of the question is made to the appropriate people, in effect, being top management's answer to the question. The system forces the Japanese to make big decisions, and to avoid the Western tendency toward "kicking the can down the road" by making small decisions that are easy to make (minutia). For example, instead of making a decision on a particular joint venture, the Japanese might consider the direction the business should go, and then this particular joint venture is then only a small aspect of the larger issue.

TERMS OF EMPLOYMENT

As noted above, the traditional corporate policy of long-term or lifetime employment is changing. First, not all workers are considered permanent. A substantial body of employees (perhaps 20 percent) is not subject to this job security. Some positions are hired and paid for by the hour. Women are generally considered in the temporary work category – Japan has often been regarded as a particularly chauvinist culture, but this is changing rapidly, especially among younger people. Some who retire at 55 may be kept on in that temporary capacity. Adjustments in workforce can be readily made using and letting go these "temporaries."

For full-time employees, pay is as a rule the basis of seniority. Pay doubles every 15 years. Retirement is a 2-year salary benefit, or severance bonus, usually at age 55. At 60, individuals qualify for social security pensions. Western pension plans are beginning to come into companies slowly, and are low in benefits.

In the past, permanent employees who left an employer had a very difficult time obtaining permanent positions with another employer. However, the new work environment places more emphasis on competence and performance.

Another standard of Japanese work life seems to be *continuous training*. This is performance-focused as opposed to promotion-focus. In scope, it involves training not only in one's own job, but in all jobs at one's level. The emphasis is on productivity, and the real burden of training is on the learner.

On the whole, Japanese believe older workers are more productive, and output per person-hour is invariably higher in a plant with an older worker population. With the new knowledge workers, that attitude is being altered.

Recognize also that the Japanese labor force is both aging and diminishing today. This has promoted the trend toward more women entering the workforce, and giving them a greater role, as well as increasing the use of robots! Realize that birth rates have plummeted, the population is shrinking drastically – possibly from 128 million now to as few as 100 million by 2050. This will affect the nation's GDP, also already on the decline. Expect Japan in the near future to become a major leader in pan-Asian cooperation, while remaining a close ally of the United States.

The Japanese are a remarkable and unique people. Their subtle, complex culture, in particular, illustrates the differences and diversity of Asian cultures in general. The Japanese have also learned and successfully applied many lessons from other countries, so other nations should be learning from their culture, especially in terms of management and organizational behavior!

Japan is not a superpower, such as the U.S.A., and China, but it is a balanced country that can support other countries, or not. The Japanese constantly reinvent themselves with technological breakthroughs, such as in robotics and nanotechnologies. But their companies must improve in collaboration with other firms around the world, like the global alliance of Renault–Nissan and Sony–Ericsson. Foreign firms going into Japan need to understand that distinctive, local market, as Starbucks did when it crafted its strategy for doing business there. Patience and determination are the keys to success in this culture. Just remember that Japan is still the world's third-largest economy, representing a substantial portion of the Asian market.

Japanese strategic thinking

Bushido. The Japanese, like the Chinese, have sources of native strategic decision-making that they employ in addition to Western strategic planning practices. Japanese strategic thinking differs from the Chinese, in its derivation from Zen Buddhism.[77] Called *bushido*,[78] the Buddhist influence represents submission to fate, stoicism in the face of danger, disdain for one's own life or success, and willingness to sacrifice oneself to ensure a successful outcome. From Zen, it acquires a method of contemplation and an understanding that, through meditation, levels of thought and action may be achieved that cannot be expressed verbally.

Bushido is organized around a series of values that its practitioner seeks to achieve simultaneously through his/her actions. Therefore, bushido is a process of deliberating and actioning strategic intention based on ethical commitments. The following are key bushido values:

1 *Rectitude or justice*. Bushido denounces dishonest and underhanded dealings. Rectitude is the ability to decide on a course of action and to pursue it without wavering, despite changing circumstances. Justice is defined in Mencian Confucian terms as benevolence towards others, righteousness in one's dealings with others, and fidelity in one's commitments to others. This value alone makes Japanese strategic thinking very different from the Chinese emphasis on deception.

2 *Courage.* Defined as doing what is right regardless of hazards including to oneself. Perceiving what is right and not doing it is considered lack of courage.

3 *Benevolence*. Defined as love, magnanimity, sympathy and affection for others. Bushido regards this as "the highest of all the attributes of the human soul."[79] One hopes to treat all relationships with kindness and magnanimity.

4 *Politeness*. This is the outward manifestation of an empathetic regard for the feelings of others. It is not based on any fear of offending another. In its highest form, politeness is like love, and is the highest form of social interaction.

5 *Veracity and sincerity*. This is telling the truth. An interesting feature of bushido values is the recognition by the Japanese that critical values may sometimes conflict. Here, veracity may conflict with politeness. Lying or equivocating are considered cowardly, and sacrificing truth for politeness is considered deception with sweet words, politeness conflicts. One must decide on situational propriety of action.

6 *Honor*. This is personal dignity and worth. Any imprecation against one's honor induces shame. Honor, however, must be tempered by magnanimity (benevolence) and patience, leading to a second value conflict.

7 *Loyalty*. This is submission to hierarchy, especially one's superiors. In China, loyalty to one's parents ahead of to one's leaders was a Confucian virtue. In Japan, loyalty to leaders took precedence.

8 *Self-control*. This is stoicism; the willingness to accept suffering and restrain natural desires and inclinations, or even (for men) expression of feelings.

SOUTH KOREA

So in Asia I want to make – I want to succeed to make a model of what is success, practicing democracy, and market economy. Then that will give a good influence over Asian countries.

Kim Dae Kung, President of South Korea, 1998–2003[80]

I will revive the legend of the economic miracle, making the country a place where people have no worry about living and young people merrily go to work.

Park Geun-hye, President of South Korea, 2012[81]

South Korea is one of the most important Asian Tiger (also including Singapore, Hong Kong and Taiwan) economies, and one of the fastest growing World economies in the 2000s. It has a market economy ranked 15th in the world by nominal GDP, and 12th by purchasing power parity (PPP). It is the only developed country included in the Goldman Sachs "Next Eleven" of countries, in addition to the Emerging Market BRICs (Brazil, Russia, India, China), likely to become the world's largest economies during the twenty-first century.[82] In 2011, four of the Next Eleven, the MIKT (Mexico, Indonesia, South Korea, Turkey) comprised 73 percent of the total Next Eleven GDP. Total BRIC GDP was US$13.5 trillion while Next Eleven total GDP was US$3.5 trillion. South Korea is evidently one of the most promising countries for future economic growth even though its credit rating has been damaged by the uncertainty caused by North Korean belligerence.[83]

The Korean Peninsula lies south of China, with the Yellow Sea to the west, and the Sea of Japan to the east. Manchuria and Russia border lie to the north. Today, the Peninsula is divided between North and South Korea. The Communist North occupies about 55 percent of the total area. Democratic South Korea is about 99,392 square kilometers (38,375 square miles). Korea is very mountainous, and Koreans proclaim that if the land could be rolled out flat, it would be as big as China.

The two political entities, North and South Korea, are separated by the Demilitarized Zone, an outcome of Korean War in 1953. This DMZ is a 4-kilometer-wide strip of land that runs along the 38th parallel for 243 kilometers, or 150 miles. There has never been a peace treaty signed between the North and the South and both sides remain militarily ready to resume the conflict at any time. The American armed forces have a real physical presence in the South intended to ensure that this does not happen.

In 688 AD, the Paekche people were in the southwest and Silla in the southeast when the latter conquered the peninsula to found a state that was the foundation of modern Korea. Over their long history, Koreans clashed with many neighbors until the Mongols conquered them in 1259 to set up a reign that lasted a hundred years.

In 1392, General Yi-Song-gye seized the Korean throne. His Choson Dynasty ruled until 1910. Previously, the country, afraid of Christian missionaries, isolated itself from the rest of the world and was known as the "Hermit Kingdom." In 1854, an American fleet under Admiral Perry defeated the Korean navy to open Korea for American trade.[84]

In the nineteenth century, both Japan and China vied for control of Korea, so the Korean king turned to Russia for assistance, but the latter sought to control the nation's warm water ports. When Koreans staged protests for independence, it led to the Sino-Japanese War of 1894–1895, resulting in Japan assuming control on the peninsula. Japan's dominance was confirmed when Japan won a war with Russia in 1905. By 1910, the Japanese abolished the Korean monarchy and treated the country as a dependent colony. When Japan again went to war with China from 1937 to 1945, it mobilized the country as a military base. The Koreans were forced to adopt the Japanese language and names, as well as Shintoism and the ideology of the divinity of the Japanese emperor.

Korea and its sufferings were virtually ignored by the rest of the world until the end of World War II. Then Russia assumed control of the peninsula north of the 38th parallel, while Americans occupied the rest of Korea in the south. In 1948, the Soviets established a Communist state in their zone and withdrew from the country. This "Democratic Republic of Korea" (DPRK) in the north is still the center of international tension in the twenty-first century. The next year, the Americans also withdrew, leaving in place the "Republic of Korea" (RFK), known today as South Korea. Efforts by the United Nations to reunite the two entities were blocked by Communist nations. Korea became a focus of world attention in a clash between the East and the West; a battleground of communist and democratic ideologies. When North Korea invaded South Korea in 1950, it led to war with both the United Nations, led by the Americans, and China's intervention on the side of the North, resulting in the battlefield death of Mao Zedong's only son. With a stalemate in this conflict, an armistice was signed in 1953, leaving Korea divided by the DMZ; two states with suspended hostilities.

Syngman Rhee was elected first President of South Korea, serving in that role from 1948 to 1960. After a period of political disorganization and rule by a military junta led by Park Chung Hee, a new constitution obtained widespread public support. When Park was officially elected President in 1963, his authoritarian regime was successful in promoting the country's development.

South Korea's economic transformation was then the wonder of the world. It took South Korea only three decades to transition from a farming nation to an industrial giant. Its quality products and energetic workers were exported around the globe, along with eager-to-learn technicians. South Korea has begun to open its market in a bid to join the big league of global competition, but some say it is having difficulty shedding its protectionist ways. Canadian Korean free trade talks have stumbled over Korean insistence that Korean cars be allowed duty free into Canada. By contrast, in Korea, foreign cars were banned until 1989. Then, Korean purchasers of foreign cars were audited – U.S. protests ended the practice. In 2009, Korean tax authorities demanded the names and personal information of any Koreans buying foreign cars. A Korean who buys a foreign car will be audited for possible tax fraud.

South Korea has renewed its cities and built satellite cities around Seoul, as well as renewing the country's west coast. While the North stagnates under totalitarianism, this dynamic society produced a first-class Olympic Games and facilities in 1988. It has experienced relatively peaceful elections as the nation transformed itself into a constitutional democracy. Its population is restless for more freedom, improved working conditions, and benefits, plus progress toward national reunification with the North.

With an economic growth rate of averaging 4.4 percent annually, South Korea has had a highly productive export market. This growth rate slumped to 2.3 percent in 2012, and 2.7 percent in 2013. The Korea Development Institute reports that the country is restructuring toward a domestic-driven economy, especially with citizens having more disposable income. There is a growing demand for domestic goods and services, along with the desire for improved housing and tourism abroad.

Doing business here requires great care and sensitivity in a land of Confucian family structure, and great respect for age-based seniority. Koreans have a passion for work and self-improvement, and are respected for their disciplined determination and entrepreneurship.

To the north, a ruthless regime abuses 23 million inhabitants, denying them freedom and food, while undermining international relations. In this failed state, with the worst human rights record and highest corruption levels in the world, one in forty have been imprisoned in *gulags*. One in twenty is in the military. Famine stalks, malnutrition spreads, mobile phones and the Internet are forbidden, and refugees attempt to flee to China or South Korea. If caught, they are imprisoned as traitors.

The former dictator, Kim Jong Il, pushed towards a global showdown over his nuclear weapons program until economic deterioration forced him to promise to dismantle his atomic bomb facilities in exchange for outside aid. He reneged. Kim Jung Il's son Kim Jong Un, age 29 or 30, succeeded to his father's position at the end of 2011. In order to secure his position as supreme commander, he threatened South Korea, Japan, and the United States with nuclear war, and positioned missiles that he claimed could reach the west coast of the United States. His belligerence was brought under control by North Korea's only ally, China, which began to refuse economic development loans critical to the North. Conditions in North Korea are described in Exhibit 13.7.

Cultural guidelines for business in South Korea

The business environment in South Korea is slowly changing from some of what is described below, because the values of Koreans are changing from generation to generation. People born in the 1950s or earlier grew up in a poor, underdeveloped, Third World country and remain committed to hard work and thrift. This generation remains in control of Korean politics and business because of the strong Korean commitment to age-based seniority. Younger generations of Koreans have grown up in a prosperous First World economy and their values are much closer to those found in other G8 countries. However, given the large number of older Koreans living or working abroad, especially in the United States, this information should prove useful in cross-cultural communication especially with senior managers and Korean expatriates.

EXHIBIT 13.7 NORTH KOREAN NIGHTMARE

In the twenty-first century, the international community has been concerned about North Korea's ability to create nuclear power and weapons. Numerous six-party negotiations by America, South Korea, Japan, China, and Russia with this rogue regime ended in discord. Despite promises of food and other aid, Kim Jong II and his militarists resisted, until recently, attempts to coax better behavior. But that is not the only problem neighbors have with this wily and cruel administration, which permits its own population to starve. There are a range of other complaints about its criminal activities, ranging from kidnappings of Japanese nationals from Japan, and production of fake drugs, to money counterfeiting and laundering, to illegal trade in endangered species, missiles, and other weapons. This racketeering state, responsible for tons of illicit goods and fake currency throughout Asia, has seen its diplomats expelled from a variety of countries. The United States slapped sanctions on North Korea for illicit weapons proliferation. Up to 40 percent of the state's exports result from its criminal sector, earning up to $1 billion in ill-gotten gains. Meanwhile, South Korea has quietly negotiated with northern officials to provide material assistance, while lessening restrictions on the exchange of citizens throughout the peninsula. Aside from North Korean elites, many face malnutrition and even starvation. These harsh realities force northerners toward improvisation in order to survive, while the elites have access to well stocked larders and foreign consumer goods in Pyongyang.

North Korea survives because it is a buffer state. China fears a unified Korea, and potentially having U.S. armed forces at the Chinese border. Also, South Korea is ill prepared for the collapse of its northern neighbor, and any eventual integration of the two Koreas will challenge the South to provide huge resources to the North. Further, their compatriots from the North will face severe culture shock when they try to acculturate to the modern world. A positive development is that the demilitarized zone (DMZ) has become a wilderness zone with flower and fauna which the Peace Forum wants to keep undeveloped as a "Peace Park."

In 2013, however, the DMZ was fully re-militarized as the new northern dictator, Kim Jong Un, solidified his position by canceling the 60-year-old ceasefire, and threatening the South, Japan, and the United States with nuclear war. Neither South Korean residents of Seoul, nor Chinese netizens were impressed by the latest North Korean bluster. A series of Mr. Kims, all North Korean dictators, have been crying wolf ever since the early 1950s.

Source: Adapted from "Asia: North Korea and Those Six-Party Talks: A Frustrating Game of Carrots and Sticks," *The Economist*, February 11, 2006, pp. 39–40. Dominic Ziegler"s "The Odd Couple: A Special Report on the Koreas," September 28, 2008, 19-page insert. Also see *The Asahi Shinbun*, "A Look at What North Korea Vow to Scrap Armistice Means" (http://ajw.asahi.com/article_korean_peninsula?AJ201303060098).

CULTURAL CHARACTERISTICS

If one were seeking a national characteristic for the Korean people, one would choose *resiliency* to describe their ability to survive hardship and to sacrifice. A vital concept to understand in Korea is *kibun*, one of the most important factors influencing the conduct and the relationship with others. The word literally means *inner feelings*. If one's *kibun* is good, then one functions smoothly and with ease. If one's *kibun* is upset or bad, then things may come to a complete halt, and one feels depressed. The word has no true English equivalent, but "mood" is close. In interpersonal relationships, keeping the *kibun* in good order often takes precedence over all other considerations.

In business situations, individuals try to operate in a manner that will enhance the *kibun* of both persons. To damage the *kibun* may effectively cut off relationships and create an enemy. One prefers not to do business with a person who has damaged one's *kibun*. Much of the disturbance of *kibun* in interpersonal relationships has to do with lower-class persons disturbing higher-class persons, or younger persons not showing sufficient respect for older persons. Thus, for example, a teacher can scold a student in the class and no individual feels hurt, so no one's *kibun* is especially disturbed. A student that resists his/her scolding will damage the teacher's *kibun*.

Proper interpersonal relationships are all important among Koreans, and there is little concept of equality in relationships. Relationships tend to be vertical rather than horizontal, and each person is in a relatively higher or lower position. It is essential for one to know the levels of society and to know one's place in the scheme of things. In relationships, it is often necessary to appear to lower oneself in selfless humility and give honor to other people. To put oneself forward is considered arrogant and worthy of scorn. Koreans will seek to determine the age of a foreign counterpart as a means of determining their proper relationship.

Confucianism's emphasis on hierarchy has also influenced relationships. Confucian thought is that one should rank the public higher than the private; one's business or government duties come before one's personal considerations. Protocol is also important to Koreans. When meeting others, if you do not appreciate a person's actual position and give it due recognition, then one might as well withdraw on some pretext and try to avoid future contacts. A representative of another person or group at a meeting is treated with great care because that representative may be sensitive to slights, either real or imagined, and report it back to his or her colleagues.

This is very difficult for Westerners to understand, but a Korean who fails to observe the basic rules of social exchange is considered by other Koreans to not even be a person. He/she is an "unperson" or "unable." Koreans show very little concern for an unperson's feelings or comfort. Thus, such an unperson is not worthy of much consideration. However, even with unpersons, every effort must be made to remain within the framework of polite relations. This need to remain within the "rules" of social exchange and interaction was forcefully demonstrated in the crash of Asiana Airlines flight 214 at San Francisco Airport in July, 2013 (see Exhibit 13.8).

Abramson[85] reported a comparative Canadian–Korean study of the independent effects of culture and personality on international buyer–seller relationships. He reported that Korean culture was significantly different from Canadian along a number of dimensions.

1   *Hierarchy and ranking considerations.* Koreans scored much higher on Hofstede's power distance work value scale.[86] Paik and Tung argued that Koreans were very hierarchical and status-conscious so that Korean negotiators were angered if the rank of American negotiators was perceived as too low.[87] Lee, Roehl, and Choe reported that Koreans resisted strongly any cultural differences that did not acknowledge their expectations about the importance and acknowledgement of hierarchical ranking.[88] Abramson reported that Koreans were far more likely than Canadians to build business relationships based on rank and hierarchy by considering a buyer's level of seniority, and behaving more respectfully to senior buyers.

2   *Business relationships and personal relationships.* Paik and Tung argued that personal relationships and mutual benefits were keys to the success of Korean–American business relationships.[89] Janelli observed that Koreans were dissatisfied with American relationship building efforts because they were too impersonal and Americans were seen as "stone-hearted, inhuman and selfish, smiling freely and greeting others politely but not extending genuine friendship."[90] Abramson found that Koreans were much more likely than Canadians to attend non-business related meals and social events to build relationships. Koreans were also far more likely to build old friends

EXHIBIT 13.8 — **EXHIBIT 13.8 KOREAN CULTURE MAY OFFER CLUES TO ASIANA CRASH-LANDING**

When Asiana's Boeing 777 flight crash-landed in San Francisco in July, 2013, initial reports suggested that Korean culture might be partly to blame. The plane was traveling too slowly and at too low an altitude on its final approach and its tail struck the seawall just before the runway. Two died and 180 were injured.

According to Thomas Kochan, a professor at Sloan School of Management, "The Korean culture has two features: (1) respect for seniority and age; and (2) quite an authoritarian style. You put those two together and you may get more one-way communication — and not a lot of it upward." Subordinates are expected to speak to superiors using honorific forms that require more words and an oblique approach. In the seconds before the crash, the cockpit voice recorders did not register any discussion about the fast-developing crisis between the pilot and co-pilot of Flight 214. It will, however, be months before a full investigation reveals exactly what happened.

Both the pilot and the co-pilot were well-qualified. However, the pilot was just learning how to fly a Boeing 777. It was his first landing of a Boeing 777 at San Francisco Airport, known to be a challenging place to land. By contrast, the senior co-pilot had considerable experience flying Boeing 777's and landing them at San Francisco.

The early speculation was that the co-pilot did not have the time to find the appropriate words and oblique approach required of him to correct his superior's unskilled landing approach.

Source: Wee, H. "Korean Culture May Offer Clues in Asiana Crash," *CNBC*, July 9, 2013 (http://www.cnbc.com/id/100869966/).

networks based on feelings of closeness, friendship, and respect that had developed over time.

3   *Handling conflicts.* Koreans were predicted not to avoid conflicts and were culturally predisposed to eventually try to *force* a solution to their own liking.[91] Abramson found that Canadians attempted to accommodate counterparts in disagreements far more often than Koreans, and were less likely to try to force a win even when they knew objectively that their positions were correct.

4   *Inhwa (harmony) and kibun.* Koreans were predicted to value feelings of harmony and positive kibun more highly than Canadians. Abramson found that Koreans were far more likely to believe that good and bad, action and reaction, balanced each other to create harmonious long-term relationships.

Abramson[92] also reported the interesting finding that Canadian companies could reduce the effect of cultural differences by selecting representatives on the basis of personality. Using the Keirsey Temperament Sorter II,[93] it was found that 77 percent of the Korean sample, and 69 percent of the Canadian sample were what Keirsey called the logistical temperament (SJ – see Chapter 7). When the Koreans and Canadians of logistical temperament were compared, there were significantly lower levels of cultural difference on certain variables. Canadian and Korean logistical personalities were more likely to trust each other. They were both more likely to build personal business relationships. They differed much less on the relative importance of hierarchical relationships. And while Korean logistical personalities were more likely to attempt to force their own ways in conflicts, Canadian logistical personalities were more likely to accommodate than Canadians of other personality types. Therefore, Canadian companies could reduce the effects of cultural differences in Korea by their selection of Canadian representatives.

RELIGION AND SPIRITUALITY

The underlying ethic of Korea is Shamanism, but the people have also been strongly influenced by Buddhism and Confucianism. Shamanism, the religion of ancient Koreans, venerates the spirit and ancestors, and considers elements of earth, mountains, rivers, etc., as sacred. Buddhism was introduced in Korea in the fourth century AD, and has the longest history among the organized religions in Korea – 22.8 percent of Koreans identified themselves as Buddhists in 2005. Confucianism also has been a strong force, and is the reason behind Koreans' strong appreciation of education. Confucianism teaches that the road to virtue is through education. The most influential of the newer native Korean religions is *Ch' ondogyo*, or religion of the Heavenly Way, founded in the mid-nineteenth century. Adherents believe they are responsible for bringing righteousness and peace to the world. It is a mixture of Confucianism, Buddhism, Taoism, shamanism, and Roman Catholicism.[94]

Christianity is also a major religion in South Korea, though banned in the North. In 2005, 29.2 percent of Koreans identified themselves as Christian (18.3 percent Protestant; 10.9

percent Catholic). Christianity is actually the largest religion given that 46.5 percent classify themselves as having no religion.[95] Christianity was not introduced through missionaries which may explain part of its appeal to a free people. In 1777, a Korean scholar in Beijing had himself baptized as Roman Catholic and introduced his new religion to his homeland. Protestantism gained a foothold in 1984 via a Korean doctor who became a royal physician diplomat and spread his religious beliefs. Presbyterianism is one of the largest Protestant denominations.

Be aware that Koreans often consult with fortune-tellers. Called a *mudang*, even executives resort to this kind of forecast, and a bad report may undermine a business undertaking. Of course, the Chinese often put considerable faith in Chinese astrology, and most American newspapers and Internet providers carry daily astrological forecasts.

DEFERENCE AND RESPECT FOR ELDERS

Elders in Korean society are always honored, respected, pampered, and appeased. One should not anger a Korean elder. It may mean serious damage, because age allows an older person in Korea to influence the opinions of others, regardless of the situational rightness or wrongness of his/her views. Like children, elders must be given special delicacies at meals, and their every wish and desire is catered to whenever possible. The custom and manner in which elderly people are sometimes sent to elder-care facilities in the United States is considered extremely barbarous and shocking to Koreans. Every home in Korea, no matter how poor, allocates the best room in the house to the honored grandfather or grandmother.

ETIQUETTE

Koreans are considered by others to be among the most naturally polite people in the world when the proper rules of etiquette are followed. In personal relationships with strangers or associates, Koreans avoid touching another person physically. This is considered an affront to his or her person, unless there is a well-established bond of close friendship or childhood ties.

In modern Korean society, many businesspersons now shake hands. However, they will very often bow at the same time that they shake a person's hand. To slap someone on the back or to put one's arms around a casual acquaintance or to be too familiar with someone in public is a serious breach that may effectively cool future relations.

To embarrass someone by making a joke at his or her expense is highly resented, even if done by a foreigner who does not understand the customs. After a few drinks, businesspeople often become very affectionate, but at the same time apologize for being a bit drunk. The next day they will tell their colleagues that they are sorry for imposing on others' good nature while being a little tipsy.

When appearing in public to speak, one bows first toward the audience and then toward the chairperson of the meeting. Businesspeople should learn the proper bowing procedures and etiquette expected here. Korean businesspersons do not seem to worry about keeping time, being on time, beginning on time, or leaving on time to the same extent as Western businesspersons. However, this is changing now, and there is more of a tendency to follow the same time schedule as in the West.

INTRODUCTIONS

Traditionally, it is not the custom among the Koreans to introduce one person to another. Instead, one would say to another, "I have never seen you before" or "I am seeing you for the first time." The other person repeats the same thing, and then usually the elder of the two persons in age or rank says, "Let us introduce ourselves." Each person then steps back a little, bows from the waist, states his or her own name, or the elder initiates a handshake. They are then formally introduced. Names are stated in a low, humble voice, and then calling cards are exchanged. One may learn the new person's name and position at leisure. Do not say, "Sorry, I did not get your name. Would you tell me again?" Business cards are very necessary in Korea and should be used by foreign or Western businesspeople at all times, beginning with the first visit.

The use of names in Korea has an entirely different connotation than in most Western cultures. To the Confucian, using a name is presumptuous and impolite, as a name is something to be honored and respected, and it should not be used casually. In Shamanism, to write a name calls up the spirit world and is considered bad luck. One's name, whether it is written or spoken, has its own special meaning and is that person's personal property. To call someone directly by his name is an affront in most social circumstances.

In Korea there are approximately 300 surnames, but more than half are Kim, Lee, or Park. When a Western businessperson uses a Korean's name to his face, one can usually observe a slight wince around the eyes of the Korean. It is almost always there. Koreans expect to be addressed by a Korean title, position, trade, profession, or some honorific title such as teacher. A polite "Good morning," or "Good morning, teacher" is much more acceptable than "Good morning, Mr. Kim."

Avoid the American custom of moving to first names. Many Koreans live next to each other for years without even knowing their full names. A Korean's name is usually made up of three characters – the family's surname is placed first, and then the given name, which is made up of one character. It is used by all members of the same generation. By knowing this name, a person's generation in the family tree can be recognized.

PRIVACY AND PROPRIETY

South Korea is one of the most densely populated, crowded nations on earth, so personal space is limited. On the street, this may result in standing or sitting close together, unintentional bumping into one another, or treading on another's foot without apology. Privacy is a luxury that few can afford in Korea, so the people have learned to make imaginary walls about themselves. A visitor calling on a hot day may find this person with his feet on the desk, fanning him/herself. The visitor coughs to announce his arrival, but he does not knock. This person does not "see" the person he/she has come to visit, nor does this individual "see" the visitor until he/she has risen. Then they "see" each other and begin the formality of greeting.

To have privacy, a Korean withdraws behind an imaginary curtain, or does what he/she has to do, not seeing or being seen by those who, by the literal Western eye, are in plain view. It is considered discourteous to violate this screen of privacy once it is drawn about a person. A discreet cough is intended to notify the person behind the screen that an interruption is impending.

Table manners are based on making the guest feel comfortable. The attitude of a servant is proper for a host with his guest. Traditionally, at meals, the hostess is at the lowest place, the farthest from the place of honor, and often will not even eat in the presence of a guest. Before beginning to eat, the host will often make a formal welcome speech, stating the purpose of the gathering and paying his respects to his guest. Often, food is served on small individual tables, each with many side dishes of food, a bowl of soup, and a bowl of rice. The soup and rice are served to remind people that at one time this was the only food available. They are usually eaten last, or simply tasted in a ritualistic way.

Korean food tends to be highly seasoned with red pepper, thus a careful sip of the soups and dishes is advisable, especially for bland American palettes, before taking a large mouthful. To lay the chopsticks or spoon on the table is to indicate that you have finished eating. To put them on top of a dish or bowl means that you are merely resting. A guest may show his appreciation for the meal by slurping soup or smacking one's lips. The host will continue to urge his guest to eat more, but a courteous refusal will be accepted. A good healthy belch after a meal is a sign that one has eaten well and enjoyed it.

Avoid writing or printing a Korean's name in red ink – this is the color that Buddhists reserve to announce death or its anniversary. It may be interpreted as a sign that the recipient should "drop dead." This is true with red ink in China as well.

GIFT GIVING

Koreans give gifts on many occasions, and the appropriate etiquette surrounding the giving of gifts is often a problem to Western businesspeople who often regard it as a corrupt practice. In this context, every gift expects something in return, and one rarely gives an expensive gift without a purpose. The purpose may be to establish an obligation, to gain a certain advantage, or merely to create an atmosphere in which the recipient will be more pliable to the request of the donor. To return a gift is considered an affront, but in some instances it may be better to return the gift than to accept it with no intention of doing a favor in return.

Some Koreans have a special ability to work their way into the affection of foreigners and form personal relationships that may later prove embarrassing and/or difficult to handle when some impossible or possibly illegal and unlawful request is made. In Korean, "yes" may merely mean "I heard you," and not agreement or intention of complying. To say "no" is an affront and could hurt the feelings, and thus is poor etiquette. Many Koreans often say "yes" to each other and to foreigners, and then do quite the opposite with little sense of breaking a promise or agreement.

BUSINESS ATTITUDES

In business, praise is a way of life. Without subtle praise, business would come to a halt. One must begin on the periphery in business relationships and gradually zero in on the main business in narrowing circles. This is called "spiral logic" and is common in Asian high-context cultures. To directly begin a discussion of some delicate business matter or new business venture is considered by Koreans to be the height of crassness and dooms the project to almost certain failure. Impatience is a major fault for Koreans. A highly skilled businessperson moves with deliberation, dignity, and studied motions, and senses the impressions and nuances being sent by the other businesspeople. One speaks of different aspects of the problem, and the listener makes the connections that the speaker has often left unsaid.

To Korean businessmen, Western businesspersons often appear to make contracts on the assumptions that all the factors will remain constant. In Korea, a written contract is becoming as important as in the West. A change in the economy, the political situation, or personal reasons of one of the contractors may invalidate the completion of the contract without any sense of misdeed. To navigate business here, an outsider needs a Korean intermediary, as well as possibly the help of the local Chamber of Commerce or one's Embassy's Commercial Division.

The economy and corporate structure in Korea are still dominated by *chaebols,* or large business conglomerates, which are closely related to the government. Some of these entities are family owned and managed, and employees tend to stay a long time with one employer. *Chaebols'* dominance is under challenge, for these big corporations have been accused of keeping wages low, sending jobs overseas, and suffocating the myriad small and middle-sized enterprises. Hyundai and Samsung are examples of Korean chaebols.

In the twenty-first century, the Korean economic emphasis is upon design as a driver of economic growth and social progress. Seoul has been called "The World Design Capital," and is redeveloping its old Yongsan district into a "Dream Hub" for international business, along with a "Digital Media City" in Jamsil, a complex for information technology innovations.

Korea is a male-oriented society, and a man rules at work and at home. The "boss" is all important in this hierarchical culture, and all defer to him. The "supervisor" is therefore treated with much respect. This trait is reflected in eye contact – persons of lower rank will avert their eyes during conversation with a higher ranked individual. Foreigners should avoid eye contact with Koreans, for this is often associated with anger or aggression. Korean managers are also very territorial about their desks. Visitors never would put information or sales literature on that desk, but give it to a lower intermediary for transfer upward. Korean society accepts centralized control, and makes a clear distinction between the ruler and subordinates.

Gradually, educated women are moving into middle management within business. Family household, financial, and child management are the female's responsibility. In public, females may appear quiet and submissive, but behind the scenes, women may exert great power. Public displays of female power or affection are unacceptable. It is notable, however, that Park Geun-hye, the elected Korean President since February 25, 2013, is a woman. Times are clearly changing even in this former bastion of chauvinism.

Because there are similarities between Korean and other Asian cultures, cross-cultural skills that are effective in this society have application elsewhere. For example, there is a large minority population of Koreans in Los Angeles, and their native language is the third largest spoken in that California city. There is a large and growing minority of Koreans in Vancouver, Canada, as well.

CONCLUSIONS

East Asia is a demonstration model of the complexity and multidimensional aspects of culture. Although we have provided cultural specifics on only a three countries, perhaps it is enough to convince global managers of the important distinctions that exist between the people of this region and Westerners. Critical matters like physical appearance, language, religion, family, social attitudes, ethics, and the building of business relations all influence business practice and differ markedly between the countries. The new market opportunities and diversity in the Pacific Basin alone should motivate us to seek further cultural information. China and Korea, especially, will become more and more important drivers of the world economy in the twenty-first century. Japan is still the third largest world economy for the foreseeable future, not quite twice as large as number four Germany.

The social situation in Asia is normally peaceful, but also very dynamic, often volatile. Traditional societies are in transition to a technological and knowledge culture. Unfortunately, historical grievances have come to muddy the relationships between China and Korea, on the one hand, and between China/Korea and Japan on the other. Chinese support for North Korea causes additional tensions between China and South Korea/Japan.

The area also benefits from the global cooperation of nations. Two examples of synergistic relationships in this region are the South Asian Free Trade Alliance, and the Asian Development Bank. Their leaders are in agreement that by 2020, the "new Asia," as well as their own organizations, will need radically different strategies with global focus.

MIND STRETCHING

1   What seemingly is involved as traditional Asian societies transition into modern ones (e.g., China, Japan, Korea)?

2   What advantages do overseas Chinese have in many Pacific Basin countries?

3   What cross-border commonalities have you observed in this study of Asian cultures?

4   Why is it important for you to increase your knowledge and skill in Asian cultures, languages, negotiation styles, and business practices?

5   How would you build guanxi relationships in China? Do you see signs that similar relationships would also be important in Japan and South Korea? How is relationship-building similar and also different in these three countries?

NOTES

1 Gao Yuan. *Lure the Tiger Out of the Mountains: The 36 Stratagems of Ancient China*. Singapore: Simon & Schuster, 1991, p. 20.

2 Zen Master Takuan, "The Inscrutable Subtlety of Immovable Wisdom," in T. Cleary (ed.), *Soul of the Samurai: Modern Translaions of Three Classic Works of Zen & Bushido*. Tokyo: Tuttle Publishing, 2005, p. 101.

3 Smambaugh, D. (ed.). *Power Shifts: China and Asia's New Dynamics*. Berkeley, CA: University of California Press, 2005. Kleveman, L. *The New Great Game: Blood and Oil in Central Asia*. New York: Atlantic Monthly Press, 2003. Ringmar, E. *The Mechanics of Modernity in Europe and East Asia: The Institutional Origins of Social Change and Stagnation*. London: Routledge, 2004. Covington, R. "Hearts of the New Silk Road," *Saudi Aramco World*, January/February 2008, pp. 18–33.

4 This is the prediction of the Organization for Economic Cooperation and Development (OECD). The OECD also predicts that by 2025 the combined GDPs of China and India will surpass that of the G7 nations (http://rt.com/usa/china-us-economic-economy-373/, November 9, 2012. Retrieved June 24, 2013).

5 Rodriguez, P. *China, India, and the United States: The Future of Economic Supremacy*. Chantilly, VA: The Great Courses, 2011.

6 Barboza, D. "China Passes Japan as Second-Largest Economy," *The New York Times*, August 15, 2010, www.nytimes.com/2010/08/16/business/global/16yuan.html?pagewanted=all&_r=0. Retrieved June 24, 2013.

7 Aston, W.G. *Nihongi: Chronicles of Japan from the Earliest Times to A.D.* 697. Boston, MA: Tuttle Publishing, 1972. Philippi, D. L. *Kojiki*. Tokyo: University of Tokyo Press, 2002.

8 Rodriguez, *China, India, and the United States*, p. 21.

9 Kissinger, H. *On China*. Toronto, ON: Allen Lane Canada (Penguin), 2011.

10 http://www.tzgpartners.com/docs/taozhugong-story.pdf. Retrieved June 24, 2013.

11 Pomfret, J. *Chinese Lessons: Five Classmates and the Story of the New China*. New York: Henry Holt and Company, 2006, p. 105.

12 Buderi, R. and Huang, G. T. *Guanxi: Microsoft, China and Bill Gates' Plan to Win the Road Ahead*. London: Random House, 2006.

13 Bell, D.A. *China's New Confucianism: Politics and Everyday Life in a Changing Society*. Princeton, NJ: Princeton University Press, 2008.

14 Pomfret, *Chinese Lessons*.

15 Twohey, M. *Authority and Welfare in China: Modern Debates in Historical Perspective*. Houndsmill: Macmillan Press, 1999.

16 Watson, B. *Xunzi: Basic Writings*. New York: Columbia University Press, 2003.

17 Yu Dan. *Confucius from the Heart: Ancient Wisdom for Today's World*. London: Macmillan, 2009.

18 Ibid.

19 For example, Ip, P. K. "Is Confucianism Good for Business Ethics in China?" *Journal of Business Ethics*, Vol. 88, 2009, pp. 463–476.

20 Abramson, N.R. "Building Effective Business Relationships in China: The Case of Richmond Engineering," in P. W. Beamish and A. E. Sefarian (eds), *North American Firms in East Asia*. Toronto, ON: Institute for International Business, University of Toronto Press, 1999, pp. 119–145.

21 For example, Fan, Y. "Guanxi's Consequences: Personal Gain at Social Cost," *Journal of Business Ethics*, Vol. 38, 2002, pp. 371–380.

22 Abramson, N. R. "Do the Chinese Seek Relationship? A Psychological Analysis of Chinese–American Business Negotiations Using the Jungian Typology," *Journal of Global Business*, Vol. 16, No. 31, 2005, pp. 7–22.

23 Sawyer, R. D. *The Seven Military Classics of Ancient China Including The Art of War*. Boulder, CO: Westview Press, 1993.

24 Gao Yuan, *Lure the Tiger*.

25 Chu, C.-N. *Thick Face, Black Heart: The Asian Path to Thriving, Winning and Succeeding*. Taipei, ROC: Nicholas Brealey Publishing, 1995.

26 Yan, X. *Ancient Chinese Thought, Modern Chinese Power*. Princeton, NJ: Princeton University Press, 2011.

27 http://en.wikipedia.org/wiki/Fuxi. Retrieved June 25, 2013.

28 Rodriguez, *China, India, and the United States.*

29 http://www.economist.com.

30 http://wn.wikipedia.org/wiki/List_of_the_largest_trading_partners_of_China. Retrieved June 27, 2013.

31 http://factsanddetails.com/china.php?itemid=303. Retrieved June 27, 2013.

32 Abramson, N. and Ai, J.X. "Richmond Engineering in China," *Harvard Case Study Analysis Solutions*, www.harvardsolution.com/Richmond-engineering-in-china-16017.

33 *The Economist*, September 20, 2008, p. 20.

34 Yeung, I. and Tung, R. "Achieving Business Success in Confucian Societies: The Importance of Guanxi (Connections)," *Organizational Dynamics*, Fall, 1996, pp. 54–65.

35 Luo, Y., Huang, Y., and Wang, S.L. "Guanxi and Organizational Performance: A Meta-Analysis," *Management and Organization Review*, Vol. 8, No. 1, 2012, pp. 139–172.

36 Abramson, N.R. and Ai, J.X. "Canadian Companies Doing Business in China: Key Success Factors," *Management International Review*, Vol. 39, No. 1, 1999, pp. 7–35.

37 Luo, Y. et al., "Guanxi and Organizational Performance."

38 Chen, C. C., Chen, X. P., and Huang, S. "Chinese Guanxi: An Integrative Review and New Directions for Future Research," *Management and Organization Review*, Vol. 9, No. 1, 2013, pp. 167–207.

39 Fei, H. *From the Soil, the Foundations of Chinese Society*. Berkeley, CA: University of California Press, 1992.

40 Wank, D. L. "Business–State Clienteleism in China: Decline or Evolution?," in T. Gold, D. Guthrie, and D. Wank (eds), *Social Connections in China: Institutions, Culture, and the Changing Nature of Guanxi*. Cambridge, MA: Cambridge University Press, 2002, pp. 97–115.

41 Chen, X.-P., Li, X., and Liang, X. "Why Do Business Leaders Pursue Political Connections in China? Economic Benefits or Psychological Placebo?" *Academy of Management* Conference Paper, San Antonio, August, 2011.

42 Abramson, N.R. and Ai, J.X. "Using Guanxi-Style Buyer–Seller Relationships in China: Reducing Uncertainty and Improving Performance Outcomes," *International Executive*, Vol. 39, No. 6, 1997, pp. 765–804.

43 Marcel, G. *The Mystery of Being Volume I: Reflection and Mystery*. South Bend, IN: St. Augustine's Press, 2001.

44 Buber, M. *I and Thou*. New York: Charles Scribner's Sons, 1986.

45 Confucius, *The Analects*. New York: Alfred A. Knopf, 2000. See also Yu Dan, op cit., 2006.

46 Hsieh, C.-H. and Jen, W. 'Great Man' (Chun-tzu) and 'Small Man' (Hsiao-jen) in the Confucian Analects: A Transformative Approach," *Journal of Applied Behavioral Research*, Vol. 27, No. 4, 1991, pp. 425–443.

47 Watson, *Xunzi*, p. 161.

48 Ibid.

49 Twohey, *Authority and Welfare in China.*

50 Bell, *China's New Confucianism.*

51 Yan, X., *Ancient Chinese Thought.*

52 Mencius, *Mencius*. London: Penguin Books, 2004.

53 Mintzberg, H., Ahlstrand, B., and Lampel, J. *Strategy Safari: A Guided Tour Through the Wilds of Strategic Management*. New York: Free Press, 1998.

54 Ibid.

55 A Western adaptation is McNeilly, M. R. *Sun Tzu and the Art of Business: Six Strategic Principles for Managers,* revised edition. Oxford: Oxford University Press, 2012.

56 Gao Yuan, *Lure the Tiger.*

57 McNeilly, *Sun Tzu.*

58 There is a very small body of Western business literature on effective punishment. The following reference summarizes it. Remington-Abramson, N. and Senyshyn, S. "Effective Punishment Through Forgiveness: Rediscovering Kierkegaard's Knight of Faith in the Abraham Story," *Organization Studies*, Vol. 31, No. 5, 2010, pp. 555–581.

59 McNeilly, *Sun Tzu*.

60 Gao Yuan, *Lure the Tiger*.

61 Ibid.

62 Abramson, "Do the Chinese."

63 Adapted with permission from Robert T. Moran's *Venturing Abroad in Asia*, published by McGraw-Hill: London, 1988.

64 Kissinger, *On China*.

65 Standage, T. "Going Hybrid: A Special Report on Japan," *The Economist*, December 1, 2007, www.economist.com/specialreports. See also Gordon, A. *A Modern History of Japan*. Oxford: Oxford University Press, 2008; Reiber, B. and Spencer, J. *Frommer's Japan*. Hoboken, NJ: John Wiley, 2008; Matsumoto, D. *The New Japan*. Boston, MA: Nicholas Brealey/Intercultural Press, 2002; Hall, E. T. and Hall, M. R. *Hidden Differences: Doing Business with the Japanese*. Garden City, NJ: Anchor/Doubleday, 1987.

66 Emmott, W. "The Sun Also Rises: A Survey of Japan," *The Economist*, October 8, 2005, 18-page insert, www.economist.com/surveys. See also Gordon, A. *A Modern History of Japan*. Oxford: Oxford University Press, 2008; Reiber, B. and Spencer, J. *Frommer's Japan*. Hoboken, NJ: John Wiley, 2008; Matsumoto, D. *The New Japan*. Boston, MA: Nicholas Brealey/Intercultural Press, 2002; Hall, E. T. and Hall, M. R. *Hidden Differences: Doing Business with the Japanese*. Garden City, NJ: Anchor/Doubleday, 1987.

67 Aston, *Nihongi*.

68 Kasulis, T. P. *Shinto: The Way Home*. Honolulu, HA: University of Hawaii, 2007.

69 Vidal, G. *Dreaming War: Blood for Oil and the Cheney-Bush Junta*. New York: Thunder's Mouth Press/Nation Books, 2002.

70 Ibid. During the war, the General in charge of Hawaii's defense was expelled from the armed forces in disgrace. When these State Department documents were disgraced, the General's surviving relatives sued, and the General's honor was restored in addition to the pension funds he would otherwise have been paid. Even though the American government knew when the Japanese would attack, and how, Roosevelt wanted an incident that would allow him to declare war on Germany, in a nation committed to peace unless first attacked.

71 De Kavanagh Boulger, D. E. *Central Asian Questions: Essays on Afghanistan, China, and Central Asia*. London: Adamant Media Corp./Elibron Classic Series, 2005; Evans, M. *Afghanistan: A Short History of its People and Politics*. New York: Harper Collins, 2002; Chayes, S. *The Punishment of Virtue: Inside Afghanistan after the Taliban*. New York: Penguin Books, 2007; Crews, R. T. and Tarzi, A. *The Taliban and the Crisis of Afghanistan*. New York: Amazon Books; Hiebert, A. *Afghanistan: Hidden Treasures*. New York: Amazon Books, 2008; Sageman, M. *Leaderless Jihad: Terrorist Networks in the Twenty-First Century*. Philadelphia, PA: University of Pennsylvania Press, 2008; Lollapally, D. *The Politics of Extremism in South Asia*. Cambridge, UK: Cambridge University Press, 2006; Post, J. *The Mind of the Terrorist*. New York: Palgrave Macmillan, 2007.

72 March, R.M. *Reading the Japanese Mind: The Realities Behind Their Thoughts and Actions*. Tokyo: Kodansha International, 2001.

73 http://en.wikipedia.org/wiki/List_of_countries_by_leading_trade_partners.

74 "Nissan Gears Up to Treble Sales in India this Year," *The Hindu*, May 23, 2013, www.thehindu.com.

75 Lie, J. *Multiethnic Japan*. Cambridge, MA: Harvard University Press, 2013.

76 The status of Confucianism as either a philosophy or a religion is debatable. While there are many temples built to Confucius in China, most have regarded it as a philosophy, or way of life intended to teach individuals to engage in ethical thinking and actions. There are those who regard Confucianism as a religion and this view seems to be becoming more common in recent times. See Sun, A. *Confucianism as a World Religion: Contested Histories and Contemporary Realities*. Princeton, NJ: Princeton University Press, 2013.

77 Cleary, *Soul of the Samurai.*

78 Nitobe, I. *Bushido: The Soul of Japan.* Tokyo: IBC Publishing, 2003.

79 Ibid, p. 49.

80 http://en.wikipedia.org/wiki/Kim_Dae-jung.

81 President Parkis the first woman elected President of South Korea. http://en.wikipedia.org/wiki/Park_Geun-hye.

82 http://en.wikipedia.org/wiki/Next_Eleven.

83 Ziegler, D. "The Odd Couple: A Special Report on the Koreas," *The Economist,* September 27, 2008, www.economist.com/specialreports; "Cool Korea," *Business Week,* June 10, 2002; "How Dangerous Is North Korea," *Time,* January 13, 2003; Hoare, J. *Korea: Culture Smart: A Quick Guide to Customs and Etiquette.* London: Kuperard, 2006; Ungoon, G. R., Sters, R. M., and Park, S. *Korean Enterprise: The Quest for Globalization,* Boston, MA: Harvard Business Press, 1997.

84 http://www.historytoday.com/wilson-strand/opening-hermit-kingdom.

85 Abramson, N.R. "Measuring the Independent Effects of National Culture and Personality on Marketing Behvior: A Canadian–Korean Comparison Using the Cognitive Theory of Strategy," *Journal of Current Research in Global Business,* Vol. 9, No. 14, 2006, pp. 1–19.

86 Hofstede, G. *Culture's Consequences: International Differences in Work-Related Values.* Beverley Hills, CA: Sage, 1980.

87 Paik, Y. and Tung, R. "Negotiating with East Asians: How to Attain 'Win-Win' Outcomes," *Management International Review,* Vol. 39, No. 2, 1999, pp. 103–122.

88 Lee, J., Roehl, T. W., and Choe, S. "What Makes Management Style Similar and Distinct Across Borders? Growth, Experience and Culture in Korean and Japanese Firms," *Journal of International Business Studies,* Vol. 31, No. 4, 2000, pp. 631–652.

89 Paik and Tung, "Nedgotiating with East Asians."

90 Janelli, R. L. with Yim, D. *Making Capitalism Work: The Social and Cultural Construction of a South Korean Conglomerate.* Stanford, CA: Stanford University Press, 1993.

91 Tjosvold, D., Cho, Y. H., Liu, W. C., and Sasaki, S. "Interdependence and Managing Conflict with Subcontractors in the Construction Industry in East Asia," *Asia Pacific Journal of Manafement,* Vol. 18, 2001, pp. 295–313.

92 Abramson, "Measuring the Independent Effects."

93 Keirsey, D. *Please Understand Me II: Temperament, Character, Intelligence.* Del Mar, CA: Prometheus Nemesis, 1998.

94 http://www.britannica.com/.

95 http://en.wikipedia.org/wiki/Religion_in_South_Korea.

ADDITIONAL FEATURES

Please visit the companion website at: www.routledge.com/cw/Moran where you will find additional case studies, study aides, and instructor resources.

14 DOING BUSINESS WITH EUROPEANS AND RUSSIANS
European Union: France, Germany, Italy; and Russia[1]

Those fusty old Europeans are engaged in a radical experiment to reinvent themselves – this bid to create a "New Europe" is more than a collection of countries, but less than a unified state. The Maastricht treaty is not yet a teenager, the common currency is barely out of its nappies, a new constitution is being debated, new members have been admitted, and new candidates are under consideration. There is agreement on a united financial recovery strategy, and still talk of a common foreign policy. The Euro is doing better than expected as a means of financial exchange. Now their European Space Agency is planning lunar missions.

The Economist, January 22, 2003

L
E
A
R
N
I
N
G

O
B
J
E
C
T
I
V
E
S

The principal objective of this chapter is to understand some of the cultural complexities and diversities in the European Union members. Specifically, two European countries, France and Italy, will be examined in some depth, providing historical perspective and cultural guidelines.

Europe is the world's second smallest continent, bounded to the west by the Atlantic Ocean, to its east by Russia, and to the southeast by Turkey. It ambles from Iceland to Gibraltar — in the north, this landmass is set apart by the Arctic Ocean and in the south by the Mediterranean, Black, and Caspian Seas. Amidst its landmass, peninsulas, and islands, it is home to more than 40 countries. Between two major mountain systems, a rolling, fertile plane stretches from the Pyrenees to the Urals. Herein are located some of the world's greatest urban centers, such as London, Paris, Berlin, and Moscow. Although set in a northern location, thanks to the influence of the Gulf Stream, Europe generally enjoys a mild climate, except for occasional winter and ice storms. The whole region, including the European part of Russia, represents 7 percent of the earth's landmass, but is only half the size of North America.

The continent has approximately 739 million people, roughly three-fourths of whom live in urban areas. Home to multiple ethnic groups, some 284 languages are spoken on the continent. (The major branches today include the Italic, Germanic, and Uralic language groups.) For millennia, Europeans have been providing humanity with ideas, ideals, and information that have nurtured the world's cultures and societies.

HISTORICAL PERSPECTIVE[2]

According to the most recent archeological evidence, the earliest fossil remains of the family of animals that includes human beings date back to approximately 1.8 million years ago. For hundreds of thousands of years, Neanderthals had preceded modern humans and shared the continent for roughly a hundred thousand years with them before becoming extinct. Recently, important fossils were uncovered in the Atapuerca Mountains of northern Spain; Hominids were living there some 600,000 years ago — these Europeans may be the last connection to both the Neanderthals and *Homo sapiens.* The wall art and artifacts in caves of northern Spain and southern France confirm the aesthetic sense and tool technology of Stone Age cultures. Migration of peoples from Central Asia some 5,000 years ago brought the Indo-European language groups into the region. Minoan civilization, an important source of Western civilization that emerged on the island of Crete, dates back to roughly 7000 BC; the Minoans produced an impressive culture that was stimulated by trade with Egypt and Asia Minor. Ancient Greece is said to begin in the eighth century BC (during its archaic period). Classical Greeks enriched the world, especially future European civilization, through philosophy, mathematics, natural sciences, political thought, arts, and architecture. The Greek legacy was bequeathed to the Romans who became masters of architecture, engineering, law, and military strategy. The Roman Empire was the first attempt at uniting the continent's peoples, and it even extended into what is now the Middle East. Although the Roman Republic survived for only 500 years, their language (Latin), infrastructure, and heritage continue to influence humankind.

As the Roman Empire declined, Christianity, coming out of Western Asia, entered Europe and became a binding force in Europe until modern times. Throughout the Middle Ages, monasteries were centers of learning, spirituality, and agriculture. A major religious split within European Christianity began in the eleventh century; as a result, Roman Catholicism under the popes dominated the west, whereas Orthodox Christianity under the patriarchs reigned in the east. European religious unity was further undermined in the fifteenth century with the introduction of Islam by the Ottoman Turks into the Balkans, and later into Spain via North Africa. The Protestant Reformation further fractured both religious and political cohesion in the sixteenth century. As medieval feudalism diminished, powerful kingdoms and nations arose, especially in Western Europe. In the second millennium provincial allegiances gave way to rising nationalism that helped to create modern states, inspiring the concepts of common language, economy, and governance that are so prevalent now.

By the eighteenth century, modern Europe arose in the aftermath of two revolutions, in the British colonies of the New World and in France. The powers of aristocracy and royalty lessened, while for the next two centuries, nationalism, socialism, and democracy flourished. Since the sixteenth century, European powers sought to colonize America, Africa, and the Middle East, as well as parts of Asia. Beginning in England some three hundred years ago, the impact of the Industrial Revolution has extended throughout the planet. In the twentieth century, after two world wars and a cold war, Europe was divided into two geopolitical spheres – Western Europe and the Eastern Bloc, which was under Soviet control. Business practices varied according to whether the capitalist or socialist system was used. The demise of communism blurred that demarcation, but complicated the situation. Despite their totalitarian conditioning for 70 years or less, nations from Central and Eastern Europe began to seek entry into the free enterprise system established in 1952 as the European Common Market. In this twenty-first century, Europe is a dynamic and exciting place to do business, although it is undergoing profound transition. The winds of economic, social, and political change are sweeping throughout the entire continent. Since 1957 the member nations of the European Economic Community (EEC), which was renamed the "European Union" in 1993, have striven to improve their standard of living and to foster closer cooperation. Their collaboration has facilitated more unified continental activities, while attempting to preserve local cultures and languages.[3]

Europeans today have a long cultural history, representing a highly diverse mixture of peoples and their governance, making generalizations difficult. Demographically, Europe's population of some 739 million is dwindling, and by 2050 that figure may be only 653 million in countries where the populations are aging. Although immigration may affect population outcomes, many inhabitants resist the EU's efforts toward the free movement of people, capital, goods, and services! The next section will provide further context to understand the Europe of the future.

EUROPEAN DIVERSITY AND SYNERGY

Late in the twentieth century, the multinational entities of Europe sought ways to unify their economic efforts through the formation of a European Common Market. As the scope of cooperation increased among the participants (e.g. European Space Agency), the term *European Community* came into use. In 1992 member countries signed the Maastricht Treaty, a road map for establishing an economic and monetary union. Under the umbrella of the European Union, three key institutions were created: a European Council, Commission, and Parliament. By 2002, a common currency called the *euro* was put into circulation and adopted by eleven member states.[4] The EU spends more than a billion dollars a year to maintain language equality by translating documents into 20 official documents!

These synergistic endeavors toward an EU resulted in formal agreements that allow goods, people, services, information, and capital to move freely among member countries. In 2010, EU membership was expanded to 27 nations. There are also three candidate countries who have applied for admission. The original members are Austria, Belgium, Denmark, Finland, France, Germany, Greece, Ireland, Italy, Luxembourg, the Netherlands, Portugal, Spain, Sweden, and the United Kingdom. President Jacques Chirac of France observed, "For nearly 50 years, the heart of our continent was split between democracy and dictatorship in a balance of terror. The fracture that started in Europe spread across the planet."[5] Now, the forces for unity and inclusion on this continent are spreading. Despite Turkey being a member of NATO and an EU applicant, it has yet to be officially admitted. Russia has sought membership, and has developed special working relationships with both NATO and the EU. These two latter countries are located in Eurasia, and will be discussed in the last section of this chapter.

Currently, the EU encompasses almost 500 million people, and has an annual GDP of about $16 trillion. Now, the central EU themes are to: (1) attain a single market economy of consumers that offers peaceful stability and wealth, as well as political and economic clout; (2) establish European-wide institutions and policies; plus (3) respect, and not fight about differences within this voluntary union. Although Europeans still cherish their diversity, not all is "smooth sailing" as different and competing visions emerge. The EU's rapid expansion has raised tensions over ethnic, religious, and cultural identity. However, many of the following issues have been solved or are in the process of resolution:

- Technical – differing national standards and regulations, conflicting business laws, and protected public procurements.

- Free flow of goods once they have cleared customs in the EU, as if national boundaries did not exist.
- Free movement of workers, so that citizens of one state may seek employment in another without discrimination relative to type of job, remunerations, or other employment conditions.
- Freedom of establishment, so a citizen or business from one state has the right to locate and conduct business elsewhere in the EU.
- Freedom to provide services to persons throughout the EU.

The efforts toward European integration and standardization have successfully led to greater economic and currency unification, as well as respect for the rule of law. Some of the benefits the new EU policies are intended to accomplish include the following:

- Ensure cost savings by removal of internal border controls.
- Increase competition and consumer demand.
- Facilitate economies of scale in production.
- Foster greater expenditures on combined research and development.
- Promote more efficient use of continental human resources.
- Decrease unemployment.
- Lower prices while increasing economic growth throughout the EU.

To manage the EU and achieve such goals, the European Commission has 27 commissioners appointed by national governments for a five-year term. With headquarters in Brussels, the Commission's administrative body consists of 20,000 officials. Political matters are left to the European Council made up of 27 heads of government; law and budgetary matters are the concern of the Council of Ministers under a six-month rotating chair under a head of a member state. These are supplemented by the European Parliament in Strasbourg of 754 members, and a Council of Justice based in Luxembourg which acts as a supreme court. The EU has a plethora of other agencies to advance its social partnership by the four freedoms of movement for goods, services, labor, and capital.

To take advantage of the single market opportunities, global corporations are establishing EU-based companies, and the Japanese are most prominent in this strategy. Many foreign enterprises are acquiring or merging with European industrial units, increasing the cross-cultural challenges at both the national and corporate levels. In addition to knowing about EU policies and regulations, global managers assigned to Europe will have to be more competitive, as well as better trained and more culturally sensitive. They also must deal with various economies and monetary systems, particularly the euro currency, which is not utilized everywhere. But they face new consumer opportunities, for Europeans increasingly buy beyond national borders, whether it is for insurance policies, bank accounts, mutual funds, or euro bonds. Europe's efforts toward synergy are not without other problems and challenges because of its very diversity, as the next section demonstrates.

Between 2000 and 2010, the EU's Lisbon Agenda sought to promote liberalized reforms, increase R&D spending, and to encourage deregulation of labor and product markets across member countries. To transform Europe by 2010, their aim was to turn the EU *into the most competitive and dynamic knowledge-based economy in the world.*

THE EUROPEAN UNION TODAY

In the opening decade of a new millennia, the optimist would declare the EU somewhat a success in achieving many of the above goals, but it is still a work in progress. The EU is one of the world's biggest markets, exporters, and foreign investors and is home to many of the largest and most successful companies; some member countries, such as Finland and Ireland, rank at the top of global competitiveness, while new Central Europe members are mainly fast-growing economies. Since the mid-twentieth century, Europe has experienced relative peace, except in the Balkans. But Gideon Rachman, in his 2004 survey of the EU, cites critics who say that far from promoting peace, prosperity, and freedom, it now threatens these achievements. Many of the unnecessary laws and regulations emanating from EU institutions in Brussels weaken some members' self-government and democracy, while engulfing the European economy. Eurosceptics fear that continuing EU enlargement distracts from the formation of an effective federation by increasing diversity of political interests and views. Further, Europe still lacks a common language, national media, and national identity. Half of the people in the EU still speak only their mother tongue. Some contend that further European integration undermines their country's nationalism, for citizens interact mainly with their own governments, not the EU. The recent failure to universally ratify the proposed constitution deterred the development of a multitier union.[6]

Yet at its fiftieth anniversary, the EU emerged at the heart of the continent's economic life, and increasingly impacts social and foreign policy. The candidates for membership, like the Balkan countries, find the benefits of EU membership so attractive that they are even willing to make peace and introduce democratic reforms – Croatia being a case in point. Negotiations are under way to admit Turkey, a secular country with Muslim inhabitants; such memberships would confirm that Islam is not incompatible with Western values. Euronationalists think that there is a distinctive European approach to global needs, such as support for multilateral institutions and antiwar demonstrations. A half-century after its birth, the EU has yet to obtain genuine popular support for "ever-closer union" which contributes to the gradual emergence of a euroculture. What may result is a more diverse EU which allows members and their inhabitants to adopt different levels of integration more attuned to their national preferences. EU expansion has been a tool for stabilizing the continent, creating new markets, and promoting interdependence through free trade and movement. The hope is that its very diversity may stimulate competition between different economic and social models within Europe! With reference to the Muslim impact on Europe, Exhibit 14.1 provides further insights. All this and more is also changing relations with North America.

EXHIBIT 14.1 INTEGRATING EUROPE'S MUSLIMS

The EU is now coping with twin challenges — acculturating a massive immigrant flow, and Islamic extremists (Spain, Great Britain, and France have already suffered the latter's destructive violence). Islamic populations are growing rapidly throughout the continent — in some cities, more go to mosques each week than churches. European countries differ on how to manage this new reality. France is strict about the integration of outsiders into their culture, and tends to keep the Muslim migrants in separate poor communities that breed radical youths; the Netherlands and Britain favor multiculturalism.

Already, with 20 million Muslims in the EU, debates go on about the admittance of Turkey with its 71 million Muslims. And the predictions are that one-tenth of Europe's population will be Muslim by 2025. Currently, there is not only economic progress among this minority, but also a rapid rise of Muslims in the workforce, including in business, politics, law enforcement, universities, as well as an increase in interracial marriages. While the average Muslim is hard-working, peaceful, and moderate, it is the *jihadists* who alarm the average citizen. Yet Euro-Muslims are changing because of their experiences in a new homeland, so they are building coalitions with non-Muslims.

Even Russia's fastest growing religious group is its Muslims, and many of its important neighbors from the ex-Soviet Bloc are Islam adherents. Actually, Russia has more Muslims than any other European state but Turkey; some 23 million, over 10 percent of its population, are followers of Mohammed. With 1,300 mosques, Russian Muslims are concentrated in Moscow, as well as Bashkoratan and Tatarstan (www.islam.ru). Thus, Euro-Islam is a factor to carefully consider in any Pan-Europe analysis.

Source: Adapted from special report, "Look Out Europe," *The Economist*, June 24, 2006, pp. 29–34. "Russia's Muslims — Benign Growth," *The Economist*, April 7, 2007, pp. 47–48.

CULTURAL GUIDELINES FOR DOING BUSINESS IN EUROPE

As Europe moves beyond national borders and national cultures toward regional cooperation, a new European identity is developing. EU youth, such as in Ireland, envision themselves as the *New Europeans.* While assimilation takes place within the Union, the cultural identity of each member country needs to be preserved as the basis for a diverse and enriched European cultural future. Latin verve and British pragmatism, for example, are viewed as strengths within the EU, rather than as divisive elements. However, the distinct cultures and enormous differences in values and outlooks among member countries must be addressed to overcome impediments to deeper unity. That being said, among the EU's burgeoning bureaucracy no research is ongoing to study the impact of cultural diversity and ways to promote more cultural synergy.

Nowhere is the latter collaboration more evident than in the field of management. Managers readily cross national boundaries not only on business, but for professional development as well. Furthermore, European managers attend courses and workshops at one another's universities, and read one another's management journals and business publications. Perhaps the transnational aspects of European management are best demonstrated in matters of partnerships, joint ventures, and acquisitions. For example, the Republic of Ireland boasts not only of its more than 200 British industries and many new American and European firms, but also of the young, well-educated workforce available for service throughout the EU.

The "internationalization" of the European workforce has been progressing for at least five decades, accelerated by the multinational corporation. Since World War II, more than 30 million workers – mostly from countries in southern Europe and North Africa – have flowed into Western and Northern Europe (the foreign-born population is now 33 million). European businesspeople have always excelled at multilingual skills. These trends are some of the reasons that cross-cultural management training is increasing within Europe.

So who is European? It is no longer the typical inhabitants of the last two centuries on that continent. The enlargement of the EU changes demographic factors, such as affluence, poverty, and fertility. Also, the ongoing mass immigration into Europe is altering the composition and culture of its peoples. Many of the new arrivals face not only discrimination, but also civil disorder caused by anti-immigrationists. The EU estimated that 500,000 illegals are being absorbed yearly. Add to that the many thousands of refugees that request political asylum, and one can see how harmony in Europe could be threatened. Regardless, the Common European Asylum System (CEAS) through legislation has established fruitful guidelines for the rights of those seeking asylum in the EU and has standardized an applicable definition of the word "refugee."

The EU is still debating the establishment of a policy on Pan-European border policing to replace national frontier controls. Furthermore, there is not a consensus in Europe as to *who is an immigrant*? The EU has not adopted the UN definition: a short-term migrant is anyone who moves to a new country and stays for 2–12 months; long-term is considered a year or more. The EU member states not only have differing policies regarding those who emigrate to their countries, but also record their population statistics differently. In Britain, acceptance or rejection of those seeking entry may take years. In Germany, automatic citizenship is bestowed on children born to foreign parents in that country. Because there may be 500,000 migrants in Italy alone, its parliament has been working on proposed legislation for controlling immigration, which may include the deportation of illegals. The country's extensive coastline has supports inflows of Albanians, Kurds, Africans, and some Asians.

European perceptions

When we analyze Europe, it is not easy to define a cultural set of beliefs, customs, values, practices, and feelings. While each country therein has its own distinctive culture, there are still commonalities that distinguish the "old world" from other regions. Below is an overview of principal themes on that continent that may alter outsiders' perceptions of them:

■ Europeans have an inherent interest in the quality of life, at all levels of society. There is a predominant humanist belief that people are to be served by progress, and not the reverse. They enjoy socialization with family and friends over beverages and meals.

■ Europeans generally have an inordinate sense of reality. When one reflects on the wars and disruptions in Europe in the twentieth century alone, one can understand how Europeans know that tragedy can be just a breath away, and that perhaps only this moment is real.

■ Europeans historically have had to fight their neighbor, whereas Americans have had to conquer the elements to develop their country. European heritage is such that they think in the context of centuries, whereas Americans' historical sense is in terms of decades.

■ Europeans have endured. They have survived plagues, atrocities, great wars, and border and government changes. They have lived through many ambiguities, and have the threads of ancient customs and traditions in the fabric of their cultures. They know the fragility of their civilization. On the one hand, it is the sense of survival, but the balance is that disaster is often not far off.

However, such perspectives may have a disadvantage in that Europeans may be less willing to take a risk on a new idea or venture with a possibly good future. For them, the concept of simply making money is not the foundation of a company; the long-term survival of the business is also important. The following are the characteristics that are representative of the overall European cultural outlook:

■ An almost cynical realism schooled by history.
■ A belief that individuals should be at the center of life.
■ A sense of social responsibility.
■ A mistrust of authority.
■ A feeling that all people have weaknesses, and sometimes one has to "muddle through" life.
■ A desire for security and continuity.
■ A belief that maximum profit is not the primary aim of business.

It has also been observed that relationships between the individual and authority in Europe are accented by differences in educational and political attitudes within the continent. The reports below would seem to substantiate this.

Education/schooling

Educational systems in Europe tend to be very traditional, somewhat rigid in offerings and organization, and resistant to change. While strong in science, engineering, literature, and languages, courses in business, management, and entrepreneurship were only recently and slowly introduced. Here is a sampling of some trends in schooling the next generation:

■ Teachers in the Netherlands and Scandinavia have far less "distance" between themselves and their pupils than their counterparts in Mediterranean countries have.

■ In one of the world's most egalitarian societies, Dutch children are taught to keep low profiles, and that being "first" at something is not necessarily a virtue; whereas in Mediterranean countries, such as Greece and Italy, children tend to be nurtured as special, unique, and implicitly superior individuals. In Britain, it is acceptable to finish first, but only if one can do it without seeming to work harder.

■ In many European countries, such as in the United Kingdom, their educational systems suffer from culture lag and need updating of their instructional systems for an "information society" and a "knowledge culture."

■ Germany's first woman chancellor, Angela Merkel, announced a plan in 2008 to modernize and renew that country's educational system at all levels.

Politics/economics

While there is diversity within Europe's political and economic systems, the EU is a force for standardization. Very gradually, the EU is fostering political integration, as demonstrated by the *euro* currency. Here are trends to observe there:

■ Countries like Britain and Denmark, with long traditions of relatively nonintrusive government but with respect for the law, have tended to resist proposals for new regulations from EU administrators in Brussels. Yet, once agreement is reached, they have the best record of implementation. But the newest EU members are less resistive and more cooperative so as to retain EU benefits.

■ On the other hand, Belgium, where bureaucracy is oppressive and evading laws/ regulations is widespread, ranks among the quickest to propose new EU rules, but has the worst record for implementing adopted regulations.

■ In France, many Arab citizens are now eligible to vote in presidential elections, thus influencing the outcome of future governmental policies.

■ While some complain that there are too many national entities in Europe, it is also home to many supranational organizations, such as NATO, UNESCO, OECD, and the European Court of Human Rights.

Kagan argues that Europe is trying to find a "post-historical paradise" – a self-contained world built on transnational rules and negotiations.[7] His point is that the fundamental cleavage is all about power. The Americans believe that world order ultimately rests on military power, whereas the Europeans envision an orderly world based on international law and multilateral institutions. The New Europe seemingly wants a more independent relationship from America, drawing on the wisdom of the old continent, while forging ahead with a more united destiny of its own creation.

Currently, Europeans are divided in their viewpoint of their world role with regard to transatlantic relations. Some argue that the EU's main weakness lies in inflexible political and economic structures that make it less capable of responding adequately to both globalization and its own enlargement challenges.[8] Yet the EU leaders announced at the turn of the twenty-first century their goals to create *the most competitive and dynamic knowledge-driven economy in the world.* With its expansion in membership, the EU's gross domestic product is some $16 trillion, better than that of the United States. Exhibit 14.2 offers one insight into the growing Pan-Europe commercial activities and their impact on the environment.

EXHIBIT 14.2 CROSS-BORDER ALPINE BUSINESS

A recent magazine feature bewailed how the Alps mountain chain is under pressure from the heavy toll of tourism, commerce, pollution, and global warming on Europe's winter playground. Along with artificial snow-making machines, synthetic blankets which reflect solar radiation are being used to slow summer melting. If current temperature trends hold, 50–80 percent of the remaining Alpine glacier ice could vanish by 2100! The whole Tyrolean culture and way of life is under threat. Arrayed across the heart of Europe, the Alps have been intensely used for centuries, but only 17 percent of its 74,000 square miles are protected. Fourteen million people live there, but usable space in Alpine valleys is limited, yet there is an orgy of multi-tasks under way there by humans — factories, train tracks, hotels, houses, churches, ski lifts, farms, parking lots, stores, boutiques, and restaurants, all bounded together by concrete roads. Every day, 4,000 tractor trailers thunder through the Mont Blanc tunnel connecting France and Italy. With the cars and buses for thousands of tourists, the small village roads are clogged, and pollution results from all that traffic. The Alps are big business, a sort of factory producing 1.6 million gallons of liquid water; millions of cubic meters of lumber; tons of iron and salt; spectacular cheese, wines, and apples; amusements, athletic challenges, and artistic inspiration; plus mining and fishing. Seventy-seven million tons of cargo move through these mountains in an average year, and trans-Alpine commercial transport is likely to double by 2020!

The Alps stretch 650 miles across 8 European nations, housing some 650 ski resorts. Scientists predict that as the permanent snow line rises along with temperatures, half of these resorts will go out of business. Furthermore, less snow and ice cover means less runoff to feed Europe's major rivers; melting permafrost destabilizes steep slopes and the structures built upon them. The mountains also concentrate fumes and noise from all the vehicle traffic, and their carbon dioxide contributes to the global warming, while the valley walls carry the maddening noise upward. Modern people are negatively impacting this unique environment

E
X
H
I
B
I
T

14.2

and culture. Alpine people — known for their stoicism and individualism, crafted for a world of isolation and avalanches — are now coping with a host of modern problems. As the awesome mountains with their beauty and tranquility are the central reality of Alpine life, humanity should cherish and protect them.

Source: Earla Zwingle, "Meltdown: The Alps Under Pressure," *National Geographic*, February 2006, Vol. 209: 2, pp. 96–115.

Immigration and labor exchange

The new EU immigration regulations and job opportunities have attracted to this continent a host of external migrants, legal and illegal. The émigrés come largely from Africa, the Middle East, and Turkey. "Destination Europe" now accounts for over 47 million immigrants from abroad (a 2010 statistic). Though the new arrivals ease labor shortages, they increase the anxieties of Europeans about cultural identities and values. EU countries have dealt with the challenge in various ways — from integrating them into society to legal containment or expulsion. For example, Austria will fine and expel immigrants who fail to attend mandated classes in the German language, while Britain requires those seeking citizenship to pass a test. As émigrés swarm into Western Europe, the nations there are tightening their immigration laws. Many of these "visitors" live together in ghettos, forming new ethnic minorities. So far, European policy has been inadequate, not facilitating integration into their societies and not encouraging assimilation. On the other hand, some of the new arrivals have resisted acculturation, refusing to learn the language and culture of the host country, and not letting their children marry the locals or outside their religious faith. When second and third generation children of immigrants are unable to enter the mainstream society, they often resort to protests and riots, such as those happening in France. Unemployment among such youths is usually higher than average, and obstacles are often in place against home ownership and adequate education.

Under the EU policies, internal migrants seeking work outside their own country in other member nations are free to do so. But such labor exchange, especially from the East, finds an open market that is curtailed, except in Britain, Ireland, and Sweden, who only delimit benefit-seekers. Most of the other original 12 members impose transitional arrangements to curb "freedom of movement," which is supposedly a right of all EU citizens. Their governments fear that Eastern Europeans will steal jobs from the locals, but in actuality, more often they take work that the locals shun. Germany and Austria are most cautious of opening their labor market, because their countries are on the border of former communist countries whose workers go west for higher wages (e.g., Austria's wages are five times higher than those of Slovakia). Globalization and an aging workforce in Europe could eventually cause greater labor mobility that will prove beneficial, forcing more workforce flexibility among the EU member states.

Multiculturalism[9]

Another EU challenge is to promote multiculturalism among its 27 members, developing a continental-wide application and understanding of Article 9 of the European Convention on Human Rights. While secularism is on the rise in Europe, and church attendance falls, new mosques are opening everywhere on the continent – the United Kingdom alone has over a thousand! The Islamic community now represents about 6 percent of the European populations, and so the term *Eurabia* arose. In several member countries, violence has erupted between a swelling Muslim minority and the majority populations. Mosque and Muslim gravesites have been vandalized, and complaints rise about discrimination against them. The Muslim global backlash, as seen in the 2006 riots and burnings because of what they perceived as blasphemous, hurtful cartoons against their founder and beliefs originating in a Danish newspaper and reprinted elsewhere, is a case in point. The growing Muslim presence is changing the "face" of Europe, more than the military invasions of the Ottoman Empire in previous centuries.

European Muslims more and more seem to be secular in outlook and supportive of liberal values – such counter stereotypes of their coreligionists. They could become leaders in promoting integration of their communities with the mainstream culture, thwarting rising contention between Muslims and other Europeans. Euro leaders, in general, are also challenged to contain resurgent xenophobic behavior across the continent, from whatever source.

With the increasing activities of global terrorism networks, EU states have new concerns about foreign visitors and migrants. Further, Europe's Muslim minorities feel stigmatized for the actions of Osama bin Laden or other criminal Islamic fundamentalists. Although many Muslims assimilate into European cultures, others choose self-segregation, and many are forced, for economic reasons, to live in impoverished "ghettos." Often, they experience cultural chauvinism and discrimination, ranging from unemployment to outright racism and violence against their person and property. Most Muslims have come to Europe seeking the opportunity to improve their lives (Exhibit 14.3).

WESTERN EUROPE

In Western Europe, we will discuss, in some detail France and Italy. Most are members of the EU. Further cultural information on all these countries is available from their embassies or on the Internet. Many books and magazines also contain cultural and country-specific information (e.g., www.economist.com/countries/cities).

EXHIBIT 14.3 GENERAL TIPS FOR DOING BUSINESS IN EUROPE

- Customer service is the key to success. The standards of Europe in this regard are not up to those of the United States, especially in matters of rapid repairs and home service.
- Publish price lists in terms of the local currency.
- Deploy Americans to Europe on the basis of a two-year minimum commitment to establish meaningful customer relations; the staying power of expatriate personnel is a subtle indicator — whenever possible, hire locals and then train them.
- Lease office equipment and computers in Europe because of the electrical differences in power outlets.
- Ensure that sales personnel know their products. Europeans are sophisticated buyers of foreign merchandise.
- Europeans gauge the forethought and commitment of a foreign firm by the way it treats its sales representatives. They perceive the salesperson as a key role, which should be judged on long-term performance; select such representatives very carefully.
- Europeans do not like change, so it is important for the foreign company to project stability and long-range commitment, yet they are attracted to "new" products, processes, and services.
- When able to properly serve the primary market in Europe, remember geographic distances are not great. Assess the secondary markets (Spain and Portugal, Greece, and the eastern European countries), and respond carefully to all inquiries from such areas.
- Beside cultural, language, and political differences in Europe, be prepared to cope with technical differences (e.g., length of stationery and forms that do not fit standard copying machines, ink that does not reproduce well, different abbreviations).
- European nomenclature and honorific titles are to be observed in oral and written communication (especially spellings in English that differ between British and North American versions).
- Europeans value personal contacts and mementos, so the token gift may create a favorable impression, as may participation in a trade fair that is part of a centuries-old tradition.

FRANCE

France is geographically the largest country in Western Europe. It lies south of Great Britain, separated by the English Channel, but connected now by an underwater tunnel, or "chunnel." The Channel gives the French nation access to the North Sea, as well as to the Irish Sea and the Atlantic Ocean on its western coast, while to the southeast France is bounded by the Mediterranean Sea. On its northeastern border are Belgium, Luxembourg, and Germany; Switzerland and Italy to the east; and Spain in the south, separated by the Pyrenees. Its natural resources include coal, iron ore, bauxite, timber, zinc, and potash. Beautiful Paris is its capital, while other major cities include Marseille, Lyon, Toulouse, Strasbourg, Nice, and Bordeaux. Apart from its advanced postindustrial economy, France is also known for its farms and vineyards.

In medieval times, French royalty and troops moved back and forth from Normandy to the British Isles, exchanging feudal domains. In the late eighteenth and early nineteenth centuries under Napoleon Bonaparte, the *grande armee* extended its control across Europe to Russia. The empire's remnants reveal the scope of France's colonial power and help us appreciate the glory that was France. Begin by looking today at what was once French East Africa, and where the French language is still spoken (Burundi, Central African Republic, the Congo, Djibouti, and, to a lesser extent, Rwanda). The same cultural impact is still evident in Northern Africa (Algeria, Chad, Egypt, Mali, Mauritania, Morocco, Niger, Tunisia, and Senegal); West Central Africa (Benin, Burkina Faso, Cameroon, Congo, Cote d'Ivoire, Gabon, Guinea, and Togo); and even in Madagascar. Recall, too, the influence of French culture and cuisine in such widely separated locations as India (Pondicherry) and Indochina (Vietnam). Today, France still administers certain Caribbean islands, such as Guadeloupe and Martinique; in addition, many islands in Oceania have special administrative arrangements with the French government.

Historical perspectives[10]

Many books have been written on the glorious history of France — from when it was known as Gaul under the Roman Empire, through the Middle Ages when France was gradually united under its own king, and then to its expansion across Europe under Emperor Napoleon. A great contribution toward the establishment of democracy came from its support of the American Revolution, and then through its own French Revolution. France helped to found both the European Common Market and Union, but has a diminished role in the world today.

The current Fifth Republic of France came into being in 1958, and has been governing by "cohabitation" — a sharing of power between the president with a seven-year term and the bicameral parliament of the National Assembly and Senate. The president appoints the prime minister, who runs the country on a daily basis, presides over the cabinet, commands the armed forces, and concludes treaties. He has the power to dissolve the National Assembly and assume full power. Two-fifths of members in that National Assembly are on leave from the civil service. Fifty-seven percent of the adult population is either civil servants or their dependents. The various ministries of government employ some two million plus in public service. Confidence is eroding in the nation's lackluster economic formula of higher taxes and higher social charges, especially during the current slowdown in economic growth. Excessive spending on healthcare, continuing widespread strikes, and the country's limited role in world affairs have disillusioned the public. Although France's colonies have diminished, it still administers Tahiti in the Pacific, and has influence in its former possessions in East Africa.

France's entrancing countryside consists of vineyards and cornfields, pastures and picturesque villages, and superb cuisine and wines. After its world-class capital of Paris and the other major five cities, Strasbourg is home to the European parliament, high-tech industrial parks, and the International Space University. Experience of bitter defeat in three devastating wars (one in Indochina and two on its own soil) has produced a strong antiwar sentiment, plus a desire for peaceful cooperation with Germany, especially through the EU. Despite long positive relations with the United States, going back to the eighteenth century, its streak of Gaullist independence prompts French politicians to often disagree publicly with American policies, particularly those regarding the Middle East.

Living in the Élysée Palace, French presidents, like the late Francois Mitterrand, have used public monies for grand schemes while fostering a top-down bureaucratic approach to governance. The modern nobility, elite graduates of grand ecoles or universities, dominate civil service and business – all supposedly based on meritocracy. But the public sector mistrusts the private sector because it often hampers initiative, creativity, and entrepreneurialism. The French market is mature and sophisticated, open to global suppliers, especially to those from within the EU community. The commercial environment is dynamic and reflects consumer trends within a world marketplace (Exhibit 14.4).

EXHIBIT 14.4 PERCEPTIONS OF FRANCE

E X H I B I T 14.4

■ The French constitute the most brilliant and the most dangerous nation in Europe, and the best qualified to become an object of admiration, hatred, pity, or terror, but never of indifference!

Alexis de Tocqueville

■ The average Frenchmen is concerned about an elite of bureaucrats, businessmen, and politicians who seemingly run the country to benefit themselves amidst corruption and public scandals.

The New York Times, August 1, 1999

■ The French themselves are horribly muddled over France's place in Europe, over the impact of globalization, and at root, over what it means to be French.... France has an identity problem. It needs the courage to redefine itself.

J. Andres, "A Divided Self – A Survey of France,"
The Economist, November 16, 2002

■ The French have a passion for engineering and technology, for research and solutions that push back the boundaries. The Ecole Polytechnique is one of the best engineering schools in the world, and French technology tends to be very sophisticated.

> Nani Becalli, CEO, GE Europe (www.thenewfrance.com)

■ As an American living in France, I personally find the quality of day-to-day life far superior to anything I could afford back home in the USA.

> Richard Chessnoff, *The Arrogance of the French*

■ The biggest lesson of the French riots is that more jobs are needed. In the deprived suburbs, a kind of soft terror rules. When too many young people see nothing ahead but unemployment after they leave school, they end up rebelling. Thus, one rational analysis of the forces that lie behind the riots, car-burning, and street battles that have broken out, first in the banlieues of Paris and then right across France for two weeks. It points to a pressing case for action to build a greater sense of identity with French society among the rioters, most of whom are second-generation Muslims of North or West African origin. There are arguments over why five to six million Muslims there feel alienated — one-third the total in the European Union and one-tenth of the country's population. But the answer surely lies in the toxic mix of poor housing, bad schools, inadequate transport, social exclusion, disaffection over discrimination, and, above all, high unemployment. French unemployment has hovered around 10 percent; the average rate among youth is over 20 percent, one of the highest in Europe; among young Muslims in the banlieues, it has been twice as high again. Most of the French elite, on the left as well as the right, have simply ignored the festering problem. There are no black or brown mainland members of the National Assembly; hardly any on television. The yawning gap between the French elite and the ordinary people was a big cause of government's loss of the referendum on the European constitution.

The unrest in French cities shows that social and policing policy has failed. France needs to acknowledge its multiracial complexion by adapting its vocabulary, rather than hiding behind "the myth of republican equality."

> "French Failure," *The Economist,* November 12,
> 2005 pp. 11–12; 24–26

■ France spends 30 percent of its budget on "social protection," and makes it possible for even an illiterate immigrant to live fairly well without having worked a day in his life. Yet shying away from reality by France's ruling class does not change the reality that one of the most civilized nations in Europe is sliding into barbarism. None of the violence was either surprising or unexpected. Indeed, it was an easily predictable denouement of the gradual transformation of hundreds of Muslim enclaves into crime-ridden, self-isolated, anti-societies that have de-facto seceded from French society in virtually every aspect, except for continuing to depend upon the welfare state.

- This is not merely a local situation, but has implications for much of Europe, in terms of socio-political and economic context. There seem to be three seemingly unstoppable trends: the implosion of the European social-market economy; an unprecedented demographic collapse of the native European populations; and the takeover of the burgeoning Muslim communities in Western Europe by radical Islam. The French and European socio-economic model had much to do with the rise of the Muslim ghetto, and its ongoing implosion will dramatically exacerbate its conflicts with society at large. The new tougher economic climate, combined with ever-present French xenophobia and racism, led to the high unemployment and progressive ghettoization of the second-generation Muslims. With a fertility rate twice that of the natives, the Muslim community in France and Western Europe is growing at 50 percent every decade. The European Union will lose nearly half its native population by 2050, while its Muslim community increases five-fold to 100 million. What is needed is a cultural revolution.

  Alex Alexiev, "France at the Brink," *The San Diego Union-Tribune,*
  January 22, 2007, pp. G3/5

- France is a stratified society in need of change, flexibility, and mobility.

  CBS Sunday Morning Report on the Student Protests
  in Paris, April 2, 2006

- A priority of my foreign policy is to further the Mediterranean Union. The goal is to create an area of solidarity involving the environment, cultural dialogue, economic growth, and security. This union should be built upon projects that are ambitious but realistic, showing all the peoples of the Mediterranean that together we can build a shared future of peace.

  Nicolas Sarkozy, President of France; President of the EuropeanUnion,
  last half of 2008, "France in a Challenging World,"
  The World in 2008, *The Economist,* 2008, p. 96.

In July 2008, a Paris summit of 40 heads of states and the EU inaugurated an unprecedented Union of the Mediterranean to achieve the goals stated by Nicolas Sarkozy above, for the benefit of southern and eastern nations bordering the Mediterranean Sea. The hope is to improve their trade with the EU members by joint programs to improve poor infrastructure, an ill-educated workforce, and unemployment. The aim also is to upgrade the environment, climate, transport, immigration procedures, and policing in the region. The summit declaration committed the participants to preventing nuclear proliferation, countering terrorism in all its forms, and promoting democratic principles, human rights, and fundamental freedoms.

Cultural guidelines for doing business in France

Idealism

The French tend to believe that the basic truths on which life is based derive from principles and immutable or universal laws. They are concerned with the essence of values. The motto of the French Republic is "Liberty, Equality, and Fraternity." To the French, values such as these should transcend everything else in life. They behave in an individualistic manner. "*Chacun defend son beef-steak*" (everyone protects his own steak). Sometimes they are frustrated and find it difficult to live by these ideals in everyday life, yet the hunger for these altruistic ideals is still present and deeply ingrained in most French people. For example, contrast the French and the American views on sex and money. The French are not easily embarrassed by sex or nudity. But they are embarrassed talking about money, how you get it, or vocational positions and salaries. To them, your job, your income, and such are personal and not the business of others.

Practicalities

Generally, except for lunch, the French time sense is casual, so people are often late and no offense is normally taken. Although the person in a subservient position is usually prompt, the executive is free to be late. Anticipate a reluctance to make commitments, leading to scheduling at the last minute. Also expect frequent rescheduling of meetings and appointments.

The French enjoy leisure and socialization, as can be seen in their two hour luncheons, seven official holidays (www.getcustoms.com), and four or five weeks of vacations (usually in August, when the nation virtually shuts down). Although a land of great medieval cathedrals, over 75 percent of citizens who call themselves Roman Catholic do not see religion as playing a large part in their lives, and may even be slightly anticlerical. While giving lip service to religious toleration, the over five million Muslims in France are treated with mistrust and often only tolerated. Realistically, the country's far-right white extremists, influenced by a colonial past, are xenophobic and hostile toward Arabs. The intensely competitive French educational system puts immigrant children of non-French-speaking backgrounds at a real disadvantage, marooning them between two cultures, even when born in France. French education does impact business – schools are rigorous and value linguistic capability.

French society is stratified with sharply defined and competing classes, where diversity is just beginning to be appreciated. Despite some female prominence in public offices and the professions, women's rights have come late, and sexual harassment only became illegal in the early 2000s. Foreigners complain of inadequate customer service. Managers and employees are "family" who often unite against outsiders.[11]

SOCIAL STRUCTURE AND STATUS

The French are very status conscious. Social status in France depends on one's social origins. Outward signs of social status are the level of education, a beautiful house with a well-designed, tasteful facade (not a gaudy one), knowledge of literature and fine arts, and the social origins of one's ancestors.

Social standing and class are very important in France as well. The French social classes are the aristocracy, the upper bourgeoisie, the upper-middle bourgeoisie, the middle, the lower-middle, and lower classes (blue-collar workers, peasants). Social classes categorize people according to their professional activities (teachers, doctors, lawyers, craftsmen, foremen, and peasants), as well as their political opinions (conservative, left-oriented). The mass influx of immigrants, an underclass, into a relatively homogeneous society is altering the situation.

Social interactions are thus affected by these social stereotypes. It is extremely difficult for a French individual to be rid of social stereotypes. They affect personal identity. Unlike an American who can theoretically attain the highest levels of social consideration by working hard and being professionally successful, the French find it difficult to do so. If professionally successful, the French can expect to climb one or two stages of the social ladder in a lifetime, but often nothing more.[12]

COOPERATIONS AND COMPETITION

The French are not basically oriented toward competition. To them, the word *competition* has a very narrow meaning – practicing a sport at the highest level of international excellence. For example, the French consider superstar professional athletes as involved in competition. The average French person does not feel affected by competition, which can be dangerous to the country's economic welfare. Some years ago during a New Year's Eve television speech, then-President Giscard d'Estaing tried to educate the French and make them face the fact that competition really should affect their lives. He said competition is not just what the French soccer team experiences during the World Cup. The economic welfare of the French people actually depends on how competitive French goods are on international markets. He tried to awaken the French to the notion of competition, so that they would motivate themselves to work harder and be more productive.

When confronted with individuals with a competitive drive, the French may interpret them as being antagonistic, ruthless, and power-hungry. They may feel threatened, and overreact or withdraw from the discussion. Yet, the pyramidal structure of the French educational system exposes French children and adolescents to competition very early.

PERSONAL CHARACTERISTICS

French people are friendly, humorous, and sardonic. The French wish to be admired. French people are more likely to be interested in a person who disagrees with them. Because they want to be liked, the French are very hard to impress and impatient with those who try. A French person, when trying to get a sense of another, looks for qualities within the person and for personality. French people tend to gain recognition and to develop their identity by thinking and acting against others.

TRUST AND RESPECT

Personal honor and integrity are valued in France. A French person trusts an individual according to an inner evaluation of the subject's personality and character. Because social stereotypes are so vivid, an average French person cannot earn respect from members of other social classes merely through work accomplishments and performance.

Regarding privacy, a foreign student living with a French family closed the door to his bedroom after dinner, not realizing that closed doors are considered rude and that the visitor was expected to socialize with the family. Furthermore, when shutters to the outside are closed, this is not a sign of distrustfulness by the French, but a desire for privacy from the passerby.

STYLE OF CONVERSATION

French speakers seldom put themselves forward or try to make themselves look good in conversations. If they accidentally do, they will usually add, "Je ne cherche pas a me vanter mais . . ." ("I do not want to boast but . . ."). Boasting is often considered a weakness, a sign of self-satisfaction and immaturity. In conversations with the French, some may ask their French counterparts questions about themselves. The French will probably shun such questions and orient the conversation toward more general subjects. To them, it is not proper to show characteristics of self-centeredness.

Further, the French are so proud of their language that they expect everyone to be able to speak it – visitors not fluent in that language are advised to apologize for lack of that knowledge and to learn a few key phrases and pronounce the words correctly. Be sure to smile when you use them. Remember that for centuries, all Western diplomats spoke French, and it was the language of the Russian Czar's royal court. The French are very sensitive about the diminishment of their language in the global market, and the introduction of English words into it.

The French, who may seem contentious, often criticize institutions, conditions, and people they live with. A disagreement can be considered stimulating to a French person. It is not uncommon to see two French people arguing with each other, their faces reddened with what seems to be anger, exchanging lively, heated, and irreconcilable arguments. Then later, they shake hands and comment, "That was a good discussion. We should do it again sometime!" The French tend to think that such arguments are interesting and stimulating. It is also a meaningful outlet for tension and appreciation of humor. They also often add a touch of cynicism to their humor and may not hesitate to make fun of institutions and people.

CONSISTENCY AND CONTRADICTIONS

The French abound in contradictions and are not overly disturbed by them; instead, they relish their complexity. They profess lofty ideals of fraternity and equality, but at times show characteristics of utmost individualism and selfish materialism. On the political scene, they seem continuously restless, verbally criticizing the government and capitalism, yet they are basically conservative.

ATTITUDES TOWARD WORK

Typically, French attitudes toward work depend on whether they are employed in the public sector or in the private sector. In the French bureaucracy and in state-owned concerns, there is little incentive to be productive. Quotas are rarely assigned, and it is virtually impossible to lay off or dismiss employees on the basis of job performance. Massive strikes have caused difficulties when companies have attempted to reform or modernize, or when government tries to pass policies and legislation that many people object to; strikes by university students have actually brought down the government in power. In the private sector, the situation is different. It is true that French workers do not respect the work ethic. They are usually not motivated by competition or by the desire to emulate fellow workers. They frown on working overtime and have four to five weeks of vacation a year. However, they usually work hard in their allotted working time. French workers have the reputation of being productive. Part of the explanation for such productiveness may lie in the French tradition of craftsmanship. A large proportion of the French workforce has traditionally been employed in small, independent businesses where there is widespread respect for a job well done, and many French people take pride in such work. This may also be explained as many have not been employed in huge, impersonal industrial concerns, where craftsmanship may not be so valued. Rather, they often have a direct stake in the work they are doing and are usually concerned with quality.

ATTITUDES TOWARD AUTHORITY

French companies contain many social reference groups that are mutually exclusive. Tight reins of authority are needed to ensure adequate job performance. The lesser emphasis on delegation of responsibility limits accountability and contributes to a more rigid organizational structure. As a consequence, decision-making is more centralized in French companies, and it may take longer before decisions are reached and applied. This may be a source of frustration for foreign executives (especially low–middle-management executives) who are working with French executives from a comparable management level. The flow of communication is improved if American executives have direct access to two or three top executives of a French company. This is where the actual decision-making power is. French subordinates tend to view an attempt to track personal progress as an infringement on their territory. The following example illustrates this point. A consultant on a project in the south of France reported the following:

> The main objective of our project was to increase sales of a high-tech product. One of the ideas to accelerate sales was to introduce the use of a daily chart to track each individual's sales progress. The goal was to focus management's and subordinates' attention on specific areas for improvement, as well as ask those who were doing well to share tips to help their colleagues' progress. Although management thought this idea was great, and many of the salespersons agreed that in theory it was a good idea, nine out of 10 salespersons loudly objected. The reason? They did not want management – or their colleagues – to be able to track their sales. This idea was never put into practice.

The highest executives of large French companies also have "different" management styles, as the French are judged on personal attributes as well as on performance. It takes poor performance for them to be challenged in their functions by a board of directors or by subordinates. Patterns of authority are stable in French industry. Therefore, because they do not need to justify their actions to the same extent, the very top French executives tend to be more autocratic in their managerial style. Executive functions also have more overtones of social leadership.

It is interesting to compare French and American business magazine interviews of executives. Along with professional experiences and activities, top French executives usually mention details concerning their personal lives, such as former professors who had an impact on them, enriching social and personal experiences, books that influenced their outlook on life, and what their convictions are on political and social issues. On the other hand, top American executives will more likely emphasize the progression of their career in terms of professional achievements. But in this arena of exercising power and authority, French management is also changing because of their involvement in the global marketplace and the foreign acquisitions, mergers, and alliances of French corporations. Obviously, there are considerable differences in the French management style as compared to the style of managers from other countries. Chapter 3 tries to explain some factors present in cross-cultural management.

ORGANIZATIONAL STRUCTURE AND STYLE

The organizational structure of French companies tends to be rigid; the French put less emphasis on control of individual performance. The decision-making process is more centralized in French companies. Important decisions are made only by the top executives, but slowly there is a trend toward team management because of consortia formed with businesses outside the country, such as Airbus.

CONFLICT

The mentally vigorous French have been aptly described as *combative libertarians*; that is, they appreciate strong argument and contradiction. The French, partly because they live in a more closed society with relatively little social mobility, are used to conflict. They are aware that some positions are irreconcilable, and that people must live with these irreconcilable opinions. They, therefore, tend not to mind conflict, and sometimes enjoy it. They even respect others who carry it off with style and get results. The French are also less concerned about negative reactions from those with whom they are in conflict.

French managers also report difficulties in adjusting to life in other countries. The French managers seem to experience problems caused by emphasis in the French culture on pride in their past cultural heritage, causing them to be too critical of people who do not benefit from that same cultural tradition. In their self-descriptions, the French managers feel handicapped by their conditioning to a formal way of thinking and a lack of actual knowledge of other cultures.

The atmosphere today in France is very diverse. There are some pessimists among the elite and intellectuals who are publishing articles and books forecasting the decline of France and its culture. For example, in 2003, Nicolas Bavez published a volume, *New World, Old France,* decrying French nihilism, which he predicts will lead to a *national crisis, unequaled since the agony of the fourth republic.* The increasing number of books and articles on such themes indicates a growing mood of melancholy, gloom, and discontent, evident in the May 2006 rejection in a national referendum of the EU constitution. The people's contrariness is reflected in a recent CSA poll when 70 percent reported that future generations would live less well than they do today, while 84 percent indicated that they were happy. More intriguing is the rise in French female fertility rate to 0.09 in 2004, the highest rate in Europe after Ireland – 1.94 children per woman.

During this decade, the French have been gripped by antiliberalism, antiglobalization, and anti-Americanism. Though these attitudes are lessening, it would seem that the present disgruntlement of French citizens is caused by the country's political ecosystem whose past elite leaders were unwilling to promote necessary change in their society. Yet the French approach to citizenship has its strengths, with its unapologetic approach to national identity, and emphasis on secularism and equality. Exhibit 14.5 lists a few business tips.

EXHIBIT 14.5 BUSINESS TIPS WITH THE FRENCH

E
X
H
I
B
I
T

14.5

1   French handshake is a FIRM, brief handclasp accompanied by a short span of eye contact. When French employees arrive at work, they usually greet their colleagues with a quick handshake, and repeat the process when they leave. Some may kiss their friends of both genders on the cheeks, but this is the exception in a business setting. A French woman offers her hand first. It is considered vulgar to snap one's fingers.

2   French conversation is not linear, and frequent interruption of each other may occur. Conversation is meant to entertain, not just inform, so expect many references to art and argument, as every possibility is explored and articulated, opinions are expressed, and need not be refuted. The French complain that Americans lecture, not converse.

3   Food is important in France, so expect to share meals enthusiastically while doing business with the locals. Whoever initiates the meal is expected to pay, and to make restaurant reservations, except in hotels and brasseries. With an invitation to a person's home for a social occasion, it is polite to bring a gift of wine or flowers (not roses or chrysanthemums, which are more appropriate for funerals).

4   Respect privacy — close doors after you, and knock on them before entering.

5   Be attentive to voices — the French expect you to recognize the person over a telephone by voice alone. As a sign of closeness, avoid saying, "Who is this?" Regulate voice volume, lest you offend with loud or boisterous talk and braying laughter.

6   Neatness and good taste are important in this culture.

Source: Morrison, T. et al. *Dun & Bradstreet Guide to Doing Business Around the World*, Upper Saddle River, NJ: Prentice-Hall, 1997.

CENTRAL EUROPE

Among the 11 nations in this geographic area, we will provide a detailed cultural analysis.

ITALY[13]

This portion of Europe has always been geographically distinctive because it is seemingly shaped like a boot. In southeastern Europe, the country lies south of France, Switzerland, and Austria, with Slovenia and Croatia on its eastern borders. It has many small islands on its eastern coastline, but the two largest are Sardinia and Sicily to the south. Generally temperate in climate, Italy's northern borders are separated from its neighbors by the snow-capped Alps mountain chain, thus enabling its city of Turin to host the 2006 Winter Olympic Games. The rest of the peninsula is surrounded by water — to the east by the Adriatic Sea;

while in the southeast, the Gulf of Taranto and the Ionian Sea; to the west, the Ligurian and Tyrrhenian Seas; and in the south, the Mediterranean Sea.

Cultural guidelines for doing business in Italy

Over millennia, this land was divided into so many independent political entities – each with autonomous governance, ruling families, language dialects, local customs and traditions, as well as cuisines – that the various parts of Italy today are unique in various ways while also sharing some common cultural values. By means of the mass media and the education system, Italy today has grown closer together into a more united country, but it is still rare to find an Italian who will say he is Italian, and not Roman, or Florentine, or Genovese. This tendency demonstrates the strong cultural value of *campanilismo*. It centers on the campanile, or bell tower, that can be found in every village in Italy. Ordinary citizens feel comfortable when they can see the campanile of their own town. The implication is that Italians prefer to stay in their city of origin and will always consider the interests of their campanile in business situations. Yet as an EU member, many cosmopolitan Italian political and business leaders find themselves more involved today in European institutions, as well as the global market. Italians have served as president of the EU and CEOs of global corporations.

What can one say about Italy? Thousands of books have been written about its cultural treasures. Anyone who visits the country falls in love with its picturesque villages and stunning countryside, its historic and beautiful cities, its poetic and dynamic language, and its incredible food and wine. It is the land of art, science, and passion, the land of "saints, scholars, and navigators" (Italian proverb). Apart from Italian contributions to art and architecture, music and literature, this creative people invented many current business practices (e.g., innovations in banking, insurance, and double-entry bookkeeping). Most people would agree that Italian fashion, food, and sports cars are the best in the world. There, we find *La Dolce Vita*, the ability to enjoy everything with art and style. But loving Italy and doing business there are two very different things.

One important thing to realize about Italy is that it has two faces, like the two-faced Roman god Janus – one looking forward and one looking backward. Italy is the vestige of the eternal Roman Empire, yet on the cutting edge of modern scientific research and many types of technology. It looks backward to its age-old traditions, and looks forward (painfully sometimes) to its position as a strong member of the EU. Italy is frequently in a state of social, economic, and political change. Such transitions attempt to cope with major challenges of immigration, European integration, globalization, and family breakdown. In addition to having two faces, Italy also has two halves. This is due in part to the historical occupations of the areas. The north is well developed into an industrial powerhouse and one of the richest areas of Europe. In contrast, the southern half of Italy starting just below Rome (known as the *Mezzogiorno*) is one of the poorest areas of Europe. The south is economically depressed and primarily agricultural. It is perhaps Italy's greatest economic problem with social issues as well. The south embodies the stereotypes that foreigners have of Italy – chaotic streets, and violently honking horns with drivers shouting at each other. Mafia criminality also undermine Naples' and Sicily's progress, whereas the north exemplifies the best rendition of Italy as a modern industrial power.

Volumes have been written on the Italian contributions to Western civilization. The West owes its essence and structure to Italy in the many areas of science, economics, navigation, art, architecture, politics, and literature. In every area of study stand many Italian geniuses, including Dante, Galileo, Michelangelo, Leonardo daVinci, Francis of Assisi, Verdi, and Marconi. Remember that Christopher Columbus (a Genovese navigator) "discovered" America, and don't forget that the name *America* comes from the Florentine cartographer, Amerigo Vespucci! Italians are very proud of their heritage, and it is advisable for businesspeople to know, appreciate, and respect it. Italians also have immigrated in large numbers abroad, especially to North America and Brazil.

The following are some insights about Italian sense of identity and cultural values that affect business. In a recent survey, Italians evaluated themselves in terms of their national character – the top three qualities reported were the art of *arrangiarsi*, creativity in art and the economy, and connection to the family. Interestingly enough, the feature that they reported as the least present was that of civic duty. Now to explain key concepts in the Italian mindset and lifestyle:

■ *Art of arrangiarsi* means to be able to make do, to get by, to work oneself out of any situation. This activity has been elevated to an art in Italy because of the fact that most systems do not function as expected. The cause of this has historical roots, owing to the numerous invaders, conquerors, and imposed systems of foreign governments. In business terms, this could be called "creative problem-solving." The Italians have learned to *arrangiarsi* as a reaction to the formidable system of government, laws, and taxes. It is hard for Americans to understand this idea because they are used to having systems that actually work as expected. Instead, Italians have developed ways to get around the system and accomplish what needs to be done in a creative way, via connections and family ties.

■ *Relationships with family and friends* emphasizes family ties, connections, and relationships as the bastions against the insecurities of life. Over the centuries, this value and system was a solution to problems imposed by foreign occupation. Today, everything flows from such relationships – from getting a job to opening a bank account; everything depends on connections. The successful foreign businessperson makes it a point to understand the connections and use them.

■ *La cordata* literally means rope or cord, referring to the practice of pulling along friends and family in the climb up the corporate ladder. It is an outgrowth of the relationship/family value explained above. People who find work in a company or government office immediately seek to be part of a *cordata,* or network. And if they also start their own enterprise, gradually their friends or relatives are involved some way in the undertaking, as the case may be. The practice is also used to form alliances between companies for buying materials or products. So Italians are very open to synergistic relationships. See Exhibit 14.6 for a few comments on Italy.

■ *Bella figura* literally means *beautiful figure*, but it can make or break a business negotiation. *Bella figura* is the desire to make a good impression, to give a good appearance, and to convey a certain image. It is somewhat like the Asian value of saving face, but encompasses appearance as well as behavior. It is responsible for the fact that Italian fashion, art, and architecture are world renowned and sought after. Italians seek to make a *bella figura* through their appearance, both physical and economic, and their behavior. It is important for managers to remember this in all areas of interaction. Proposals and presentations must look good. Image is the key in all areas, including dress and behavior. Status and prestige also matter. The foreign businessperson is advised to imitate the Italians on this one. And be careful not to present a *brutta figura* (ugly figure) – that can mean being obviously drunk, looking slovenly, arriving late, being unprepared, giving an unattractive presentation.

EXHIBIT 14.6 OBSERVATIONS ON ITALY

E X H I B I T 14.6

"The first thing to say about Italy is that, however grubby its politics or flaky its economics, it is still for most of its inhabitants and visitors, one of the most delightful countries of the world. Its confection of man-made and natural beauty, cultural heritage, and clement climate is second to none. Its people are blessed with charm, humor, and the ability to enjoy, let alone let others enjoy, life. Few have so brilliant a sense of style and fashion, so sumptuous a cuisine and cellar, so strong a tradition of melding hard work with pleasure."

This survey is filled with praise for the globe's sixth largest economy; its relatively strong family life and social cohesion; its top-flight universities and scientists; its manufacturing and high-tech pursuits. Then it points up Italy's continuing problems – government instability and turnovers; Western's Europe's worst performing economy; business failure to be competitive and to effectively use new communications technologies; slow pace of reform in labor markets and in overcoming the North–South income gap; inadequate probity in battling corruption and criminal behavior (e.g., the Mafia); lack of foreign investor trust because of the country's rickety and opaque legal system; need for faster decentralization and privatization, as well as for constitutional, electoral, and welfare reforms by the state.

But the report concludes that Italy is still one of the world's most dynamic, enjoyable, and, in many ways, admirable countries.

Source: Jan Smiley, "A Survey of Italy – What a Lovely Odd Place," *The Economist*, July 7, 2001, p. 18. Also see the update by John Peet, "Addio, Dolce Vita: A Survey of Italy," *The Economist*, November 26, 2005 (www.economist.com/surveys).

■ *Furbo* is an Italian word that is very hard to translate. It can have negative or positive connotations. It has evolved as a concept that describes how to outsmart one's adversary or beat the system. A funny example is that of the seat belt law. Seat belts are now required everywhere in Italy, and the police will fine motorists if they aren't wearing them. Someone in Naples started producing a sweater that was made with a black diagonal stripe from the neck to the stomach, so that when you wear it, it appears that you are wearing a seat belt. So you outsmart the police. This is being a *furbo*. In business, it is very important to be on your guard, because often someone will try to outsmart you in some way. Beware of the well-developed *furbo*, because he is waiting to rip you off.

Foreigners also need to be aware of the following value orientations among the Italian people.

DETERMINISM

Italians are basically fatalistic, *che sarà, sarà*. Because of their long history of natural and political disasters, as well as their experiences with Catholicism, they tend to believe that nothing can be done to prevent things from happening the way they are destined to happen. Insecurity is viewed as a fact of life. This conviction may explain why they tend to live in the moment. Remember that the famous Latin quote *carpe diem* (seize the day) came from Italy; thus, they will take opportunities in the moment without thinking that they have control over their actual success. One source of frustration in business stems from this fatalism. Foreign managers will find it difficult to extract detailed objectives and plans from their Italian counterparts, as the practice of setting precise objectives goes against this deterministic philosophy. Besides believing that they do not control their destiny, they also hate to make mistakes (it causes *brutta figura*), so they do not like to commit themselves too tightly to objectives they are not sure that they can complete.

TIME SENSE

Italians are often multitasking. Conducting a meeting, taking a phone call, and signing papers all at the same time are quite common. It can be very stressful for foreigners to be in a meeting that is constantly being interrupted with knocks on the door and phone calls. As far as punctuality is concerned, the north is much closer to Northern Europe in its adherence to meeting times and time allocation; but in the south, time flows at a slower pace, and people tend to be much more relaxed with appointments and schedules. It is common to have many changes of schedule, shifting, canceling, reinstating, and so forth. The best way to handle this is to be flexible and patient. Anticipate schedule changes as a matter of course. However, foreigners are expected to be on time for business and social engagements, while Italians have more latitude in this regard. Again, North Americans and northern

Europeans will discover the business environment in the south to be less time conscious, even more relationship-oriented, and more relaxed.

Normal business hours range from 8–9 a.m. to 1 p.m., and then from 3–6 or 7 p.m. There are 12 national, plus regional holidays; a city can shut down to celebrate the feast of the local patron saint. July and August are vacation months for firms, and many close during this period.

ACTION ORIENTATION

Italians tend more toward *being* than doing, because of their long past, their traditions, and their propensity to form relationships. They identify themselves with their region, their family, or their soccer team more than with their job. Italians define themselves also by their network of relationships and the connections they enjoy.

Again, there is a pronounced difference between north and south. The north has a greater focus on activity and is more dynamic; the south has an even greater focus on relationships and operates at a slower pace. The key difference between outsiders and the Italian is that individuals do not value themselves here by what they do, but by how well they, their families, and their friends can live on their financial and professional successes.

COMMUNICATION

Italian culture is high context, although the north is somewhat less than the south. The Italian language is very colorful and musical. One of the favorite pastimes of Italians is that of talking and engaging in polemical discussions. For visitors, the natives seem to waste a lot of time talking. They usually speak rapidly, in high volume, all at the same time, and in very heated discussions. They are known for their buoyant style, combining emotion, gestures, and volume that create an overall impression of a theatrical presentation. One of their most admired abilities is that of being able to put on a spectacle or show. They tend to keep one eye on the other members of the group so that they can gauge their performance. They are very expressive, or *esternazione*, meaning *expressing* or *venting*, or *letting it all out*. *Esternazione* is reflected in every communication situation. In politics and the media, it means press releases. In private life, it means telling it all. There is no word for *privacy* in the Italian language. For some companies, this can pose a problem, because secret policies, etc., are never secret and are often discussed at the local cappuccino bar with the family, and even with the press. However, it must never be assumed that the Italian businessperson will tell you everything. There is also another Italian quality, *omertà*, which means silence. Here are some communication behaviors to look for in Italians:

■　　*Indirect versus direct.* In spite of *esternazione*, personal and business relationships can be quite indirect, on the basis of unspoken (high context) values that everyone (Italian) is supposed to know. Third parties are often used to communicate important messages, especially unpleasant ones. A foreign businessperson must be aware of the hidden cultural assumptions. The best solution for this is to have a bilingual, bicultural person to advise you.

■ *Expressive.* Italians have an incredibly well-developed system of gestures. They also have an uncanny ability to yell at each other simultaneously, while somehow communicating a message.

■ *Formal.* In spite of whatever stereotypes foreigners may have about the informality of Italians (e.g., drivers screaming and gesturing at each other in traffic jams), the Italians are initially quite formal, both in personal and business relationships. They adore the spectacle of form and ritual, even in business situations. Appropriate titles are always used, such as *Dottore/Dottoressa* (person with a university degree). The businessperson must be sure to know in advance the appropriate titles. When speaking in Italian, the formal style is always used unless otherwise specified. The above tendencies are evident in business cards, which may be of three kinds: formal with all the necessary business information, including titles and degrees; informal without extensive titles, but which indicates that one has formed a less formal professional relationship; social or visiting card with just the person's name.

PHYSICAL CONTACT

Italians are very warm, and it is quite normal to see men hugging each other or sitting or leaning close. Women greet each other with a kiss on both cheeks, usually after the first time they meet. Men shake hands with men and will kiss women who they know on both cheeks. However, Italians have a smaller spatial radius than many foreigners. Part of this is due to the nature of the culture, very relationship-oriented, but also because in many areas space is actually very limited.

POWER DISTANCE

Italians tend to follow more traditional roles of hierarchy. They seem to be very egalitarian in their communication style, but they respect hierarchical structure. Status and titles are important. Foreign managers who are more informal must remember to project themselves in terms of their perceived status.

INDIVIDUALISM

Italians pride themselves on being highly individualistic. This comes out repeatedly as being a very important cultural value. But individualism does not mean independent. They are very social and prefer to be in groups, as long as they are still viewed as unique individuals. In negotiating, it often happens that each individual wants to speak, and basically repeats everything that has already been said. If the individuals are denied the opportunity to speak, they go away feeling resentful and undervalued. The result of this individualism is the fact that Italians find it difficult to truly work as part of a team.

COMPETITIVENESS

Italians are competitive even though they put a high stress on relationships. Probably the biggest areas of competition are physical appearance and lifestyle. But Italian business does not have the same drive toward competition that many foreign businesses do, probably because business is based on relationships, which means that client relationships take precedence. It is not common practice in Italian business to give individual awards or single out one individual for commendation. This trait is very much evident in the field of sports.

STRUCTURE

Italian life is seemingly highly chaotic, perhaps as a result of the bureaucracy and the lack of overall communication between government offices. Thousands of laws are made in the hope of imposing some sort of control. But as one writer said succinctly, the Italians are unpredictable, but they love routine. They are highly risk-aversive, but they go out of their way to circumvent regulations. Italian companies do not like to take risks. However, experience has shown that if a company is willing to take a risk, it will do very well in Italy.

THINKING

Italians are *deductive* in academic situations, but pragmatic in business negotiations. They tend to decide on the basis of separate situations, and often refer back to other similar situations and results.

Italian systems' orientation

ECONOMY

Italy has the eighth largest economy in the world (a 2011 statistic), despite its problems. The government seems to favor privatization and less state control of the economy, though it is required to meet EU standards and regulations. For all its attractions and successful firms, Italy is caught in a slow economic decline, requiring bold political leadership to push needed reforms. The single *euro* currency has broken the country's habit of frequent devaluation, but it is also forcing Italy to change its whole economic model while promoting structural reforms. Some of the biggest economic challenges facing Italy are the following:

- Living standards are falling in spite of increasing costs.
- Too many small, privately and family-owned companies, which contribute to low female participation in the workforce and are often in the wrong industries.

- Backward southern regional economy that is poorly performing and too dependent on the public sector.
- Corruption and violent crime (e.g., Naples), aided by Mafia activities somewhat delimited by prosecutions by dedicated magistrates.
- Underdeveloped tourism industry despite the gains the country can make from tourism.
- High unemployment rate, heavy business tax burden, and unwieldy government bureaucracy – the high rate of unemployment is caused by the heavy employment taxes that businesses must pay to employ people legally; high business taxes and red tape discourage foreign investment.
- A very strong black market, whose dimension is really not known. This means that the Italian economy is probably a lot stronger than it appears on paper because of the size of the *mercato nero*.

Further, the amount of foreign investment is significantly less than in other European countries, for several reasons. First, communism exerted a strong influence on the government after World War II, discouraging foreign business. Second, the distribution system of Italy has a long way to go before it can compete effectively with other European countries. Third, the practice of delayed payment discourages business in all areas. Italian companies usually pay on a 60- to 120-day basis, which ends up frequently translating into 120–160 days. This can cause a significant cash flow problem for foreign companies who are waiting for payment and must finance the delay. As can well be imagined, there is an ensuing snowball effect. Delayed payment is rampant in Italy. Currently, the government is trying to solve such problems, but it is unlikely that solutions will be found very soon.

SOCIO-POLITICAL FORCES

The Catholic Church continues to be a significant political and cultural force in Italy, even though it has declined in power in the past few years. Italy is primarily Catholic, but a great percentage of the population does not actually regularly practice that ancient religion. However, the Vatican has a strong presence in the formation of government policy, especially in the moral and ethical areas.

GOVERNMENT AND POLITICAL FORCES

Mussolini once said, "It is not impossible to govern Italians. It is merely useless." Italy is a multiparty parliamentary republic. Because of the large number of political parties (approximately 50 or more), Italy is basically governed by coalitions formed by various parties. One can only imagine the challenge of developing policies with so many parties. There is both a president and a prime minister. Government plays a heavy role in business, as do the labor unions. Foreign managers must be very aware of this added dimension to doing business in Italy, especially its complex justice system.

LEGAL SYSTEM

The Italian legal system and bureaucracy is infamously torturous and slow, as well as contradictory. It has been estimated that there are over 500,000 laws in Italy, many of which have never been canceled since Roman and medieval times, as well as the hundreds of new ones that are made every year. This makes the law profession quite attractive as it is necessary for every business to have a competent lawyer on call. Similarly, tax codes are perilous. The situation is further complicated by the overlay of EU rules and regulations. Such a high number of laws, laughed one Italian businessman, and nobody follows any of them! Thus, the cultural value of *arrangiarsi* flourishes in response to an overloaded system.

WOMEN IN BUSINESS

Traditionally, Italy and its business world were male-dominated, despite great respect for women and matriarchal figures. Since the 1990s, women have been challenging such attitudes. Although women in commerce and the professions are more prevalent and accepted, their salaries and perks usually are not yet comparable to their male colleagues, even when the women have superior education. However, they are making rapid progress, especially when such career women develop their own personalized management style.

BUSINESS–FAMILY CAPITALISM

As a great number of businesses in Italy are family-owned, many businesses lack management professionals. The head of the family wants to maintain control over the business. This widespread phenomenon weakens Italy because these businesses do not want to be publicly traded. Because they finance through debt, and because they want to maintain control at all costs, they limit their growth, and subsequently cannot compete in the global market. Yet the genial, amiable, and volatile Italian people will endure and move ahead in the twenty-first century — by most standards, they are wealthy, live long, and their families work together! The tips in Exhibit 14.7 will be helpful for all travelers to consider.

EXHIBIT 14.7 CONCLUDING TIPS FOR DOING BUSINESS IN ITALY

EXHIBIT 14.7

- Start-up: Be aware of possible problems — involving laws and taxes.
- Learn Italian.
- Try to find an Italian counterpart to help you through the bureaucracy.
- For the initial contact, a third-party introduction is very helpful; if you can't get that, write directly in Italian.
- Print materials in Italian.

E
X
H
I
B
I
T

14.7

- Meeting: Try to build a relationship. This is a relationship-oriented country, and if you form a relationship, you have a better chance. You do that by taking time, finding out about the other person, and building trust. It is perfectly acceptable to ask questions about family, and expect to answer questions about yours.
- Dress code: Look your best.
- Forms of address: Be formal until the other person indicates that you may speak in the familiar (that is, if you are speaking in Italian).
- Access the *cordata*.
- Get a good lawyer and a good *commercialista*.
- Be flexible.
- Make connections.
- Be patient (things go along at what seems to be a standstill, and suddenly the ball starts rolling).

EAST EUROPE/RUSSIA

Europe borders on Russia and Turkey, both of which provide entry into Asia. In ancient times, they connected to a series of trade routes with multiple branches through the heart of Europe and Asia, such as the Asian Silk Road.

The eastern region of the European continent tends to be landlocked, but for the European–Asian connection we consider in the section on Eurasia. However, this region is also punctuated by mountain systems like the Urals, and rivers such as the Deniester, Dnieper, and Don and Volga, which also empty into the Black Sea. The area also marks where Finland meets Russia, and where in past centuries, there were great westward migrations of peoples and their flocks.

From the geopolitical entity known as the U.S.S.R., the Russian Federation has emerged since the turn of the millennium, along with its neighbors in the Commonwealth of Independent States (CIS). Together, the CIS has sought to (1) repeal all Soviet laws and assume the powers of that former regime; (2) launch radical economic reforms, including the freeing of most prices; (3) retain the ruble, while allowing new currencies to be adopted in some countries; (4) establish a European-style free trade zone; (5) create joint control of all nuclear weapons; and (6) fulfil all foreign treaties and other obligations of the former communist regime.

Since the Soviet breakup, the countries immediately surrounding the Russian Federation have been in turmoil. Once part of the Czar's empire in the Caucasus, these entities struggle to be nations, like Belarus, Georgia, and the Ukraine. They seek a new identity and more independence, while coping with dictators, internal conflict, and serious economic problems. Besides the Russian Federation, the other key Commonwealth player is ancient Ukraine, populated with Slavic peoples since at least 2000 BC. Its name means *borderland*, and its beautiful capital is Kiev, the mother city of the Old Russian Empire, famous for Slavic Orthodox churches, and Cossacks.

Historical perspective on Eastern Europe[14]

To understand what is happening in contemporary Russia, its regions, and satellite countries, one has to comprehend that vast country's recent history, especially its 1918 revolution. Figes, who did a sweeping cultural survey of Russia for the past three centuries, raised an astute question: "How can this nation, whose elites have consistently looked to foreign countries for their cultural examples, be held together by the unseen threads of native sensibility?" Yet, for much of the twentieth century, its totalitarian mindset and policies dominated political, social, and economic life throughout both Central Europe and Eurasia. When the Union of Soviet Socialist Republics was founded in 1922, Russia, and eventually its Eastern Bloc allies, ensured that all major government and economic decision-making posts were filled by Communist Party members. These enforced its doctrine of centralism, requiring that decisions made at the top not be questioned by the lower echelons. This led to a situation in which a few people at the peak of the pyramid made almost every significant decision, and local initiative was practically nonexistent. The system restricted enterprise and meaningful contact with world market demand and supply. Its state monopoly sought to prevent capitalist countries from influencing the course of economic activities in the whole geographic area, except for what Western science and technologies its spies could steal.

Yet, under this repressive regime, the U.S.S.R. did survive World War II, becoming a superpower that achieved some impressive accomplishments. These ranged from education and healthcare to industrialization and an innovative space program. Before its decline, the Soviet empire had 450 million inhabitants, including some 140 national groups with a mix of European/Asian cultures, and religions including 50 million Muslims. The U.S.S.R.'s 31 so-called autonomous republics and regions stretched from the Gulf of Finland to the Pacific Ocean. As this great monolith disintegrated, the people of Russia and its satellite countries endured disruptions in their lives, such as the following:

- Widespread unemployment and massive amounts of unpaid work.
- Rapid rise in penury and beggary, stress and alcoholism, and corruption and crime.
- Deterioration in public services and the economy, especially currency speculation.
- Chaos in political, social, and family life.
- Initial failure with capitalism, while the "new aristocracy" made up of greedy oligarchs or tycoons mainly prospered.

Since the collapse of the U.S.S.R. in 1991, the peoples of Central and Eastern Europe identify themselves increasingly with Western culture and free-market enterprises. Their traditional institutions are trying to transform themselves, as new entities, missions, and roles are being formulated. There is growing emphasis on protection of freedom, human rights, and the rule of law, as well as on improving the environment and quality of life. Many of today's inhabitants are not only victims of communist cultural conditioning, but also suffered the effects from the former Cold War between East and West.

The trends, depending on where you are in that area of Europe, are toward reviving the private sector, so that businesspeople can not only own property, but also get access to labor, capital, machinery, and raw materials. Increasingly, within their huge, inefficient public sector, governments have undertaken a number of reform experiments, such as the following:

- Downsizing bureaucracies to more efficient entities.
- Modernizing legal systems and procedures, especially regarding private property.
- Changing legislation to privatize state-owned businesses and to subsidize enterprises that are private or cooperatives.
- Permitting market forces, instead of the government, to set prices.
- Creating more flexible and open banking systems that lend money on the basis of fiscal soundness instead of merely connections.
- Innovating to attract Western investment, credit, and joint ventures.

Each of these countries is in transition, having troubles institutionalizing reforms and countering widespread corruption. But global managers with vision see new market possibilities in both Central and Eastern Europe, and seek to develop links there with representatives from governments, unions, businesses, churches, environmentalists, and students. Aware of the cultural and intellectual heritage of the region, as well as its potential, they network and encourage entrepreneurs, provide training and services, while promoting diversification and outside investment. Trade and education, especially involving the exchange of people, can be a powerful means of facilitating the reform of obsolete systems and practices. The twenty-first century provides a rare chance to work towards peaceful prosperity in this part of Europe for those bold enough to participate in the improvement process.

To acculturate the peoples of former communist countries to real democracy and a market economy is a massive reeducation challenge that will take many decades. George Soros, investment broker, has made the case for this. Through his Soros Foundation, this billionaire funds practical projects in this region (and China) initiated by dissenters, journalists, educators, and entrepreneurs. He supports those seeking to bolster battered economies in their transition from socialism to free enterprise systems. In 1991, for example, at the start of an aborted Soviet coup, his foundation gave photocopiers to then-Russian President Boris Yeltsin, so fliers could be printed to rally Moscow citizens to support the embattled reformers. Since then, this Quantum Fund founder spends both time and money in development of modern management within Central and Eastern Europe, cultivating entrepreneurial job skills, as well as basic market and consumer literacy. This philanthropist also founded and endowed Central European University, a private graduate school located in Budapest, Hungary, and Warsaw, Poland. Hopefully, it will inspire other Western institutions and foundations to emulate such endeavors.

CONCLUSIONS

In the opening section of this chapter, we have presented both a historical and a contemporary analysis of Europe as it enters the new millennium. The overview includes the ongoing developments within the EU expansion to 27 members, as well as its accomplishments and ambitions. Some countries who have expressed interest in EU membership have been given no timetable for admittance, such as the mini-Balkan states. Others, like Iceland, are conflicted about potential admittance – they would like the *euro* for currency stability, but are uncertain about other membership obligations. Yet Iceland had been one of Europe's richest countries and fastest growing economies before its financial meltdown in 2008; it has since recovered significantly in both economic and political terms. Some key dimensions of European diversity and synergy have been examined here – from languages and demographics to immigration and identity. One new EU strategy for nonmembers is the *European Neighborhood Policy* – this offers countries of North Africa, the Mediterranean, the Caucasus, and Eastern Europe, graduated access to the single EU market. The aim is to provide financial and technical aid to these neighbors, in exchange for reforms that bring them closer to the Union's political and economic models.

To help global leaders become more effective on this important continent, this chapter then devoted its coverage to historical context, plus insights into diverse cultural and business practices in different geographies of Europe. Profiles were provided for most countries in these locations, while culture-specific information was shared about select countries. This sampling of the continent's complex cultural groupings and national entities may help readers avoid the trap of overgeneralized assumptions about Europeans. If more cooperative relationships are to be developed with their citizens and leaders, we recommend further data gathering, especially via the Internet. Information collection is the initial step in developing a personal file of business intelligence about countries and cultures if one wishes to perform well. Whether in Europe or elsewhere, such learning should be continually verified for validity in specific times and places, as well as with different individuals and organizations.

At this opening decade of the twenty-first century, profound economic, social, political, and cultural changes are under way throughout the whole of Europe. Peaceful trade, commerce, and travel there undergird that transformation process. But the EU is the key mechanism for furthering free enterprise and democracy, as well as the preservation of human rights while respecting diversity among all its inhabitants.

Well into the twenty-first century, Europeans are likely to be engaged in struggles to (1) gain continental identity; (2) cope with fertility issues of lower birth rates among the traditional inhabitants, and higher ones among the immigrants; (3) control the flow and acculturate these new arrivals from abroad, especially among the Muslim populations; (4) transform their agricultural and industrial cultures to a continental knowledge culture; and (5) operate more effectively within the realities of the global market. Currently 20 European nations collaborate in space investment and exploration through the European Space Agency.

MIND STRETCHING

1   Why is some understanding of European history so important to comprehending EU and related continental developments today?

2   What are the implications of changes in the balance of religious adherents within Europe (e.g., Christianity, Muslims, and Jews)?

3   How is the development of a single continental market strategy in Europe going to affect the global market?

4   Why are the nations in northern Europe concerned about the less economically developed countries in southern Europe?

5   What are some of the specific European countries whose cultures facilitate synergistic relations with their neighbors, and which ones are seemingly unsynergistic (e.g., more combative, less cooperative)?

6   What impact do geography and climate in various parts of Europe have on a people's culture and economy?

NOTES

1   Cultural profiles of France, Italy, and Russia are included in the book. Additional country profiles are on the Managing Cultural Differences website.

2   *Europe in Transition: Reshaping a Continent* (a map insert). Washington, DC: National Geographic, 2008; *Family Reference Atlas of the World*. Washington, DC: National Geographic Society, 2002, "Europe," pp. 126–141; Davis, W., Harrison, K., and Howell, C. H. *Book of Peoples of the World: A Guide to Cultures*. Washington, DC: National Geographic, 2008, "Europe," pp. 192–255; refer to website, www.nationalgeographic.com; Morrison, T., Conway, W. A., and Douress, J. J. *Dun & Bradstreet Guide to Doing Business Around the World*. Upper Saddle River, NJ: Prentice-Hall, 2009.

3   *Europe: The State of the Union*. New York: Atlantic Monthly Press, 2008; Pinder, J. and Usherwood, S. *The European Union: A Very Short Guide*. Oxford: Oxford University Press, 2007; *Guide to the European Union*. South Burlington, VT: Bloomberg Press/Economist Books, 2004, www.bloomberg.com/economistbooks; Beech, D. *The Dynamics of European Integration: Why and When EU Institutions Matter*. London: Palgrave Macmillan, 2005.

4   Ibid.

5 This quote can be found in the following articles: Rennie, D. "In the Nick of Time: A Special Report on EU Enlargement," *The Economist*, May 31, 2008, p. 16; Peet, J. "Fit at 50: A Special Report on the European Union," *The Economist*, March 17, 2007, p. 20, www.economst.com/specialreports; Rachman, G. "Outgrowing the Union: Survey of European Union," *The Economist*, September 24, 2004, www.economist.com/surveys.

6 Norman, P. *The Accidental Constitution: The Story of the European Convention*. London: Palgrave Macmillan, 2005; Leonard, M. *Why Europe Will Run the 21st Century*. London: Fourth Estate, 2006.

7 Kagan, R. *Of Paradise and Power: America versus Europe in the New World Order*. New York: Knopf Publishing, 2003; Simons, G. F. *Eurodiversity: A Business Guide to Managing Differences*. Burlington, MA: Elsevier/Butterworth-Heinemann, 2002.

8 Storti, C. *Old World/New World: Bridging Cultural Differences: Britain, France, Germany, and the U.S.* Boston, MA: Nicholas Brealey/Intercultural Press, 2003; Brittan, S. "Europe Is Not So Backward After All," *Financial Times*, July 30, 2004; Roger, P. *The American Enemy: The History of French Anti-Americanism*. Chicago, IL: University of Chicago Press, 2005; Chesnoff, R. Z. *The Arrogance of the French: Why They Can't Stand Us and Why the Feeling Is Mutual*. New York: Sentinel Press, 2005; Ver Berkmoes, R. *Western Europe (Multi Country Guide)*. New York: Amazon.com/books, 2007.

9 Klausen, J. *The Islamic Challenge: Politics and Religion in Western Europe*. Oxford: Oxford University Press, 2005; Burleigh, M. *Earthly Power: The Clash of Religion and Politics in Europe from the French Revolution to the Great War*. New York: HarperCollins, 2006; Baker, R. W. *Islam without Fear: Egypt and the New Islamists*. Boston, MA: Harvard University Press, 2003.

10 Guizot, P. G. *A Popular History of France from Earliest Times*, Vol. 1. London: BiblioBazaar, 2008; Porter, D. and Prince, D. *Frommer's France 2008*. Hoboken, NJ: Wiley Publishing Inc., 2007; Asselin, G. and Mastron, R. *Au Contraire! Figuring Out the French*. Boston, MA: Nicholas Brealey/Intercultural Press, 2001; "The Art of the Impossible: A Survey of France," *The Economist*, October 28, 2006, p. 16; "French Decline: Predators and Prophets," *The Economist*, February 4, 2006, p. 6.

11 For the insights which follow, the authors express appreciation to Gerd-Peter E. Lotao, who first wrote on "Doing Business in France" in the World Trade Notes of *Credit and Financial Management Magazine* (June 1987, p. 10).

12 A previous edition of our book, *Managing Cultural Differences,* was translated into French under the title, *Au-Dela Des Cultures,* in 1994 by InterEditions, Centre francaise d'exploitation du droit de copie, 3, Hautefeuille, 75006 Paris, France.

13 The authors are grateful to Maryellen Toffle, MIM, a graduate of the Thunderbird School of Global Management, who wrote this section on Italy. Her work resulted, in part, from interviews with Italian professionals, such as management consultant, Dr. Luigi Giannitrapani; managing director, Marina Zacco; and operations director, Dr. Annalisa Bardi. We have updated this material with special acknowledgment to "Audio, Dolce Vita: A Survey of Italy," *The Economist,* November 26, 2005, p. 16, www.economist.com/surveys.

14 Kitchen, M. *A History of Modern Germany 1800–2000*. Malden, MA: Blackwell Publishing, 2006; Porter, D. and Prince, D. *Frommer's Germany 2008*. Hoken, NJ: Wiley Publishing Inc, 2007; Bigham, G. *German Survival Guide*. Shell Rock, IA: World Prospect Press, 2008, www.worldprospectpress.com; "A Survey of Germany," *The Economist*, November 19, 1996; "Waiting for Wunder – A Survey of Germany," *The Economist*, February 11, 2006, www.economist.com/surveys; "An Uncertain Giant," *The Economist*, December 7, 2002, p. 20; Neiman, S. *Foreigners See It Differently*. Potsdam, Germany: Einstein Forum, 2005.

Resources for the Future: MCD9e readers concerned about the future of the world or a specific region or country will find useful these three sources of information:

1 The annual *State of the Future* report and CD (www.StateOfTheFuture.org). This is an outcome of The Millennium Project sponsored by the World Federation of UN Associations (emailemail: jglenn@igc.org).

2   The Foundation for the Future (www.futurefoundation.org). Request information about publications, proceedings, awards, and symposia (email: info@ futurefoundation.org).

3   The World Future Society (www.worldfuturesociety.org). Request membership for access to their annual forecasts, publications, online exchanges, and conferences (email: jcornish@wfs.org).

Resources on Europe: Periodically, *The Economist* magazine publishes special country surveys which are also available in reprints. For latest surveys on any country, see www. economist.com/surveys.

ADDITIONAL FEATURES

Please visit the companion website at: www.routledge.com/cw/Moran where you will find additional case studies, study aides, and instructor resources.

15 DOING BUSINESS WITH AFRICANS

Northern Africa, East Africa, West Central Africa, and Southern Africa

One of Africa's nicknames is "the continent of beginnings." Fossil and records there of the earliest humans go back more than 4 million years. What can be considered our early upright ancestor, *Homo erectus*, departed Africa on the long journey that eventually peopled the Earth. It now seems likely that every person in today's world comes from a lineage that derives from the ancient Africans. Innumerable cave paintings and petroglyphs, from the Sahara to South Africa, provide clues to the beliefs and ways of life of these age-old hominids.[1]

We need to appreciate Africa as the cradle of human civilization, not just as a continent of economically developing countries. After an overview of African history, this chapter will examine the nations and peoples on this diverse continent and will provide specifics regarding their respective cultures, so as to not only facilitate communications and business with Africans, but also to better understand Africans and some of the challenges they face.

INSIGHTS INTO AFRICA

Two-hundred million years ago, this landmass split off from the ancient supercontinent of Pangea. Africa is the cradle of all humanity, for we all trace our DNA heritage to this area. *Homo sapiens* first appeared in Africa in an anatomically mature state some 200,000 years ago, probably in what is today known as Omo Kibish in Ethiopia. Genetic data indicate that there were two human migrations out of this continent. The first group went no further than what is now Israel, dying out some 90,000 years ago. Descendants of modern humans left Africa some 70,000–50,000 years ago. By 50,000 years ago, following a coastal route along southern Asia, they reached what is now Australia and became a people known today as Aborigines. Some 40,000–30,000 years ago, human inland migration, apparently via Asia, populated the continent known as Europe. During roughly the same period, these humans migrated into Central Asia, arriving on the grassy steppes north of the Himalayas. They also traveled through Southeast Asia and China, eventually reaching Japan and Siberia. Genetic clues lead us to believe that humans in northern Asia eventually migrated to the Americas. Between 20,000 and 15,000 years ago, sea levels were low, and so were lands that connected Siberia to Alaska; the new arrivals trekked southward down the west coast of what is now America. The DNA marker M168 among today's non-Africans is one indicator used to prove that we all trace our origins to the *mother of the human family –* Africa! Our diverse faces and races ultimately trace their origins through genes back to the first hunter-gatherers.

Africa has largely remained a mystery to the outside world, marked perhaps more by its isolation than by any other feature. This stubborn reality can be traced to the earliest times, and is reflected in the hopelessly misrepresented images of ancient cartographers, whose graphic distortions were as errant as the half myths and false science that passed for knowledge about the "dark continent." Yet, ancient civilizations flourished in Africa from Carthage in the north to "empires" in the south. Among these was the Kingdom of Zimbabwe, which flourished in the thirteenth to fifteenth centuries; and, in the Niger area, the grand states of the Yoruba, the Ashanti, and the Hausa people prospered. From 900 AD onward, the eastern coastal plains were the homeland of the Swahili culture and language that flourished in the area stretching from Somalia to Zanzibar, including a mix of local peoples,

Arabs, and immigrants. From the fifteenth to nineteenth centuries, the search for riches and a route to India brought European explorers and occupiers, beginning with the Portuguese, with the British, French, Belgians, and Germans following their lead. Unfortunately, few Europeans appreciated the civilizations and cultures already functioning there, imposing their own ways on the indigenous inhabitants. Although Africans dispersed by natural migration, they were also forcefully introduced into the Americas, Europe, Latin America, and the Middle East as a result of the inhumane slave trade. The last half of the twentieth century has been Africa's postcolonial period of independence. As the people of the world scramble to utilize African resources, may a mature continental civilization finally come into its own in this twenty-first century!

Historical perspective on modern Africa[2]

At the time of publication 54 countries are located on the continent, from Algeria in the Islamic north to South Africa. National identities are diverse for peoples assembled within borders imposed by departed European imperialists. The outsiders' partitioning of Africa in the past two centuries made little attempt to make national borders coincide with on-site ethnic groups and tribes; boundaries on this continent are continuously being reconfigured as new states emerge. In 1993, Eritrea officially achieved independence from its neighbor, Ethiopia. National names also change frequently: for instance, Rhodesia became Zimbabwe, and Tanganyika became Tanzania. Africa is home to roughly one-third of the world's sovereign states, but only 19 of them here have democratic governments, depending on how the word "democracy" is defined. At least four are routinely classified as failed states – the Congo, Somalia, the Sudan, and Zimbabwe. The World Bank and the IMF currently classifies 39 countries worldwide as heavily indebted poor countries (HIPC) – 33 of these are in Sub-Saharan Africa. Most of these countries came into existence in the twentieth century, and currently about half of the governments were formed as the result of coups, principally by the military. In too many African states, the rule of law has been displaced by the rule of the autocrat who seizes power and control. The redrawing of former colonial boundaries need not mean smaller African states; it could simply mean more rational and viable political communities. The long-term scenario emerging from continuing crises may be the gradual change of boundaries between the DRC (Democratic Republic of the Congo), Rwanda, and Burundi. Unless the Hutu and Tutsi are partitioned into separate countries or federated into a larger, stable, and democratic political community, they are likely to engage in endless conflict. One solution for the problems in the region calls for the international community to put together a large package of incentives to persuade Rwanda, Burundi, and Tanzania to create the United States of Central Africa; that way, parts of the DRC could one day seek admission into the new federation. Currently, the African Union acts as a coordinating medium for the continental countries, which strives to encourage regional cooperation, trading, and political stability. Sovereign states with bureaucratic controls are the hallmark of Western European civilization. But such historical experience was largely absent in sub-Saharan kingdoms before the arrival of European colonialism during the past three centuries.

Although Africans had learned to smelt iron by the year 1500 AD, the industrial stage of development was not experienced by most Africans. They were mainly hunter-gatherers, farmers, and herders; only a small minority lived in urban areas. After a few hundred years of predatory slave-raiding and direct European influence or rule, all African countries have regained their independence from European control since the mid- to late twentieth century. Thus, a dynamic process is under way throughout Africa to develop modern mass societies with the accompanying political, economic, and technological systems. One needs an *Afrocentric* approach to appreciate fully this heritage and experience. Africans in diaspora may be found on every continent, but there are large populations of them in both North and Latin America, as well as in Europe. Barack Obama, it's worth noting, became the President of the United States of America in 2009; his father was a Kenyan from the *luo*-speaking Nyanza Province in Kenya.

Africa is a land of great promise and potential, a continent of immense natural beauty and resources, most of which is still undeveloped. It is a region of contrasts between the primitive and the ultramodern, a place where new industries, technologies, and cities emerge gradually. Yet, in this postcolonial period, it is the misfortune of Africa, which birthed civilization, to remain mired in human suffering and carnage in this twenty-first century. Although this collective of countries is somewhat disconnected from the world by its unmatched sorrows, its rich mixture of people has a distinctly African sense of brotherhood and humor.

For global leaders to be effective in their trade and development efforts within Africa, they must be realistic in their analysis of its peoples and possibilities. First, there is great diversity of tribes, languages, customs, religions, education, and governments. Second, most of the people here are generous, eager to learn, and hardworking. Their natural buoyancy and flexibility have been dampened by widespread famine, epidemics, exploitation, and social unrest. The world media often distorts the external image of Africa by its emphasis on African tragedies – the horror of the mass poverty, the AIDS epidemic, the extensive droughts, the many civil wars, and the millions of refugees. Often overlooked in these reports are the success stories – World Bank and UNESCO projects that work at the local levels, the green revolution that expands agricultural production, the many business enterprises that flourish, the African foreign students who return to apply their Western education, and the shift from failed socialism to democratic and market-oriented policies.

Africa entered this new millennium in a state of intense transition. The changes under way can also be summed up in three words: *tribalism, chaos*, and *development*. To illustrate our choice of this terminology, consider the following observations:

Tribalism

The tribe is the basic sociological unit of Africa that provides one's sense of identity, belonging, and responsibility. When tribal members leave rural areas to go to the city for a job or to study, traditionally their enhanced stature brings with it responsibility for assisting their tribal brothers and sisters at home. Such social pressure on successful Africans may impose a burden to augment income by any means, legal or otherwise. Tribal bonds also lead to intergroup conflict, destruction, and corruption. As the force of tribalism deteriorates in modern, urban environments, Africans search for other substitutes, new institutional loyalties such as membership in a religion, cooperatives, and political parties, often formed along ethnic lines.

For many, tribalism is the bane of independent Africa with its many tribes and clans involving more than 2,000 living languages. Left over from the colonialists are areas where French, English, Portuguese, and a dialect of Dutch are widely spoken. National leaders seek to transform intertribal hostility into collaborative community endeavors. Tribalism is evident in elections when the voting favors the largest tribes, while the winners are only slowly learning that power should be shared with the minority losers. It is also behind failed attempts at ethnic cleansing, authoritarian regimes, and political corruption. The challenge for many Africans is to build upon tribal heritage, while moving beyond narrow tribal loyalties and constraints for the greater common good of the nation and its economic development.

This issue is closely connected to ethnicity. Perhaps this definition will make our point: *An ethnic group is a distinct population whose members identify with each other based on a common ancestry. Such groups are distinguished by common cultural, linguistic, or religious traits.* Ethnicity is different from the concept of *race*, which divides people on the basis of physical or biological traits, such as skin color, which in Africa protects the inhabitants from a strong sun. The point for cosmopolitans to remember is that many African "leaders" exploit tribal and ethnic ties over national interests. Both are used by the "big boys" as a means of staying in power!

Chaos

As Africans seek to move beyond their colonial dependency, while rapidly creating appropriate cultural institutions and opportunities, tumult abounds. The destabilization process is compounded by a combination of factors. Sometimes, it is caused by nature, when lack of rain triggers mass famine, or a monkey virus infects entire East African populations through the plague of acquired immunodeficiency syndrome, caused by the HIV virus that continues to kill many thousands each day. Because of poor or inadequate water systems, other infectious diseases devastate African communities, such as malaria. In June 2003, a group of African presidents appealed for greater help from the rich G8 nations meeting in Evian, France. Foreign governments have spent billions to fight disease in Africa, mainly through the Global Fund, an organization supporting 150 programs to fight AIDS, tuberculosis, and malaria. But other nations have to match that commitment, which the G8 leaders promised to do. But in some African states, such as in South Africa, the governments have been unable to use the external resources effectively. Other countries on the continent lack a well-organized and functioning healthcare system. Many immature political entities do not use donor funds effectively because of a lack of medical personnel and inadequate road and communications infrastructure. Sometimes, the disarray and the obstacles to African development come from the following:[3]

- The rise of extremist Muslim militants and terrorists as in North Africa, Sudan, Somalia, and more recently elsewhere, as in Kenya.

- Tribal conflicts that escalated into civil wars, as in Rwanda when the Hutu army oversaw the murder of a million Tutsi; in Somalia where tribal warfare led to the collapse of the government and anarchy; and in the Congo and Sudan where genocide prevailed and millions died. Distorted ambitions and ideologies of local dictators and guerrillas to crush their opposition in other tribes have led to new tyrannies, such as that which occurred in Uganda, Nigeria, Liberia, Angola, and elsewhere.

- African infighting and the resultant destruction are sometimes attributed to religion, such as when brown-skinned, Muslim Arabs from the north of Somalia raid and destroy dark-skinned, Christians in the south of a country with hopeless governance.

- Incompetent strongmen who take political power through coups or rigged elections, and use their positions as head of state to benefit only themselves and their cronies. This lack of authentic leaders has contributed to undermining of national economies and exploitation of the citizenry. Hence, the rule of the "big man" replaces the rule of law, while the average person suffers. The deterioration of Rhodesia when it became Zimbabwe under its dictator, Robert Mugabe; the DRC when ruled by Mobutu Sese Seko; or Uganda under its despot, Idi Amin, are cases in point.

- Failure of the current states in terms of borders, governance, and infrastructure. Before the nineteenth century, Africa had been divided into thousands of kingdoms and chiefdoms whose systems of government developed over hundreds of years. For administrative purposes, European colonialists created a few dozen nation-states whose borders often divided tribal lands. On all this was grafted European governance models, such as parliamentary democracy, that were alien to Africans, lacking in educated leadership, to make it all work. The new regimes proved unstable and dysfunctional, with elected governments giving way to authoritarianism, military take-overs, and assignations. The result has undermined any democratic free-enterprise system from growing, while incumbents became rich and powerful with their private militias and suppressed media, unless they were killed, jailed, or driven into exile.[4]

Often, such internal troubles are exacerbated by outside intervention, as when in past centuries, Europeans imposed their controls on the locals, so that today the influence of European cultures and dependency still may be found in former African colonies of Britain, France, Germany, and Portugal. In the twentieth century, Western powers twice involved Africans in their world wars, as well as in the cold war between the United States and the former U.S.S.R. Africans have been involved again, when the United Nations sends relief efforts, but with inadequate peacekeeping troops to such places as the Sudan, Liberia, Rwanda, and Somalia.

The combination of such problems worsens because of overpopulation, the need for food because of disruption in farming and fishing, systemic corruption, and widespread unemployment. Mass poverty engenders desperation, which may feed political extremity. All of the above factors contribute to the displacement of millions of Africans from their homelands. Many end up as refugees amid poverty on a gigantic scale. One effect of this chaos is the threat it poses to the ecological environment of the continent. Deserts are widening, broad savannas and their communities struggle to survive. Sometimes the confusion is simply *future shock* as tribal cultures and rural peoples try to cope with the demands of an urban, postindustrial way of life. Finally, too many postcolonial nation-states and their political leaders in Africa are failing to liberate, protect, and service their own citizens, as well as their country's resources.

But the situation is not all bad – Africans are survivors with remarkable resilience and "make do" capacities. Entrepreneurs abound, humanitarian efforts progress, and some countries are justly and successfully ruled by elected leaders. Peacekeepers and peace enforcers in many cases produce positive results, as in Cote d'Ivoire; the African Union is training regional brigades.

Development

Africa has been classified as the Third World in economic terms – it contributes only 1 percent of the global economic output. This poor continent is often viewed as a land of tragedy or promise because of its rich natural and human resources that have not been fully developed. The nations here are being crippled by debt to foreign interests. The cause of the current woes goes with past European colonialism and inadequate education of the African people. Because of this historical influence, when the majority of Africa gained independence after the 1960s, many of its "leaders" were ill-prepared to lead their countries. They turned toward state socialism, favoring government intervention in the economy with bureaucratic controls that stifled initiative, killed incentive, and created chronic, artificial shortages. The situation represents a rejection of the continent's heritage of consensual and participatory democracy, which should embrace *free* markets, trade, and enterprise. The full potential of Africa may be realized in this century if Africans are empowered to build an infrastructure on the basis of their own uniqueness and cultures. Development increases opportunity for people. But to actualize these prospects, Africans will have to learn how to: (1) practice synergy among themselves; (2) control their populations; (3) advance their literacy, education, and productivity; (4) build infrastructure, especially roads and transportation; (5) promote conservation and ecotourism; and (6) connect with the information age and its technologies. Consider just one reality to be rectified – less than 10 percent of the continent's land is formally owned, and only 1 in

10 Africans lives in a house with formal deeds or titles. But Africa's biggest need is for effective, indigenous leadership at all levels of their society, yet no institution is effectively addressing this need.

There have been promising developments toward progress in Africa, as the next four reports indicate:

■ *Continental synergy.* In the 1980s, 16 countries joined together to form the Economic Community of West African States while in the 1990s, nine more countries launched the Southern African Coordination Conference. In a sense, the current African Union (AU) is a case study illustrating in its short history the challenge and the promise of the future, as it evolved from prior attempts at unified action. First, there was the Organization of African States founded in 1963, then later the Organization of African Unity. Such institutions have been both a disappointment and modest success – too often their officials used their positions there for demagoguery, posturing, and travel junkets. Yet these unifying efforts also have achieved, through their economic and technical projects, the improvement of the continent's communication and banking systems and the maintenance of interstate peace. The hope is that the renewed African Union, with UN assistance, will become the forum and mechanism for continental recovery and renewal. Today, booming economies in Uganda, Mauritania, Ghana, and Mozambique demonstrate that African countries can thrive, given some measure of peace, stability, and governance. In the year 2000, total foreign investments in Africa were about $6 billion, only 3 percent of the $235 billion that flowed into Third World economies. By 2006, that investment by outsiders had gone up considerably, thanks to establishment of the Millennium Fund. For this decade, the 48th sub-Saharan countries have been growing at a rate of 5 percent or more.

■ *Rebuilding failed states.* The World Bank frets about 30 "low income countries under stress," while the U.K.'s Department of International Development worries about 46 "fragile states." Many of these today are in Africa, such as Angola, Central African Republic, both Congos, Nigeria, Somalia, Sudan, and Zimbabwe. For example, a third of the African countries are trapped in civil wars or cycles of unrest. But some are recovering – after a civil war, Liberia came back from misrule, violence, and famine a few years ago. While its former gangsterish president, Charles Taylor, along with other African warlords, is being tried by the International Criminal Court in The Hague, the Liberian electorate chose its first female head of state. A large UN peacekeeping force keeps the nation calm and safe while reconstruction goes forward with external humanitarian aid. Another failed state, Sierra Leone, again with UN help, is holding accountable those war criminals who despoiled it. Ultimately, restoring peace and a measure of prosperity is the responsibility of local citizens.[5] Following are some hopeful signs: two-thirds of African countries now limit presidential terms; multiparty political systems are growing; media coverage is improving, thanks to television and the Internet; the mobile phone revolution has helped many people, especially poor peasants and traders; banking systems are modernizing and attracting more international investment; mortgages are more available to a growing middle class; farmers are being helped by the issuance of individual land titles; creation of mechanisms like the Extractive Industries Transparency Initiative, a code for opening up agreements of governments and foreign investors; establishment of savings or sovereign funds in commodity-flush countries.

■ *Private sector initiatives.* If foreign aid, debt forgiveness, and trade reform are to help this continent, then a 2005 World Bank Annual, *Doing Business in Africa*, suggests the private sector must provide leadership. Public sector bureaucracy, ineptness, regulatory obstacles, and red tape contribute to undermining the business climate there. Investors, whether corporate or foundations, realize that if entrepreneurs are to flourish, programs must be undertaken to improve infrastructure, train skilled workers, provide capital support, and curb disease. Yet this report points to 14 sub-Saharan countries where healthy economic growth is under way, because their GNP has increased at least 5 percent a year since 1990. Botswana and South Africa are at the top when it comes to the "best business environment." So, a group of multinational companies have formed "Business Action of Africa" to improve business conditions on that continent. In addition, 24 countries outside the region have signed up to a "New Partnership for Africa's Development," aimed at bringing together both the African public and private sectors to improve investment conditions on the continent. Yet, the UN Economic Commission on Africa calculates that already the foreign direct investment in Africa has on average a four times better return than in G7 countries, and twice as much as in Asia![6]

■ *African optimism.* They may not be the richest, but Africans remain the world's staunchest optimists. An annual world survey by Gallup International found that 60 percent of the African respondents think that the present year will be better than the last – twice as many as reported in Europe. Despite two million Africans killed by AIDS in 2005, these people are upbeat and hopeful. One speculation for this is that 9 out of 10 Africans are religious, and know how to transform suffering into recovery.

For foreigners to be more effective in their business and professional relationships with Africans, it is helpful to have some insights into the diverse cultures of this continent. In the previous chapter, we described the Islamic culture, which also dominates North Africa and the Muslim states elsewhere in this area. Within black Africa, there are some common cultural characteristics. The next section will review five dimensions of those African cultures – family, trust/friendship, time, corruption, and respect for elders. This selected analysis may increase awareness and improve interaction not only with Africans, but with the millions of descendants from this heritage who are found throughout North, Central, and South America, as well as in the Caribbean, the United Kingdom, and the Middle

East. Be cautious with African generalizations, because African cultures are not only diverse, but dynamic, changing to ensure survival, as well as to adapt to new times and circumstances.

Exhibits 15.1 and 15.2 illustrate how quickly the situation can change in Africa, especially when private enterprise is allowed to work.

EXHIBIT 15.1 IMPACT OF TELECOMMUNICATIONS IN AFRICA

First radio, then television, and now mobile telephones are transforming African communications and business. The wireless age is overcoming the obstacles on this huge continent caused by poor roads, unreliable energy, political instability, and corruption that prevented the wiring of landline telephones. The new technologies bypass all this, giving regions and people access to phones they never had before. But Africans use this new communication tool for more than mere talking — shepherds in drought-ridden Sahel are using handheld GPS units and cell phones to alert others to good grazing; in Nairobi, customers avoid long lines at their bank by monitoring their accounts by text messaging; in Ethiopia, teachers are being trained to use solar-powered satellite radios to receive lessons broadcast to their classes; in South Africa, wives at home use mobile phones to talk in the evening with their husbands who work hundreds of miles away; healthcare workers use their phones to summon ambulances; fisherwomen who can't read tell their customers to call their cell numbers to order fish; and retailers in the slums can take delivery orders from affluent suburbanites. On a continent where some remote villages communicate by beating drums, cell phones are a technological revolution. Cell operators can't put up phone towers fast enough. This phenomenon is causing a sociological and economic godsend for Africans at large. Today, Africa is the world's fastest growing cell phone market — in 2012, in fact, there were 648.4 million cell phone subscriptions on the continent. Others simply buy cell phone time to make each call — buying wireless phone time is like using the grocery list. Used handsets are sold for $50 or less. All this from a people who typically live on $2 or less a day! Domestic cell companies, like MTB and Conteh, are not only building telecommunications networks, but providing much-needed jobs and national income. International firms, like Vodacom, have 1.1 million subscribers in the Congo, adding a thousand new customers daily, and logging 10,000 calls a day. Bicycle-driven battery chargers are being used in rural areas to provide sufficient electricity to charge the phones. It's all been a boon, not only to business throughout Africa, but also to families who want to connect with one another.

Source: "Making the Connection in Africa — Whatever You Thought, Think Again," *National Geographic*, September 2005. "Africa Calling," *The Economist*, May 26, 2007, p. 74.

E
X
H
I
B
I
T

15.2

EXHIBIT 15.2 CHINA'S AFRICAN PARTNERSHIP

China takes a long view of its relationship to the continent of Africa and its people. It began in 1414 when Emperor Ming sent Admiral Zing He to East Africa. He took his vast fleet of 62 galleons for 7 voyages there to engage in trade and establish diplomatic relations. After 1431, the Chinese did not return until the 1960s when Chairman Mao Zedong supported liberation movements and newly independent states. This time, the Chinese built roads, bridges, stadiums, water systems, and even the Tanzum railroad from Tanzania to Zambia — all with thousands of Chinese laborers! They also established farms and factories, provided materials and loans — all with a view to obtaining political support from Africa's 54 nations for China in the United Nations, World Trade Organization, and elsewhere. They also sent doctors, nurses, and medical aid. It is no wonder that, in 2000, governments in both China and Africa formed the China–Africa Conference (POCAC). By the China–Africa Summit in 2003, China was writing off billions in Africa debts. Their managers in Africa live at the level of their workers, buying local products and selling their own wares made in China. Even traditional African fabrics are now made in Guangdong for export to Africa and elsewhere.

The center for Chinese Studies at Stellenbosch, South Africa, monitors considerable Chinese activities on the continent. China treats Africa as an equal, so their leaders appreciate that China presents itself as a neutral, nonimperialist, value-free outsider simply wanting a friendly trade relationship. Chinese there emphasize the best in Africa, avoiding references to its failures. Further, the Chinese keep their promises, building infrastructure on time and often under budget. But the Chinese employ their own, providing little training or limited jobs for the locals. In their African projects, the Chinese do not show much regard for environmental damage, human rights, combating poverty, nor the Charter of the African Union. The African governments have yet to successfully manage their business relationships with China, which views them as business opportunities. But it is the new professional middle class in Pan Africa that is taking control of the continent's development and transformation.

Source: Adapted from Richard Dowden's *Africa: Altered States and Ordinary Miracles*, London, UK: Portobello Publishing, 2008, Chapter 17.

Humanitarian role in Africa[7]

According to the latest estimates, there are some 2.3 million refugees spread across Africa, along with 12.7 million internally displaced persons who did not flee across borders. Those figures alone justify that humanity elsewhere seeks to help such unfortunate people whose lives have been disrupted by wars and ethnic cleansing. All of Africa benefits from the exceptional service of international humanitarian organizations, some of which are UN/ UNESCO or government-sponsored, while others are under private auspices, foundations, or nongovernmental organizations (NGOs). Exhibit 15.4 provides some insights into the dedication of such volunteers. The first item concerns the tiny country of Benin, the most underdeveloped nation in the world. In West Africa, it is situated between Togo and Nigeria. Although French is the official medium of communication, there are 54 local languages used by the average person, who is largely uneducated. Radio is the means for creating public awareness in this new capitalistic society, especially concerning issues such as malnutrition, healthcare, and education.

CULTURAL CHARACTERISTICS OF AFRICA[8]

We must always be cautious about cultural generalizations, and in Africa there is no one culture. The northern African states of Mauritania, Morocco, Algeria, Libya, and part of Sudan are closer to the Middle Eastern cultures. The descriptions that follow best apply to sub-Sahara, home of black Africans, like the peoples of Mali, Senegal, Ghana, Congo, Benin, Tanzania, and South Africa. Yet, even their music and musical instruments reflect the diversity of their culture. The African diaspora also brought to the West the popular music that is known today as blues, jazz, R&B, rumba, reggae, and even hip-hop![9]

Family and kinship

The basic unit of African society is the family, which includes the nuclear family and the extended family, or tribe. In traditional African society, the tribe is the ultimate community; no unit has more importance. There may be some loose confederations, but they are temporary and limited in scope. In political terms, the tribe is the equivalent of a nation. It does not have fixed boundaries, but on its sanction rests the law (customary law like the English Common Law). All wars were fought on the tribe's behalf, and the division between "them" and "us" lay in tribal boundaries.

Africans center their communities around villages for food gathering and cultivation. The village elders become judges, mediators, trade masters, and leaders within both religious and tribal life. In some ways, the tribe is more than a nation. In Europe and America, ethical and moral standards are not given by national sanctions, but rest on religious and cultural traditions common to the whole continent. But in traditional Africa, except for areas under Islamic control, the family tribe provides the guidelines for accepted behavior. The tribe bears a moral connotation and provides an emotional security. It is also a source of social and moral sanctions, as well as political and physical security. The tribe provides its members with rules governing responsibilities, explanations of the responsibilities, and guidelines for organizing the society, and, hence, the culture.

The tribe is broken down into different kinship lines. The concept of kinship is important to understanding African societies. It constitutes the primary basis for an individual's rights, duties, rules of residence, marriage, inheritance, and succession. Kinship refers to blood relationships between individuals, and is used to describe relationships in both a narrow and a broad sense. Parents and their children are a special kind of kin group. The social significance of kinship covers a wide social field in most African societies. In Western culture, its significance usually does not extend beyond the nuclear family, but in the African culture, it embraces a network of people, including those that left the village for urban areas.

The family – father, mother, children – is the ultimate basis of the tribe. But the tribal and family unit organization is being disrupted by changes in the economic organizational structure. The economic organization has tied reward to individual effort, and developed road, rail, water, and air communication networks that have increased the range and speed of contact – thereby increasing the rate of intercultural contact and change. The reorganization has also brought tribes together as territorial units, with greater opportunities for migration from one area to another, but with a corresponding weakening of family bonds and behavior control.

As this newfound mobility moves more people to the large urban areas, they try to maintain some family ties. This involves a responsibility to support family members still in the villages. It also affects Africans' business relationships with managers from abroad in terms of hiring practices and the need for extra income to support those at home. Earnings from business transactions are often used for this purpose.

Trust and friendship

Trust and confidence are essential elements needed for successful enterprise in Africa. It is very important to get to know coworkers as individuals before getting down to actual business activities. With Africans, after family, friendship comes next in importance. Often, a friendship continues after specific business activities end. Socializing outside of the office is common. It is under those relaxed conditions that managers talk politics, sports, and sometimes business.

In Africa, interpersonal relationships are based on sincerity. African societies are normally warm and friendly. People generally assume that everyone is a friend until proven otherwise. When Africans smile, it means they like you. When smiles are not seen, it is a clear sign of distrust. Once a person is accepted as a friend, that person is automatically an "adopted" member of the family. A friend can pop into a friend's place anytime. In African societies, formal invitations and appointment making are not common.

One of the most important factors to remember when doing business in Africa is the concept of friendship before business. Normally, before a meeting begins, there is general talk about events that have little or nothing to do with the business at hand. This can go on for some time. If the meeting involves people coming together who have never met, but who are trying to strike a deal (an African and a foreigner), the African will try to reach out for friendship first. If, in doing so, the African receives a cold response, he may become suspicious and lose interest in the deal.

In the traditional village culture, Africans share good fortune and food with other members of the community. This is an example of the wonderful values that modernization may unfortunately change. Society's predators – in the form of rebels and terrorists, greedy politicians, and abusive militias – undermine this cultural quality.

Time and time consciousness

The way an individual views the concept of time has a major impact on any business relationship. If two businesspeople enter into a situation with complementary goals, abilities, and needs, a successful arrangement can be thwarted if each has different ideas about time. In Africa, time is viewed as flexible, not rigid or segmented. People come first, then time. Anyone in a hurry is viewed with suspicion and distrust. Because trust is very important, individuals who follow inflexible time schedules will have little success. The African wants to sit and talk – to get to know the person before discussing business. Normally, time is not seen as a limited commodity. What cannot be done today can always be accomplished tomorrow. Meetings are not held promptly, and people may arrive several hours late. Often, foreigners misinterpret this as laziness, untrustworthiness, lack of seriousness in doing business, or even lack of interest in the venture. However, lateness in meetings should be perceived as part of African life. It is understood among friends that even though everybody agrees to meet at a given time, they will not actually gather until much later.

However, when Africans are dealing with foreigners, they normally try to be on time out of respect for the non-Africans' concept of time. But in the larger cities of Africa, the concept of time is changing. Punctuality is becoming more important. Contact with Western businesspersons has brought an increasing awareness and acceptance of the segmentation of time and its consequent inflexibility. But away from the capital city, time is still viewed in a relaxed and easygoing manner.

Corruption

Corruption in Africa sometimes is related to its poverty, and often results from tribal responsibilities that individuals carry with them when leaving the village for a job or schooling in the city. The enhanced stature of city life brings a responsibility of assisting one's tribal family. This obligation often imposes a financial burden on the successful member far in excess of income. The worker is unlikely to resist the pressures of society, and is thus forced to augment income, often by means regarded by foreigners as bribery or corruption. However, to the African, it is not. As long as great disparities in income and standards of living continue, the bribe system is likely to continue, as it has in many developing economies. In Africa, extra income is swiftly distributed through the extended family system to remote relations living in remote places. The tradition of sharing continues even as individuals move away from their tribal origins.

Corruption may arise because of inadequate compensation for work, causing laborers to seek additional income. Many African state governments have been corrupted by greedy political and military rulers who use public monies and offices to enrich themselves and their families at the expense of citizens and foreign business persons. Exhibit 15.3 on Jones & Smith Food Company gives readers some appreciation for the payment of gratuities.

E
X
H
I
B
I
T

15.3

EXHIBIT 15.3 JONES & SMITH FOOD COMPANY

The Jones & Smith Food Company is located in the capital of a large African country. However, they want to expand their headquarters to another state capital. To do this, they need approval from both the federal and the state government. The company sent a written application a few months ago, but did not get any response.

The manager of the project went several times to the Federal Ministry of Trade and Economic Development, but was always told to come back the next day. Mr. Jones became frustrated and mad at the clerks and officials involved. However, in the process of the argument, one of them said, "This is not America. It's Africa. If you want anything done on time, you've got to give a bribe. Kind of like a gratuity tendered before, rather than after, a service is performed."

Mr. Jones, who is not accustomed to such practices, angrily stormed out of the office. In the car, he narrated the incident to the driver, who advised him to give the "gratuity" or have the proposal denied.

In an emergency meeting, the company's board of directors decided to offer the gratuity. To the company's surprise, the proposal was approved the next day.

But back in Mr. Jones' home culture, a board of directors may frown upon such payments, and home country laws may consider such bribes illegal.

Respect for elders

Age is another important factor to consider in Africa. It is believed that the older one gets, the wiser one becomes – life has seasoned the individual with varied experience. Hence, in Africa, age is an asset. The older the person, the more respect the person receives within the traditional community, especially from the young. Thus, if a foreigner is considerably younger than the African, the latter will have little confidence in the outsider. However, if sincerity, respect, and empathy are shown, the person will receive a positive response. Respect for elders tends to be the key for harmony in African cultures and village life.

Young Africans normally do not oppose the opinion of their elders. They may not agree, but they must respect the opinion. In some cases, especially in rural areas, young people are not expected to offer opinions in meetings. The informal and formal interpersonal relationships in Africa are on the basis of cultural norms of various African societies. As Africa modernizes – nearly 40 of its cities have over a million inhabitants – some of the old ways, such as respect and care for seniors, may unfortunately diminish, as is happening with other traditional cultures in transition. African cultural characteristics vary in an urban area, in contrast to classical village life.

CULTURAL SPECIFICS BY GEOGRAPHIC REGIONS[10]

It is impossible here to cover all the cultural aspects of doing business or humanitarian work in all 50 African states. Instead, four major geographic areas of Africa will be profiled. In each region, we have selected one country for in-depth analysis for one or more of these reasons: (1) representative of a grouping; (2) economic implications for all of Africa; and (3) insights into what is happening in their societies. We will also consider a particular cultural dimension of Africa — business customs, protocols, and prospects.

NORTHERN AFRICA[11]

This region contains seven countries: Algeria, Egypt, Libya, Morocco, the Sudan, Tunisia, and Western Sahara. Many classify themselves as republics. Libya, moreover, is a provisional parliamentary republic, and was once a subsumed sphere of Italian influence. Morocco is the only kingdom. Except for the coastal countries, the area can be characterized as one of high temperatures, vast deserts, Muslim religious practice, and French colonial cultural influence. The economies are developing, centered on textiles, food processing, agriculture, and mining; several are better off for producing or processing crude oil and petroleum.

The history of North Africa has been impacted significantly by the Middle East, especially by the culture of the Arabs and the Muslim religion. The latter defines the region's ethnicity and languages, particularly among the Semitic-speaking Arabs. From Morocco to East Africa, Arabic is the unifying common cultural influence. Up to 10,000 years ago, we already learned, Egypt gave rise to agriculture and a civilization based upon it. The area has also been known in the past for its nomadic herding, with life centered around the oases, still evident in today's Libya. The sea and the camel became the means for development of North African trading routes. Since ancient times, the making and distribution of bread is a common factor which the Arabs call *aish*, or life. Other regional foods include rice, yogurt, and meat kebabs, along with Mediterranean dishes that feature eggplant, beans, olives, pickles, and pastries. Extended families with arranged marriages are traditional, but are changing with urbanization and modernization, especially with regard to the role of women in society. Oral verse, poetry, and literature are common here as ways of expressing feelings. Pan-Arab movements have occurred in both the past and present, but generally have not succeeded because Arab leaders prefer decentralized power, avoiding domination by others. Abdul Nasser's attempt in 1958 to found a United Arab Republic lasted about four years. The region resists national unity and federalism, as evident in Algeria, Libya, Yemen, and other parts of Africa, such as the Sudan and Somalia.

EAST AFRICA[12]

This eastern region encompasses a dozen states, just south of Libya and Egypt, and bordering on the Red Sea, Gulf of Aden, and the Indian Ocean. The states include Burundi, Central African Republic, Congo, Djibouti, Eritrea, Ethiopia, Kenya, Rwanda, Somalia, Sudan, Tanzania, and Uganda. The area starts in the north with the Sahara Desert of Sudan and ends in the south with the Congo and Tanzania. Except for Eritrea and Somalia, the other ten countries style themselves as "republics," despite the presence of dictators or military coup commanders. Although Ethiopia was an ancient empire, most East African states were created as national entities by Britain, France, Germany, and Italy during the nineteenth century. Their borders and names have frequently changed as a result of civil wars and other conflicts. Some geographers place Sudan as part of North Africa, but we prefer to consider it within East Africa, sometimes called the Horn of Africa.

East Africa is a landmass of great natural diversity and beauty, with its deserts and mountains, rivers, and lakes, as well as a long, stunning coastline. It has temperatures and precipitation – from 73 to 89°F in the north, and from 64 to 69°F in the south. Except for deserts and barren lands in five northeastern countries, the predominant land use is grassland, woodland, and forest, with some cropland and wetlands. Agriculture is the primary regional industry, along with mining of copper, gold, fluorite, and diamonds. Two manufacturing centers are in Khartoum, Sudan, and Kinshasa, Congo; as well as one processing plant near Lubumbashi, Congo. Resplendent with spectacular landscape, Tanzania has one of the largest populations in the area. The region boasts the natural wonders of Mount Kilimanjaro and Mount Kenya, Africa's highest peaks, as well as Lake Victoria, the second largest lake in the world and the largest on this continent. The latter is the source of the White Nile, the largest branch of the Nile River, which flows northward until it empties into the Mediterranean Sea.

Some of these countries are landlocked – Central African Republic, Congo, and Democratic Republic of the Congo, but the latter does border on Lake Tanganyika. The remainder have coastlines along the Indian Ocean, Gulf of Aden, and the Red Sea. The land is defined by the Great Rift Valley, a 3000-mile-long fault that runs north to south, and was originally formed when massive tectonic plates shifted millions of years ago.

It was from East Africa that humanity spread beyond its origins, moving to all five continents.

WEST CENTRAL AFRICA

On the Atlantic side of the African continent, the Gulf of Guinea defines the region. Its coastline has a series of exotic names that reveal something of its history – Grain Coast, Ivory Coast, Gold Coast, and Slave Coast. This is an equatorial area of high precipitation (20–40 inches of rain), and high temperatures (75–80°F). It is a land mass primarily of forest, woodlands, and grasslands, plus mixed use cropland, and wetland. It is an expanse filled with

EXHIBIT 15.4 AFRICAN HUMANITARIAN SERVICES

Not all foreigners in Africa are there to despoil her — for centuries, outsiders have also come to help its people and solve their problems, as the next four examples will confirm:

The Peace Corps (PC) has a 45-year legacy of American service to those in need at home and abroad. One such idealistic representative was Benedict Moran of Scottsdale, Arizona. Each day, 7,000 PC volunteers like him work in the developing world to fight hunger and disease, to further basic education, and promote economic security. Motivated by a strong work ethic, these unpaid, optimistic Corps members have a commitment to human service, as well as a pragmatic approach in problem-solving. After graduation from college, Ben had joined and was assigned to a very undeveloped Benin in West Africa. There he worked with local community leaders to bring the benefits of information technology to some 6.6 million people who earn on average less than $2 a day. To assist its largely impoverished and uneducated population, his project in the Peace Corps Partnership program was improving and upgrading *Radio Rural Locale de Quake*, founded in 1996.

Note: After his Peace Corps service, Ben Moran, son of our senior author, volunteered with a French humanitarian organization for two more years of working in Darfur, Sudan. He recently completed dual degree graduate studies in the Schools of International Public Affairs and Journalism at Columbia University.

Media broadcasting in the French and major local languages has a significant impact toward improving healthcare, in girl school enrollment, and in use of sustainable agro-forestry techniques. In his time there, Ben's project replaced deteriorating technical equipment in the Quake station, especially computers, music library, information database, and sound quality. By using the Internet, they were able to reach a larger number of citizens to cover a wide range of subjects for community development purposes. Through computer workshops for employees, the Beninese learned new skills, which further empowered them in their business careers. Moran and other volunteers worked closely with the natives to raise funds, obtain and install new equipment, and manage and evaluate this innovative project for maximum benefit of the people, so as to enrich their lives and self-worth.

Source: Paul D. Civerdell, Peace Corps Headquarters, 1111 20th St. NW, Washington, D.C. 20526, U.S.A. (www.peacecorps.gov/project#680-120).

In 1999, Médecins Sans Frontières (MSF), or Doctors Without Borders (DWB), was awarded the Nobel Peace Prize for their exceptional, global humanitarian service! In 2005, within 72 hours, their healthcare teams responded to disasters in Southeast Asia. MSF provided two-hundred international volunteers and two-hundred metric tons of aid supplies to assist people in five countries who were suffering from tsunami damage. Another of their campaigns is *Access to Essential Medicines*, which offers generic drugs to assist 25,000 patients in 27 countries who are coping with the HIV/AIDS — many of these recipients are in Africa.

Among its many projects on that continent is one to support the healthcare system of Uganda, where conflict has raged for 18 years. For example, in the Lira District, MSF runs a 350-bed therapeutic feeding center and program, as well as four clinics and two mobile clinics. In the Gulu District, this non-profit organization administers a night shelter for 4,000 children in need of a safe place to sleep in the grounds of Lacor Hospital. From their experience, DWB identified ten top humanitarian stories that were most unreported by the global media. Six trouble spots were in Africa — displaced inhabitants of Somalia due to violence; healthcare crisis in Zimbabwe due to political and economic turmoil; need for effective drugs to combat tuberculosis, as in Kenya and Uganda; combating malnutrition with nutrient-dense ready-to-use foods; worsening conditions in eastern Democratic Republic of the Congo requiring expanded medical services; and civilians caught between government troops and rebel groups in northern Central African Republic are being displaced from their homes. Doctors without Borders are addressing these multiple human needs of Africans.

Source: Doctors Without Borders, 333 Seventh Ave., 2nd Fl., New York, N.Y. 1001, U.S.A. (www.doctorswithoutborders.org).

New York's Fordham University established an Institute of International Humanitarian Affairs in 2001. Its founding director is an alumnus, Kevin M. Cahill, M.D., who has undertaken medical humanitarian missions for more than 45 years in 60 countries as a member of the above MSF. Recently, this "visionary grounded in human realities" wrote a book, *To Bear Witness: A Journey of Healing and Solidarity* (Fordham University Press, 2005). Among Cahill's many true stories, it describes how this physician of Irish heritage treated John Paul II after the 1981 assassination attempt on the Pope's life. Dr. Cahill also pays tribute to his late wife, Kathryn, who often worked with him on his DWB undertakings, saying: *Ours was a marriage made in heaven, and honed to perfection in some of the hell holes on Earth!* Such humanitarian efforts took him to many African countries, such as drought-plagued Somalia; and more recently to serve victims in need after the devastation of U.S. Gulf Coast hurricanes, the earthquake in Kashmir, Pakistan, and India, as well from the Iraq war. Here is an excerpt from his new volume: *Those of us privileged to participate in great humanitarian dramas have the opportunity that adversity offers to build a new frame-work — using and sometimes rediscovering the best of old structures, but realizing that a new spirit and innovative methods are necessary for international discourse in a new millennium.*

Source: "Nota Bene," *Fordham Alumni Magazine*, Fall/Winter 2005/6, Vol. 39:1 (www.fordhamedu/instituteofinternational humanitarianaffairs).

The Heifer Foundation operates worldwide from its international headquarters in Little Rock, Arkansas. This non-profit humanitarian entity works with communities who seek to end hunger and poverty, while caring for the Earth and its environment. Since 1944, it has helped 9.2 million families move toward greater self-reliance through the gift of livestock, plus training in environmentally sound agriculture. The impact of each original gift is multiplied by recipients who agree to "pass on the gift" by giving one or more of their animals, or the equivalent, to a neighbor in need. For example, an 11-year civil war in Sierra Leone fought over rich natural resources plunged this West African country into destitution. Many people lost their livestock in the conflict. So, in 2008, Heifer International opened an office in Freetown where they are working with poor Sierra Leoneans to establish programs that develop animal and agricultural projects so as to help the locals to rebuild self-sustaining communities.

Source: George Bugbee and Sherri Nelson's "Sierra Leone on the Mend," *WorldArk*, November/December 2008, pp. 21–26 (www. heiferinternational.org/worldark).

wildlife and fauna – the major crops being bananas, cassava, cattle, citrus fruit, cocoa, coffee, corn, fish, forest products, millet, oil palm fruit, pineapple, rice, rubber, sesame seed, sheep, sorghum, sugarcane, swine, tea, and tobacco. The area is also rich in industry and mining – aluminum, gold, manganese, titanium, diamonds, manufacturing, petroleum, and processing. West Africa is in the midst of an oil boom today, but, unfortunately, too many corrupt elite benefit, instead of improving the masses. These natural resources are why so many non-Africans have come here, and why it is a target of foreign investment.

Centuries ago, this region experienced the rise and fall of great African empires, like the Mali from the thirteenth century and the Songhay from the fifteenth. Great rivers, such as the Gambia and Niger, flow from the mountains to the shores through forests, savannahs, and arid plains to an often swampy coastline.

The region is home to some 14 nation-states, all of which describe themselves as republics. However, their rulers range from democratically elected presidents to dictators and military coup masters. The locale extends from Guinea-Bissau in the northwest corner, south of Senegal, to another Congo in the southwest that abuts the Democratic Republic of the Congo. Alphabetically, these countries are called: Benin, Burkina Faso, Cameroon, Congo, Cote d'Ivoire, Equatorial Guinea, Gabon, Ghana, Guinea, Guinea-Bissau, Liberia, Nigeria, Sierra Leone, and Togo. The biggest urban center is Lagos, Nigeria, with a population of approximately five million. One country in the region, Nigeria, has been chosen for a cultural analysis. Unfortunately, West Africa is a region of political instability and even civil war, often originating from rebel groups in neighboring countries.

SOUTHERN AFRICA[13]

The southern tip of the African continent encompasses some 11 nations. On the West Coast facing the Atlantic Ocean are Angola, Namibia, and South Africa. The latter is the most modern state bordering on the Indian Ocean, and will be the target for our analysis which follows. Within that country are the small kingdoms of Lesotho and Swaziland. In the region's interior are Zambia, Malawi, Zimbabwe, and Botswana. On the east coast facing the Indian

Ocean are Mozambique, plus the island of Madagascar. In this southern area, the largest population centers are along the northwest and southwest coastlines, as well as in the north.

The area's peace and prosperity has been severely constricted by a 30-year civil war in Angola; a lengthy, costly, but successful struggle to overturn the all-white, Afrikaner apartheid government; and the ongoing civil unrest, killings, land grabs, and economic disasters of President Robert Mugabe's administration in Zimbabwe. An exception to this pattern is Botswana, a small peaceful country of only 1.8 million people, just north of South Africa. It has used its vast diamond wealth wisely to foster education, one of the best on the continent, as well as tourism and a friendly business environment. This country is known to be the least corrupt state, but its sparkling image is marred by a high rate of AIDS, and its mistreatment of a most vulnerable ethnic group, the Bushmen, or San, a hunter-gatherer tribal people.

Off the coast of Mozambique is the island of Madagascar, also a part of Southern Africa. Further east in the Indian Ocean are three small other islands. The second is called Mauritius, an independent republic of some 1.3 million inhabitants (Exhibit 15.5).

EXHIBIT 15.5 MAURITIUS: MULTIDIVERSITY PROGRESS

E X H I B I T 15.5

This isolated island state of only 1,100 square miles gained its independence from Britain in 1968. Then, it was a sugar-based economy with a GDP of $200 per person. But with freedom, the country's GDP has jumped to $7,000 per person and ranks first for good governance on the above Ibrahim index! The World Bank has also given the republic a high ranking as the best African country for ease of doing business. With over a hundred hotels, it is now a peaceful and popular place with tourists who crave sun, palm trees, and good service. Its capital of Port Louis is an attractive place for offshore banking, hosting 19 global banks. Furthermore, Mauritius is a low-tax gateway for investment into Asia, especially India. The economy also includes food processing, sugar milling, chemical and textile manufacturing, fishing, as well as cattle raising plus the exporting of cut flowers and molasses.

With an economic mindset that welcomes competition, its government has slashed commercial red tape and cut taxes, while reforming labor legislation and promoting itself as a desirable business destination. As a result, unemployment and budget deficits are down, and foreign investments are up. Unfortunately, the republic has to import most of its food and energy, while too much of the economy is concentrated in the hands of a few local conglomerates. These factors are being diminished by a new competition commission and development of new industries. With an independent judiciary and democratic elections, three political parties agree on broad policy directions.

A pluralistic population mix of Africans, Chinese, Europeans, and Indians has religious and cultural differences, but has avoided communal divisions. They speak some seven languages, ranging from English, Creole, and French to Hindi, Urdu, Hakka, and Bojoori. Further, adherents of Christianity, Hinduism, and Muslim religions have learned to tolerate one anothers' beliefs. Surely, a demonstration model for other African nations to emulate!

Source: Adapted from "Beyond Beaches and Palm Trees," *The Economist*, October 18, 2008, p. 58.

South Africa[14]

There are multiple visions of what South Africa has been and should be. One vision is that it is a land of promise – the most advanced economy on the continent, a country with enormous natural beauty and resources. In the twenty-first century, the African continent needs a strong and prosperous South Africa.

South African society is in the midst of a transformation that could lead to prosperity, if both the white citizen minority who had been in control and the oppressed black majority now ruling truly share their nation's socio-political institutions and power. By their practice of cultural synergy, both may create a multicultural society of equal opportunity.[15] One small indicator of progress is the "Buppies," the growing, upwardly mobile, black professionals. In this multiracial democracy, they can even be found at gatherings of "high society," such as the J&B Met Horse Race, an annual sports and fashion extravaganza, formerly the exclusive domain of middle-aged white suburbia.

HISTORICAL PERSPECTIVE

South Africa has a heritage of pioneering, colonization, wars, and building a modern infrastructure. Thankfully, now, *apartheid* is gone – a failed policy of separation of white and blacks that was internationally condemned and finally abandoned in the 1990s. Three centuries ago, this land became home to Bushmen and Hottentots, Bantu-speaking black tribes. In the mid-seventeenth century, the European whites arrived. First were the Dutch, who built a trading settlement at the Cape of Good Hope. They were joined by Germans and French Huguenot refugees in 1688. Together, these colonists would become known as Boers (farmers). The British invaded and captured the Cape in 1806, gaining formal possession of the colony in 1814 as the result of the Napoleonic wars. To avoid English rule, the Boers migrated to the undeveloped interior of the country from 1835 to 1848, defeating the indigenous Zulu and other black tribes in the process. With the discovery of gold and diamonds in that territory, Britain annexed parts of that area that led to the Boer War, which they won in 1902. The British then combined their colonies of Cape and Natal with the Boer Republics of Orange Free State and Transvaal, creating in 1910 the Union of South Africa, today called the Republic of South Africa (RSA).

Thus, this is a nation of four cultural influences or ethnic groups: the native African majority, the minority populations consisting of the Dutch who were to become known as Boers and *Afrikaners*, along with the British and Asian immigrants, the latter mostly from India and designated later as the *Coloureds*. As British power waned, the Afrikaners increasingly took control of the government after the election of their National Party in 1948. During the 1960s, Afrikaners introduced the oppressive apartheid system separating blacks from whites, creating two unequal communities. Another flawed policy was launched that forced settlement for the majority black African population in separate and supposedly independent homelands (e.g., Lesotho and Swaziland). Since the 1960s, domestic turmoil and violence caused by these inhumane political actions brought international protests and boycotts, including trade sanctions by the United States and condemnation by the United Nations.

To fight for black human rights, the African National Congress (ANC) was formed in 1955 and eventually coalesced with other black groups' campaigns against the white power government. Finally, the economic and social impact of multinational sanctions led to the resignation in 1989 of the president of the RSA, P. W. Botha. His replacement, F. W. de Klerk, implemented a series of democratic reforms, beginning with the freeing of political prisoners, the desegregating of institutions, and the legal recognition of the ANC as a political party. The outcome was the signing of a peace agreement between the latter and the ruling elite providing for power sharing, the dismantling of apartheid, and the holding of open elections. In the 1994 election, all RSA citizens voted for the first time, electing ANC leader and former political prisoner, Nelson Mandela as president, and de Klerk as vice president of a multiethnic government. For their peace-keeping success, both men were awarded the Nobel Peace Prize. Since then, a political evolution, not revolution, has been under way. Nelson Mandela, or Madiba, died in December 2013. He was a remarkable person and should be a model for other leaders, political or business, throughout Africa and the world.

The RSA is a laboratory of social experimentation that has implications for the whole continent. With the ascendancy of the ANC leadership to the national government in 1994, and a new approach to white/black power sharing, the inequitable, segregated, apartheid political and social system is very slowly being transformed into a more democratic, multiparty one. Despite an odious and corrosive historical legacy, here the change process and progress are under way. Suffrage policy was at first limited to whites only, and then extended to the *coloureds*, and now finally includes the blacks, formerly restricted to voting in local "homeland" or township elections. The shift in political parties and power has been from the National Party and Conservative Party to the ANC, the Inkatha Freedom Party (Zulu), and the Democratic Party. Overall, the current government is striving to meet educational and training needs for a global economy and a knowledge society.

Postapartheid presidents have all been from the ANC, and struggle with human resource and economic improvements for all. They have been slow to counter the AIDS epidemic in the country, and to provide human rights' leadership relative to nasty regimes elsewhere. With refugees flocking in from nearby Zimbabwe, they have been reluctant to confront its failed president, Robert Mugabe, or to endorse the International Criminal Courts prosecution of Omar al-Bashir, Sudan's president accused of genocide. They have not implemented the vision of the revered Nelson Mandela when he was elected president: *Human rights will be the light that guides our foreign affairs*. Africa's richest nation has yet to become a "beacon of hope" to the world's oppressed. However, the government has been a leading peace-maker in the New Partnership for Africa's Development, which promotes continental democracy and effective governance through a peer-review system. South Africa has sent troops to mediate conflicts in Darfur, Burundi, the Central African Republic, and Congo. At home, it has adopted a progressive constitution, prohibiting discrimination, and promoting civil liberties. Its officials have sought to provide more adequate housing and reproductive healthcare for citizens. But South Africa must do more to exercise moral leadership in Africa, while contributing to a more equitable world order. As their Nobel prize winner, Archbishop Desmond Tutu observed that turning a blind eye to oppression outside South Africa is *a betrayal of our noble past. . . . If others had used the arguments we are using today when we asked them for support against apartheid, we might have still have been unfree.*[16]

CULTURAL GUIDELINES FOR BUSINESS IN SOUTH AFRICA

Today, there are some 47 million South Africans, equally divided between men and women, who have a life expectancy of only 48 years. This is a relatively young population, about 70 percent or more are under 50 years of age, with 26 percent under the age of 10. Approximately 37 million are black Africans (79.3 percent); 4.4 million are white (9.3 percent); 1.2 million are Asian (2.5 percent); and 4.1 million are colored (8.8 percent). The black Africans consist of 9 tribal groups − Zulu (the largest), Xhosas, North and South Sothos, Tswanas, Shangaan-Tsongas, Swazis, South Ndebeles, and Vendas. Each has its own special cultural heritage, language, and sense of identity. During the apartheid period, tribal groups had been assigned by the racist government to 10 ethnic "homelands" that were supposed to have self-rule, but actually were dependent on the white statecraft − these are being dismantled under the new regime. Although English and Afrikaans (a Dutch derivation) are the official languages, the blacks among the four major tribes speak varying forms of Bantu. The whites have zero population growth, but were reserved 85 percent of the land under the old system. The whites are divided into two groups − the English-speaking descendants of English, Scottish, and Irish settlers, and the Afrikaan-speaking offspring of the Dutch, German, and French colonials; there are also the English-speaking *coloureds* descendants of early white setters, native Hottentots, imported Dutch East Indian slaves, and indentured laborers from India (Hindi speakers).

Religion. In terms of religious affiliations, most South Africans are Christians, divided among the Dutch Reformed Church of the Afrikaners, and other denominations, such as Anglican, Methodist, Presbyterian, Roman Catholic, as well as African Charismatic, a combination of Christian and traditional African rituals. The Indian community consists of both Hindus and Muslims. There are also a small number of Jews.

Literacy/education. Compared to most other African nations, the overall literacy rate is high but deceptive. The overall literacy rate is 84.6 percent, which is among the highest in Africa, but 99 percent of whites as compared to 50 percent of blacks are literate. (The other two highest African literacy rates are also in the south − Lesotho, 82 percent, and Zimbabwe, 85 percent; all three countries are former British colonies in which English is widely spoken.)

Among the black population, 22.3 percent have no schooling; 25.4 percent have some or completed primary school; 30.4 percent have some secondary schooling; while only 16.8 percent have completed their "metrics"; 5.2 percent has had higher education. Generally, the Indians (41 percent), the whites (36 percent), and the coloreds (7 percent) benefit by passing metric exams, and moving on to university or college. Formerly all-white institutions, such as Witwatersrand and Cape Town universities, are still excellent. Historically, black universities have been described as atrocious with serious security problems, so reforms are under way among them. Until recently, when Africans replaced Afrikaners in the education ministry, only 3.8 percent of the GDP was devoted to education and 85 percent of that went to whites; now, 20 percent of the national budget is spent on education regardless of color. Today, nearly all children attend primary school – over eight million students enrolled in elementary schools, one million plus in secondary, and 282,000 or so in third or higher levels of education. But the quality of that education is questionable – the new education minister claims 30 percent of the schools are not fit for use, and there is an acute shortage of qualified teachers. The school system is an adaptation of the British educational model, but is in transition to integrate more black Africans at all levels. Fifty-eight percent of students matriculating in secondary school do graduate. The situation improves in independent schools, the majority of which charge fees – 2,000 of them enroll 4 percent of the student population. The proportion of blacks in them has risen to 60 percent, and this system is the best racially integrated. Furthermore, parents are becoming educational entrepreneurs, creating their own avenues of learning opportunities for economic and social mobility. Private business is involved in funding initiatives to improve all types of schooling. Overall, South Africa has one educational advantage – its school systems are flexible and opening to customizing programs to meet national and student needs.

SOCIAL CONDITIONS

Consider these cultural insights about contemporary South Africa, especially among the black African majority:

- *Family structure* in the black community has been destabilized by past apartheid policies and its constraints; dislocation caused by job searches contributes to seven million people living in poverty. In the black extended family, there is normally great respect manifested toward the elderly and obedience to parents. In contrast, the white community's family is nuclear, close-knit, and privileged, though declining in affluence and influence. The Truth and Reconciliation Commission enabled families from both sides to testify or confess about the brutality of 40 years of the apartheid regime, and to try to move on with reconstruction.

- *Emerging middle class* is slowly happening among the black community – up to 40 percent of the total population. Africans have taken over downtown urban centers, formerly only open to them by day. Affirmative action and black empowerment programs have opened up the job market and management positions, but only one black-owned company is a real success – Johnnic Holds, an entertainment, media, and telecommunications group. Today, some 70 percent of the workforce is black

Africans, of which 45 percent are women and 5 percent disabled. The black share of personal income has climbed and is rising, whereas that of the whites is declining, falling from 71 percent (1970) to 50 percent (2000). With all of the country's problems, including a 36 percent unemployment rate, the trends point toward greater prosperity for black Africans, even with a 2 percent annual growth rate in population.

- *Lifestyle* is better for many black Africans since the early 2000s – their society is humming with activity and opportunity amidst poverty. Among the blacks, one can find more vibrancy, naturalness, and brotherhood, but it is sometimes marred by intertribal conflict and power struggles. The government is spending 21 percent of the national budget on education now, which is 5.7 percent of the GDP. But the rates of crime, violence, and alcohol abuse are up, again partially because of past Afrikaner practices of uprooting people (e.g., putting migrant laborers into hostels, and paying too many wages in *papsak*, or wine). The dying white-dominated culture kept Africans subordinate, called men *boys*, and undermined their role as protectors, often dumping their wives and children in so-called "homelands." Realistically, postapartheid South Africa is experiencing serious threats to family life, which is increasingly breaking down with male violence.

- *Sports* are a positive influence among the masses. While a prisoner, Nelson Mandela taught himself about rugby because his Afrikaner jailors were so mad about it.[17] When he was released from jail, Mandela inspired black Africans in many ways, including sports; he coaxed all his countrymen towards more civilized government and behavior. Having studied the culture of his opponents, he promoted rugby as a bridge across the racial chasm. Thus, he overcame some of the tensions between the two racial groups that ultimately resulted in the destruction of apartheid. In 2010, South Africa hosted the FIFA World Cup (soccer).

- *Work environment* is gradually improving for all employees. However, in government, the ANC, a former revolutionary party, is still authoritarian and prizes political loyalty over competence. Its officials have not mastered the art of administration and science of management, while being deployed from one job position to another. Their public servants are not open to new ideas outside their own bureaucracy. Their current policies discourage blacks from becoming entrepreneurs, so small and medium enterprises languish. Also, there is a severe shortage of native skilled workers, and protectionism in place to prevent the import of technicians from abroad. This shortage of qualified personnel has led to thousands of job vacancies, especially in the financial and banking sectors, as well as in delivering services. Presently a plan is under way – Joint Initiative for Priority Skills Acquisition – to develop the needed skill base by recruiting and training more engineers, technicians, and other skilled professionals.

- *Healthcare and social services* are beginning to deteriorate, though the country has the most organized and functioning healthcare system in Africa. The quality of life for average citizens is being severely undermined by the spread of diseases, especially AIDS. UNAIDS estimates that nearly 4.7 million people here are HIV-positive, yet government "leaders" often live in denial. The administration of President Mbeki was absurdly slow in responding to the epidemic of 5.2 million HIV-infected citizens. With 40 percent so infected, forecasts are that AIDS deaths will be up to 635,000 by 2010, bringing a vast increase in orphaned children and dysfunctional families. As a result, by 2020, the public health costs are likely to approach 38 billion rand. The healthcare and social services systems, until recently, had no effective plan in place to cope with growing numbers of patients and dying people, no less their youthful offspring, who may end up truants, street gang members, and eventually criminals. Within that context, the UN expects South Africa's GDP by the 2020s to be lowered by 17 percent. With about 1,000 dying daily from this illness, the government is finally waking up to the scourge of AIDS and its implications – a comprehensive regime is under way to combat the pandemic with antiretroviral drugs. But the whole healthcare system is inadequate for coping with this plague, which now infects 5.5 million people in South Africa.

■ *Criminal justice* is weak in South Africa – the system suffers from too many unemployed criminals who either do not get caught, or when they are arrested, are not likely to be convicted. Although the government is spending more on law enforcement, crime statistics show the country to be among the most violent in the world with 50 people killed every day. With a loss of cases by prosecutors of 500 out of 1,800 prosecuted, half of the 2.2 million crimes reported go unsolved. However, private investment and research into the processing of accused criminals has produced reforms in the justice system and higher conviction rates. The old hatred of police lingers, along with a legacy of firearms. Poorly paid police ranks are riddled by corruption, inadequate equipment, insufficient training, and ineptness (about a quarter are functionally illiterate, and large numbers do not even have a driver's license to drive themselves to crime scenes). The cost of crime to business is up approximately to 12 billion rand, while the national police budget is about 16 billion rand. Reforms under way include the appointment of a new national prosecutor, establishment of a new elite investigation force, legislation to mandate minimum sentences, and bail. Poverty and the shantytowns it produced, such as Soweto outside of Cape Town and Forman Road in Durban, are home to thousands of struggling black Africans and their uneducated and unemployed youth, many of whom turn to criminal activities to survive. In the 1990s, there was a crime wave, and Johannesburg became known as the "crime capital of the world." But there has been a remarkable turnaround in that municipality with the formation of Business Against Crime (BAC) – it has reduced street crime by 80 percent after installing 200 surveillance cameras in that city's central business district. Other cities, like Cape Town, have also had success in curbing crime with closed-circuit television monitoring. With a mixture of both private and public sector funding in crime prevention, young professionals have begun to move back into the inner cities, contributing to their renewal. Private security firms have increased and employ some 250,000 people, twice as many as in the regular police force. There are other positive signs, such as an efficient constitutional court and vocal think-tanks. The nation has become a leader in conflict resolution within Africa and the founding of the African Union.

ECONOMIC AND SOCIAL CHALLENGES

Economic development. South Africa still has the strongest and most diversified economy on the African continent. Although it has only 6 percent of the sub-Saharan people, it accounts for one-third of its GDP. With a diversified economy and first-world financial services, the economy has structurally changed and is more internationally competitive. It is strong not only in minerals and raw materials, but increasingly in high technologies. A strong central bank and an improving legal system, as well as a fair road and transport infrastructure, all contribute to development. Although foreign investments did not grow as anticipated with the lifting of global economic sanctions and diminishing civil protests, the global companies that have come are pleased overall with their experience and are expanding.

The government has succeeded in reducing the national budget, debt, and inflation, through disciplined, responsible fiscal and monetary policies. It aims to promote growth, employment, and redistribution. The challenge is whether the high standard of living enjoyed by the whites can be shared somewhat by the masses of black citizens, developing in the process a broader middle class. The GDP average is obviously much higher for whites than for blacks, but the GDP is growing too slowly overall. With an employment rate between 25 percent and 35 percent, three million inhabitants are looking for work. Reducing unemployment and job creation are critical, along with new enterprises, for growth within a new multiracial society. In the past, the economy was largely based on varied agriculture, as well as the mining of diamonds and gold, until the manufacturing industries took hold. South Africa has vast natural resources, including chromite, coal, uranium, platinum, natural gas, and fish. Today, this mixed economy has a large industrial base – from metal products, chemicals, and foodstuffs, to machinery, vehicles, and textiles – all part of a strong exporting program. With a good infrastructure in transportation and communication already in place, as well as a relatively well educated population, this nation has great potential for development.

The economic situation is well summarized in the township of Soweto, Johannesburg. In what was once a byword for violence and black deprivation, shiny new cars are parked in front of elegant houses protected by security systems. Shopping malls, banks, and tourists are now visible. Black economic empowerment is evident throughout the country. Although it creates a half-million jobs every year, unemployment ranges from 25 percent to 40 percent, and half the total population is classified as poor, with a quarter of them on government handouts. Yes, South Africa is still a young, vulnerable economy.

Twenty-first century needs. This country produced two of the greatest modern African leaders: namely, Nelson Mandela and Desmond Tutu, both Nobel Peace Prize winners. Mandela, as the first African president, and Archbishop Tutu personified the vision of creating a country with a nonracial future. Together, they established a Truth and

Reconciliation Commission, engaging enlightened leadership like theirs, in both the public and private sector. Leadership is South Africa's primary need; leadership that is concerned for the whole citizenry, not just for his or her racial community. That type of leadership would address challenges, such as promoting the following:

- *Pluralism and inclusiveness*, which allows for reasonable dissent, compromise, give and take, and protection of human rights.
- *Educational and training improvements* at all levels for the development of a more knowledgeable and competent workforce.
- *Rebuilding strong family life and childcare*, especially in those African homes and villages devastated by past apartheid policies and currently by AIDS.
- *Economic development* without graft and corruption that improves the whole society, especially the black African and colored poor.
- *Political diversity and inclusiveness* so that all citizens participate in voting, and parties other than the ANC are given the opportunity for more leadership participation in a government that is less centralized (e.g., Democratic Alliance). As former President Thabo Mbeki stated in 2007, the country needs to pursue a *commonly defined national agenda*, something he was unable to accomplish during his administration. If such a new mission statement for South Africa is ever written, it should emphasize "bridge building" among the many elements needed in a still divided society (Exhibit 15.6).

Those observations written a number of years ago are still valid for the most part. Today, there are too much division, factionalism, stagnation, and patronage.[18] The country's potential is being undermined by a high crime rate, high food and petrol prices, power cuts, strikes, and the economic downturn. The deteriorating situation is fueling a white diaspora among the English-speaking and Afrikaan-speaking population who make up only 9 percent of the richest and best-educated people. How long these talented émigrés, including mixed race and black inhabitants, will stay abroad depend on how much improvement occurs in the land of their birth. Some professionals are attracted by higher salaries paid in foreign places. But people of all races are put off by myopic regimes which promote greed, corruption, nepotism, and incompetence. The new South African leadership needs to "nurture" Mandela's rainbow vision to build a vibrant, pluralistic society that cares for all its citizens and their progress. South Africa possesses the assets to realize this vision – an energetic people who live in a beautiful country; a model constitution which protects individual rights; a free press and judiciary; a democratic parliament and separation of powers; and a good infrastructure and banking system.

BUSINESS TIPS IN SOUTH AFRICA

With a continent as vast and diverse as this, it is impossible to generalize on the preferred business and trade practices. South African business customs, for example, require some

EXHIBIT 15.6 THE NEW SOUTH AFRICA

Since the 1990s when African National Congress triumphantly took power in South Africa's first multiracial democratic elections, the country has plotted its course to relative stability, democracy, and prosperity. It is even beginning to lead the continent in an entirely new way, urging other nations there to emulate its example. Under Nelson Mandela's leadership, the ANC government campaigned to alleviate poverty and degradation of apartheid victims, without resorting to counterproductive populism. While there have been some improvements, there is growing impatience over the pace of change in South Africa. Mandela's vision of a "rainbow nation" has slowed to a crawl.

Yet, from education to foreign policy to crime-fighting, the inhabitants have found creative solutions to their problems. The government has presided over 87 months of economic growth (currently 5 percent a year), low budget deficits, and low inflation, while trying to encourage free enterprise. Buoyant domestic demand has been accompanied by the sort of foreign investment that some thought would never come. But despite a 5 percent GDP growth, the unemployment rate has risen and has affected 27 percent of the population. Governance policy has provided more money for social program grants, mainly for child support and pensions to some 10 million people, as well as for public works, mainly to stimulate job creation, consumer demand, and tourism.

Furthermore, there are hopeful experiments to benefit children from squatters' camps, such as an extraordinary school called *Sekolo Sa Bonrokgo* in the northern suburbs of Johannesburg. There, 25 dedicated teachers inspire black students to achieve remarkable academic progress. As the lack of quality education is the single most important factor holding back the country's development, such innovations need to be multiplied.

The continent needs a strong South Africa, one prepared to go beyond traditional agendas, and to make a commitment to good governance, human rights, and democracy as enshrined in the goals of the African Union.

Source: Excerpted and adapted from Richard Crokett's "Chasing the Rainbow – A Survey of South Africa," *The Economist*, April 8, 2006, 12-page insert (www.economist.com/surveys).

flexibility, depending on which ethnic group you are dealing with. The white business protocols are comparable to those of Europe and North America, whereas those of Indian heritage may seem more like the commercial environment found in India. However, in what is typically referred to as *Black Africa*, whether in the west, east, or south, the following observations may prove useful. These observations supplement those made earlier in this chapter on "Cultural Characteristics of Africa."

- *Meetings*. Business is normally discussed in an office, bar, or restaurant, but always outside the home. What happens in the home is considered private. When invited to someone's residence for a meal, do not discuss business. When an African is the host of such meetings, he or she will pay for everyone. If a foreigner is the host, he or she should pay. If a foreigner receives an invitation to a *braaivlets*, or barbecue, it is an important part of getting to know business associates better without discussing business per se. It is customary for outsiders to bring a token gift, such as beverage or candy.

- *Communications*. Most businesspeople have business cards which are exchanged readily. After some small talk on encountering a foreigner, white South Africans tend to get down to the purpose or agenda for meeting, whereas those of other races may make long inquiries about your health and family before getting down to business.

- *Attitudes*. South Africans generally are more low key in their business discussion, searching for "win-win" opportunities for both parties. They are wary of foreigners who try to take advantage of them, so resist high-pressure and cut-throat tactics, and emotional appeals. Ordinarily, in the world of commerce and government, people do not like to be rushed into decisions about a deal. The local merchants of Indian or Chinese heritage are experienced and shrewd traders, and may be more aggressive in their negotiations.

- *Seniority*. As indicated previously, traditionally, age commands respect. Age and wisdom are seen as identical, and the norms of the elders must be followed to ensure smooth business dealings. Some of this tribal heritage is retained in some business environments.

- *Gender*. As women become better educated and involved in business life, the traditional precedent of man before woman is giving way to a more equalitarian approach. This is confirmed by the national policy of affirmative action to ensure equal opportunity.

PROSPECTS FOR PAN-AFRICAN SYNERGY[19]

In general, Africans are in transition from their traditional cultures based on a rural, agricultural, and tribal way of life. Rapidly, they are moving toward an urban lifestyle that is based on industrial and technological development. Since the 1950s, international business, professionals, and humanitarian workers have done much to promote greater African prosperity, whether through the United Nation's agencies, their own governments, multinational corporations, foundations, or other financial investment. Some foreigners and their governments have long contributed to the exploitation of Africa's enormous resources for their own greedy purposes, and now there are new players seeking to benefit from the continent's rich resources (Exhibit 15.7).

EXHIBIT 15.7 CHINA IN AFRICA

During the cold war, China entered Africa to encourage solidarity with socialistic states there by aiding with infrastructure projects, as well as supporting liberation movements. Now, China rapidly buys up African oil, metals, and farm products to fuel its own economic growth. Chinese officials, businesspeople, and laborers are flocking into this continent in ever-increasing numbers. For example, in 1991 only 300 Chinese foreigners lived in Zambia; by 2008, the number had jumped to 3,000. Similar trends can be seen in other African states, such as Algeria, Angola, Congo, Kenya, Morocco, Nigeria, and even South Africa. In 2008, the PRC President, Hu Jintao, not only visited some of these countries, but invited 30 African leaders to a Sino-African summit in Beijing!

With China's economy growing on average 9 percent annually, and its foreign trade increasing five-fold, it needs African natural resources, more than just ideology and influence. Thus, its trade and investment in Africa is $50 billion or more. China looks for copper and cobalt in the DRC and Zambia; for iron ore and platinum in South Africa; for timber in Cameroon, Congo-Brazzaville, and Gabon; for oil primarily in Nigeria, as well as Congo, Equatorial Guinea, Gabon. Thus, Chinese trade with African sources continually expands (about 10 percent of all African trade). By 2010, estimates are that these numbers will double. China also contributes aid and investment into this continent (over $10 million yearly), as well as canceling African debt, thus assisting there the development of infrastructure and housing. Further, China aid is straightforward without the bureaucratic demands of the IMF and World Bank. China builds strategic relationships and agreement with African states. Its assistance includes investments, professional training, and providing Chinese doctors, technicians, and workers to Africa. In sharing its technology, many African states benefit, such as building and launching a satellite for Nigeria. Also, China is becoming a processor of commodities, cheaper goods services, and military hardware to the continent. By buying African, the PRC reduces its own trade deficits, and offers competition to Westerners there. Yet, there are concerns for human and economic rights in China's projects — for example, alleged mistreatment of workers in a Chinese-owned mine in Zambia; technical assistance, which necessitates the Chinese remain to maintain railways and pipelines built mainly with Chinese laborers; support for the Sudan government when it commits genocide against its own people in Darfur; resisting democratic reforms in countries ruled by the "big man"; and blocking UN reforms and sanctions against failed administrations, such as that of Robert Mugabe in Zimbabwe. It would appear that this new interloper is no more altruistic than its colonial predecessors on this great continent. In the long term, the ultimate question is: will China contribute to lifting Africa from the Third to the First World civilization? There can be synergy between China and its African partners that is "win-win" for both partners.

Source: Adapted from "China in Africa: Never Too Late to Scramble," *The Economist*, October 28, 2006, pp. 53–56. Parag Khanna, "China Moves In," *The Second World*, New York: Random House, 2008, pp. 188–190.

For this new millennium, there is much discussion of an *African Renaissance* and rediscovery of its creative past, led by South Africa. If non-Africans wish to participate in that renewal, consider the following arenas to promote:

- *Effective leadership* – replacement with twenty-first-century leaders who are better educated and more competent and honest, as well as more socially responsible and foresighted, aware of international interdependence. Such new leadership in governance and public service will promote democratic government, and respect for human and environmental rights. This will require massive cultural changes so that Africans become more goal-oriented and less fatalistic. It means the heads of the 53 states must learn to work together synergistically through the African Union.
- *Environmental protection/rural development* – preserving the natural beauty and resources, while stopping further degradation of land and forests. The goal is to manage natural resources for sustainable development and more equitable sharing by the whole population. Less emphasis on urban development and more efforts directed to creating rural opportunity and agricultural production, including providing basic infrastructure for smaller towns and villages (e.g., clean water, electricity, transportation, jobs, education, and health services).
- *Population control* – traditional large families that enlarge tribal power bases have to be regulated, while social security provisions are made for the aged and orphan children. Only then can tough problems related to infant mortality, child abuse, illiteracy, nutrition, and healthcare be solved in Africa. The internal refugee crisis needs continental solutions.
- *Continental health crusade* – an African Union initiative to control and conquer, with the help of global organizations, the scourges of HIV/AIDS and malaria, to improve water systems and medical treatment, and to provide cheaper drugs. Within Africa, multinational synergistic efforts are needed to defeat the HIV/AIDS epidemic that is devastating Southern Africa, the epicenter of this Pan-African tragedy.
- *Education and training* – promote education and skill development throughout the continent suitable for a technological work environment and the knowledge culture. Such human resource development should include environmental education, civic responsibilities and competencies, intertribal and interracial tolerance, as well as management and administrative skills. The aim would be empowerment of the people, particularly of women and minorities.

If synergy is to occur between the more modern, developed world and Africa, there are lessons to be learned from the observations in Exhibit 15.8.

Africa covers 20 percent of the world's landmass and has 10 percent of its people. Yes, it has problems, but nothing that a North–South dialogue and collaboration cannot resolve, for Africa is a rich continent with great resources. That may explain why the People's Republic of China has stepped up its involvement there. Remember that six centuries ago,

EXHIBIT 15.8 AFRICA'S POVERTY

Humanitarian assistance should not be confused with economic development assistance. A rampaging disease that respects no international border threatens the survival of Africa. About 70 percent of AIDS sufferers worldwide are African, and fighting the disease has overwhelmed African budgets. At a United Nations Conference on AIDS last June, UN Secretary General, Kofi Annan, called for a global war chest of $7–10 billion to battle AIDS.

The state of postcolonial leadership in Africa is not pretty – a hideous assortment of "Swiss bank account" socialists, military vagabonds, quack revolutionaries, and briefcase bandits. Their overriding preoccupation is not to develop their economies, but to perpetuate themselves in office, loot the treasury, and brutally suppress all dissent and opposition.

Africa is not poor for lack of resources. Its mineral wealth is immense: hydro-electric power potential; the bulk of the world's diamonds and chromium; substantial deposits of uranium; and gold, cobalt, phosphates, platinum, manganese, copper, and vast bauxite deposits, plus nickel and lead resources. There is also vast oil and natural gas wealth. Yet paradoxically, a continent with such abundance and potential is mired in squalor, misery, deprivation, and chaos.

African leaders often prefer to blame the West for Africa's poverty. But, in fact, it has little to do with colonial legacies, the slave trade, imperialism, or other external factors. At the 2000 Summit of the Organization of African Unity in Lomé, Tongo, Kofi Annan told African leaders they are to blame for most of the continent's problems: "Instead of being exploited for the benefit of the people, Africa's mineral resources have been so mismanaged and plundered that they are now a source of our misery."

The way out of Africa's economic miasma is through investment. Aid to rogue regimes helps nobody. And to trade, a country must first produce the goods required for international commerce. In 1990, only 4 out of 44 African countries were democratic; this number has now grown to 15. Target aid only to those countries that are democratic. To establish a democratic order, these are most critical: an independent central bank; an independent judiciary; an independent free press and media; an independent electoral commission; a neutral and professional armed or security force; and an efficient civil service.

Source: Ayittey, B. N: "Africa's Poverty," *San Diego Union-Tribune*, INSIGHT, June 16, 2002, pp. G1, G6.

Ming Dynasty seafarers reached African shores for trade purposes, and today, Chinese vessels ply those same sea lanes to bring back oil, iron ore, and other commodities to satisfy the voracious needs of its huge, expanding economy. Meanwhile, the West makes insufficient investments in African human and natural resources, while wondering if the Chinese presence will undermine their own efforts there on behalf of human rights, democracy, peace-keeping, healthcare, and anticorruption. But Africa should be of global concern for humanity, not just of Eastern and Western nations.

The continent's emerging middle class is taking advantage of technology to improve communications among diverse African people, especially through satellite television and mobile phones. Hopefully, this century will find Africa moving beyond its colonial past and contemporary problems toward self-sufficiency in a more peaceful environment that protects and develops its vast natural and human resources. Recall that it took centuries for another continent to move from feudalism to an effective European Union – here, a comparable African Union may be created in decades!

CONCLUSIONS

Africa is the cradle of our civilizations, home to every person in the human family, whether they come to this continent as tourists, professionals, humanitarians, or businesspersons. Accept the diversity among Africans, while seeking to understand its inhabitants in an atmosphere of nonjudgmental acceptance.

In this chapter, we examined the immense continent of Africa in terms of its four geographic regions and the multitude of states within it. Profiles of selected countries with the larger populations in each area were presented, along with four in-depth regional case studies. Overall, we also provided general insights into Africa, its current problems and promise, as well as characteristics of its diverse peoples. As a result, global leaders may appreciate the possibilities in Africa. Then, with respect and sensitivity to its inhabitants, synergistic partnerships, such as joint ventures and humanitarian projects, can do much toward contributing to the proper development of the area and its resources.

When comparing cultures, such as the American and African, and how they affect the business environment or humanitarian service, it is necessary to understand that the United States is a low-context culture. It is technologically and futuristically oriented with an emphasis on individual achievement rather than on group participation. In the communication process, a low-context culture places meaning in the exact verbal description of an event. Individuals in such a culture rely on the spoken word. In contrast, Africa's culture is high context. In the communication process, much of the meaning comes not from the words, but is internalized in the person. Meaning comes from the environment and is sought in the relationships between the ideas expressed in the communication process. High-context cultures, more so than low-context cultures, tend to be more human-oriented and to value the extended family. Perhaps this closing quotation may stimulate readers' thinking about Africa: "No other continent has endured such an unspeakably bizarre combination of foreign thievery and foreign goodwill" (B. Kingsolver, *The Poisonwood Bible*, New York: HarperCollins, 1998). The outside world needs to appreciate and give back to Africa for its enormous contributions to humanity and multiple nations, as confirmed by the election of Barak Obama, the first American president of African heritage.

MIND STRETCHING

1   Why is it important for all members of the human family, now consisting of 7 billion people, to understand and appreciate Africa's past, present, and future potential?

2   How has past European colonialism impacted today's Africans, in contrast to present Asian influence on them?

3   What and where is Sub-Sahara Africa, and how does it differ from the rest of the continent?

4   What is the implication of the fact that in Africa, 900 million inhabitants live in the countryside, while rapid urbanization is under way?

5   How can those who live outside of Africa contribute to development of its human and natural resources, to combating poverty and disease on this continent, and to promoting peace and better governance?

6   What is the connection, if any, between a third of Africa's countries with soaring oil revenues, and cycles of unrest, violence, and civil wars on the continent?

7   Discuss Acemoglu and Robinson's theory described in Chapter 1, *Why Nations Fail*, as it applies to Africa.

NOTES

1 *Family Reference Guide to the Future Book of the Peoples of the World: A Guide to Cultures.* Washington, DC: National Geographic, 2002, 2008.

2 Dowden, R. *Africa: Altered States, Ordinary Miracles.* London: Portobello Books, 2008; Meredith, M. *The Future of Africa: A History of Fifty Years of Independence.* New York: Perseus Books/Public Affairs, 2006; Iliffe, J. *Africans: The History of a Continent.* Cambridge, UK: Cambridge University Press, 2007; Pitcher, G. *Lonely Planet's Africa* (A Travel Guide). New York: Lonely Planet Publisher, 2007; "Africa: Whatever You Thought, Think Again," *National Geographic Magazine*, Special Issue, September 2005; Guest, R. "How to Make Africa Smile: A Survey of Sub-Saharan Africa," *The Economist*, January 17, 2004, p. 16, www.economist.com/surveys; Oldfield, S. (ed.). *The Trade in Wildlife: Regulation for Conservation.* New York: Earthscan, 2003; Peterson, D. *Eating Apes.* Berkeley, CA: University of California Press, 2003.

3 Painter, N. I. *Creating Black America: African-American History and Its Meaning.* Oxford: Oxford University Press, 2006; Hill, K. H. *Religious Education in the African-American Tradition.* Danvers, MA: Chalice Press, 2007, www.chalicepress.com.

4 Salgado, S. *Africa.* New York: Tachen, 2007, www.amazon.com/books; Obradovic, N. (ed.). *The Anchor Book of Modern African Stories*, 2nd edn. New York: Anchor, 2003; Richmond, Y. and Gestrin, P. *Into Africa: Intercultural Insights.* Boston, MA: Nicholas Brealey/Intercultural Press, 1998; Wiredu, K. *Cultural Universals and Particulars: An African Perspective.* Bloomington, IN: Indiana University Press, 1997; Arnold, M. J., Geary, G. M., and Hardin, K. L. (eds). *African Material Culture.* Bloomington, IN: Indiana University Press, 1996; Ojisku, U. J. *Surviving the Iron Curtain: A Microscopic View of What It Was Like in a War-Torn Region.* Baltimore, MD: PublishAmerica, 2007, www. publioshamerica. com; Lovejoy, P. E. *Transitions in Slavery: A History of Slavery in Africa.* Cambridge, UK: Cambridge University Press, 2000.

5 Refer to "Rebuilding Failed States: From Chaos, Order," *The Economist*, March 5, 2005, pp. 45–47.

6 Refer to "Doing Business in Africa: Different Skills Required," *The Economist*, July 2, 2005, p. 61; and "African Optimism: The Hopeful Continent," *The Economist*, January 7, 2006, p. 50.

7 Bass, G. J. *Freedom's Battle: The Origins of Humanitarian Intervention*. New York: Knopf, 2008; Obrinski, J. *An Imperfect Offering: Humanitarian Actions for the Twenty-First Century*. London: Walker and Company, 2008; Bolton, G. *Africa Doesn't Matter: How the West Failed the Poorest Continent and What We Can Do About It*. New York: Arcade, 2008; Ginn, J. K. *Circle of Giving*. Little Rock, AR: Heifer International, www. heiferfoundation.org.

8 Salgado, *Africa*; Obradovic, *The Anchor Book of Modern African Stories*; Richmond and Gestrin, *Into Africa*; Wiredo, *Cultural Universals and Particulars*; Arnold et al., *African Material Culture*; Ojisku, *Surviving the Iron Curtain*; Lovejoy, *Transitions in Slavery*.

9 Painter, *Creating Black America*; Hill, *Religious Education in the African-American Tradition*.

10 Ham, A. *West Africa* (Multi Country Guide). New York: Lonely Planet, 2006; Vansina, J. *How Societies Are Born: Governance in West Central Africa before 1600*. Charlottesville, VA: University of Virginia Press, 2005; Falola, T. and Heston, M. *A History of Nigeria*. Cambridge, UK: Cambridge University Press, 2008.

11 Diagram Group, *North Africa: Islam, and the Mediterranean World*. New York: Frank Cass Publications, 2005; Davis, D. *Resurrecting the Granary of Rome: Environmental History and French Colonial Expansion in North Africa*. Athens, OH: Ohio New University Press, 2007.

12 Diagram Group. *History of East Africa*. New York: Frank Cass Publications, 2003; Fitzpatrick, M. and Parkinson, T. *Lonely Planet's East Africa*. New York: Lonely Planet, 2009; Davitt, N. *Kenya: A Country in the Making*. New York: W. G. Norton, 2008; Marcus, H. G. *History of Ethiopia*. Berkeley, CA: University of California Press, 2008; Johnson, D. H. *The Root Causes of Sudan's Civil Wars*. Bloomington, IN: University of Indiana Press, 2002; Flint, J. and deWaal, A. *Darfur: A New History of a Long War*. New York: Zed Books, 2008; Barz, G. *Music in East Africa: Experience Music, Expressing Culture*. Oxford, UK: Oxford University Press, 2004.

13 Meredith, M. *Diamonds, Gold, and War: The British, the Boers, and the Making of South Africa*. New York: Public Affairs/Perseus Group, 2008; Murphy, A., Armstrong, K., Firestone, M., and Fitzpatrick, M. *Southern Africa* (Multi Country Guide). New York: Lonely Planet, 2007; Ehret, C. *An African Classical Age: Eastern and Central Africa in World History, 1000 B.C. to A.D. 400*. Charlottesville, VA: University of Virginia Press, 2001.

14 Cockett, R. "Chasing the Rainbow: A Survey of South Africa," *The Economist*, April 8, 2006, p. 12; Grimond, J. "A Survey of South Africa: Africa's Great Black Hope," *The Economist*, February 24, 2001, p. 16; Sadiman, J. *South Africa's "Black" Market: How to Do Business with Africans*. Boston, MA: Nicholas Brealey/Intercultural Press, 2000. The authors acknowledge that the insights for this profile were partially obtained from a "Culturegram for the Republic of South Africa," *Culturegrams*, David, M. Kennedy Center for International Studies, Brigham Young University, 280 HRCB, Provo, Utah 84602, USA (Tel: 801/378-6528); Carlin, J. *Playing the Enemy: Nelson Mandela and the Game That Made a Nation*. New York: Penguin Books, 2008. For further information about this nation and its culture, contact the Embassy of South Africa (3051 Massachusetts Ave., NW, Washington, DC 20008, USA) and the South African Tourism Board (747 Third Ave., 20th Floor, New York, NY 10017 or 9841 Airport Blvd., Ste. 1524, Los Angeles, CA 90045, USA).

15 Lewis, R. D. *The Cultural Imperative: Global Trends in the 21st Century*. Boston, MA: Nicholas Brealey/Intercultural Press, 2003; Khanna, P. *The Second World: Empires and Influence in the New Global Order*. New York: Random House, 2008, chapter 21.

16 "South Africa and the World: The See-No-Evil Foreign Policy," *The Economist*, November 15, 2008, pp. 55–56.

17 Note in chapter reference 12, John Carlin's book, *Playing the Enemy: Nelson Mandela and the Game That Made the Nation*, Penguin Books, 2008. Also see "Briefing South Africa: The Long Journey of a Young Democracy," *The Economist*, March 3, 2007, pp. 32–34.

18 "South Africa: A Future of Division, Factionalism, Stagnation, and Patronage," *The Economist*, August 9, 2008, pp. 43–44; "White Flight from South Africa: Between Staying and Going," *The Economist*, September 27, 2008, pp. 35–36.

19 Lewis, *The Cultural Imperative*; Khanna, *The Second World*, chapter 21.

AFRICAN RESOURCES

Beside a search on the Internet for Africa or any country therein, consult www.africaguide.com; www.joeant. com/DIR/info/get/7375/18588; and www.sul.stanford.edu/ depts/ssrg/africa/ guide.html. A very useful learning system is Africa, produced by Palm World Voices (www.palmworldvoices.com). This compact packet focuses on African peoples and their business. Each package contains a National Geographic map of African peoples and their music; a booklet with pictures entitled Africa the Musical Continent; a visual DVD; and an audio CD on the music of Africa. Inquire about other productions, such as BabbaMaal: Senegal. Specific country reports are available from Reprints Department, *The Economist* Newspaper Group, Inc., 111 W. 57th St., 10019. New York, NY 10019, USA (www.economist.com/surveys).

Details on every country in the world, including those in Africa, are available in the CIA Fact Book (www.cia. gov/cia/publications/factbook/geos/ct.html). The National Geographic Society periodically publishes updated maps on Africa (www.nationalgeographic/africa). For example, the map supplement to their maga-zine in September 2001 was entitled "Africa Today," and in September 2005, "Africa the Human Footprint." National Trade Data Bank, International Trade Administration, U.S. Department of Commerce, Washington, DC, 20230 (Tel: 1/800-USA TRADE #4/5; www. export.gov; click on "market research" and then "country commercial guide" choosing a particular African state). For hard copy or diskette of any African country guide, call National Technical Information Service (1–800/553-NTIS). There is a country code for informa-tion on all nations of Chapters 10–16 and this chapter on Africa (telephone hotline, 1–202/482–1064 or 1860). Major U.S. cities also have local offices of USDC with commercial advisors to provide counseling and resources to businesspersons seeking data or connections abroad in a specific country or area within that target culture. Also consult the local telephone directory under "Government Pages" for the nearest listing of the United States Government Offices and the Federal Commerce Department.

ADDITIONAL FEATURES

Please visit the companion website at: www.routledge.com/cw/Moran where you will find additional case studies, study aides, and instructor resources.

16 DOING BUSINESS WITH NORTH AMERICANS

A cardinal principle of Total Quality escapes too many managers: you cannot continuously improve interdependent systems and processes until you progressively perfect interdependent, interpersonal relationships.

Steven Covey[1]

Americans should never underestimate the constant pressure on Canada the mere presence of the United States has produced.... Living next to you is in some ways like sleeping with an elephant. No matter how friendly and even-tempered the beast ... one is affected by every twitch and grunt. It should not therefore be expected that ... this Canada, should project itself as a mirror image of the United States.

Pierre Trudeau[2]

The United States and Canada have often been thought to have very similar national and business cultures.[3] This assumption may have been based on older studies showing that American and Canadian values and attitudes were more similar to each other and together more distinct from those of other cultural groupings or clusters of nations.[4] Certainly, the two nations have long shared a very close trade relationship. Since the signing of the Free Trade Agreement (FTA) in 1988, and the inclusion of Mexico in the North American Free Trade Agreement (NAFTA) that superseded the FTA in 1994, Canada and the United States have each been the other's top trading partner. For 2012, Canada accounted for 16.1 percent of total American trade (exports + imports), ahead of China (14.0 percent), Mexico (12.9 percent), and Japan (5.9 percent).[5] In 2010, trade with the United States accounted for 74.9 percent of total Canadian trade.[6]

However, these days Canada is actively seeking to reduce its trade dependence on American markets. It is predicted that by 2020, the United States will receive only about 66 percent of Canadian direct exports, down from 85 percent in 2002.[7] This reduction in trade has resulted from relative parity in the value of American and Canadian currency, greater American imports from China, and new free trade agreements with other countries. In addition, The United States is beginning to seem an unreliable trading partner, placing its domestic politics ahead of its trade relationship with Canada. The long delayed approval process for the Keystone XL Pipeline,[8] intended to pipe landlocked Alberta oil sands oil to the Gulf of Mexico, has the Canadian government seriously considering selling the oil to East Asia instead, by way of an all Canadian route.[9] There are also perennial disputes about softwood lumber and Canadian meat products.

Certainly, Canadian businesspeople have thought of U.S. markets as natural extensions of Canadian markets and have not worried about the possibility of cultural differences. Americans and Canadians have similar democratic political systems, and free-enterprise economies. They have similar lifestyles based on similar levels of income. They watch the same television and movies, and access the same Internet based social media. A small Canadian software manufacturer would be more likely to expand from English-speaking Ontario, the Prairies, or British Columbia to the United States, than to French-speaking Quebec (a province of Canada).[10] Cultural differences within Canada, between English and French-speaking Canada, seem more difficult to overcome than differences between English Canada and the United States.

There is evidence, however, that this assessment has been proven incorrect. Over and over, well-known Canadian retailers have utterly failed when they attempted to enter American markets using business strategies that had been very successful in Canada.[11] In the 1990s, the success rate was only 20 percent, and now it is only 50 percent.[12] O'Grady and Lane[13] argued that cultural differences were an "unobtrusive" barrier. Canadians and Americans encountered difficulties doing business in each other's countries because the assumption of cultural similarity prevented them from identifying critical differences. As a result, Canadians and Americans had unanticipated difficulties establishing the rapport for effective business relationships.

The purpose of this chapter was to discuss how culture impacted doing business both in, and between, the United States and Canada. It was our view that in understanding the differences between American and Canadian approaches to building business relationships, the preferences of both Americans and Canadians would become clearer.

Although North America geographically includes three major nations — Canada, the United States, and Mexico, Chapter 16 covers only the two countries north of the Rio Grande River. Since Mexico is culturally and linguistically aligned with Latin America (Central/South America), Mexico has been covered in Chapter 11. Recognize that the term "American" can be used by everyone living in North and South America, but, colloquially, American is more often used to refer to those living in the United States. Specific objectives included understanding:

1   The cultural context of the United States.
2   The cultural context of Canada.
3   The First Nations' cultural context of both the United States and Canada. The Aboriginal First Nations of Canada, for example, are an Emerging Market (see Chapter 7) internal to Canada.
4   Similarities and differences between Americans and Canadians seeking to build business relationships with each other.

We believe that these discussions will prove valuable not only for those seeking to do business with Americans and Canadians, but also for the many who seek to invest. The United States has long been considered a "safe port" for business investments because of its relative political and economic security. American consumers have long been the principal sparkplug for world economic growth through their willingness to buy vast quantities of imports from around the world.

While First World economies such as the United States, European Union, and Japan have languished from the effects of the 2008–2009 world recession and subsequent debt crisis, emerging markets have continued to grow. Chinese, Indian, and Brazilian Emerging Market companies are becoming ever more prosperous. They see the United States as an ideal location for safe and dynamic investment. And thanks to the NAFTA agreement, companies from around the world may choose to invest in Canada and achieve the same free access to American markets that Canadian companies have enjoyed. Honda, for example, supplies Civic cars to Canada and the United States from its Ontario plant. We hope that the discussions in this chapter will be of help for companies with these goals.

THE UNITED STATES OF AMERICA

America is great, not because it is perfect, but because it can always be made better – and that unfinished work of perfecting our nation falls to each of us. It's a charge we pass on to our children, coming closer with each new generation to do what we know America should be.

Barak Obama[14]

The United States is the most technologically advanced and largest economy in the world.[15] It is a free-market economy in the sense that private individuals and businesses make most economic decisions, and governments, both federal and state, buy most of their goods and services from the marketplace. American companies have greater flexibility than companies from Western Europe or Japan in making expansion plans, laying off unneeded employees, and developing new products. American firms are at the technological leading edge especially in the computer, medical technology, aerospace, and military industries. Other industries of note include petroleum, steel, motor vehicles, telecommunications, chemicals, electronics, food processing, consumer goods, lumber, and mining. The industrial production growth rate in 2011 was 4.1 percent.[16]

United States industries exported US$1.61 trillion in 2012. U.S. exports were the third greatest amount of all countries. Principal exports included, in order of dollar volume, capital goods (49.0 percent, including transistors, aircraft, motor vehicle parts, computers, telecommunication equipment), industrial supplies (26.8 percent), consumer goods (15.0 percent, including automobiles, medicines), and agricultural products (9.2 percent). The main recipients of U.S. exports in 2011 included Canada (19.0 percent), Mexico (13.3 percent), China (7.0 percent), and Japan (4.5 percent).

The United States imported US$2.36 trillion in 2012, the second greatest amount of any countries. Principal imports included industrial supplies (32.9 percent) including oil (8.0 percent), consumer goods (31.8 percent, including automobiles, clothing, medicines, furniture, and toys), and capital goods (30.4 percent, including computers, telecommunications equipment, motor vehicle parts, office machines, and electric power equipment). Main exporters to the United States in 2011 included China (18.4 percent), Canada (14.2 percent), Mexico (11.7 percent), Japan (5.8 percent), and Germany (4.4 percent).

While it appears that the United States ran a significant current exchange deficit due to the much higher level of imports to exports, this is only partially true. Foreign companies that set up wholly owned manufacturing plants in the United States are allowed to import parts and assemblies from their foreign suppliers for products to be sold either in the United States as American products, or for re-export to foreign markets. In 2012, the United States had US$2.82 trillion in foreign investment, and had invested US$4.77 trillion outside the United States. The government held US$148 billion in foreign exchange and gold, the 17th largest amount of any country.

Governmental context

The United States of America is a constitutional republic, a federation of 50 states and other territories. It is a representative democracy in which the rule of the majority is tempered by laws protecting minority rights. The U.S. Constitution is both the supreme legal dictate and a social contract with the American people.

This document regulates a governance system of checks and balances centered on three branches of government, each with inherent powers that limit the others. The nationally elected President ("White House" Administration) provides leadership. There is also an elected Congress (Legislature) consisting of the Senate (100 members, or 2 per state) and House of Representatives (435 apportioned by population) responsible for legislated policies and laws. The Supreme Court (judiciary of nine), whose judges are appointed by the President with approval of the Senate, is the final arbiter of justice. They rule on the constitutionality of laws, which are passed both nationally and by states. The President can initiate or veto legislation by the Congress, and is the Commander-in-Chief of the military forces.

This federalist system is the model for government activities at the regional, state, and local levels; the latter powers may be split between county and municipal administrations. State governors and other officials are elected by popular vote. The United States follows the rule of laws, subject to review and the possibility that laws may be declared unconstitutional. Governments are subject to laws in the same way as individual citizens – for example, when the major city of Detroit cannot pay its bills, it declares bankruptcy, the same as an individual person.[17] The Constitution, amended 27 times, has articles structuring the role and responsibilities of the federal government in relation to the state governments. It also protects citizen rights, such as in the Bill of Rights and the writ of "habeas corpus." The two major political parties are the Democrats and Republicans, although citizens may vote as Independents or form other political parties.

Geographical context

The mainland of the United States is situated in the central part of North America, south of Canada, and north of Mexico, Cuba, and the Bahamas. It is bound on its west coast by the Pacific Ocean, and on its east coast by the Atlantic Ocean. Its northernmost state is Alaska, which lies above the Arctic Circle and above Canada. Hawaii is the furthest away state, west of the mainland in the Pacific Ocean.

The United States is the fourth largest country in the world by area (3.72 million square miles or 9.63 million square kilometers), somewhat smaller than Canada, the second largest (3.86 million square miles or 9.98 million square kilometers). The United States was the third most populous country in the world in 2013 (315.59 million), much bigger than Canada (35.00 million in 2012).[18] It is located in the Western Hemisphere on the North American continent.

The United States consists of 50 states – 48 contiguous ones are on the mainland, plus the state of Alaska in the northwestern tip of the hemisphere, and the state of Hawaii located west of California in the Pacific Ocean. Washington, D.C. (District of Columbia) is the federal capital of the United States. Puerto Rico is a self-governing commonwealth. The U.S. Virgin Islands are a territory. Since the end of World War II, the United States has administered 11 trust territories in the South Pacifific, gradually relinquishing control. Between 1975 and 1980, accords were negotiated with the native islanders to establish the commonwealths of the northern Marianas, the Marshall Islands, the Federated States of Micronesia, and the Republic of Palau. The federal government supervises the national highway and transportation systems, national park and forest systems, national wildlife refuges and grasslands, national marine sanctuaries, national energy and environmental systems, as well as reservations for First Nations, and the military.

Historical context

The United States originally consisted of 13 British colonies located along the eastern seaboard of what is now the United States. In the course of a Revolution (1776–1783), the British were expelled and the current republican government was initiated. A major cultural difference between the United States and Canada was that Canada at that time consisted of British colonies that remained loyal to Britain. Americans who had supported the British crown during the Revolution emigrated to Canada and were known as Empire Loyalists.

A number of wars were fought in the eighteenth and nineteenth centuries between the United States and what became Canada. In both the Revolution, and the War of 1812, the United States tried and failed to liberate Canada from the British. In the latter war, British troops from Canada burned Washington, D.C., and American troops burned Toronto, currently Canada's largest city. However, since the Pork and Beans War of 1838–1839 over Maine's northern boundaries, the American/Canadian border was demilitarized until recent patrols for illegal drugs and aliens.

Military collaboration commenced in World War II and has continued bilaterally through the NORAD treaty, and multilaterally through NATO, to the present day. Today, Canada and the United States are the world's largest trading partners, sharing the world's longest border.

The twentieth century witnessed America becoming a world power, the deciding force in both in World Wars I and II. That twentieth century saw the United States swing from isolationism and non-ratification of the League of Nations to internationalism and formation of the United Nations with its headquarters in New York City. During this time, citizen movements ensured:

1   The guarantee of women's suffrage by a constitutional amendment granting females the right to vote.
2   The end of prohibition laws against alcohol consumption.

3   The protection of African-American citizens in the Civil Rights Act of 1964 and the Voting Rights Act of 1965.

During World War II, the United States and its democratic allies overcame Nazi, Fascist, and Japanese powers, ending the war in the Pacific by developing and using two nuclear or atomic bombs against Japan (1945). The nation then led in establishing international structures and economic policies, such as the International Monetary Fund, the World Bank, and NATO. During the postwar period, the United States initiated the Marshall plan to help Europe recover. It undertook through NASA an Apollo space program that placed satellites in orbit and two American astronauts on the moon on six different occasions. It engaged in a geopolitical cold war with the U.S.S.R. that resulted in the demise of that Communist government in 1991.

Unfortunately, the United States, during that period, like Russia, conducted "witch-hunts" against supposed Communist infiltrators during the McCarthy period (1947–1954) that questioned the loyalty of anyone with leftist political sympathies.[19] It supported dictatorships and proxy governments in unwise attempts to defeat Communism or other anti-American interests. The United States was also involved in a series of regional wars in Korea (1950–1953); Vietnam (1961–1973); Iraq (1991; 2003–2012); and Afghanistan (2001–?). In America, these major military conflicts not only weakened the nation's economy, and vastly increased American federal debt, but also resulted in significant countercultural movements and public protests. These anti-war movements contributed to altering American behavior, attitudes, and foreign policy to some extent.

In the twenty-first century, the attack of Middle Eastern terrorists on September 11, 2001, against New York City's Trade Center and Washington, D.C.'s Pentagon building became a significant force, changing the nation and its citizens. Most Americans believed that the events of 9/11 were the most serious terrorist acts ever committed against the United States. That event led to a declaration of war on terrorism worldwide, and against the Al Qaeda global network of radical Islamic anarchists, in particular. It contributed to the nation's concern about improving security for its citizens, limitations on immigration and human rights, as well as neglect of domestic concerns (e.g., natural disasters). Another consequence was the United States' invasion of Afghanistan, and later Iraq. These bloody conflicts diminished both the national treasury and the image of the world's only superpower, which was no longer held in high esteem by many foreigners.[20]

Amidst the severe economic recession of 2008–2009, a new President was elected in 2008, and reelected in 2012. Barack Obama was the first African American in that powerful office. He focused somewhat more on domestic American issues such as providing medicare for all Americans, and ending the Iraq conflict. At the same time, he kept up the war on terror with escalations in Afghanistan, and succeeded in killing Osama bin Laden, the 9/11 mastermind.[21]

Today, the United States seems less eager to be involved in a role as "world policeman."[22] It ceded leadership in recent conflicts in Libya, Syria, and Mali to its allies. It remains, however, the leading world exporter of advanced military arms and equipment, and this remains a major American industry.[23]

American cultural insights[24]

The citizens of the United States of America refer to themselves as "Americans." The United States has been referred to as a "melting pot" culture, where people come from many places and meld into the mainstream European cultures of the United States. The "salad bowl" metaphor is perhaps more appropriate and accurate. It recognizes the contributions of the Native American, African, Asian, and Latin cultures, each maintaining its unique cultural markers, while striving to work and live in harmony.

It is true that the United States is a land of immigrants – from the time of colonists (British/French/Spanish), plus the African slaves, and nineteenth- and twentieth-century European influx. More recent waves of refugees are from Japan, Indochina, China, Cuba, Haiti, Latin America, and the Philippines. German-Americans are the largest grouping at 49.8 million.[25] In 2000,[26] the Irish (30.5 million), English (24.5 million), African American (24.9 million), Mexican (18.4 million), Italian (15.6 million), and First Nations (7.8 million) were the major ethnicities. The last census confirmed that nearly 40 million people now in the United States were foreign born. Many of these cultural immigrants try to preserve their beliefs and traditions.

By 2050, the U.S. census forecasts that minorities in this country will become the majority. By then, the American population is expected to number 438 million, including some 40 million of Asian heritage. It is estimated that "whites" will make up only 46 percent of the U.S. population, while one in three Americans will be Hispanic or Latino. In Canada, Hispanics would be considered by many to be "whites" as well. An element of American culture is a rather morbid fascination with dividing ethnicities by "race" as a basis for ascribing status.

Like the rest of the world, there are more aging Americans due to fewer childbirths and longer lifespans. Recent surveys reveal that among 450,000 centenarians worldwide, 50,000 now live in the United States. Such demographic changes have a significant impact on American culture and society.

Obviously, then, the United States is a multicultural society with many microcultures. In addition to the American form of English, Spanish is emerging as a second language, especially in the Southwest, California, Florida, and Puerto Rico. American speech is as varied as the country's geography. French is still spoken by many in the state of Louisiana and parts of New England.

American cultural profile

There are some general cultural characteristics associated with most Americans. The overview of the dominant culture mainstream culture reveals that citizens of the United States tend to be:

- *Goal- and achievement-oriented*: Americans are optimistic, and think they can accomplish just about anything, given enough time, money, and technology.
- *Highly organized*: Americans prefer a society that is strong institutionally, well organized, and secure.
- *Freedom-loving and self-reliant*: Americans fought a revolution and subsequent wars to preserve their concept of democracy, so they resent too much control or interference, especially by government or external forces. They believe the ideal that all persons are created equal, though they sometimes fail to live that ideal fully, especially in the context of "race." They strive through law to promote equal opportunity and to confront their own racism or prejudice. Americans also idealize the self-made person who rises from poverty and adversity. Control of one's destiny is popularly expressed as "doing your own thing." Americans think, for the most part, that with determination and initiative, one can achieve whatever he or she sets out to do, and can thus fulfill individual human potential.
- *Work-oriented and efficient*: Americans possess a strong work ethic, though they are learning in the present generation to enjoy leisure time constructively through social media. They are very time-conscious and efficient in doing things. They tinker with gadgets and technological systems, always searching for easier, better, more efficient ways of accomplishment.
- *Friendly and informal*: Americans reject the ascribed privileges of royalty and class, but do defer to those with affluence and power. Media celebrities impress many Americans. Although informal in greeting and dress, they are a noncontact culture (e.g., they usually avoid embracing in public).
- *Competitive and assertive*: Americans in play or business generally are so oriented because of their drives to achieve and succeed. This is partially traced to their heritage, having overcome wilderness and hostile elements in their environment. The expectation is that people are free to achieve any dream in America, and can go "from rags to riches."
- *Values in transition*: America is a dynamic and open society. Traditional American values of family loyalty, respect and care of the aged, marriage and the nuclear family, patriotism, material acquisition, forthrightness, and the like are undergoing profound re-evaluation.
- *Generous and altruistic*: Although Americans seemingly emphasize material values, they are a sharing people, as has been demonstrated in the Marshall Fund, foreign aid programs, refugee assistance, and their willingness at home and abroad to espouse a good cause and to help neighbors in need. They tend to be altruistic and, some would say, naive as a people. Volunteerism is alive and well in the United States.

American social institutions

In terms of U.S. social institutions, three are worth noting here.

Education: Education is viewed as a means of self-development, so participation in the process and within the classroom is encouraged. Education is mandatory until age 16, and 97 percent finish at least elementary school, so the literacy rate is high. There is a public system (largely free of cost) with charter schools that focus on innovation and specialization. There is an independent private school system, which in some cases is sponsored by religious institutions. These schools extend from the elementary and secondary levels through college and university level. Two-year community or junior colleges are popular for the learning of technical and professional skills, as well as for transitioning into four-year college degree studies.

Family: The average family has been nuclear, consisting of only parents and children. However, the number of single-parent and extended families is increasing. Growing pluralism has also led to rising numbers of intercultural marriages. There is a strong movement in some areas toward same-sex marriages or legal partnerships with or without children. Fifty percent or more of all marriages in this country end in divorce. More than half of American women work outside the home. Women have considerable and improving opportunities for personal and professional growth, guaranteed by law. The society is youth-oriented, and usually cares for the elderly outside the home, in institutions. It is experimenting with new family arrangements, including unmarried couples living together, or even in communes.

Politically: The government operates based on the Constitution of 1787, providing a three-branch approach of checks and balances, and two or more political parties as described above. Currently, there is much disillusionment with political leaders, bureaucracy, corruption in public offices, and a counter push towards decentralization or the confederation of states for regional action (i.e., emphasis on states' rights and less government regulation over individual lives, or regional plans to respond to natural disasters). Increasingly, high-tech communications and Internet based social media are altering traditional politics. Popular politicians communicate with supporters using Facebook and Twitter.

Cultural challenges and changes in the United States

Americans are in the midst of profound social change, and even an identity crisis. The following factors have contributed to this maturation challenge.

NATIONAL IMAGE

The American national self-image is being challenged. It has been the world's most significant driver of world prosperity but this is a time of slow world economic growth. Continuous recession and debt load especially within the United States, European Union, and Japan have curtailed growth. For many years, exporting nations have relied on American consumerism to purchase their goods but now, with the decline in American housing values, Americans have had to cut back.

After much success in its wars abroad, military conflicts in Korea, Vietnam, Iraq, and Afghanistan proved to be costly and questionable. Public support for such military actions is declining. And the focus is more upon international diplomatic solutions, such as cooperation with the United Nations. Critics have argued that the United States has not afforded social programs available in the European Union, Canada, and Japan because of the costs of these conflicts. Now, it seems many European countries, the PIIGS (Portugal, Iceland, Ireland, Italy, Greece, Spain) for example, cannot afford them either.

The country's social fabric was undermined by the assassinations of the country's leaders in the 1960s leading to growing violence and social protests at that time in the streets. Acts of both domestic and foreign terrorism, and absurd racist policies and practices in light of growing pluralism and "latinization" of the country have caused division. The recent recession caused by the subprime mortgage scandals have increased homelessness and the creation of an underclass. And the many foreign wars seem to have caused an erosion of American values, and a sharp decline in positive international perceptions about the United States. Now, America is challenged by gun violence. These and many other factors are causing people in the United States to reassess their national image.

Transition into a postindustrial society happened first and faster in the United States than in most other countries because of scientific and technological advances. The values and lifestyles brought on by the industrial stage of development are being re-examined, and new replacements are being sought for more effective coping in a knowledge culture.

The impact of such contemporary trends depends on where you live in America, for there are considerable regional differences and subcultures. There is also a big difference between eastern, western, southern, and central lifestyles and attitudes. The eastern United States is thought to be more established, liberal in thinking, over-organized, and deteriorating industrially. The southern and central areas are thought to be more conservative. The western part of the nation is seen as more casual, innovative, and flexible. Certainly there are regional cultures when it comes to "taste." Pepsi outsells Coke in the United States because Pepsi has been engineered to satisfy the different flavor preferences of regional cultures, while Coke is a consistent flavor everywhere.

As a result of the 9/11 attacks, more Americans are becoming isolationist, nationalistic, and provincial in their thinking and actions. In an era of globalization, corporate acquisitions, and property purchases in the United States by Canadians, Japanese, Chinese, Europeans, Middle Easterners, and South Africans are considerable. This has caused some fear and backlash. The increased influx of refugees, along with legal and illegal immigrants, has strained existing social systems. But most of the newcomers, like Mexicans, Somalis, and Iraqis, are communities of strivers who want only to advance themselves in their new

EXHIBIT 16.1 AMERICA'S CHANGING CULTURE

5.2   million Americans are estimated to be living overseas.

5.7   million unmarried, heterosexual couples live together.

65   percent of population is urban, 33.6 percent suburban, and remainder other (e.g., rural).

27   percent of the high-income males report a work week up to 50 hours.

33   percent of the females are college graduates; 25 percent of the males in age group 25–29.

77   percent work in the service sector; 20 percent in industry; 3 percent in agriculture.

46   percent of the workforce are civilian women.

67   percent of children live with two parents; 28 percent with one parent; 5 percent other.

31   percent of college freshmen describe themselves as liberal in their political/social outlook.

20   percent of the population will be age 65 or older in 2050.

45   percent of population by 2050 will be white, 31 percent Hispanic, 14 percent black. 10 percent Asian.

80   percent today accept interracial marriage among Americans, while 45 percent of voters under 30 accept gay marriage rights.

Source: *Newsweek Magazine* Special Inaugural Issue, January, 2009, entitled "Obama's America: Where We are Now," 78 pp. The data are based on a Newsweek poll, plus information from Pew Research Center, U.S. Census Bureau, Congressional Research Center, and Environmental Systems Research Institute.

homeland, hoping to find the "American dream." Exhibit 16.1 summarizes insights on the changing American culture.

Obviously, from the brief summary above, it is evident that America is changing almost beyond recognition. Non-Americans need to revise their image of a "typical" American! Assimilation into the United States is not easy, but the constant inflow of immigrants produces a vibrant society with a fluid culture, breaking down barriers among previously estranged groups. The country, on the whole, is also becoming more tolerant on social issues that previously divided its citizens.

The increasing numbers who travel, study, work, or live abroad also foster a population more global and open to different perspectives, and less self-satisfied. Americans are becoming more "borderless" in their attitudes toward environment, energy, trade, and human rights. They are more resilient in coping with climate and weather changes, economic setbacks, and in creating a work environment in which home and office are more integrated.

Today's Americans still have a sense of affinity, but are creating new associations and communities based more upon common causes, issues, interests of concern that go beyond the traditional organizations. Knowledge and expertise divide these people more than class

EXHIBIT 16.2 CULTURE CONTRAST

Host country value	United States value
Japan: Group orientation	Individualism
Guatemala: Flexible time sense	Punctuality
Saudi Arabia: Relationship focus	Task/goal orientation
Switzerland: Formality	Informality
India: Stratified class structure	Egalitarianism
China: Long-term view	Short-term
Germany: Structured orderliness	Flexible pragmatic
France: Deductive thinking	Inductive thinking
Sweden: Individual cooperation	Individual competition
Malaysia: Modesty	Self-promotion

Source: Wederspahn, G. M. *Intercultural Services: A Worldwide Buyer's Guide and Sourcebook*. Burlington, MA: Butterworth-Heinemann/Gulf, 2000, pp. 41–42.

or wealth. Rebuilding the ladder of upward mobility and historic optimism in hard economic times is a challenge.

In business agreements or partnerships with Americans, Exhibit 16.2 illustrates how cultural values and assumptions may potentially clash with those from other international cultures.

Microcultures in the United States[27]

Thus far, the emphasis has been on the majority American macroculture. In mainstream American society, for example, most people are concerned with "doing." Americans have a preoccupation with time, organization, and the use of resources. In American social relationships, everyone is assumed equal, thus removing the need for elaborate forms of social address. Social relationships are characterized by informality, and social reciprocities are much less clearly defined. In the majority culture, citizens are motivated by achievement and accomplishment. American personal identity and, to a certain extent, one's self-worth are measured by what the individual achieves. What is valued is generally material rather than spiritual, and Americans also see themselves as individual and unique.

However, American culture is in transition. For economic and social change reasons, many American families are in crisis, especially in the inner cities and suburbs. Some also fear that America's large middle class is being eroded through increasing economic disparities that have increased the wealth of the upper class but not the middle class.

Violence is increasing, especially among the young gang members, many of whom lack adequate character education and supervision, as well as job opportunities. Their parents' attention is directed toward work and earning a living, and many times there is only a single parent, usually female. Under these circumstances, an expanding segment of the population is prone to homelessness, child or spousal abuse, substance abuse, crime, and intolerance. This distressed underclass is balanced by a majority of Americans who are relatively affluent and well-educated, in contrast to the rest of the world's population.

The exceptional uniformity that characterized American society in the post-World War II period has been supplanted by extreme diversity. The most integrated national market in the history of the world is splintering into an array of niches. Immigration, legal and illegal, has eroded the homogeneity of the U.S. population while multiplying commonalities and connections between American society and other societies around the world. There are multiple minorities or subcultures in this large country that have their own unique needs and concerns. The emergence of a polyethnic society is most evident in Los Angeles, where a cacophony of 160 languages is spoken today. California is now home to up to 2.4 percent illegal immigrants. The transformation of minorities into majorities is also taking place in Texas, Arizona, New York, Nevada, New Jersey, and Maryland.

In the United States, these microcultures – such as those of African Americans, Aboriginal First Nations, Hispanics, Chinese-Americans, Vietnamese-Americans, Muslim-Americans – are socially, economically, and physically challenged by the mainstream culture. Furthermore, there are subcultures that cross national boundaries, such as First Nations, youth, and senior citizens. Each of these groups has aspects of their lives, priorities, or values that may differ in part from mainstream America. To work effectively together and develop authentic relationships among all Americans, it is helpful to be aware, accept, appreciate, and respect the uniqueness of these various subcultures.

Those who have been part of the majority will have to change their sense of identity as they themselves become minorities and find themselves sharing power and influence with "people of color" if American institutions are to retain their effectiveness.[28] Mainstream cultural norms and standards are being altered as minorities move up into full equality.

There are three substantial minority groups distinguished by their physical, as opposed to cultural, characteristics. According to Gudykjunst and Kim,[29] there are five characteristics of minority group membership:

1   Members of minority groups are treated differently from members of a majority group by members of the majority group. This inequality usually takes the form of prejudice, discrimination, and even segregation.
2   Members of minority groups have either physical or cultural characteristics that make them stand out from the majority group.
3   Because minority groups stand out from the majority, membership in them is not voluntary.
4   Members of a minority group tend to associate with and marry other members of their group.

5   Members of a minority group are aware of their subordinate status, which leads to strong group solidarity and gaining a sense of ethnic identity.

In the past, each new wave of immigrants to the United States became a minority group and was discriminated against until subsequent generations became subsumed into the great American "melting pot." The Irish, the Germans, the Italians – all these groups suffered when they first immigrated. There are, however, three minority microcultures that have persisted for generations because their skin color made them easy targets for members of the "white" majority. These include African Americans, Aboriginal First Nations, and Hispanic Americans.

African Americans

Since colonial times in America, people from Africa were here as either slaves or freemen, many of whom served gallantly in the Revolutionary War. They became the backbone of the Southern plantation economy; in return for this subservient status, their human rights were denied and their families broken apart. The Civil War was fought to give blacks full citizenship. Although African Americans today still struggle to maintain their full civil rights and equal opportunity under the law, their economic and social position has advanced. Yet racism against them has become subtler within institutions, housing, or educational opportunities. Despite their accomplishments and the growth of the black middle and upper classes, unemployment among black teens and deaths from violence within black communities has also risen. There is much to be done together if all African-American citizens are to share in the American dream. Power is not equally shared, and economic access is limited, not equal. Yet, the election of the first African-American president in 2008, re-elected in 2012, has brought new hope to this oppressed community.

Racism entered global consciousness in World War II with the Holocaust and the racist philosophy of Nazi Germany that resulted in the imprisonment and death of millions of Jews. Today, world events have convinced most that racism is a significant problem in all countries, as the ethnic cleansing in former Yugoslavia and genocide in Rwanda exemplify. Law enforcement has also utilized questionable "racial profiling" in world security systems. Whether one focuses on individual, institutional, cultural, or symbolic racism, it is a phenomenon that is deeply ingrained throughout many cultures.

Racism is an explosive issue in American life today. To begin a serious dialogue regarding race, one must establish the terms for racial issues. As long as African Americans are viewed as "them," the burden falls on the persons of color to do all the "cultural" and "moral" compromising, so healthy race relations are hampered. It is not acceptable under the U.S. Bill of Rights that only certain Americans can define what it means to be American – and the rest must simply "fit in."

Obviously, African Americans are made visible by their skin color, but that is simply an example of human adaptability to environmental circumstances. They have made unusual contributions to American military and economic history, as African studies in U.S. colleges and universities underscore. They have enriched American culture in music, dance, art, education, entertainment, and sports. Other Americans need to share their unique qualities for joy and survival, and be transformed by experiencing them as friends, neighbors, and co-workers. Consider these indicators of progress in the African-American community:

- Since 1970, the proportion of African-American households living in poverty has shrunk from 70 percent to 46 percent, while the "black" middle class has grown from 27 percent to 37 percent.
- The percentage considered prosperous – earning more than $107,000 a year in 2007 dollars – rose from 3 percent to 17 percent.
- The racial wage gap between "blacks" and "whites" is diminishing because of increasing deregulation and competition in financial institutions.
- The number of "blacks" elected or appointed to office at all levels of government has increased dramatically, including to the U.S. Supreme Court and Attorney General, as well as the presidency itself.
- The number of "blacks" completing secondary school, college, and post-graduate studies is rising steadily.
- African Americans can be found everywhere in the United States, but their population concentration by states is centered in six southern states – Mississippi, Louisiana, South Carolina, Georgia, Maryland, and Alabama, as well as the District of Columbia.
- The African refugees from Somalia, Sudan, and Ethiopia are spreading from urban areas to smaller towns, such as Lewiston, Maine, and prospering while infusing more diversity into these communities.

With an African American elected to the Presidency of the United States, Civil Rights leaders have had to develop new strategies to fit within the President's own priorities for economic uplift. They need to learn how to take advantage of new administration programs that will address these long-standing, unresolved concerns of the African-American community: (1) unequal schools; (2) segregated housing; (3) lagging economic opportunities; (4) disproportionate number of black males incarcerated in prisons; (5) too many single-mother families and absent fathers. Yet, a 2008 opinion poll conducted after the Obama election reported that 42 percent of African Americans now believe that American society is fair and decent toward them.

Aboriginal First Nations

The Aboriginal First Nations' people lived in North and South America before the Europeans began to arrive with the Vikings in about 1000 AD and Columbus in 1493. They are known as First Nations because they were the original inhabitants, possibly having arrived from Asia over a land bridge from Siberia more than 20,000 years ago. In the Americas, First

Nations' groups created high civilizations as advanced in social organization as those in Europe. These included the Maya (2000 BC to 900 AD), Aztec (thirteenth century AD to 1521), Inca (thirteenth century to 1533; destroyed by the Spanish), and Iroquois.

When Columbus arrived, it is possible that there were as many as 100 million First Nations' people, though 99 percent of them died within a few generations from diseases inadvertently brought from Europe – like smallpox.[30] Columbus misnamed them the "Indians" because he thought he had arrived in India, and the name stuck. Organized into some 1,000 indigenous tribes, they had about 300 original languages, of which 175 living languages survive. Since 1493, they have experienced their worlds turned upside down – spiritually, physically, socially – by migrants, primarily from Europe, Asia, and Africa. Among them, whole communities were and are wiped out by the diseases, wars, and segregationist policies brought by newcomers.

The U.S. government, which came into existence with the adoption of the Constitution in 1787, found the First Nations blocking U.S. expansion across the North American continent. So began its imperialistic relationship with the First Nations, treating the various tribes as national entities and either negotiating with them for land or defeating them in battle and taking their land. For the past few centuries, relations between Americans and Aboriginals have been both cordial and hostile. First Nations' people have suffered many injustices through wrong or questionable government policies, such as the establishment of the reservation system to relocate Aboriginals to relatively undesirable land.

There are many fundamental differences between tribal culture and the dominant U.S. culture. The following contrasts five of these differences between the mainstream culture and that of Native Americans:

- In the mainstream, time is to be used, saved, and spent. People are paid for their time and generally view time as a commodity and a continuum. For Aboriginals, time is relative traditionally to the rising and setting of the sun, and to the changes in the seasons.
- In the mainstream, decision-making is based on authority. Some have authority to make decisions and others do not. Authority in Native American cultures is more horizontal than vertical because of the necessity of reaching group unanimity on a decision before any action will be taken.
- In the mainstream, people are generally future oriented and believe strongly in progress. Virtually any technological advance is greeted with enthusiasm. No opportunity for development is eschewed. First Nations seek to maintain their traditional culture and values. They prefer to live in harmony with, and preserving the quality of, their natural environments. First Nations will generally not support development that interferes with their traditional cultural values.
- In the mainstream, Americans have come to prefer to live in urban settings believing there to be greater opportunities for economic advancement, social welfare, and entertainment. Aboriginals tend to prefer to live in rural settings far away from mainstream development as a means of protecting their cultural integrity.

■   In the mainstream, people make decisions by confronting those that disagree. It is not uncommon for interested parties to interrupt each other, and to battle over areas of disagreement. In First Nations' culture, people are careful to share speaking time, speaking calmly, and often it is only the person holding the "talking stick" who is allowed to speak until s/he is finished and passes the stick to the next person in the circle.

Understanding the Native American way of life provides outsiders with a challenge and an opportunity. For thousands of years, First Nations' children have listened and learned from tribal elders who pass down tradition, wisdom, and experience. The connection between the sacred and the real world is important to them. They believe that creative forces formed the universe, and humans are only a small part of that creation. The spirits and power are to be found in nature. Aboriginals can learn to develop new skills, and many want to, but need modern work and practices that do not destroy their dignity, so they can change at their own pace. An understanding of Native American history, values, and cultural differences facilitates communication and business with these remarkable First People.

Within the continental United States, many Native Americans have passed into the mainstream culture. Those still living on reservations are extracting oil and other minerals, and starting entrepreneurial businesses. Today, in many states, gaming and casino operations are managed and owned by Native Americans. Some, like the Sycuans in San Diego County, have also built hotels and shopping centers. They not only offer education, jobs, and training to their own, but make significant financial contributions and investments in their neighboring communities. For those who still live on government reservations, painful progress is being made to gain greater control and administration of their own affairs, whether this be in schools and services or within the Federal Bureau of Indian Affairs. With recent financial settlements through the courts over abrogated treaty rights and lost lands, some tribes have established modern corporations to manage their natural resources. They enter into joint ventures with major companies for economic development purposes, even in the field of high technology on the reservations. Native North Americans never had the "white man's" sense of private property. Tribal culture thinks in terms of the collective, and assumes responsibility for the preservation of the land and nature's gifts. Today, mainstream ecology and environmental movements are catching up to the aboriginal concern for nature.

It is impossible to provide information presented on all the Native American nations because of their number and diversity. However, those planning to engage in business relations with a specific tribe or band should research the specific cultural elements of those potential partners. Your efforts will not go unnoticed.

Hispanic Americans

Hispanics are moving up in every American business area. Their cultural passion and adaptability with emphasis on family is ideally suited to both the American and global business scene.[31]

Recall the insights on Latin American culture provided in Chapter 11 before this examination of an emerging majority. Broadly defined, a Latino or Hispanic is an immigrant to the United States, or one whose ancestors came from Spain or Latin America. Most still speak Spanish and reflect the cultural images of both Spain and the indigenous peoples of Mexico, Central, and South America.

From a Canadian point-of-view, Spanish would be considered "white." People of mixed European and indigenous ancestry would be considered Metis (usually English or French and First Nation in Canada). They could easily "pass" for "white" in Canadian society unless they preferred to pursue their newly granted First Nation treaty rights to land and social assistance. These rights were established in a landmark Canadian Supreme Court decision in 2013.

The Hispanic cultural influence in the United States is most evident in California, Florida, Nevada, Arizona, Texas, Puerto Rico, and Guam. However, Hispanics have also been migrating to the Midwest and Northeastern states. From the viewpoint of creating synergy from cultural differences, the Latino expansion and integration into U.S. culture is also in major urban centers such as Denver, Chicago, and New York, as well as in Miami, Los Angeles, and San Diego.

Many Latinos, whose communities here go back to the sixteenth century, consider themselves "native" Americans. Less than 200 years have passed since the United States annexed the southwest after the Mexican–American War, and only a century since it occupied Puerto Rico.

In 2011, Latinos represent 16.3 percent of the U.S. population,[32] having grown by 43 percent over the previous decade. Census forecasters expect the total U.S. population of 438 million to be 29 percent Hispanic in 2050.[33] Spanish-speaking Americans are heterogeneous in terms of skin color and in terms of origin. Approximately 65 percent are from Mexico, 12 percent Puerto Ricans, 12 percent Central Americans and other Latin countries, 8 percent Cubans, and 5 percent Dominicans. Hispanics are most diverse in terms of histories, loyalties, and class. Some come from elite and wealthy backgrounds or ancestry in Mexico, Latin America, or Spain. Many others have come as migrant workers, legally or illegally, willing to work hard and long, yet many can find only low-paying and low-status jobs. Once established, they take advantage of American public education and the ability to move ahead economically and socially.

It is difficult to generalize about Latino-Americans, but they are gaining political power and representation as greater numbers of them vote. Although many are bilingual, they gain some cohesiveness through the Spanish language, Roman Catholicism, and family values. They are moving rapidly into middle-class status and home ownership. In most states, the number of Hispanic-owned businesses has doubled, and their purchasing power is likely to triple by the end of this decade. The Hispanic buying power in the United States reached $1 trillion by 2012 and is predicted to rise to $1.5 billion in the next five years.[34] The Latino consumer market – large and growing – has a reputation for brand loyalty, particularly when shopping for food and clothing.

As they become more assimilated, Latinos are slowly entering the mainstream of cultural and performing arts, the professions, and law enforcement. People of Hispanic background bring a distinct, joyous flavor to the American mainstream, especially in terms of food and music. They comprise a varied tapestry of Spanish, Indian, African American, and Metis heritages.

Tips for doing business and negotiating with Americans

The following is a profile of an American negotiator, reflecting some of the variables that can be important for business and negotiations:

Basic concept of negotiation: American negotiators view conflict and confrontation as an opportunity to exchange viewpoints and as part of the process in resolution, negotiation, and agreement. Americans prefer outlining the issues or problems and a direct approach to determining possible solutions. They are motivated to further the interests of their corporation or government, and have a highly competitive nature regarding the outcome or settlement. They tend to confront areas of difference rather than identifying points of similarity.

Dualistic thinking: In common with Western Europeans, and different from Japanese, Chinese, and other Asians, American negotiators tend dualistically to believe in opposites; one is right and the other must be wrong. They are not skillful in finding complementarity between conflicting positions.

Selection of negotiators: American negotiators are usually chosen for a negotiating team based on their record of success in past negotiations and their knowledge and expertise in the area to be negotiated. Negotiations that are technical in nature require Americans with very specifific knowledge and the ability to communicate their expertise. Individual differences, gender, age, and social class are not generally criteria for selection, but individual differences in character (cooperative, authoritarian, trustworthy) can determine whether one is chosen for an American negotiating team.

Role of individual aspirations: As a rule, Americans encourage individual aspirations and individual achievements. When representing her/his corporation or country, Americans temper their individualism and seek to accomplish and/or represent the positions of their company or country. Americans are generally unlikely to accept personal gifts or favors, and to feel offended, regarding them as questionable practices.

Concern with protocol: Generally, Americans are friendly and open. Their etiquette is largely informal, and so is their basic concern for protocol. They are relaxed in their business conduct, and do not often adhere to strict or explicit codes of behavior and ceremony. They may engage in what some ethnicities regard as inappropriate touching, like back-slapping. They do, however, tend to prefer to get down to business as soon as possible.

Significance of type of issue: The popular American expression "getting the job done" reflects their desire to assess the situation and get results quickly. In negotiations, Americans may focus on the tangible aspects of the negotiation without spending enough time on the more intangible aspects, such as building relationships during the process.

Complexity of language: Americans are low-context communicators. The message is primarily in the words spoken, and is not overridden by nonverbal communication – the cues of gesture, eye contact, and silence. Americans may require more background information than a high-context person is expecting to provide. Nonverbal expressions may inadvertently offend – Americans are not skilled in nonverbal communications.

Nature of persuasive argument: Americans usually attempt a rational presentation with detailed facts and figures accompanied by logical and analytical arguments when persuading one's counterparts.

Value of time: Every culture has different ways of organizing time and using it. Some cultures are rigidly bound by their schedules and deadlines, while other cultures have a relaxed attitude about detailed plans and schedules. Monochronic time emphasizes schedules, segmentation, and promptness. Polychronic time stresses involvement with people and completion of transactions rather than an adherence to a preset schedule. Americans generally have a monochronic time orientation, and for most Americans "time is money." Some American minorities, such as First Nations and Hispanic, may be more polychromic. In negotiations, Americans set schedules and appointments and tend to prioritize events and move through the process "controlling" the time allotted them.

Bases of trust: In negotiations, Americans generally trust the accuracy of the information being communicated and negotiated, and they assume that the negotiations will have a desirable outcome. If, however, Americans have had a past experience with a counterpart who has not been trustworthy, they will withhold their trust.

Risk-taking propensity: Americans are risk-takers. In light of their history, their perception of themselves as rugged individualists, and the rewards of capitalism, Americans have embraced risk and are not risk avoiding.

Internal decision-making systems: Decision-making is becoming more and more decentralized with authority, within predetermined limits, being given to those with negotiating experience. Most of the final decisions must be cleared with senior executives in the organization.

Form of satisfactory agreement: Because the American culture is legalistic, Americans prefer and expect detailed contractual agreements to formalize negotiations. A handshake may conclude negotiations, but the attorneys are always involved.

Dominion of Canada

Canada[35] is very similar to the United States in being a democratic, affluent, high-technology oriented, industrial society with a US$1.45 trillion plus economy (GDP measured as Purchasing Power Parity) in 2012. As a rule-of-thumb, Canada is almost exactly one tenth the population of the United States, and Canadians measure how they are doing economically by multiplying Canadian figures by a factor of 10. Since the U.S. GDP was US$15.66 trillion in 2012, Canadian commentators report that there is a productivity gap between American and Canadian workers.[36]

However, Canada is a very successful trading nation – possibly more so than the United States. While the United States was the third most successful world exporter in 2011 (US$1,497 billion), and Canada the eleventh (US$463 billion),[37] Canada exported about three times more per capita. Canada's principal trading partner was the United States (73.7 percent of exports) followed by the United Kingdom (4.7 percent). Principal Canadian exports included motor vehicles and parts, industrial machinery, aircraft, telecommunications equipment, chemicals, plastics, fertilizers, wood pulp, timber, crude petroleum, natural gas, electricity, and aluminum.

Canada achieved a balance of payments surplus in 2012, exporting US$481.7 billion while importing US$480.9 billion. Canada's principal import sources were the United States (49.5 percent), China (10.8 percent), and Mexico (5.5 percent). Principal imports included machinery and equipment, motor vehicles and parts, crude oil, chemicals, electricity, and durable consumer products.

The reason Canada both imported and exported crude oil is because of the tight integration between U.S. and Canadian economies. Most Canadian oil is produced in the western prairie regions of Alberta and Saskatchewan. Existing pipelines flow north/south to Texas where the bitumen oil is processed. Eastern Canada is supplied by sea from the Middle East because there is no east/west pipeline. Such a pipeline is currently being considered, as is one from Alberta through British Columbia to the west coast for shipment to China and Japan. This latter pipeline would reduce Canadian trade dependence on the United States, a Canadian governmental goal. Supplying eastern Canada by pipeline would also reduce Canadian dependence on U.S. oil purchases. This is a good idea since the United States is becoming self-sufficient in oil production by 2015 due to "fracking" technology.[38] The United States may no longer need Canadian oil in the near future.

There are regional differences in trade orientation within Canada. The province of Ontario has always been the industrial and manufacturing heartland of Canada. Most Ontario trade has historically been with the United States. For much of the twentieth century, the *U.S.–Canada Auto Pact* guaranteed that Canada would produce as many automobiles for the Big Three Auto Makers (General Motors, Ford, Chrysler) as they sold in Canada. That pact is history, but it resulted in a major automotive industry in Ontario that still supplies the United States with specific models of cars.

By contrast, British Columbia on Canada's West coast has become very Pacific Rim oriented in its trade focus. This has been facilitated by British Columbia's major city, Vancouver, being a popular spot for Asian immigration (approximately 42 percent visible minorities; including 20 percent ethnic Chinese, and 10 percent various South Asian).[39] In 2012, only 45.8 percent of British Columbia's exports went to the United States, while the rest went to China (19.4 percent), Japan (13.5 percent), Europe (6.5 percent), and South Korea (6.1 percent). Recently, the British Columbia government announced the opening of a provincial trade office in London, UK, to build off the Canadian government's about-to-be-concluded EU Free Trade Agreement.[40] However, there are already 13 existing offices located in Asia and the United States including four in China. The new B.C. provincial government is actively organizing to supply liquid natural gas (LNG) to customers in China and Japan.

Governmental context

The Canadian federal government is based on the British parliamentary system. The Prime Minister of Canada is the leader of the party with the greatest number of seats elected in the Parliament. The American equivalent of Parliament is the Congressional House of Representatives. There is a Senate in Canada as well, but its members are appointed by the sitting Prime Minister for terms that end at age 75. Its powers are to facilitate "sober second thought" and while it may delay Parliamentary legislation, it cannot do so indefinitely. Canada also has an independent judiciary as in the United States. While Canadians complain that a prime minister with a majority in Parliament may act as a dictator during his/her four- to five-year term, the Canadian system generally prevents the logjam between Democrats and Republicans, and between Congress, Senate, President, and judiciary that currently exists in the United States.

Provincial governments in Canada have significantly more powers than state governments in the United States. Generally, government powers have been divided between the federal and provincial governments and the courts uphold that the federal government cannot take unilateral action in an area of provincial responsibility. For example, Medicare is a provincial area. The federal government has offered to pay 10 percent of the costs if provincial governments provide similar levels of care in each province. Most provinces cannot afford to eschew this deal, but are not legally required to take the money and enforce the standards.

This system of devolved powers has been the result of the fact that the Province of Quebec is the primary seat of Francophone influence in Canada. And since the 1970s, a sizable minority of Francophones have desired, and elected provincial governments to facilitate, independence from Canada. There is currently a separatist government in Quebec, elected in 2012.

Francophone Quebecers do have legitimate historical grievances with the rest of Canada (ROC). From the time of the British victory on the Plains of Abraham in 1763, until the last third of the twentieth century, Anglophones ruled Francophones politically and economically in their own province as if they were second-class citizens. These days, successive Quebec governments have made Quebec basically a unilingual French-speaking province, attempting to preserve French culture. By contrast, the ROC is officially a bilingual English and French country, though little French is spoken elsewhere except in northern New Brunswick, Ottawa (Canada's capital), and parts of Manitoba. In Vancouver (British Columbia) and Toronto (Ontario), Canada's third and first largest cities where most Asian immigrants have settled, Mandarin would be a more likely second language than French – certainly it is an unofficial second language.

In any event, the federal government has attempted over the years to appease French nationalists by devolving more and more power to Quebec. And the other nine provinces have successfully argued that they also should receive any additional powers delegated to Quebec. The provinces are so independent from federal authority that they have enacted trade barriers between each other's products and services to protect their local markets. When Canada negotiated its Free Trade Agreement with the United States in 1987, further negotiations were needed to ensure that interprovincial trade barriers would not impede American investments in Canada.

Social context

Canada is also a multicultural society, perhaps more intentionally so than the United States. While the United States prided itself for many years as a cultural "melting pot" and only recently found itself a "salad bowl," Canada has long regarded itself as a "cultural mosaic." Originally, this attitude stemmed from Canada's origins as a combination of British and French colonies that united by force when the British army defeated the French army on the Plains of Abraham near Quebec City in 1763. Only a few years later, during the American Revolution of 1776–1783, many Empire Loyalists fled the United States and settled primarily in Nova Scotia and the Maritimes.

Canada's most defining feature is its ethical diversity. Up to the present day, the British (Anglophones) and French (Francophones) have maintained their separate cultural identities, and when Canada gained its independence from Britain in 1867, English and French both became official languages of the Dominion. In recent times, the Anglophones and Francophones have been joined by a vast influx of immigrants (Allophones) and Canada currently accepts upwards of 300,000 to 350,000 new immigrants per year – approximately 1 percent of its total population. Statistics Canada reported that according to the 2001 census, Canada had 34 ethnic groups with at least 100,000 members, and 10 of these had memberships of 1 million plus (see Exhibit 16.3). In 2006, 20 percent of the Canadian population was foreign born, and this element of the population was increasing four times faster than the native born population.[41]

EXHIBIT 16.3 LARGEST ETHNIC IDENTITY GROUPS IN CANADA

Ethnic origin	%	Population	Area of largest proportion (%)
English	21.03	6.57 M	Newfoundland (43.2)
French	15.82	4.94 M	Quebec (28.9)
Scottish	15.11	4.72 M	Prince Edward Island (40.5)
Irish	13.94	4.35 M	Prince Edward Island (29.2)
German	10.18	3.18 M	Saskatchewan (30.0)
Italian	4.63	1.45 M	Ontario (7.2)
Chinese	4.31	1.35 M	British Columbia (10.6)
First Nations	4.01	1.25 M	Northwest Territories (36.5)
Ukrainian	3.87	1.21 M	Manitoba (14.8)
Dutch	3.32	1.04 M	Alberta (5.3)

Source: Wikipedia: Demographics of Canada, 2011.

Microcultures: First Nations

In the context of business opportunities, Canada contains several micro-communities of interest. The First Nations are a genuine Emerging Market (see Chapter 7) within Canada. One and a quarter million Canadians are classified as having native ancestry. Three-quarters of these people live on reservations. The federal government groups First Nations' classified people into four categories – status (registered formally under the Indian Act); non-status persons who have not registered with the government; Metis (descendants of mixed aboriginal and European ancestry); and Inuit, a distinct cultural group, who generally live in the far north and speak primarily their own language Inuktitut.

A 1985 change in Canadian law has caused a dramatic rise in Indian population figures, now including Indian women who marry Canadians of non-Indian ancestry. In the past, Native men who married non-Native women retained their status, but Native women in the same circumstances did not.

Canadian courts have held that First Nations' people deserve compensation for guarantees made to them by the British crown in treaties that were subsequently not honored. In addition, the federal government confiscated some tribes' hereditary lands in the past without legal ratification in the form of treaties. Courts have held that treaties must be agreed to, and compensation paid to address these ancient wrongs. There were, for example, no treaties ever signed between the federal government and the First Nations of British Columbia. First Nations' groups have consequently claimed practically the entire province as part of their ongoing treaty negotiations.

Conditions on First Nations' reserves are generally terrible, with high unemployment, substance abuse, high rates of suicide, poor housing conditions, poor schooling resources, and so on. Many reserves are located in rural and/or wilderness locations where it is difficult for the federal government to provide adequate services. Many First Nations' people want to put their full efforts into negotiating treaties as a means of obtaining the financial compensation needed to develop their resources and improve their living conditions. The *Idle No More* movement that began in 2012 and continues today has been an effort by Aboriginal leadership and young Aboriginals to pressure a government believed to be insincere in its negotiating strategies, and not committed to finding equitable solutions.

For example, in the Nisga'a treaty, the federal government allocated lands to the Nisga'a that were also claimed by another First Nations' group which promptly stated it would go to court to sue the Nisga'a for the return of the land. Some suggested that this was a deliberate strategy to turn the tribes against each other. And the First Nations' do not have a central authority that speaks for all the 700+ bands in Canada. Ultimately, each pursues its own interests, independently if necessary.

A smaller number of First Nations' people believe that their social and economic conditions need to be addressed with whatever resources are available to them currently. Each band receives annual financial allocations from Indian and Northern Affairs Canada (INAC), the government department responsible for managing the Indian Act. In 2011–2012,

INAC's budget was CAN$7.3 billion.[42] If a band chief is elected that supports the goal of immediate development, then that band will initiate plans to attempt to build a piece of infrastructure, or support local business initiatives to develop the band economy.[43] Generally, such bands find that in addition to inadequate financial resources, they lack managerial and organizational capabilities necessary for an effective business.

The serious needs of bands and the desire to address them, plus the lack of First Nations' managerial resources, and substantial government funding have spawned an industry in Canada. Many consultants have found opportunities doing needs assessment, planning projects, providing managerial capabilities, and even supporting the treaty negotiations from the Aboriginal side.

Microcultures: Asian

Vancouver, British Columbia, is Canada's third largest city. Of a total population in the Greater Vancouver Regional District of 2.3 million, 52 percent do not speak English as their first language due to the effects of immigration. Almost 30 percent of the city's population is of Chinese heritage. Many of these Chinese people emigrated from Hong Kong prior to the return of the British colony to China in 1997. Other significant Asian groupings include South Asian (mostly Punjabi, 5.7 percent), Filipino (5.0 percent), Japanese (1.7 percent), Korean (1.5 percent), as well as sizable numbers of Vietnamese, Indonesians, and Cambodians. In Vancouver, the second language after English is Mandarin or Cantonese. French is almost never heard except for tourists from eastern Canada.

Some neighborhoods are more Asian than others. Richmond's population would make it the fourth-largest city in British Columbia, and its 60 percent immigrant population is the highest in Canada. More than half its population of 190,000 is South Asian, including Chinese (43.6 percent, mostly originally from Hong Kong, Taiwan, and China), South Asian (8.0 percent), and Filipino (5.5 percent). Richmond has two Buddhist temples.

This strong Asian representation has produced a remarkably multicultural city. It has also produced many opportunities for doing business in China or India, and for attracting Asian businesspeople to Vancouver. This explains why British Columbia exports significantly more to China, Japan, and South Korea, and significantly less to the United States and Europe, than the rest of Canada.

Tips for doing business with Canadians

Years ago, it was easy to pick out Canadian businesspersons. They were the ones with red maple leaf pins on their suit lapels, or tags attached to their briefcases or suitcases. With the advent of global terrorism, American businesspeople were advised to wear red maple leaf tags and pins so as to appear Canadian. *WorldBusinessCulture*[44] has offered some tips for doing business with Canadians, if they can be successfully identified.

1   Although there are similarities between American and Canadian approaches to doing business, there are also enormous differences. Be aware of Canadian sensitivities in this area.

2   Canada is officially a bilingual country (English and French). It is a good idea to recognize the linguistic and cultural heritage of the French-speaking minority when they are encountered.

3   Cultural diversity is a valued aspect of Canadian culture, reinforced by its multicultural immigration policy. It is likely you will encounter people from a wide variety of cultural backgrounds. You should avoid initial judgments about their status and competency.

4   Business structures vary enormously as they do in the United States. Do your homework or contact organizations for information before visiting.

5   Business meetings in Canada tend to be more formal than in the United States. First names are not always preferred. A more restrained approach is advisable.

6   People expect to be heard and listened to at meetings regardless of their rank or standing.

7   Detailed preparation before meetings is advisable. Decisions are not usually made until all necessary facts are revealed and inspected.

8   Communication styles are reserved and often understated. Canadians may be suspicious of grand gestures and hyperbole.

9   Canadians tend to be direct in their communication style. They can usually be taken at face value rather than needing to be decoded looking for underlying meanings.

10   Women visitors should have no difficulty being treated with deference and respect. Visitors may negotiate with businesswomen who expect to be treated the same as men.

Canada's multicultural environment means Canadian business counterparts may be from almost any culture. While these general tips may be helpful, you must be careful to observe appropriate cultural niceties – many other chapters in this text offer relevant tips for handling negotiations with Canadian minority ethnicities. For example, First Nations' culture does not necessarily value direct and/or continuous eye contact. Nor does Japanese culture. Chinese culture has concerns for saving face (respect). It isn't a good idea to confront points of disagreement, but rather to focus on extending areas of agreement. A book on Chinese business etiquette[45] would not be out-of-place as a business resource for Vancouver or Toronto.

AMERICAN–CANADIAN COMPARISONS

A useful way to understand American and Canadian business attitudes and practices is through directly comparing how they differ from each other. There are a number of studies that compare the two economies, and the ease of doing business in each country. There are studies comparing how Americans and Canadians approach decision-making, and how they are different in the ways that they prefer to build effective business relationships. There are even differences in the ways they define and regulate business ethics.

EXHIBIT 16.4 COMPARATIVE ECONOMIC AND SOCIAL INDICES

Index	Canadian economy	American economy
Economic freedom	Ranked 18th	Ranked 7th
Economic importance	Ranked 7th	Ranked 1st
GDP	Ranked 13th	Ranked 2nd
GDP per capita	Ranked 8th	Ranked 3rd
Human Development Index	Ranked 5th	Ranked 10th
Child poverty	Ranked 7th	45% more than Canada
Big Mac Index	$3.01	$3.15

Source: "Economy Stats: Canada vs. United States," www.nationmaster.com/compare/Canada/United-States/Economy.

Economic comparisons

Economically speaking, the United States has a stronger and better performing economy than Canada. See selected indices in Exhibit 16.4. Using world nations' ranks, the United States has greater economic freedom and more economic importance. Both GDP and GDP per capita are higher suggesting both a richer country and better-off citizens.

Canadians would, however, argue that their country had sacrificed economically to produce a better and more supportive social environment for all its citizens. Universal Medicare is an obvious example that the United States is only lately beginning to address with much opposition. More effort is made in Canada to develop people. There is less child poverty. And the Big Mac Index, a fun index created by *The Economist*, to show how far one's currency goes in different countries, shows the Big Mac is cheaper in Canada. Americans have more money than Canadians but money doesn't go quite as far in the United States.

Ease of doing business

The World Bank compares a number of statistics on an annual basis, ranking all 185 nations in the world on various criteria related to doing business. The 2013 rankings for the United States and Canada are found in Exhibit 16.5.

This exhibit is useful for predicting the kinds of problems Americans would face coming to do business in Canada and vice versa. A problem is surely a situation that is unexpected based on one's existing experience. The United States seems to generally be an easier place to do business than most other countries, including Canada. Getting electricity seems likely to be a Third World experience in Canada. On the other hand, Canada is an easier business environment for start-up, investor protection, resolving insolvency, and especially dealing with taxes. Canada's total tax load, however, is 38.4 percent of GDP

EXHIBIT 16.5 WORLD BANK: EASE OF DOING BUSINESS

EXHIBIT 16.5

Topic rankings (of 185)	Canadian rank	American rank
Starting a business	3	13
Dealing with construction permits	69	17
Getting electricity	152	19
Registering property	54	25
Getting credit	23	4
Protecting investors	4	6
Paying taxes	8	69
Trading across borders	44	22
Enforcing contracts	62	6
Resolving insolvency	4	16
Average score	38.5	17.9

Source: World Bank Group: Doing Business: Measuring Business Regulations (www.doingbusiness.org/data/exploreeconomies/).

compared with 28.2 percent in the United States. However, Canadian business taxes may be quite low – 10 percent in Alberta and 11 percent in British Columbia, for example. So, personal taxation is higher, but business taxation is lower.

Cognitive and cultural problem-solving differences

There have been relatively few management studies of cross-cultural differences between Americans and Canadians, and how these might affect business outcomes. Evans, Lane, and O'Grady[46] observed that successful Canadian business strategies usually did not work in the United States. They also observed interesting differences in business practices. For example, Canadian customers were satisfied with stores that carried a wide range of product assortment without much product variety and depth in terms of sizes, styles, and options. Americans preferred specialty stores with relatively limited product range but considerable variety and depth of assortment within that range. They did not, however, offer reasons for why these differences existed.

Later, O'Grady and Lane[47] attributed the differences in practices to cultural differences that were an unobtrusive barrier because they were unrecognized. Adler and Graham[48] argued that English Canadians behaved very much as Americans in negotiations, but French Canadian negotiators behaved quite differently.

One of the first studies to compare the cognitive problem-solving and decision-making preferences of American and Canadian businesspeople was Abramson, Keating, and Lane.[49] This research measured samples of American and Canadian business students using the Jungian based Myers-Briggs Type Indicator (MBTI) instrument. Significant differences were found on two of the four scales – *Sensing versus Intuiting*, and *Judging versus Perceiving*. These are described in detail below. No significant differences were found on the *Extravert versus Introvert* or *Thinking versus Feeling* scales.

1   *Sensing versus intuiting*: A *sensing* person focuses primarily on immediate sensory experience and tends to be more realistic and practical. S/he develops acute powers of observation and a good memory for details. An *intuiting* person is more concerned with possibilities and meanings than sensory information. She/he may not have such an acute memory for details but is likely to be more imaginative, innovative, theoretical, and abstract. Sensing and intuiting are, according to Jung,[50] two primary modes of gathering information regarded by an individual as relevant to problem-solving.

2   *Judging versus perceiving*: A *judging* person prefers to make relatively quick decisions based on a more limited data-set. She/he is well organized and makes the most of the information s/he has. She/he tends to seek closure as soon as possible. A judging person would appear decisive and confident. A *perceiving* person values the constant possibility of receiving new information relevant to a decision. Closure and decision-making is delayed to allow time for further information to manifest. A perceiving person would appear curious and adaptable, but relatively slow to commit him/herself.

The study found that American managers were more *sensing* and *judging*. The Canadians were more *intuiting* and *perceiving*. The differences on the sensing versus perceiving scale were especially acute. It predicted that Americans and Canadians would face a number of serious potential interaction problems because the Americans would perceive the Canadians as very slow to make up their minds, and not entirely accurate in their understanding and interpretation of physical evidence. The Canadians would perceive the Americans as always in a rush, willing to make ill-considered decisions, and relatively unimaginative and un-innovative.

A second interesting study was that of van Oudenthoven.[51] American and Canadian managers were surveyed using Hofstede's[52] work values instrument. The Americans and Canadians were very similar on the *power distance* and *uncertainty avoidance* scales but not on *individualism* or *masculinity*. The Americans were closer to the British than the Canadians on *individualism*, and closer to the Belgians and Greeks on *masculinity* (or task versus relationship orientation). On the *individualism versus collectivism* scale, Americans would perceive Canadians as less concerned with personal achievements and individual rights, and less likely than Americans to stand up for themselves and their beliefs. On the *masculinity versus femininity* scale, Americans would perceive Canadians as less competitive, assertive, and materialistic, and less interested in personal ambition and power.

Cross-national differences in relationship building activities

Abramson[53] conducted a study to determine the activities that Americans and Canadians preferred to use to build and maintain effective buyer–seller relationships. These results are summarized in Exhibit 16.6. Considerable differences were found, both on marketing mix (product, promotion, price, direct sales and service) and relationship marketing variables. The Americans were much more committed to relational activities. They built and maintained relationships by focusing on developing mutual respect, shared goals, personal trust, and making sure everyone received the expected benefits. Canadians also valued these activities highly but Americans valued them much more highly. By contrast, Canadians were more likely to focus on sharp pricing, and helping out a customer if asked to do so. In the Exhibit, a significant difference is shown as either (>) or (>>) depending how much more. Similarly, less and very less are (<) and (<<).

EXHIBIT 16.6 BUYER–SELLER RELATIONSHIP BUILDING ACTIVITIES BY MEAN SCORE

Mean score	American	Canadian
4.6	Build respect — U.S. >	
4.5		
4.4		
4.3		Build respect — Can.
4.2		
4.1	Advertising and Promotion — U.S. >> Build shared goals — U.S. >> Build trust — U.S. >	
4.0		Sharp pricing — Can. >>
3.9	Ensure mutual benefits — U.S. >	Help if asked — Can. >>
3.8		Build trust — Can. <
3.7	Sharp pricing — U.S. <<	Advertising and Promotion — Can. << Build shared goals — Can. << Ensure mutual benefits — Can. < Product R&D — Can. >
3.6		
3.5	Help if asked — U.S. << Product R&D — U.S. <	
3.4		Ask for small favors — Can. >>
3.3		
2.9		
2.8	Ask for small favors — U.S. <<	

Source: Abramson, N. R. "Building and Maintaining Effective Buyer–Seller Relationships: A Comparative Study of American and Canadian Expectations," *Journal of Promotion Management*, Vol. 12, No. 1, 2005, pp. 129–150.

Exhibit 16.6 shows that even though the top activity for both Americans and Canadians was building mutual respect, the Americans worked at it considerably more. They built shared goals to a much greater extent, and did much more to build trust and ensure everyone achieved the mutual benefits expected. Americans also engaged in considerably more advertising and promotion. In contrast, the Canadians were very much more likely to rely on sharp pricing, being helpful, and developing their products at the request of their customers. It was interesting that the Canadians were much more likely to ask for small favors whereas this was an unlikely approach for the Americans.

Business ethics and bribery[54]

Bribing government officials is a criminal offense in both Canadian and American law. Under the Canadian *Corruption of Foreign Public Officials* Act, a bribe is defined as a payment of value to a foreign official intended to obtain, either directly or indirectly, a business advantage or opportunity by inducing the official to use his/her position to decide in favor of the bribe-giver. Items of value could include cash, computer equipment, travel, medical supplies, entertainment, or vehicles. A foreign official is a person who holds a legislative, administrative, or judicial position, or performs public duties for a state. This definition includes foreign military officers responsible for procurement decisions. The American equivalent of this Act is the *U.S. Foreign Corrupt Practices Act*.

Not all payments are, however, considered bribes. Public officials in many foreign nations, especially in the Third World, control the granting of licenses. It is a normal practice for they, or their superiors, to increase their income with payments for their favors. Reasonable payments to foreign officials to promote products or to facilitate the performance of contracts are not illegal.

It is similarly legal to offer facilitation payments to induce officials to perform routine acts within the scope of their normal duties. One may pay officials to perform routine functions that they are supposed to be performing as part of their jobs. For example, one may legally bribe an official to receive a visa or work permit. One may pay a harbormaster to unload a cargo from a ship. Such bribery is expensive because it cannot be used as a tax deduction and must use after-tax dollars.

There is, however, no established standard for what constitutes an illegal bribe. Businesses are on their own judging on the basis of circumstances and local culture. A gift of a bottle of whiskey costing $300 may be appropriate for a senior official, but a collector bottle worth $100,000 is likely not. The Canadian Revenue Agency does not provide acceptable guidelines as to what constitutes a reasonable payment. Businesses must use their judgment, and that of their lawyers.

By contrast, U.S. authorities provide 120 pages of guidelines defining proper gifts, travel and entertainment expenses, and facilitation payments. These guidelines say, for example, that wining and dining a foreign official is completely acceptable, but spending $10,000 doing so would likely lead to prosecution.

EXHIBIT 16.7 A PERSONAL RECOLLECTION, TRAVELING IN CHINA

When I was traveling in China doing research in the 1990s, I met a senior Chinese official who tried to explain to me about Chinese foreign policy. He said, "We love the Americans — they are far away. We hate the Japanese — they are very close. It's easier to get along harmoniously with those far enough away that they can't make trouble for us too easily." I said, "I know how you feel. We Canadians love China. You are far away. But the Americans are very close."

CONCLUSIONS

Despite their many similarities, there are also many differences between the United States and Canada. Many of those differences may stem from the fact that the United States has been a world superpower — political, military, and economic — for most of the past century. For a large part of that time, Canada stood in America's shadow, largely invisible beyond the North American continent. Former Prime Minister Trudeau's comment, at the beginning of this chapter, about Canada being in bed with an elephant is very insightful about Canadian identity. Canadians are very sensitive about what is going on in the U.S. At the same time, they assert themselves by feeling superior whenever the United States suffers some setback. Exhibit 16.7 is suggestive of this very Canadian attitude.

Canada is a staunch ally of the United States. It always will be because their interests are completely intertwined. On the one hand, Canada sometimes feels forgotten as America pursues its other friends. On the other hand, it may be a blessing when the elephant isn't thinking of you and goes off on his way.

Americans and Canadians do more business together than any other two nations in the world. Too often difficulties arise in their relationships because both parties mistake the other for themselves. We hope the contents of this chapter will help you recognize how Americans and Canadians are different, as an aid to building even stronger relationships.

MIND STRETCHING

1   Many Americans seem to be anxious about how the world perceives them, and are disturbed by what seems to be its declining image and position in many countries. Some wonder if the end is near for U.S. dominance or influence. The following are some quotations from recently published materials that are worth considering:

■ "In Muslim and developing countries, the image of America is skewed by north/south, east/west economic inequality; by longstanding, direct grievances over foreign policy…"

■ "On the surface, President Bush's week-long swing through northeast Asia has been a strong contrast with his recent storming (and, some say, stumbling) excursion with Latin America. While no foreign leader will openly oppose American leadership … beneath the polite appearance, however, there is no less a challenge to American leadership in Asia…"

■ "In developing countries … there is much greater awareness now than there used to be of the nature and pervasiveness of imperialism. As a result, in some countries there is mounting reluctance to conform to ideals 'born in the USA'…"

■ "One of the trickiest files for the prime minister (of Canada) will be relations with the United States. The two countries are drifting apart."

2   Consider how a typical American businessperson would be received in Canada? How is s/he likely to be treated? What must the Canadians be thinking of him/her? How should an American businessperson behave to receive the best results in a negotiation with Canadians.

3   Now consider how a Canadian businessperson will be received in the United States. How should s/he behave differently than usual in order to be effective?

NOTES

1   www.brainyquote.com/quotes/topics/topic_business.html.

2   www.canada4life.ca/quotes.php. Pierre Trudeau was Prime Minister of Canada, 1968–1979, 1980–1984.

3   Root, F. R. *Entry Strategies for International Markets.* Lexington, MA: Lexington, 1987.

4   See Ronen, S. and Kraut, A. J. "Similarities among Countries Based on Employee Work Values and Attitudes," *Columbia Journal of World Business*, Vol. 12, 1977, pp. 89–96. Also see Hofstede, G. *Culture's Consequences: International Differences in Work Related Values.* Beverly Hills, CA: Sage. Both studies observed that national cultures could be grouped into clusters of cultures that were more alike than cultures grouped into other clusters.

5   www.census.gov/foreign-trade/statistics/highlights/top/.

6   "Canada's State of Trade: Trade and Investment Update 2011," *Foreign Affairs and Investment Trade Canada*, www.international.gc.ca.

7   Lam, E. "Canada–U.S. Trade Relationship Drifting Apart: TD," *Financial Post*, February 1, 2012.

8   Potter, M. "Keystone XL: How Canada's Pipeline Splits the U.S.," *Toronto Star*, June 9, 2012, thestar.com.

9   O', P. "Canadian Business Lobby Pressures B.C. to Approve Northern Gateway, Kinder Morgan Pipelines: Province Urged to Consider 'National Interest' as It Weighs Northern Gateway, Kinder Morgan Proposals," *The Vancouver Sun*, February 12, 2013.

10 Abramson, N. R. "Configuration, Coordination, Learning and Foreign Market Entry: A Study of Canadian Software Companies Entering the United States," University of Western Ontario Doctoral Dissertation, 1992.

11 Evans, W., Lane, H., and O'Grady, S. *Bordercrossings: Doing Business in the US*. Toronto, ON: Prentice Hall Canada, 1992.

12 Pitts, G. "Jean Coutu Goes Where Others Fear to Tread," *The Globe and Mail*, April 7, 2004, pp. B1, 17.

13 O'Grady, S. and Lane, H. W. "The Psychic Distance Paradox," *Journal of International Business Studies*, Vol. 27, No. 2, 1996, pp. 309–333.

14 Obama, B. "What I Want for You and Every Child in America: A Letter to My Daughters," *Parade – The San Diego Union Tribune*, January 18, 2009, pp. 4–5. Barack Obama is the 44th President of the United States.

15 Central Intelligence Agency, *CIA World Factbook*, 2013, www.cia.gov/library/publications/the-world-factbook/geos/us.html.

16 Ibid.

17 Riley, R., "Bankruptcy a Chance for Detroit to Begin Anew," *The Detroit Free Press*, July 19, 2013.

18 en.wikipedia.org/wiki/List_of_countries_by_population.

19 Fariello, G. *Red Scare: Memories of the American Inquisition: An Oral History*. New York: Avon, 1995; May, G. *Un-American Activities: The Trials of William Remington*. New York: Oxford University Press, 1994; Schrecker, E. *Many Are the Crimes: McCarthyism in America*. Princeton, NJ: Princeton University Press, 1998. Some Americans still defend the memory of McCarthy and there is evidence there were some Soviet infiltrators. See Weinstein, A. and Vassiliev, A. *The Haunted Wood: Soviet Espionage in America: The Stalin Era*. New York: Modern Library, 2000.

20 Maddox, B. *In Defense of America*. New York: Little Brown, 2008; Tyler, P. *A World of Trouble: The White House and the Middle East – From Cold War to the War on Terror*. New York: Farrar, Strauss and Giroux, 2009.

21 Rodriguez, J. A. "The Path to bin Laden's Death Didn't Start with Obama," *The Washington Post*, April 30, 2012.

22 Gottlieb, S. "What If U.S. Stops Policing the World?" *CNN Opinion*, September 19, 2012, www.cnn.com/2012/09/18/opinion/gottlieb-us-retrenchment.

23 This information is from the *Stockholm International Peace Research Institute* (http://www.sipri.org/databases/armstransfers).

24 Campbell, J. *U.S.A. (Country Guide)*. New York: Lonely Planet, 2009. For U.S. Census Information, visit http://www.census.gov/main. Also see Sayre, A. P. *Welcome to North Amertica*. Brookfield, CT: Millbrook, 2003.

25 Bass, F. "U.S. Ethnic Mix Boasts German Accent Amid Surge of Hispanics," *Bloomberg*, March 5, 2012, www.bloomberg.com/news/2012–03–06/.

26 http://names.mongabay.com/ancestry/ancestry-population.html.

27 Gudykunst, W. B. and Kim, K. Y. *Communicating with Strangers: An Approach to Intercultural Communication*, 3rd edn. New York: McGraw-Hill, 1994.

28 Hewlett, S. A. "Too Many People of Color Feel Uncomfortable at Work," *Harvard Business Review – HBR Blog Network*, October 18, 2012.

29 Gudykunst and Kim, *Communicating with Strangers*.

30 Zinn, H. *A People's History of the United States*. New York: Harper Perennial, 2005.

31 Failde, A. and Doyle, W. *Latino Success: Insights from 100 of America's Most Powerful Business Professionals*. New York: Simon and Shuster, 1996.

32 Pew Research Center, "Hispanic Population in the U.S.," March 30, 2011.

33 Passel, J. and Cohn, D. V. "U.S. Population Projections: 2005–2050," Pew Research Hispanic Center, February 11, 2008.

34 Nhan, D. "Buying Power of Hispanics Worth $1 Trillion, Report Says," *National Journal: The Next America*, May 10, 2012.

35 Central Intelligence Agency, *CIA World Factbook*, 2013, www.cia.gov/library/publications/the-world-factbook/geos/ca.html.

36 Simpson, S. "Innovation Key to Close Canada's Productivity Gap," *Calgary Herald*, February 19, 2013, www.calgaryherald.com/business/.

37 http://en.wikipedia.org/wiki/List_of_countries_by_exports. These figures are based on the *CIA World Factbook*.

38 "US Shale Oil Supply Shock Shifts Global Power Balance," *BBC News*, May 14, 2013, www.bbc.co.uk/news/business−22524597.

39 Roy, R. "Vancouver's Multi-Ethnic Population," *Vancouver.com*, http://2vancouver.com/en/articles/vancouvers-multi-ethnic-population.

40 O'Neil, P. "Some Experts Puzzled by B.C.'s Decision to Open Trade Office in London," *The Vancouver Sun*, February 28, 2013, pp. B1, B3.

41 Statistics Canada. "Study: Projections of the Diversity of the Canadian Population," March 9, 2010, www.statcan.gc.ca.

42 Assembly of First Nations; British Columbia Assembly of First Nations, "First Nations' Revenues," www.bcafn.ca/toolkit/.

43 See Abramson, N. R. and Ai, J. X. *Royal Bank: Hagwilget Band Case Series* in the instructor online teaching materials. These cases detail negotiations initiated by the Hagwilget Band in Hazelton, B.C., to obtain a Royal Bank branch on the Hagwilget Reserve.

44 www.worldbusinessculture.com/Doing-Business-in-Canada.html.

45 De Mente, B. *Chinese Etiquette & Ethics in Business*. Lincolnwood, IL: NTC Business Books, 1990.

46 Evans, Lane, and O'Grady, *Bordercrossings*.

47 O'Grady and Lane, "The Psychic Distance Paradox."

48 Adler, N. J. and Graham, J. L. "Business Negotiations: Canadians Are Not Just Like Americans," *Canadian Journal of Administrative Sciences*, Vol. 4, No. 3, 1987, pp. 11−238.

49 Abramson, N. R., Keating, R. J., and Lane, H. W. "Cross-national Cognitive Process Differences: A Comparison of Canadian, American and Japanese Managers," *Management International Review*, Vol. 36, No. 2, 1996, pp. 123−147.

50 Jung, C. G. *Personality Types*. Princeton, NJ: Princeton University, Bollingen Series XX, 1976.

51 van Oudenhoven, J. P. "Do Organizations Reflect National Cultures? A 10-Nation Study," *International Journal of Intercultural Relations*, Vol. 25, 2001, pp. 89−107.

52 Hofstede, G. *Culture's Consequences: International Differences in Work-Related Values*. Beverley Hills, CA: Sage, 1980.

53 Abramson, N. R. "Building and Maintaining Effective Buyer–Seller Relationships: A Comparative Study of American and Canadian Expectations," *Journal of Promotion Management*, Vol. 12, No. 1, 2005, pp. 129−150.

54 Krishna, V. "The Dangers of Bribery," *Financial Post*, February 14, 2013, p. D4.

ADDITIONAL FEATURES

Please visit the companion website at: www.routledge.com/cw/Moran where you will find additional case studies, study aides, and instructor resources.

INDEX

Page numbers in *italics* denotes a table/figure